C

SAN FRANCISCO

LEGEND

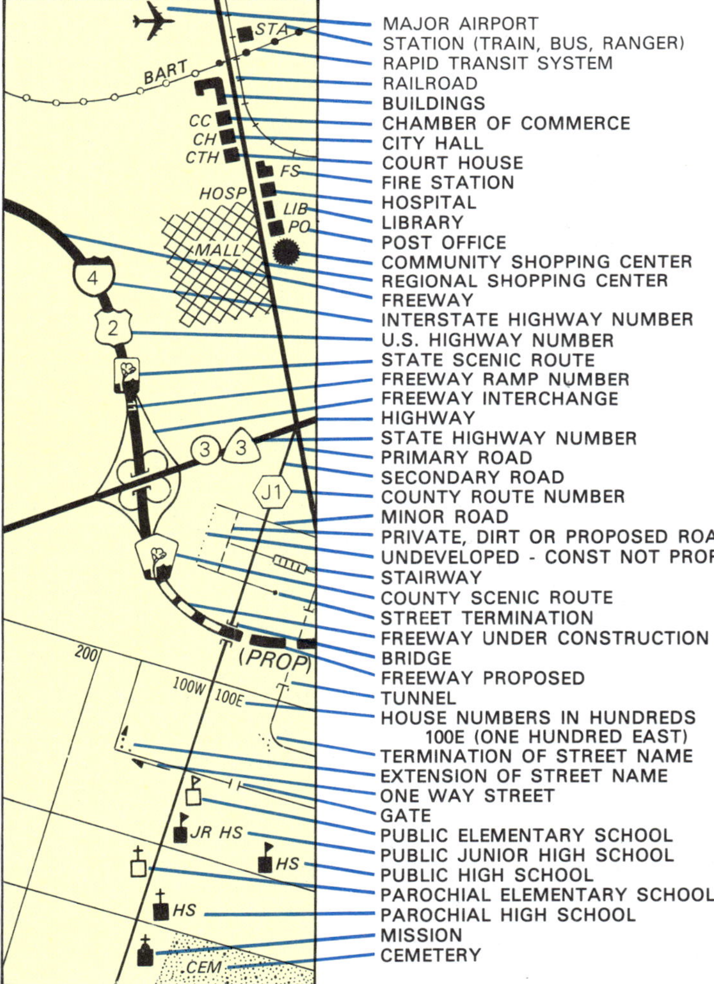

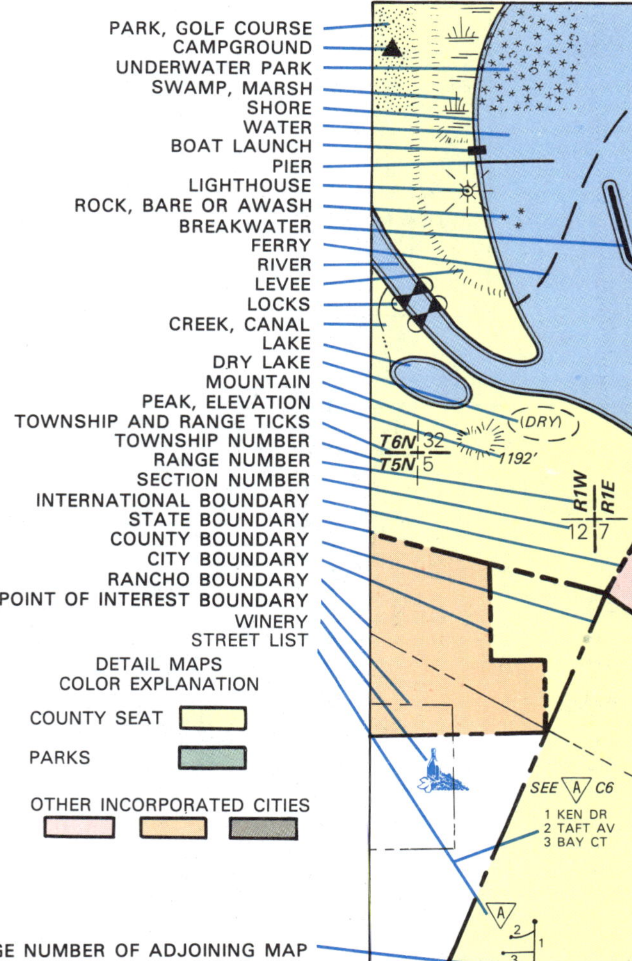

DETAIL MAPS
COLOR EXPLANATION

COUNTY SEAT

PARKS

OTHER INCORPORATED CITIES

SCALE OF MAP PAGES
1 INCH TO ¼ MILE

MAJOR DEPARTMENT STORES

BK	BULLOCKS
EC	EMPORIUM CAPWELL
MA	MACYS
NM	NEIMAN MARCUS

LEGEND

1988 SAN FRANCISCO COUNTY COMMUNITIES

ESTIMATED POPULATION 742,700 *AREA IN SQUARE MILES 44.75

COMMUNITY	ZIP CODE	MAP
BAYVIEW	94124	21
BERNAL HEIGHTS	94110	14
CHINATOWN	94108	3
COW HOLLOW	94123	2
DIAMOND HEIGHTS	94131	14
EUREKA VALLEY	94114	10
EXCELSIOR	94112	20
FOREST HILL	94116	13
GLEN PARK	94131	14
HAIGHT-ASHBURY	94117	9
HUNTER'S POINT	94124	17
INGLESIDE	94112	19
LAKESIDE	94132	12
LAUREL HEIGHTS	94118	5

COMMUNITY	ZIP CODE	MAP
MARINA	94123	1
MIRALOMA PARK	94127	13
MISSION DISTRICT	94110	11
NOB HILL	94108	7
NOE VALLEY	94114	14
NORTH BEACH	94133	3
PACIFIC HEIGHTS	94115	6
PARK MERCED	94132	19
PARKSIDE	94116	12
PORTOLA	94134	20
POTRERO HILL	94107	11
PRESIDIO HEIGHTS	94118	5
PRESDIO OF SN FRANCSCO	94129	5
RICHMOND	94121	8

COMMUNITY	ZIP CODE	MAP
RUSSIAN HILL	94133	2
ST FRANCIS WOOD	94127	13
SAN FRANCISCO -SAN FRANCISCO COUNTY	94101	3
SEACLIFF	94121	4
SOUTH OF MARKET	94103	7
STONESTOWN	94132	19
SUNSET	94122	8
TELEGRAPH HILL	94133	3
VISITACION VALLEY	94134	21
WESTERN ADDITION	94115	6
WEST OF TWIN PEAKS	94122	9
WEST PORTAL	94127	13
WESTWOOD PARK	94127	13

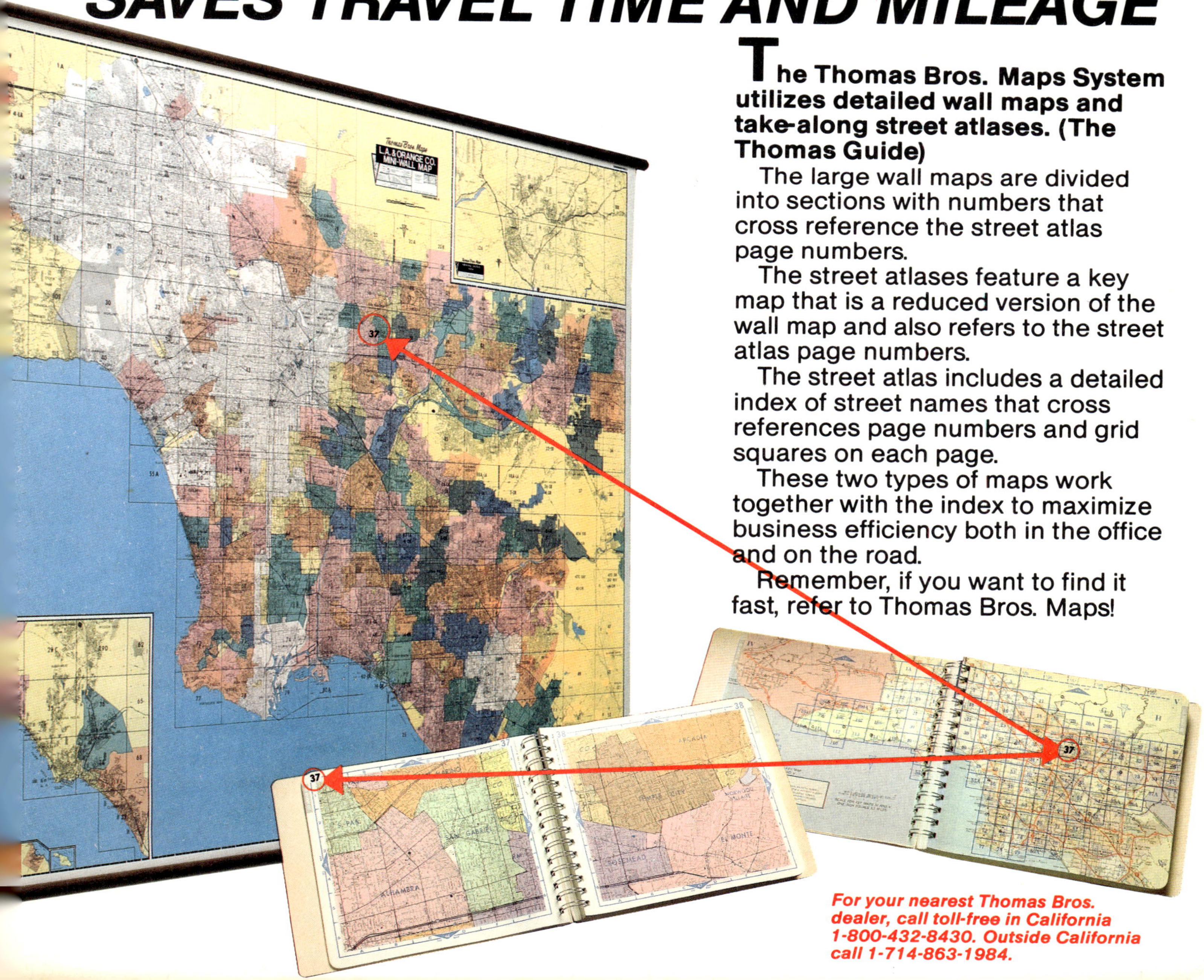

The Thomas Bros. Maps System utilizes detailed wall maps and take-along street atlases. (The Thomas Guide)

The large wall maps are divided into sections with numbers that cross reference the street atlas page numbers.

The street atlases feature a key map that is a reduced version of the wall map and also refers to the street atlas page numbers.

The street atlas includes a detailed index of street names that cross references page numbers and grid squares on each page.

These two types of maps work together with the index to maximize business efficiency both in the office and on the road.

Remember, if you want to find it fast, refer to Thomas Bros. Maps!

For your nearest Thomas Bros. dealer, call toll-free in California 1-800-432-8430. Outside California call 1-714-863-1984.

SAN FRANCISCO COUNTY

SAN FRANCISCO

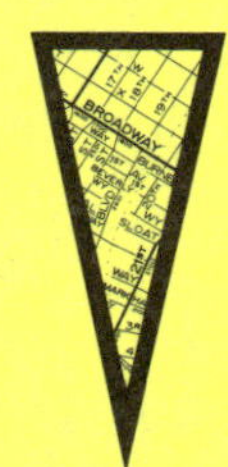

1988 *Thomas Guide*®

TABLE OF CONTENTS

		PAGE	
HOW TO USE THIS GUIDE	Includes information on the use of this guide, along with a list of abbreviations.	**B**	USE
LEGEND OF MAP SYMBOLS	Includes map scales and explanation of symbols.	**C**	LEGEND
DOWNTOWN MAPS AND COMMUNITIES INDEX	Downtown maps include civic center points of interest list. Communities are are listed with zip code numbers.	**D-E**	DOWN-TOWN
KEY MAP	Shows relationship of all detail maps in this guide.	**F**	AREA
DETAIL MAPS	Highly detailed pages of urban areas.	**1-21**	DETAIL
IP CODE MAPS AND LARGE CALE DOWNTOWN MAPS	Zip maps show boundaries of area zip codes. Large scale maps highlight one-way streets and points of interest.	**22-29**	ZIP
TREET INDEX & ROSS STREET INDEX	Alphabetical listing of all streets. Also includes points of interest and cross street index.	**30-89**	INDEX
IRPORT ACCESS MAP	The San Francisco International Airport access map includes airline terminal lists.	**90**	SFX

Corporate Office & Showroom
17731 Cowan, Irvine, CA 92714 (714) 863-1984
Retail Stores
603 W. 7th St., Los Angeles, CA 90017 (213) 627-4018
550 Jackson St., San Francisco, CA 94133 (415) 981-7520

GOLDEN GATE TBM 4025	***$29.95***
SAN FRANCISCO TBM 3035	***$10.95***

SAN FRANCISCO

B

HOW TO USE THIS GUIDE

Planning Your Route

- Use the Key Map in front of the Guide or the Fold-out Map to get an overall picture of the area and to determine the most direct route from one community to another.

- Turn to the individual map pages which correspond to the numbered areas shown on the Key Map.

- Follow a street from one page to another by turning to the "See Map" number shown in each margin which indicates continuation of the map.

Finding a Street

- When you know the street name use the Street Index to find its page and grid.

Other Features in Your Guide

- Use the Cities & Communities Index to find the location of a city or community.

- Use the Points of Interest Index when you know the name of a prominent feature you want to locate. This index is divided into many categories such as hospitals, chambers of commerce, colleges and universities, shopping centers, parks, and many other points of interest.

Cross Street Index

- A special index has been prepared for all streets in San Francisco. This index lists each street, followed by all the cross streets in block number order. Most cross street names include the lowest house address starting at the intersection.

USE

LIST OF ABBREVIATIONS

AL ALLEY
AR ARROYO
ARR ARROYO
AV AVENUE
AVD AVENIDA
AVD D LS AVENIDA DE LOS
BCH BEACH
BL BOULEVARD
BLVD BOULEVARD
CEM CEMETERY
CIR CIRCLE
CK CREEK
CL CALLE
CL DL CALLE DEL
CL D LS CALLE DE LAS, CALLE DE LOS
CL EL CALLE EL
CLJ CALLEJON
CL LA CALLE LA
CL LS CALLE LAS, CALLE LOS
CM CAMINO
CM D CAMINO DE
CM D LA CAMINO DE LA
CM D LS CAMINO DE LAS, CAMINO DE LOS
CMTO CAMINITO
CN CANAL
COM COMMON
CR CRESCENT
CRES CRESCENT
CSWY CAUSEWAY
CT COURT
CTE CORTE
CTO CUT OFF
CTR CENTER
CV COVE
CY CANYON
CYN CANYON
D DE
DL DEL
DR DRIVE
DS DOS
E EAST
EST ESTATE
EXPWY EXPRESSWAY
EXT EXTENSION
FRWY FREEWAY
FRW FREEWAY
FY FREEWAY
GN GLEN
GRDS GROUNDS
GRN GREEN
GRV GROVE
HTS HEIGHTS
HWY HIGHWAY
HY HIGHWAY
JCT JUNCTION
KPN KEY PENINSULA NORTH
KPS KEY PENINSULA SOUTH
L LA
LN LANE
LP LOOP
LS LAS, LOS
MDW MEADOW
MHP MOBILE HOME PARK
MNR MANOR
MT MOUNT
MTN MOUNTAIN
MTWY MOTORWAY
MTY MOTORWAY
N NORTH
PAS PASEO
PAS DE PASEO DE
PAS DL PASEO DEL
PAS D LS PASEO DE LAS, PASEO DE LOS
PGD PLAYGROUND
PK PARK
PK PEAK
PKWY PARKWAY
PL PLACE
PT POINT
PY PARKWAY
PZ PLAZA
RCH RANCH
RCHO RANCHO
RD ROAD
RDG RIDGE
RES RESERVOIR
RIV RIVER
RV RIVER
RO RANCHO
S SOUTH
SN SAN
SPG SPRING
SPGS SPRINGS
SQ SQUARE
SRA SIERRA
ST SAINT
ST STREET
STA SANTA
STA STATION
TER TERRACE
THTR THEATER
TK TR TRUCK TRAIL
TR TRAIL
VIA D VIA DE
VIA D LS VIA DE LAS, VIA DE LOS
VIA DL VIA DEL
VIS VISTA
VLG VILLAGE
VLY VALLEY
VW VIEW
W WEST
WK WALK
WY WAY

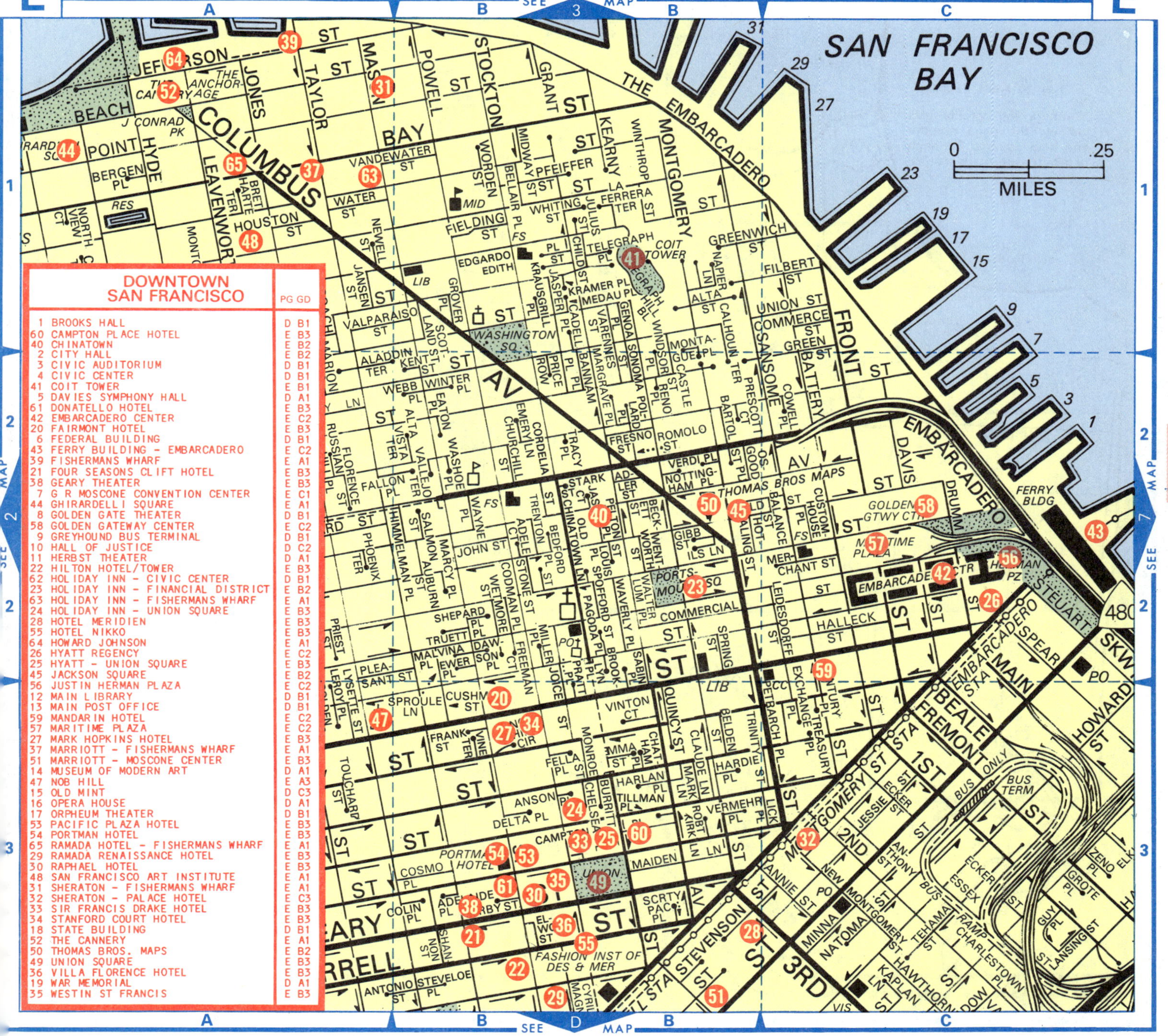

DOWNTOWN SAN FRANCISCO

		PG	GD
1	BROOKS HALL	D	B1
60	CAMPTON PLACE HOTEL	E	B3
40	CHINATOWN	E	B2
2	CITY HALL	E	B2
3	CIVIC AUDITORIUM	D	B1
4	CIVIC CENTER	D	B1
41	COIT TOWER	E	B1
5	DAVIES SYMPHONY HALL	D	A1
61	DONATELLO HOTEL	E	B3
42	EMBARCADERO CENTER	E	C2
20	FAIRMONT HOTEL	E	B3
6	FEDERAL BUILDING	D	B1
43	FERRY BUILDING - EMBARCADERO	E	C2
39	FISHERMANS WHARF	E	A1
21	FOUR SEASONS CLIFT HOTEL	E	B3
38	GEARY THEATER	E	B3
7	G R MOSCONE CONVENTION CENTER	E	C1
44	GHIRARDELLI SQUARE	E	A1
8	GOLDEN GATE THEATER	D	B1
58	GOLDEN GATEWAY CENTER	E	C2
9	GREYHOUND BUS TERMINAL	D	B1
10	HALL OF JUSTICE	D	C2
11	HERBST THEATER	D	A1
22	HILTON HOTEL/TOWER	E	B3
62	HOLIDAY INN - CIVIC CENTER	D	B1
23	HOLIDAY INN - FINANCIAL DISTRICT	E	B2
63	HOLIDAY INN - FISHERMANS WHARF	E	A1
24	HOLIDAY INN - UNION SQUARE	E	B3
28	HOTEL MERIDIEN	E	B3
55	HOTEL NIKKO	E	B3
64	HOWARD JOHNSON	E	A1
26	HYATT REGENCY	E	C2
25	HYATT - UNION SQUARE	E	B3
45	JACKSON SQUARE	E	B2
56	JUSTIN HERMAN PLAZA	E	C2
12	MAIN LIBRARY	D	B1
13	MAIN POST OFFICE	D	B1
59	MANDARIN HOTEL	E	C2
57	MARITIME PLAZA	E	C2
27	MARK HOPKINS HOTEL	E	B3
37	MARRIOTT - FISHERMANS WHARF	E	A1
51	MARRIOTT - MOSCONE CENTER	E	B3
14	MUSEUM OF MODERN ART	D	A1
47	NOB HILL	E	A3
15	OLD MINT	D	C3
16	OPERA HOUSE	D	A1
17	ORPHEUM THEATER	D	B1
53	PACIFIC PLAZA HOTEL	E	B3
54	PORTMAN HOTEL	E	B3
65	RAMADA HOTEL - FISHERMANS WHARF	E	A1
29	RAMADA RENAISSANCE HOTEL	E	B3
30	RAPHAEL HOTEL	E	B3
48	SAN FRANCISCO ART INSTITUTE	E	A1
31	SHERATON - FISHERMANS WHARF	E	A1
32	SHERATON - PALACE HOTEL	E	C3
33	SIR FRANCIS DRAKE HOTEL	E	B3
34	STANFORD COURT HOTEL	E	B3
18	STATE BUILDING	D	B1
52	THE CANNERY	E	A1
50	THOMAS BROS. MAPS	E	B2
49	UNION SQUARE	E	B3
36	VILLA FLORENCE HOTEL	E	B3
19	WAR MEMORIAL	D	A1
35	WESTIN ST FRANCIS	E	B3

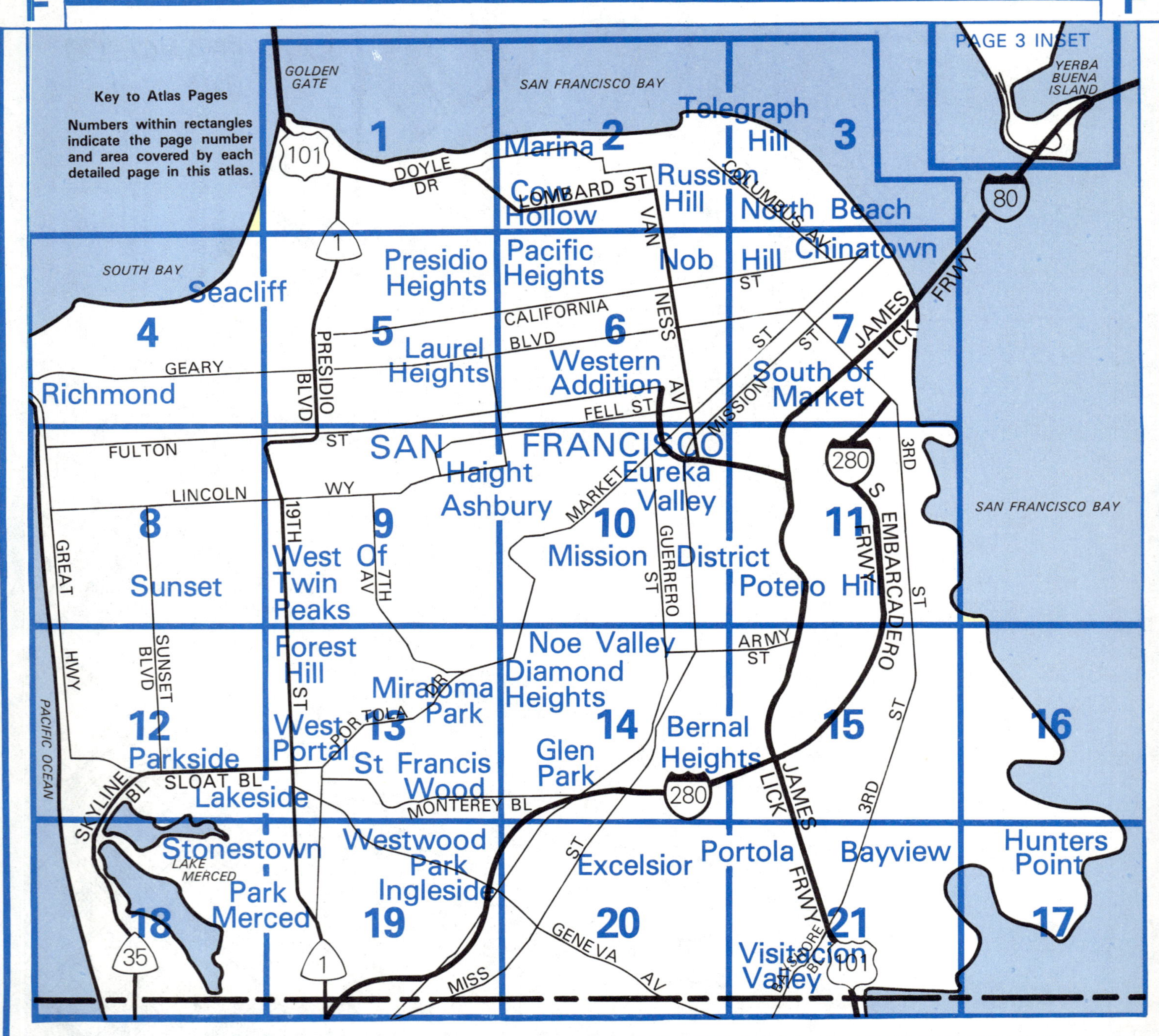
F
F
Key to Atlas Pages
Numbers within rectangles indicate the page number and area covered by each detailed page in this atlas.
PAGE 3 INSET
YERBA BUENA ISLAND
GOLDEN GATE
SAN FRANCISCO BAY
SOUTH BAY
PACIFIC OCEAN
LAKE MERCED
1
2
3
4
5
6
7
8
9
10
11
12
13
14
15
16
17
18
19
20
21
Marina
Telegraph Hill
Russian Hill
North Beach
Cow Hollow
Presidio Heights
Pacific Heights
Nob Hill
Chinatown
Seacliff
Laurel Heights
Western Addition
South of Market
Richmond
SAN FRANCISCO
Haight Ashbury
Eureka Valley
Sunset
West Of Twin Peaks
Mission District
Potero Hill
Forest Hill
Noe Valley
Diamond Heights
Miraloma Park
West Portal
St Francis Wood
Glen Park
Bernal Heights
Parkside
Lakeside
Stonestown
Park Merced
Westwood Park
Ingleside
Excelsior
Portola
Bayview
Hunters Point
Visitacion Valley
DOYLE DR
LOMBARD ST
VAN NESS AV
COLUMBUS AV
CALIFORNIA BLVD
GEARY
FELL ST
FULTON ST
LINCOLN WY
PRESIDIO BLVD
MISSION ST
MARKET ST
JAMES LICK FRWY
3RD ST
S EMBARCADERO
GUERRERO ST
19TH AV
7TH AV
ARMY ST
GREAT HWY
SUNSET BLVD
PORTOLA DR
SLOAT BL
SKYLINE BL
MONTEREY BL
GENEVA AV
MISS ST
BAYSHORE BL
101
1
80
280
35

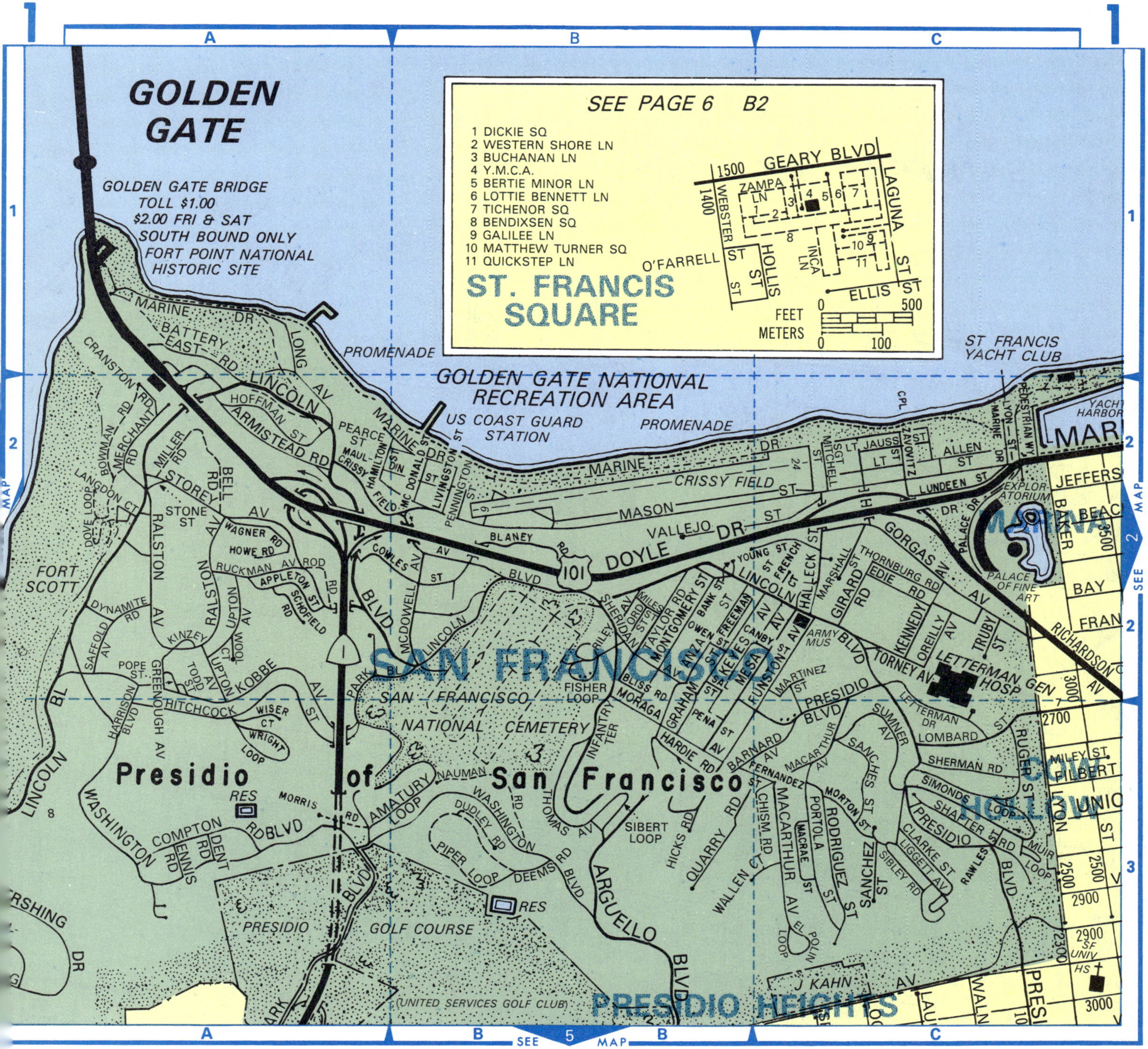
GOLDEN GATE
GOLDEN GATE BRIDGE
TOLL $1.00
$2.00 FRI & SAT
SOUTH BOUND ONLY
FORT POINT NATIONAL
HISTORIC SITE
SEE PAGE 6 B2
1 DICKIE SQ
2 WESTERN SHORE LN
3 BUCHANAN LN
4 Y.M.C.A.
5 BERTIE MINOR LN
6 LOTTIE BENNETT LN
7 TICHENOR SQ
8 BENDIXSEN SQ
9 GALILEE LN
10 MATTHEW TURNER SQ
11 QUICKSTEP LN
ST. FRANCIS SQUARE
GEARY BLVD
LAGUNA ST
WEBSTER ST
O'FARRELL ST
HOLLIS ST
ELLIS ST
FEET
METERS
ST FRANCIS YACHT CLUB
PROMENADE
GOLDEN GATE NATIONAL RECREATION AREA
US COAST GUARD STATION
MARINE DR
CRISSY FIELD
MASON ST
DOYLE DR
101
LINCOLN BLVD
SAN FRANCISCO
SAN FRANCISCO NATIONAL CEMETERY
Presidio of San Francisco
FORT SCOTT
PRESIDIO GOLF COURSE
(UNITED SERVICES GOLF CLUB)
PRESIDIO HEIGHTS
COW HOLLOW
MARINA
EXPLORATORIUM
PALACE OF FINE ART
LETTERMAN GEN HOSP
ARMY MUS
RICHARDSON AV
LOMBARD ST
ARGUELLO BLVD
PARK PRESIDIO BLVD
WASHINGTON BLVD
YACHT HARBOR
SF UNIV
SEE MAP 2
SEE MAP 5

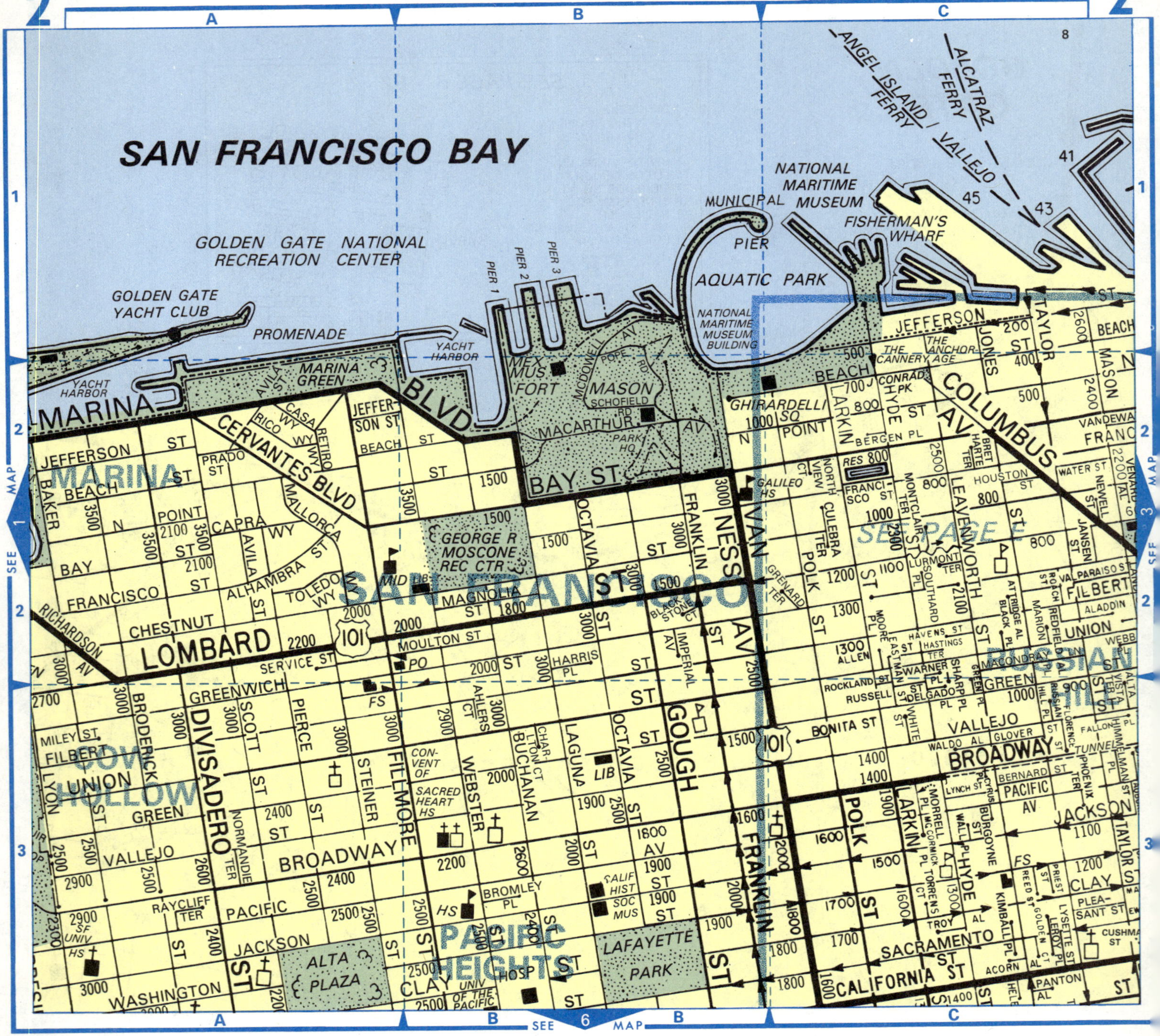
SAN FRANCISCO BAY
GOLDEN GATE NATIONAL RECREATION CENTER
GOLDEN GATE YACHT CLUB
PROMENADE
YACHT HARBOR
MARINA GREEN
MARINA BLVD
PIER 1
PIER 2
PIER 3
FORT MASON
MEX MUS
MACARTHUR AV
PARK HQ
MUNICIPAL PIER
AQUATIC PARK
NATIONAL MARITIME MUSEUM
NATIONAL MARITIME MUSEUM BUILDING
FISHERMAN'S WHARF
ANGEL ISLAND FERRY
ALCATRAZ FERRY
VALLEJO
GHIRARDELLI SQ
THE CANNERY
THE ANCHORAGE
COLUMBUS AV
MARINA
CERVANTES BLVD
GEORGE R MOSCONE REC CTR
SAN FRANCISCO
LOMBARD ST
RICHARDSON AV
SEE PAGE 1
RUSSIAN HILL
COW HOLLOW
BROADWAY
DIVISADERO
FILLMORE
VAN NESS AV
FRANKLIN
GOUGH
POLK
LARKIN
HYDE
LEAVENWORTH
CALIFORNIA ST
SACRAMENTO
PACIFIC HEIGHTS
LAFAYETTE PARK
ALTA PLAZA
CONVENT OF SACRED HEART HS
CALIF HIST SOC MUS
UNIV OF THE PACIFIC
SEE 6 MAP
SEE 1 MAP
SEE 3 MAP

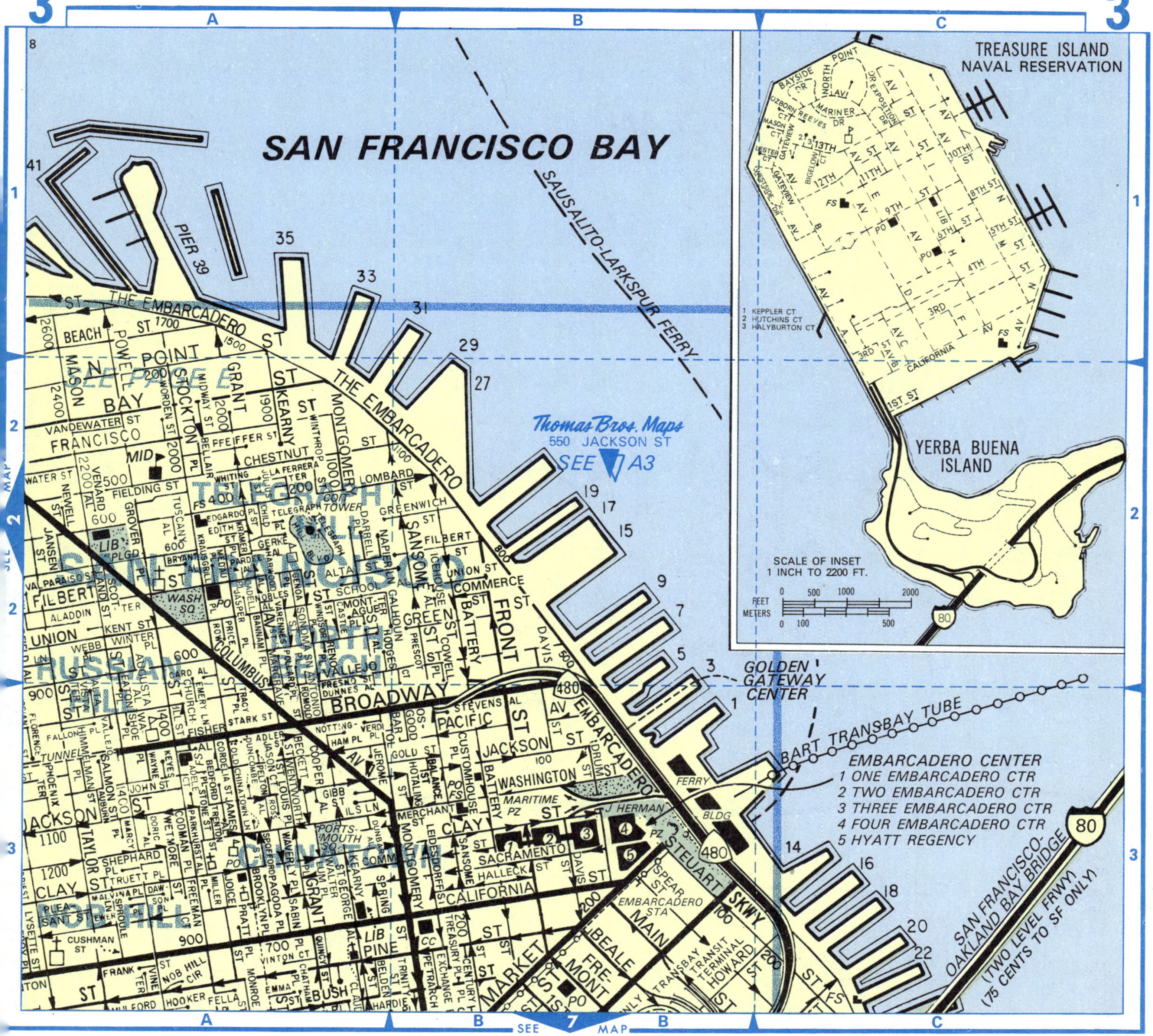
SAN FRANCISCO BAY
SAUSALITO-LARKSPUR FERRY
PIER 39
THE EMBARCADERO
Thomas Bros. Maps
550 JACKSON ST
SEE A3
TREASURE ISLAND NAVAL RESERVATION
YERBA BUENA ISLAND
1 KEPPLER CT
2 HUTCHINS CT
3 HALYBURTON CT
SCALE OF INSET
1 INCH TO 2200 FT.
FEET
METERS
GOLDEN GATEWAY CENTER
BART TRANSBAY TUBE
EMBARCADERO CENTER
1 ONE EMBARCADERO CTR
2 TWO EMBARCADERO CTR
3 THREE EMBARCADERO CTR
4 FOUR EMBARCADERO CTR
5 HYATT REGENCY
FERRY BLDG
SAN FRANCISCO-OAKLAND BAY BRIDGE
(TWO LEVEL FRWY)
(75 CENTS TO SF ONLY)
TELEGRAPH HILL
SAN FRANCISCO
NORTH BEACH
RUSSIAN HILL
CHINATOWN
NOB HILL
SEE PAGE E
BROADWAY
COLUMBUS
MARKET
CALIFORNIA
PACIFIC
JACKSON
WASHINGTON
CLAY
SACRAMENTO
PINE
BUSH
LOMBARD
GREENWICH
FILBERT
UNION
VALLEJO
GREEN
CHESTNUT
FRANCISCO
BAY
NORTH POINT
BEACH
TRANSBAY TRANSIT TERMINAL
EMBARCADERO STA
STEUART
SKWY
SEE 7 MAP

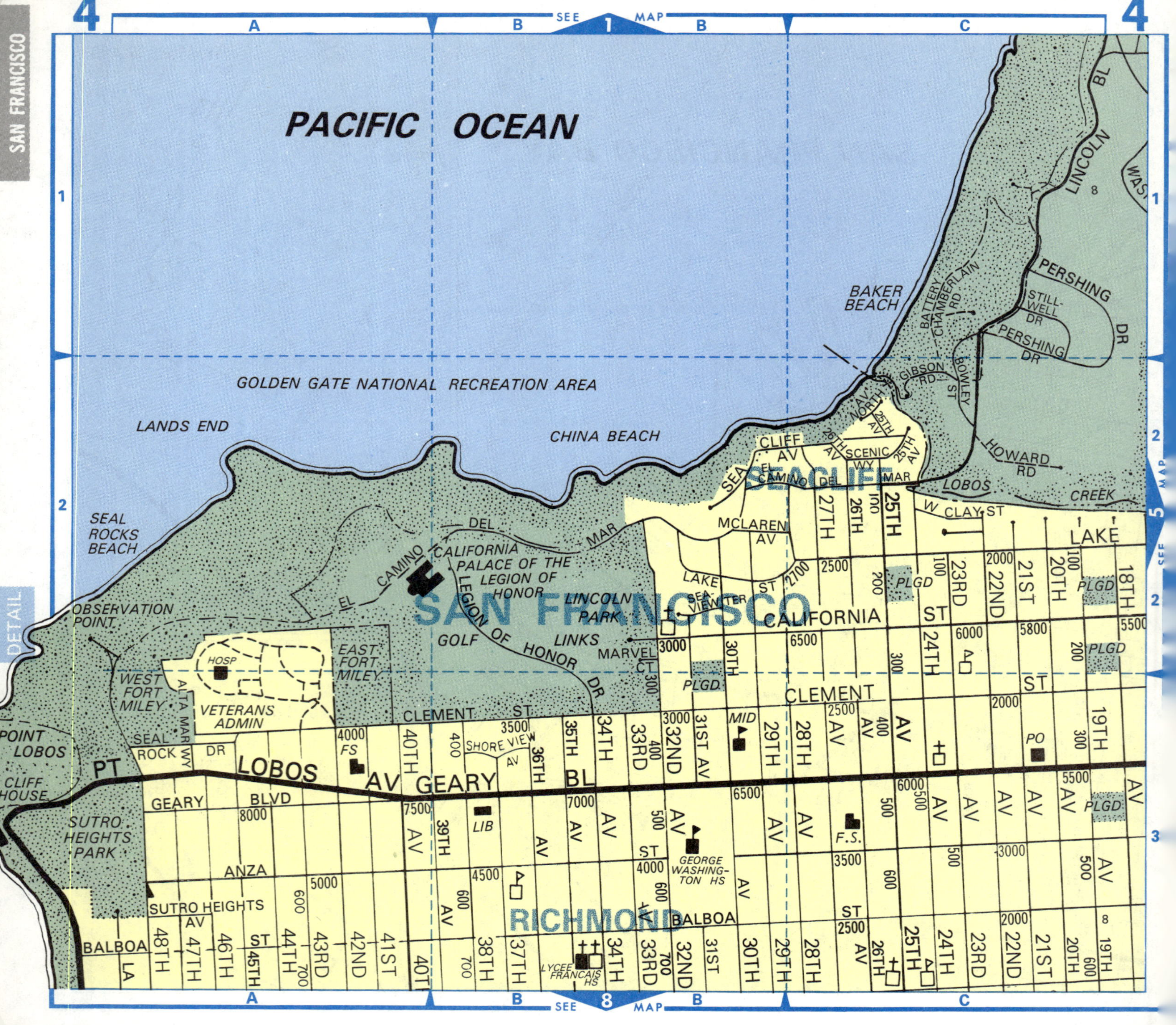
SAN FRANCISCO
PACIFIC OCEAN
GOLDEN GATE NATIONAL RECREATION AREA
LANDS END
CHINA BEACH
BAKER BEACH
SEAL ROCKS BEACH
OBSERVATION POINT
POINT LOBOS
CLIFF HOUSE
SUTRO HEIGHTS PARK
WEST FORT MILEY
EAST FORT MILEY
VETERANS ADMIN
HOSP
CALIFORNIA PALACE OF THE LEGION OF HONOR
LINCOLN PARK
GOLF
LINKS
SEACLIFF
SAN FRANCISCO
RICHMOND
GEORGE WASHINGTON HS
LYCEE FRANCAIS HS
LIB
MID
FS
F.S.
PO
PLGD
EL CAMINO DEL MAR
LEGION OF HONOR DR
PT LOBOS AV
GEARY BL
GEARY BLVD
CLEMENT ST
CALIFORNIA ST
LAKE ST
ANZA ST
BALBOA ST
SUTRO HEIGHTS AV
SEAL ROCK DR
ALTA MAR WY
SHORE VIEW AV
SEA VIEW TER
MARVEL CT
MCLAREN AV
CLIFF AV
SCENIC WY
SEA CLIFF AV
W CLAY ST
LOBOS CREEK
PERSHING DR
STILLWELL DR
BATTERY CHAMBERLAIN RD
GIBSON RD
BOWLEY ST
HOWARD RD
LINCOLN BL
WASH
48TH
47TH
46TH
45TH
44TH
43RD
42ND
41ST
40TH
39TH
38TH
37TH
36TH
35TH
34TH
33RD
32ND
31ST
30TH
29TH
28TH
27TH
26TH
25TH
24TH
23RD
22ND
21ST
20TH
19TH
18TH
LA
SEE MAP 1
SEE MAP 5
SEE MAP 8
DETAIL

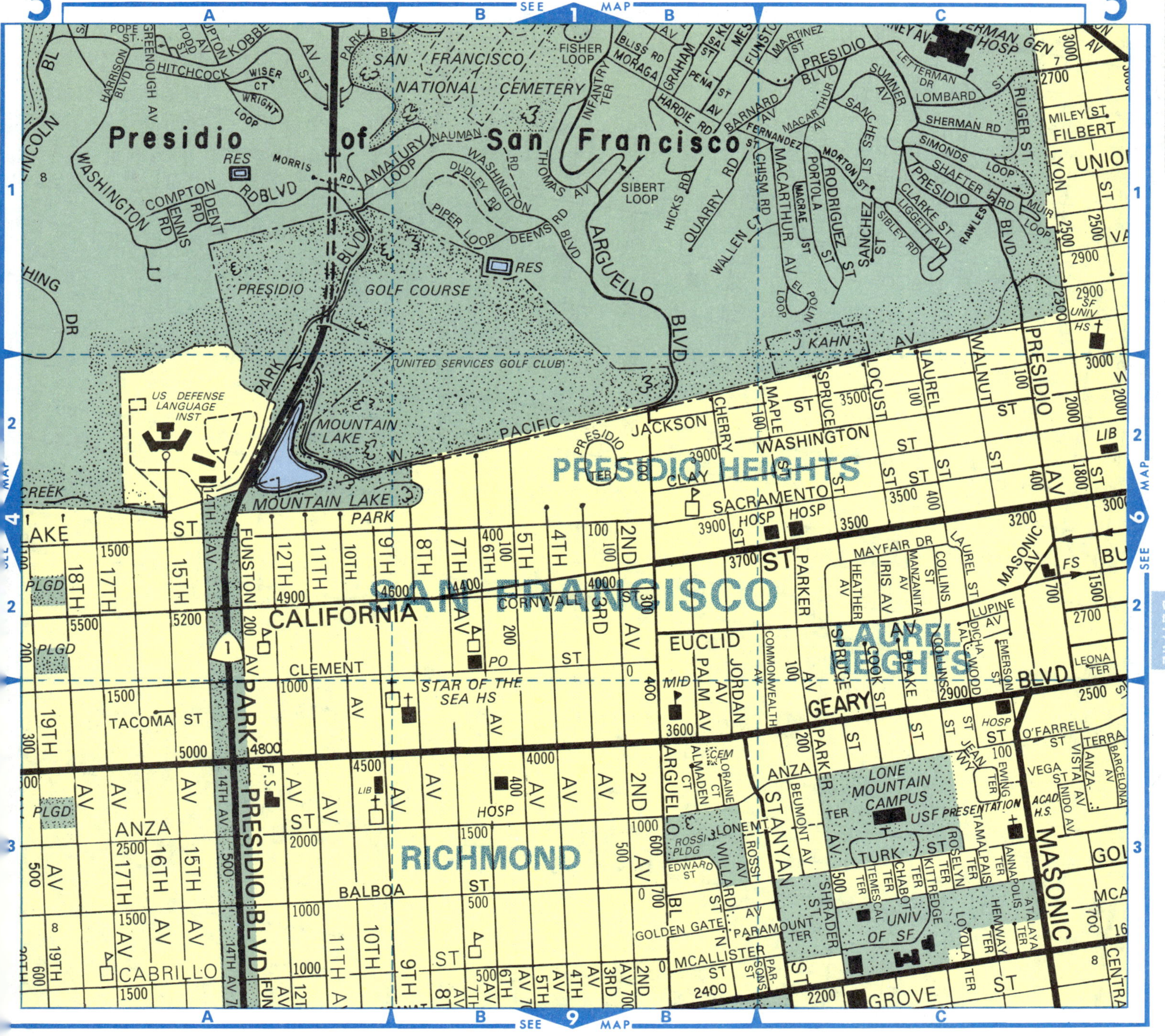

SEE 1 MAP
SEE 9 MAP
SEE 4 MAP
SEE 6 MAP

DETAIL

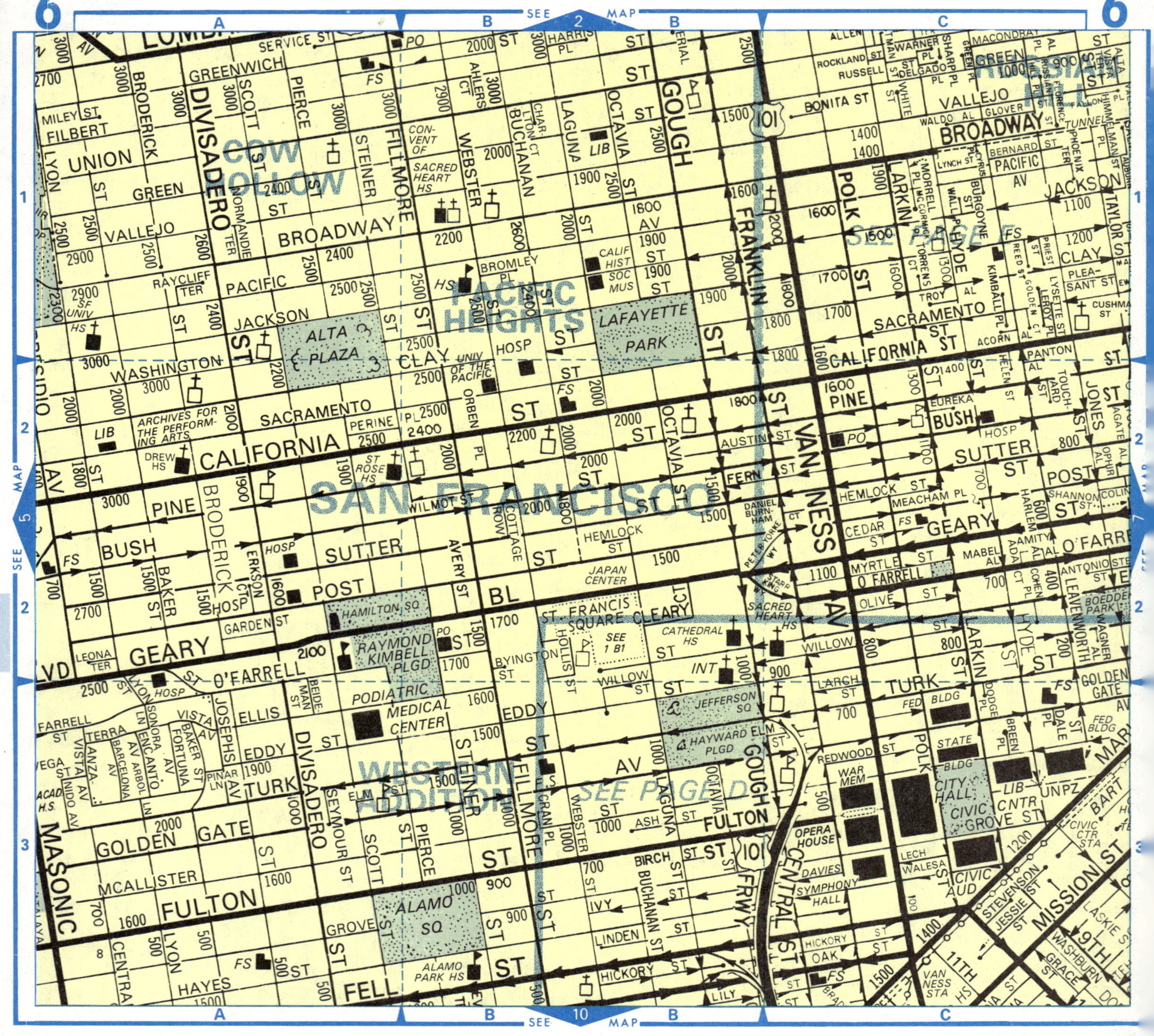
SEE MAP 2
SEE MAP 10
SEE MAP 5
SEE MAP 7
A
B
C
1
2
3
DETAIL
COW HOLLOW
PACIFIC HEIGHTS
SAN FRANCISCO
WESTERN ADDITION
RUSSIAN HILL
SEE PAGE F
SEE PAGE D
SEE 1 B1
ALTA PLAZA
LAFAYETTE PARK
HAMILTON SQ
RAYMOND KIMBELL PLGD
JEFFERSON SQ
HAYWARD PLGD
ALAMO SQ
CIVIC CNTR
CIVIC CTR STA
VAN NESS STA
CITY HALL
OPERA HOUSE
WAR MEM
DAVIES SYMPHONY HALL
CIVIC AUD
UNPZ
BART
PODIATRIC MEDICAL CENTER
JAPAN CENTER
ST FRANCIS SQUARE
CATHEDRAL HS
SACRED HEART HS
CONVENT OF SACRED HEART HS
CALIF HIST SOC MUS
UNIV OF THE PACIFIC
ARCHIVES FOR THE PERFORMING ARTS
ALAMO PARK HS
SF UNIV HS
DREW HS
ST ROSE HS
LOMBARD
GREENWICH
FILBERT
UNION
GREEN
VALLEJO
BROADWAY
PACIFIC
JACKSON
WASHINGTON
CLAY
SACRAMENTO
CALIFORNIA
PINE
BUSH
SUTTER
POST
GEARY BL
O'FARRELL
ELLIS
EDDY
TURK
GOLDEN GATE
McALLISTER
FULTON
GROVE
HAYES
FELL
DIVISADERO
BRODERICK
SCOTT
PIERCE
STEINER
FILLMORE
WEBSTER
BUCHANAN
LAGUNA
OCTAVIA
GOUGH
FRANKLIN
VAN NESS AV
POLK
LARKIN
HYDE
LEAVENWORTH
JONES
TAYLOR
MASONIC
LYON
BAKER
MISSION
MARKET
CENTRAL FRWY
101

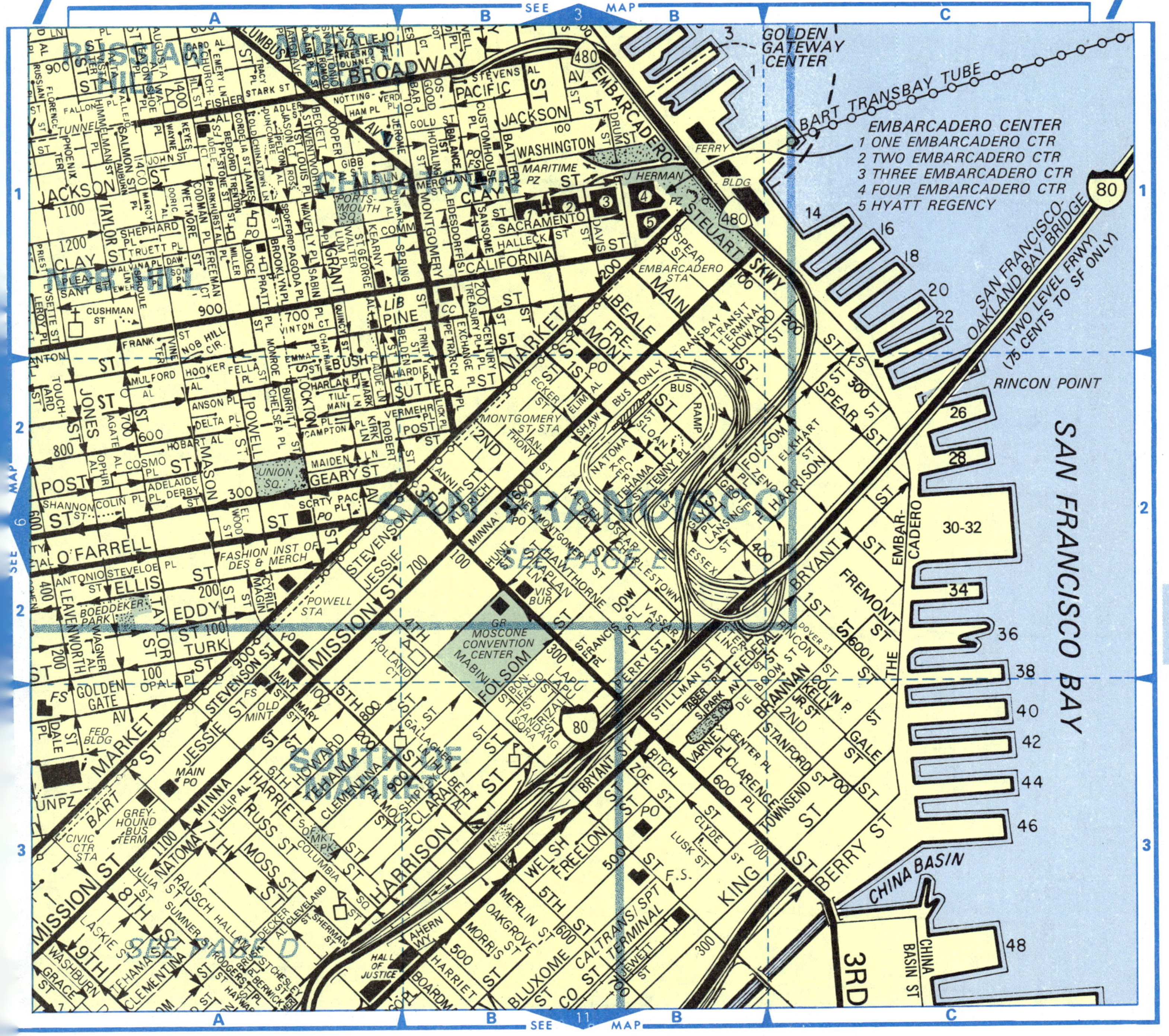
7
A
B
SEE 3 MAP
C
SAN FRANCISCO
GOLDEN GATEWAY CENTER
BART TRANSBAY TUBE
EMBARCADERO CENTER
1 ONE EMBARCADERO CTR
2 TWO EMBARCADERO CTR
3 THREE EMBARCADERO CTR
4 FOUR EMBARCADERO CTR
5 HYATT REGENCY
80
SAN FRANCISCO-OAKLAND BAY BRIDGE
(TWO LEVEL FRWY)
(75 CENTS TO SF ONLY)
RINCON POINT
SAN FRANCISCO BAY
CHINA BASIN
RUSSIAN HILL
NOB HILL
CHINATOWN
SAN FRANCISCO
SOUTH OF MARKET
SEE PAGE E
SEE PAGE D
BROADWAY
PACIFIC
JACKSON
WASHINGTON
CLAY
SACRAMENTO
CALIFORNIA
PINE
BUSH
SUTTER
POST
GEARY ST
O'FARRELL
ELLIS
EDDY
TURK
GOLDEN GATE
MARKET
MISSION
HOWARD
FOLSOM
HARRISON
BRYANT
BRANNAN
TOWNSEND
KING
BERRY ST
EMBARCADERO
STEUART
SPEAR
MAIN
BEALE
FREMONT
1ST
2ND
3RD
4TH
5TH
6TH
7TH
8TH
9TH
JONES
TAYLOR
MASON
POWELL
STOCKTON
GRANT
KEARNY
MONTGOMERY
SANSOME
BATTERY
FRONT
DAVIS
DRUMM
TRANSBAY TRANSIT TERMINAL
MOSCONE CONVENTION CENTER
UNION SQ.
PORTSMOUTH SQ.
FERRY BLDG
MARITIME PZ
J HERMAN PZ
EMBARCADERO STA
MONTGOMERY ST STA
POWELL STA
CIVIC CTR STA
GREYHOUND BUS TERM
MAIN PO
FED BLDG
OLD MINT
HALL OF JUSTICE
CALTRANS/SPT TERMINAL
FASHION INST OF DES & MERCH
14
16
18
20
22
26
28
30-32
34
36
38
40
42
44
46
48
1
2
3
SEE 6 MAP
SEE 11 MAP
DETAIL

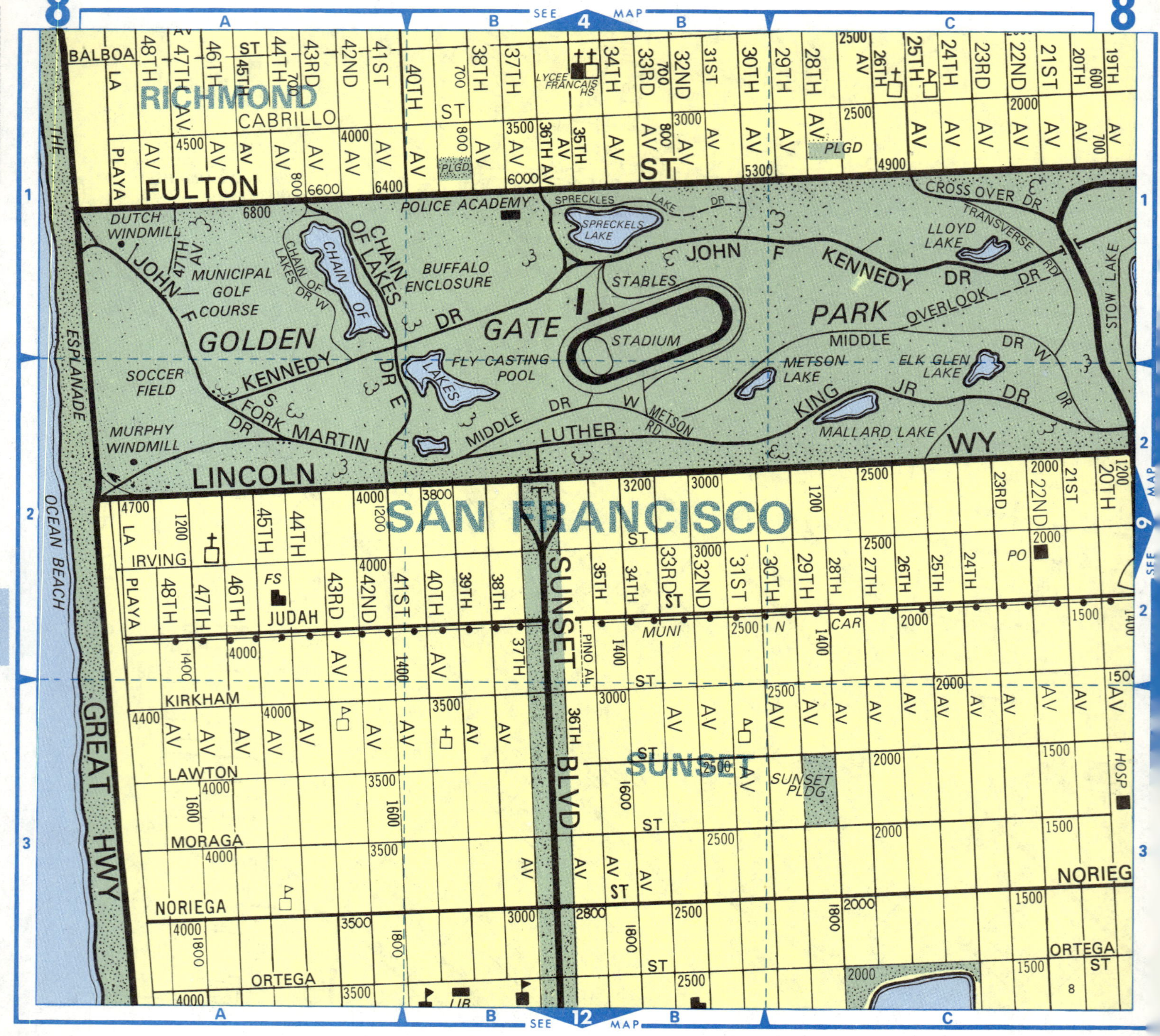
8
8
SEE 4 MAP
SEE 12 MAP
SEE 9 MAP
DETAIL
A
B
C
1
2
3
RICHMOND
SAN FRANCISCO
SUNSET
BALBOA
CABRILLO
FULTON
ST
PLAYA
LA
48TH
47TH
46TH
45TH
44TH
43RD
42ND
41ST
40TH
38TH
37TH
36TH AV
35TH
34TH
33RD
32ND
31ST
30TH
29TH
28TH
26TH
25TH
24TH
23RD
22ND
21ST
20TH
19TH
AV
LYCEE FRANCAIS HS
PLGD
GOLDEN GATE PARK
JOHN F KENNEDY DR
MARTIN LUTHER KING JR DR
DUTCH WINDMILL
MURPHY WINDMILL
MUNICIPAL GOLF COURSE
SOCCER FIELD
CHAIN OF LAKES
CHAIN OF LAKES DR W
CHAIN OF LAKES DR E
BUFFALO ENCLOSURE
POLICE ACADEMY
SPRECKLES LAKE
SPRECKLES LAKE DR
STABLES
STADIUM
FLY CASTING POOL
LAKES
METSON LAKE
METSON RD
MIDDLE DR W
MIDDLE DR
S FORK DR
CROSS OVER DR
TRANSVERSE RD
LLOYD LAKE
OVERLOOK DR
ELK GLEN LAKE
MALLARD LAKE
STOW LAKE DR
WY
THE ESPLANADE
OCEAN BEACH
GREAT HWY
LINCOLN
IRVING
JUDAH
KIRKHAM
LAWTON
MORAGA
NORIEGA
ORTEGA
SUNSET BLVD
PINO AL
MUNI N CAR
SUNSET PLDG
FS
PO
HOSP
LIB

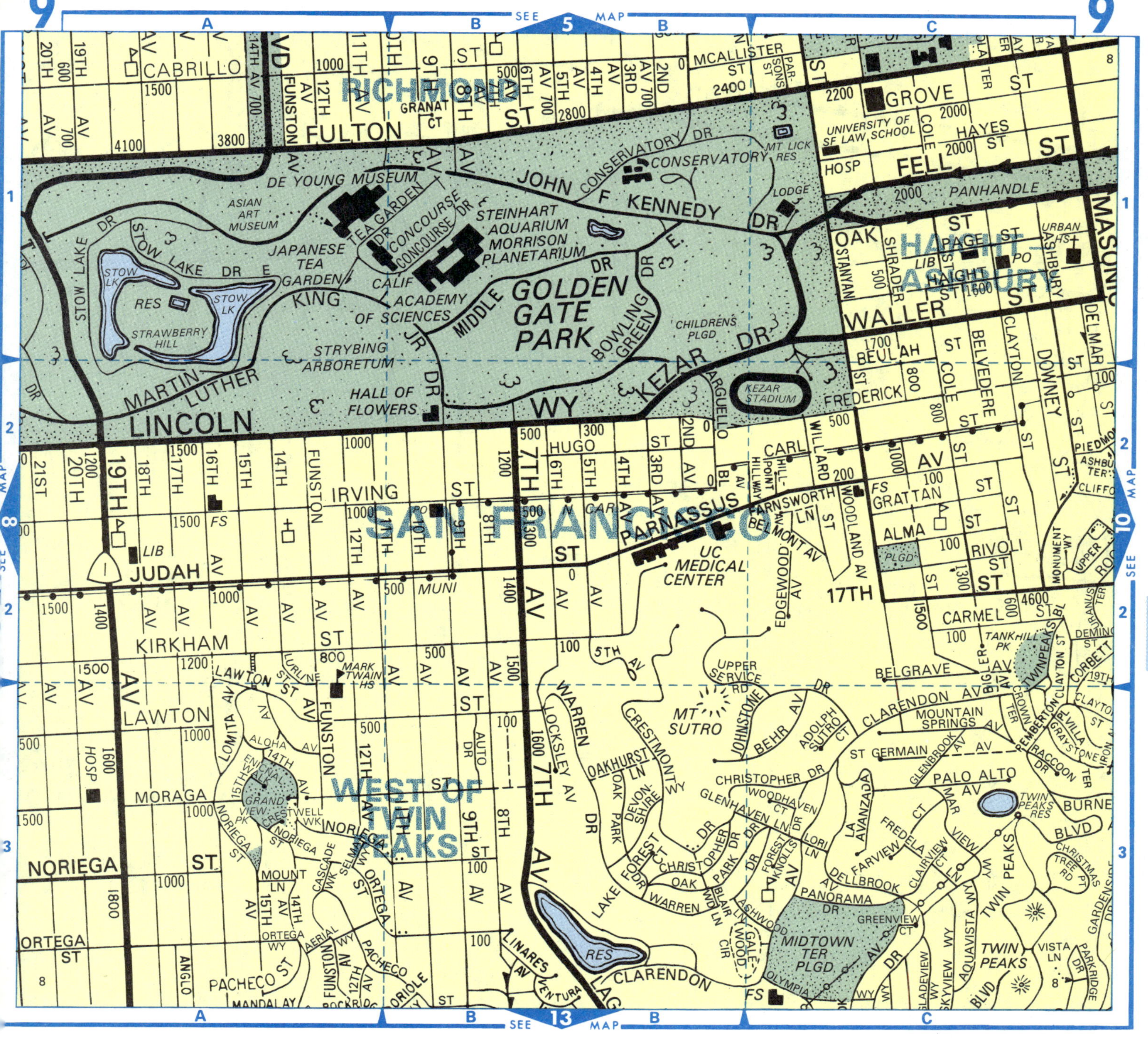

SEE MAP 5
SEE MAP 13
SEE MAP 8
SEE MAP 10
SAN FRANCISCO
DETAIL
RICHMOND
GOLDEN GATE PARK
HAIGHT-ASHBURY
SAN FRANCISCO
WEST OF TWIN PEAKS
FULTON
LINCOLN
JUDAH
KIRKHAM
LAWTON
MORAGA
NORIEGA
ORTEGA
IRVING
PARNASSUS
JOHN F KENNEDY DR
MARTIN LUTHER KING JR DR
KEZAR DR
DE YOUNG MUSEUM
ASIAN ART MUSEUM
JAPANESE TEA GARDEN
STEINHART AQUARIUM
MORRISON PLANETARIUM
CALIF ACADEMY OF SCIENCES
STRYBING ARBORETUM
HALL OF FLOWERS
CONSERVATORY
KEZAR STADIUM
STRAWBERRY HILL
STOW LAKE DR
CHILDRENS PLGD
UNIVERSITY OF SF LAW SCHOOL
UC MEDICAL CENTER
MT SUTRO
MIDTOWN TER PLGD
TWIN PEAKS
TWIN PEAKS RES
TANK HILL PK
GROVE
HAYES
FELL
OAK
PAGE
HAIGHT
WALLER
FREDERICK
CARL
GRATTAN
ALMA
RIVOLI
17TH
CARMEL
CLARENDON AV
PALO ALTO AV
PANORAMA DR
LAGUNA HONDA BLVD
19TH AV
7TH AV

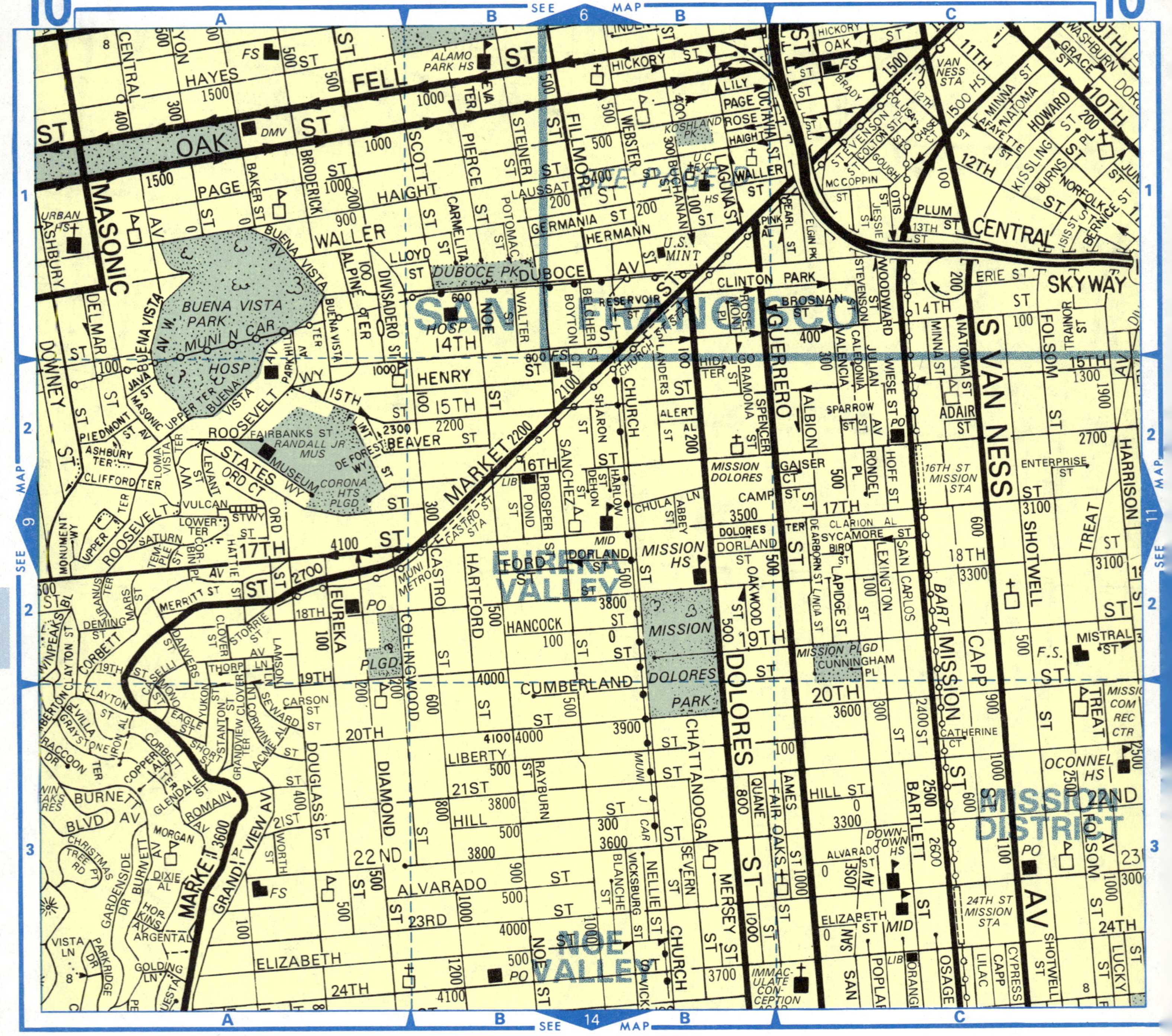

SEE 6 MAP
SEE 14 MAP
SEE 9 MAP
SEE 11 MAP
A
B
C
1
2
3
HAYES ST
FELL ST
OAK ST
DMV
ALAMO PARK HS
FS
PAGE ST
HAIGHT ST
WALLER ST
MASONIC
CENTRAL
ASHBURY
URBAN HS
BAKER ST
BRODERICK
DIVISADERO ST
SCOTT ST
PIERCE ST
STEINER ST
FILLMORE ST
WEBSTER ST
BUCHANAN
LAGUNA ST
OCTAVIA ST
HICKORY
LILY
ROSE
HAIGHT
KOSHLAND PK
U C EXT
HERMANN
GERMANIA ST
LAUSSAT
U.S. MINT
DUBOCE PK
DUBOCE AV
LLOYD
ALPINE TER
CARMELITA
POTOMAC
BUENA VISTA PARK
BUENA VISTA AV W.
MUNI N CAR
HOSP
SAN FRANCISCO
NOE
WALTER
BOYTON
BELCHER
RESERVOIR
CLINTON PARK
BROSNAN
14TH
15TH
HENRY
ROOSEVELT
BEAVER
FAIRBANKS ST
RANDALL JR MUS
MUSEUM WY
STATES ST
CORONA HTS PLGD
DE FOREST WY
FLINT
MARKET
16TH
LIB
PROSPER
SANCHEZ
CHURCH
DOLORES
GUERRERO
VALENCIA
JULIAN
MISSION
S VAN NESS
FOLSOM
HARRISON
SHOTWELL
TREAT
CAPP
NATOMA
MINNA ST
SKYWAY
ERIE ST
CENTRAL
VAN NESS STA
11TH
12TH
13TH
10TH
HOWARD
KISSLING
MCCOPPIN
PLUM
ALBION
SPARROW
ADAIR
ALERT AL
HIDALGO TER
RAMONA
SPENCER
MISSION DOLORES
GAISER CT
CAMP
17TH
CLARION AL
SYCAMORE
16TH ST MISSION STA
ENTERPRISE ST
CHULA
ABBEY
DORLAND
MISSION HS
EUREKA VALLEY
CASTRO
CASTRO ST STA
17TH
ORD CT
CLIFFORD TER
VULCAN STWY
LOWER TER
SATURN
MUNI METRO
HARTFORD
FORD
DOLORES
18TH
LEXINGTON
SAN CARLOS
BART
PO
EUREKA
DOUGLASS
DIAMOND
COLLINGWOOD
HANCOCK
MISSION DOLORES PARK
19TH
MISSION PLGD
CUNNINGHAM PL
MISTRAL
F.S.
CUMBERLAND
20TH
CORBETT
CLAYTON
DEMING
MERRITT ST
PLGD
LIBERTY
CATHERINE CT
MISSION COM REC CTR
OCONNEL HS
21ST
HILL
RAYBURN
CHATTANOOGA
FAIR OAKS
QUANE
AMES
HILL ST
BARTLETT
22ND
MISSION DISTRICT
22 ND
DOWNTOWN HS
ALVARADO
23RD
VICKSBURG
BLANCHE
NELLIE
SEVERN
MERSEY ST
ELIZABETH
MID
24TH ST MISSION STA
24TH
NOE VALLEY
IMMACULATE CONCEPTION
POPLAR
ORANGE
OSAGE
LILAC
CYPRESS
LUCKY
GRAND VIEW AV
MARKET
BURNETT AV
ROMAIN
GLENDALE
DIXIE AL
GARDENSIDE DR
PARKRIDGE DR
GOLDING LN
VISTA LN
ARGENTAL
HOPKINS AV
DOWNEY
PIEDMONT
DELMAR
UPPER TER

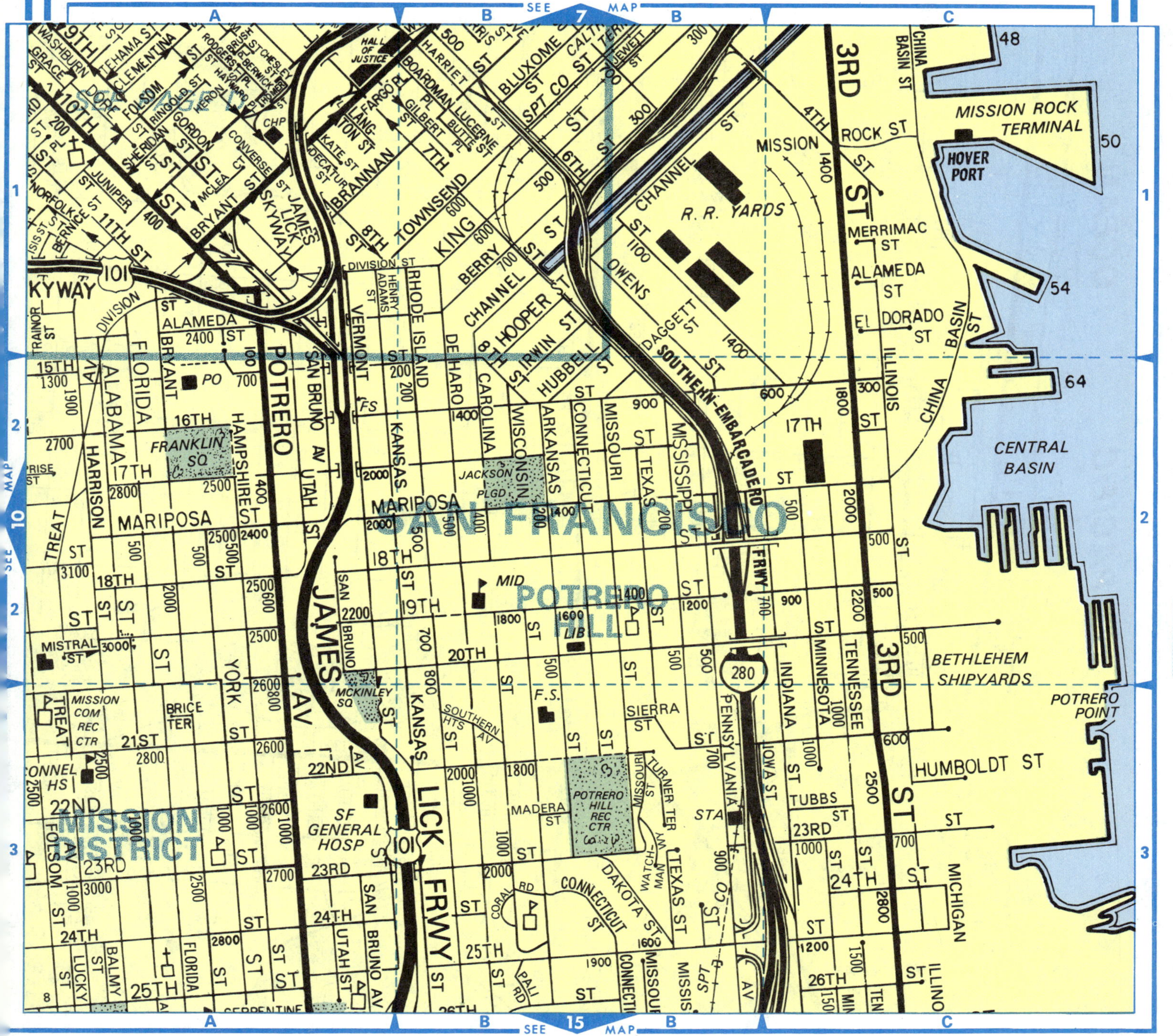
SEE MAP 7
SEE MAP 15
SEE MAP 10
SAN FRANCISCO
DETAIL
SAN FRANCISCO
POTRERO HILL
MISSION DISTRICT
MISSION ROCK TERMINAL
HOVER PORT
R. R. YARDS
CENTRAL BASIN
BETHLEHEM SHIPYARDS
POTRERO POINT
CHINA BASIN ST
3RD ST
SOUTHERN EMBARCADERO FRWY
JAMES LICK FRWY
JAMES LICK SKYWAY
POTRERO AV
FRANKLIN SQ
JACKSON PLGD
MCKINLEY SQ
POTRERO HILL REC CTR
SF GENERAL HOSP
HALL OF JUSTICE
MISSION COM REC CTR
MID
LIB
STA
PO
CHP
F.S.
101
280
HUMBOLDT ST
MARIPOSA
TOWNSEND
KING
BRANNAN
BRYANT
CHANNEL
DIVISION ST
ALAMEDA ST
16TH
17TH
18TH
19TH
20TH
21ST
22ND
23RD
24TH
25TH
26TH

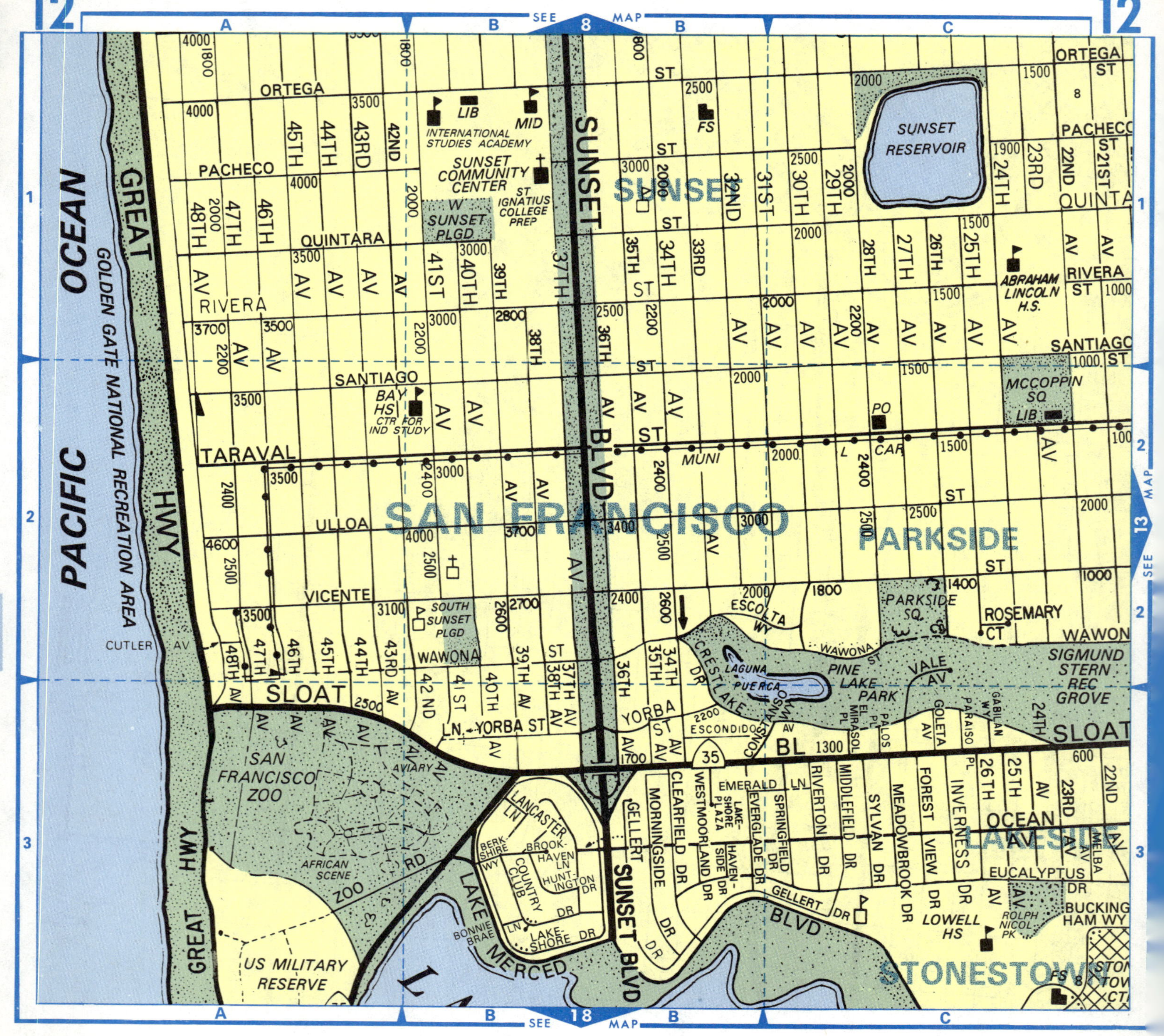
SEE 8 MAP
A
B
B
C
PACIFIC
OCEAN
GOLDEN GATE NATIONAL RECREATION AREA
GREAT HWY
ORTEGA
PACHECO
QUINTARA
RIVERA
SANTIAGO
TARAVAL
ULLOA
VICENTE
WAWONA
SLOAT
CUTLER AV
48TH
47TH
46TH
45TH
44TH
43RD
42ND
41ST
40TH
39TH
38TH
37TH
36TH
35TH
34TH
33RD
32ND
31ST
30TH
29TH
28TH
27TH
26TH
25TH
24TH
23RD
22ND
21ST
AV
ST
LIB
MID
INTERNATIONAL STUDIES ACADEMY
SUNSET COMMUNITY CENTER
ST IGNATIUS COLLEGE PREP
W SUNSET PLGD
FS
SUNSET
SUNSET RESERVOIR
SUNSET BLVD
ABRAHAM LINCOLN H.S.
MCCOPPIN SQ
LIB
PO
BAY HS
CTR FOR IND STUDY
MUNI
L CAR
SAN FRANCISCO
PARKSIDE
SOUTH SUNSET PLGD
ESCOLTA WY
PARKSIDE SQ
ROSEMARY CT
SIGMUND STERN REC GROVE
PINE LAKE PARK
LAGUNA PUERCA
CRESTLAKE DR
VALE AV
YORBA ST
ESCONDIDO
CONSTANSO WY
EL MIRASOL PL
PALOS PL
GOLETA AV
PARAISO PL
GABILAN WY
SLOAT BL
35
SAN FRANCISCO ZOO
AVIARY
AFRICAN SCENE
ZOO RD
US MILITARY RESERVE
LAKE MERCED
LANCASTER LN
BERKSHIRE WY
BROOKHAVEN LN
COUNTRY CLUB DR
HUNTINGTON DR
BONNIE BRAE LN
LAKESHORE DR
GELLERT
MORNINGSIDE DR
CLEARFIELD DR
WESTMOORLAND DR
EMERALD LN
LAKESHORE PLAZA
LAKESIDE DR
HAVENSIDE DR
EVERGLADE DR
SPRINGFIELD DR
RIVERTON DR
MIDDLEFIELD DR
SYLVAN DR
MEADOWBROOK DR
FOREST VIEW DR
INVERNESS DR
LOWELL HS
GELLERT BLVD
OCEAN AV
LAKESIDE
EUCALYPTUS DR
MELBA AV
BUCKINGHAM WY
ROLPH NICOL PK
STONESTOWN
FS 8
SEE 13 MAP
SEE 18 MAP

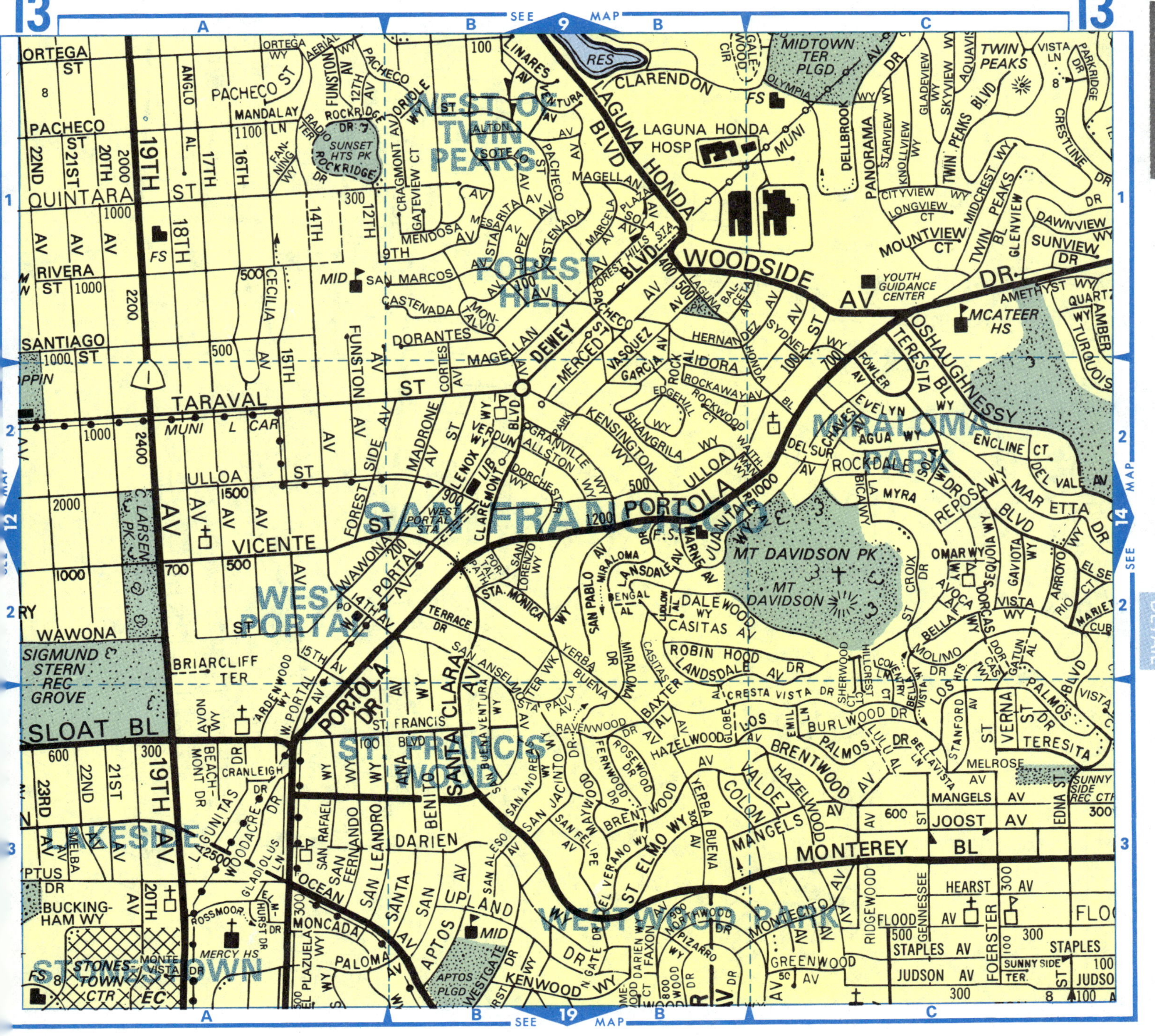
SEE MAP 9
SEE MAP 19
SEE MAP 14
SEE MAP 12
DETAIL
A
B
C
WEST OF TWIN PEAKS
FOREST HILL
MIRALOMA PARK
SAN FRANCISCO
WEST PORTAL
ST. FRANCIS WOOD
WESTWOOD PARK
LAKESIDE
STONESTOWN
MIDTOWN TER PLGD
LAGUNA HONDA HOSP
YOUTH GUIDANCE CENTER
MCATEER HS
MT DAVIDSON PK
MT DAVIDSON
SIGMUND STERN REC GROVE
SUNNY SIDE REC CTR
APTOS PLGD
MERCY HS
SUNSET HTS PK
RES
ORTEGA ST
PACHECO ST
QUINTARA ST
RIVERA ST
SANTIAGO ST
TARAVAL ST
ULLOA ST
VICENTE ST
WAWONA
SLOAT BL
19TH AV
LAGUNA HONDA BLVD
WOODSIDE AV
PORTOLA DR
O'SHAUGHNESSY BL
MONTEREY BL
OCEAN AV
JUNIPERO SERRA
DEWEY BLVD
CLARENDON
MAGELLAN
DORANTES
CASTENADA
SAN MARCOS
TWIN PEAKS BLVD
MUNI
MUNI L CAR
JOOST AV
MANGELS AV
HEARST AV
FLOOD AV
STAPLES AV
JUDSON AV
BRENTWOOD AV
HAZELWOOD AV
ROBIN HOOD DR
DALEWOOD WY
SANTA CLARA AV
SAN FERNANDO
SAN LEANDRO
UPLAND DR
KENWOOD WY
PLYMOUTH AV
TERESITA BL
REPOSA WY
MAR ETTA DR
GAVIOTA WY
MYRA WY
ROCKDALE DR
KENSINGTON WY
WEST PORTAL STA
FOREST HILLS STA
FS
MID

SEE MAP 10

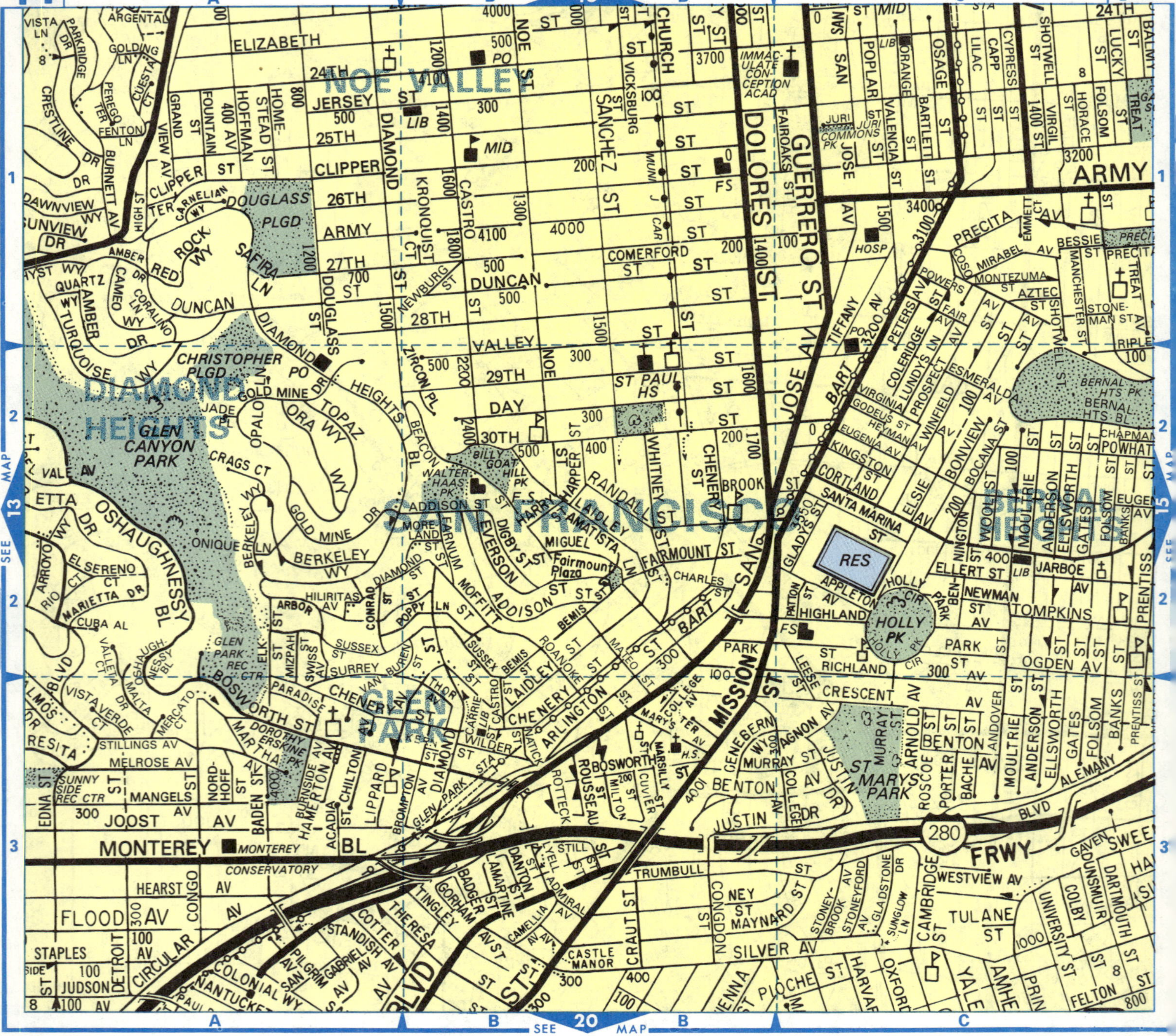

A B B C

NOE VALLEY
DIAMOND HEIGHTS
GLEN CANYON PARK
SAN FRANCISCO
GLEN PARK
BERNAL HEIGHTS
HOLLY PK
ST MARYS PARK
DOUGLASS PLGD
CHRISTOPHER PLGD
BILLY GOAT HILL PK
WALTER HAAS PK
GLEN PARK REC CTR
SUNNYSIDE REC CTR
BERNAL HTS PK
JURI COMMONS PK
FAIRMOUNT PLAZA
RES
IMMACULATE CONCEPTION ACAD
ST PAUL HS
MONTEREY
CONSERVATORY

ELIZABETH ST
24TH ST
JERSEY ST
25TH ST
CLIPPER ST
26TH ST
ARMY ST
27TH ST
DUNCAN ST
28TH ST
VALLEY ST
29TH ST
DAY ST
30TH ST
CHURCH ST
SANCHEZ ST
NOE ST
CASTRO ST
DIAMOND ST
DOUGLASS ST
DOLORES ST
GUERRERO ST
SAN JOSE AV
MISSION ST
VALENCIA ST
BARTLETT ST
OSAGE ST
HOFFMAN AV
FOUNTAIN ST
GRAND VIEW AV
DIAMOND HEIGHTS BL
GOLD MINE DR
CHENERY ST
BOSWORTH ST
MONTEREY BL
280 FRWY
ALEMANY BLVD
PRECITA AV
CORTLAND AV
HOLLY PARK CIR
RICHLAND AV
CRESCENT AV
OGDEN AV
SILVER AV
CIRCULAR AV
O'SHAUGHNESSY BL
PORTOLA DR
RANDALL ST
MIGUEL ST
FAIRMOUNT ST
BEMIS ST
ARLINGTON ST
JUSTIN DR
TRUMBULL ST
HEARST AV
FLOOD AV
JOOST AV
MANGELS AV
MELROSE AV
STAPLES AV
JUDSON AV
TULANE ST
FELTON ST
WESTVIEW AV

1 2 3

SEE MAP 13

SEE MAP 15

DETAIL

SEE MAP 20

A B B C

15

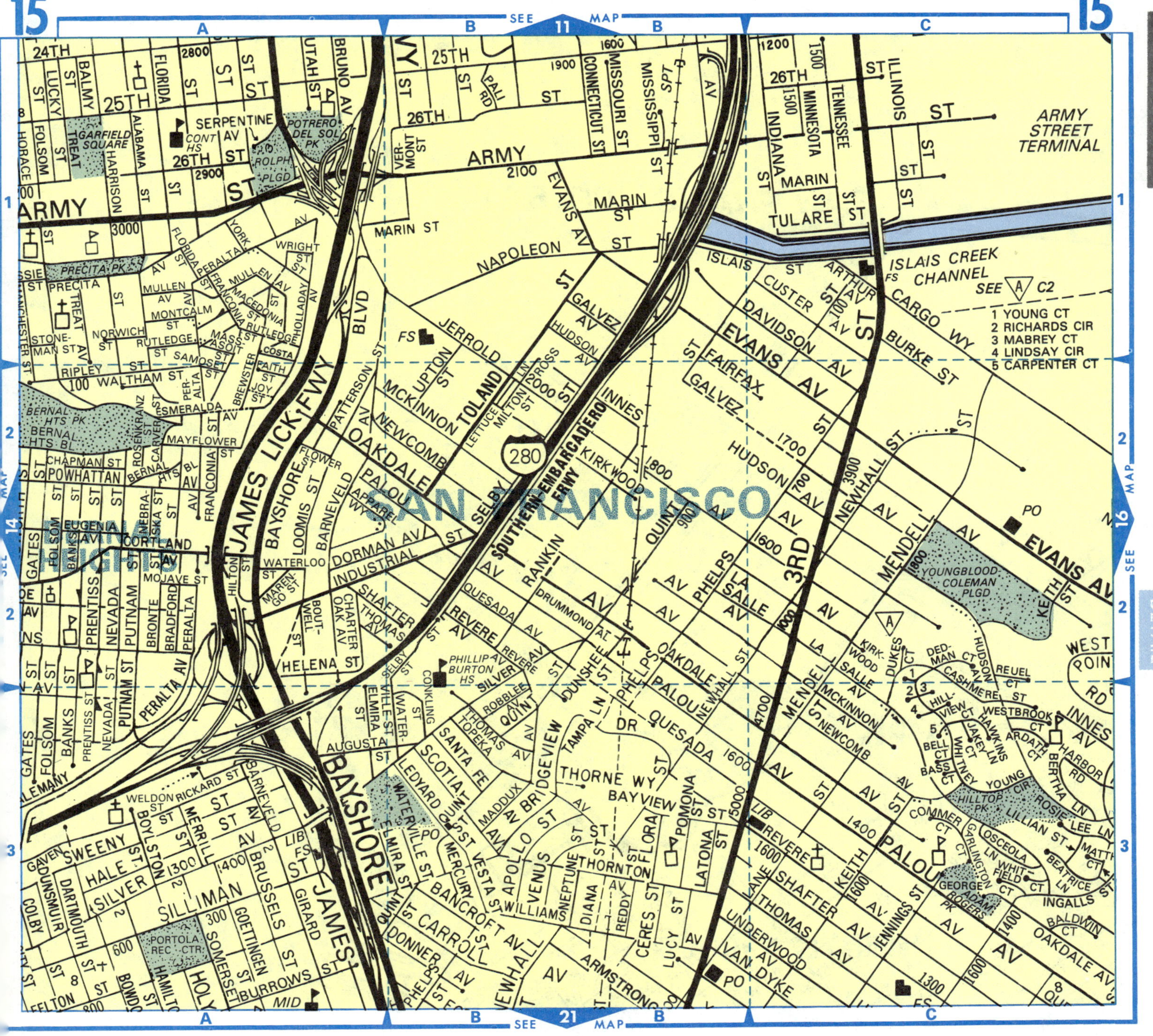
SEE 11 MAP
SEE 21 MAP
SEE 14 MAP
SEE 16 MAP
SAN FRANCISCO
BERNAL HEIGHTS
ARMY STREET TERMINAL
ISLAIS CREEK CHANNEL
SEE A C2
1 YOUNG CT
2 RICHARDS CIR
3 MABREY CT
4 LINDSAY CIR
5 CARPENTER CT
JAMES LICK FWY
SOUTHERN EMBARCADERO FWY
280
BAYSHORE BLVD
3RD ST
EVANS AV
ARMY ST
GARFIELD SQUARE
POTRERO DEL SOL PK
PRECITA PK
BERNAL HTS PK
YOUNGBLOOD-COLEMAN PLGD
HILLTOP PK
GEORGE ADAM ROGERS PK
PORTOLA REC CTR
PHILLIP BURTON HS
DETAIL

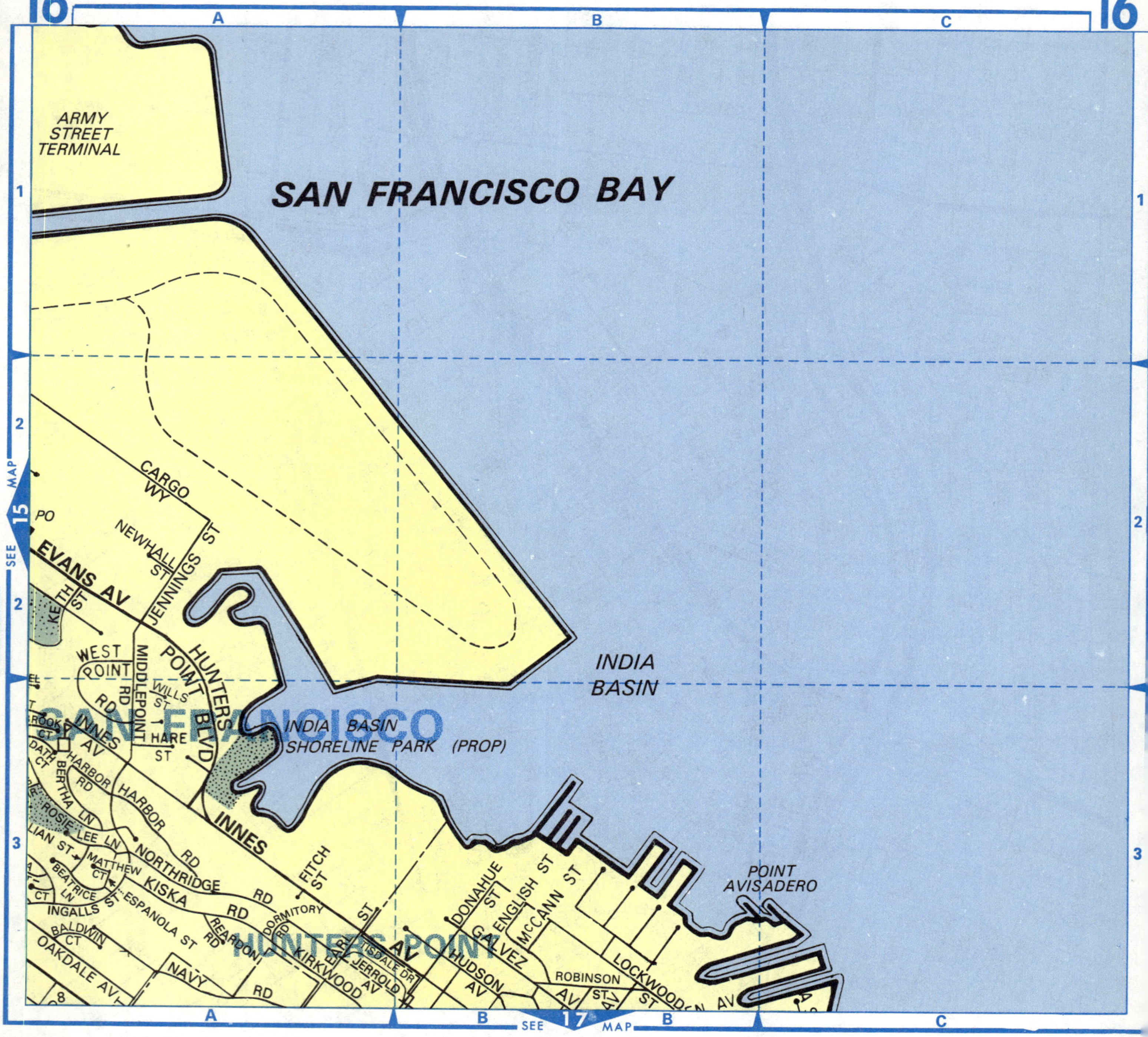

A B C

ARMY STREET TERMINAL

SAN FRANCISCO BAY

INDIA BASIN

INDIA BASIN SHORELINE PARK (PROP)

SAN FRANCISCO

HUNTERS POINT

POINT AVISADERO

CARGO WY
NEWHALL ST
JENNINGS ST
EVANS AV
KEITH ST
WEST POINT RD
MIDDLEPOINT RD
HUNTERS POINT BLVD
WILLS ST
HARE ST
INNES AV
HARBOR RD
BERTHA LN
ROSIE LEE LN
LILLIAN ST
MATTHEW CT
BEATRICE LN
NORTHRIDGE RD
KISKA RD
ESPANOLA ST
INGALLS ST
BALDWIN CT
OAKDALE AV
NAVY RD
REARDON RD
DORMITORY RD
KIRKWOOD AV
JERROLD AV
FITCH ST
EARL ST
DONAHUE ST
ENGLISH ST
McCANN ST
GALVEZ AV
HUDSON AV
ROBINSON ST
LOCKWOOD ST
INNES AV
PO

SEE 15 MAP
DETAIL 2
SEE 17 MAP

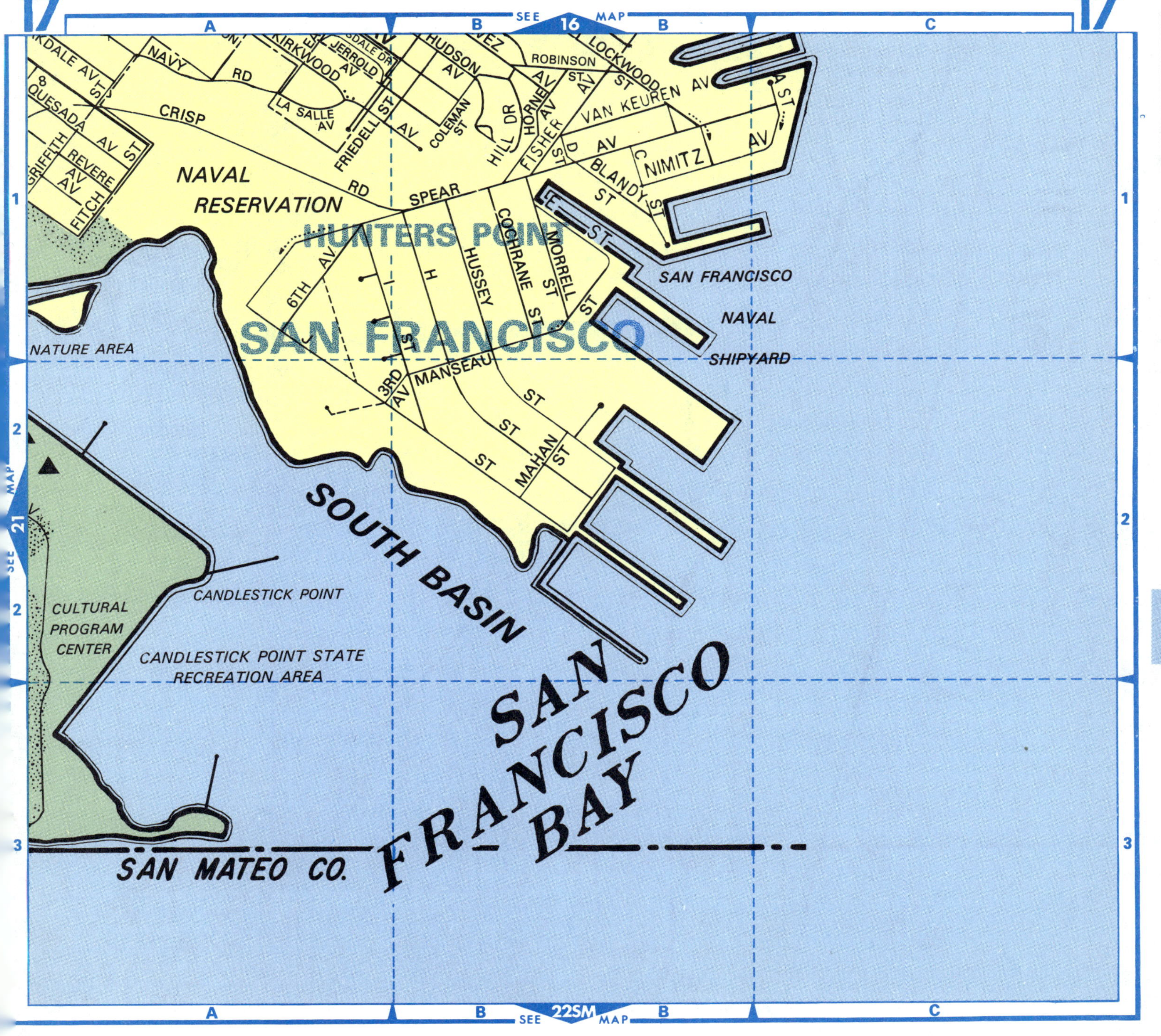
SEE 16 MAP
SEE 22SM MAP
SEE 21 MAP
SAN FRANCISCO
DETAIL
HUNTERS POINT
SAN FRANCISCO
NAVAL RESERVATION
SAN FRANCISCO NAVAL SHIPYARD
NATURE AREA
SOUTH BASIN
CANDLESTICK POINT
CULTURAL PROGRAM CENTER
CANDLESTICK POINT STATE RECREATION AREA
SAN FRANCISCO BAY
SAN MATEO CO.
CRISP RD
SPEAR
NAVY RD
HUDSON AV
ROBINSON
LOCKWOOD ST
VAN KEUREN AV
NIMITZ AV
BLANDY ST
HILL DR
FISHER AV
HORNE AV
COLEMAN ST
FRIEDELL ST
LA SALLE AV
KIRKWOOD AV
JERROLD AV
QUESADA AV
REVERE AV
GRIFFITH ST
FITCH ST
6TH AV
HUSSEY ST
COCHRANE ST
MORRELL ST
MANSEAU ST
MAHAN ST
3RD AV
E ST
A ST

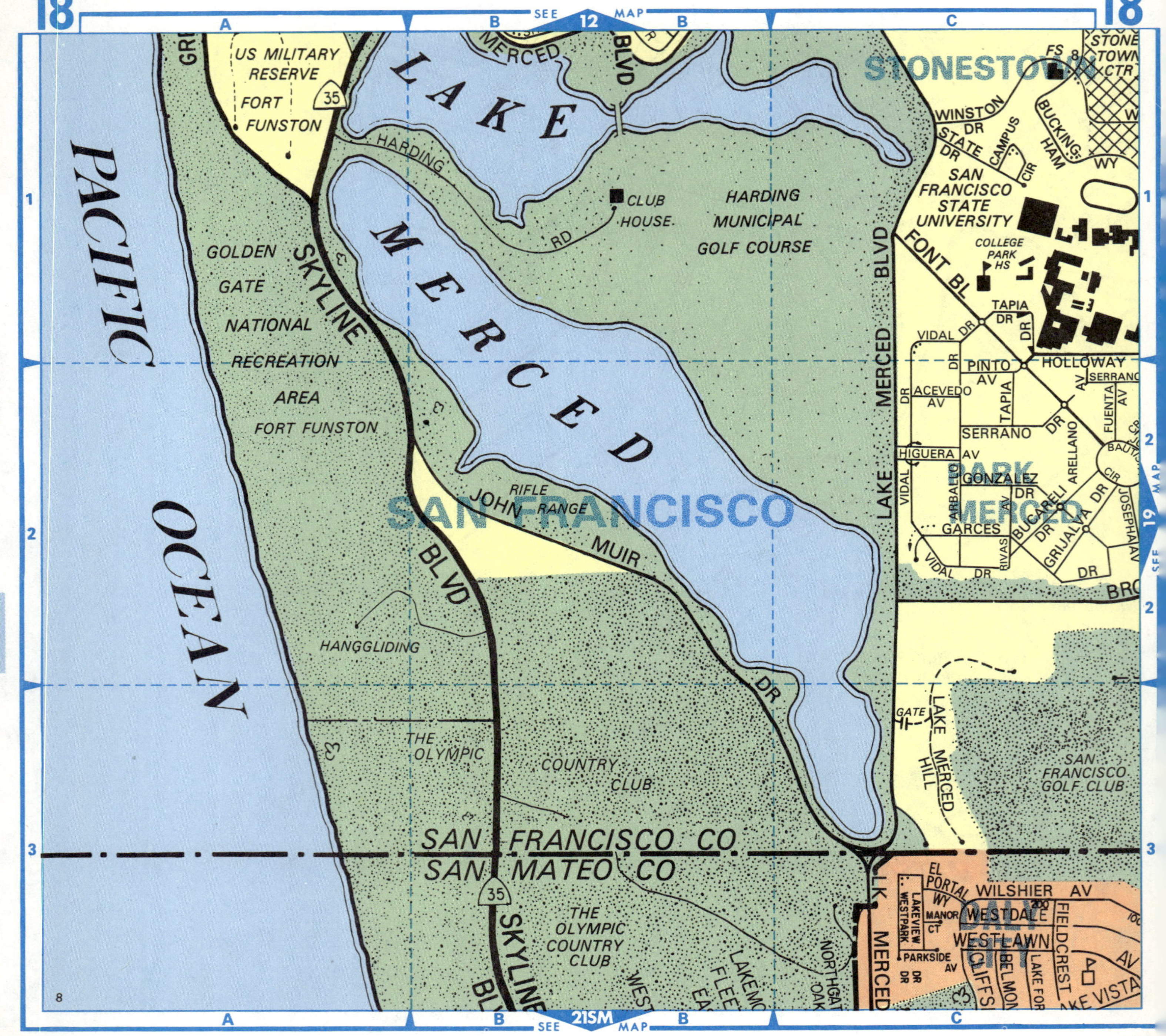
SEE 12 MAP
PACIFIC OCEAN
LAKE MERCED
US MILITARY RESERVE
FORT FUNSTON
GOLDEN GATE NATIONAL RECREATION AREA
FORT FUNSTON
SKYLINE BLVD
HARDING RD
CLUB HOUSE
HARDING MUNICIPAL GOLF COURSE
STONESTOWN
STONESTOWN CTR
SAN FRANCISCO STATE UNIVERSITY
COLLEGE PARK HS
FONT BL
WINSTON DR
STATE DR
CAMPUS CIR
BUCKINGHAM WY
TAPIA DR
VIDAL DR
HOLLOWAY
PINTO AV
ACEVEDO AV
SERRANO DR
HIGUERA AV
GONZALEZ DR
PARK MERCED
GARCES DR
BUCARELI DR
GRIJALVA DR
ARELLANO
FUENTA AV
JOSEPHA AV
ARBALLO DR
RIVAS AV
BAUTISTA CIR
LAKE MERCED BLVD
SAN FRANCISCO
JOHN MUIR DR
RIFLE RANGE
HANGGLIDING
THE OLYMPIC COUNTRY CLUB
GATE
LAKE MERCED HILL
SAN FRANCISCO GOLF CLUB
SAN FRANCISCO CO
SAN MATEO CO
THE OLYMPIC COUNTRY CLUB
35
EL PORTAL WY
WILSHIER AV
MANOR CT
WESTDALE
WESTLAWN
LAKEVIEW
WESTPARK DR
PARKSIDE AV
DALY CITY
FIELDCREST
LAKE VISTA
CLIFFS
BELMONT
LK MERCED
NORTHGATE
SEE 21SM MAP
SEE 19 MAP
A
B
C
1
2
3

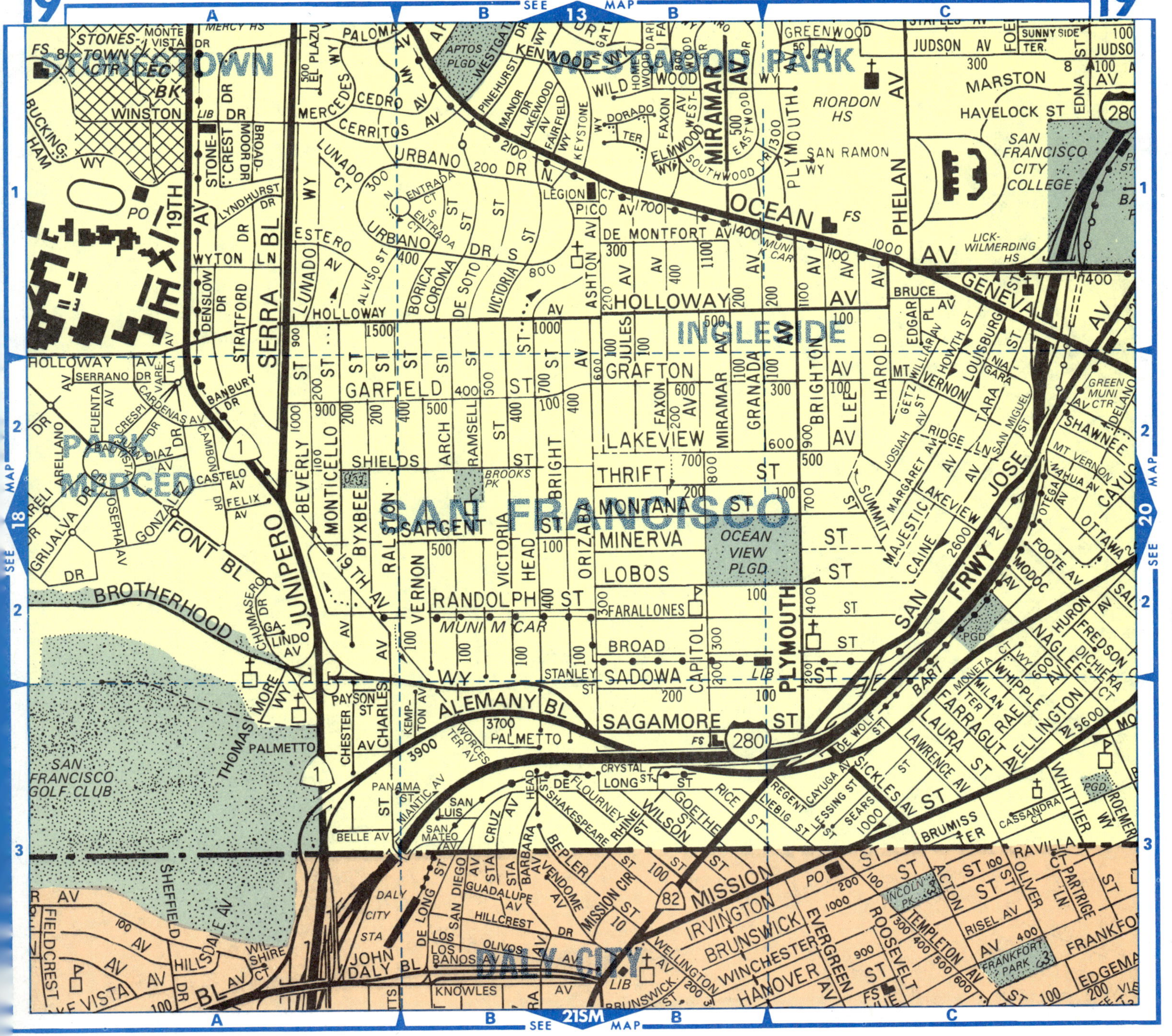
SEE MAP 13
SAN FRANCISCO
STONESTOWN
WESTWOOD PARK
INGLESIDE
PARK MERCED
SAN FRANCISCO GOLF CLUB
DALY CITY
SAN FRANCISCO CITY COLLEGE
OCEAN VIEW PLGD
RIORDON HS
LICK-WILMERDING HS
OCEAN AV
HOLLOWAY AV
JUNIPERO SERRA BL
ALEMANY BL
SAN JOSE AV
MISSION ST
GENEVA AV
BROTHERHOOD WY
SEE MAP 18
SEE MAP 20
SEE 215M MAP

DETAIL

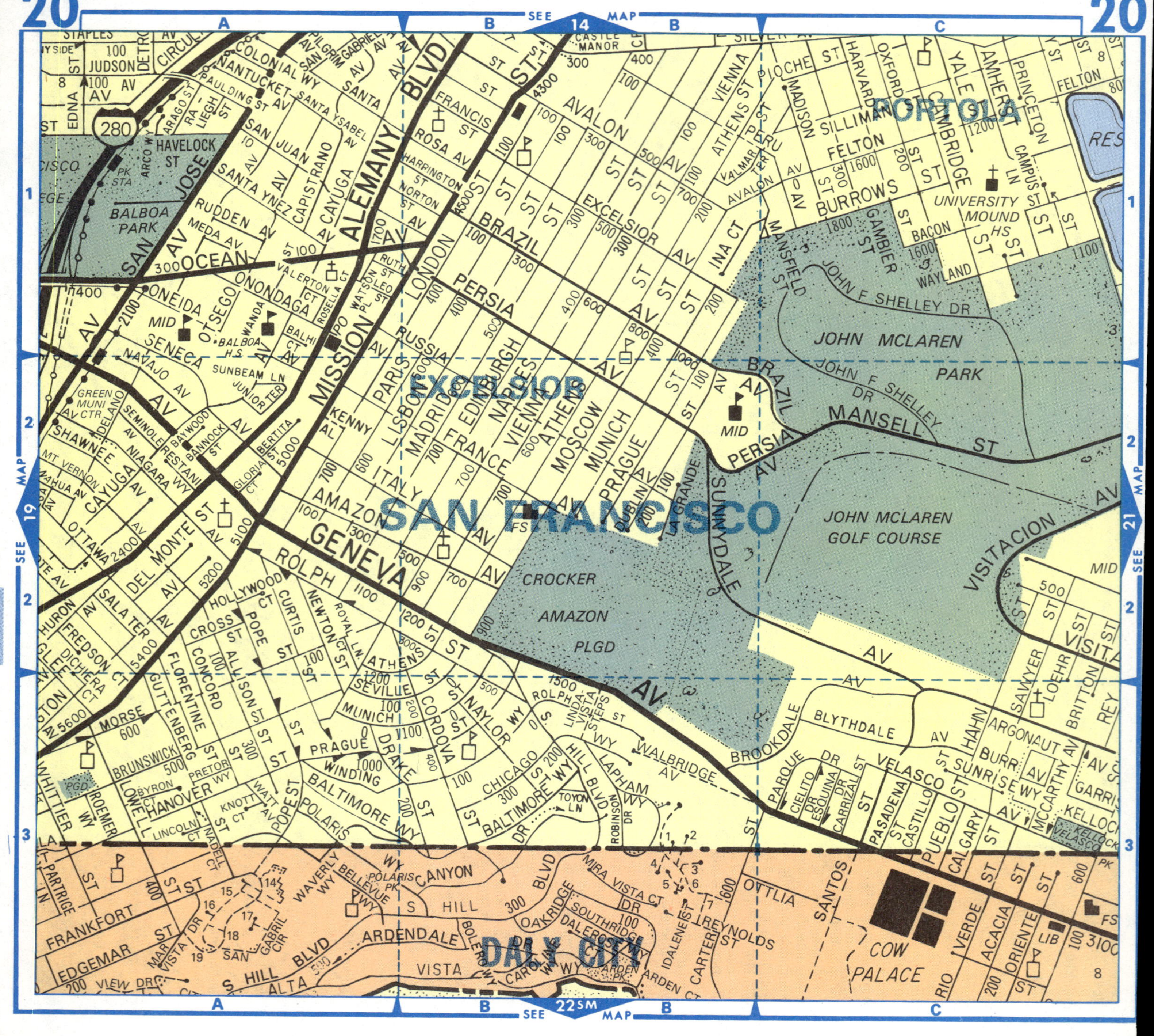
SEE 14 MAP
SEE 22SM MAP
SEE 19 MAP
SEE 21 MAP
DETAIL
A
B
C
1
2
3
PORTOLA
EXCELSIOR
SAN FRANCISCO
DALY CITY
JOHN MCLAREN PARK
JOHN MCLAREN GOLF COURSE
CROCKER AMAZON PLGD
BALBOA PARK
UNIVERSITY MOUND HS
COW PALACE
BALBOA H.S.
GREEN MUNI CTR
MISSION
ALEMANY BLVD
SAN JOSE AV
GENEVA AV
OCEAN AV
PERSIA AV
BRAZIL AV
EXCELSIOR AV
AVALON AV
MANSELL ST
SUNNYDALE AV
VISITACION AV
JOHN F SHELLEY DR
ROLPH ST
BURROWS
FELTON
SILLIMAN
CAMBRIDGE
YALE
PRINCETON
AMHERST
OXFORD
HARVARD
LONDON
PARIS
LISBON
MADRID
EDINBURGH
NAPLES
VIENNA
ATHENS
MOSCOW
MUNICH
PRAGUE
DUBLIN
LA GRANDE
RUSSIA
FRANCE
ITALY
AMAZON
KENNY AL
ONEIDA
OTSEGO
ONONDAGA
SENECA
NAVAJO AV
CAYUGA
SHAWNEE
NIAGARA
OTTAWA
SEMINOLE
DELANO
DEL MONTE ST
HURON
SALA TER
FREDSON CT
MORSE
GUTTENBERG
FLORENTINE
CONCORD
ALLISON ST
CROSS
POPE
CURTIS
NEWTON
HOLLYWOOD CT
BRUNSWICK
HANOVER
LOWELL
ROEMER WY
WHITTIER
POPE ST
POLARIS
BALTIMORE WY
WINDING
SEVILLE
CORDOVA
NAYLOR
DRAKE
CHICAGO
HILL BLVD
LAPHAM WY
WALBRIDGE AV
BROOKDALE
BLYTHDALE AV
VELASCO
PASADENA
CASTILLO
PUEBLO ST
CALGARY ST
ORIENTE
ACACIA
VERDE
RIO
ARGONAUT
SAWYER
LOEHR
BRITTON
REY
SANTOS
OTTLIA
REYNOLDS
CARTER ST
IDALENE ST
MIRA VISTA CT
SOUTHRIDGE
DALEROSE
OAKRIDGE
ARDENDALE
VISTA
CANYON
S HILL BLVD
ALTA
EDGEMAR
FRANKFORT
PARTRIDGE
STAPLES AV
JUDSON
EDNA
CIRCULAR
HAVELOCK ST
SANTA YNEZ
CAPISTRANO
CAYUGA
RUDDEN
SAN JUAN
COLONIAL WY
NANTUCKET
PILGRIM
SANTA YSABEL
FRANCIS ST
ROSA AV
HARRINGTON ST
NORTON ST
CASTLE MANOR
SILVER AV
PIOCHE
MADISON
BACON
WAYLAND
GAMBIER
MANSFIELD ST
INA CT
PERU
280
MID
FS
LIB
PK
PLGD.

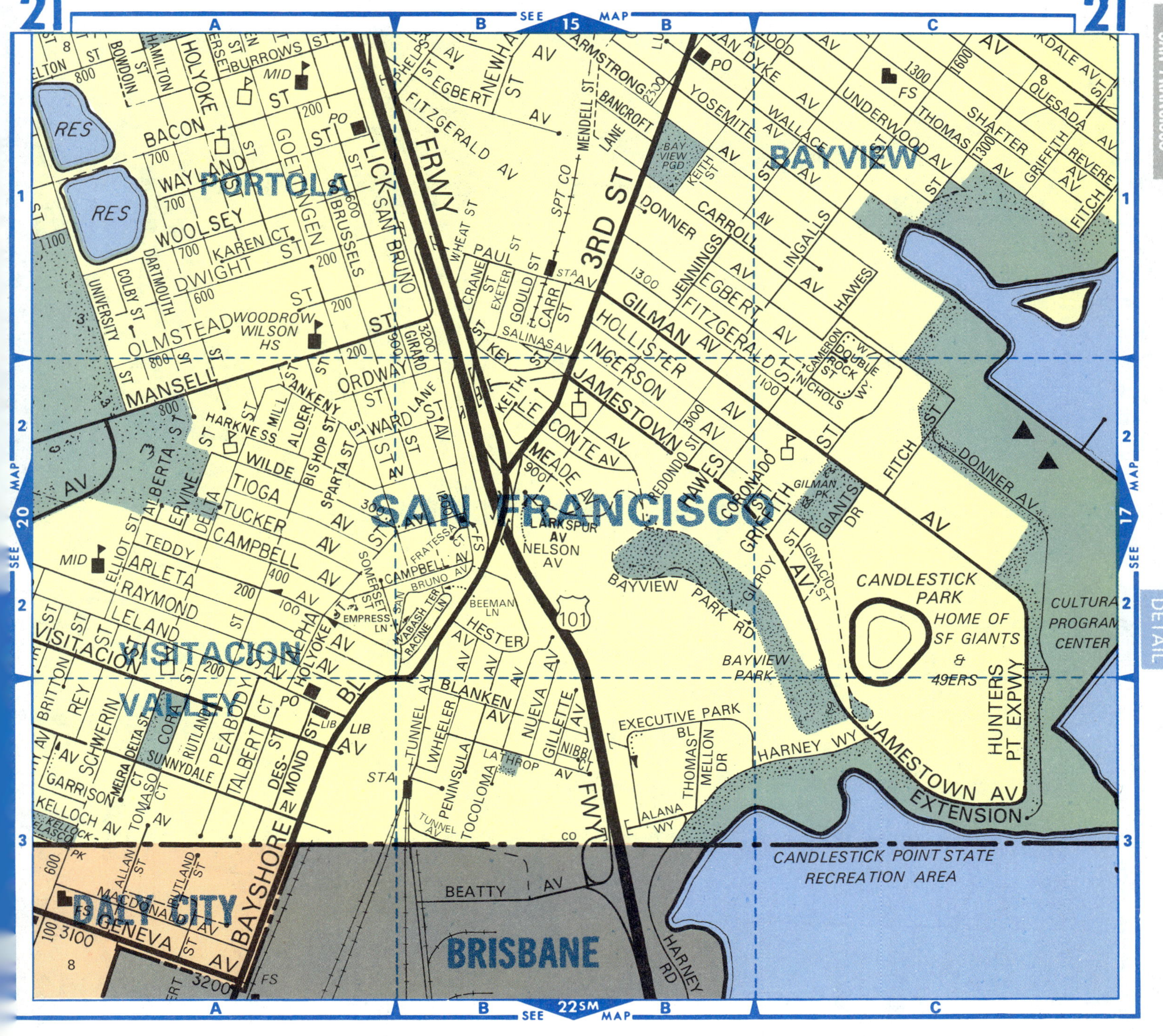

SEE MAP 15
PORTOLA
BAYVIEW
SAN FRANCISCO
VISITACION VALLEY
DALY CITY
BRISBANE
CANDLESTICK PARK
HOME OF SF GIANTS & 49ERS
CULTURAL PROGRAM CENTER
CANDLESTICK POINT STATE RECREATION AREA
BAYVIEW PARK
EXECUTIVE PARK
SAN FRANCISCO
DETAIL
SEE MAP 20
SEE MAP 17
SEE 22SM MAP

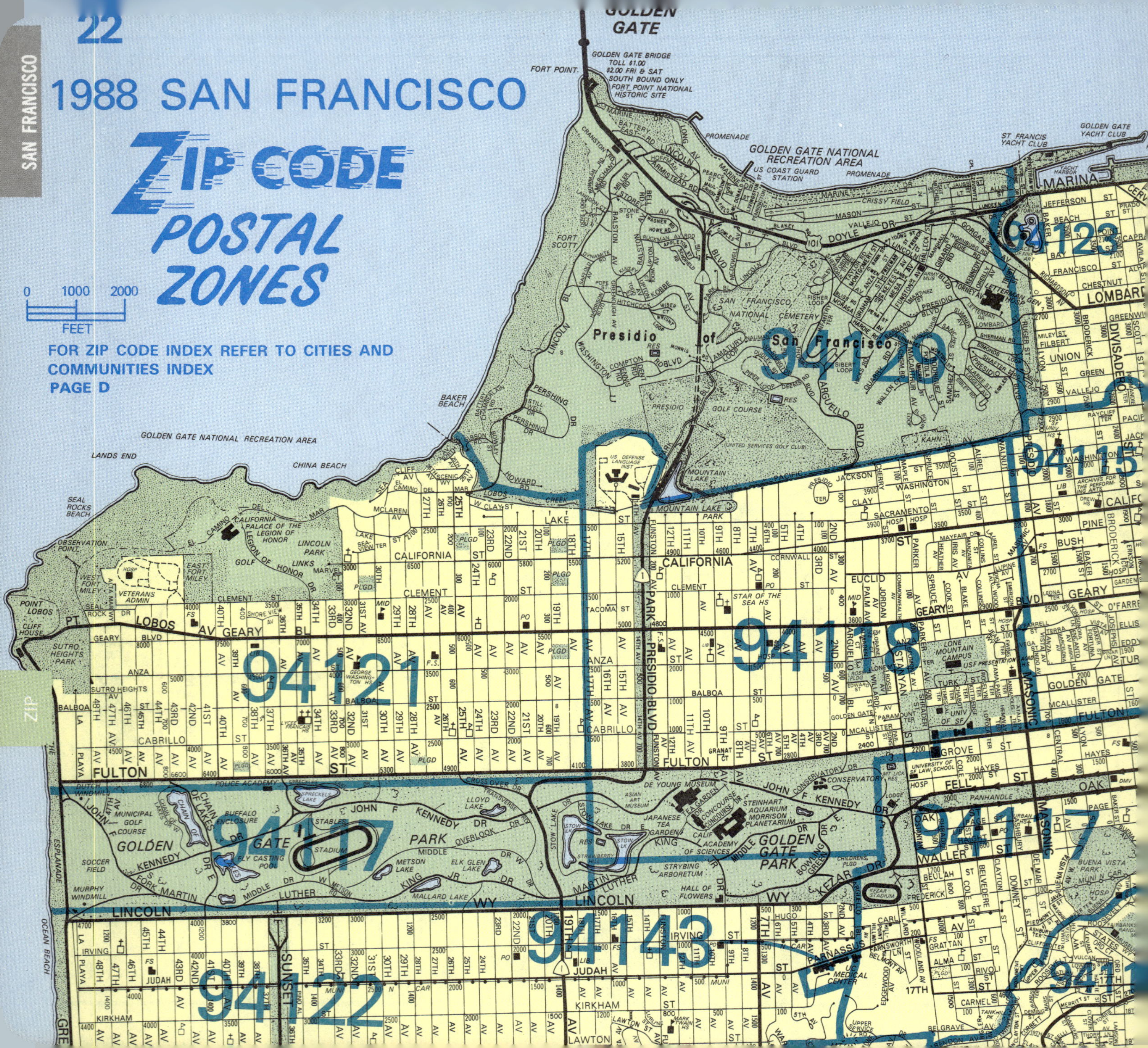
1988 SAN FRANCISCO
ZIP CODE
POSTAL
ZONES
0 1000 2000
FEET
FOR ZIP CODE INDEX REFER TO CITIES AND COMMUNITIES INDEX PAGE D
GOLDEN GATE
GOLDEN GATE BRIDGE
TOLL $1.00
$2.00 FRI & SAT
SOUTH BOUND ONLY
FORT POINT NATIONAL HISTORIC SITE
FORT POINT
GOLDEN GATE NATIONAL RECREATION AREA
US COAST GUARD STATION
PROMENADE
CRISSY FIELD
ST FRANCIS YACHT CLUB
GOLDEN GATE YACHT CLUB
MARINA
FORT SCOTT
Presidio of San Francisco
SAN FRANCISCO NATIONAL CEMETERY
GOLF COURSE
MOUNTAIN LAKE
MOUNTAIN LAKE PARK
BAKER BEACH
LANDS END
CHINA BEACH
SEAL ROCKS BEACH
OBSERVATION POINT
POINT LOBOS
CLIFF HOUSE
SUTRO HEIGHTS PARK
CALIFORNIA PALACE OF THE LEGION OF HONOR
LINCOLN PARK GOLF LINKS
FORT MILEY
94123
94129
94115
94118
94121
94117
94122
94143
94114
GOLDEN GATE PARK
JOHN F KENNEDY DR
DE YOUNG MUSEUM
ASIAN ART MUSEUM
JAPANESE TEA GARDEN
CALIF ACADEMY OF SCIENCES
STEINHART AQUARIUM
MORRISON PLANETARIUM
CONSERVATORY
STRYBING ARBORETUM
HALL OF FLOWERS
KEZAR STADIUM
POLICE ACADEMY
DUTCH WINDMILL
MUNICIPAL GOLF COURSE
BUFFALO ENCLOSURE
CHAIN OF LAKES
SPRECKELS LAKE
STADIUM
LLOYD LAKE
STOW LAKE
STRAWBERRY HILL
METSON LAKE
ELK GLEN LAKE
MALLARD LAKE
SOCCER FIELD
MURPHY WINDMILL
MARTIN LUTHER KING JR DR
OCEAN BEACH
ESPLANADE
LINCOLN WY
FULTON ST
GEARY BLVD
CALIFORNIA ST
CLEMENT ST
BALBOA ST
CABRILLO ST
ANZA ST
LAKE ST
SUNSET BLVD
PARK PRESIDIO BLVD
IRVING ST
JUDAH ST
KIRKHAM ST
LAWTON ST
MEDICAL CENTER
LONE MOUNTAIN CAMPUS
UNIV OF SF
MASONIC AV
DIVISADERO
LOMBARD ST
FELL ST
OAK ST
HAYES ST
GROVE ST
PANHANDLE
BUENA VISTA PARK
PARNASSUS

SAN FRANCISCO BAY
THOMAS BROS. MAPS
550 JACKSON ST
94133
94111
94104
94123
94108
94109
94105
94102
94103
94141
P.O. BOXES
94107
94110
94130
EMBARCADERO CENTER
1 ONE EMBARCADERO CTR
2 TWO EMBARCADERO CTR
3 THREE EMBARCADERO CTR
4 FOUR EMBARCADERO CTR
5 HYATT REGENCY
GOLDEN GATEWAY CENTER
BART TRANSBAY TUBE
SAN FRANCISCO OAKLAND BAY BRIDGE
RINCON POINT
CHINA BASIN
MISSION ROCK TERMINAL
CENTRAL BASIN
AQUATIC PARK
NATIONAL MARITIME MUSEUM
FISHERMAN'S WHARF
INSET OF
TREASURE ISLAND
NAVAL RESERVATION
YERBA BUENA
ISLAND
SCALE OF INSET
1 INCH TO 2200 FT.
1 KEPPLER CT
2 HUTCHINS CT
3 HALYBURTON CT
SEE SAN FRANCISCO ATLAS PAGE 3 GRID C2

94122
94116
94131
94127
94132
94112

PACIFIC OCEAN
GOLDEN GATE NATIONAL RECREATION AREA
GREAT HWY
SUNSET BLVD
SUNSET RESERVOIR
SUNSET COMMUNITY CENTER
ABRAHAM LINCOLN H.S.
MCCOPPIN SQ
SAN FRANCISCO ZOO
PINE LAKE PARK
SIGMUND STERN REC GROVE
LAKE MERCED
HARDING MUNICIPAL GOLF COURSE
US MILITARY RESERVE
FORT FUNSTON
GOLDEN GATE NATIONAL RECREATION AREA FORT FUNSTON
SKYLINE BLVD
JOHN MUIR DR
RIFLE RANGE
HANGGLIDING
THE OLYMPIC COUNTRY CLUB
SAN FRANCISCO GOLF CLUB
SAN FRANCISCO STATE UNIVERSITY
STONESTOWN CTR
LAGUNA HONDA HOSP
MT DAVIDSON PK
GLEN CANYON PARK
SAN FRANCISCO CITY COLLEGE
BALBOA PARK
OCEAN VIEW PLGD
JUNIPERO SERRA BL
PORTOLA DR
MONTEREY BL
OCEAN AV
SLOAT BL
TARAVAL ST
NORIEGA ST
WOODSIDE AV
ALEMANY BL
SAN JOSE AV
MISSION ST
SAN FRANCISCO CO
SAN MATEO CO

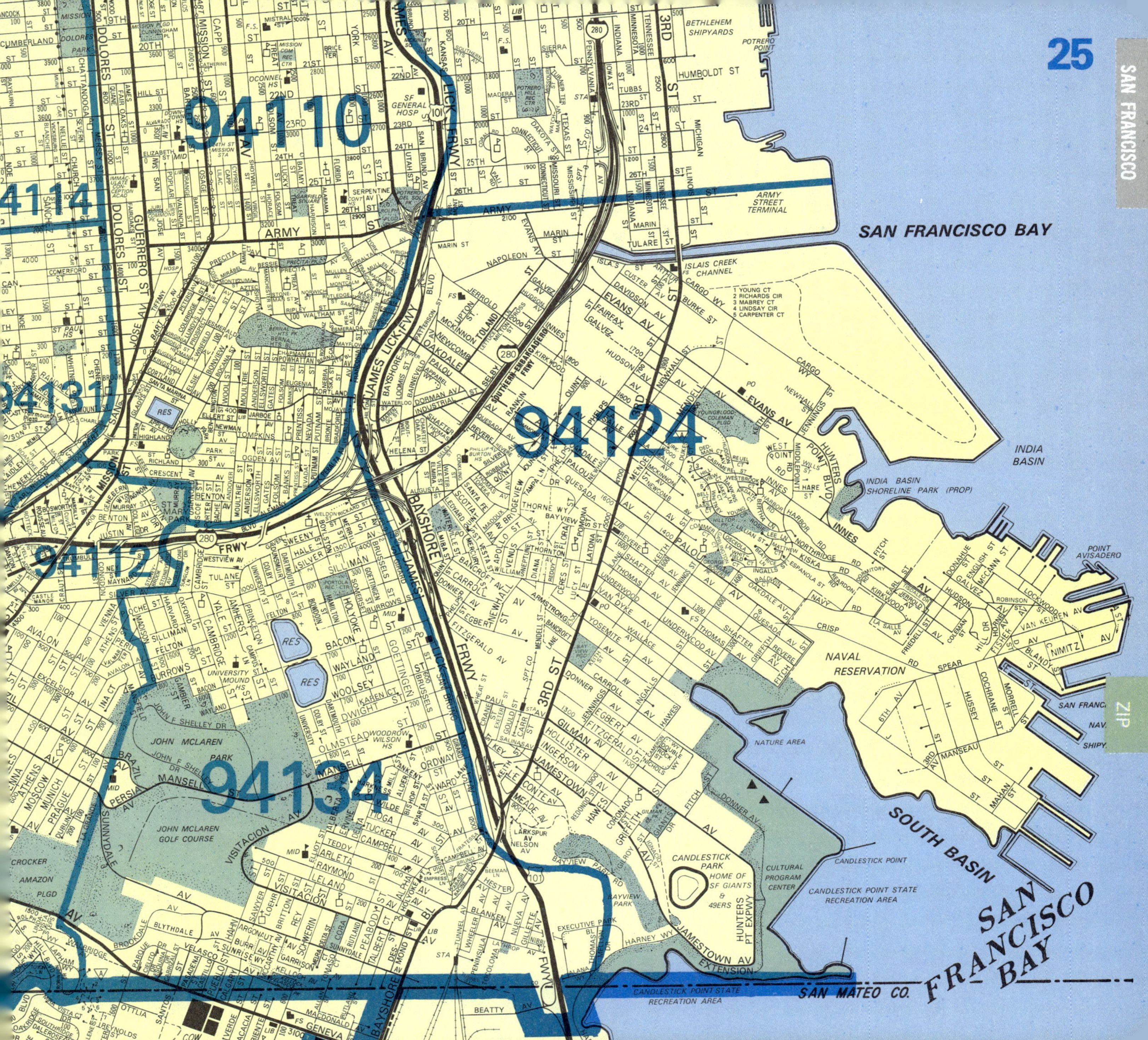
94110
94114
94131
94112
94124
94134
SAN FRANCISCO BAY
BETHLEHEM SHIPYARDS
POTRERO POINT
ARMY STREET TERMINAL
ISLAIS CREEK CHANNEL
1 YOUNG CT
2 RICHARDS CIR
3 MABREY CT
4 LINDSAY CIR
5 CARPENTER CT
INDIA BASIN
INDIA BASIN SHORELINE PARK (PROP)
POINT AVISADERO
NAVAL RESERVATION
NATURE AREA
SOUTH BASIN
CANDLESTICK POINT
CANDLESTICK POINT STATE RECREATION AREA
CULTURAL PROGRAM CENTER
CANDLESTICK PARK
HOME OF SF GIANTS & 49ERS
HUNTERS PT EXPWY
JAMESTOWN AV EXTENSION
BAYVIEW PARK
EXECUTIVE PARK
SAN MATEO CO.
SAN FRANCISCO BAY
JOHN McLAREN PARK
JOHN McLAREN GOLF COURSE
CROCKER AMAZON PLGD
SF GENERAL HOSP
JAMES LICK FRWY
SOUTHERN EMBARCADERO FRWY
BAYSHORE FRWY
ARMY
MISSION
DOLORES
GUERRERO ST
3RD ST
EVANS AV
CARGO WY
HUNTERS POINT BLVD
INNES
PALOU
QUESADA
SILVER AV
MANSELL
VISITACION
GENEVA
SUNNYDALE
GILMAN AV
CRISP
SPEAR
RES

MUNICIPAL PIER
MARITIME MUSEUM
AQUATIC PARK
45
43
35
PIER 39
BALCLUTHA SHIP
THE EMBARCADERO
FISHERMAN'S WHARF
ST
GRANT
MCDOWELL AV
FORT MASON
POPE
RD
SCHOFIELD RD
MACARTHUR AV
JEFFERSON
THE CANNERY
THE ANCORAGE
MARITIME MUSEUM BUILDING
BEACH
GHIRARDELLI SQUARE
NORTH
POINT
JONES
TAYLOR
MASON
POWELL
STOCKTON
KEARNY
MIDWAY ST
BERGEN PL
COLUMBUS
VANDEWATER ST
WORDEN ST
BAY
NORTHVIEW CT
BRET HARTE TER
PFEIFFER ST
BELLAIR PL
JULIUS
RES
60
59
WATER ST
HOUSTON ST
VENARD ST
NEWELL ST
WHITING ST
LA FERRERA TER
WINTHROP ST
FIELDING ST
FRANCISCO
CULEBRA TER
LARKIN
HYDE
MONTCLAIR TER
LEAVENWORTH
LOMBARD
TUSCANY AL
EDGARDO PL
KRAMER PL
ST CHILD ST
TELEGRAPH PL
TELEGRAPH
EDITH ST
CHESTNUT
POLK
LIB
PLGD
JANSEN ST
GERKE AL
PARDEE AL
GOUGH
FRANKLIN
CROOKEDEST ST
LURMONT TER
ROACH ST
GROVER PL
BRYANT AL
KRAUSGRILL PL
MEDAU PL
HARWOOD AL
GENOA PL
BLACKSTONE CT
VAN NESS
101
SOUTHARD PL
VALPARAISO ST
SCOTLAND ST
FILBERT
WASHINGTON SQ
JASPER PL
CADELL PL
NOBLES AL
SONOMA ST
VARENNES
GRENARD TER
GREENWICH
ATTRIDGE AL
ALADDIN TER
KENT ST
AUGUST AL
PO
UNION
BANNAM PL
AV
POLLARD PL
SAN ANTONIO PL
MOORE PL
SHARP PL
HAVENS ST
BLACK PL
MARION PL
REDFIELD AL
WEBB PL
WINTER PL
PRICE ROW
GREEN
MARGRAVE PL
IMPERIAL AV
FILBERT
ALLEN ST
HASTINGS TER
MACONDRAY
ALTA VISTA TER
CLUB FUGAZI
CARD AL
NORTH BEACH MUSEUM
ROMOLO PL
UNION
EASTMAN ST
RUSSELL ST
WARNER PL
DELGADO PL
GREEN PL
RUSSIAN HILL PL
EATON PL
CHURCHILL ST
EMERY LN
CORDELIA ST
TRACY PL
ROCKLAND ST
UNION ST
OCTAGON HOUSE
GREEN
WHITE ST
FLORENCE ST
FALLON PL
VALLEJO TER
WASHOE PL
ADLER ST
BONITA ST
WALDO AL
GLOVER ST
SALMON ST
WAYNE PL
FISHER AL
STARK ST
BECKETT ST
VALLEJO
TUNNEL
MORRELL PL
CYRUS PL
CHARING CROSS
BERNARD ST
HIMMELMAN PL
KEYES
ADELE CT
BEDFORD PL
DUNCOMBE
PELTON PL
JASON CT
CHINATOWN
COOPER AL
BROADWAY
LYNCH ST
PHOENIX TER
AUBURN ST
JOHN ST
STONE ST
TRENTON ST
CHINATOWN LN
ROSS AL
ST LOUIS PL
WENTWORTH PL
MARCY PL
DORIC AL
CODMAN PL
OLD CHINATOWN LN
SPOFFORD LN
WAVERLY PL
WALTER LUM PL
PACIFIC
MCCORMICK PL
WALL PL
BURGOYNE ST
CABLE CAR BARN
WETMORE
PARKHURST AL
STOCKTON
JACKSON
REED
PRIEST
SPROULE
TRUETT PL
SHEPHARD PL
ZIP

DOWNTOWN
SAN FRANCISCO
LEGEND
Cable Car Track/Route No.
Bay Area Rapid Transit (BART)
Tunnels
One Way Streets
SCALE: ONE INCH EQUALS 830 FEET
SAN FRANCISCO BAY
TIBURON FERRY
SAUSALITO-LARKSPUR FERRY
BART TRANSBAY TUBE
THE EMBARCADERO
EMBARCADERO SKYWAY
FERRY BLDG
GOLDEN GATEWAY CENTER
MARITIME PZ
JUSTIN HERMAN PLAZA
EMBARCADERO CENTER
HYATT REGENCY HOTEL
MANDARIN HOTEL
TRANSAMERICA PYRAMID
JACKSON SQ
SANSOME
BATTERY
FRONT
DAVIS
DRUMM
MONTGOMERY
COMMERCE ST
ICEHOUSE AL
COWELL PL
STEVENS AL
JACKSON
PACIFIC
MERCHANT
HALLECK ST
LEIDESDORFF
CUSTOM HOUSE PL
HOTALING
GOLD ST
BALANCE ST
OSGOOD PL
PRESCOTT CT
BARTOL
HODGES AL
CALHOUN TER
NAPIER LN
DARRELL PL
VERDI PL
JEROME
DUNBAR AL
SPRING
480
PO
33
31
29
27
23
19
17
9
7
5
3
1
14
16

LAFAYETTE PARK
HASS-LILIENTHAL HOUSE
WASHINGTON
CLAY
SACRAMENTO
CALIFORNIA
61
PINE
BUSH
SUTTER
POST
GEARY
O'FARRELL
ELLIS
EDDY
TURK
GOLDEN GATE
MCALLISTER
FULTON
GROVE
HAYES
FELL
OCTAVIA
GOUGH
FRANKLIN
VAN NESS
POLK
LARKIN
HYDE
LEAVENWORTH
JONES
MASON
POWELL
LAGUNA
AUSTIN
FERN
DANIEL BURHAM CT
PETER YORKE WY
CATHEDRAL HILL HOTEL
ST MARYS CATHEDRAL
STARR KING WY
MYRTLE
OLIVE
CLEARY CT
WILLOW
WILLOW ST
LARCH ST
JEFFERSON SQUARE
HAYWARD PLGD
ELM
REDWOOD
ASH
BIRCH ST
CENTRAL FRWY
101
FEDERAL BLDG
STATE BLDG
MUSEUM OF MODERN ART
HERBST THTR
WAR MEMORIAL
OPERA HOUSE
CITY HALL
PO
JAMES ROLPH JR CIVIC CENTER
BROOKS HALL
CIVIC AUDITORIUM
DAVIES SYMPHONY HALL
LECH WALESA
LINDEN ST
MAIN LIB
FED BLDG
ORPHEUM THTR
BREEN PL
DALE PL
DODGE PL
MEACHAM PL
HARLEM AL
ADA CT
AMITY AL
MABEL AL
COHEN PL
WAGNER AL
EUREKA PL
HEMLOCK
CEDAR
TROY AL
ACORN AL
HELEN ST
PANTON AL
TOUCHARD ST
GOLDEN CT
LEROY PL
LYSETTE ST
GRACE CATHEDRAL
PLEASANT ST
EWER PL
CUSHMAN ST
FAIRMONT HOTEL
MARK HOPKINS
STANFORD COURT
FRANK ST
NOB HILL CIR
VINE TER
MULFORD AL
HOOKER AL
FELLA PL
ANSON PL
HOLIDAY INN
DELTA PL
SUTTER
HYATT HOTEL
SIR FRANCIS DRAKE HOTEL
PORTMAN HOTEL
SAKS
HOBART AL
COSMO PL
OPHIR AL
AGATE AL
ADELAIDE PL
COLIN PL
SHANNON ST
DERBY
CURRAN THTR
GEARY THTR
ELWOOD ST
CLIFT HOTEL
HOTEL NIKKO
HILTON HOTEL
ST FRANCIS HOTEL
UNION SQUARE
MAIDEN
FRANK LLOYD WRIGHT BLDG
GUMPS
CAMPTON PL
TILLMAN
HARLAN
EMMA ST
CHATHAM PL
VINTON CT
MONROE ST
CHELSEA PL
BURRITT ST
TUNNEL
BROOKLYN PL
SABIN PL
PRATT PL
QUINCY
N-M
MA
60
C MAGNIN ST
STEVELOE PL
ANTONIO ST
AIRLINES BUS TERMINAL
VISITOR INFO CENTER
RAMADA RENAISSANCE
HALLIDIE PLAZA
POWELL ST STATION
PIONEER
PO EC
OLD MINT
MINT ST
GOLDEN GATE THTR
OPAL PL
BART & MUNI METRO
MARY ST
5TH
6TH
7TH
8TH
9TH
MARKET
JESSIE
MAIN POST OFFICE
STEVENSON
CIVIC CENTER STATION
GREYHOUND BUS TERMINAL
MINNA
NATOMA
TULIP AL
RUSS
HOWARD
TEHAMA
CLEMENTINA
S OF MKT PK
HARRIET
JULIA ST
LASKE ST
LANGTON ST
MOSS ST
RAUSCH ST
SUMNER ST
DECKER AL
CLEVELAND ST
SHERMAN ST
COLUMBIA
AV
ST

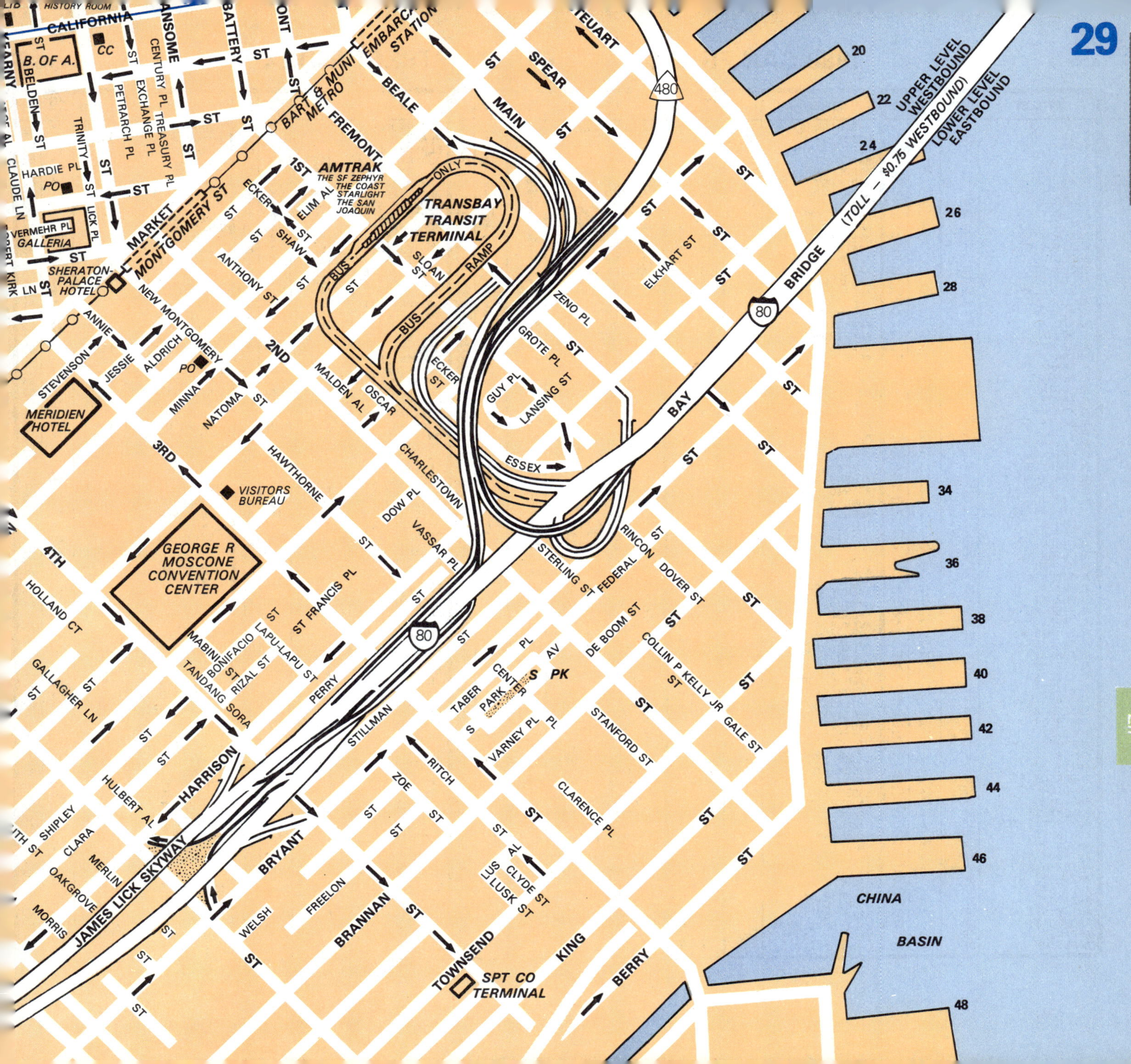
CALIFORNIA
HISTORY ROOM
B. OF A.
CC
SANSOME
BATTERY
STEUART
SPEAR
MAIN
BEALE
FREMONT
EMBARCADERO STATION
BART & MUNI METRO
CENTURY PL
TREASURY PL
EXCHANGE PL
PETRARCH PL
TRINITY
BELDEN
HARDIE PL
PO
CLAUDE LN
LICK PL
VERMEHR PL
GALLERIA
MARKET
MONTGOMERY ST
SHERATON-PALACE HOTEL
KIRK
1ST
AMTRAK
THE SF ZEPHYR
THE COAST STARLIGHT
THE SAN JOAQUIN
ECKER
ELIM AL
SHAW
ANTHONY
TRANSBAY TRANSIT TERMINAL
BUS ONLY
BUS RAMP
SLOAN ST
ELKHART ST
ZENO PL
GROTE PL
GUY PL
LANSING ST
ECKER ST
ESSEX
NEW MONTGOMERY
ANNIE
STEVENSON
JESSIE
ALDRICH
PO
2ND
MINNA
NATOMA
MALDEN AL
OSCAR
MERIDIEN HOTEL
3RD
HAWTHORNE
CHARLESTOWN
VISITORS BUREAU
DOW PL
VASSAR PL
GEORGE R MOSCONE CONVENTION CENTER
4TH
HOLLAND CT
ST FRANCIS PL
MABINI
BONIFACIO
LAPU-LAPU ST
RIZAL ST
TANDANG SORA
PERRY
GALLAGHER LN
HARRISON
HULBERT AL
STILLMAN
RITCH
ZOE
TABER
PARK
CENTER
S PK
VARNEY PL
STERLING ST
FEDERAL
RINCON
DOVER ST
DE BOOM ST
COLLIN P KELLY JR
GALE ST
STANFORD ST
CLARENCE PL
BRYANT
JAMES LICK SKYWAY
SHIPLEY
CLARA
MERLIN
OAKGROVE
MORRIS
WELSH
FREELON
BRANNAN
LUSK ST
CLYDE ST
TOWNSEND
SPT CO TERMINAL
KING
BERRY
480
80
BAY BRIDGE (TOLL — $0.75 WESTBOUND)
UPPER LEVEL WESTBOUND
LOWER LEVEL EASTBOUND
20
22
24
26
28
34
36
38
40
42
44
46
48
CHINA BASIN

1988 SAN FRANCISCO COUNTY STREET INDEX

STREET	CITY	PG. NO.	SEE
A			
A ST	SF	17	C1
A ST	SF	10	B2
A ST	SF	14	A3
A ST	SF	20	C3
A ST	SF	18	C2
A ST	SF	10	A3
ACORN AL	SF	6	C1
ACTNO ST	SF	19	C3
ADA CT	SF	6	C2
ADAIR ST	SF	10	C2
ADDISON ST	SF	14	B2
ADELAIDE PL	SF	7	A2
ADELE CT	SF	3	A3
ADLER ST	SF	3	A3
ADMIRAL AV	SF	14	B3
ADOLPH SUTRO CT	SF	9	C3
AERIAL WY	SF	9	A3
AGATE AL	SF	7	A2
AGNON AV	SF	14	C3
AGUA WY	SF	13	C2
AHERN WY	SF	7	B3
ALABAMA ST	SF	11	A1
ALABAMA ST	SF	15	A1
ALADDIN TER	SF	3	A2
ALAMEDA ST	SF	11	A1
ALANA WY	SF	21	B3
ALBERTA ST	SF	21	A2
ALBION ST	SF	10	C2
ALDER ST	SF	21	A2
ALDRICH AL	SF	7	B2
ALEMANY BLVD	SF	14	C3
ALEMANY BLVD	SF	19	B3
ALEMANY BLVD	SF	20	A1
ALERT AL	SF	10	B2
ALHAMBRA ST	SF	2	A2
ALLAN ST	SF	21	A3
ALLEN ST	SF	2	C3
ALLISON ST	SF	20	A2
ALLSTON WY	SF	13	B2
ALMA ST	SF	9	C2
ALMADEN CT	SF	5	B3
ALOHA AV	SF	9	A3
ALPHA ST	SF	21	A2
ALPINE TER	SF	10	A1
ALTA ST	SF	3	A2
ALTA MAR WY	SF	4	A3
ALTA VISTA TER	SF	2	C3
ALTON AV	SF	13	B1
ALVARADO ST	SF	10	A3
ALVISO ST	SF	19	A1
AMATISTA LN	SF	14	B2
AMATURY LOOP	SF	1	B3
AMAZON AV	SF	20	A2
AMBER DR	SF	14	A1
AMES ST	SF	10	C3
AMETHYST WY	SF	13	C1
AMHERST ST	SF	20	C1
AMITY AL	SF	6	C2
ANDERSON ST	SF	14	C2
ANDOVER ST	SF	14	C3
ANGLO AL	SF	13	A1
ANKENY ST	SF	21	A2
ANNAPOLIS TER	SF	5	C3
ANNIE ST	SF	7	B2
ANSON PL	SF	7	A2
ANTHONY ST	SF	7	B2
ANTONIO ST	SF	6	C2
ANZA ST	SF	1	B2
ANZA ST	SF	4	A3
ANZA ST	SF	5	C3
ANZAVISTA AV	SF	6	A3
APOLLO ST	SF	15	B3
APPAREL WY	SF	15	A2
APPLETON AV	SF	14	C2

STREET	CITY	PG. NO.	SEE
APPLETON ST	SF	1	A2
APTOS AV	SF	13	B3
AQUAVISTA WY	SF	9	C3
ARAGO ST	SF	20	A1
ARBOL LN	SF	6	A3
ARBOR ST	SF	14	A2
ARCH ST	SF	19	B1
ARCO WY	SF	20	A1
ARDATH CT	SF	15	C3
ARDENWOOD WY	SF	13	A3
ARELLANO AV	SF	19	A2
ARGENT AL	SF	10	A3
ARGONAUT AV	SF	20	C3
ARGUELLO BLVD	SF	5	B1
ARGUELLO BLVD	SF	9	B2
ARKANSAS ST	SF	11	B2
ARLETA AV	SF	21	A2
ARLINGTON ST	SF	14	B3
ARMISTEAD RD	SF	1	A2
ARMSTRONG AV	SF	21	B1
ARMY ST	SF	14	A1
ARMY ST	SF	15	A1
ARNOLD AV	SF	14	C3
ARROYO WY	SF	13	C2
ARTHUR AV	SF	15	C1
ASH ST	SF	6	B3
ASHBURTON PL	SF	7	A2
ASHBURY ST	SF	9	C1
ASHBURY TER	SF	10	A2
ASHTON AV	SF	19	B1
ASHWOOD LN	SF	9	C3
ATALAYA TER	SF	5	C3
ATHENS ST	SF	20	B2
ATTRIDGE AL	SF	2	C2
AUBURN ST	SF	3	A3
AUGUST AL	SF	3	A2
AUGUSTA ST	SF	15	A3
AUSTIN ST	SF	6	B2
AUTO DR	SF	9	B3
AVALON AV	SF	20	B1
AVENUE A	SF	3	C1
AVENUE B	SF	3	C2
AVENUE C	SF	3	C1
AVENUE D	SF	3	C1
AVENUE E	SF	3	C1
AVENUE F	SF	3	C1
AVENUE H	SF	3	C1
AVENUE I	SF	3	C1
AVENUE M	SF	3	C1
AVENUE N	SF	3	C1
AVENUE NORTH	SF	4	C2
AVERY ST	SF	6	B2
AVILA ST	SF	2	A2
AVOCA AL	SF	13	C2
AVON WY	SF	13	A3
AZTEC ST	SF	14	C1
B			
BACHE ST	SF	14	C3
BACON ST	SF	20	C1
BACON ST	SF	21	A1
BADEN ST	SF	14	A3
BADGER ST	SF	14	B3
BAKER ST	SF	2	A2
BAKER ST	SF	6	A2
BAKER ST	SF	10	A1
BALANCE ST	SF	3	A3
BALBOA ST	SF	4	B3
BALBOA ST	SF	5	A3
BALCETA AV	SF	13	B1
BALDWIN CT	SF	15	C3
BALHI CT	SF	20	A1
BALMY ST	SF	11	A3
BALTIMORE WY	SF	20	B3
BANBURY DR	SF	19	A2
BANCROFT AV	SF	15	B3

STREET	CITY	PG. NO.	SEE
BANCROFT AV	SF	21	B1
BANK ST	SF	1	B2
BANKS ST	SF	15	A2
BANNAM PL	SF	3	A2
BANNOCK ST	SF	20	A2
BARCELONA AV	SF	6	A3
BARNARD AV	SF	1	C3
BARNEVELD AV	SF	15	A2
BARTLETT ST	SF	10	C3
BARTLETT ST	SF	14	C1
BARTOL ST	SF	3	A2
BASS CT	SF	15	C3
BATTERY ST	SF	3	B2
BATTERY CMBR RD	SF	4	C1
BATTERY EAST RD	SF	1	A1
BAXTER AL	SF	13	B3
BAY ST	SF	2	B2
BAY ST	SF	3	A2
BAYSHORE BLVD	SF	15	A2
BAYSHORE BLVD	SF	21	A3
BAYSIDE DR	SF	3	C1
BAYVIEW ST	SF	15	B3
BAYVIEW PARK RD	SF	21	B2
BAYWOOD CT	SF	20	A2
BEACH ST	SF	2	A2
BEACH ST	SF	3	A2
BEACHMONT DR	SF	13	A3
BEACON ST	SF	14	B2
BEALE ST	SF	7	B1
BEATRICE LN	SF	15	C3
BEAUMONT AV	SF	5	C3
BEAVER ST	SF	10	A2
BECKETT ST	SF	3	A2
BEDFORD PL	SF	3	A3
BEEMAN LN	SF	21	B2
BEHR AV	SF	9	C3
BEIDEMAN ST	SF	6	A3
BELCHER ST	SF	10	B1
BELDEN ST	SF	7	A1
BELGRAVE AV	SF	9	C2
BELL CT	SF	15	C3
BELL RD	SF	1	A2
BELLAIR PL	SF	3	A2
BELLAVISTA LN	SF	13	C3
BELLA VISTA WY	SF	13	C2
BELLE AV	SF	19	A3
BELLEVUE AV	SF	20	A3
BELMONT AV	SF	9	C2
BELVEDERE ST	SF	9	C1
BEMIS ST	SF	14	B2
BENGAL AL	SF	13	B2
BENNINGTON ST	SF	14	C2
BENTON AV	SF	14	B3
BEPLER ST	SF	19	B3
BERGEN PL	SF	2	C2
BERKELEY WY	SF	14	A2
BERKSHIRE WY	SF	12	B3
BERNAL HTS BLVD	SF	14	C2
BERNARD ST	SF	2	C3
BERNICE ST	SF	11	A1
BERRY ST	SF	7	C3
BERRY ST	SF	11	B1
BERTHA LN	SF	15	C3
BERTITA ST	SF	20	A2
BERWICK PL	SF	11	A1
BESSIE ST	SF	14	C1
BEULAH ST	SF	9	C2
BEVERLY ST	SF	19	A2
BIGELOW CT	SF	3	C1
BIGLER AV	SF	9	C3
BIRCH ST	SF	6	B3
BIRD ST	SF	10	C2
BISHOP ST	SF	21	A2
BLACK PL	SF	2	C2
BLACKSTONE CT	SF	2	B2

STREET	CITY	PG. NO.	SEE
BLAIRWOOD LN	SF	9	B3
BLAKE ST	SF	5	C2
BLANCHE ST	SF	10	B3
BLANDY ST	SF	17	B1
BLANEY RD	SF	1	B2
BLANKEN AV	SF	21	B3
BLISS RD	SF	1	B3
BLUXOME ST	SF	7	B3
BLYTHDALE AV	SF	20	C3
BOARDMAN PL	SF	11	B1
BOCANA ST	SF	14	C2
BONIFACIO ST	SF	7	B3
BONITA ST	SF	2	C3
BONNIE BRAE LN	SF	12	B3
BONVIEW ST	SF	14	C2
BORICA ST	SF	19	B1
BOSWORTH ST	SF	14	A3
BOUTWELL ST	SF	15	A2
BOWDOIN ST	SF	21	A1
BOWLEY ST	SF	4	C1
BOWLING GRN DR	SF	9	B1
BOWMAN RD	SF	1	A2
BOYLSTON ST	SF	15	A3
BOYNTON CT	SF	10	B1
BRADFORD ST	SF	15	A2
BRADY ST	SF	10	C1
BRANNAN ST	SF	7	B3
BRANNAN ST	SF	11	A1
BRANT AL	SF	3	A2
BRAZIL AV	SF	20	B1
BREEN PL	SF	6	C3
BRENTWOOD AV	SF	13	C3
BRET HARTE TER	SF	2	C2
BREWSTER ST	SF	15	A2
BRIARCLIFF TER	SF	13	A2
BRICE TER	SF	11	A3
BRIDGEVIEW DR	SF	15	B3
BRIGHT ST	SF	19	B1
BRIGHTON AV	SF	19	C2
BRITTON ST	SF	21	A3
BROAD ST	SF	19	B2
BROADMOOR DR	SF	19	A1
BROADWAY	SF	2	A3
BROADWAY	SF	3	A3
BRODERICK ST	SF	2	A3
BRODERICK ST	SF	6	A2
BRODERICK ST	SF	10	A1
BROMLEY PL	SF	2	B3
BROMPTON AV	SF	14	A3
BRONTE ST	SF	15	A2
BROOK ST	SF	14	B2
BROOKDALE AV	SF	20	B3
BROOKHAVEN LN	SF	12	B3
BROOKLYN PL	SF	3	A3
BROSNAN ST	SF	10	C1
BROTHERHOOD WY	SF	19	A2
BRUCE AV	SF	19	C1
BRUMISS TER	SF	19	C3
BRUNSWICK ST	SF	19	B3
BRUNSWICK ST	SF	20	A3
BRUSH PL	SF	11	A1
BRUSSELS ST	SF	15	A3
BRYANT ST	SF	7	C2
BRYANT ST	SF	11	A1
BUCARELI DR	SF	18	C2
BUCHANAN ST	SF	2	B3
BUCHANAN ST	SF	6	B3
BUCKINGHAM WY	SF	19	A1
BUENA VISTA AV	SF	10	A1
BUENA VISTA TER	SF	10	A1
BURGOYNE ST	SF	2	C3
BURKE ST	SF	15	C2
BURLWOOD DR	SF	13	C3
BURNETT AV	SF	10	A3
BURNETT AV	SF	14	A1

STREET	CITY	PG. NO.	SEE
BURNHAM DANL CT	SF	6	B2
BURNS PL	SF	10	C1
BURNSIDE AV	SF	14	A3
BURR AV	SF	20	C3
BURRITT ST	SF	7	A2
BURROWS ST	SF	20	C1
BURROWS ST	SF	21	A1
BUSH ST	SF	6	A2
BUSH ST	SF	7	A1
BUTTE PL	SF	11	B1
BYINGTON ST	SF	6	B2
BYRON CT	SF	20	A3
BYXBEE ST	SF	19	A2
C			
C ST	SF	17	B1
CABRILLO ST	SF	8	A1
CABRILLO ST	SF	9	A1
CADELL PL	SF	3	A2
CAINE AV	SF	19	C2
CALEDONIA ST	SF	10	C1
CALGARY ST	SF	20	C3
CALHOUN TER	SF	3	A2
CALIFORNIA AV	SF	3	C2
CALIFORNIA ST	SF	3	B3
CALIFORNIA ST	SF	4	C2
CALIFORNIA ST	SF	5	A2
CALIFORNIA ST	SF	6	A2
CAMBON DR	SF	19	A2
CAMBRIDGE ST	SF	14	C3
CAMBRIDGE ST	SF	20	C1
CAMELLIA AV	SF	14	B3
CAMEO WY	SF	14	A1
CAMERON WY	SF	21	C2
CAMP ST	SF	10	B2
CAMPBELL AV	SF	21	A2
CAMPTON PL	SF	7	A2
CAMPUS CIR	SF	18	C1
CAMPUS LN	SF	20	C1
CANBY ST	SF	1	C2
CANYON DR	SF	20	B3
CAPISTRANO AV	SF	20	A1
CAPITOL AV	SF	19	B3
CAPP ST	SF	10	C2
CAPP ST	SF	14	C1
CAPRA WY	SF	2	A2
CARD AL	SF	3	A3
CARDENAS AV	SF	19	A2
CARGO WY	SF	15	C1
CARL ST	SF	9	C2
CARMEL ST	SF	9	C2
CARMELITA ST	SF	10	B1
CARNELIAN WY	SF	14	A1
CAROLINA ST	SF	11	B2
CARPENTER CT	SF	15	C1
CARR ST	SF	21	B1
CARRIE ST	SF	14	B3
CARRIZAL ST	SF	20	C3
CARROLL AV	SF	15	B3
CARROLL AV	SF	21	B1
CARSON ST	SF	10	A3
CARTER ST	SF	20	B3
CARVER ST	SF	15	A2
CASA WY	SF	2	A2
CASCADE WK	SF	13	A1
CASELLI AV	SF	10	A3
CASHMERE ST	SF	15	C3
CASITAS AV	SF	13	B2
CASSANDRA CT	SF	19	C3
CASTELO AV	SF	19	A2
CASTENADA AV	SF	13	B1
CASTILLO ST	SF	20	C3
CASTLE ST	SF	3	A2
CASTLE MANOR AV	SF	14	B3
CASTRO ST	SF	10	B2
CASTRO ST	SF	14	B1

1988 SAN FRANCISCO COUNTY STREET INDEX

STREET	CITY	PG. NO.	SEE
CATHERINE CT	SF	10	C3
CAYUGA AV	SF	19	C3
CAYUGA AV	SF	20	A2
CECILIA AV	SF	13	A1
CEDAR ST	SF	6	C2
CEDRO AV	SF	19	A1
CENTER PL	SF	7	B3
CENTRAL AV	SF	10	A1
CENTRAL FRWY	SF	6	C3
CENTRAL SKWY	SF	10	C1
CENTURY PL	SF	7	B1
CERES ST	SF	15	B3
CERRITOS AV	SF	19	A1
CERVANTES BLVD	SF	2	A2
CHABOT TER	SF	5	C3
CHAIN OF L DR E	SF	8	A1
CHAIN OF L DR W	SF	8	A1
CHANNEL ST	SF	11	B1
CHAPMAN ST	SF	15	A2
CHARING CRSS ST	SF	2	C3
CHARLES ST	SF	14	B2
CHARLESTOWN PL	SF	7	B2
CHARLTON CT	SF	2	B3
CHARTER OAK AV	SF	15	A2
CHASE CT	SF	10	C1
CHATHAM PL	SF	7	A1
CHATTANOOGA ST	SF	10	B3
CHAVES AV	SF	13	C2
CHELSEA PL	SF	7	A2
CHENERY ST	SF	14	B2
CHERRY ST	SF	5	B2
CHESLEY ST	SF	11	A1
CHESTER AV	SF	19	A3
CHESTNUT ST	SF	2	A2
CHESTNUT ST	SF	3	A2
CHICAGO WY	SF	20	B3
CHILD ST	SF	3	A2
CHILTON AV	SF	14	A3
CHINA BASIN ST	SF	11	C1
CHISM RD	SF	1	C3
CHRISTMAS TR PT	SF	10	A3
CHRISTOPHER DR	SF	9	B3
CHULA LN	SF	10	B2
CHUMASERO DR	SF	19	A2
CHURCH ST	SF	10	B2
CHURCH ST	SF	14	B1
CHURCHILL ST	SF	3	A3
CIELITO DR	SF	20	C3
CIRCULAR AV	SF	14	A3
CITY VIEW WY	SF	13	C1
CLAIRVIEW CT	SF	9	C3
CLARA ST	SF	7	B3
CLAREMONT BLVD	SF	13	B2
CLARENCE PL	SF	7	B3
CLARENDON AV	SF	9	C3
CLARION AL	SF	10	C2
CLARKE ST	SF	1	C3
CLAUDE LN	SF	7	A1
CLAY ST	SF	3	A3
CLAY ST	SF	5	C2
CLAYTON ST	SF	9	C1
CLAYTON ST	SF	10	A3
CLEARFIELD DR	SF	12	B3
CLEARY CT	SF	6	B2
CLEMENT ST	SF	4	A3
CLEMENT ST	SF	5	A2
CLEMENTINA ST	SF	7	B2
CLEMENTINA ST	SF	11	A1
CLEVELAND ST	SF	7	A3
CLIFFORD TER	SF	10	A2
CLINTON PARK	SF	10	B1
CLIPPER ST	SF	14	A1
CLIPPER TER	SF	14	A1
CLOVER LN	SF	10	A3
CLOVER ST	SF	10	A2
CLYDE ST	SF	11	A1
COCHRANE ST	SF	17	B1
CODMAN PL	SF	3	A3
COHEN PL	SF	6	C2
COLBY ST	SF	15	A3
COLBY ST	SF	21	A1
COLE ST	SF	9	C2
COLEMAN ST	SF	17	B1
COLERIDGE ST	SF	14	C2
COLIN PL	SF	7	A2
COLIN KELLY ST	SF	7	C3
COLLEGE AV	SF	14	B3
COLLEGE TER	SF	14	B3
COLLIER	SF	3	A3
COLLINGWOOD ST	SF	10	A2
COLLINS ST	SF	5	C2
COLON AV	SF	13	B3
COLONIAL WY	SF	20	A1
COLTON ST	SF	10	C1
COLUMBIA SQ ST	SF	7	A3
COLUMBUS AV	SF	2	C2
COLUSA PL	SF	10	C1
COMERFORD ST	SF	14	B1
COMMER CT	SF	15	C3
COMMERCE ST	SF	3	B2
COMMERCIAL ST	SF	3	A3
COMMONWEALTH AV	SF	5	C2
COMPTON RD	SF	1	A3
CONCORD ST	SF	20	A2
CONCOURSE DR	SF	9	B1
CONGDON	SF	14	B3
CONGO ST	SF	14	A3
CONKLING ST	SF	15	B3
CONNECTICUT ST	SF	11	B2
CONRAD ST	SF	14	A2
CONSERVATORY DR	SF	9	B1
CONSTANSO WY	SF	12	C3
CONVERSE ST	SF	11	A1
COOK ST	SF	5	C2
COOPER AL	SF	3	A3
COPPER AL	SF	10	A3
CORA ST	SF	21	A3
CORAL RD	SF	11	B3
CORALINO LN	SF	14	A1
CORBETT AV	SF	10	A3
CORBIN PL	SF	10	A2
CORDELIA ST	SF	3	A3
CORDOVA ST	SF	20	B3
CORNWALL ST	SF	5	B2
CORONA ST	SF	19	B1
CORONADO ST	SF	21	B2
CORP ZAVOVTZ ST	SF	1	C2
CORTES AV	SF	13	B2
CORTLAND AV	SF	14	C2
CORTLAND AV	SF	15	A2
CORWIN ST	SF	10	A3
COSMO PL	SF	7	A2
COSO AV	SF	14	C1
COSTA ST	SF	15	A1
COTTAGE ROW	SF	6	B2
COTTER ST	SF	14	A3
COUNTRY CLUB DR	SF	12	B3
COVENTRY CT	SF	13	C2
COVENTRY LN	SF	13	C2
COWELL PL	SF	3	B2
COWLES ST	SF	1	A2
CRAGMONT AV	SF	13	B1
CRAGS CT	SF	14	A2
CRAN PL	SF	6	B3
CRANE ST	SF	21	B1
CRANLEIGH DR	SF	13	A3
CRANSTON RD	SF	1	A2
CRAUT ST	SF	14	B3
CRESCENT AV	SF	14	C3
CRESPI DR	SF	19	A2
CRESTA VISTA DR	SF	13	B3
CRESTLAKE DR	SF	12	B2
CRESTLINE DR	SF	13	C1
CRESTMONT DR	SF	9	B3
CRESTWELL WK	SF	9	A3
CRISP RD	SF	17	A1
CRISSY FIELD AV	SF	1	A2
CROSS ST	SF	20	A2
CROSS OVER DR	SF	8	C1
CROWN TER	SF	9	C3
CRYSTAL ST	SF	19	B3
CUBA AL	SF	14	A2
CUESTA CT	SF	14	A1
CULEBRA TER	SF	2	C2
CUMBERLAND ST	SF	10	B3
CUNNINGHAM PL	SF	10	C3
CURTIS ST	SF	20	A2
CUSHMAN ST	SF	3	A3
CUSTER AV	SF	15	C1
CUSTOM HOUSE PL	SF	3	A3
CUTLER AV	SF	12	A2
CUVIER ST	SF	14	B3
CYPRESS ST	SF	14	C1
CYRIL MAGIN ST	SF	7	A2
CYRUS PL	SF	2	C3
D			
D ST	SF	17	B1
DAGGETT ST	SF	11	B1
DAKOTA ST	SF	11	B3
DALE PL	SF	6	C3
DALEWOOD WY	SF	13	B2
DANL BURNHAM CT	SF	6	B2
DANTON ST	SF	14	B3
DANVERS ST	SF	10	A2
DARIEN WY	SF	13	B3
DARRELL PL	SF	3	A2
DARTMOUTH ST	SF	15	A3
DARTMOUTH ST	SF	21	A1
DAVIDSON AV	SF	15	C1
DAVIS ST	SF	3	B3
DAWNVIEW WY	SF	14	A1
DAWSON PL	SF	3	A3
DAY ST	SF	14	B2
DEARBORN ST	SF	10	C2
DE BOOM ST	SF	7	B3
DECATUR ST	SF	11	A1
DECKER AL	SF	7	A3
DEDMAN CT	SF	15	C2
DEEMS RD	SF	1	B3
DEFOREST WY	SF	10	A2
DE HARO ST	SF	11	B1
DEHON ST	SF	10	B2
DELANO AV	SF	20	A2
DELGADO PL	SF	2	C3
DELLBROOK AV	SF	9	C3
DELLBROOK AV	SF	13	C1
DELMAR ST	SF	10	A1
DEL MONTE ST	SF	20	A2
DE LONG ST	SF	19	B3
DEL SUR AV	SF	13	C2
DELTA PL	SF	7	A2
DELTA ST	SF	21	A2
DEL VALE AV	SF	13	C2
DEMING ST	SF	10	A2
DEMONTFORT AV	SF	19	B1
DENSLOWE DR	SF	19	A2
DENT RD	SF	1	A3
DERBY ST	SF	7	A2
DESMOND ST	SF	21	A3
DE SOTO ST	SF	19	B1
DETROIT ST	SF	14	A3
DEVONSHIRE WY	SF	9	B3
DEWEY BLVD	SF	13	B1
DE WOLF ST	SF	19	C3
DIAMOND ST	SF	10	A2
DIAMOND ST	SF	14	A2
DIAMOND HTS BL	SF	14	A1
DIANA ST	SF	15	B3
DIAZ AV	SF	19	A2
DICHA AL	SF	5	C2
DICHIERA CT	SF	19	C3
DIGBY ST	SF	14	B2
DIVISADERO ST	SF	2	A3
DIVISADERO ST	SF	6	A3
DIVISADERO ST	SF	10	A1
DIVISION ST	SF	11	A1
DIXIE AL	SF	10	A3
DODGE PL	SF	6	C2
DOLORES ST	SF	10	B1
DOLORES ST	SF	14	B1
DOLORES TER	SF	10	B2
DONAHUE ST	SF	16	B3
DONAHUE ST	SF	17	A1
DONNER AV	SF	15	B3
DONNER AV	SF	21	B1
DORADO TER	SF	19	B1
DORANTES AV	SF	13	B1
DORCAS WY	SF	13	C2
DORCHESTER WY	SF	13	B2
DORE ST	SF	11	A1
DORIC AL	SF	3	A3
DORLAND ST	SF	10	B2
DORMAN AV	SF	15	A2
DORMITORY RD	SF	16	A3
DOUBLE ROCK ST	SF	21	C1
DOUGLASS ST	SF	10	A3
DOUGLASS ST	SF	14	A1
DOVE LOOP	SF	1	A2
DOVER ST	SF	7	C2
DOW PL	SF	7	B2
DOWNEY ST	SF	9	C2
DOYLE DR	SF	1	B2
DRAKE ST	SF	20	A3
DRUMM ST	SF	3	B3
DRUMMOND AL	SF	15	B2
DUBLIN ST	SF	20	B2
DUBOCE AV	SF	10	B1
DUDLEY RD	SF	1	B3
DUKES CT	SF	15	C2
DUNBAR AL	SF	3	A3
DUNCAN ST	SF	14	B1
DUNCOMBE AL	SF	3	A3
DUNNES AL	SF	3	A3
DUNSHEE AL	SF	15	B3
DUNSMUIR ST	SF	15	A3
DWIGHT ST	SF	21	A1
DYNAMITE RD	SF	1	A2
E			
E ST	SF	17	B1
EAGLE ST	SF	10	A3
EARL ST	SF	17	A1
EASTMAN ST	SF	2	C2
EASTWOOD DR	SF	19	B1
EATON PL	SF	3	A3
ECKER ST	SF	7	B1
EDDY ST	SF	6	A3
EDDY ST	SF	7	A2
EDGAR PL	SF	19	C1
EDGARDO PL	SF	3	A2
EDGEHILL WY	SF	13	B2
EDGEWOOD AV	SF	9	C2
EDIE RD	SF	1	C2
EDINBURGH ST	SF	20	B2
EDITH ST	SF	3	A2
EDNA ST	SF	19	C1
EDWARD ST	SF	5	B3
EGBERT AV	SF	21	B1
EL CAMINO D MAR	SF	4	A2
EL DORADO ST	SF	11	C1
ELGIN PARK	SF	10	C1
ELIM AL	SF	7	B1
ELIZABETH ST	SF	10	A3
ELIZABETH ST	SF	14	A1
ELK ST	SF	14	A3
ELKHART ST	SF	7	C2
ELLERT ST	SF	14	C2
ELLICK LN	SF	3	A3
ELLINGTON AV	SF	19	C3
ELLIOT ST	SF	21	A2
ELLIS ST	SF	6	A3
ELLIS ST	SF	7	A2
ELLSWORTH ST	SF	14	C2
ELM ST	SF	6	B3
ELMHURST DR	SF	13	A3
ELMIRA ST	SF	15	A2
EL MIRASOL PL	SF	12	C3
ELMWOOD WY	SF	19	B1
EL PLAZUELA WY	SF	19	A1
EL POLIN LOOP	SF	1	C3
EL SERENO CT	SF	14	A2
ELSIE ST	SF	14	C2
EL VERANO WY	SF	13	B3
ELWOOD ST	SF	7	A2
EMBARCADERO SWY	SF	3	B3
EMBARCADERO THE	SF	3	A2
EMERALD LN	SF	12	B3
EMERSON ST	SF	5	C2
EMERY LN	SF	3	A3
EMIL LN	SF	13	C3
EMMA ST	SF	7	A1
EMMET PL	SF	3	A3
EMMETT CT	SF	14	C1
EMPRESS LN	SF	21	A2
ENCANTO AV	SF	6	A3
ENCINAL WK	SF	9	A3
ENCLINE CT	SF	13	C2
ENGLISH ST	SF	16	B3
ENNIS RD	SF	1	A3
ENTERPRISE ST	SF	10	C2
ENTRADA CT N	SF	19	B1
ENTRADA CT S	SF	19	B1
ERIE ST	SF	10	C1
ERKSON CT	SF	6	A2
ERVINE ST	SF	21	A2
ESCOLTA WY	SF	12	B2
ESCONDIDO AV	SF	12	B3
ESMERALDA AV	SF	14	C2
ESMERALDA AV	SF	15	A2
ESPANOLA ST	SF	16	A3
ESPLANADE THE	SF	8	A1
ESQUINA DR	SF	20	C3
ESSEX ST	SF	7	B2
ESTERO AV	SF	19	A1
EUCALYPTUS DR	SF	12	C3
EUCLID AV	SF	5	B2
EUGENIA AV	SF	14	C2
EUREKA PL	SF	6	C2
EUREKA ST	SF	10	A2
EVA TER	SF	10	B1
EVANS AV	SF	15	C2
EVELYN WY	SF	13	C2
EVERGLADE DR	SF	12	B3
EVERSON ST	SF	14	B2
EWER PL	SF	3	A3
EWING TER	SF	5	C3
EXCELSIOR AV	SF	20	B1
EXCHANGE PL	SF	7	B1
EXECUTIVE PK BL	SF	21	B3
EXETER ST	SF	21	B1
EXPOSITION DR	SF	3	C1
F			
FAIR AV	SF	14	C1
FAIRBANKS ST	SF	10	A2
FAIRFAX AV	SF	15	B1
FAIRFIELD WY	SF	19	B1

1988 SAN FRANCISCO COUNTY STREET INDEX

STREET	CITY	PG. NO.	SEE
FAIRMOUNT ST	SF	14	B2
FAIR OAKS ST	SF	10	B3
FAITH ST	SF	15	A1
FALLON PL	SF	3	A3
FALMOUTH ST	SF	7	A3
FANNING WY	SF	13	A1
FARALLONES ST	SF	19	B2
FARGO PL	SF	11	A1
FARNSWORTH LN	SF	9	C2
FARNUM ST	SF	14	B2
FARRAGUT AV	SF	19	C3
FARVIEW CT	SF	9	C3
FAXON AV	SF	19	B1
FEDERAL ST	SF	7	B2
FELIX AV	SF	19	A2
FELL ST	SF	6	C3
FELL ST	SF	9	C1
FELL ST	SF	10	A1
FELLA PL	SF	7	A1
FELTON ST	SF	20	C1
FENTON LN	SF	14	A1
FERN ST	SF	6	B2
FERNANDEZ ST	SF	1	C3
FERNWOOD DR	SF	13	B3
FIELDING ST	SF	3	A2
FILBERT ST	SF	2	A3
FILBERT ST	SF	3	A2
FILLMORE ST	SF	2	A3
FILLMORE ST	SF	6	B3
FILLMORE ST	SF	10	B1
FISHER AL	SF	3	A3
FISHER AV	SF	17	B1
FISHER LOOP	SF	1	B3
FITCH ST	SF	21	C2
FITZGERALD AV	SF	21	B1
FLINT ST	SF	10	A2
FLOOD AV	SF	14	A3
FLORA ST	SF	15	B3
FLORENCE ST	SF	3	A3
FLORENTINE ST	SF	20	A2
FLORIDA ST	SF	11	A1
FLORIDA ST	SF	15	A1
FLOURNOY ST	SF	19	B3
FLOWER ST	SF	15	A2
FOERSTER ST	SF	13	C3
FOLGER AL	SF	6	B2
FOLSOM ST	SF	7	B2
FOLSOM ST	SF	10	C1
FOLSOM ST	SF	11	A1
FOLSOM ST	SF	15	A2
FONT BLVD	SF	18	C1
FONT BLVD	SF	19	A2
FOOTE AV	SF	19	C2
FORD ST	SF	10	B2
FOREST KNLS DR	SF	9	C3
FOREST SIDE AV	SF	13	A2
FOREST VIEW DR	SF	12	C3
FORTUNA AV	SF	6	A3
FOUNTAIN ST	SF	14	A1
FOWLER AV	SF	13	C1
FRANCE AV	SF	20	B2
FRANCIS ST	SF	20	B1
FRANCISCO ST	SF	2	A2
FRANCISCO ST	SF	3	A2
FRANCONIA ST	SF	15	A2
FRANK ST	SF	7	A1
FRANKLIN ST	SF	2	B2
FRANKLIN ST	SF	6	B1
FRATESSA CT	SF	21	B2
FREDELA LN	SF	9	C3
FREDERICK ST	SF	9	C2
FREDSON CT	SF	20	A2
FREELON ST	SF	7	B3
FREEMAN CT	SF	3	A3
FREEMAN ST	SF	1	B2
FREMONT ST	SF	7	B1
FRENCH CT	SF	1	C2
FRESNO ST	SF	3	A3
FRIEDELL ST	SF	17	A1
FRONT ST	SF	3	B2
FUENTE AV	SF	19	A2
FULTON ST	SF	6	A3
FULTON ST	SF	8	A1
FULTON ST	SF	9	A1
FUNSTON AV	SF	1	C3
FUNSTON AV	SF	5	A2
FUNSTON AV	SF	9	A2
FUNSTON AV	SF	13	A1
G			
GABILAN WY	SF	12	C3
GAISER CT	SF	10	B2
GALE ST	SF	7	C3
GALEWOOD CIR	SF	9	C3
GALINDO AV	SF	19	A2
GALLAGHER LN	SF	7	A3
GALVEZ AV	SF	15	B2
GALVEZ AV	SF	16	A3
GAMBIER ST	SF	20	C1
GARCES DR	SF	18	C2
GARCIA AV	SF	13	B2
GARDEN ST	SF	6	A2
GARDENSIDE DR	SF	10	A3
GARDNER PL	SF	7	A2
GARFIELD ST	SF	19	A2
GARLINGTON CT	SF	15	C3
GARRISON AV	SF	21	A3
GATES ST	SF	15	A2
GATEVIEW AV	SF	3	C1
GATEVIEW CT	SF	13	B1
GATUN AL	SF	13	C2
GAVEN ST	SF	15	A3
GAVIOTA WY	SF	13	C2
GEARY BLVD	SF	5	C3
GEARY BLVD	SF	6	A2
GEARY ST	SF	6	C2
GEARY ST	SF	7	A2
GELLERT DR	SF	12	B3
GENEBERN WY	SF	14	B3
GENEVA AV	SF	19	C1
GENEVA AV	SF	20	A2
GENNESSEE ST	SF	13	C3
GENOA PL	SF	3	A2
GEORGE CT	SF	15	C3
GERKE AL	SF	3	A2
GERMANIA ST	SF	10	B1
GETZ ST	SF	19	C2
GIANTS DR	SF	21	C2
GIBB ST	SF	3	A3
GIBSON RD	SF	4	C2
GILBERT ST	SF	11	A1
GILLETTE AV	SF	21	B3
GILMAN AV	SF	21	B1
GILROY ST	SF	21	B2
GIRARD RD	SF	1	C2
GIRARD ST	SF	15	A2
GLADEVIEW WY	SF	13	C1
GLADIOLUS LN	SF	13	A3
GLADSTONE DR	SF	14	C3
GLADYS ST	SF	14	C2
GLENBROOK AV	SF	9	C3
GLENDALE ST	SF	10	A3
GLENHAVEN LN	SF	10	A3
GLENVIEW DR	SF	13	C1
GLOBE AL	SF	13	B3
GLORIA CT	SF	20	A2
GLOVER ST	SF	2	C3
GODEUS ST	SF	14	C2
GOETHE ST	SF	19	B3
GOETTINGEN ST	SF	15	A3
GOETTINGEN ST	SF	21	A1
GOLD ST	SF	3	A3
GOLDEN CT	SF	2	C3
GOLDEN GATE AV	SF	5	B3
GOLDEN GATE AV	SF	6	A3
GOLDING LN	SF	10	A3
GOLD MINE DR	SF	14	A2
GOLETA AV	SF	12	C3
GONZALEZ DR	SF	18	C2
GONZALEZ DR	SF	19	A2
GORDON ST	SF	11	A1
GORGAS AV	SF	1	C2
GORHAM ST	SF	14	B3
GOUGH ST	SF	6	B1
GOUGH ST	SF	10	C1
GOULD ST	SF	21	B1
GRACE ST	SF	10	C1
GRAFTON AV	SF	19	B2
GRAHAM ST	SF	1	B3
GRANADA AV	SF	19	B2
GRANAT CT	SF	9	B1
GRAND VIEW AV	SF	10	A3
GRAND VIEW AV	SF	14	A1
GRANDVIEW TER	SF	10	A3
GRANT AV	SF	3	A2
GRANT AV	SF	7	A1
GRANVILLE WY	SF	13	B2
GRATTAN ST	SF	9	C2
GRAYSTONE TER	SF	9	C3
GREAT HWY	SF	8	A3
GREAT HWY	SF	12	A1
GREEN PL	SF	2	C3
GREEN ST	SF	2	A3
GREEN ST	SF	3	B2
GREENOUGH AV	SF	1	A2
GREENVIEW CT	SF	9	B3
GREENWICH ST	SF	2	A3
GREENWICH ST	SF	3	B2
GREENWICH TER	SF	2	C2
GREENWOOD AV	SF	19	C1
GRENARD TER	SF	2	B2
GRIFFITH ST	SF	21	C2
GRIJALVA DR	SF	19	A2
GROTE PL	SF	7	B2
GROVE ST	SF	6	A3
GROVE ST	SF	9	C1
GROVER PL	SF	3	A2
GUERRERO ST	SF	10	C1
GUERRERO ST	SF	14	C1
GUTTENBERG ST	SF	20	A3
GUY PL	SF	7	B2
H			
H ST	SF	17	B1
HAHN ST	SF	20	C3
HAIGHT ST	SF	9	C1
HAIGHT ST	SF	10	A1
HALE ST	SF	15	A3
HALLAM ST	SF	7	A3
HALLECK ST	SF	1	C2
HALLECK ST	SF	3	B3
HALYBURTON CT	SF	3	C1
HAMERTON AV	SF	14	A3
HAMILTON ST	SF	1	A2
HAMILTON ST	SF	21	A1
HAMPSHIRE ST	SF	11	A2
HANCOCK ST	SF	10	B2
HANOVER ST	SF	20	A3
HARBOR RD	SF	16	A3
HARDIE PL	SF	7	A1
HARDIE RD	SF	1	B3
HARDING RD	SF	18	A1
HARE ST	SF	16	A3
HARKNESS AV	SF	21	A2
HARLAN PL	SF	7	A1
HARLEM AL	SF	6	C2
HARLOW ST	SF	10	B2
HARNEY WY	SF	21	B3
HAROLD AV	SF	19	C2
HARPER ST	SF	14	B2
HARRIET ST	SF	7	A3
HARRIET ST	SF	11	B1
HARRINGTON ST	SF	20	A1
HARRIS PL	SF	2	B2
HARRISON BLVD	SF	1	A3
HARRISON ST	SF	7	A3
HARRISON ST	SF	11	A2
HARRISON ST	SF	15	A1
HARRY ST	SF	14	B2
HARTFORD ST	SF	10	B2
HARVARD ST	SF	20	C1
HARWOOD AL	SF	3	A2
HASTINGS TER	SF	2	C2
HATTIE ST	SF	10	A2
HAVELOCK ST	SF	19	C1
HAVENS ST	SF	2	C2
HAVENSIDE DR	SF	12	B3
HAWES ST	SF	21	C1
HAWKINS LN	SF	15	C3
HAWTHORNE ST	SF	7	B2
HAYES ST	SF	6	A3
HAYES ST	SF	9	C1
HAYWARD PL	SF	11	A1
HAZELWOOD AV	SF	13	C3
HEAD ST	SF	19	B2
HEARST AV	SF	13	C3
HEATHER AV	SF	5	C2
HELEN ST	SF	6	C1
HELENA ST	SF	15	A2
HEMLOCK ST	SF	6	B2
HEMWAY TER	SF	5	C3
HENRY ST	SF	10	B2
HENRY ADAMS ST	SF	11	A1
HERMANN ST	SF	10	B1
HERNANDEZ AV	SF	13	B1
HERON ST	SF	11	A1
HESTER AV	SF	21	B2
HEYMAN AV	SF	14	C2
HICKORY ST	SF	10	B1
HICKS RD	SF	1	B3
HIDALGO TER	SF	10	B2
HIGH ST	SF	14	A1
HIGHLAND AV	SF	14	B2
HIGUERA AV	SF	18	C2
HILIRITAS AV	SF	14	A2
HILL BLVD S	SF	20	B3
HILL DR	SF	17	B1
HILL ST	SF	10	B3
HILLCREST CT	SF	13	C3
HILLPOINT AV	SF	9	C2
HILLVIEW CT	SF	15	C3
HILLWAY AV	SF	9	C2
HILTON ST	SF	15	A2
HIMMELMAN PL	SF	2	C3
HITCHCOCK ST	SF	1	A2
HOBART AL	SF	7	A2
HODGES AL	SF	3	A2
HOFF ST	SF	10	C2
HOFFMAN AV	SF	14	A1
HOFFMAN ST	SF	1	A2
HOLLADAY AV	SF	15	A1
HOLLAND CT	SF	7	A2
HOLLIS ST	SF	6	B2
HOLLISTER AV	SF	21	B1
HOLLOWAY AV	SF	19	B1
HOLLY PARK CIR	SF	14	C2
HOLLYWOOD CT	SF	20	A2
HOLYOKE ST	SF	21	A1
HOMER ST	SF	11	A1
HOMESTEAD ST	SF	14	A1
HOMEWOOD CT	SF	19	B1
HOOKER AL	SF	7	A1
HOOPER ST	SF	11	B1
HOPKINS AV	SF	10	A3
HORACE ST	SF	15	A1
HORNE AV	SF	17	B1
HOTALING PL	SF	3	B3
HOUSTON ST	SF	2	C2
HOWARD RD	SF	4	C2
HOWARD ST	SF	7	A3
HOWARD ST	SF	10	C1
HOWE RD	SF	1	A2
HOWTH ST	SF	19	C2
HUBBELL ST	SF	11	B2
HUDSON AV	SF	15	B1
HUDSON AV	SF	16	C3
HUGO ST	SF	9	B2
HULBERT AL	SF	7	B3
HUMBOLDT ST	SF	11	C3
HUNT ST	SF	7	B2
HUNTERS PT BLVD	SF	16	A2
HUNTERS PT EXWY	SF	21	C2
HUNTINGTON DR	SF	12	B3
HURON AV	SF	19	C2
HUSSEY ST	SF	17	B1
HUTCHINS CT	SF	3	C1
HYDE ST	SF	2	C2
HYDE ST	SF	6	C2
I			
I ST	SF	17	A1
ICEHOUSE AL	SF	3	B2
IDORA AV	SF	13	B2
IGNACIO ST	SF	21	C2
ILLINOIS ST	SF	11	C1
ILLINOIS ST	SF	15	C1
ILS LN	SF	3	A3
IMPERIAL AV	SF	2	B2
INA CT	SF	20	B1
INDIANA ST	SF	11	C2
INDIANA ST	SF	15	C1
INDUSTRIAL ST	SF	15	A2
INFANTRY TER	SF	1	B3
INGALLS ST	SF	16	A3
INGALLS ST	SF	21	C1
INGERSON AV	SF	21	B1
INNES AV	SF	15	B1
INNES AV	SF	16	A3
INVERNESS DR	SF	12	C3
IOWA ST	SF	11	C3
IRIS AV	SF	5	C2
IRON AL	SF	10	A3
IRVING ST	SF	8	A2
IRVING ST	SF	9	A2
IRWIN ST	SF	11	B2
ISIS ST	SF	10	C1
ISLAIS ST	SF	15	C1
ISOLA WY	SF	13	C2
ITALY AV	SF	20	A2
IVY ST	SF	6	B3
J			
J ST	SF	17	A1
JACKSON PL	SF	3	B3
JACKSON ST	SF	2	A3
JACKSON ST	SF	3	A3
JACKSON ST	SF	5	B2
JADE PL	SF	14	A2
JAKEY CT	SF	15	C3
JAMES AL	SF	3	A3
JAMES LICK FRWY	SF	15	A2
JAMES LICK FRWY	SF	21	A1
JAMES LICK SKWY	SF	11	A1
JAMESTOWN AV	SF	21	B2
JANSEN ST	SF	2	C2
JARBOE AV	SF	14	C2
JASON CT	SF	3	A3
JASPER PL	SF	3	A2
JAVA ST	SF	10	A2

1988 SAN FRANCISCO COUNTY STREET INDEX

STREET	CITY	PG. NO.	SEE
JEAN WY	SF	5	C3
JEFFERSON ST	SF	2	A2
JENNINGS ST	SF	15	C3
JENNINGS ST	SF	16	A2
JENNINGS ST	SF	21	B1
JEROME AL	SF	3	A3
JERROLD AV	SF	15	B1
JERROLD AV	SF	16	A3
JERSEY ST	SF	14	A1
JESSIE ST	SF	6	C3
JESSIE ST	SF	7	A2
JESSIE ST	SF	10	C1
JEWETT ST	SF	11	B1
JOHN ST	SF	3	A3
JOHN F KNNDY DR	SF	8	A1
J F KENNEDY DR	SF	9	A1
J F SHELLEY DR	SF	20	C1
JOHN MUIR DR	SF	18	B2
JOHNSTONE DR	SF	9	C3
JOICE ST	SF	3	A3
JONES ST	SF	2	C2
JONES ST	SF	7	A2
JOOST AV	SF	13	C3
JORDAN AV	SF	5	C2
JOSEPHA AV	SF	19	A2
JOSIAH AV	SF	19	C2
JOY ST	SF	15	A2
JUAN BATSTA CIR	SF	19	A2
JUANITA WY	SF	13	B2
JUDAH ST	SF	8	A2
JUDAH ST	SF	9	A2
JUDSON AV	SF	19	C1
JULES AV	SF	19	B1
JULIA ST	SF	7	A3
JULIAN AV	SF	10	C1
JULIUS ST	SF	3	A2
JUNIOR TER	SF	20	A2
JUNIPER ST	SF	11	A1
JUNIPRO SRRA BL	SF	19	A2
JURI ST	SF	14	C1
JUSTIN DR	SF	14	B3
K			
KANSAS ST	SF	11	A1
KAPLAN LN	SF	7	B2
KAREN CT	SF	21	A1
KATE ST	SF	11	A1
KEARNY ST	SF	3	A2
KEARNY ST	SF	7	A1
KEITH ST	SF	15	C2
KEITH ST	SF	21	B2
KELLOCH AV	SF	21	A3
KEMPTON AV	SF	19	B3
KENNEDY AV	SF	1	C2
KENNY AL	SF	20	A2
KENSINGTON WY	SF	13	B2
KENT ST	SF	3	A2
KENWOOD WY	SF	19	B1
KEPPLER CT	SF	3	C1
KERN ST	SF	14	B3
KEY AV	SF	21	B2
KEYES AL	SF	3	A3
KEYES AV	SF	1	B2
KEYSTONE WY	SF	19	B1
KEZAR DR	SF	9	B2
KIMBALL PL	SF	2	C3
KING ST	SF	7	B3
KING ST	SF	11	B1
KINGSTON ST	SF	14	C2
KINZEY ST	SF	1	A2
KIRKHAM ST	SF	8	A3
KIRKHAM ST	SF	9	A2
KIRKWOOD AV	SF	15	B2
KIRKWOOD AV	SF	17	A1
KISKA RD	SF	16	A3
KISSLING ST	SF	10	C1
KITTREDGE TER	SF	5	C3
KNOLLVIEW WY	SF	13	C1
KNOTT CT	SF	20	A3
KOBBE AV	SF	1	A3
KOHLER	SF	3	A2
KRAMER PL	SF	3	A2
KRAUSGRILL PL	SF	3	A2
KRONQUIST CT	SF	14	B1
L			
LA AVANZADA	SF	9	C3
LA BICA WY	SF	13	C2
LAFAYETTE ST	SF	10	C1
LA FERRERA TER	SF	3	A2
LA GRANDE AV	SF	20	B2
LAGUNA ST	SF	2	B3
LAGUNA ST	SF	6	B3
LAGUNA ST	SF	10	B1
LAGUNA HONDA BL	SF	13	B1
LAGUNITAS DR	SF	13	A3
LAIDLEY ST	SF	14	B2
LAKE ST	SF	4	B2
LAKE ST	SF	5	A2
LAKE FOREST CT	SF	9	B3
LAKE MERCED BL	SF	12	B3
LAKE MERCED BL	SF	18	C2
LAKE MERCED HLL	SF	18	C3
LAKE SHORE DR	SF	12	B3
LAKE SHORE PLZA	SF	12	B3
LAKEVIEW AV	SF	19	B2
LAKEWOOD AV	SF	19	B1
LAMARTINE ST	SF	14	B3
LAMSON LN	SF	10	A3
LANCASTER LN	SF	12	B3
LANDERS ST	SF	10	B2
LANE ST	SF	15	C3
LANE ST	SF	21	B2
LANGDON CT	SF	1	A2
LANGTON ST	SF	7	A3
LANSDALE AV	SF	13	B2
LANSING ST	SF	7	B2
LAPHAM WY	SF	20	B3
LAPIDGE ST	SF	10	C2
LA PLAYA	SF	8	A1
LAPU LAPU ST	SF	7	B3
LARCH ST	SF	6	A3
LARKIN ST	SF	2	C2
LARKIN ST	SF	6	C2
LARKSPUR AV	SF	21	B2
LA SALLE AV	SF	15	C2
LA SALLE AV	SF	17	A1
LASKIE ST	SF	7	A3
LATHROP AV	SF	21	B3
LATONA ST	SF	15	B3
LAURA ST	SF	19	C3
LAUREL ST	SF	5	C1
LAUSSAT ST	SF	10	B1
LAWRENCE AV	SF	19	C3
LAWTON ST	SF	8	A3
LAWTON ST	SF	9	A3
LEAVENWORTH ST	SF	2	C2
LEAVENWORTH ST	SF	6	C2
LEAVENWORTH ST	SF	7	A3
LECH WALESA	SF	6	C3
LE CONTE AV	SF	21	B2
LEDYARD ST	SF	15	B3
LEE AV	SF	19	C2
LEESE ST	SF	14	C2
LEGION CT	SF	19	B1
LEGION HONOR DR	SF	4	C1
LEIDESDORFF ST	SF	3	B3
LELAND AV	SF	21	A2
LENOX WY	SF	13	B2
LEO ST	SF	20	B1
LEONA TER	SF	6	A2
LEROY PL	SF	2	C3
LESSING ST	SF	19	C3
LESTER CT	SF	3	C1
LETTERMAN DR	SF	1	C2
LETTUCE LN	SF	15	B2
LEVANT ST	SF	10	A2
LEXINGTON ST	SF	10	C2
LIBERTY ST	SF	10	B3
LICK PL	SF	7	B2
LIEBIG ST	SF	19	C3
LIEUT ALLEN ST	SF	1	C2
LIEUT JAUSS ST	SF	1	C2
LIGGETT AV	SF	1	C3
LILAC ST	SF	14	C1
LILLIAN ST	SF	15	C3
LILY ST	SF	10	B1
LINARES AV	SF	9	B3
LINCOLN BLVD	SF	1	A3
LINCOLN BLVD	SF	4	C1
LINCOLN CT	SF	20	A3
LINCOLN WY	SF	8	A2
LINCOLN WY	SF	9	A2
LINDA ST	SF	10	C2
LINDA VIS STEPS	SF	7	B3
LINDEN ST	SF	6	B3
LINDSAY CIR	SF	15	C1
LIPPARD AV	SF	14	A3
LISBON ST	SF	20	A2
LIVINGSTON ST	SF	1	B2
LLOYD ST	SF	10	A1
LOBOS ST	SF	19	B2
LOCKSLEY AV	SF	9	B3
LOCKWOOD ST	SF	17	B1
LOCUST ST	SF	5	C2
LOEHR ST	SF	20	C3
LOMA VISTA TER	SF	10	A2
LOMBARD ST	SF	1	C3
LOMBARD ST	SF	2	A2
LOMBARD ST	SF	3	A2
LOMITA AV	SF	9	A3
LONDON ST	SF	20	A1
LONE MTN TER	SF	5	C3
LONG AV	SF	1	A2
LONGVIEW CT	SF	13	C1
LOOMIS ST	SF	15	A2
LOPEZ AV	SF	13	B1
LORAINE CT	SF	5	B3
LORI LN	SF	9	C3
LOS PALMOS DR	SF	13	C3
LOUISBURG ST	SF	19	C2
LOWELL ST	SF	20	A3
LOWER TER	SF	10	A2
LOYOLA TER	SF	5	C3
LUCERNE ST	SF	11	B1
LUCKY ST	SF	15	A1
LUCY ST	SF	15	B3
LUDLOW AL	SF	13	B2
LULU AL	SF	13	C3
LUM, WALTER PL	SF	3	A3
LUM, WALTER PL	SF	7	A1
LUNADO CT	SF	19	A1
LUNADO WY	SF	19	A1
LUNDEEN ST	SF	1	C2
LUNDYS LN	SF	14	C2
LUPINE AV	SF	5	C2
LURLINE ST	SF	9	A3
LURMONT TER	SF	2	C2
LUSK ST	SF	7	B3
LYELL ST	SF	14	B3
LYNCH ST	SF	2	C3
LYNDHURST DR.	SF	19	A1
LYON ST	SF	1	C3
LYON ST	SF	6	A1
LYON ST	SF	10	A1
LYSETTE ST	SF	2	C3
MABEL AL	SF	6	C2
MABINI ST	SF	7	B2
MABREY CT	SF	15	C1
MACARTHUR AV	SF	1	C3
MAC ARTHUR AV	SF	2	B2
MACEDONIA ST	SF	15	A1
MACONDRAY LN	SF	2	C3
MACRAE ST	SF	1	C2
MADDUX AV	SF	15	B3
MADERA ST	SF	11	B3
MADISON ST	SF	20	C1
MADRID ST	SF	20	B2
MADRONE AV	SF	13	B2
MAGELLAN AV	SF	13	B1
MAGNOLIA ST	SF	2	B2
MAHAN ST	SF	17	B2
MAIDEN LN	SF	7	A2
MAIN ST	SF	7	B1
MAJESTIC AV	SF	19	C2
MALDEN AL	SF	7	B2
MALLORCA WY	SF	2	A2
MALTA DR	SF	14	A3
MALVINA PL	SF	3	A3
MANCHESTER ST	SF	14	C1
MANDALAY LN	SF	13	A1
MANGELS AV	SF	13	C3
MANOR DR	SF	19	B1
MANSEAU ST	SF	17	B2
MANSELL ST	SF	20	C2
MANSELL ST	SF	21	A2
MANSFIELD ST	SF	20	C3
MANZANITA AV	SF	5	C2
MAPLE ST	SF	5	C2
MARCELA AV	SF	13	B1
MARCY PL	SF	3	A3
MARENGO ST	SF	15	A2
MARGARET AV	SF	19	C2
MARGRAVE PL	SF	3	A2
MARIETTA DR	SF	13	C2
MARIETTA DR	SF	14	A2
MARIN ST	SF	15	C1
MARINA BLVD	SF	2	A2
MARINE DR	SF	1	B2
MARINER DR	SF	3	C1
MARION PL	SF	2	C2
MARIPOSA ST	SF	11	A2
MARK LN	SF	7	A1
MARKET ST	SF	7	A3
MARKET ST	SF	10	B2
MARNE AV	SF	13	B2
MARS ST	SF	10	A2
MARSHALL ST	SF	1	C2
MARSILLY ST	SF	14	B3
MARSTON AV	SF	19	C1
MARTHA AV	SF	14	A3
MARTINEZ ST	SF	1	C3
MARTN L KING DR	SF	8	A2
MARTN L KING DR	SF	9	A2
MARVEL CT	SF	4	B2
MAR VIEW WY	SF	9	C3
MARX MEADOW DR	SF	8	C1
MARY ST	SF	7	A3
MASON CT	SF	3	C1
MASON ST	SF	1	B2
MASON ST	SF	3	A2
MASON ST	SF	7	A2
MASONIC AV	SF	5	C3
MASONIC AV	SF	10	A1
MASSASOIT ST	SF	15	A1
MASSETT PL	SF	7	B2
MATEO ST	SF	14	B2
MATTHEW CT	SF	16	A3
MAULDIN ST	SF	1	A2
MAYFAIR DR	SF	5	C2
MAYFLOWER ST	SF	15	A2
MAYNARD ST	SF	14	B3
MAYWOOD DR	SF	13	B3
MCALLISTER ST	SF	5	C3
MCALLISTER ST	SF	6	A3
MCCANN ST	SF	16	B3
MCCARTHY AV	SF	20	C3
MCCOPPIN ST	SF	10	C1
MCCORMICK PL	SF	2	C3
MCDONALD ST	SF	1	B2
MCDOWELL AV	SF	1	B2
MCDOWELL AV	SF	2	B2
MCKINNON AV	SF	15	B2
MCLAREN AV	SF	4	B2
MCLEA CT	SF	11	A1
MEACHAM PL	SF	6	C2
MEADE AV	SF	21	B2
MEADOWBROOK DR	SF	12	C3
MEDA AV	SF	20	A1
MEDAU PL	SF	3	A2
MELBA AV	SF	13	A3
MELRA CT	SF	21	A3
MELROSE AV	SF	13	C3
MENDELL ST	SF	15	B2
MENDELL ST	SF	21	B1
MENDOSA AV	SF	13	B1
MERCATO CT	SF	14	A3
MERCED AV	SF	13	B2
MERCEDES WY	SF	19	A1
MERCHANT RD	SF	1	A2
MERCHANT ST	SF	3	B3
MERCURY ST	SF	15	B3
MERLIN ST	SF	7	B3
MERRILL ST	SF	15	A3
MERRIMAC ST	SF	11	C1
MERRITT ST	SF	10	A2
MERSEY ST	SF	10	B3
MESA AV	SF	1	C2
MESA AV	SF	13	B1
METSON RD	SF	8	C2
MICHIGAN ST	SF	11	C3
MIDCREST WY	SF	13	C1
MIDDLE DR E	SF	9	B1
MIDDLE DR W	SF	8	C2
MIDDLEFIELD DR	SF	12	C3
MIDDLE POINT RD	SF	16	A2
MIDWAY ST	SF	3	A2
MIGUEL ST	SF	14	B2
MILAN TER	SF	19	C3
MILES ST	SF	1	B2
MILEY ST	SF	5	C1
MILL ST	SF	21	A2
MILLER PL	SF	3	A3
MILLER RD	SF	1	A2
MILTON ST	SF	14	B3
MILTON ROSS ST	SF	15	B2
MINERVA ST	SF	19	B2
MINNA ST	SF	7	A3
MINNA ST	SF	10	C1
MINNESOTA ST	SF	11	C2
MINNESOTA ST	SF	15	C1
MINT ST	SF	7	A3
MIRABEL AV	SF	14	C1
MIRALOMA DR	SF	13	B2
MIRAMAR AV	SF	19	B2
MISSION ST	SF	6	C3
MISSION ST	SF	7	A2
MISSION ST	SF	10	C2
MISSION ST	SF	14	B3
MISSION ST	SF	20	A2
MISSION ROCK ST	SF	11	B1
MISSISSIPPI ST	SF	11	B2
MISSISSIPPI ST	SF	15	B1
MISSOURI ST	SF	11	B2
MISSOURI ST	SF	15	B1
MISTRAL ST	SF	11	A2

STREET	CITY	PG. NO.	SEE
MIZPAH ST	SF	14	A3
MODOC AV	SF	19	C2
MOFFITT ST	SF	14	B2
MOJAVE ST	SF	15	A2
MOLIMO DR	SF	13	C2
MONCADA WY	SF	13	A3
MONETA CT	SF	19	C3
MONETA WY	SF	19	C3
MONO ST	SF	10	A3
MONROE ST	SF	7	A1
MONTAGUE PL	SF	3	A2
MONTALVO AV	SF	13	B1
MONTANA ST	SF	19	B2
MONTCALM AV	SF	15	A1
MONTCLAIR TER	SF	2	C2
MONTECITO AV	SF	13	C3
MONTEREY BLVD	SF	13	C3
MONTE VISTA DR	SF	19	A1
MONTEZUMA ST	SF	14	C1
MONTGOMERY ST	SF	1	B2
MONTGOMERY ST	SF	3	A2
MONTGOMERY ST	SF	7	B1
MONTICELLO ST	SF	19	A2
MONUMENT WY	SF	9	C2
MOORE PL	SF	2	C2
MORAGA AV	SF	1	B3
MORAGA ST	SF	8	A3
MORAGA ST	SF	9	A3
MORELAND ST	SF	14	B2
MORGAN AL	SF	10	A3
MORNINGSIDE DR	SF	12	B3
MORRELL PL	SF	2	C3
MORRELL ST	SF	17	B1
MORRIS RD	SF	1	A3
MORRIS ST	SF	7	B3
MORSE ST	SF	20	A3
MORTON ST	SF	1	C2
MOSCOW ST	SF	20	B2
MOSS ST	SF	7	A3
MOULTON ST	SF	2	A2
MOULTRIE ST	SF	14	C2
MOUNT LN	SF	9	A3
MOUNTN SPGS AV	SF	9	C3
MOUNT VERNON AV	SF	19	C2
MOUNTVIEW CT	SF	13	C1
MUIR LOOP	SF	1	C3
MULFORD AL	SF	7	A1
MULLEN AV	SF	15	A1
MUNICH ST	SF	20	B2
MURRAY ST	SF	14	B3
MUSEUM WY	SF	10	A2
MYRA WY	SF	13	C2
MYRTLE ST	SF	6	C2
N			
NADELL CT	SF	20	A3
NAGLEE AV	SF	19	C2
NAHUA AV	SF	19	C2
NANTUCKET AV	SF	20	A1
NAPIER LN	SF	3	A2
NAPLES ST	SF	20	B2
NAPOLEON ST	SF	15	B1
NATICK ST	SF	14	B3
NATOMA ST	SF	7	A3
NATOMA ST	SF	10	C1
NAUMAN RD	SF	1	B3
NAVAJO AV	SF	20	A1
NAVY RD	SF	16	A3
NAYLOR ST	SF	20	B3
NEBRASKA ST	SF	15	A2
NELLIE ST	SF	10	B3
NELSON AV	SF	21	B2
NEPTUNE ST	SF	15	B3
NEVADA ST	SF	15	A2
NEWBURG ST	SF	14	A1
NEWCOMB AV	SF	15	B2

STREET	CITY	PG. NO.	SEE
NEWELL ST	SF	2	C2
NEWHALL ST	SF	15	B3
NEWHALL ST	SF	21	B1
NEWMAN ST	SF	14	C2
NEW MONTGMRY ST	SF	7	B2
NEWTON ST	SF	20	A2
NEY ST	SF	14	B3
NIAGARA AV	SF	19	C2
NIANTIC AV	SF	19	B3
NIBBI CT	SF	21	B3
NICHOLS WY	SF	21	C2
NIDO AV	SF	5	C3
NIMITZ AV	SF	17	B1
NOB HILL CIR	SF	7	A1
NOBLES AL	SF	3	A2
NOE ST	SF	10	B1
NOE ST	SF	14	B1
NORDHOFF ST	SF	14	A3
NORFOLK ST	SF	10	C1
NORIEGA ST	SF	8	A3
NORIEGA ST	SF	9	A3
NORMANDIE TER	SF	2	A3
NORTH GATE DR	SF	13	B3
NORTH POINT DR	SF	3	C1
NORTH POINT ST	SF	2	A2
NORTH POINT ST	SF	3	A2
NORTHRIDGE RD	SF	16	A3
NORTH VIEW CT	SF	2	C2
NORTHWOOD DR	SF	13	B3
NORTON ST	SF	20	A1
NORWICH ST	SF	15	A1
NOTTINGHAM PL	SF	3	A3
NUEVA AV	SF	21	B3
O			
OAK ST	SF	10	A1
OAKDALE AV	SF	15	B2
OAK GROVE ST	SF	7	B3
OAKHURST LN	SF	9	B3
OAK PARK DR	SF	9	B3
OAKWOOD ST	SF	10	B2
OCEAN AV	SF	19	B1
OCTAVIA ST	SF	2	B2
OCTAVIA ST	SF	6	B3
OCTAVIA ST	SF	10	B1
OFARRELL ST	SF	6	A3
OFARRELL ST	SF	7	A2
OGDEN AV	SF	14	C2
OLD CHINATWN LN	SF	3	A3
OLIVE ST	SF	6	C2
OLIVER ST	SF	19	C3
OLMSTEAD ST	SF	21	A2
OLYMPIA WY	SF	13	C1
OMAR WY	SF	13	C2
ONEIDA AV	SF	20	A1
ONIQUE LN	SF	14	A2
ONONDAGA AV	SF	20	A1
OPAL PL	SF	7	A2
OPALO LN	SF	14	A2
OPHIR AL	SF	6	C2
ORA WY	SF	14	A2
ORANGE ST	SF	14	C1
ORBEN PL	SF	6	B1
ORD CT	SF	10	A2
ORD ST	SF	1	B2
ORD ST	SF	10	A2
ORDWAY ST	SF	21	A2
OREILLY AV	SF	1	C2
ORIENTE ST	SF	20	C3
ORIOLE WY	SF	13	B1
ORIZABA AV	SF	19	B2
ORTEGA ST	SF	12	A1
ORTEGA ST	SF	14	C1
ORTEGA WY	SF	9	A3
OSAGE ST	SF	14	C1
OSCAR AL	SF	7	B2

STREET	CITY	PG. NO.	SEE
OSCEOLA LN	SF	15	C3
OSGOOD PL	SF	3	B3
OSHAUGHNESSY BL	SF	13	C1
OSHAUGHNESSY BL	SF	14	A2
OTEGA AV	SF	19	C2
OTIS ST	SF	10	C1
OTSEGO AV	SF	20	A1
OTTAWA AV	SF	20	A2
OVERLOOK DR	SF	8	C1
OWEN ST	SF	1	B2
OWENS ST	SF	11	B1
OXFORD ST	SF	20	C1
OZBORN CT	SF	3	C1
P			
PACHECO ST	SF	9	A3
PACHECO ST	SF	12	A1
PACHECO ST	SF	13	A1
PACIFIC AV	SF	2	A3
PACIFIC AV	SF	3	B3
PACIFIC AV W	SF	5	B2
PAGE ST	SF	9	C1
PAGE ST	SF	10	B1
PAGODA PL	SF	7	A1
PALACE DR	SF	1	C2
PALI RD	SF	15	B1
PALM AV	SF	5	B2
PALMETTO AV	SF	19	B3
PALO ALTO AV	SF	9	C3
PALOMA AV	SF	19	A1
PALOS PL	SF	12	C3
PALOU AV	SF	15	B2
PANAMA ST	SF	19	A3
PANORAMA DR	SF	9	C3
PANORAMA DR	SF	13	C1
PANTON AL	SF	6	C1
PARADISE AV	SF	14	A3
PARAISO PL	SF	12	C3
PARAMOUNT TER	SF	5	C3
PARDEE AL	SF	3	A2
PARIS ST	SF	20	A2
PARK BLVD	SF	1	A3
PARK ST	SF	14	B2
PARKER AV	SF	5	C2
PARK HILL AV	SF	10	A2
PARKHURST AL	SF	3	A3
PARK PRSIDIO BL	SF	5	A3
PARKRIDGE DR	SF	14	A1
PARNASSUS AV	SF	9	B2
PARQUE DR	SF	20	C3
PARSONS ST	SF	9	C1
PASADENA ST	SF	20	C3
PATTEN RD	SF	1	B2
PATTERSON ST	SF	15	A2
PATTON ST	SF	14	C2
PAUL AV	SF	21	B1
PAULDING ST	SF	20	A1
PAYSON ST	SF	19	A3
PEABODY ST	SF	21	A3
PEARCE ST	SF	1	A2
PEARL ST	SF	10	C1
PEDESTRIAN WY	SF	1	C2
PELTON PL	SF	3	A3
PEMBERTON PL	SF	9	C3
PENA ST	SF	1	B3
PENINSULA AV	SF	21	B3
PENNINGTON ST	SF	1	B2
PENNSYLVANIA AV	SF	11	B3
PERALTA AV	SF	15	A2
PEREGO TER	SF	14	A1
PERINE PL	SF	6	A2
PERRY ST	SF	7	B2
PERSHING DR	SF	4	C1
PERSIA AV	SF	20	B1
PERU AV	SF	20	B1
PETERS AV	SF	14	C2

STREET	CITY	PG. NO.	SEE
PETER YORKE WY	SF	6	B2
PETRARCH PL	SF	7	B1
PFEIFFER ST	SF	3	A2
PHELAN AV	SF	19	C1
PHELPS ST	SF	15	B2
PHELPS ST	SF	21	B1
PHOENIX TER	SF	2	C3
PICO AV	SF	19	B1
PIEDMONT ST	SF	10	A2
PIERCE ST	SF	2	A3
PIERCE ST	SF	6	A3
PIERCE ST	SF	10	B1
PILGRIM AV	SF	14	A3
PINAR LN	SF	6	A3
PINE ST	SF	3	B3
PINE ST	SF	6	A2
PINEHURST WY	SF	19	B1
PINK AL	SF	10	B1
PINO AL	SF	8	C2
PINTO AV	SF	18	C2
PIOCHE ST	SF	20	B1
PIPER LOOP	SF	1	B3
PIXLEY ST	SF	2	A3
PIZARRO WY	SF	13	B3
PLAZA ST	SF	13	B1
PLEASANT ST	SF	2	C3
PLUM ST	SF	10	C1
PLYMOUTH AV	SF	19	C3
POINT LOBOS AV	SF	4	A3
POLARIS WY	SF	20	A3
POLK ST	SF	2	C2
POLK ST	SF	6	A3
POLLARD PL	SF	3	A2
POMONA ST	SF	15	B3
POND ST	SF	10	B2
POPE RD	SF	2	B2
POPE ST	SF	1	A3
POPE ST	SF	20	A2
POPLAR ST	SF	14	C1
POPPY LN	SF	14	A2
PORTAL PATH	SF	13	B2
PORTER ST	SF	14	C3
PORTOLA DR	SF	13	B2
PORTOLA ST	SF	1	C2
POST ST	SF	6	A2
POST ST	SF	7	A2
POTOMAC ST	SF	10	B1
POTRERO AV	SF	11	A3
POWELL ST	SF	3	A1
POWELL ST	SF	7	A2
POWERS AV	SF	14	C1
POWHATTAN AV	SF	15	A2
PRADO ST	SF	2	A2
PRAGUE ST	SF	20	B2
PRECITA AV	SF	14	C1
PRENTISS ST	SF	15	A2
PRESCOTT CT	SF	3	B2
PRESIDIO AV	SF	5	C1
PRESIDIO BLVD	SF	1	C3
PRESIDIO TER	SF	5	B2
PRETOR WY	SF	20	A3
PRICE ROW	SF	3	A2
PRIEST ST	SF	2	C3
PRINCETON ST	SF	20	C1
PROSPECT AV	SF	14	C2
PROSPER ST	SF	10	B2
PUEBLO ST	SF	20	C3
PUTNAM ST	SF	15	A2
Q			
QUANE ST	SF	10	B3
QUARRY RD	SF	5	B3
QUARTZ WY	SF	14	A1
QUESADA AV	SF	15	B2
QUINCY ST	SF	3	A3
QUINT ST	SF	15	B2

STREET	CITY	PG. NO.	SEE
QUINTARA ST	SF	12	A1
QUINTARA ST	SF	13	A1
R			
RACCOON DR	SF	9	C3
RACINE LN	SF	21	B2
RADIO TER	SF	13	A1
RAE AV	SF	19	C3
RALEIGH ST	SF	20	A1
RALSTON AV	SF	1	A2
RALSTON ST	SF	19	A2
RAMONA ST	SF	10	B2
RAMSELL ST	SF	19	B2
RANDALL ST	SF	14	B2
RANDOLPH ST	SF	19	B2
RANKIN ST	SF	15	B2
RAUSCH ST	SF	7	A3
RAVENWOOD DR	SF	13	B3
RAWLES ST	SF	1	C3
RAYBURN ST	SF	10	B3
RAYCLIFF TER	SF	2	A3
RAYMOND AV	SF	21	A2
REARDON RD	SF	16	A3
REDDY ST	SF	15	B3
REDFIELD AL	SF	2	C2
REDONDO ST	SF	21	B2
RED ROCK WY	SF	14	A1
REDWOOD ST	SF	6	B3
REED ST	SF	2	C3
REEVES CT	SF	3	C1
REGENT ST	SF	19	C3
RENO PL	SF	3	A2
REPOSA WY	SF	13	C2
RESERVOIR ST	SF	10	B1
RESTANI WY	SF	20	A2
RETIRO WY	SF	2	A2
REUEL CT	SF	15	C2
REVERE AV	SF	15	B2
REX AV	SF	13	B2
REY ST	SF	21	A3
RHINE ST	SF	19	B3
RHODE ISLAND ST	SF	11	B1
RICE ST	SF	19	B3
RICHARDS CIR	SF	15	C1
RICHARDSON AV	SF	1	C2
RICHLAND AV	SF	14	C2
RICKARD ST	SF	15	A3
RICO WY	SF	2	A2
RIDGE LN	SF	19	C2
RIDGEWOOD AV	SF	13	C3
RILEY AV	SF	1	B2
RINCON ST	SF	7	C2
RINGOLD ST	SF	11	A1
RIO CT	SF	13	C2
RIO VERDE ST	SF	20	C3
RIPLEY ST	SF	15	A1
RITCH ST	SF	7	B3
RIVAS AV	SF	18	C2
RIVERA ST	SF	12	A1
RIVERA ST	SF	13	A1
RIVERTON DR	SF	12	C3
RIVOLI ST	SF	9	C2
RIZAL ST	SF	7	B3
ROACH ST	SF	2	C2
ROANOKE ST	SF	14	B2
ROBBLEE AV	SF	15	B3
ROBINHOOD DR	SF	13	B2
ROBINSON DR	SF	20	B3
ROBINSON ST	SF	17	B1
ROCK AL	SF	13	B2
ROCKAWAY AV	SF	13	B2
ROCKDALE DR	SF	13	C2
ROCKLAND ST	SF	2	C3
ROCKRIDGE DR	SF	13	A1
ROCKWOOD CT	SF	13	B2
ROD RD	SF	1	A2

1988 SAN FRANCISCO COUNTY STREET INDEX

STREET	CITY	PG. NO.	SEE
RODGERS ST	SF	11	A1
RODRIGUEZ ST	SF	1	C3
ROEMER WY	SF	19	C3
ROLPH ST	SF	20	A2
ROMAIN ST	SF	10	A3
ROME ST	SF	19	C2
ROME ST	SF	20	C2
ROMOLO ST	SF	3	A3
RONDEL PL	SF	10	C2
ROOSEVELT WY	SF	10	A2
ROSCOE ST	SF	14	C3
ROSE ST	SF	10	B1
ROSELLA CT	SF	20	A1
ROSELYN TER	SF	5	C3
ROSEMARY CT	SF	12	C2
ROSEMONT PL	SF	10	B1
ROSENKRANZ ST	SF	15	A2
ROSEWOOD DR	SF	13	B3
ROSIE LEE LN	SF	15	C3
ROSS AL	SF	3	A3
ROSSI AV	SF	5	C3
ROSSMOOR DR	SF	13	A3
ROTTECK ST	SF	14	B3
ROUSSEAU ST	SF	14	B3
ROYAL LANE CT	SF	20	A2
RUCKMAN AV	SF	1	A2
RUDDEN AV	SF	20	A1
RUGER ST	SF	1	C3
RUSS ST	SF	7	A3
RUSSELL ST	SF	2	C3
RUSSIA AV	SF	20	A1
RUSSIAN HILL PL	SF	2	C3
RUTH ST	SF	20	A1
RUTLAND ST	SF	21	A3
RUTLEDGE ST	SF	15	A1
S			
SABIN PL	SF	3	A3
SACRAMENTO ST	SF	2	C3
SACRAMENTO ST	SF	3	A3
SACRAMENTO ST	SF	5	B2
SACRAMENTO ST	SF	6	A3
SADOWA ST	SF	19	B3
SAFFOLD RD	SF	1	A3
SAFIRA LN	SF	14	A1
SAGAMORE ST	SF	19	B3
ST CHARLES AV	SF	19	A3
ST CROIX DR	SF	13	C2
ST ELMO WY	SF	13	B3
ST FRANCIS BLVD	SF	13	B3
ST GEORGE AL	SF	3	A3
ST GERMAIN AV	SF	9	C3
ST JOSEPHS AV	SF	6	A3
ST LOUIS PL	SF	3	A3
ST MARYS AV	SF	14	B3
SAL ST	SF	1	B3
SALA TER	SF	20	A2
SALINAS AV	SF	21	B1
SALMON ST	SF	3	A3
SAMOSET ST	SF	15	A1
SAMPSON AV	SF	21	B3
SAN ALESO AV	SF	13	B3
SAN ANDREAS WY	SF	13	B3
SAN ANSELMO AV	SF	13	B2
SAN ANTONIO PL	SF	3	A2
SAN BENITO WY	SF	13	B3
SAN BRUNO AV	SF	11	A2
SAN BRUNO AV	SF	15	A3
SAN BRUNO AV	SF	21	A1
SN BUENAVNTR WY	SF	13	B3
SAN CARLOS ST	SF	10	C2
SANCHEZ ST	SF	1	C3
SANCHEZ ST	SF	5	C1
SANCHEZ ST	SF	10	B2
SAN DIEGO AV	SF	19	B3
SAN FELIPE AV	SF	13	B3
SAN FERNANDO WY	SF	13	A3
SAN GABRIEL AV	SF	20	A1
SAN JACINTO WY	SF	13	B3
SAN JOSE AV	SF	14	B2
SAN JOSE AV	SF	19	C2
SAN JOSE AV	SF	20	A1
SAN JUAN AV	SF	20	A1
SAN LEANDRO WY	SF	13	A3
SAN LORENZO WY	SF	13	B2
SAN LUIS AV	SF	19	B3
SAN MARCOS AV	SF	13	B1
SAN MATEO AV	SF	19	B3
SAN MIGUEL ST	SF	19	C2
SAN PABLO AV	SF	13	B2
SAN RAFAEL WY	SF	13	A3
SAN RAMON WY	SF	19	C1
SANSOME ST	SF	3	B2
SANTA ANA AV	SF	13	B3
STA BARBARA AV	SF	19	B3
SANTA CLARA AV	SF	13	B3
SANTA CRUZ AV	SF	19	B3
SANTA FE AV	SF	15	B3
SANTA MARINA ST	SF	14	C2
SANTA MONICA WY	SF	13	B2
SANTA PAULA AV	SF	13	B3
SANTA RITA AV	SF	13	B1
SANTA ROSA AV	SF	20	A1
SANTA YNEZ AV	SF	20	A1
SANTA YSABEL AV	SF	20	A1
SANTIAGO ST	SF	12	A1
SANTIAGO ST	SF	13	A1
SANTOS ST	SF	20	C3
SARGENT ST	SF	19	B2
SATURN ST	SF	10	A2
SAWYER ST	SF	20	C3
SCENIC WY	SF	4	C2
SCHOFIELD RD	SF	1	A2
SCHOFIELD RD	SF	2	B2
SCHOOL AL	SF	3	A2
SCHWERIN ST	SF	21	A3
SCOTIA AV	SF	15	B3
SCOTLAND ST	SF	3	A2
SCOTT ST	SF	2	A3
SCOTT ST	SF	6	A3
SCOTT ST	SF	10	A1
SEA CLIFF AV	SF	4	B2
SEAL ROCK DR	SF	4	A3
SEARS ST	SF	19	C3
SEAVIEW TER	SF	4	B2
SECURITY PAC PL	SF	7	A2
SELBY ST	SF	15	B2
SELMA WY	SF	9	A3
SEMINOLE AV	SF	20	A2
SENECA AV	SF	20	A1
SEQUOIA WY	SF	13	C2
SGT MITCHELL	SF	1	C3
SGT MITCHELL ST	SF	1	C2
SERPENTINE AV	SF	15	A1
SERRANO DR	SF	18	C2
SERRANO DR	SF	19	A2
SERVICE ST	SF	2	A3
SEVERN ST	SF	10	B3
SEVILLE ST	SF	20	A3
SEWARD ST	SF	10	A3
SEYMOUR ST	SF	6	A3
SHAFTER AV	SF	15	C3
SHAFTER AV	SF	21	C1
SHAFTER RD	SF	1	C3
SHAKESPEARE ST	SF	19	B3
SHANGRILA WY	SF	13	B2
SHANNON ST	SF	7	A2
SHARON ST	SF	10	B2
SHARP PL	SF	2	C3
SHAW AL	SF	7	B2
SHAWNEE AV	SF	20	A2
SHEPHARD PL	SF	3	A3
SHERIDAN AV	SF	1	B2
SHERIDAN ST	SF	11	A1
SHERMAN RD	SF	1	C3
SHERMAN ST	SF	7	A3
SHERWOOD CT	SF	13	C3
SHIELDS ST	SF	19	A2
SHIPLEY ST	SF	7	A3
SHORE VIEW AV	SF	4	B3
SHORT ST	SF	10	A3
SHOTWELL ST	SF	10	C2
SHOTWELL ST	SF	14	C1
SHRADER ST	SF	5	C3
SHRADER ST	SF	9	C1
SIBERT LOOP	SF	1	B3
SIBLEY RD	SF	1	C3
SICKLES AV	SF	19	C3
SIERRA ST	SF	11	B3
SILLIMAN ST	SF	15	A3
SILLIMAN ST	SF	20	C1
SILVER AV	SF	14	B3
SILVER AV	SF	15	A3
SIMONDS LOOP	SF	1	C3
SKYLINE BLVD	SF	18	A1
SKYVIEW WY	SF	9	C3
SLOAN AL	SF	7	B2
SLOAT BLVD	SF	12	A3
SOLA AV	SF	13	B1
SOMERSET ST	SF	15	C3
SOMERSET ST	SF	21	A1
SONOMA ST	SF	3	A2
SONORA LN	SF	6	A3
SOTELO AV	SF	13	B1
SOUTH DR	SF	8	A2
SOUTHERN HTS AV	SF	11	B3
SOUTH HILL BLVD	SF	20	B3
SOUTH PARK AV	SF	7	B3
S VAN NESS AV	SF	10	C1
SOUTHWOOD DR	SF	19	B1
SPARROW ST	SF	10	C2
SPARTA ST	SF	21	A2
SPEAR AV	SF	17	B1
SPEAR ST	SF	7	B1
SPENCE ST	SF	10	B2
SPOFFORD ST	SF	3	A3
SPRECKLES LK DR	SF	8	C1
SPRING ST	SF	3	A3
SPRINGFIELD DR	SF	12	C3
SPROULE LN	SF	3	A3
SPRUCE ST	SF	5	C2
STANDISH AV	SF	14	A3
STANFORD ST	SF	7	C3
STANFORD HTS AV	SF	13	C3
STANLEY ST	SF	19	B2
STANTON ST	SF	10	A3
STANYAN ST	SF	5	C3
STANYAN ST	SF	9	C1
STAPLES AV	SF	13	C3
STARK ST	SF	3	A3
STARR KING WY	SF	6	C2
STARVIEW WY	SF	13	C1
STATE DR	SF	18	C1
STATES ST	SF	10	A2
STEINER ST	SF	2	A3
STEINER ST	SF	6	B3
STEINER ST	SF	10	B1
STERLING ST	SF	7	B2
STEUART ST	SF	7	B1
STEVELOE PL	SF	7	A2
STEVENS AL	SF	3	B3
STEVENSON ST	SF	6	C3
STEVENSON ST	SF	7	A3
STEVENSON ST	SF	10	C1
STILL ST	SF	14	B3
STILLINGS AV	SF	14	A3
STILLMAN ST	SF	7	B3
STILWELL DR	SF	4	C1
STOCKTON ST	SF	3	A2
STOCKTON ST	SF	7	A1
STONE ST	SF	1	A2
STONE ST	SF	3	A3
STONECREST DR	SF	19	A1
STONEMAN ST	SF	15	A1
STONEYBROOK AV	SF	14	C3
STONEYFORD AV	SF	14	C3
STOREY AV	SF	1	A2
STORRIE ST	SF	10	A2
STOW LAKE DR	SF	9	A1
STOW LAKE DR E	SF	9	A1
STRATFORD DR	SF	19	A2
SUMMIT ST	SF	19	C2
SUMNER AV	SF	1	C3
SUMNER ST	SF	7	A3
SUNBEAM LN	SF	20	A2
SUNGLOW LN	SF	14	C3
SUNNYDALE AV	SF	20	B2
SUNNYDALE AV	SF	21	A3
SUNNYSIDE TER	SF	19	C1
SUNRISE WY	SF	20	C3
SUNSET BLVD	SF	8	B2
SUNSET BLVD	SF	12	B1
SUNVIEW DR	SF	14	A1
SURREY ST	SF	14	A3
SUSSEX ST	SF	14	B2
SUTRO HTS AV	SF	4	A3
SUTTER ST	SF	6	A3
SUTTER ST	SF	7	A2
SWEENY ST	SF	15	A3
SWISS AV	SF	14	A3
SYCAMORE ST	SF	10	C2
SYDNEY WY	SF	13	C1
SYLVAN DR	SF	12	C3
T			
TABER PL	SF	7	B3
TACOMA ST	SF	5	A3
TALBERT CT	SF	21	A3
TALBERT ST	SF	21	A3
TAMALPAIS TER	SF	5	C3
TAMPA LN	SF	15	B3
TANDANG SORA	SF	7	B3
TAPIA DR	SF	18	C1
TARA ST	SF	19	C2
TARAVAL ST	SF	12	A2
TARAVAL ST	SF	13	A2
TAYLOR RD	SF	1	B2
TAYLOR ST	SF	2	C1
TAYLOR ST	SF	7	A1
TAYLOR ST	SF	7	A2
TEDDY AV	SF	21	A2
TEHAMA ST	SF	7	A3
TELEGRAPH PL	SF	3	A2
TELEGRAPH HL BL	SF	3	A2
TEMESCAL TER	SF	5	C3
TEMPLE ST	SF	10	A2
TENNESSEE ST	SF	11	C2
TENNESSEE ST	SF	15	C1
TENNY PL	SF	7	B2
TERESITA BLVD	SF	13	C1
TERRACE DR	SF	13	B2
TERRACE WALK	SF	13	B2
TERRA VISTA AV	SF	6	A3
TEXAS ST	SF	11	B2
THE ESPLANADE	SF	8	A1
THERESA ST	SF	14	A3
THOMAS AV	SF	1	B3
THOMAS AV	SF	15	A2
THOMAS AV	SF	15	C3
THOMAS MELLN DR	SF	21	B3
THOMAS MORE WY	SF	19	A3
THOR AV	SF	14	B3
THORNBURG RD	SF	1	C2
THORNE WY	SF	15	B3
THORNTON AV	SF	15	B3
THORP LN	SF	10	A3
THRIFT ST	SF	19	B2
TIFFANY AV	SF	14	C1
TILLMAN PL	SF	7	A2
TINGLEY ST	SF	14	B3
TIOGA AV	SF	21	A2
TISDALE RD	SF	16	A3
TOCOLOMA AV	SF	21	B3
TODD ST	SF	1	A2
TOLAND ST	SF	15	B2
TOLEDO WY	SF	2	A2
TOMASO CT	SF	21	A3
TOMPKINS AV	SF	14	C2
TOPAZ WY	SF	14	A2
TOPEKA AV	SF	15	B3
TORNEY AV	SF	1	C2
TORRENS CT	SF	2	C3
TOUCHARD ST	SF	6	C1
TOWNSEND ST	SF	7	C3
TOWNSEND ST	SF	11	A1
TOYON LN	SF	20	B3
TRACY PL	SF	3	A3
TRAINOR ST	SF	10	C1
TRANSVERSE RD	SF	8	C1
TREASURY PL	SF	3	B3
TREAT AV	SF	11	A2
TREAT AV	SF	15	A1
TRENTON ST	SF	3	A3
TRINITY ST	SF	7	B1
TROY AL	SF	2	C3
TRUBY ST	SF	1	C2
TRUETT PL	SF	3	A3
TRUMBULL ST	SF	14	B3
TUBBS ST	SF	11	C3
TUCKER AV	SF	21	A2
TULANE ST	SF	14	C3
TULARE ST	SF	15	C1
TULIP AL	SF	7	A3
TUNNEL AV	SF	21	B3
TURK ST	SF	5	C3
TURK ST	SF	6	A3
TURK ST	SF	7	A2
TURNER TER	SF	11	B3
TURQUOISE WY	SF	14	A2
TUSCANY AL	SF	3	A2
TWIN PEAKS BLVD	SF	9	C3
U			
ULLOA ST	SF	12	A2
ULLOA ST	SF	13	A2
UNDERWOOD AV	SF	21	C1
UNION ST	SF	2	A3
UNION ST	SF	3	A2
UNITED NATNS PZ	SF	6	C3
UNIVERSITY ST	SF	20	C1
UNIVERSITY ST	SF	21	A1
UPLAND DR	SF	13	B3
UPPER TER	SF	10	A2
UPR SERVICE RD	SF	9	B2
UPTON AV	SF	1	A2
UPTON ST	SF	15	B2
URANUS TER	SF	9	C2
URBANO DR N	SF	19	B1
URBANO DR S	SF	19	B1
UTAH ST	SF	11	A3
V			
VALDEZ AV	SF	13	C3
VALE AV	SF	12	C3
VALENCIA ST	SF	10	C1
VALENCIA ST	SF	14	C1
VALERTON CT	SF	20	A1
VALLEJO ST	SF	1	B2
VALLEJO ST	SF	2	C3

1988 SAN FRANCISCO COUNTY STREET INDEX

STREET	CITY	PG. NO.	SEE
VALLEJO ST	SF	3	A3
VALLEJO TER	SF	3	A3
VALLETA CT	SF	14	A2
VALLEY ST	SF	14	B1
VALMAR TER	SF	20	B1
VALPARAISO ST	SF	2	C2
VAN BUREN ST	SF	14	A3
VANDEWATER ST	SF	3	A2
VAN DYKE AV	SF	21	B1
VAN KEUREN AV	SF	17	B1
VAN NESS AV	SF	2	B2
VAN NESS AV	SF	6	C2
VARELA AV	SF	19	A1
VARENNES ST	SF	3	A2
VARNEY PL	SF	7	B3
VASQUEZ AV	SF	13	B2
VASSAR PL	SF	7	B2
VEGA ST	SF	5	C3
VELASCO AV	SF	20	C3
VENARD AL	SF	3	A2
VENTURA AV	SF	13	B1
VENUS ST	SF	15	B3
VERDI PL	SF	3	A3
VERDUN WY	SF	13	B2
VERMEHR PL	SF	7	A2
VERMONT ST	SF	11	A1
VERMONT ST	SF	15	B1
VERNA ST	SF	13	C3
VERNON ST	SF	19	B2
VERONA PL	SF	7	B2
VESTA ST	SF	15	B3
VICENTE ST	SF	12	A2
VICENTE ST	SF	13	A2
VICKSBURG ST	SF	10	B3
VICKSBURG ST	SF	14	B1
VICTORIA ST	SF	19	B2
VIDAL DR	SF	18	C2
VIENNA ST	SF	20	B2
VILLA TER	SF	10	A3
VINE TER	SF	7	A1
VINTON CT	SF	3	A3
VIRGIL ST	SF	14	C1
VIRGINIA AV	SF	14	C2
VISITACION AV	SF	20	C2
VISITACION AV	SF	21	A3
VISTA LN	SF	10	A3
VISTA VERDE CT	SF	14	A3
VULCAN STAIRWAY	SF	10	A2
W			
WABASH TER	SF	21	B2
WAGNER AL	SF	6	C2
WAGNER AL	SF	7	A3
WAGNER RD	SF	1	A2
WAITHMAN WY	SF	13	B2
WALBRIDGE ST	SF	20	B3
WALDO AL	SF	3	C3
WALESA, LECH	SF	6	C3
WALL PL	SF	3	C3
WALLACE AV	SF	21	B1
WALLEN CT	SF	1	C3
WALLER ST	SF	9	C1
WALLER ST	SF	10	A1
WALNUT ST	SF	5	C1
WALTER ST	SF	10	B1
WALTER LUM PL	SF	3	A3
WALTER LUM PL	SF	7	A1
WALTHAM ST	SF	15	A1
WANDA ST	SF	20	A1
WARD ST	SF	21	A2
WARNER PL	SF	3	C3
WARREN DR	SF	9	B3
WASHBURN ST	SF	11	A1
WASHINGTON BLVD	SF	1	B3
WASHINGTON ST	SF	3	B3
WASHINGTON ST	SF	5	C2

STREET	CITY	PG. NO.	SEE
WASHINGTON ST	SF	6	A2
WASHOE PL	SF	3	A3
WATCHMAN WY	SF	11	B3
WATER ST	SF	2	C2
WATERLOO ST	SF	15	A2
WATERVILLE ST	SF	15	B2
WATSON PL	SF	20	A1
WATT AV	SF	20	A3
WAVERLY PL	SF	3	A3
WAWONA ST	SF	12	B3
WAWONA ST	SF	13	A2
WAYLAND ST	SF	20	C1
WAYLAND ST	SF	21	A1
WAYNE PL	SF	3	A3
WEBB PL	SF	3	A2
WEBSTER ST	SF	2	B3
WEBSTER ST	SF	6	B3
WEBSTER ST	SF	10	B1
WELDON ST	SF	15	A3
WELSH ST	SF	7	B3
WENTWORTH PL	SF	3	A3
WESTBROOK CT	SF	15	C3
WEST CLAY ST	SF	4	C2
WESTGATE DR	SF	13	B3
WESTMOORLAND DR	SF	12	B3
WEST POINT RD	SF	16	A2
WEST PORTAL AV	SF	13	A2
WESTSIDE DR	SF	3	C1
WEST VIEW AV	SF	14	C3
WESTWOOD DR	SF	19	B1
WETMORE ST	SF	3	A3
WHEAT ST	SF	21	B1
WHEELER AV	SF	21	B3
WHIPPLE AV	SF	19	C3
WHITE ST	SF	2	C3
WHITFIELD CT	SF	15	C3
WHITING ST	SF	3	A2
WHITNEY ST	SF	14	B2
WHITNEY YNG CIR	SF	15	C3
WHITTIER ST	SF	19	C3
WIESE ST	SF	10	C2
WILDE AV	SF	21	A2
WILDER ST	SF	14	B3
WILDWOOD WY	SF	19	B1
WILLARD ST	SF	9	C2
WILLARD ST N	SF	5	B3
WILLIAMS AV	SF	15	B3
WILLIAR AV	SF	19	C2
WILLOW ST	SF	6	B3
WILLS ST	SF	16	A2
WILMOT ST	SF	6	B2
WILSON ST	SF	19	B3
WINDING WY	SF	20	A3
WINDSOR PL	SF	3	A2
WINFIELD ST	SF	14	C2
WINSTON DR	SF	19	A1
WINTER PL	SF	3	A2
WINTHROP ST	SF	3	A2
WISCONSIN ST	SF	11	B2
WISER CT	SF	1	A3
WOOD ST	SF	5	C2
WOODACRE DR	SF	13	A3
WOODHAVEN CT	SF	9	C3
WOODLAND AV	SF	9	C2
WOODSIDE AV	SF	13	B1
WOODWARD ST	SF	10	C1
WOOL CT	SF	1	A2
WOOL ST	SF	14	C2
WOOLSEY ST	SF	21	A1
WORCESTER AV	SF	19	B3
WORDEN ST	SF	3	A2
WORTH ST	SF	10	A3
WRIGHT LOOP	SF	1	A3
WRIGHT ST	SF	15	A1
WYTON LN	SF	19	A1

STREET	CITY	PG. NO.	SEE
Y			
YALE ST	SF	20	C1
YERBA BUENA AV	SF	13	B2
YORBA LN	SF	12	B3
YORBA ST	SF	12	B3
YORK ST	SF	11	A2
YORK ST	SF	15	A1
YOSEMITE AV	SF	21	B1
YOUNG ST	SF	1	C2
YOUNG CT	SF	15	C1
YUKON ST	SF	10	A3
Z			
ZENO PL	SF	7	B2
ZIRCON PL	SF	14	B2
ZOE ST	SF	7	B3
ZOO RD	SF	12	A3
NUMERIC STREETS			
1ST ST	SF	3	C2
1ST ST	SF	7	B1
2ND AV	SF	5	B2
2ND AV	SF	9	B2
2ND ST	SF	3	C1
2ND ST	SF	7	B2
3RD AV	SF	5	B2
3RD AV	SF	9	B2
3RD AV	SF	17	A2
3RD ST	SF	3	C1
3RD ST	SF	7	B2
3RD ST	SF	11	C1
3RD ST	SF	15	C2
3RD ST	SF	21	B1
4TH AV	SF	5	B2
4TH AV	SF	9	B2
4TH ST	SF	3	C1
4TH ST	SF	7	B2
4TH ST	SF	11	C1
5TH AV	SF	5	B2
5TH AV	SF	9	B2
5TH ST	SF	3	C1
5TH ST	SF	7	A2
6TH AV	SF	5	B2
6TH AV	SF	9	B2
6TH AV	SF	17	A1
6TH ST	SF	3	C1
6TH ST	SF	7	A3
6TH ST	SF	11	B1
7TH AV	SF	5	B2
7TH AV	SF	9	B2
7TH ST	SF	7	A3
7TH ST	SF	11	B1
8TH AV	SF	5	B2
8TH AV	SF	9	B2
8TH ST	SF	3	C1
8TH ST	SF	7	A3
8TH ST	SF	11	A1
9TH AV	SF	5	B2
9TH AV	SF	9	B3
9TH AV	SF	13	B1
9TH ST	SF	3	C1
9TH ST	SF	11	A1
10TH AV	SF	5	A2
10TH AV	SF	9	B2
10TH AV	SF	13	B1
10TH ST	SF	3	C1
10TH ST	SF	11	A1
11TH AV	SF	5	A2
11TH AV	SF	9	B2
11TH ST	SF	3	C1
11TH ST	SF	10	C1
12TH AV	SF	5	A2
12TH AV	SF	9	A3
12TH AV	SF	13	B1
12TH ST	SF	3	C1
12TH ST	SF	10	C1
13TH ST	SF	3	C1

STREET	CITY	PG. NO.	SEE
13TH ST	SF	10	C1
14TH AV	SF	5	A2
14TH AV	SF	9	A2
14TH AV	SF	13	A1
14TH ST	SF	10	B1
15TH AV	SF	5	A2
15TH AV	SF	9	A3
15TH AV	SF	13	A1
15TH ST	SF	10	A2
15TH ST	SF	11	A2
16TH AV	SF	5	A2
16TH AV	SF	9	A2
16TH AV	SF	13	A1
16TH ST	SF	10	B2
16TH ST	SF	11	A2
17TH AV	SF	5	A2
17TH AV	SF	9	A2
17TH ST	SF	9	C2
17TH ST	SF	10	A2
17TH ST	SF	11	A2
18TH AV	SF	5	A3
18TH AV	SF	9	A2
18TH AV	SF	13	A1
18TH ST	SF	10	A2
18TH ST	SF	11	A2
19TH AV	SF	5	A3
19TH AV	SF	9	A2
19TH AV	SF	13	A1
19TH AV	SF	19	A1
19TH ST	SF	10	A2
19TH ST	SF	11	A2
20TH AV	SF	4	C2
20TH AV	SF	9	A2
20TH AV	SF	13	A1
20TH ST	SF	10	A3
20TH ST	SF	11	A2
21ST AV	SF	4	C2
21ST AV	SF	9	A2
21ST AV	SF	13	A1
21ST ST	SF	10	B3
21ST ST	SF	11	A3
22ND AV	SF	4	C2
22ND AV	SF	8	C3
22ND AV	SF	13	A1
22ND ST	SF	10	A3
22ND ST	SF	11	A3
23RD AV	SF	4	C2
23RD AV	SF	8	C2
23RD AV	SF	12	C1
23RD AV	SF	13	A3
23RD ST	SF	10	B3
23RD ST	SF	11	A3
24TH AV	SF	4	C2
24TH AV	SF	8	C3
24TH AV	SF	12	C1
24TH ST	SF	10	A3
24TH ST	SF	11	A3
24TH ST	SF	14	A1
25TH AV	SF	4	C2
25TH AV	SF	8	C3
25TH AV	SF	12	C1
25TH ST	SF	14	A1
25TH ST	SF	15	A1
26TH AV	SF	4	C2
26TH AV	SF	8	C3
26TH AV	SF	12	C1
26TH ST	SF	14	A1
26TH ST	SF	15	A1
27TH AV	SF	4	C2
27TH AV	SF	8	C3
27TH AV	SF	12	C1
27TH ST	SF	14	A1
28TH AV	SF	4	C3
28TH AV	SF	8	C3
28TH AV	SF	12	C1

STREET	CITY	PG. NO.	SEE
28TH ST	SF	14	B1
29TH AV	SF	4	C3
29TH AV	SF	8	C3
29TH AV	SF	12	C1
29TH ST	SF	14	B2
30TH AV	SF	4	B3
30TH AV	SF	8	C2
30TH AV	SF	12	C1
30TH ST	SF	14	B2
31ST AV	SF	4	B2
31ST AV	SF	8	B2
31ST AV	SF	12	C1
32ND AV	SF	4	B3
32ND AV	SF	8	B2
32ND AV	SF	12	B1
33RD AV	SF	4	B3
33RD AV	SF	8	B2
33RD AV	SF	12	B1
34TH AV	SF	4	B3
34TH AV	SF	8	B2
34TH AV	SF	12	B1
35TH AV	SF	4	B3
35TH AV	SF	8	B2
35TH AV	SF	12	B1
36TH AV	SF	4	B3
36TH AV	SF	8	B3
36TH AV	SF	12	B1
37TH AV	SF	4	B3
37TH AV	SF	8	B2
37TH AV	SF	12	B1
38TH AV	SF	4	B3
38TH AV	SF	8	B2
38TH AV	SF	12	B1
39TH AV	SF	4	B3
39TH AV	SF	8	B2
39TH AV	SF	12	B1
40TH AV	SF	4	A3
40TH AV	SF	8	B2
40TH AV	SF	12	B1
41ST AV	SF	4	A3
41ST AV	SF	8	A1
41ST AV	SF	12	B1
42ND AV	SF	4	A3
42ND AV	SF	8	A2
42ND AV	SF	12	A1
43RD AV	SF	4	A3
43RD AV	SF	8	A2
43RD AV	SF	12	A1
44TH AV	SF	4	A3
44TH AV	SF	8	A1
44TH AV	SF	12	A1
45TH AV	SF	4	A3
45TH AV	SF	8	A1
45TH AV	SF	12	A1
46TH AV	SF	4	A3
46TH AV	SF	8	A1
46TH AV	SF	12	A1
47TH AV	SF	4	A3
47TH AV	SF	8	A1
47TH AV	SF	12	A1
48TH AV	SF	4	A3
48TH AV	SF	8	A2
48TH AV	SF	12	A1

1988 SAN FRANCISCO COUNTY POINTS OF INTEREST

PAGE & GRID	NAME	ADDRESS	CITY	PHONE
	AIRPORTS & AIRLINES			
7 A2	AIR CALIFORNIA	460 POST ST		433 2660
7 A2	AIR CANADA	350 POST ST		761 0733
7 A2	ALASKA AIRLINES	275 POST ST		931 8888
7 A2	AMERICAN AIRLINES	CALIFORNIA & POWELL ST		398 4434
7 A2	BRITISH AIRWAYS	345 POWELL ST		877 0622
7 A2	CANADIAN PACIFIC AIR	343 POWELL ST		877 5960
7 A2	CHINA AIRLINES	391 SUTTER ST		989 3300
7 B1	CONTINENTAL AIRLINES	433 CALIFORNIA ST		397 8818
7 A2	DELTA AIRLINES	250 STOCKTON ST		552 5700
7 A1	EASTERN AIRLINES	CALIFORNIA & POWELL ST		474 5858
7 A2	JAPAN AIRLINES	POWELL & O FARRELL STS		982 8141
7 A2	LTU	360 POST ST		989 6640
7 A2	LUFTHANSA	360 POST ST		645 3880
7 A2	MEXICANA AIRLINES	421 POWELL ST		982 1424
7 A2	NORTHWEST ORIENT	350 POST ST		392 2163
7 A2	PACIFIC SOUTHWEST, PSA	212 STOCKTON ST		956 8636
7 A2	PAN AMERICAN	222 STOCKTON ST		221 1111
7 A2	PHILIPPINE AIRLINES	447 SUTTER		391 0470
6 C3	PUBLIC UTILITIES COMM	505 VAN NESS AV		
7 A2	QANTAS AIRWAYS	360 POST ST		761 8000
	S F INT AIRPORT	AIRPORT WY	SSF	761 0800
7 A2	SINGAPORE AIRLINES	476 POST ST		781 7304
7 A2	TRANS WORLD AIRLINES	433 CALIFORNIA		864 5731
7 A2	UNITED AIRLINES	POST & POWELL		397 2100
7 A2	WESTERN	287 GEARY ST		761 3300
7 A2	WORLD AIRWAYS	320 20TH ST		577 2500
	BUILDINGS			
7 A2	A/AARON BUSINESS SERV	260 KEARNY ST		
7 B1	ADAM GRANT	114 SANSOME ST		981 0375
7 B2	AETNA LIFE & CASUALTY	600 MARKET ST		
7 B1	ALCOA, THE	1 MARITIME PLAZA		434 2000
7 B2	ALEXANDER	155 MONTGOMERY ST		981 5074
7 B1	AMERICAN INTERNATIONAL	206 SANSOME ST		
7 B2	AMERICAN SAVINGS	MARKET & KEARNY STS		362 8220
7 B2	BANKERS INVESTMENT	742 MARKET ST		781 2836
7 B1	BANK OF AMERICA CENTER	555 CALIFORNIA ST		765 3174
7 B1	BECHTEL	50 BEALE ST		768 1234
7 A2	BOARD OF TRADE	989 MARKET ST		421 6302
7 A2	BROOKS BROTHERS	209 POST ST		
6 C3	BROOKS HALL	HYDE & FULTON STS		974 4000
6 C2	BUILDERS EXCHANGE	850 S VAN NESS AV		282 8220
7 B1	CAL COMMERCIAL UNION	315 MONTGOMERY ST		
7 B2	CALIFORNIA PACIFIC	105 MONTGOMERY ST		
6 C3	CALIFORNIA STATE	350 MCALLISTER ST		
7 B2	CALL	74 NEW MONTGOMERY ST		
6 C2	CATHEDRAL HILL	1255 POST ST		776 8200
7 B2	CENTRAL TOWER	703 MARKET ST		982 1935
7 B2	CHANCERY	564 MARKET ST		
3 A3	CHINESE CULTURAL CTR	750 KEARNY ST		
7 A2	CHRONICLE	5TH & MISSION STS		777 1111
6 C3	CITY HALL	400 VAN NESS AV		554 4000
6 C3	CIVIC AUDITORIUM	99 GROVE ST		974 4000
6 C3	CIVIC CENTER	VAN NESS & POLK ST		
3 A2	CLUB FUGAZI	678 GREEN ST		
7 A2	COMMERCIAL	833 MARKET ST		362 4915
7 B1	COMMERCIAL BLOCK	149 CALIFORNIA ST		
7 A2	CORDES, W F	126 POST ST		
20 C3	COW PALACE	GENEVA AV & SANTOS ST		469 6000
7 A2	CROCKER CENTER	POST ST & KEARNY ST		
7 B2	CROCKER NATIONAL BANK	1 MONTGOMERY ST		399 7564
7 B2	CROCKER PLAZA	600 MARKET ST		434 4753
7 B1	CROWN ZELLERBACH	1 BUSH ST		951 5209
7 A2	CURRAN THEATER	445 GEARY ST		
7 B1	CUSTOMS HOUSE	555 BATTERY ST		556 4440
7 B1	DANT MANAGEMENT CORP	260 CALIFORNIA ST		397 5404
6 C3	DAVIES SYMPHONY HALL	GROVE ST & VAN NESS AV		431 5400
5 A2	DEFENSE LANGUAGE INST	1804 14TH AV-PRESIDIO		221 0369
7 A1	DE MARIA ENTERPRISES	222 COLUMBUS AV		
10 A1	DEPT MOTOR VEHICLES	1377 FELL ST		557 1179
7 B1	DOLLAR, J HAROLD	351 CALIFORNIA ST		
3 B3	DOLLAR, ROBERT	311 CALIFORNIA ST		392 8454
7 A2	EIGHT THIRTY MARKET	830 MARKET ST		
7 A2	ELEVATED SHOPS	150 POWELL ST		781 5185
7 B1	1 EMBARCADERO CENTER	EMBARCADERO CENTER		772 0500
7 B1	2 EMBARCADERO CENTER	EMBARCADERO CENTER		772 0500
7 B1	3 EMBARCADERO CENTER	EMBARCADERO CENTER		772 0500
7 B2	EQUITABLE LIFE ASSUR	120 MONTGOMERY ST		781 6200
7 B1	EXCHANGE BLOCK	369 PINE ST		421 0422
7 B1	EXECUTIVE TOWERS	503 MARKET ST		
6 C3	FEDERAL	450 MCALLISTER		556 6600
7 B1	FERRY	FOOT OF MARKET ST		
7 B1	FIFTEEN CALIFORNIA ST	15 CALIFORNIA ST		
7 B2	FIFTY HAWTHORNE	50 HAWTHORNE ST		
7 B1	FIRST INTERSTATE BANK	405 MONTGOMERY ST		544 5000
7 B2	FIVE FREMONT CENTER	MISSION & FREMONT STS		
7 A2	FLOOD	870 MARKET ST		982 3298
7 B2	FORTY FOUR MONTGOMERY	44 MONTGOMERY ST		392 2433
7 A2	FOUR FIFTY SUTTER	450 SUTTER ST		421 7221
7 B1	FOUR SEVENTEEN MONTGMY	417 MONTGOMERY ST		392 2470
6 C3	FOX PLAZA	1390 MARKET ST		626 6900
11 A1	GALLERIA	101 HENRY ADAMS ST		863 3388
7 A2	GEARY THEATER	450 GEARY ST		771 3880
7 A3	GOLDEN GATE	25 TAYLOR ST		775 3890
7 A3	GOLDEN GATE THEATER	GOLDEN GT AV&TAYLOR ST		775 8800
7 A3	GRANT	1095 MARKET ST		621 8139
7 A2	GUNST, ELKAN	323 GEARY ST		421 4762
7 A1	HARTFORD OFFICES	650 CALIFORNIA ST		781 0260
6 C3	HEALTH CENTER	260 KEARNY ST		
7 B2	HEARST	3RD & MARKET STS		777 0600
6 C3	HERBST THEATER	VAN NESS & GROVE ST		392 4400
7 B2	HOBART	582 MARKET ST		362 8783
7 B2	HOLBROOK	58 SUTTER ST		
7 A2	HOWARD	209 POST ST		
7 B1	INSURANCE CENTER CORP	450 SANSOME ST		981 0660
7 B1	INSURANCE EXCHANGE	433 CALIFORNIA ST		362 0529
7 A1	INTERNATIONAL	601 CALIFORNIA ST		981 7878
7 B1	KOHL	400 MONTGOMERY ST		392 2470
7 A2	KOHLER & CHASE	26 O'FARRELL ST		
7 A3	LOEW'S WARFIELD	988 MARKET ST		771 9858
7 B2	MACK MILTON ASSOC LTD	116 NEW MONTGOMERY ST		546 9380
7 B1	MFG'S AGENTS EXHIBIT	200 DAVIS ST		
6 C3	MARSHALL SQUARE	1182 MARKET ST		
7 B1	MARVIN	24 CALIFORNIA ST		
15 C3	MASONIC	1111 CALIFORNIA ST		776 4702
6 C2	MEDICAL	909 HYDE ST		673 1317
6 C1	MEDICAL ARTS	2000 VAN NESS AV		474 9292
7 A2	MEDICO/DENTAL	490 POST ST		781 1427
7 B2	MERCANTILEL CENTER	86 3RD ST		
7 B2	MERCHANTS' EXCHANGE	465 CALIFORNIA ST		421 7730
7 B1	MILLS	220 MONTGOMERY ST		421 1444
7 B1	MILLS TOWER	200 BUSH ST		
10 C3	MISSION MEDICAL/DENTAL	2480 MISSION		
7 B2	MONADNOCK	681 MARKET ST		781 1361
7 B2	MOSCONE CONVENTION CTR	747 HOWARD ST		974 4000
7 A2	NATIVE SONS	414 MASON ST		392 0943
7 B2	ONE ELEVEN SUTTER	111 SUTTER ST		477 3274
7 B1	ONE JACKSON PLACE	633 BATTERY ST		362 1800
7 B1	ONE METROPOLITAN PLAZA	425 MARKET ST		495 7333
7 A2	ONE SIXTY FIVE POST	165 POST ST		
6 C3	ORPHEUM THEATER	1192 MARKET ST		
7 A2	PACIFIC	821 MARKET ST		
7 B2	PACIFIC BELL	140 NEW MONTGOMERY ST		811 9000
7 A1	PACIFIC MUTUAL LIFE	600 CALIFORNIA ST		
6 C3	PERFORMING ARTS CENTER	GROVE ST & VAN NESS AV		621 6600
7 A2	PHELAN	760 MARKET ST		392 7552
3 A3	PHOENIX THEATER	430 BROADWAY		
7 A2	PHYSICIANS'	516 SUTTER ST		
7 A2	POETZ	449 POWELL ST		
6 C3	PROFESSIONAL/LEGAL CTR	335 HAYES ST		
7 B2	RIALTO	116 NEW MONTGOMERY ST		421 0704
7 B1	RITCHIE & RITCHIE	120 BUSH ST		
7 B1	ROYAL INSURANCE	201 SANSOME ST		
7 B1	RUSS	235 MONTGOMERY ST		421 7424
7 A2	SACHS	133 GEARY ST		
7 A2	ST PAUL	285 GEARY ST		421 7454
21 B1	SALES MART	1485 BAYSHORE BLVD		467 0707
7 A3	SAN CHRISTINA	1026 MARKET ST		
7 B2	S F FEDERAL SAVINGS	POST ST & KEARNY ST		
7 B1	S F STOCK EXCHANGE	301 PINE ST		
7 B1	SANTA MARINA	112 MARKET ST		
7 A2	SCHROTH	240 STOCKTON ST		
7 B2	SEVENTY NINE NEW MONTG	79 NEW MONTGOMERY ST		
7 B2	SHARON	55 NEW MONTGOMERY ST		982 9281
7 B2	SHELDON	9 FIRST ST		
7 B1	SHELL	100 BUSH ST		986 0647

1988 SAN FRANCISCO COUNTY POINTS OF INTEREST

PAGE & GRID	NAME	ADDRESS	CITY	PHONE
7 A2	SHREVE & CO	POST ST & GRANT AV		781 2065
7 B2	605 MARKET STREET	605 MARKET ST		495 0239
7 B2	SIX SIXTY MARKET ST	660 MARKET ST		788 4820
7 B2	SIXTY EIGHT POST	80 POST ST		
7 B1	SIXTY FOUR PINE ST	64 PINE ST		
7 B1	SOUTHERN PACIFIC	1 MARKET ST		541 1000
7 B1	STANDARD OIL	225 BUSH ST		894 7700
7 B1	THREE FORTY MARKET ST	340 MARKET ST		
7 B1	343 SANSOME	343 SONSOME ST		
7 B1	THREE TWENTY CALIF ST	320 CALIFORNIA ST		397 6943
7 B2	TIDEWATER	55 NEW MONTGOMERY ST		
11 A1	TRADE SHOW CENTER	2 HENRY ADAMS ST		864 1500
7 B1	TRANSAMERICA (PYRAMID)	600 MONTGOMERY ST		983 4000
6 A2	2299 POST MEDICAL CTR	2299 POST ST		
7 B1	200 BUSH INVENTMENT CO	200 BUSH ST		
3 B3	UNION BANK	50 CALIFORNIA ST		774 6000
3 B3	UNION CARBIDE	1 CALIFORNIA ST		
6 B1	UNION STREET PLAZA	2001 UNION ST		931 2445
6 C1	VAN NESS PACIFIC MED	2107 VAN NESS AV		885 6808
6 C2	VAN NESS POST CENTER	1255 POST ST		
6 C3	VETERANS' WAR MEMORIAL	MCALLISTER & VAN NESS		
21 A3	VISITACION MED & DENTL	5 PEABODY ST		239 5500
6 C3	WAR MEMRL OPERA HOUSE	VAN NESS AV & GROVE ST		864 3330
7 B1	WELLS FARGO	464 CALIFORNIA ST		396 0123
7 B2	WESIX	390 FIRST ST		
6 C3	WEST COAST LIFE	1275 MARKET ST		552 6200
7 A2	WESTPHAL	545 SUTTER ST		
7 A2	WILSON	973 MARKET ST		
6 C3	WOODBRIDGE	228 MCALLISTER ST		
	CHAMBER OF COMMERCE			
7 B2	SAN FRANCISCO	465 CALIFORNIA ST		392 4511
7 B2	SF CONVENTION/VIS BUR	201 3RD ST		976 6900
	COLLEGES & UNIVERSITIES			
19 C1	CITY COLLEGE OF S F	50 PHELAN AV		239 3000
7 B2	GOLDEN GATE UNIVERSITY	550 MISSION ST		442 7225
18 C1	SAN FRANCISCO STATE U	1600 HOLLOWAY AV		469 1111
14 B3	SIMPSON COLLEGE	801 SILVER AV		334 7400
9 B2	UNIVERSITY OF CAL, S F	501 PARNASSUS AV		476 9000
10 B1	UC EXTENSION CENTER	55 LAGUNA ST		552 3016
6 C3	UC/HASTINGS COL OF LAW	198 MCALLISTER ST		565 4600
6 B2	UNIV OF THE PACIFIC	2155 WEBSTER ST		929 6450
5 C3	UNIVERSITY OF S F	PARKER&GOLDEN GATE AVS		666 6886
	GOLF COURSES			
18 B1	FLEMING (PUBLIC)	HARDING & SKYLINE BLVD		661 1865
8 A1	GOLDEN GATE PARK (PUB)	47TH AV & FULTON ST		751 8987
18 B1	HARDING PARK (PUBLIC)	HARDING & SKYLINE BLVD		664 4690
21 E5	LAKE MERCED GOLF CLUB	2300 JUNIPERO SERRA BL	DALY CITY	755 2233
4 B3	LINCOLN PARK (PUBLIC)	CLEMENT ST & 33RD AV		221 9911
20 C2	MCLAREN, JOHN (PUBLIC)	MCLAREN PARK		587 2425
5 A1	PRESIDIO GOLF CLUB	PARK PRESIDIO BLVD		751 1322
19 A3	S F GOLF & COUNTRY CLB	JUNIPERO SERRA BLVD		585 0480
	HOSPITALS			
	*EMERGENCY SERVICES AVAILABLE			
5 C2	*CHILDREN'S HOSPITAL	3700 CALIFORNIA ST		387 8700
3 A3	CHINESE HOSPITAL	835 JACKSON ST		982 2400
5 B3	*FRENCH HOSPITAL	4131 GEARY BLVD		386 9000
6 A3	*KAISER FOUNDATION HOS	2425 GEARY BLVD		929 4000
13 B1	*LAGUNA HONDA HOSP	375 LAGUNA HONDA BL		664 1580
5 C2	*MARSHAL HALE MEM HOSP	3773 SACRAMENTO ST		386 7000
6 A2	*MOUNT ZION HOSPITAL	1600 DIVISADERO ST		567 6600
5 C3	*PACIFIC PRESBYTERIAN	2750 GEARY BLVD		921 6171
2 B3	*PRESBYTERIAN HOSPITAL	2333 BUCHANAN ST		563 4321
10 B1	*RALPH DAVIES MED CTR	CASTRO & DUBOCE		565 6779
6 C2	*ST FRANCIS MEMORIAL	900 HYDE ST		775 4321
14 C1	*ST LUKE'S HOSPITAL	3555 ARMY ST		647 8600
9 C1	*ST MARY'S HOSPITAL	450 STANYAN ST		668 1000
11 A3	*S F GENERAL HOSPITAL	1001 POTRERO AV		821 8200
9 A3	SHRINERS CRIPLD CHILD	1701 19TH AV		665 1100
9 B2	*UCSF MEDICAL CENTER	501 PARNASSUS AV		476 1000
4 A2	V A MEDICAL CENTER	4150 CLEMENT ST		221 4810

PAGE & GRID	NAME	ADDRESS	CITY	PHONE
	HOTELS & MOTELS			
7 A3	AMERICANIA	121 7TH ST		626 0200
7 A2	BELLEVUE	505 GEARY ST		474 3600
7 A2	CAMPTON PLACE	340 STOCKTON ST		781 5555
6 C2	CATHEDRAL HILL	VAN NESS AV & GEARY ST		776 8200
7 A2	DONATELLO, THE	POST ST & MASON		441 7100
7 A1	FAIRMONT	CALIFORNIA & MASON STS		772 5000
7 A2	FOUR SEASONS CLIFT	GEARY & TAYLOR STS		775 4700
6 C2	GROSVENOR INN	1050 VAN NESS AV		673 4711
	HILTON	SN FRANCISCO INT AIRPT		589 0770
7 A2	HILTON HOTEL & TOWER	333 O'FARRELL ST		771 1400
	HOLIDAY INN, AIRPORT	245 S AIRPORT BL	S SF	589 7200
7 A3	HOLIDAY INN, CIVIC CTR	50 8TH ST		626 6103
7 A1	HOLIDAY INN, FINAN DIS	750 KEARNY ST		433 6600
2 C2	HOLIDAY INN,FISHERMN W	1300 COLUMBUS AV		771 9000
6 C2	HOLIDAY INN,GOLDEN GTE	1500 VAN NESS AV		441 4000
7 A2	HOLIDAY INN, UNION SQ	480 SUTTER ST		398 8900
2 C2	HOWARD JOHNSONS	580 BEACH ST		775 3800
7 A2	HOTEL NIKKO OF S F	150 POWELL ST		421 9037
7 A2	HYATT ON UNION SQ	345 STOCKTON ST		398 1234
7 B1	HYATT REGENCY	5 EMBARCADERO CENTER		788 1234
6 B2	KYOTO INN	1800 SUTTER ST		921 4000
7 B1	MANDARIN OF S F	222 SANSOME ST		885 0999
2 C2	MARRIOTT-FISHERMNS WHF	1250 COLUMBUS AV		775 7555
7 A2	MARRIOTT-MOSCONE CTR	785 MARKET ST		896 1600
6 B2	MIYAKO	1625 POST ST		922 3200
7 A1	MARK HOPKINS	CALIFORNIA & MASON STS		392 3434
7 B2	MERIDIEN	50 THIRD ST		974 6400
7 A2	PACIFIC PLAZA HOTEL	POST & MASON ST		441 7100
7 A2	PORTMAN HOTEL	414 MASON ST		398 2525
2 C2	RAMADA FISHRMN'S WHARF	590 BAY ST		885 4700
7 A2	RAMADA RENAISSANCE	55 CYRL MAGNIN ST/EDDY		392 8000
7 A2	RAPHAEL	386 GEARY ST		986 2000
3 A1	SHERATON FISHERMNS WHF	2500 MASON ST		362 5500
7 B2	SHERATON PALACE	2 NEW MONTGOMERY ST		392 8600
7 A2	SIR FRANCIS DRAKE	SUTTER & POWELL STS		392 7755
7 A1	STANFORD COURT	905 CALIFORNIA ST		989 3500
9 C1	STANYAN PARK HOTEL	750 STANYAN ST		751 1000
3 A1	TRAVELODGE AT WHARF	250 BEACH ST		392 6700
6 C2	TRAVELODGE CIVIC CTR	655 ELLIS ST		771 3000
6 C2	TRAVELODGE DOWNTOWN	790 ELLIS ST		775 7612
2 C2	TRAVELODGE FISHERM WHF	1201 COLUMBUS AV		776 7070
2 A2	TRAVELODGE GOLDEN GATE	2230 LOMBARD ST		922 3900
2 A3	TRAVELODGE PRESIDIO	2755 LOMBARD ST		931 8581
10 C1	TRAVELODGE S F CENTRAL	1707 MARKET ST		621 6775
7 A3	TRAVELODGE YERBA BUENA	240 7TH ST		861 6469
2 B2	VAGABOND INN - MIDTOWN	2550 VAN NESS AV		776 7500
7 A2	VILLA FLORENCE	225 POWELL ST		397 7700
7 A2	WESTIN ST FRANCIS	POWELL & GEARY STS		397 7000
	LIBRARIES			
15 C3	ANNA WADEN	5075 3RD ST		468 1323
4 B3	ANZA	550 37TH AV		752 1960
14 C2	BERNAL	500 CORTLAND AV		285 1744
7 A1	BUSINESS	530 KEARNY ST		558 3946
7 A1	CHINATOWN	1135 POWELL ST		989 6770
6 A2	COMMUNICATIONS CTR	3150 SACRAMENTO ST		558 5035
10 B2	EUREKA VALLEY	3555 16TH ST		626 1132
20 B1	EXCELSIOR	4400 MISSION ST		586 4075
14 B3	GLEN PARK	653 CHENERY ST		586 4144
2 B3	GOLDEN GATE	1801 GREEN ST		346 9273
19 B1	INGLESIDE	387 ASHTON ST		586 4156
6 C3	MAIN LIBRARY	CIVIC CENTER		558 3191
2 B2	MARINA	CHESTNUT & WEBSTER		346 9336
19 A1	MERCED	155 WINSTON DR		586 4246
10 C3	MISSION	3359 24TH ST		824 2810
14 B1	NOE VALLEY	451 JERSEY ST		285 2788
3 A2	NORTH BEACH	2000 MASON ST		391 9473
19 B2	OCEAN VIEW	111 BROAD ST		586 4193
12 B1	ORTEGA	3223 ORTEGA ST		681 1848
9 C1	PARK	1833 PAGE ST		752 4620
12 C2	PARKSIDE	1200 TARAVAL ST		566 4647
15 A3	PORTOLA	2434 SAN BRUNO AV		468 2232
11 B2	POTRERO	1616 20TH ST		285 3022
5 A3	RICHMOND	351 9TH AV		752 1240
9 A2	SUNSET	1305 18TH AV		566 4552
21 A3	VISITACION	45 LELAND AV		239 5270

1988 SAN FRANCISCO COUNTY POINTS OF INTEREST

PAGE & GRID	NAME	ADDRESS	CITY	PHONE
6 A2	WESTERN ADDITION	1550 SCOTT		346 9531
13 B2	WEST PORTAL	190 LENOX WY		566 4584
	POST OFFICES			
15 B3	BAYVIEW	2111 LANE ST		822 7619
14 C2	BERNAL	30 29TH ST		695 1703
7 A1	CHINATOWN	867 STOCKTON ST		956 3566
6 C3	CITY HALL	CIVIC CENTER		621 6325
14 A1	DIAMOND HEIGHTS	5262 DIAMOND HTS BLVD		550 6412
6 C3	FEDERAL BUILDING	450 GOLDEN GATE AV		621 7505
9 B2	FISK	1317 9TH AV		759 1901
4 C3	GEARY	5654 GEARY BL		752 0231
15 C2	GENERAL MAIL FACILITY	1300 EVANS AV		550 5247
1 C2	LETTERMAN	PRESIDIO MILITARY		563 7195
7 A3	MAIN OFFICE	7TH & MISSION STS		621 6792
2 A2	MARINA	3225 FILLMORE ST		563 4674
21 A1	MCLAREN	2755 SAN BRUNO AV		467 3560
11 A2	MISSION ANNEX	1600 BRYANT ST		621 8646
10 B3	NOE VALLEY	4083 24TH ST		821 0776
3 A2	NORTH BEACH	1640 STOCKTON ST		956 3581
12 C2	PARKSIDE	1800 TARAVAL ST		759 1601
1 C2	PRESIDIO	PRESIDIO MILITARY		563 4975
7 B1	RINCON ANNEX	50 1ST ST		543 3340
19 A1	STONESTOWN	565 BUCKINGHAM WY		759 1660
8 C2	SUNSET	1314 22ND AV		759 1707
7 A2	SUTTER	150 SUTTER ST		956 3169
3 C1	TREASURE ISLAND	TREASURE ISLAND		956 1520
21 A3	VISITACION	68 LELAND AV		331 1150
13 A2	WEST PORTAL	317 W PORTAL AV		759 1811
7 A2	NO 23 THE EMPORIUM	835 MARKET ST		543 2606
10 C2	NO 40 BELL BAZAAR	3030 16TH ST		621 6053
7 A2	NO 57 MACYS	STOCKTON & O'FARRELL		956 3570
6 B2	A	1550 STEINER ST		563 5954
3 B3	B	555 BATTERY ST		956 3140
6 C2	C	1198 S VAN NESS AV		285 7382
7 B3	E	460 BRANNAN ST		543 7729
20 A1	F	15 ONONDAGA AV		334 0709
10 A2	G	4304 18TH ST		621 5317
9 C1	J	554 CLAYTON ST		621 7445
7 B2	K	137 NEW MONTGOMERY ST		543 4125
5 B2	M	275 6TH AV		668 2092
6 C2	O	1414 VAN NESS AV		441 6941
	SCHOOLS - PRIVATE ELEMENTARY			
15 C3	ALL HALLOWS	1601 LANE ST		822 8780
19 A2	BRANDEIS-HILLEL DAY	655 BROTHERHOOD WY		334 9841
4 B2	BURKE, KATHERINE D	7070 CALIFORNIA ST		751 0177
6 B3	CATHEDRAL INTERMEDIATE	1016 EDDY ST		567 1082
7 A1	CATHEDRAL SCH FOR BOYS	1275 SACRAMENTO ST		771 6600
6 B1	CONVENT SACRED HEART	2200 BROADWAY ST		563 2900
20 B1	CORPUS CHRISTI	75 FRANCIS ST		587 7014
20 A1	DISCOVERY CENTER	65 OCEAN AV		333 6609
20 B2	EPIPHANY	600 ITALY AV		587 6900
10 B1	FIRST BAPTIST CHURCH	42 WALLER ST		863 1691
10 B1	FRENCH AMER INTERNATL	220 BUCHANAN ST		626 8564
6 B1	HAMLIN	2129 VALLEJO ST		922 0600
8 C1	HEBREW ACADEMY OF S F	763 25TH AV		752 7490
8 B3	HOLY NAME	1560 40TH AV		731 4077
15 A1	IMMACULATE CONCEPTION	1550 TREAT AV		824 6860
8 A2	LITTLE LIGHTS BAPTIST	4508 IRVING ST		564 8357
4 B3	LYCEE FRANCAIS DE S F	3301 BALBOA ST		668 1833
10 B2	MISSION DOLORES	3371 16TH ST		861 7673
6 B2	MORNING STAR	1911 PINE ST		921 4436
10 B2	NOTRE DAME ELEMENTARY	333 DOLORES ST		552 3590
7 A1	NOTRE DAME VICTOIRES	659 PINE ST		421 0069
20 C3	OUR LADY OF VISITACION	785 SUNNYDALE AV		239 7840
10 B1	SACRED HEART ELEM	660 OAK ST		621 8035
9 A2	ST ANNE	1320 14TH AV		664 7977
14 C1	ST ANTHONY	299 PRECITA AV		648 2008
13 C2	ST BRENDAN	234 ULLOA ST		731 2665
2 C3	ST BRIGID	2250 FRANKLIN ST		673 4523
13 A2	ST CECILIA	660 VICENTE ST		731 8400
10 C2	ST CHARLES	3250 18TH ST		861 7652
6 B2	ST DOMINIC	2445 PINE ST		346 9500
21 A1	ST ELIZABETH	450 SOMERSET ST		468 3247
19 B1	ST EMYDIUS	301 DE MONTFORT AV		333 4877
13 C3	ST FINN BARR	419 HEARST AV		333 1800
12 B2	ST GABRIEL	2550 41ST AV		566 0314

PAGE & GRID	NAME	ADDRESS	CITY	PHONE
10 B3	ST JAMES	321 FAIR OAKS ST		647 8972
14 A3	ST JOHN	925 CHENERY ST		584 8383
10 C1	ST JOSEPH	220 10TH ST		431 1206
7 A1	ST MARY CHINESE DAY	902 STOCKTON ST		362 7394
19 C2	ST MICHAEL	55 FARALLONES ST		585 4781
4 C3	ST MONICA	5920 GEARY BLVD		751 9564
14 B2	ST PAUL	1660 CHURCH ST		648 2055
21 B2	ST PAUL OF SHIPWRECK	6475 3RD ST		467 1798
6 C3	ST PAULUS LUTHERAN	888 TURK ST		673 0497
15 A1	ST PETER	1266 FLORIDA ST		647 8662
3 A2	SAINTS PETER & PAUL	632 FILBERT ST		421 5219
10 A3	ST PHILIP	665 ELIZABETH ST		824 8467
13 A3	ST STEPHEN	401 EUCALYPTUS DR		664 8331
4 B3	ST THOMAS THE APOSTLE	3801 BALBOA ST		221 2711
19 A3	ST THOMAS MORE	50 THOMAS MORE WY		585 1963
2 A3	ST VINCENT DE PAUL	2356 GREEN ST		346 5505
7 A1	SF CHINESE PARENT COMM	843 STOCKTON ST		391 5564
19 C3	S F CHRISTIAN ELEM	25 WHITTIER ST		586 1117
6 B2	SAN FRANCISCO DAY	2266 CALIFORNIA ST		563 6355
20 A2	S F JUNIOR ACADEMY	66 GENEVA AV		585 5550
15 A3	S F MONTESSORI	300 GAVEN ST		239 5065
6 A2	SAN FRANCISCO WALDORF	2938 WASHINGTON ST		931 2750
2 A3	TOWN SCHOOL FOR BOYS	2750 JACKSON ST		921 3747
5 B3	STAR OF THE SEA ELEM	360 9TH AV		221 8558
6 B1	STUART HALL FOR BOYS	2252 BROADWAY		563 2900
13 A3	WEST PORTAL LUTHERAN	200 SLOAT BLVD		665 6330
5 B3	ZION LUTHERAN	495 9TH AV		221 7500
	SCHOOLS - PRIVATE HIGH			
6 B2	CATHEDRAL HIGH SCHOOL	1100 ELLIS ST		567 7400
6 B1	CONVENT SACRED HT HIGH	2222 BROADWAY ST		563 2900
10 B1	FRENCH AMERICAN INTNL	220 BUCHANAN ST		626 8564
6 A2	DREW COLLEGE PREP	2901 CALIFORNIA ST		346 4831
14 C1	IMMAC CONCEPTION ACAD	3625 24TH ST		824 2052
19 C1	LICK-WILMERDING	775 OCEAN AV		333 4021
4 B3	LYCEE FRANCAIS DE SF	3301 BALBOA ST		668 1833
13 A3	MERCY HIGH (GIRLS)	3250 19TH AV		334 0525
5 C3	PRESENTATION HIGH	2350 TURK ST		387 4720
19 C1	RIORDAN HIGH (BOYS)	175 PHELAN AV		586 8200
6 C2	SACRED HEART BOYS HS	1075 ELLIS ST		775 6626
12 B1	ST IGNATIUS (BOYS)	2001 37TH AV		731 7500
14 B3	ST JOHN URSULINE HIGH	4056 MISSION ST		586 6333
14 B2	ST PAUL'S GIRLS HIGH	317 29TH ST		648 0505
6 A2	ST ROSE ACADEMY	2475 PINE ST		346 7035
5 C1	SF UNIVERSITY HS	3065 JACKSON ST		346 8400
5 B3	STAR OF THE SEA ACAD	350 9TH AV		752 6024
10 A1	URBAN	1563 PAGE ST		626 2919
	SCHOOLS - PUBLIC ELEMENTARY			
4 C2	ALAMO	250 23RD AV		752 8244
10 A3	ALVARADO	625 DOUGLASS ST		826 1650
9 A1	ARGONNE	675 17TH AV		751 6717
11 A3	BRYANT	1050 YORK ST		647 4959
15 A1	BUENA VISTA	2641 25TH ST		821 1852
8 C1	CABRILLO	735 24TH AV		752 9237
7 A3	CARMICHAEL, BESSIE	55 SHERMAN ST		863 2442
15 C3	CARVER, GEO WASHINGTON	1360 OAKDALE AV		822 6391
7 B1	CHINESE EDUCATION CTR	657 MERCHANT ST		982 9550
9 C3	CLARENDON	500 CLARENDON AV		661 0770
20 B1	CLEVELAND	455 ATHENS ST		585 0845
6 A2	COBB, WILLIAM L	2725 CALIFORNIA ST		567 0700
13 A3	COMMODORE SLOAT	50 DARIEN WY		564 0311
7 A1	COMMODORE STOCKTON	950 CLAY ST		781 7045
10 A1	DE AVILA, WILLIAM	1351 HAIGHT ST		626 0181
10 A3	DOUGLAS	4235 19TH ST		863 5184
15 C3	DRAKE, SIR FRANCIS	350 HARBOR RD		282 8390
15 B3	DREW, CHARLES R	50 POMONA ST		822 9770
10 B3	EDISON	3531 22ND ST		821 4510
21 A2	EL DORADO	70 DELTA ST		467 6050
14 B2	FAIRMOUNT	65 CHENERY ST		285 3828
7 B3	FILIPINO EDUCATION CTR	824 HARRISON ST		543 8430
15 A1	FLYNN, LEONARD	3125 ARMY ST		648 8727
3 A2	GARFIELD	420 FILBERT ST		982 2823
14 A3	GLEN PARK	151 LIPPARD AV		333 6388
6 A3	GOLDEN GATE	1601 TURK ST		931 0449
9 C2	GRATTAN	165 GRATTAN ST		681 8822
20 B3	GUADALUPE	859 PRAGUE ST		334 1975
21 C2	HARTE, BRET	1035 GILMAN AV		822 5271

1988 SAN FRANCISCO COUNTY POINTS OF INTEREST

PAGE & GRID	NAME	ADDRESS	CITY	PHONE
10 C3	HAWTHORNE	825 SHOTWELL ST		824 0896
14 C3	HILLCREST	810 SILVER AV		585 3202
9 A2	JEFFERSON	1725 IRVING ST		664 0342
8 A3	KEY, FRANCIS SCOTT	1530 43RD AV		664 2062
11 B3	KING, STARR	1215 CAROLINA ST		282 8615
4 B3	LAFAYETTE	4545 ANZA ST		387 3322
12 C3	LAKESHORE	220 MIDDLEFIELD DR		664 6768
8 B3	LAWTON	1570 31ST AV		564 5500
5 B2	LILIENTHAL, CLAIRE	3950 SACRAMENTO ST		751 9630
20 A3	LONGFELLOW	755 MORSE ST		587 2400
10 C2	MARSHALL	1575 15TH ST		626 9180
5 B3	MCCOPPIN, FRANK	651 6TH AV		752 9825
10 A2	MCKINLEY	1025 14TH ST		626 3055
13 C2	MIRALOMA	175 OMAR WY		587 4028
11 A3	MISSION EDUCATION CTR	2641 25TH ST		826 8330
20 B1	MONROE	260 MADRID ST		334 0754
10 C3	MOSCONE, GEORGE R	2355 FOLSOM ST		647 8526
10 B1	MUIR, JOHN	380 WEBSTER ST		621 0600
6 B2	NEW TRADITIONS CTR	1501 OFARRELL ST		922 1850
19 B2	ORTEGA, JOSE	400 SARGENT ST		587 7529
3 A3	PARKER, JEAN	840 BROADWAY		421 2988
5 B2	PEABODY, GEORGE	251 6TH AV		565 9574
6 C2	REDDING	1421 PINE ST		673 7931
14 C2	REVERE, PAUL	555 TOMPKINS AV		282 2875
14 C2	REVERE, PAUL ANNEX	610 TOMPKINS AV		648 1776
10 A3	ROOFTOP ALT	445 BURNETT ST		285 1977
10 B2	SANCHEZ	325 SANCHEZ ST		626 4527
20 B1	SN FRANCISCO COMMUNITY	125 EXCELSIOR ST		239 1870
14 C2	SERRA, JUNIPERO	625 HOLLY PARK CIR		285 0252
19 B2	SHERIDAN	431 CAPITOL AV		586 2200
2 B3	SHERMAN	1651 UNION ST		776 5500
6 C1	SPRING VALLEY	1451 JACKSON ST		474 5637
12 B1	STEVENSON, ROBT LOUIS	2051 34TH AV		564 4159
13 C3	SUNNYSIDE	250 FOERSTER ST		585 8127
5 A2	SUTRO	235 12TH AV		752 4203
6 C3	SWETT, JOHN	727 GOLDEN GATE AV		863 6474
21 A1	TAYLOR, E R	423 BURROWS ST		468 1912
3 C1	TREASURE ISLAND	13TH ST & AV E	TREASURE ISL	421 5412
12 B2	ULLOA	2650 42ND AV		564 4240
21 A2	VISITACION VALLEY	55 SCHWERIN ST		239 7396
11 B2	WEBSTER, DANIEL	465 MISSOURI ST		826 6195
6 B2	WEILL, RAPHAEL	1501 O'FARRELL ST		922 0757
13 B2	WEST PORTAL	5 LENOX WY		731 0340
2 C2	YICK WO	2245 JONES ST		474 2833
	SCHOOLS - PUBLIC MIDDLE			
13 B3	APTOS	105 APTOS AV		586 6194
20 B2	BURBANK, LUTHER	325 LA GRANDE AV		586 1650
20 A1	DENMAN, JAMES	241 ONEIDA AV		586 0840
10 B2	EVERETT	450 CHURCH ST		431 0822
3 A2	FRANCISCO	2190 POWELL ST		392 8214
6 A2	FRANKLIN, BENJAMIN	1430 SCOTT ST		565 9654
12 B1	GIANNINI, A P	3151 ORTEGA ST		664 4575
13 A1	HOOVER, HERBERT	2290 14TH AV		564 1226
21 A1	KING, MARTIN LUTHER	350 GIRARD ST		468 7290
14 B1	LICK, JAMES	1220 NOE ST		648 8080
10 C3	MANN, HORACE	3351 23RD ST		826 4504
2 A2	MARINA	3500 FILLMORE ST		565 9577
11 B2	POTRERO HILL	655 DE HARO ST		647 1011
4 B3	PRESIDIO	450 30TH AV		752 9696
5 B3	ROOSEVELT	460 ARGUELLO BL		386 1600
20 C2	VISITACION VALLEY	450 RAYMOND AV		239 6550
	SCHOOLS - PUBLIC HIGH			
6 B3	ALAMO PARK	1099 HAYES ST		565 9756
20 A1	BALBOA	1000 CAYUGA AV		333 2777
12 A2	BAY	2325 41ST AV		753 8703
12 A2	CTR INDEPENDENT STUDY	3045 SANTIAGO ST		546 7717
18 C1	COLLEGE PARK	700 FONT BLVD		334 5601
15 B3	BURTON, PHILLIP	45 CONKLING ST		826 9090
10 C3	DOWNTOWN	110 BARTLETT ST		565 9610
2 B2	GALILEO	1150 FRANCISCO ST		771 3150
12 B1	INTERNTL STUDIES ACAD	1920 41ST AV		566 3800
20 C2	JOHN MCLAREN PARK	2055 SUNNYDALE AV		333 6410
12 C1	LINCOLN, ABRAHAM	2162 24TH AV		566 1618
12 C3	LOWELL	1101 EUCALYPTUS DR		566 7900
9 A2	MARK TWAIN	1541 12TH AV		731 3380
13 C1	MCATEER, J EUGENE	555 PORTOLA DR		824 6001

PAGE & GRID	NAME	ADDRESS	CITY	PHONE
10 B2	MISSION	3750 18TH ST		552 5800
2 B3	NEWCOMER	2340 JACKSON ST		922 1190
10 C3	O'CONNELL, JOHN	2905 21ST ST		648 1326
15 A1	SUNSHINE	2730 BRYANT ST		647 1516
5 C3	WALLENBERG, RAOUL	40 VEGA ST		346 7466
4 B3	WASHINGTON, GEORGE	600 32ND AV		387 0550
21 A1	WILSON, WOODROW	400 MANSELL ST		239 6200
	SHOPPING CENTERS			
2 C2	ANCHORAGE, THE	2800 LEAVENWORTH ST		775 6000
2 C2	CANNERY, THE	2801 LEAVENWORTH ST		771 3112
7 B2	CROCKER GALLERIA	50 POST ST		
3 B3	EMBARCADERO CENTER	SACRAMENTO & CLAY		772 0500
2 C2	GHIRARDELLI SQUARE	POLK & NORTH POINT		775 5500
6 B2	JAPAN CENTER	POST & LAGUNA		567 6076
3 A1	PIER 39	EMBARCADERO		981 7437
19 A1	STONESTOWN CENTER	EUCALYPTUS DR&19TH AV		564 4000
	U S GOVERNMENT OFFICES			
7 B1	AGRICULTURE DEPT	630 SANSOME ST		556 6464
1 C2	ARMY DEPT	PRESIDIO OF S F		561 2211
6 C3	CIVIL SERVICE COM	450 GOLDEN GATE AV		556 6667
7 B1	COAST GUARD	630 SANSOME ST		556 3530
3 B3	CUSTOMS HOUSE	555 BATTERY ST		556 4440
6 C3	FED BUREAU INVESTIGATN	450 GOLDEN GATE AV		553 7400
6 C3	FEDERAL OFFICE BLDG	450 GOLDEN GATE AV		556 6600
6 C3	FEDERAL OFC BLDG (OLD)	50 FULTON ST		
6 C3	INTERNAL REVENUE SERV	450 GOLDEN GATE AV		839 1040
3 C1	MARINES	TREASURE ISLAND		765 6074
7 B2	MARITIME COMMISSION	525 MARKET ST		974 9756
3 C1	NAVY DEPT	TREASURE ISLAND		765 9111
6 C3	SOCIAL SECURITY BOARD	FEDERAL OFFICE BLDG		956 3000
7 B2	VETERANS ADMINISTRATN	211 MAIN ST		495 8900
6 C3	WEATHER BUREAU	FEDERAL OFFICE BLDG		936 1212

1988 SAN FRANCISCO COUNTY POINTS OF INTEREST

ALCATRAZ ISLAND....................................S.F. BAY
1-3/4 miles from the San Francisco shoreline. Until recently visitors could only look at Alcatraz or sail by at a cautious distance, speculating on what the inside of the legendary federal prison was actually like. 'The Rock' has been a fortification, a U.S. military prison, an Army disciplinary barracks, and finally a maximum security federal penitentiary before it was 'phased out' in 1963.
TOUR HOURS: 9am to 3pm May thru September. 9am to 5pm other months.
CLOSED: Thanksgiving, Christmas and New Year's Day.
ADMISSION: $4.00 Adults, $2.50 children (5 to 11 years), includes transportation.
RESERVATIONS: Ticketron or in person, Pier 41, San Francisco (415) 546-2805.

AQUATIC PARK.......................................2 B1
The Aquatic Park, three blocks west of Fisherman's Wharf and north of Ghirardelli Square, contains the Hyde Street Pier and the architecturally unique Maritime Museum building.

BAKER BEACH..4 C1

BALCLUTHA..3 A1
A steel hulled, square rigged vessel, built in Scotland in 1886, now survives as the last of the Cape Horn Fleet.

BART...3 B2
75 mile transbay Bay Area Rapid Transit links San Francisco's subway stations with East Bay terminals. For information telephone 788-BART.

CABLE CAR BARN AND MUSEUM..........................7 A1
This red brick building, built in 1887, is the control center for the cable car system, and is also a museum and visitors' gallery with exhibits and photos of 19th century cable car operations. Located at Washington and Mason Streets.
For information telephone 474-1887.
HOURS: 10am to 6pm daily. Closed Thanksgiving, Christmas and New Year's Day.

CALIFORNIA ACADEMY OF SCIENCES........See Golden Gate Park

CALIFORNIA PALACE OF THE LEGION OF HONOR...........4 B2
This unique collection, displaying 16th to 20th century French art works, features paintings of prominent 18th & 19th century French artists. The sculpture collection of Rodin is of special significance. Decorative arts of Medieval & Renaissance periods are on display in the new gallery. Lincoln Park. 750-3614.
HOURS: 10am to 5pm Wednesday thru Sunday. Free first Wednesday of each month and Saturday morning from 10am to 12 noon.
ADMISSION: $3.00 Adults; $1.00 Children (5 to 17 years) and seniors.

CHINATOWN..7 A1
This bustling community is the largest Chinese settlement in the United States and a delight for tourists. A multitude of curio bazaars, exotic shops, restaurants, and food markets line its main street, Grant Avenue, and continue for eight blocks between Bush and Columbus.

CIVIC CENTER.......................................6 C3
Located at Van Ness Avenue and McAllister Street.

A. City Hall
B. Federal Building
C. Brooks Hall
D. Civic Auditorium
E. Public Library
F. Performing Arts Center
   1. Davies Symphony Hall
   2. Opera House
   3. Herbst Theatre
G. War Memorial Veterans Building and the San Francisco Museum of Modern Art. A selection of 20th century contemporary art is shown in the many galleries on the spacious third and fourth floors of the Veterans Building.
   HOURS: 10am to 5pm Tuesday thru Friday, Saturday & Sunday 11am to 5pm, & Thursday until 10pm. Closed Mondays and major holidays.
   ADMISSION: Adults $3.50 unless special events; seniors & juniors (under 16 years) $1.50. Free Thursday evenings 6pm to 10pm.

CLIFF HOUSE..4 A3
The famous Cliff House, a restaurant and gift shop, offers a magnificent view of the Seal Rocks and the Pacific Ocean. Located at 1066 to 1090 Point Lobos Avenue, Ocean Beach.

COIT TOWER...3 A2
The Tower, located on Telegraph Hill, was built as a memorial to the City's volunteer firefighters. Elevator ride to the top provides magnificent views of the skyline and bay.
HOURS: 11am to 4pm.

EMBARCADERO CENTER.................................3 C2
Four spectacular buildings designed by architect John Portman tower above three interconnecting levels of shops, restaurants, services & entertainment. Pedestrian bridges link the buildings with the Golden Gateway Center. The architecturally innovative Hyatt Regency and sculptures by Willi Gutmann, Louise Nevelson and Nicolas Schoffer create a visually exciting environment.

FERRY BUILDING.....................................3 B2
A former commuter terminal building is now occupied by the Port Commission, the World Trade Center, a mineral exhibit, and library.

FISHERMAN'S WHARF..................................2 C1
This is the headquarters for the fishing fleet, harbor cruise boats, and sightseeing tours. Visitors enjoy outstanding seafood restaurants, shops, and outdoor seafood stores. Located at the foot of Taylor Street at Jefferson, on the northern waterfront.

FORT POINT NATIONAL HISTORIC SITE..................1 A1
A three tiered fort which required eight years to complete (1853-1861) surrounds a large courtyard. Guided tours provided. Presidio of San Francisco reached via Lincoln Boulevard to Long Avenue. 556-1693. Admission free.
HOURS: 10am to 5pm daily; closed Christmas.

GOLDEN GATE BRIDGE.................................1 A1
One of the longest single span suspension bridges in the world.
ADMISSION: Auto toll collected southbound only, $1.00., $2.00 Friday & Saturday; pedestrians free.

GOLDEN GATE PARK...................................8 C1

A. California Academy of Sciences.......................9 A1
   'It's in Golden Gate Park But It's Out of This World' can identify only one place in San Francisco...the California Academy of Sciences. This magnet annually attracts more than 1,000,000 visitors of every age and interest, and it keeps luring them back year after year. All under one roof are the STEINHART AQUARIUM, the FISH ROUNDABOUT, the MORRISON PLANETARIUM and the HALLS OF SCIENCE. The WATTIS HALL OF MAN, depicting a series of life-like cultural habitat scenes, is a worthwhile exhibit for those with an interest in ecology, anthropology, or the exotic. The Fish Roundabout is unique in the United States. 752-8268.
   HOURS: 10am to 5pm daily (open later in summer months).
   ADMISSION: $3.00 Adults (18-64); $1.50 seniors & students (12-17); 75c for children (6-11). First day of the month is free. Planetarium shows: $2.00 adults, $1.00 children 7 to 17. Children 6 and under are free. 750-7145.
B. Strybing Arboretum and Botanical Gardens..............9 A1
   Sixty acres of more than six thousand species and varieties of plants.
   HOURS: Weekdays 8am to 4:30pm. Weekends 10am to 5pm.
C. Asian Art Museum......................................9 A1
   The Avery Brundage Collection contains objects of art from Oriental civilizations. Special exhibits.
   HOURS: 10am to 5pm Tuesday thru Sunday. 668-8921.
   ADMISSION: $3.00 Adults (18-65); $1.00 seniors and juniors (5-17).
D. Conservatory..9 B1
   Tropical plants and flower shows.
   HOURS: Open 8am to 4:30pm.
E. M. H. De Young Museum.................................9 A1
   This is the city's most diversified art museum. With more than 1,000,000 visitors annually, it is one of America's most popular. Permanent exhibition of fine and applied arts, special exhibits, and educational services. 750-3659.

1988 SAN FRANCISCO COUNTY POINTS OF INTEREST

HOURS: 10am to 5pm Wednesday thru Sunday.
ADMISSION: $3.00 Adults (18-65); $1.00 seniors & young adults (12-18); all others free. One admission charge for Asian Art, De Young and Legion of Honor Museums on same day.

F. Japanese Tea Garden..................9 A1
Superb example of a Japanese garden. The fragile blossoms of 200 cherry trees are at their peak blooming period the first week of April.
HOURS: Open daily from 8am to dusk.
ADMISSION: 75c.

G. Music Concourse..................9 A1
Sunday afternoon concerts held in a peaceful, tree-sheltered setting.

H. Kezar Stadium..................9 B1

I. Stow Lake..................9 A1
Row boats, paddle boats, and electric boats for rent.

J. Golden Gate Equestrian Center..................8 B1
Horseback riding.

K. Golden Gate Golf Course..................8 A1
Nine hole golf course, par 3. No reservations.

L. Children's Playground..................9 B2
All types of playground equipment and an animal farm. Visitors of all ages are delighted by a 1912 Hershel-Spillman carousel.

GUINESS MUSEUM OF WORLD RECORDS..................2 C1
Tallest, fastest, greatest and smallest of literally hundreds of people, animals, things, whatever. 235 Jefferson Street, Fisherman's Wharf. 771-9890.
HOURS: Sunday thru Thursday 10am to 10pm, Friday & Saturday 10am to midnight.
ADMISSION: $4.95 Adults, $2.50 children (6-12); under 6 free.

JACKSON SQUARE..................3 A2
This Square, originally known as the Barbary Coast, is entered from Jackson and Montgmery Streets. Decorator and specialty shops now occupy the 19th century buildings which have been preserved.

JAPAN CENTER..................6 B2
Bounded by Geary, Laguna, Fillmore and Post Streets, this area includes a hotel, shopping center, restaurants and many interesting gift shops.

MISSION DOLORES..................10 B2
Mission San Francisco de Asis. Dolores and 16th Sts. 621-8203
Sixth in a chain of missions established by Father Junipero Serra in 1776.
HOURS: May thru October, 9am to 5pm; November thru April, 9am to 4pm. Closed on major holidays. Restoration fee 50c.

GEORGE R. MOSCONE CONVENTION CENTER..................7 B2
Third and Howard Streets.

NATIONAL MARITIME MUSEUM..................2 C1
Hyde Street Pier, Hyde and Jefferson Streets, 556-6435. The four vessels moored here have much in common: they all played a significant part in Pacific Maritime History. Now part of the National Park Service. Fully restored and afloat.
HOURS: 10am to 6pm June thru August; 10am to 5pm the rest of the year. Closed Christmas and New Year's Day.
ADMISSION: Free.

NATIONAL MARITIME MUSEUM BUILDING..................2 B1
The Maritime Museum Building, now part of the National Park Service, is located at the foot of Polk Street, Aquatic Park. 556-8177. It contains an exciting historical display of ship models, photographs, relics, paintings, maps and sailors' handicrafts.
HOURS: 10am to 5pm daily.
ADMISSION: Free.

OCTAGON HOUSE..................2 B2
2645 Gough Street at Union Street. 885-9796. Built in 1861, this house was one of five such residences in early San Francisco. Now the residence of the National Society of Colonial Dames of America, it is one of the few remaining examples of this style.
HOURS: Open the first Sunday of the month and the second and fourth Thursday, 1pm to 4pm. Admission by donation.

OLD UNITED STATES MINT..................7 A2
The mint opened in 1874 to serve the West during the Gold Rush. Having survived the 1906 earthquake, this building now houses a museum of western exhibits and a solid gold bear. 974-0788.
HOURS: 10am to 4pm Monday thru Friday. Closed holidays and weekends.
ADMISSION: Free.

PALACE OF FINE ARTS..................1 C2
Built for the 1915 Panama Pacific International Exposition and later restored, this building now houses a science museum, 'The Exploratorium' and a theater.

PERFORMING ARTS CENTER..................(See Civic Center)

PIER 39..................3 A1
A unique shopping and restaurant complex on the waterfront, designed in the manner of a San Francisco street scene at the turn of the century.

PRESIDIO..................1 A2
Sixth Army Headquarters, established in 1776 by Spaniards.

PRESIDIO ARMY MUSEUM..................1 C2
Lincoln Boulevard and Funston Avenue in the Presidio of San Francisco. 561-4115. The museum focuses on the role of the military in the history and development of San Francisco from 1776 to the present.
HOURS: 10am to 4pm, closed Mondays and major holidays.
ADMISSION: Free.

RIPLEY'S 'BELIEVE IT OR NOT' MUSEUM..................2 C1
175 Jefferson Street, Fisherman's Wharf. 771-6188. Cartoonist Robert L. Ripley's fascination with the unbelievable and unimaginable resulted in an enormous collection of oddities that is now on view in San Francisco.
HOURS: During summer months - 9am to 11pm, until midnight Friday & Saturday. All other months - 10am to 10pm, until midnight Friday & Saturday.
ADMISSION: $4.95 for Adults, $2.50 for Children (under 5 free).

SAN FRANCISCO VISITOR INFORMATION CENTER..................7 A2
(Service of San Francisco Convention & Visitors Bureau)
The place to contact for anything you need to know about San Francisco. Brochures and information supplied free. Located in the Hallidie Plaza (Powell and Market Streets). 391-2000. Business office: 201 Third Street 974-6900. For a two minute recorded summary of daily activities and events, telephone 391-2001. Benhamin H. Swig Pavilion.
HOURS: Daily except Thanksgiving, Christmas and New Year's Day.

SAN FRANCISCO ZOO..................12 A3
Colorful and unusual animals, Zebra Zephyr Guided Tours, a Children's Zoo and picnic areas provide enjoyment for young and old.
HOURS: 10am to 5pm daily, all year round.
ADMISSION: Adults & children not accompanied by adults $3.50. Children (15 years and under with an adult) free. Seniors $1.00. Handicapped & school groups free. Church groups & other groups $2.50 per adult. Children's Zoo $1.00.

SEAL ROCKS..................4 A3
400 feet off shore from the Cliff House Restaurant and Gift Shop, these miniature islands of the Sea Lions can be enjoyed all year round. Point Lobos Avenue, Ocean Beach.

SIGMUND STERN GROVE..................12 C2
Sloat Boulevard and 19th Avenue. Natural Amphitheater sheltered by eucalyptus trees. Summer concerts Sunday, 2pm. Free.

THOMAS BROS. MAPS..................3 A3
Since 1915. Unique 'Old English Map House' featuring everything in maps. It is located at the entrance to Jackson Square which is noted for antique and decorator shops. Jackson at Columbus. 981-7520.
HOURS: Daily 9am to 5pm. Closed Saturday and Sunday.

YACHT HARBOR..................1 C1
St. Francis Yacht Club. Foot of Divisadero Street. Regattas held during the summer months.

HOW TO USE THE CROSS STREET INDEX

A special index has been prepared for all streets in San Francisco. This index lists each street, followed by all the crossing streets in house address order. Most crossing streets include the lowest house address starting at the intersection.

1988 SAN FRANCISCO COUNTY CROSS STREET INDEX

A ST SF 17 C1
N FROM NIMITZ AV E OF LOCKWOOD ST
ABBEY ST SF 10 B2
N FROM 17TH ST BETWEEN
DOLORES ST AND CHURCH ST
N TO CHULA LANE
ACADIA ST SF 14 A3
FROM MONTEREY BLVD TO A POINT
N OF JOOST AV
100 MONTEREY BLVD
200 JOOST AV
END PT N OF JOOST AV
ACCACIA ST SF 20 C3
FROM VELASCO AV TO COUNTY LINE
ACEVEDO AV SF 18 C2
W FROM ARBALLO DR N OF
HIGUERA AV TO VIDAL DR
ACME AL SF 10 A3
FROM SEWARD ST NEAR DOUGLASS ST
SW TO GRAND VIEW AV
ACORN AL SF 6 C1
SW FROM LEAVENWORTH ST BETWEEN
CALIFORNIA ST AND SACRAMENTO ST
ACTON ST SF 19 C3
FROM 5900 MISSION ST S TO
COUNTY LINE
ADA CT SF 6 C2
N FROM O'FARRELL ST TO AMITY AL
BETWEEN LEAVENWORTH ST
AND HYDE ST
ADAIR ST SF 10 C2
W FROM SOUTH VAN NESS AV BETWEEN
15TH ST AND 16TH ST W TO CAPP ST
ADDISON ST SF 14 B2
FROM BEMIS ST W TO
DIAMOND HEIGHTS BLVD
ADELAIDE PL SF 7 A2
W FROM TAYLOR ST BETWEEN
GEARY ST AND POST ST
ADELE CT SF 3 A3
N FROM JACKSON ST BETWEEN
STOCKTON ST AND POWELL ST
ADLER ST SF 3 A3
E FROM GRANT AV BETWEEN
PACIFIC AV AND BROADWAY
TO COLUMBUS AV
ADMIRAL AV SF 14 B3
FROM 4150 MISSION ST W TO
ALEMANY BLVD
DOLPH SUTRO CT SF 9 C3
W FROM JOHNSTONE DR
W BLK N OF CLARENDON AV
ERIAL WY SF 9 A3
W FROM ORTEGA ST TO 14TH AV
ORTEGA ST
PACHECO ST
FUNSTON AVE
END 14TH AV
GATE AL SF 7 A2
N FROM POST ST BETWEEN JONES
ST AND TAYLOR ST
AGNON AV SF 14 C3
FROM 100 CRESCENT AV SW
TO JUSTIN DR
AGUA WY SF 13 C2
FROM TERESITA BLVD W TO
CHAVES AV
AHERN WY SF 7 B3
W OF SIXTH ST BETWEEN HARRISON
AND BRYANT ST
AHLERS CT SF 2 B3
S FROM FILBERT ST BETWEEN WEBSTER
AND BUCHANAN STS
AILEEN ST SF 10 B2
N FROM 15TH ST BETWEEN
RAMONA ST AND DOLORES ST
ALABAMA ST SF 11 A2
ALABAMA ST SF 15 A1
FROM ALAMEDA ST BETWEEN
FLORIDA ST AND HARRISON ST
S TO ESMERALDA AV
100 ALAMEDA ST
TREAT AV
200 15TH ST
300 16TH ST
400 17TH ST
500 MARIPOSA ST
600 18TH ST
700 19TH ST
800 20TH ST
900 21ST ST
1000 22ND ST
1100 23RD ST
1200 24TH ST
1300 25TH ST
1400 26TH ST
1500 ARMY ST
1600 PRECITA AV
MULLEN AV
MONTCALM ST
1700 NORWICH ST
RUTLEDGE ST
1800 RIPLEY ST
WALTHAM ST
END ESMERALDA AV
ALADDIN TER SF 2 C2
FROM TAYLOR E & W BETWEEN
UNION ST AND FILBERT ST
ALAMEDA ST SF 11 A1
W FROM ILLINOIS ST TO A POINT
E OF 3RD ST
FROM DEHARO ST W TO
HARRISON ST N OF 15TH ST
1700 DE HARO ST
1800 RHODE ISLAND ST
1900 KANSAS ST
2000 VERMONT ST
2100 SAN BRUNO AV
2200 UTAH ST
2300 POTRERO AV
2400 HAMPSHIRE ST
END BRYANT ST
FROM FLORIDA ST W
TREAT AV
2800 ALABAMA ST
END HARRISON ST
ALANA WY SF 21 B3
W FROM HARNEY WY
E OF JAMES LICK FWY (HWY 101)
ALBATROSS CT SF 16 A3
S FROM KISKA RD IN
HUNTERS PT NAVAL RES
ALBERTA ST SF 21 A2
N FROM CAMPBELL AV NEAR ELLIOT ST
ALBION ST SF 10 C2
S FROM 15TH ST BETWEEN
VALENCIA ST AND GUERRERO ST
S TO 17TH ST
2 15TH ST
100 16TH ST
END 17TH ST
ALDER ST SF 21 A2
FROM ANKENY ST S TO HARKNESS AV
BETWEEN MILL ST & BISHOP ST
ALDRICH AL SF 7 B2
SW FROM NEW MONTGOMERY ST
BETWEEN JESSIE ST AND MISSION
ST W TO ANNIE ST
ALEMANY BLVD SF 14 C3
ALEMANY BLVD SF 19 B3
ALEMANY BLVD SF 20 A1
SW FROM BAYSHORE BLVD
TO JUNIPERO SERRA BLVD
BAYSHORE BLVD
JAMES LICK FRWY
PUTNAM ST
FOLSOM ST
ELLSWORTH ST
I-280 FRWY
TRUMBULL ST
JUSTIN DR
CONGDON ST
ROUSSEAU ST
ADMIRAL AV
LYELL ST
SILVER AV
TINGLEY ST
THERESA ST
COTTER ST
FRANCIS ST
1600 SANTA ROSA AV
HARRINGTON ST
NORTON ST
1700 SAN JUAN AV
OCEAN AV
LEO ST
1900 ONONDAGA ST
2000 ONEIDA AV
2100 SENECA AV
2200 GENEVA AV
2300 NIAGARA AV
2400 MOUNT VERNON AV
HURON AV
OTTAWA AV
FOOTE AV
NAGLEE AV
FARRAGUT AV
LAURA ST
LAWRENCE AV
CAYUGA AV
DE WOLF ST
3100 SICKLES AV
REGENT ST
3150 SAN JOSE AV
SAGAMORE ST
ORIZABA AV
BROTHERHOOD WY
BRIGHT ST
HEAD ST
VICTORIA ST
RAMSELL ST
WORCESTER AV
ARCH ST
KEMPTON AV
ST CHARLES AV
END JUNIPERO SERRA BLVD
ALERT AL SF 10 B2
W FROM DOLORES ST BETWEEN
15TH ST AND 16TH ST TO
LANDERS ST
ALHAMBRA ST SF 2 A2
FROM CERVANTES BLVD NEAR
FILLMORE ST W TO AVILA ST
2 CERVANTES BLVD
100 MALLORCA WY
200 PIERCE ST
END AVILA ST
ALLAN ST SF 21 A3
N FROM 3100 GENEVA AV
2 BLKS W OF BAYSHORE BLVD
ALLEN ST SF 2 C2
W FROM WS HYDE ST BETWEEN UNION
ST AND FILBERT ST TO
EASTMAN ST
ALLISON ST SF 20 A2
SE FROM 5301 MISSION ST TO A
POINT NEAR THE COUNTY LINE
2 MISSION ST
100 CROSS ST
200 MORSE ST
300 BRUNSWICK ST
400 HANOVER ST
END PT S OF HANOVER ST
ALLSTON WY SF 13 B2
FROM 650 ULLOA ST NW TO
CLAREMONT BLVD
VASQUEZ AV END CLAREMONT BLVD
ALMA ST SF 9 C2
SW FROM BELVEDERE ST BETWEEN
GRATTAN ST AND RIVOLI ST
TO SANYAN ST
2 BELVEDERE ST
100 COLE ST
200 SHRADER ST
END STANYAN ST
ALMADEN CT SF 5 B3
N FROM ANZA ST BETWEEN
LORAINE CT AND ARGUELLO BLVD
TO A POINT S OF GEARY BLVD
ALOHA AV SF 9 A3
FROM 1601 FUNSTON AV W TO
LOMITA AVE
ALPHA ST SF 21 A2
W FROM SAN BRUNO AV S FROM
GOETTINGEN ST TO LELAND AV
GOETTINGEN ST
GIRARD AV
BRUSSELS ST
34 TIOGA AV
58 TUCKER AV
CAMPBELL AV
200 TEDDY AV
300 ARLETA AV
400 RAYMOND AV
END LELAND AV
ALPINE TER SF 10 A1
S FROM WALLER ST BETWEEN BUENA
VISTA AV AND DIVISADERO
ST TO 14TH ST
2 WALLER ST
100 DUBOCE AV
END 14TH ST
ALTA ST SF 3 A2
E & W FROM MONTGOMERY ST BETWEEN
UNION AND FILBERT STS
ALTA MAR WY SF 4 A3
N FROM PT LOBOS AV BETWEEN EL
CAMINO DEL MAR ST AND 45TH
AV TO SEAL ROCK DR
ALTA VISTA TER SF 3 A2
N FROM VALLEJO ST BETWEEN
MASON ST AND TAYLOR ST
ALTON AV SF 13 B1
W FROM CASTENADA AV TO 9TH AV
2 CASTENADA AV
100 PACHECO ST
END 9TH AV
ALVARADO ST SF 10 B3
W FROM SAN JOSE AV BETWEEN
22ND AND 23RD STS TO
GUERRERO ST AND W FROM
SANCHEZ ST TO DIAMOND ST AND
W FROM DOUGLASS ST TO
GRAND VIEW AV
2 SAN JOSE AV

GUERRERO ST
400 SANCHEZ ST
500 NOE ST
CASTRO ST
DIAMOND ST
ALVISO ST SF 19 A1
N FROM HOLLOWAY AV BETWEEN
MONTICELLO ST AND BORICA ST
AMATISTA LN SF 14 B2
N FROM BEMIS ONE BLK
W OF MIGUEL ST
AMATURY LOOP SF 1 B3
N OF WASHINGTON BLVD
IN PRESIDIO
AMAZON AV SF 20 A2
E FROM 5101 MISSION ST BETWEEN
ITALY AV AND GENEVA AV
TO MOSCOW ST
2 MISSION ST
100 LONDON ST
200 PARIS ST
300 LISBON ST
400 MADRID ST
500 EDINBURGH ST
600 NAPLES ST
700 VIENNA ST
800 ATHENS ST
END MOSCOW ST
AMBER DR SF 14 A1
W FROM DUNCAN 2 BLKS W OF
DOUGLASS
CAMEO WY
AMES ST SF 10 C3
S FROM 21ST ST BETWEEN FAIR
OAKS AND GUERRERO STS TO
23RD ST
AMETHYST WY SF 13 C1
W FROM AMBER DR
AMHERST ST SF 20 C1
S FROM SILVER AV BETWEEN
YALE STS TO WAYLAND ST
BURROWS ST S FROM BACON ST
TO WAYLAND ST
2 SILVER AV
100 SILLIMAN ST
200 FELTON ST
BURROWS ST
BACON ST
END WAYLAND ST
AMITY AL SF 6 C2
E FROM ADA CT NEAR HYDE ST
AND O'FARRELL ST
ANDERSON ST SF 14 C2
S FROM BERNAL HEIGHTS BLVD
BETWEEN ELLSWORTH & MOULTRIE STS
TO A POINT S OF CRESCENT AV
2 ESMERALDA AVE
100 POWHATTAN AV
200 EUGENIA AV
300 CORTLAND AV
400 JARBOE AV
500 TOMPKINS AV
600 OGDEN AV
700 CRESCENT AV
END PT S OF CRESCENT AV
ANDOVER ST SF 14 C3
S FROM A POINT N OF POWHATTAN ST
BETWEEN WOOL ST AND MOULTRIE ST
TO A POINT S OF BENTON AV
2 ESMERALDA AVE
BERNAL HEIGHTS AVE
100 POWHATTAN AV
200 EUGENIA AV
300 CORTLAND AV
400 ELLERT ST
450 NEWMAN ST
TOMPKINS AV
500 HIGHLAND AV
600 PARK ST
OGDEN AV

RICHLAND AV
700 CRESCENT AV
BENTON AV
END PT S OF BENTON AV
ANGLO AL SF 13 A1
S FROM ORTEGA ST BETWEEN 17TH AV
AND 18TH AV TO A POINT S
OF PACHECO ST
ANKENY ST SF 21 A2
FROM DELTA ST E TO SPARTA ST
ANNAPOLIS TER SF 5 C3
S FROM TURK ST BETWEEN MASONIC
AV AND TAMALPAIS TER TO
GOLDEN GATE AV
ANNIE ST SF 7 B2
SE FROM MARKET ST BETWEEN NEW
MONTGOMERY ST AND 3RD ST
TO MISSION ST
ANSON PL SF 7 A2
E FROM POWELL ST BETWEEN SUTTER
ST AND BUSH ST
ANTHONY ST SF 7 B2
FROM POINT N OF JESSIE ST
BETWEEN ECKER AND 2ND STS SE
TO MISSION ST
ANTONIO ST SF 6 C2
W FROM JONES ST BETWEEN
ELLIS AND O'FARRELL STS
ANZA ST SF 1 B2
IN PRESIDIO
ANZA ST SF 4 A3
ANZA ST SF 5 C3
FROM MASONIC AV BETWEEN GEARY
BLVD AND BALBOA ST W TO
48TH AV
100 MASONIC AV
WOOD ST
JEAN WY
COLLINS ST
BLAKE ST
COOK ST
SPRUCE ST
PARKER AV
BEAUMONT AV
STANYAN ST
ROSSI AV
LORAINE CT
ALMADEN CT
1000 ARGUELLO BLVD
1100 2ND AV
1200 3RD AV
1300 4TH AV
1400 5TH AV
1500 6TH AV
1600 7TH AV
1700 8TH AV
1800 9TH AV
1900 10TH AV
2000 11TH AV
2100 12TH AV
2000 FUNSTON AV
PARK PRESIDIO BLVD
2300 14TH AV
2400 15TH AV
2500 16TH AV
2600 17TH AV
2700 18TH AV
2800 19TH AV
2900 20TH AV
3000 21ST AV
3100 22ND AV
3200 23RD AV
3300 24TH AV
3400 25TH AV
3500 26TH AV
3600 27TH AV
3700 28TH AV
3800 29TH AV
30TH AV
4000 32ND AV

4100 33RD AV
4200 34TH AV
4300 35TH AV
4400 36TH AV
4500 37TH AV
4600 38TH AV
4700 39TH AV
4800 40TH AV
4900 41ST AV
5000 42ND AV
5100 43RD AV
5200 44TH AV
5300 45TH AV
5400 46TH AV
5500 47TH AV
END 48TH AV
ANZAVISTA AV SF 6 A3
S FROM O'FARRELL ST TO
BAKER ST
O'FARRELL ST
TERRA VISTA AV
VEGA ST
BARCELONA AV
ARBOL LN
ENCANTO AV
FORTUNA AV
END BAKER ST
APOLLO ST SF 15 B3
S FROM TOPEKA AV TO
WILLIAMS AV
APPAREL WY SF 15 A2
E FROM BARNEVELD AV BETWEEN
PALOU AV AND DORMAN AV
APPLETON AV SF 14 C2
SE FROM 3601 MISSION ST BETWEEN
SANTA MARINA ST AND HIGHLAND AV
TO HOLLY PARK CIR
APPLETON ST SF 1 A2
IN PRESIDIO S AND W
FROM RUCKMAN AV
APTOS AV SF 13 B3
N FROM 2200 OCEAN AV TO DARIEN WY
2 OCEAN AV
200 UPLAND DR
END DARIEN WY
AQUAVISTA WY SF 9 C3
S FROM MAR VIEW WY TO SKYVIEW WY
ARAGO ST SF 20 A1
S FROM PAULDING ST W OF
SAN JOSE AV TO HAVELOCK ST
ARBALLO DR SF 18 C2
N FROM TAPIA DR ENDING AT A POINT
N OF TAPIA DR CONTINUING SW FROM
TAPIA DR TO VIDAL DR
TAPIA DR
VIDAL DR
PINTO ST
ACEVEDO AV
SERRANO DR
HIGUERA AV
GONZALEZ DR
GARCES DR
END VIDAL DR
ARBOL LN SF 6 A3
N FROM TURK ST BETWEEN BAKER ST
AND CENTRAL AV TO A POINT S OF
ANZAVISTA AV
ARBOR ST SF 14 A2
W FROM DIAMOND ST TO BERKELY WY
ARCH ST SF 19 B2
S FROM ALEMANY BLVD BETWEEN
VERNON ST AND RAMSELL ST
N TO HOLLOWAY AV
ALEMANY BLVD
100 BROTHERHOOD WY
200 RANDOLPH ST
300 SARGENT ST
400 SHIELDS ST
500 GARFIELD ST
END HOLLOWAY AV

ARCO WY SF 20 A1
N FROM HAVELOCK ST BETWEEN
ARAGO ST AND 280 FREEWAY
ARDATH CT SF 15 C3
E FROM HUDSON AV BETWEEN
WESTBROOK CT AND
WHITNEY YOUNG CIR
ARDENWOOD WY SF 13 A3
N FROM SLOAT BLVD BETWEEN 19TH
AV AND WEST PORTAL AV
ARELLANO AV SF 19 A2
S FROM HOLLOWAY AV BETWEEN
CARDENAS AV AND TAPIA DR
TO SERRANO DR
ARGENT AL SF 10 A3
W FROM MARKET ST N OF 23RD
ST TO CORBETT AV
ARGONAUT AV SF 20 C3
W FROM GARRISON AV S OF
SUNNYDALE AV TO VELASCO AV
MC CARTHY AV
BURR AV
END VELASCO AV
ARGUELLO BLVD SF 1 B3
ARGUELLO BLVD SF 5 B1
ARGUELLO BLVD SF 9 B2
S FROM SHERIDAN AV
IN THE PRESIDIO TO PARNASSUS
BETWEEN 3RD AV AND HILLWAY AV
2 PACIFIC AV
SHERIDAN AV
MORAGA AV
HARDIE RD
SIBERT LOOP
WASHINGTON BLVD
RACH
50 JACKSON ST
100 WASHINGTON ST
PRESIDIO TER
150 CLAY ST
LAKE ST
200 SACRAMENTO ST
300 CALIFORNIA ST
CORNWALL ST
400 EUCLID AV
CLEMENT ST
500 GEARY BLVD
ANZA ST
600 EDWARD ST
BALBOA ST
700 TURK ST
750 GOLDEN GATE AV
CABRILLO ST
800 MCALLISTER ST
FULTON ST
END CONSERVATORY DR E
CONTINUING S FROM KEZAR DR IN
GOLDEN GATE PARK
KEZAR DR
LINCOLN WY
1200 FREDERICK ST
HUGO ST
1300 CARL ST
IRVING ST
END PARNASSUS AV
ARKANSAS ST SF 11 B2
S FROM 16TH ST BETWEEN
CONNECTICUT ST AND WISCONSIN ST
TO 23RD ST
2 16TH ST
100 17TH ST
200 MARIPOSA ST
300 18TH ST
400 19TH ST
500 20TH ST
700 22ND ST
MADERA ST
END 23RD ST
ARLETA AV SF 21 A2
NW FROM BAYSHORE BLVD TO

ELLIOTT ST BETWEEN TEDDY AV &
RAYMOND AV
BAYSHORE BLVD
100 ALPHA ST
200 RUTLAND ST
300 DELTA ST
END ELLIOT ST
ARLINGTON ST SF 14 B3
SW FROM RANDALL ST BETWEEN
SAN JOSE AV AND CHENERY ST TO
BOSWORTH ST
RANDALL ST
FAIRMOUNT ST
CHARLES ST
300 MIGUEL ST
MATEO ST
ST MARYS AV
ROANOKE ST
NATICK ST
END BOSWORTH ST
ARMISTEAD RD SF 1 A2
IN THE PRESIDIO
ARMSTRONG AV SF 21 B1
FROM HAWES ST BETWEEN YOSEMITE AV
AND BANCROFT AV NW TO NEWHALL ST
HAWES ST
INGALLS ST
JENNINGS ST
KEITH ST
3RD ST
LANE ST
END MENDELL ST
FROM RAILROAD TRACKS
END NEWHALL ST
ARMY ST SF 14 A1
ARMY ST SF 15 A1
FROM A POINT E OF MICHIGAN ST
W TO DOUGLASS ST
1000 3RD ST
TENNESSEE ST
MINNESOTA ST
INDIANA ST
PENNSYLVANIA ST
MISSOURI ST
CONNECTICUT ST
EVANS AV
KANSAS ST
VERMONT ST
JAMES LICK FRWY
2800 POTRERO AV
2850 HAMPSHIRE ST
2900 YORK ST
2950 BRYANT ST
3000 FLORIDA ST
3050 ALABAMA ST
3100 HARRISON ST
3200 FOLSOM ST
SHOTWELL ST
3300 SOUTH VAN NESS
CAPP ST
3400 MISSION ST
3450 BARTLETT ST
3500 VALENCIA ST
3600 SAN JOSE AV
3700 GUERRERO ST
3800 DOLORES ST
3900 CHURCH ST
4000 SANCHEZ ST
4100 NOE ST
4200 CASTRO ST
4300 DIAMOND ST
END DOUGLASS ST
ARNOLD AV SF 14 C3
S FROM CRESCENT AV BETWEEN
ROSCOE ST AND AGNON AV
ARROYO WY SF 13 C2
S FROM MARIETTA DR TO
BELLA VISTA WY
ARTHUR AV SF 15 C1
SE FROM ISLAIS ST TO 3RD ST

ASH ST SF 6 B3
W FROM GOUGH ST BETWEEN
FULTON ST AND MCALLISTER ST
W TO BUCHANAN ST
BUCHANAN ST
GOUGH ST
500 OCTAVIA ST
600 LAGUNA ST
END BUCHANAN ST
ASHBURTON PL SF 7 A2
E FROM GRANT AV BETWEEN
POST ST AND SUTTER ST
ASHBURY ST SF 9 C1
S FROM FULTON ST BETWEEN
MASONIC AV AND CLAYTON ST
ENDING AT CLAYTON ST
2 FULTON ST
100 GROVE ST
200 HAYES ST
FELL ST
400 OAK ST
500 PAGE ST
600 HAIGHT ST
WALLER ST
800 FREDERICK ST
930 PIEDMONT ST
1000 CLIFFORD ST
DOWNEY ST
END CLAYTON ST
ASHBURY TER SF 10 A2
S FROM PIEDMONT ST AND E TO
UPPER TER
ASHTON AV SF 19 B1
BETWEEN JULES ST AND
ORIZABA ST N FROM
LAKEVIEW AV TO OCEAN AV
2 LAKEVIEW AV
100 GRAFTON AV
200 HOLLOWAY AV
HEAD ST
300 DE MONTFORD AV
PICO AV
END OCEAN AV
ASHWOOD LN SF 9 C3
NW FROM CLARENDON AV BETWEEN
OLYMPIC WY AND PANORAMA DR
ATALAYA TER SF 5 C3
N FROM 1850 FULTON ST
ATHENS ST SF 20 B2
W FROM MADISON ST CONTINUING
TO NAPLES ST
2 MADISON ST
100 PERU AV
200 AVALON AV
300 EXCELSIOR AV
400 BRAZIL AV
500 PERSIA AV
600 RUSSIA AV
700 FRANCE AV
800 ITALY AV
900 AMAZON AV
1000 GENEVA AV
1100 ROLPH ST
1200 CORDOVA ST
END NAPLES ST
ATTRIDGE AL SF 2 C2
N FROM FILBERT ST BETWEEN
JONES ST AND LEAVENWORTH ST
AUBURN ST SF 3 A3
N FROM JACKSON ST BETWEEN
MASON ST AND TAYLOR ST
N TO PACIFIC AV
AUGUST AL SF 3 A2
N FROM GREEN ST BETWEEN
POWELL ST AND MASON ST
AUGUSTA ST SF 15 A3
FROM SILVER AV BETWEEN
SILVER AV AND HELENA ST
W TO SAN BRUNO AV
2 SILVER AV
WATERVILLE ST
100 EL MIRA ST
200 CHARTER OAK AV
300 BOUTWELL ST
BAY SHORE BLVD
400 STEUBEN ST
END SAN BRUNO AV
AUSTIN ST SF 6 B2
W FROM S LARKIN ST BETWEEN
BUSH ST AND PINE ST CONTINUING
TO OCTAVIA ST
2 LARKIN ST
100 POLK ST
200 VAN NESS AV
300 FRANKLIN ST
400 GOUGH ST
END OCTAVIA ST
AUTO DR SF 9 B3
S FROM LAWTON TO MORAGA ST
BETWEEN 8TH AV AND 9TH AV
AVALON AV SF 20 B1
FROM MISSION ST 1 BLK N OF
EXCELSIOR AV SE TO PERU AV
2 MISSION ST
100 LONDON ST
200 PARIS ST
300 LISBON ST
400 MADRID ST
500 EDINBURGH ST
600 NAPLES ST
700 VIENNA ST
800 ATHENS ST
MOSCOW ST
LA GRANDE AV
END PERU ST
AVENUE A SF 3 C1
NW FROM 1ST ST AT ENTRANCE OF
TREASURE ISLAND, TO 9TH ST
1ST ST
CALIFORNIA AV
3RD ST
END 9TH ST
AVENUE B SF 3 C2
NW FROM CALIFORNIA AV TO 3RD ST,
BETWEEN AV A & AV C,
TREASURE ISLAND
AVENUE C SF 3 C1
NW FROM CALIFORNIA AV TO SW
EXTENSION OF 4TH ST BETWEEN
AV B & AV D, TREASURE ISLAND
AVENUE D SF 3 C1
NW FROM CALIFORNIA AV TO 12TH ST
BETWEEN AV C & AV F,
TREASURE ISLAND
CALIFORNIA AV
3RD ST
9TH ST
11TH ST
END 12TH ST
AVENUE E SF 3 C1
NW FROM 9TH ST TO 13TH ST BETWEEN
AV D & AV H, TREASURE ISLAND
9TH ST
11TH ST
12TH ST
END 13TH ST
AVENUE F SF 3 C1
NW FROM CALIFORNIA AV TO 3RD ST,
& FROM UNNAMED ST TO 9TH ST
BETWEEN AV D & AV H,
TREASURE ISLAND
AVENUE H SF 3 C1
NW FROM CALIFORNIA AV TO 13TH ST,
TREASURE ISLAND
CALIFORNIA AV
3RD ST
4TH ST
6TH ST
9TH ST
11TH ST
12TH ST
END 13TH ST
AVENUE I SF 3 C1
NW FROM 6TH ST TO PARKING LOT
ADJOINING AV M, TREASURE ISLAND
6TH ST
9TH ST
11TH ST
13TH ST
END AV M
AVENUE M SF 3 C1
NW FROM CALIFORNIA AV TO
PARKING LOT ADJOINING AV I,
TREASURE ISLAND
CALIFORNIA AV
3RD ST
4TH ST
5TH ST
6TH ST
8TH ST
9TH ST
10TH ST
11TH ST
13TH ST
END AV I
AVENUE N SF 3 C1
N FROM SE CORNER OF TREASURE
ISLAND TO 3RD ST THEN NW TO POINT
N OF 13TH ST
CALIFORNIA AV
3RD ST
4TH ST
5TH ST
8TH ST
10TH ST
13TH ST
AVENUE NORTH SF 4 C2
N FROM 25TH AV
AVERY ST SF 6 B2
N FROM GEARY ST BETWEEN
FILLMORE ST AND
STEINER ST TO POST ST
AVILA ST SF 2 A2
N FROM 2250 CHESTNUT ST
TO MARINA BLVD
2 CHESTNUT ST
100 ALHAMBRA ST
200 CAPRA WY
300 PRADO ST
END MARINA BLVD
AVOCA AL SF 13 C2
SE FROM CRESTA VISTA DR BETWEEN
OMAR WY AND MYRA WY TO
ROCKDALE DR
AVON WY SF 13 A3
N FROM SLOAT BLVD BETWEEN
JUNIPERO SERRA & 19TH AV
AZTEC ST SF 14 C1
FROM COSO AV E TO SHOTWELL ST
BACHE ST SF 14 C3
S FROM CRESCENT AV BETWEEN
ANDOVER ST AND PORTER ST
BACON ST SF 20 C1
BACON ST SF 21 A1
FROM BAYSHORE BLVD BETWEEN
BURROWS ST & WAYLAND ST W TO
HARVARD ST
BAYSHORE BLVD
100 SAN BRUNO AV
200 GIRARD ST
300 BRUSSELS ST
400 GOETTINGEN ST
500 SOMERSET ST
600 HOLYOKE ST
HAMILTON ST
BOWDOIN ST
UNIVERSITY ST
PRINCETON ST
CAMPUS LN
AMHERST ST
1500 CAMBRIDGE ST
1600 OXFORD ST
END HARVARD ST
BADEN ST SF 14 A3
FROM CIRCULAR AV BETWEEN
ACADIA ST AND CONGO ST
N TO MARTHA ST
2 CIRCULAR AV
100 HEARST AV
200 MONTEREY BLVD
300 JOOST AV
400 MANGELS AV
END MARTHA ST
BADGER ST SF 14 B3
N FROM CAYUGA AV BETWEEN
LAMARTINE ST & GORMAN ST
BAKER ST SF 2 A2
BAKER ST SF 6 A2
BAKER ST SF 10 A1
N FROM S HAIGHT ST BETWEEN
BRODERICK ST AND LYON ST
N TO THE BAY
2 HAIGHT ST
100 PAGE ST
200 OAK ST
300 FELL ST
400 HAYES ST
500 GROVE ST
600 FULTON ST
700 MCALLISTER ST
800 GOLDEN GATE AV
TURK ST
ANZAVISTA AV
PINAR LN
ELLIS ST
1300 GEARY ST
1400 POST ST
1500 SUTTER ST
1600 BUSH ST
1700 PINE ST
1800 CALIFORNIA ST
1900 SACRAMENTO ST
2000 CLAY ST
2100 WASHINGTON ST
2200 JACKSON ST
2300 PACIFIC AV
END BROADWAY
2500 VALLEJO ST
2600 GREEN ST
2700 UNION ST
2800 FILBERT ST
MILEY ST
2900 GREENWICH ST
3000 LOMBARD ST
3100 CHESTNUT ST
RICHARDSON AV
3200 FRANCISCO ST
3300 BAY ST
3400 NORTH POINT ST
3500 BEACH ST
3600 JEFFERSON ST
3700 MARINA BLVD
BALANCE ST SF 3 B3
N FROM S JACKSON ST BETWEEN
SANSOME ST AND
MONTGOMERY ST N TO GOLD ST
BALBOA ST SF 4 B3
BALBOA ST SF 5 A3
FROM ARGUELLO BLVD BETWEEN
ANZA ST AND CABRILLO ST W
TO GREAT HIGHWAY
2 ARGUELLO BLVD
100 2ND AV
200 3RD AV
300 4TH AV
400 5TH AV
500 6TH AV
600 7TH AV
700 8TH AV
800 9TH AV
900 10TH AV
1000 11TH AV
1100 12TH AV
FUNSTON AV
PARK PRESIDIO BL
1300 14TH AV
1400 15TH AV
1500 16TH AV
1600 17TH AV
1700 18TH AV
1800 19TH AV
1900 20TH AV
2000 21ST AV
2100 22ND AV
2200 23RD AV
2300 24TH AV
2400 25TH AV
2500 26TH AV
2600 27TH AV
2700 28TH AV
2800 29TH AV
2900 30TH AV
3000 31ST AV
3100 32ND AV
3200 33RD AV
3300 34TH AV
3400 35TH AV
3500 36TH AV
3600 37TH AV
3700 38TH AV
3800 39TH AV
3900 40TH AV
4000 41ST AV
4100 42ND AV
4200 43RD AV
4300 44TH AV
4400 45TH AV
4500 46TH AV
4600 47TH AV
4700 48TH AV
4800 LA PLAYA ST
END THE GREAT HIGHWAY
BALCETA AV SF 13 B1
FROM LAGUNA HONDA ST NE
TO WOODSIDE AV
BALDWIN CT SF 15 C3
NE OFF OAKDALE AV S OF INGALLS ST
BALHI CT SF 20 A1
E FROM CAYUGA AV BETWEEN
ONEIDA AV AND ONONDAGA AV
BALMY ST SF 11 A3
S FROM S 24TH ST BETWEEN
HARRISON ST AND TREAT AV
S TO 25TH ST
BALTIMORE WY SF 20 B3
NE FROM S CORDOVA ST TO
SOUTH HILL BLVD
BANBURY DR SF 19 A2
E FROM 19TH AV TO
STRATFORD DR S OF
HOLLOWAY AV
BANCROFT AV SF 15 B3
BANCROFT AV SF 21 B1
NW FROM HAWES ST BETWEEN
ARMSTRONG ST & CARROLL ST TO
MENDELL ST & NEWHALL ST
TO QUINT ST
HAWES ST
INGALLS ST
JENNINGS ST
KEITH ST
3RD ST
MENDELL ST
NEWHALL ST
PHELPS ST
END QUINT ST
BANK ST SF 1 B2
N FROM LINCOLN BLVD S OF DOYLE DR
BANKS ST SF 15 A2
S FROM BERNAL HTS BLVD BETWEEN

PRENTISS ST AND FOLSOM ST TO A
POINT S OF CRESCENT AV
2 BERNAL HTS BLVD
CHAPMAN ST
100 POWHATTAN AV
200 EUGENIA AV
300 CORTLAND AV
400 JARBOE AV
500 TOMPKINS AV
600 OGDEN AV
700 CRESCENT AV
END PT S OF CRESCENT

BANNAM PL SF 3 A2
N FROM S GREEN ST BETWEEN
GRANT AV AND STOCKSTON ST
N TO UNION ST

BANNOCK ST SF 20 A2
N OFF S GENEVA AV TO
SENECA AV BETWEEN CAYUGA AV
AND ALEMANY BLVD

BARCELONA AV SF 6 A3
N FROM ANZAVISTA AV BETWEEN
ENCANTO AV AND ANZAVISTA AV TO
TERRA VISTA AV

BARNARD AV SF 1 C3
S OFF OF PRESIDIO BLVD

BARNEVELD AV SF 15 A2
S FROM JERROLD AV AND
SW TO SILVER AV
JERROLD AV
LOOMIS ST
MCKINNON AV
NEWCOMB AV
OAKDALE AV
PALOU AV
APPAREL WY
DORMAN AV
INDUSTRIAL ST
DICKENSON ST
600 SAN BRUNO AV
700 RICKARD ST
750 GAVEN ST
800 SWEENY ST
850 HALE ST
END SILVER AV

BARTLETT ST SF 10 C3
S FROM S 21ST ST BETWEEN
MISSION ST AND VALENCIA ST
TO ARMY ST
2 21ST ST
100 22ND ST
200 23RD ST
300 24TH ST
400 25TH ST
500 26TH ST
END ARMY ST

BARTOL ST SF 3 A2
FROM A POINT S OF
BROADWAY BETWEEN SANSOME ST
AND MONTGOMERY ST N TO
VALLEJO ST

BATTERY ST SF 3 B2
N FROM S MARKET ST BETWEEN
FRONT ST AND SANSOME ST
TO THE EMBARCADERO
2 MARKET ST
BUSH ST
100 PINE ST
200 CALIFORNIA ST
HALLECK ST
300 SACRAMENTO ST
COMMERCIAL ST
400 CLAY ST
MERCHANT ST
500 WASHINGTON ST
600 JACKSON ST
700 PACIFIC AV
800 BROADWAY
900 VALLEJO ST
1000 GREEN ST
COMMERCE ST
1100 UNION ST
1200 FILBERT ST
1300 GREENWICH ST
LOMBARD ST
END THE EMBARCADERO

BTRY CHMBRLN RD SF 4 C1
N FROM GIBSON RD AND NE
TO LINCOLN BLVD

BATTERY EAST RD SF 1 A1

BAXTER AL SF 13 B3
NE FROM YERBA BUENA AV
TO CASITAS AV BETWEEN
MIRALOMA DR AND HAZELWOOD AV

BAY ST SF 2 B2
BAY ST SF 3 A2
FROM THE EMBARCADERO BETWEEN
NORTH POINT AND FRANCISCO STS
W TO BAKER ST
2 THE EMBARCADERO
50 KEARNY ST
MIDWAY ST
200 STOCKTON ST
300 POWELL ST
400 MASON ST
500 TAYLOR ST
COLUMBUS AV
JONES ST
700 LEAVENWORTH ST
800 HYDE ST
900 LARKIN ST
1000 POLK ST
VAN NESS AV
FRANKLIN ST
GOUGH ST
OCTAVIA ST
1500 LAGUNA ST
1600 BUCHANAN ST
1700 WEBSTER ST
END FILLMORE ST
2100 SCOTT ST
2200 DIVISADERO ST
2300 BRODERICK ST
END BAKER ST

BAYSHORE BLVD SF 11 B3
BAYSHORE BLVD SF 15 A2
BAYSHORE BLVD SF 21 A3
S FROM ARMY TO CITY LIMITS
ARMY ST
MARIN ST
JERROLD AV
OAKDALE AV
COSGROVE ST
FLOWER ST
CORTLAND AV
WATERLOO ST
MARENGO ST
INDUSTRIAL ST
HELENA ST
LOOMIS ST
I-280 FRWY RAMPS
800 AUGUSTA ST
900 SILVER AV
1100 FELTON ST
QUINT ST
DONNER AV
EGBERT AV
1300 BACON ST
PHELPS ST
FITZGERALD AV
PAUL AV
WHEAT ST
CRANE ST
SALINAS AV
KEY AVE
LANE ST
3RD ST
JAMES LICK FRWY
2100 HESTER AV
TUNNEL AV
2400 BLANKEN AV
SOMERSET ST
ARLETA AV
RAYMOND AV
LELAND AV
2500 VISITACION AV
SUNNYDALE AV
CITY LIMITS

BAYSIDE DR SF 3 C1
LOOP EXTENDING NW FROM GATEVIEW
AV, TREASURE ISLAND

BAYVIEW ST SF 15 B3
W FROM S 3RD ST AT REVERE AV
TO NEWHALL ST
LATONA ST
POMONA ST
FLORA ST

BAYVIEW PARK RD SF 21 B2
S FROM KEY AV

BAYWOOD CT SF 20 A2
NE FROM GENEVA AV BETWEEN
BANNOCK ST AND CAYUGA AV

BEACH ST SF 2 A2
BEACH ST SF 3 A1
FROM THE EMBARCADERO BET
NORTH POINT ST AND
JEFFERSON ST W TO BAKER ST
THE EMBARCADERO
2 GRANT AV
100 STOCKTON ST
200 POWELL ST
300 MASON ST
400 TAYLOR ST
500 JONES ST
600 LEAVENWORTH ST
COLUMBUS AV
700 HYDE ST
800 LARKIN ST
END W OF POLK ST
1400 LAGUNA ST
1500 BUCHANAN ST
1600 WEBSTER ST
1700 FILLMORE ST
1800 RETIRO ST
1900 CERVANTES BLVD
MALLORCA WY
PIERCE ST
AVILA ST
2000 SCOTT ST
2100 DIVISADERO ST
2200 BRODERICK ST
END BAKER ST

BEACHMONT DR SF 13 A3
N FROM LAGUNITAS DR BETWEEN
19TH AV AND LAGUNITAS DR
TO SLOAT BLVD

BEACON ST SF 14 B2
E FROM DIAMOND BETWEEN
29TH ST AND ADDISON ST

BEALE ST SF 7 B1
SE FROM S MARKET ST BETWEEN
MAIN ST AND FREMONT ST
TO THE EMBARCADERO
2 MARKET ST
100 MISSION ST
200 HOWARD ST
300 FOLSOM ST
400 HARRISON ST
500 BRYANT ST
BRANNAN ST
END THE EMBARCADERO

BEATRICE LN SF 15 C3
TO KEYES AV S OF PRESIDIO BLVD
OFF INGALLS ST BETWEEN
LA SALLE AV & ROSIE LEE LN

BEAUMONT AV SF 5 C3
S FROM GEARY BLVD TO
TURK ST

BEAVER ST SF 10 A2
W FROM NOE ST BETWEEN
15TH ST & 16TH ST TO 15TH ST
WAY

BECKETT ST SF 3 A3
N FROM S JACKSON ST BETWEEN
KEARNY ST AND GRANT AV TO
PACIFIC AV

BEDFORD PL SF 3 A3
N FROM S JACKSON ST BETWEEN
STOCKTON ST AND POWELL ST
TO PACIFIC AV

BEEMAN LN SF 21 B2
S FROM SAN BRUNO AV TO
WABASH TER NEAR BAY SHORE BLVD

BEHR AV SF 9 C3
SE OF JOHNSTONE DR CIRCLES BACK
TO JOHNSTONE DR

BEIDEMAN ST SF 6 A3
N FROM S ELLIS ST BETWEEN
SCOTT ST AND DIVISADERO ST
N TO O'FARRELL ST

BELCHER ST SF 10 B1
S FROM S DUBOCE AV BETWEEN
CHURCH ST AND SANCHEZ ST
S TO 14TH ST

BELDEN ST SF 7 A1
N FROM S BUSH ST BETWEEN
MONTGOMERY ST AND KEARNY
ST TO PINE ST

BELGRAVE AV SF 9 C2
FROM POINT E OF COLE ST W TO
A POINT W OF STANYAN ST

BELL RD SF 1 A2
NW OFF STOREY AV TO MILLER RD

BELLAIR PL SF 3 A2
N FROM S CHESTNUT ST BETWEEN
GRANT AV AND STOCKTON ST
TO FRANCISCO ST

BELLAVISTA LN SF 13 C3
SE FROM LOS PALMOS DR TO
BELLA VISTA WY AT MELROSE AV
PALMOS DR

BELLA VISTA WY SF 13 C2
W FROM TERESITA BLVD TO
MELROSE AV

BELLE AV SF 19 A3
W FROM ST CHARLES AV BETWEEN
PALMETTO AV AND COUNTY LINE

BELLEVUE AV SF 20 A3
E OFF GUTENBERG ST TO WAVERLY WY
NEAR COUNTY LINE

BELMONT AV SF 9 C2
S OF PARNASSUS AV SE
FROM EDGEWOOD AV TO
WILLARD ST

BELVEDERE ST SF 9 C1
S FROM S HAIGHT ST BETWEEN
CLAYTON ST AND COLE ST S
TO CARMEL ST
2 HAIGHT ST
100 WALLER ST
FREDERICK ST
400 PARNASSUS AV
GRATTAN ST
ALMA ST
RIVOLI ST
600 17TH ST
END CARMEL ST

BEMIS ST SF 14 B2
FROM MIGUEL ST SE TO CASTRO ST
MIGUEL ST
100 ADDISON ST
MATEO ST
ROANOKE ST
END CASTRO ST

BENGAL AL SF 13 B2
E FROM MIRALOMA DR TO
LANSDALE AV S OF PORTOLA DR

BENNINGTON ST SF 14 C2
TO SIMONDS LOOP
S FROM EUGENIA AV TO HIGHLAND AV
2 EUGENIA AV
100 CORTLAND AV
200 ELLERT ST
300 NEWMAN ST
END HIGHLAND AV

BENTON AV SF 14 B3
NE FROM A POINT SW OF GENEBERN WY
TO ANDOVER ST
100 GENEBERN WY
200 COLLEGE AV
END JUSTIN DR
ARNOLD AV
400 ROSCOE ST
500 PORTER ST
600 BACHE ST
END ANDOVER ST

BEPLER ST SF 19 B3
NW FROM RHINE ST AT THE
COUNTY LINE

BERGEN PL SF 2 C2
W FROM S HYDE ST BETWEEN
BAY ST AND NORTH PT ST

BERKELEY WY SF 14 A2
W FROM DIAMOND HGTS BLVD
S OF GOLD MINE DR

BERKSHIRE WY SF 12 B3
E OFF LAKESHORE DR TO
COUNTRY CLUB DR

BERNAL HTS BLVD SF 14 C2
W S E AND N FROM
CARVER ST TO CARVER ST
CARVER ST
ESMERALDA AV
FOLSOM ST
MOULTRIE ST
ANDERSON ST
ELLSWORTH ST
GATES ST
FOLSOM ST
BANKS ST
PRENTISS ST
NEVADA ST
ROSENKRANZ ST
END CARVER ST

BERNARD ST SF 2 C3
W FROM S TAYLOR ST BETWEEN
PACIFIC AV AND BROADWAY
TO LEAVENWORTH ST
2 TAYLOR ST
100 JONES ST
END LEAVENWORTH ST

BERNICE ST SF 11 A1
S FROM S 12TH ST BETWEEN
FOLSOM ST AND HARRISON ST

BERRY ST SF 7 C3
BERRY ST SF 11 B1
FROM THE EMBARCADERO BETWEEN
KING ST AND CHANNEL ST SW TO
DE HARO ST
THE EMBARCADERO
2 2ND ST
100 3RD ST
200 4TH ST
300 5TH ST
400 6TH ST
500 7TH ST
END DE HARO ST

BERTHA LN SF 15 C3
N FROM HUDSON AV BETWEEN INGALLS
ST AND WHITNERY YOUNG CIR
TO HARBOR RD

BERTITA ST SF 20 A2
N FROM S SENECA AV BETWEEN
ALEMANY BLVD AND MISSION ST

BERWICK PL SF 11 A1
FROM A POINT NEAR HERON ST
BETWEEN 7TH ST AND 8TH ST SE
TO HARRISON ST

BESSIE ST SF 14 C3
S OF PRECITA AV FROM

1988 SAN FRANCISCO COUNTY CROSS STREET INDEX

FOLSOM ST W TO A POINT W OF
MANCHESTER ST
BEULAH ST SF 9 C2
FROM COLE ST BETWEEN WALLER ST
AND FREDERICK ST W TO
STANYAN ST
2 COLE ST
100 SHRADER ST
END STANYAN ST
BEVERLY ST SF 19 A2
N FROM 19TH AV BETWEEN
MONTICELLO ST AND JUNIPERO
SERRA BLVD TO HOLLOWAY AV
19TH AV
100 SHIELDS ST
200 GARFIELD ST
END HOLLOWAY AV
BIGELOW CT SF 3 C1
S FROM 13TH ST BETWEEN
HALYBURTON CT & AV E,
TREASURE ISLAND
BIGLER AV SF 9 C3
S FROM BELGRAVE AV TO TWIN
PEAKS BLVD
BIRCH ST SF 6 B3
W FROM S OCTAVIA ST BETWEEN
GROVE ST AND FULTON ST TO
LAGUNA ST
BIRD ST SF 10 C2
E FROM DEARBORN ST BETWEEN
17TH ST AND 18TH ST
BISHOP ST SF 21 A2
SW OF ANKENY ST BETWEEN
ALDER ST AND SPARTA ST TO
HARKNESS AV
BLACK PL SF 2 C2
N FROM S UNION ST BETWEEN
LEAVENWORTH ST & JONES ST
BLACKSTONE CT SF 2 B2
W FROM FRANKLIN ST BETWEEN
GREENWICH ST AND LOMBARD ST
BLACKWOOD ST SF 11 A1
E OFF S 9TH ST BETWEEN MCLEA CT
AND HARRISON ST
BLAIRWOOD LN SF 9 B3
N FROM WARREN DR BETWEEN
CHRISTOPHER DR AND ASHWOOD
LANE TO CRESTMONT DR
BLAKE ST SF 5 C2
FROM A POINT N OF GEARY BLVD
BETWEEN COLLINS ST AND COOK ST
TO ANZA ST
BLANCHE ST SF 10 B3
FROM A POINT N OF 23RD ST BETWEEN
VICKSBURG ST AND SANCHEZ ST
TO ELIZABETH ST
BLANDY ST SF 17 B1
SE FROM SPEAR AV BETWEEN
C ST AND E ST TO C ST
BLANEY RD SF 1 B2
S FROM A POINT N OF DOYLE DR
E OF CRISSY FIELD AV TO PATTEN RD
DOYLE DR
BLANKEN AV SF 21 B3
E FROM BAY SHORE BLVD TO
EXECUTIVE PARK BLVD
CRISSY FIELD AV
COWLES ST
END PATTEN RD
BAY SHORE BLVD
TUNNEL AV
WHEELER AV
PENINSULA AV
TOCOLOMA AV
NUEVA AV
GILLETTE AV
END EXECUTIVE PARK BL
BLISS RD SF 1 B3
E FROM TAYLOR RD BETWEEN
SHERIDAN AV & MORAGA AV

TO MONTGOMERY ST
BLUXOME ST SF 7 B3
SW FROM 4TH ST BETWEEN BRANNAN ST
AND TOWNSEND ST TO 6TH ST
BLYTHDALE AV SF 20 C3
E FROM BROOKDALE AV TO
HAHN ST N OF VELASCO AV
BOARDMAN PL SF 11 B1
SE FROM BRYANT ST BETWEEN 6TH ST
& 7TH ST TO BRANNAN ST
BOCANA ST SF 14 C2
SW FROM A POINT N OF POWHATTAN AV
TO HOLLY PARK CIRCLE
POWHATTAN AV
200 EUGENIA AV
300 CORTLAND AV
ELLERT ST
END HOLLY PARK CIR
BONIFACIO ST SF 7 B3
SW FROM LAPU LAPU ST TO TANDANG
SORA BETWEEN FOLSOM ST
AND HARRISON ST
LAPU LAPU ST
MABINI ST
END TANDANG SORA
BONITA ST SF 2 C3
W FROM S POLK ST BETWEEN GREEN ST
AND VALLEJO ST
BONNIE BRAE LN SF 12 B3
NE OFF LAKESHORE DR TO
COUNTRY CLUB DR
BONVIEW ST SF 14 C2
SW FROM COO AV E OF ELSIE ST
TO CORTLAND AV
2 COSO AV
200 EUGENIA AV
END CORTLAND AV
BORICA ST SF 19 B1
N FROM HOLLOWAY AV BETWEEN
ALVISO ST AND CORONA ST TO
URBANO DR N
HOLLOWAY AV
URBANO DR S
N ENTRADA CT
END URBANO DR N
BOSWORTH ST SF 14 A3
W FROM MISSION ST S OF
ST MARYS AV TO A POINT NE OF
O'SHAUGNESSY BLVD
2 MISSION ST
100 MARSILLY ST
200 CUVIER ST
300 MILTON ST
400 ROSSEAU ST
ROTTECK ST
LYELL ST
500 ARLINGTON ST
600 DIAMOND ST
700 BROMPTON AV
800 LIPPARD AV
900 CHILTON AV
1000 HAMERTON AV
1100 BURNSIDE AV
CONGO ST
END O'SHAUGHNESSY BLVD
BOUTWELL ST SF 15 A2
S FROM INDUSTRIAL ST TO
BAY SHORE BLVD
BOWDOIN ST SF 15 A3
BOWDOIN ST SF 15 A3
BOWDOIN ST SF 21 A1
SE FROM A POINT N OF GAVEN ST W
OF BOYLSTON ST TO A POINT SE OF
MANSELL ST
GAVEN ST
SWEENY ST
HALE ST
400 SILVER AV
500 SILLIMAN ST
600 FELTON ST

END BURROWS ST
800 BACON ST
900 WAYLAND ST
1000 WOOLSEY ST
1100 DWIGHT ST
1200 OLMSTEAD ST
1300 MANSELL ST
END SE OF MANSELL ST
BOWLEY ST SF 4 C1
W FROM LINCOLN BLVD THEN CIRCLE
BACK TO LINCOLN BLVD
BOWLING GREEN DR SF 9 B1
SW FROM MIDDLE DR E TO SOUTH DR
BOWMAN RD SF 1 A2
W OF MERCHANT RD
BOYLSTON ST SF 15 A3
S FROM A POINT N OF GAVEN ST W OF
MERRILL ST TO SILLIMAN ST
GAVEN ST
SWEENEY ST
HALE ST
SILVER AV
END SILLIMAN ST
BOYNTON CT SF 10 B1
S FROM S 14TH ST BETWEEN
CHURCH ST AND SANCHEZ ST
BRADFORD ST SF 15 A2
S FROM ESMERALDA AV BETWEEN
PERALTA AV AND CARVER ST TO
TOMPKINS AV
2 ESMERALDA AV
MAYFLOWER ST
100 POWHATTAN AV
200 CORTLAND AV
MOJAVE ST
300 JARBOE AV
END TOMPKINS AV
BRADY ST SF 10 C1
SE FROM MARKET ST BETWEEN 12TH ST
AND GOUGH ST TO OTIS ST
BRANNAN ST SF 7 C3
BRANNAN ST SF 11 A1
FROM THE EMBARCADERO BETWEEN
BRYANT ST AND TOWNSEND ST
SW TO DIVISION ST
THE EMBARCADERO
2 BEALE ST
100 FREMONT ST
200 1ST ST
COLIN P KELLY JR ST
300 2ND ST
STANFORD ST
CENTER PL
400 3RD ST
420 RITCH ST
ZOE ST
500 4TH ST
600 5TH ST
700 6TH ST
722 HARRIET ST
LUCERNE ST
BOARDMAN PL
BUTTE PL
GILBERT ST
800 7TH ST
900 8TH ST
1000 9TH ST
DORE ST
END DIVISION ST
BRANT AL SF 3 A2
S FROM S GREENWICH ST BETWEEN
STOCKTON ST AND POWELL ST
BRAZIL AV SF 20 B1
SE FROM S MISSION ST BETWEEN
EXCELSIOR AV AND PERSIA AV
TO MANSELL ST
2 MISSION ST
100 LONDON ST
200 PARIS ST
300 LISBON ST

400 MADRID ST
500 EDINBURGH ST
600 NAPLES ST
700 VIENNA ST
800 ATHENS ST
900 MOSCOW ST
1000 MUNICH ST
1100 PRAGUE ST
DUBLIN ST
END MANSELL ST
BREEN PL SF 6 C3
N FROM MCALLISTEER ST BETWEEN
HYDE ST AND LARKIN ST
BRENTWOOD AV SF 13 C3
W FROM MELROSE AV TO MAYWOOD DR
MELROSE AV
MANGELS ST
100 HAZELWOOD AV
VALDEZ AV
COLON AV
200 YERBA BUENA AV
300 FERNWOOD DR
END MAYWOOD AV
BRET HARTE TER SF 2 C2
N FROM FRANCISCO ST BETWEEN
LEAVENWORTH ST AND JONES ST
BREWSTER ST SF 15 A2
SW FROM MONTCALM ST TO
ESMERALDA AV
2 MONTCALM ST
MACEDONIA ST
100 RUTLEDGE ST
COSTA ST
JOY ST
END ESMERALDA AV
BRIARCLIFF TER SF 13 A2
E FROM 19TH AV ONE BLK
N OF SLOAT BLVD
BRICE TER SF 11 A3
W FROM S BRYANT ST BETWEEN
20TH ST AND 21ST ST
BRIDGEVIEW DR SF 15 B3
N AND E FROM THORNTON AV
TO NEWHALL ST
THORNTON AV
TOPEKA AV
THORNE WY
TAMPA LN
END NEWHALL ST
BRIGHT ST SF 19 B2
S FROM ALEMANY BLVD, & N FROM
STANLEY ST TO HOLLOWAY AV BETWEEN
ORIZABA AV AND HEAD ST
ALEMANY BLVD
100 STANLEY ST
200 RANDOLPH ST
300 SARGENT ST
400 SHIELDS ST
500 GARFIELD ST
END HOLLOWAY AV
BRIGHTON AV SF 19 C2
N FROM LAKE VIEW AV BETWEEN LEE
AV AND PLYMOUTH AV TO OCEAN AV
2 LAKE VIEW AV
100 GRAFTON AV
200 HOLLOWAY AV
END OCEAN AV
BRITTON ST SF 21 A3
S FROM LELAND TO A POINT S OF
BROAD VISITACION AV
BROAD ST SF 19 B2
W FROM SAN JOSE AV BETWEEN
SADOWA ST AND FARRALLONES ST TO
ORIZABA AV
2 SAN JOSE AV
100 PLYMOUTH AV
200 CAPITOL AV
END ORIZABA AV
BROADMOOR DR SF 19 A1
S FROM STONECREST DR TO

STONECREST DR W OF
JUNIPERO SERRA BLVD
BROADWAY SF 2 A3
BROADWAY SF 3 A3
FROM THE EMBARCADERO BETWEEN
PACIFIC AV AND VALLEJO ST
W TO LYON ST
2 THE EMBARCADERO
50 DAVIS ST
100 FRONT ST
200 BATTERY ST
300 SANSOME ST
OSGOOD PL
BARTOL ST
400 MONTGOMERY ST
500 KEARNY ST
ROMOLO ST
COLUMBUS AV
600 GRANT AV
700 STOCKTON ST
CORDELIA ST
CHURCHILL ST
800 POWELL ST
WAYNE PL
900 MASON ST
HIMMELMAN PL
1000 TAYLOR ST
1100 JONES ST
1200 LEAVENWORTH ST
CYRUS PL
1300 HYDE ST
MORRELL PL
1400 LARKIN ST
1500 POLK ST
1600 VAN NESS AV
1700 FRANKLIN ST
1800 GOUGH ST
1900 OCTAVIA ST
2000 LAGUNA ST
2100 BUCHANAN ST
2200 WEBSTER ST
2300 FILLMORE ST
2400 STEINER ST
2500 PIERCE ST
2600 SCOTT ST
2700 DIVISADERO ST
2800 BRODERICK ST
2900 BAKER ST
END LYON ST
BRODERICK ST SF 2 A3
BRODERICK ST SF 6 A2
BRODERICK ST SF 10 A1
N FROM WALLER ST BETWEEN
DIVISADERO ST & BAKER ST
TO THE BAY
2 WALLER ST
100 HAIGHT ST
200 PAGE ST
300 OAK ST
400 FELL ST
500 HAYES ST
600 GROVE ST
700 FULTON ST
800 MCALLISTER ST
900 GOLDEN GATE AV
1000 TURK ST
1100 EDDY ST
1200 ELLIS ST
1300 O'FARRELL ST
1400 GEARY BLVD
1500 GARDEN ST
1500 POST ST
1600 SUTTER ST
1700 BUSH ST
1800 PINE ST
1900 CALIFORNIA ST
2000 SACRAMENTO ST
2100 CLAY ST
2200 WASHINGTON ST
2300 JACKSON ST

1988 SAN FRANCISCO COUNTY CROSS STREET INDEX

2400 PACIFIC AV
2500 BROADWAY
2600 VALLEJO ST
2700 GREEN ST
2800 UNION ST
2900 FILBERT ST
3000 GREENWICH ST
3100 LOMBARD ST
3200 CHESTNUT ST
3300 FRANCISCO ST
3400 BAY ST
3500 NORTH POINT ST
3600 BEACH ST
3700 JEFFERSON ST
END MARINA BLVD
BROMLEY PL SF 2 B3
E FROM S WEBSTER ST BETWEEN
JACKSON ST AND PACIFIC AV
BROMPTON AV SF 14 A3
S FROM CHENERY ST BETWEEN
DIAMOND ST AND LIPPARD AV
TO JOOST AV
2 CHENERY ST
KERN ST
100 BOSWORTH ST
END JOOST AVE
BRONTE ST SF 15 A2
S FROM S CORTLAND AV BETWEEN
BRADFORD ST AND PUTNAM ST
S TO TOMPKINS AV
2 CORTLAND AV
MOJAVE ST
100 JARBOE AV
END TOMPKINS AV
BROOK ST SF 14 B2
W FROM S MISSION ST BETWEEN
KINGSTON ST & RANDALL ST
TO JOSE AV
BROOKDALE AV SF 20 B3
NE FROM GENEVA AV TO
SANTOS ST N OF BLYTHDALE AV
BROOKHAVEN LN SF 12 B3
OFF HUNTINGTON DR E AND W
BROOKLYN PL SF 3 A3
S FROM S SACRAMENTO ST BETWEEN
GRANT AV & STOCKTON ST
BROSNAN ST SF 10 C1
W FROM S VALENCIA ST BETWEEN
CLINTON PARK AND 14TH ST
TO GUERRERO ST
BROTHERHOOD WY SF 19 A2
NW FROM ALEMANY BLVD TO
LAKE MERCED BLVD
ALEMANY BLVD
100 STANLEY ST
400 ARCH ST
ST CHARLES AV
JUNIPERO SERRA BL (HY 1)
CHUMASERO DR
THOMAS MORE WY
END LAKE MERCED BLVD
BRUCE AV SF 19 C1
E FROM 200 BLOCK OF HAROLD AV
BRUMISS TER SF 19 C3
E FROM ACTON ST BETWEEN
MISSION ST & BRUNSWICK ST
BRUNSWICK ST SF 19 B3
BRUNSWICK ST SF 20 A3
SW FROM NEWTON ST BETWEEN
MORSE ST & HANOVER ST
TO THE COUNTY LINE
2 NEWTON ST
100 CURTIS ST
200 POPE ST
300 ALLISON ST
400 CONCORD ST
FLORENTINE AV
500 GUTTENBERG ST
600 LOWELL ST
ROEMER WY
700 WHITTIER ST
800 OLIVER ST
END COUNTY LINE
BRUSH PL SF 11 A1
SW FROM HALLAM ST NEAR FOLSOM ST
BETWEEN 7TH ST AND 8TH ST
8TH ST
BRUSSELS ST SF 15 A3
BRUSSELS ST SF 21 A1
SE FROM SILVER AV BETWEEN
GIRARD ST AND GOETTINGEN
ST S TO CAMPBELL AV
2 SILVER AV
100 SILLIMAN ST
200 FELTON ST
END BURROWS ST
400 BACON ST
500 WAYLAND ST
600 WOOLSEY ST
700 DWIGHT ST
800 OLMSTEAD ST
900 MANSELL ST
1000 ORDWAY ST
1100 WARD ST
1200 HARKNESS ST
1300 WILDE ST
END CAMPBELL ST
BRYANT ST SF 7 C2
BRYANT ST SF 11 A1
BRYANT ST SF 15 A1
SW FROM THE EMBARCADERO BETWEEN
HARRISON ST AND BRANNAN ST
TO 11TH ST THEN S TO PRECITA AV
THE EMBARCADERO
50 MAIN ST
100 BEALE ST
300 1ST ST
RINCON ST
STERLING ST
400 2ND ST
CENTER PL
500 3RD ST
RITCH ST
600 ZOE ST
600 4TH ST
STILLMAN ST
700 5TH ST
OAK GROVE ST
MORRIS ST
800 6TH ST
HARRIET ST
BOARDMAN PL
GILBERT ST
900 7TH ST
LANGTON ST
KATE ST
DECATUR ST
1000 8TH ST
CONVERSE ST
1100 9TH ST
DORE ST
1200 10TH ST
JUNIPER ST
1300 11TH ST
1400 DIVISION ST
1500 ALAMEDA ST
1600 15TH ST
1700 16TH ST
1800 17TH ST
1900 MARIPOSA ST
2000 18TH ST
2100 19TH ST
2200 20TH ST
BRICE TER
2300 21ST ST
2400 22ND ST
2500 23RD ST
2600 24TH ST
2700 25TH ST
2800 26TH ST
2900 ARMY ST
END PRECITA AV
BUCARELI DR SF 18 C2
SW FROM JUAN BAUTIISTA
CIRCLE TO RIVAS AV N OF
BROTHERHOOD WY
BUCHANAN ST SF 2 B3
BUCHANAN ST SF 6 B3
BUCHANAN ST SF 10 B1
N FROM S MARKET ST AND
DUBOCE AV BETWEEN LAGUNA ST AND
WEBSTER ST TO MARINA BLVD
2 MARKET ST
DUBOCE AV
100 HERMANN ST
200 WALLER ST
250 LAUSSAT ST
300 HAIGHT ST
400 PAGE ST
LILY ST
500 OAK ST
550 HICKORY ST
600 FELL ST
638 LINDEN ST
700 HAYES ST
726 IVY ST
END GROVE ST
1300 EDDY ST
END WILLOW ST
1700 POST ST
1800 SUTTER ST
FERN ST
1900 BUSH ST
2000 PINE ST
2100 CALIFORNIA ST
2200 SACRAMENTO ST
2300 CLAY ST
2400 WASHINGTON ST
2500 JACKSON ST
2600 PACIFIC AV
2700 BROADWAY
2800 VALLEJO ST
2900 GREEN ST
3000 UNION ST
3100 FILBERT ST
HARRIS PL
3200 GREENWICH ST
MOULTON ST
3300 LOMBARD ST
MAGNOLIA ST
END CHESTNUT ST
GEORGE MOSCONE REC CTR
3600 BAY ST
3700 NORTH POINT ST
3800 BEACH ST
END MARINA BLVD
BUCKINGHAM WY SF 19 A1
NW FROM 19TH AV TO WINSTON DR
BUENA VISTA AV SF 10 A1
SURROUNDING BUENA VISTA PARK S
OF HAIGHT ST E OF MASONIC AV
EAST
HAIGHT ST
WALLER ST
DUBOCE AV
BUENA VISTA TER
PARK HILL AV
BUENA VISTA TER SF 10 A1
S FROM JUNCTION BUENA VISTA AV
& DUBOCE AV TO 15TH ST
2 BUENA VISTA AV
DUBOCE AV
100 14TH ST
ROOSEVELT WY
END 15TH ST
BURGOYNE ST SF 2 C3
S FROM S PACIFIC AV BETWEEN
LEAVENWORTH ST AND HYDE ST
BURKE ST SF 15 C2
FROM 3600 3RD ST
BURLWOOD DR SF 13 C3
E FROM LOS PALMOS DR BETWEEN
LOS PALMOS DR AND CRESTA VISTA DR
TO BELLA VISTA WY
BURNETT AV SF 10 A3
BURNETT AV SF 14 A1
SE FROM TWIN PEAKS BLVD
TO PORTOLA
TWIN PEAKS BLVD
GARDENSIDE DR
450 DIXIE AL
HOPKINS AV
GOLDING LN
FENTON LN
CRESTLINE DR
GLENVIEW DR
DAWNVIEW WY
END PORTOLA DR
BURNS PL SF 10 C1
W FROM S 11TH ST N OF FOLSOM ST
BURNSIDE AV SF 14 A3
N FROM MANGELS AV TO CHENERY ST
2 CHENERY ST
PARADISE AV
100 BOSWORTH ST
END MANGELS AV
BURR AV SF 20 C3
E FROM ARGONAUT AV N OF
VELASCO AV
BURRITT ST SF 7 A2
S FROM S BUSH ST BETWEEN
STOCKTON ST AND POWELL ST
BURROWS ST SF 20 C1
BURROWS ST SF 21 A1
E FROM LA GRANDE AV BETWEEN
FELTON & BACON ST TO A POINT
E OF SAN BRUNO AV
100 SAN BRUNO AV
200 GIRARD ST
300 BRUSSELS ST
400 GOETTINGEN ST
500 SOMERSET ST
600 HOLYOKE ST
700 HAMILTON ST
END BOWDOIN ST
RESERVOIR
UNIVERSITY ST
CAMPUS LN
END AMHERST ST
1500 CAMBRIDGE ST
1600 OXFORD ST
1700 HARVARD ST
1800 GAMBIER ST
1900 MADISON ST
PERU AV
MANSFIELD ST
END LA GRANDE AV
BUSH ST SF 6 A2
BUSH ST SF 7 A2
W FROM S MARKET ST BETWEEN
SUTTER ST AND PINE ST TO
PRESIDIO AV
2 MARKET ST
100 BATTERY ST
200 SANSOME ST
TREASURY PL
PETRARCH PL
300 MONTGOMERY ST
TRINITY ST
BELDEN ST
400 KEARNY ST
ST GEORGE AL
CLAUDE LN
MARK LN
500 GRANT AV
CHATHAM PL
600 STOCKTON ST
BURRITT ST
650 MONROE ST
CHELSEA PL
700 POWELL ST
800 MASON ST
900 TAYLOR ST
1000 JONES ST
1100 LEAVENWORTH ST
1200 HYDE ST
1300 LARKIN ST
1400 POLK ST
1500 VAN NESS AV
1600 FRANKLIN ST
1700 GOUGH ST
1800 OCTAVIA ST
1900 LAGUNA ST
2000 BUCHANAN ST
2100 WEBSTER ST
COTTAGE ROW
2200 FILLMORE ST
2300 STEINER ST
2400 PIERCE ST
2500 SCOTT ST
2600 DIVISADERO ST
2700 BRODERICK ST
2800 BAKER ST
2900 LYON ST
END PRESIDIO AV
BUTTE PL SF 11 B1
S FROM S BRANNAN ST BETWEEN
6TH ST AND 7TH ST
BYINGTON ST SF 6 B2
E FROM S FILLMORE ST BETWEEN
ELLIS ST AND O'FARRELL
BYRON CT SF 20 A3
E FROM LOWELL ST BETWEEN
BRUNSWICK ST AND HANOVER ST
BYXBEE ST SF 19 A2
N FROM RANDOLPH ST BETWEEN
MONTICELLO ST & RALSTON ST TO
HOLLOWAY AV
2 RANDOLPH ST
19TH AV
100 SARGENT ST
200 SHIELDS ST
300 GARFIELD ST
END HOLLOWAY AV
C ST SF 17 B1
S FROM SPEAR AV BETWEEN LOCKWOOD
AND BLANDY ST TO A POINT S OF
NIMITZ AV
SPEAR AV
NIMITZ AV
END BLANDY ST
CABRILLO ST SF 8 A1
CABRILLO ST SF 9 A1
W FROM ARGUELLO BLVD BETWEEN
BALBOA ST AND FULTON ST
W TO LA PLAYA
2 ARGUELLO BLVD
100 2ND AV
200 3RD AV
300 4TH AV
400 5TH AV
500 6TH AV
600 7TH AV
700 8TH AV
800 9TH AV
900 10TH AV
1000 11TH AV
1100 12TH AV
FUNSTON AV
PARK PRESIDIO BLVD
1300 14TH AV
1400 15TH AV
1500 16TH AV
1600 17TH AV
1700 18TH AV
1800 19TH AV
1900 20TH AV
2000 21ST AV
2100 22ND AV
2200 23RD AV

2300 24TH AV
2400 25TH AV
2500 26TH AV
2600 27TH AV
2700 28TH AV
2800 29TH AV
2900 30TH AV
3000 31ST AV
3100 32ND AV
3200 33RD AV
3300 34TH AV
3400 35TH AV
3500 36TH AV
3600 37TH AV
3700 38TH AV
3800 39TH AV
3900 40TH AV
4000 41ST AV
4100 42ND AV
4200 43RD AV
4300 44TH AV
4400 45TH AV
4500 46TH AV
4600 47TH AV
4700 48TH AV
END LA PLAYA ST

CADELL PL SF 3 A2
N FROM S S UNION ST BETWEEN
GRANT AV & STOCKTON ST

CAINE AV SF 19 C2
NE FROM LOBOS ST BETWEEN
MAJESTIC AV AND SAN JOSE AV
TO RIDGE LN
2 RIDGE LANE ST
100 LAKE VIEW AV
END LOBOS ST

CALEDONIA ST SF 10 C1
FROM A POINT N OF 15TH ST
BETWEEN JULIAN AV AND
VALENCIA ST S TO 16TH ST

CALGARY ST SF 20 C3
S FROM VELASCO AV TO
COUNTY LINE E OF PUEBLO ST

CALHOUN TER SF 3 A2
SANSOME ST AND MONTGOMERY ST TO
GREEN ST

CALIFORNIA AV SF 3 C2
NE FROM AV A TO AV N, TREASURE IS
AVENUE A
AVENUE B
AVENUE C
AVENUE D
AVENUE F
AVENUE H
AVENUE M
END AVENUE N

CALIFORNIA ST SF 3 B3
CALIFORNIA ST SF 4 C2
CALIFORNIA ST SF 5 A2
CALIFORNIA ST SF 6 A2
W FROM MARKET ST BETWEEN
PINE ST AND SACRAMENTO ST
A POINT W OF 32ND ST
2 MARKET ST
DRUMM ST
100 DAVIS ST
200 FRONT ST
300 BATTERY ST
400 SANSOME ST
LEIDESDORFF ST
500 MONTGOMERY ST
SPRING ST
600 KEARNY ST
QUINCY ST
700 GRANT AV
SABIN PL
800 STOCKTON ST
PRATT PL
JOICE ST
900 POWELL ST
1000 MASON ST
SPROULE LN
1100 TAYLOR ST
1200 JONES ST
LYSETTE ST
1300 LEAVENWORTH ST
HELEN ST
1400 HYDE ST
1500 LARKIN ST
1600 POLK ST
1700 VAN NESS AV
1800 FRANKLIN ST
1900 GOUGH ST
2000 OCTAVIA ST
2100 LAGUNA ST
2200 BUCHANAN ST
2300 WEBSTER ST
ORBEN PL
2400 FILLMORE ST
2500 STEINER ST
2600 PIERCE ST
2700 SCOTT ST
2800 DIVISADERO ST
2900 BRODERICK ST
3000 BAKER ST
3100 LYON ST
3200 PRESIDIO AV
3300 WALNUT ST
3400 LAUREL ST
3500 LOCUST ST
3600 SPRUCE ST
PARKER AV
3700 MAPLE ST
COMMONWEALTH AV
3800 CHERRY ST
JORDAN AV
PALM AV
3900 ARGUELLO BLVD
4000 2ND AV
4100 3RD AV
4200 4TH AV
4300 5TH AV
CORNWALL ST
4400 6TH AV
4500 7TH AV
4600 8TH AV
4700 9TH AV
4800 10TH AV
4900 11TH AV
5000 12TH AV
FUNSTON AV
PARK PRESIDIO BLVD
5200 14TH AV
5300 15TH AV
5400 16TH AV
5500 57TH AV
5600 18TH AV
5700 19TH AV
5800 20TH AV
5900 21ST AV
6000 22ND AV
6100 23RD AV
6200 24TH AV
6300 25TH AV
6400 26TH AV
6500 27TH AV
6600 28TH AV
6700 29TH AV
6800 30TH AV
6900 31ST AV
7000 32ND AV
END 33RD AV

CAMBON DR SF 19 A2
N FROM FONT BLVD BETWEEN
JUNIPERO SERRA BLVD AND
GONZALES DR

CAMBRIDGE ST SF 14 C3
CAMBRIDGE ST SF 20 C1
E FROM STONEYBROOK AV PARALLEL
TO I-280, THEN S TO
JOHN F SHELLEY DR
TRUMBULL ST
STONEYBROOK AV
STONEYFORD AV
GLADSTONE DR
WEST VIEW AV
SWEENY ST
SILVER AVE
PIOCHE ST
SILLIMAN ST
FELTON ST
BURROWS ST
BACON ST
WAYLAND ST
END JOHN F SHELLEY DR

CAMELLIA AV SF 14 B3
N FROM SILVER AV N TO
ADMIRAL AV
ADMIRAL AV
CASTLE MANOR AV
END SILVER AV

CAMEO WY SF 14 A1
SE FROM AMBER DR TO DUNCAN ST

CAMERON WY SF 21 C2
N FROM FITZGERALD AV BETWEEN
HAWES ST AND GRIFFITH ST
FITZGERALD AV
NICHOLS WY
DOUBLE ROCK ST
NICHOLS WY
END GRIFFITH ST

CAMP ST SF 10 B2
E FROM GUERRO ST BETWEEN
16TH ST AND 17TH ST TO
ALBION ST

CAMPBELL AV SF 21 A2
SW FROM SAN BRUNO AV TO
HOLLYOKE DR THEN NW TO ELLIOT ST
2 SAN BRUNO AV
100 BRUSSELS ST
200 GOETTINGEN ST
SOMERSET ST
HOLYOKE ST
400 ALPHA ST
500 RUTLAND ST
600 DELTA ST
ERVINE ST
ALBERTA ST
END ELLIOT ST

CAMPTON PL SF 7 A2
W FROM S GRANT AV BETWEEN
POST ST AND SUTTER ST
TO STOCKTON ST

CAMPUS CIR SF 18 C1
OFF STATE DR-SAN
FRANCISCO STATE UNIVERSITY

CAMPUS LN SF 20 C1
NORTH EXTENSION OF PRICETON ST

CANBY BETWEEN AMHERST

CANBY ST SF 1 C2
NW FROM MESA AV TO KEYES AV

CANYON DR SF 20 B3
SW FROM SOUTH HILL BLVD TO
THE COUNTY LINE

CAPISTRANO AV SF 20 A1
SE FROM SAN JOSE AV AND THEN
S TO SANTA YNEZ ST BETWEEN
LOTTER ST & SANTA ROSA AV
AND SANTA ROSA AVE
2 SAN JOSE AV
100 SAN GABRIEL AV
200 SANTA ROSA AV
300 SANTA YSABEL AV
400 SAN JUAN AV
END SANTA YNEZ AV

CAPITOL AV SF 19 B3
FROM A POINT S OF SAGAMORE ST
BETWEEN PLYMOUTH AV & ORIZABA AV
N TO OCEAN AV
100 SAGAMORE ST
200 SADOWA ST
300 BROAD ST
400 FARALLONES ST
500 LOBOS ST
600 MINERVA ST
700 MONTANA ST
800 THRIFT ST
900 LAKE VIEW AV
1000 GRAFTON AV
1100 HOLLOWAY AV
1200 DE MONTFORD AV
END OCEAN AV

CAPP ST SF 10 C2
CAPP ST SF 14 C1
S FROM S 15TH ST BETWEEN
SO VAN NESS AV AND MISSION
ST TO MISSION ST
2 15TH ST
ADAIR ST
100 16TH ST
200 17TH ST
300 18TH ST
400 19TH ST
500 20TH ST
600 21ST ST
700 22ND ST
800 23RD ST
900 24TH ST
1000 25TH ST
1100 26TH ST
END MISSION ST

CAPRA WY SF 2 A2
W FROM MALLORCA WY TO SCOTT ST
2 MALLORCA WY
100 PIERCE ST
150 AVILA ST
END SCOTT ST

CARD AL SF 3 A3
W FROM S STOCKTON ST BETWEEN
VALLEJO ST AND GREEN ST

CARDENAS AV SF 19 A2
SE FROM HOLLOWAY AV BETWEEN
VARELA AV AND FUENTE AV
TO 19TH AV

CARGO WY SF 15 C1
CARGO WY SF 16 A2
SE FROM 3RD ST TO JENNINGS ST

CARL ST SF 9 C2
W FROM 857 CLAYTON ST S OF
FREDERICK ST TO ARGUELLO BLVD
2 CLAYTON ST
100 COLE ST
152 SHRADER ST
200 STANYAN ST
300 WILLARD ST
HILLWAY ST
END ARGUELLO BLVD

CARMEL ST SF 9 C2
W FROM CLAYTON ST TO SHRADER ST
2 CLAYTON ST
64 BELVEDERE ST
100 COLE ST
END SHRADER ST

CARMELITA ST SF 10 B1
S FROM WALLER ST BETWEEN
PIERCE ST AND SCOTT ST
TO DUBOCE PARK

CARNELIAN WY SF 14 A1
N FROM DIAMOND HEIGHTS BLVD
2 BLKS E OF PORTOLA DR

CAROLINA ST SF 11 B2
S FROM CHANNEL ST BETWEEN
WISCONSIT ST AND DE HARO ST
S TO KONA RD
2 CHANNEL ST
100 15TH ST
200 16TH ST
300 17TH ST
400 MARIPOSA ST
500 18TH ST
KOHALA RD
600 19TH ST
700 20TH ST
SOUTHERN HTS AV
900 22ND ST
1100 23RD ST
CORAL RD
END WISCONSIN ST

CARR ST SF 21 B1
S FROM PAUL AV BETWEEN 3RD ST
AND GOULD ST TO SALINAS AV

CARRIE ST SF 14 B3
S FROM CHENERY ST W OF
CASTRO ST TO WILDER ST

CARRIZAL ST SF 20 C3
S FROM VELASCO AV TO GENEVA AV

CARROLL AV SF 15 B3
CARROLL AV SF 21 B1
FROM FITCH ST NW TO THORNTON AV
FITCH ST
HAWES ST
INGALLS ST
JENNINGS ST
KEITH ST
3RD ST
MENDELL ST
NEWHALL ST
PHELPS ST
QUINT ST
END THORNTON AVE

CARSON ST SF 10 A3
W FROM S DOUGLASS ST BETWEEN
19TH ST AND SEWARD ST

CARTER ST SF 20 B3
SW FROM GENEVA AV TO COUNTY LINE

CARVER ST SF 15 A2
S FROM BERNAL HEIGHTS BLVD

CASA WY SF 2 A2
NW FROM RETIRO WY TO MARINA BLVD

CASCADE WK SF 19 A3
SW FROM ORTEGA ST TO FUNSTON AV

CASELLI AV SF 10 A3
FROM DOUGLASS ST NEAR
19TH ST TO MARKET ST
2 DOUGLASS ST
LAMSON LANE
CLOVER LN
100 CLOVER ST
YUKON ST
200 DANVERS ST
300 MONO ST
END MARKET ST

CASHMERE ST SF 15 C3
N FROM LA SALLE AV N TO A POINT
E OF HUDSON AV

CASITAS AV SF 13 B2
E FROM LANDSDALE AV BETWEEN
OAKDALE WY & ROBINHOOD DR

CASSANDRA CT SF 19 C3
SE OFF S WHITTIER ST BETWEEN
MISSION ST & BRUNSWICK ST

CASTELO AV SF 19 A2
E FROM GONZALES DR BETWEEN
CARDENAS AV AND FONT BLVD
TO CAMBON DR

CASTENADA AV SF 13 B1
SW FROM S VENTURA AV TO A POINT
W OF MONTALVO
2 VENTURA AVE
100 ALTON AVE
MAGELLAN AVE
200 PACHECO AVE
LOPEZ AVE
SAN MARCOS AVE
300 SANTA RITA AVE
MONTALVO AVE
END 12TH AVE

CASTILLO ST SF 20 C3
S FROM VELASCO AV TO COUNTY LINE

CASTLE ST SF 3 A2

1988 SAN FRANCISCO COUNTY CROSS STREET INDEX

N FROM S GREEN ST BETWEEN
MONTGOMERY ST AND KEARNY ST
TO UNION ST
CASTLE MANOR AV SF 14 B3
W FROM 4200 MISSION ST
TO CAMMELLIA AV
CASTRO ST SF 10 B2
CASTRO ST SF 14 B1
S FROM S WALLER ST W OF
NOE ST S TO CHENERY ST
2 DUBOCE AVE
100 14TH ST
HENRY ST
200 15TH ST
250 BEAVER ST
300 16TH ST
340 STATES ST
MARKET ST
400 17TH ST
500 18TH ST
600 19TH ST
700 20TH ST
LIBERTY ST
800 21ST ST
HILL ST
900 22ND ST
1000 ALVARADO ST
1100 23RD ST
1200 ELIZABETH ST
1300 24TH ST
1400 JERSEY ST
1500 25TH ST
1600 CLIPPER ST
1700 26TH ST
1800 ARMY ST
1900 27TH ST
2000 DUNCAN ST
2100 28TH ST
2200 VALLEY
2300 29TH ST
2400 DAY ST
2500 30TH ST
CONTINUED AT SUSSEX TO
CHENERY
CATHERINE CT SF 10 C3
E OFF 2425 MISSION ST
CAYUGA AV SF 19 C3
CAYUGA AV SF 20 A2
SW FROM A POINT NE OF ROUSSEAU ST
MISSION ST SW TO REGENT ST
REGENT ST
2 CUVIER ST
36 MILTON ST
68 ROSSEAU ST
S FROM UNION ST BETWEEN
100 ROTTECK ST
LYELL ST
DANTON ST
200 LAMARTINE ST
BADGER ST
300 GORHAM ST
400 TINGLEY ST
THERESA ST
COTTER ST
600 SANTA ROSA AVE
800 SAN JUAN AVE
SANTA YNEZ AVE
900 OCEAN AVE
VALERTON CT
ONONDAGA AVE
BALHI CT
ONEIDA AVE
SUNBEAM LN
JUNIOR TERR
SENECA AVE
NAVAJO AVE
GENEVA AVE
SEMINOLE AVE
NIAGARA AVE
SHAWNEE ST

MT VERNON AVE
1600 OTTAWA AVE
ROME ST
1700 FOOTE AVE
MODOC AVE
NAGLEE AVE
MANDAN AVE
WHIPPLE AVE
LIPANI AVE
2200 ALEMANY BLVD
SICKLES AVE
END REGENT ST
CECILIA AV SF 13 A1
S FROM RIVERA ST ACROSS
SANTIAGO ST TO A POINT
ON 16TH AV N OF TARAVAL
CEDAR ST SF 6 C2
W FROM S LARKIN ST BETWEEN
GEARY ST AND POST ST TO
TO VAN NESS AV
600 LARKIN ST
100 POLK ST
END VAN NESS AVE
CEDRO AV SF 19 A1
SW FROM S OCEAN AV TO MERCEDES WY
CENTER PL SF 7 B3
S FROM S BRYANT ST BETWEEN
2ND ST AND 3RD ST TO BRANNAN ST
CENTRAL AV SF 6 A3
CENTRAL AV SF 10 A1
N FROM BUENA VISTA AV W
OF LYON ST TO TURK ST
2 BUENA VISTA AVE
50 WALLER ST
100 HAIGHT ST
200 PAGE ST
OAK ST
400 FELL ST
500 HAYES ST
600 GROVE ST
700 FULTON ST
800 MCALLISTER ST
900 GOLDEN GATE AVE
END TURK ST
CENTRAL FRWY SF 6 C3
CENTRAL SKYWAY SF 10 C1
CENTURY PL SF 7 B1
S FROM PINE ST BETWEEN
SANSOME ST & MONTGOMERY ST
CERES ST SF 15 B3
S FROM THORNTON AV TO WILLIAMS AV
CERRITOS AV SF 19 A1
SW FROM OCEAN AV SW TO
MERCEDES WY
2 OCEAN AVE
100 MONCADA WAY
END MERCEDES WAY
CERVANTES BLVD SF 2 A2
NW FROM FILLMORE ST AND
BAY ST TO MARINA BLVD
2 FILLMORE ST
ALHAMBRA ST
100 BEACH ST
200 PRADO ST
AVILA ST
END MARINA BLVD
CHABOT TER SF 5 C3
S FROM TURK ST BETWEEN
TEMESCAL TER AND
KITTREDGE TER TO
GOLDEN GATE AV
CHAIN OF L DR E SF 8 A1
IN GOLDEN GATE PARK
CHAIN OF L DR W SF 8 A1
IN GOLDEN GATE PARK
CHANNEL ST SF 11 B1
SW FROM THE BAY BETWEEN BERRY ST
AND HOOPER ST TO CAROLINA ST
CHAPMAN ST SF 15 A2
W FROM NEVADA ST BETWEEN

BERNAL HEIGHTS BLVD AND
POWHATTAN AV TO FOLSOM ST
CHARLES ST SF 14 B2
W FROM S ARLINGTONS ST
NEAR HIGHLAND AV TO CHENERY ST
CHARLESTOWN PL SF 7 B2
NW FROM S HARRISON ST BETWEEN
ESSEX ST AND 2ND ST
CHARLTON CT SF 2 B3
S FROM S UNION ST BETWEEN
LAGUNA ST AND BUCHANAN ST
CHARTER OAK AV SF 15 A2
S FROM INDUSTRIAL TO SILVER AV
BRUNO AVE S TO SILVER AV
2 INDUSTRIAL ST
100 HELENA ST
200 AUGUSTA ST
END SILVER AVE
CHASE CT SF 10 C1
NE FROM COLUSA PL BETWEEN
OTIS ST AND COLTON ST W
CHATHAM PL SF 7 A1
N FROM W BUSH ST BETWEEN
GRANT AV & STOCKTON ST
CHATTANOOGA ST SF 10 B3
S FROM S 21ST ST BETWEEN
DOLORES ST AND CHURCH ST
TO JERSEY ST
2 21ST ST
100 22ND ST
200 23RD ST
300 24TH ST
400 JERSEY ST
CHAVES AV SF 13 C2
SW FROM EVELYN WY TO A POINT
SW OF ROCKDALE DR
CHELSEA PL SF 7 A2
S FROM S BUSH ST BETWEEN
STOCKTON ST AND POWELL ST
CHENERY ST SF 14 B2
S FROM 30TH ST NEAR CHURCH TO
CHARLES ST AND SW TO ELK ST
ST S AND S W TO ELK ST
2 30TH ST
100 RANDALL ST
200 FAIRMOUNT ST
CHARLES ST
300 MIGUEL ST
400 MATEO ST
500 ROANOKE ST
NATICK ST
600 CASTRO ST
CARRIE ST
700 DIAMOND ST
THOR ST
BROMPTON AVE
LIPPARD AVE
CHILTON AVE
942 HAMERTON AVE
BURNSIDE AVE
1000 MIZPAH ST
END ELK ST
CHERRY ST SF 5 B2
S FROM A POINT N OF JACKSON ST
BETWEEN MAPLE ST AND
ARGUELLO BLVD TO CALIFORNIA ST
2 PRESIDIO
RESERVATION
100 JACKSON ST
200 WASHINGTON ST
300 CLAY ST
400 SACRAMENTO ST
END CALIFORNIA ST
CHESLEY ST SF 11 A1
SE FROM S HARRISON ST BETWEEN
7TH ST AND 8TH ST TO HOMER ST
BRYANT ST
CHESTER AV SF 19 A3
S FROM 19TH AV BETWEEN
ST CHARLES ST AND

JUNIPERO SERRA BLVD TO BELL AV
CHESTNUT ST SF 2 A2
CHESTNUT ST SF 3 A2
W FROM THE EMBARCADERO BETWEEN
LOMBARD ST AND FRANCISCO ST
TO LYON ST
2 SANSOME ST
100 MONTGOMERY ST
WINTHROP ST
200 KEARNY ST
300 GRANT AVE
MIDWAY ST
BELLAIR PL
400 STOCKTON ST
500 POWELL ST
VENARD AL
600 MASON ST
700 COLUMBUS AVE
TAYLOR ST
800 JONES ST
MONTCLAIR TER
1000 HYDE ST
1100 LARKIN ST
CULEBRA TER
1200 POLK ST
1300 VAN NESS AVE
1400 FRANKLIN ST
1500 GOUGH ST
1600 OCTAVIA ST
LAGUNA ST
BUCHANAN ST
1900 WEBSTER ST
2000 FILLMORE ST
MALLORCA WAY
2100 STEINER ST
2200 PIERCE ST
2300 SCOTT ST
2400 DIVISADERO ST
2500 BRODERICK ST
RICHARDSON AVE
2600 BAKER ST
END LYON ST
CHICAGO WY SF 20 B3
FROM A POINT E OF LINDA
VISTA LN W AND SW TO CORDOVA ST
2 PT E OF LINDA
VISTA STEPS
100 LINDA VISTA STEPS
200 SOUTH HILL BLVD
300 NAYLOR ST
END CORDOVA ST
CHILD ST SF 3 A2
N FROM NS GREENWICH ST BETWEEN
KEARNY ST AND GRANT AV
TO LOMBARD ST
CHILTON AV SF 14 A3
SW FROM CHENERY ST BETWEEN
HAMERTON AV AND LIPPARD AV
TO A POINT N OF JOOST AV
2 CHENERY ST
100 BOSWORTH ST
END ACADIA ST
CHINA BASIN ST SF 11 C1
E FROM 3RD ST S OF CHANNEL
THEN S TO ILLINOIS ST
CHISM RD SF 1 C3
IN PRESIDIO
CHRISTMAS TR PT SF 9 C3
NE FROM TWIN PEAKS BLVD
CHRISTOPHER DR SF 9 B3
NE FROM WARREN DR BETWEEN
DEVONSHIRE WY & BLAIRWOOD LN
TO CLARENDON AV
CHULA LN SF 10 B2
W FROM S DOLORES ST BETWEEN
16TH ST AND 17TH ST TO CHURCH ST
CHUMASERO DR SF 19 A2
SE FROM FONT BLVD TO
BROTHERHOOD WY
CHURCH ST SF 10 B2

CHURCH ST SF 14 B1
S FROM HERMANN ST BETWEEN
DOLORES ST AND SANCHEZ ST
TO RANDALL ST
2 HERMANN ST
100 DUBOCE AVE
RESERVOIR ST
200 14TH ST
MARKET ST
300 15TH ST
400 16TH ST
CHULA LANE
500 17TH ST
550 DORLAND ST
600 18TH ST
650 HANCOCK ST
700 19TH ST
748 CUMBERLAND ST
800 20TH ST
850 LIBERTY ST
900 21ST ST
950 HILL ST
1000 22ND ST
1100 23RD ST
1150 ELIZABETH ST
1200 24TH ST
1250 JERSEY ST
1300 25TH ST
1332 CLIPPER ST
1400 26TH ST
1450 ARMY ST
1500 27TH ST
1550 DUNCAN ST
1600 28TH ST
1650 VALLEY ST
1700 29TH ST
1750 DAY ST
1800 30TH ST
END RANDALL ST
CHURCHILL ST SF 3 A3
N FROM S BROADWAY BETWEEN
STOCKTON ST AND POWELL ST
TO VALLEJO ST
CIELITO DR SF 20 C3
S FROM PARQUE DR BETWEEN
PARQUE DR AND ESQUINA DR
TO GENEVA AV
CIRCULAR AV SF 14 A3
FROM JOOST AV AND DIAMOND ST
SW TO HAVELOCK ST
2 JOOST AVE
100 MONTEREY BLVD
ACADIA ST
200 HEARST AV
BADEN ST
300 FLOOD AVE
350 CONGO ST
400 STAPLES AVE
DETROIT ST
600 MARSTON AVE
END HAVELOCK ST
CITY VIEW WY SF 13 C1
E FROM PANORAMA DR AT
MIDCREST WY
CLAIRVIEW CT SF 9 C3
N FROM PANORAMA DR AT
DELLBROOK AV
CLARA ST SF 7 B3
SW FROM 4TH ST BETWEEN
FOLSOM ST & HARRISON ST TO 6TH ST
100 4TH ST
HULBERT AL
200 5TH ST
END 6TH ST
CLAREMONT BLVD SF 13 B2
S FROM JUNCTION OF TARAVAL ST AND
DEWEY BOLD TO PORTOLA DR
2 TARAVAL ST
GRANVILLE WAY
ALLSTON WAY

VERDUN WAY
DORCHESTER WAY
300 ULLOA ST
END PORTOLA DR
CLARENCE PL SF 7 B3
NW FROM TOWNSEND ST BETWEEN
2ND ST AND 3RD ST
CLARENDON AV SF 9 C3
SW FROM BIGLER AV TO
LAGUNA HONDA BLVD
CLARION AL SF 10 C2
W FROM S MISSION ST BETWEEN
17TH ST AND SYCAMORE ST
W TO VALENCIA ST
CLARKE ST SF 1 C3
IN PRESIDIO
CLAUDE LN SF 7 A1
N FROM S SUTTER ST BETWEEN
KEARNY ST AND GRANT AV
TO BUSH ST
CLAY ST SF 2 C3
CLAY ST SF 3 A3
CLAY ST SF 5 C2
W FROM THE EMBARCADERO BETWEEN
SACRAMENTO ST AND WASHINGTON ST
TO ARGUELLO BLVD
2 THE EMBARCADERO
100 DRUMM ST
200 DAVIS ST
400 BATTERY ST
500 SANSOME ST
LEIDESDORFF ST
600 MONTGOMERY ST
700 KEARNY ST
760 WALTER LUM PL
800 GRANT AVE
WAVERLY PL
SPOFFORD ST
900 STOCKTON ST
JOICE ST
PARKHURST AL
1000 POWELL ST
FREEMAN CT
CODMAN PL
TAY ST
WESTMORE PL
1100 MASON ST
YERBA BUENA ST
1200 TAYLOR ST
1300 JONES ST
PRIEST ST
REED ST
1400 LEAVENWORTH ST
1500 HYDE ST
TORRENS CT
1600 LARKIN ST
1700 POLK ST
1800 VAN NESS AVE
1900 FRANKLIN ST
GOUGH ST
LAFAYETTE PARK
2200 LAGUNA ST
2300 BUCHANAN ST
2400 WEBSTER ST
2500 FILLMORE ST
STEINER ST
PIERCE ST
2800 SCOTT ST
2900 DIVISADERO ST
3000 BRODERICK ST
3100 BAKER ST
3200 LYON ST
3300 PRESIDIO AVE
3400 WALNUT ST
3500 LAUREL ST
3600 LOCUST ST
3700 SPRUCE ST
3800 MAPLE ST
3900 CHERRY ST
END ARGUELLO BLVD

CLAYTON ST SF 9 C1
CLAYTON ST SF 10 A3
S FROM FULTON ST BETWEEN COLE ST
AND ASHBURY ST TO MARKET ST
2 FULTON ST
100 GROVE ST
200 HAYES ST
FELL ST
400 OAK ST
500 PAGE ST
600 HAIGHT ST
700 WALLER ST
800 FREDERICK ST
CARL ST
PARNASSUS AVE
1100 ASHBURY ST
1200 17TH ST
1300 DEMING ST
1400 PEMBERTON PL
CORBETT ST
END MARKET ST
CLEARFIELD DR SF 12 B3
S FROM SLOAT BLVD BETWEEN
WESTMOORLAND DR & MORNINGSIDE DR
TO LAKE MERCED BLVD
CLEARY CT SF 6 B2
S FROM 1400 GEARY ST
S AND W TO LAGUNA ST
CLEMENT ST SF 4 A3
CLEMENT ST SF 5 A2
W FROM ARGUELLO BLVD BETWEEN
GEARY BLVD AND CORNWALL
ST TO 45TH AV
2 ARGUELLO BLVD
100 2ND AVE
200 3RD AVE
300 4TH AVE
400 5TH AVE
500 6TH AVE
600 7TH AVE
700 8TH AVE
800 9TH AVE
900 10TH AVE
1000 11TH AVE
1100 12TH AVE
FUNSTON AVE
PARK PRESIDIO BLVD
1300 14TH AVE
1400 15TH AVE
1500 16TH AVE
1600 17TH AVE
1700 18TH AVE
1800 19TH AVE
1900 20TH AVE
2000 21ST AVE
2100 22ND AVE
2200 23RD AVE
2300 24TH AVE
2400 25TH AVE
2500 26TH AVE
2600 27TH AVE
2700 28TH AVE
2800 29TH AVE
2900 30TH AVE
3000 31ST AVE
3100 32ND AVE
3200 33RD AVE
3300 34TH AVE
3400 35TH AVE
3500 36TH AVE
3600 37TH AVE
3700 38TH AVE
3800 39TH AVE
3900 40TH AVE
4000 41ST AVE
4100 42ND AVE
4200 43RD AVE
4300 44TH AVE
END 45TH AVE
CLEMENTINA ST SF 7 B2

CLEMENTINA ST SF 11 A1
W FROM S 1ST ST BETWEEN
TEHAMA ST AND FOLSOM ST
TO 9TH ST
2 1ST ST
ECKER ST
OSCAR AL
132 2ND ST
200 3RD ST
300 4TH ST
400 5TH ST
6TH ST
600 SUMNER ST
700 8TH ST
END 9TH ST
CLEVELAND ST SF 7 A3
SW FROM S SHERMAN ST BETWEEN
FOLSOM ST AND HARRISON ST
TO 7TH ST
CLIFFORD TER SF 10 A2
NW FROM ROOSEVELT WY TO
ASHBURY ST
2 ROOSEVELT WAY
100 UPPER TERR
END ASHBURY ST
CLINTON PARK SF 10 C1
W FROM S STEVENSON ST
BETWEEN DUBOCE AV AND 14TH ST
TO DOLORES ST
2 STEVENSON ST
100 VALENCIA ST
200 GUERRERO ST
END DOLORES ST
CLIPPER ST SF 14 A1
W FROM S DOLORES BETWEEN
25TH ST AND 26TH ST TO PORTOLA DR
2 DOLORES ST
100 CHURCH ST
200 SANCHEZ ST
300 NOE ST
400 CASTRO ST
500 DIAMOND ST
600 DOUGLASS ST
HOMESTEAD ST
700 HOFFMAN AVE
FOUNTAIN ST
800 GRAND VIEW AVE
HIGH ST
END PORTOLA DR
CLIPPER TER SF 14 A1
OFF CLIPPER ST BETWEEN
GRAND VIEW AV AND HIGH ST
CLOVER LN SF 10 A3
S FROM CASSELLI AV W OF
DOUGLASS ST TO CORWIN ST
CLOVER ST SF 10 A2
S FROM 18TH ST W OF
DOUGLASS ST TO CASSELLI AV
CLYDE ST SF 7 A1
N FROM TOWNSEND ST BETWEEN
3RD ST AND 4TH ST TO BLUXOME ST
COCHRANE ST SF 17 B1
NW FROM MANSEAU ST TO SPEAR AV
CODMAN PL SF 3 A3
S FROM WASHINGTON ST BETWEEN
POWELL ST AND MASON ST TO CLAY ST
COHEN PL SF 6 C2
S FROM ELLIS ST BETWEEN
LEAVENWORTH ST AND HYDE ST
COLBY ST SF 15 A3
COLBY ST SF 21 A1
S FROM SWEENY ST BETWEEN
DARTMOUTH ST AND UNIVERSITY ST
TO MANSELL ST
SWEENY ST
SILVER AVE
100 SILLIMAN ST
FELTON ST
600 WOOLSEY ST
700 DWIGHT ST

800 OLMSTEAD ST
END MANSELL ST
COLE ST SF 9 C2
S FROM FULTON ST BETWEEN
CLAYTON ST AND SHRADER ST
TO POINT S OF CARMEL ST
2 FULTON ST
100 GROVE ST
200 HAYES ST
FELL ST
400 OAK ST
500 PAGE ST
600 HAIGHT ST
700 WALLER ST
BEULAH ST
800 FREDERICK ST
900 CARL ST
1000 PARNASSUS ST
1100 GRATTAN ST
1200 ALMA ST
1300 RIVOLI ST
1400 17TH ST
1500 CARMEL ST
END PT S OF CARMEL ST
COLEMAN ST SF 17 B1
SW FROM HUDSON ST E OF
FRIEDELL ST TO JERROLD AV
HUDSON ST
INNES AVE
END JERROLD AVE
COLERIDGE AV SF 14 C2
SW FROM COSO AV BETWEEN
MISSION ST AND PROSPECT AV
TO CORTLAND AV
2 COSO AVE
POWERS AVE
100 FAIR AVE
ESMERALDA AVE
200 VIRGINIA AVE
250 GODEUS ST
HEYMAN ST
300 EUGENIA AVE
KINGSTON AVE
END CORTLAND AVE
COLIN PL SF 7 A2
NE FROM JONES ST BETWEEN
GEARY ST AND POST ST
COLIN P KELLY ST SF 7 C3
NW FROM TOWNSEND ST BETWEEN
1ST ST AND 2ND ST TO BRANNAN ST
COLLEGE AV SF 14 B3
N FROM JUSTIN DR TO MISSION ST
TO E OF SAN JOSE AV
S TO ST MARYS AV
2 ST MARYS AVE
200 MISSION ST
300 GENEBERN WAY
JUSTIN DR
400 MURRAY ST
500 BENTON AVE
END JUSTIN DR
COLLEGE TER SF 14 B3
NW FROM 3900 MISSION ST BETWEEN
COLLEGE AV AND ST MARY AV
COLLINGWOOD ST SF 10 A2
S FROM 17TH ST BETWEEN
CASTRO ST AND DIAMOND ST
S TO 22ND ST
2 MARKET ST
100 18TH ST
200 19TH ST
300 20TH ST
400 21ST ST
END 22ND ST
COLLINS ST SF 5 C2
S FROM MAYFAIR DR BETWEEN
WOOD ST AND BLAKE ST TO ANZA ST
COLON AV SF 13 B3
N FROM POINT S OF GREENWOOD AV
TO BRENTWOOD AV

2 PT S OF GREENWOOD
100 GREENWOOD AVE
200 MONTECITO AVE
300 MONTEREY BLVD
400 MANGELS AVE
END BRENTWOOD ST
COLONIAL WY SF 20 A1
NW FROM 1800 SAN JOSE AV
COLTON ST SF 10 C1
NE FROM GOUGH ST BETWEEN
MARKET ST AND OTIS ST
COLUMBIA SQ ST SF 7 A3
SE FROM S FOLSOM ST BETWEEN
6TH ST AND 7TH ST TO
HARRISON ST
COLUMBUS AV SF 2 C2
COLUMBUS AV SF 3 A2
NW FROM JUCTION MONTGOMERY
ST AND WASHINGTON ST
TO BEACH ST
2 MONTGOMERY ST
WASHINGTON ST
GIBB ST
100 JACKSON ST
KEARNY ST
200 PACIFIC AV
ALDER ST
300 BROADWAY
338 GRANT AVE
400 VALLEJO ST
500 STOCKTON ST
GREEN ST
UNION ST
POWELL ST
GROVER PL
700 FILBERT ST
800 GREENWICH ST
830 MASON ST
900 LOMBARD ST
NEWELL ST
1000 TAYLOR ST
CHESTNUT ST
HOUSTON ST
1100 FRANCISCO ST
JONES ST
1200 BAY ST
1300 NORTH POINT ST
END BEACH ST
COLUSA PL SF 10 C1
SE FROM COLTON ST BETWEEN 12TH ST
AND BRADY ST TO CHASE ST
COMERFORD ST SF 14 B1
E FROM SANCHEZ ST BETWEEN
27TH ST & DUNCAN ST TO CHURCH ST
COMMER CT SF 15 C3
SOUTH FROM NEWCOMB AV TO
GARLINGTON CT
COMMERCE ST SF 3 B2
W FROM S FRONT ST BETWEEN
GREEN ST AND UNION ST
TO BATTERY ST
COMMERCIAL ST SF 3 A3
W FROM BATTERY ST BETWEEN
SACRAMENTO ST AND CLAY ST
TO GRANT AV
2 THE EMBARCADERO
100 DRUMM ST
200 DAVIS ST
300 FRONT ST
400 BATTERY ST
500 SANSOME ST
LEIDESDORFF ST
600 MONTGOMERY ST
700 KEARNY ST
END GRANT AVE
COMMONWEALTH AV SF 5 C2
S FROM CALIFORNIA ST TO
GEARY BLVD BETWEEN PARKER AV
AND JORDAN AV
2 CALIFORNIA ST

1988 SAN FRANCISCO COUNTY CROSS STREET INDEX

100 EUCLID AVE
END GEARY BLVD
COMPTON RD SF 1 A3
NE FROM WASHINGTON BLVD
CONCORTHEN SE TO WASHINGTON BLVD
CONCORD ST SF 20 A2
SW FROM MISSION ST BETWEEN
ALLISON ST AND FLORENTINE ST
TO HANOVER ST
2 MISSION ST
CROSS ST
100 MORSE ST
200 BRUNSWICK ST
END WATT AVE
CONCOURSE DR SF 9 B1
IN GOLDEN GATE PARK
CONGDON AV SF 14 B3
E OF CRAUT ST FROM CANAL
ST TO SILVER AV
2 CANAL ST
100 TRUMBULL ST
200 NEY ST
300 MAYNARD ST
END SILVER AVE
CONGO ST SF 14 A3
N FROM CIRCULAR AV AND
E TO BOSWORTH ST
2 CIRCULAR AVE
100 FLOOD AVE
200 HEARST AVE
300 MONTEREY BLVD
400 JOOST AVE
500 MANGELS AVE
MELROSE AVE
600 STILLINGS ST
END BOSWORTH ST
CONKLING ST SF 15 B3
N FROM SILVER AV NEAR AUGUSTA ST
CONNECTICUT ST SF 11 B2
S FROM 16TH ST BETWEEN
MISSOURI ST AND ARKANSAS ST
TO ARMY ST
2 16TH ST
100 17TH ST
200 MARIPOSA ST
300 18TH ST
400 19TH ST
500 20TH ST
700 22ND ST
WISCONSIN ST
1100 25TH ST
26TH ST
1300 ARMY ST
CONRAD ST SF 14 A2
W OF DIAMOND ST FROM
SUSSEX ST N TO DIAMOND
CONSERVATORY DR SF 9 B1
IN GOLDEN GATE PARK
CONSTANSO WY SF 12 C3
N FROM 1500 SLOAT BLVD
TO CRESTLAKE DR
CONVERSE ST SF 11 A1
NW FROM S BRYANT ST BETWEEN
8TH ST AND 9TH ST
COOK ST SF 5 C2
S FROM POINT N OF GEARY BLVD
BETWEEN BLAKE ST AND
SPRUCE ST TO ANZA ST
COOPER AL SF 3 A3
S FROM S JACKSON ST BETWEEN
KEARNY AND GRANT AV
COPPER AL SF 10 A3
FROM MARKET ST NEAR
SHORT ST SW TO BURNETT ST
2 MARKET ST
100 CORBETT ST
GRAYSTONE TER
END BURNETT ST
CORA ST SF 21 A3
S FROM LELAND AV BETWEEN
DELTA ST AND RUTLAND ST
TO A POINT N OF COUNTY LINE
CORAL CT SF 17 A1
N FROM KIRKWOOD AV IN
HUNTERS PT NAVAL RES
CORAL RD SF 11 B3
W OF CAROLINA ST BETWEEN
23RD ST AND 25TH ST
CORALINO LN SF 14 A1
S FROM CAMEO WY TO AMBER DR
CORBETT AV SF 10 A3
SW FROM 17TH ST AND
DOUGLASS ST AND S TO MARKET ST
2 DOUGLASS ST
17TH ST
100 ORD ST
130 HATTIE ST
200 CORBIN PL
DANVERS ST
300 MARS ST
19TH ST
400 PEMBERTON PL
CLAYTON ST
500 IRON AL
600 COPPER AL
YUKON ST
GLENDALE ST
GRAYSTONE TER
700 ROMAIN ST
MORGAN ST
800 DIXIE AL
ARGENT AL
900 HOPKINS ST
23RD ST
956 GOLDING AL
END 24TH ST
CORBIN PL SF 10 A2
S FROM 17TH ST E OF
TEMPLE ST TO CORBETT AV
CORDELIA ST SF 3 A3
N FROM S PACIFIC AV BETWEEN
STOCKTON ST AND POWELL ST
TO BROADWAY
CORDOVA ST SF 20 B3
SE FROM S ROLPH ST E OF
NAPLES ST TO BALTIMORE WY
2 ROLPH ST
100 ATHENS ST
200 SEVILLE ST
300 MUNICH ST
400 PRAGUE ST
CHICAGO WY
500 WINDING WY
END COUNTY LINE
CORNWALL ST SF 5 B2
W FROM ARGUELLO BLVD BETWEEN
CLLEMENT ST AND CALIFORNIA ST
TO CALIFORNIA ST
CALIFORNIA ST
2 ARGUELLO BLVD
100 2ND AVE
200 3RD AVE
300 4TH AVE
400 5TH AVE
END CALIFORNIA ST
CORONA ST SF 19 B1
N FROM HOLLOWAY AV TO
OCEAN AV BETWEEN DE SOTO ST
AND BORICO ST
2 HOLLOWAY AVE
100 URBANO DR
END PT N OF URBANO DR
CORONADO ST SF 21 B2
SW FROM INGERSON AV TO
JAMESTOWN AV BETWEEN HAWES AND
GRIFFITH ST
CPL ZAVOVITZ ST SF 1 C2
N FROM LUNDEEN ST
CORTES AV SF 13 B2
N FROM 100 TARAVAL ST TO
DORANTES ST
CORTLAND AV SF 14 C2
CORTLAND AV SF 15 A2
E FROM 3501 MISSION ST BETWEEN
KINGSTON AV AND SANTA MARINA ST
TO BAY SHORE BLVD
2 MISSION ST
COLERIDGE ST
100 PROSPECT ST
WINFIELD ST
200 ELSIE ST
BONVIEW ST
300 BOCANA ST
400 BENNINGTON ST
WOOL ST
500 ANDOVER ST
600 MOULTRIE ST
700 ANDERSON ST
800 ELLSWORTH ST
900 GATES ST
1000 FOLSOM ST
1100 BANKS ST
1200 PRENTISS ST
1300 NEVADA ST
1400 PUTNAM ST
NEBRASKA ST
BRONTE ST
1500 BRADFORD ST
1600 PERALTA ST
1700 HOLLADAY AVE
HILTON ST
END BAY SHORE BLVD
CORWIN ST SF 10 A3
NW FROM DOUGLASS ST S OF 20TH ST
TO CLOVER LN
2 DOUGLASS ST
100 ACME AL
END CLOVER LN
COSGROVE ST SF 15 A2
SW FROM BAY SHORE BLVD
S OF OAKDALE AV
COSMO PL SF 7 A2
W FROM S TAYLOR ST BETWEEN
POST ST AND SUTTER ST
TO JONES ST
COSO AV SF 14 C1
FROM MISSION ST SE TO BOCANA AV
MISSION ST
PRECITA AVE
BERNAL AVE
MONTEZUMA ST
LUNDY LANE
150 PROSPECT ST
200 WINFIELD ST
AZTEC ST
ELSIE ST
BONVIEW ST
SHOTWELL ST
END BOCANA ST
COSTA ST SF 15 A1
SE FROM BREWSTER ST BETWEEN
RUTLEDGE ST AND FAITH ST
TO A POINT E OF HOLLADAY AV
COTTAGE ROW SF 6 B2
N FROM S SUTTER ST BETWEEN
WEBSTER ST AND FILLMORE ST
TO BUSH ST
COTTER ST SF 14 A3
SE FROM 4400 MISSION ST BETWEEN
THERESA ST AND FRANCIS ST
2 MISSION ST
100 ALEMANY BLVD
200 CAYUGA AVE
END SAN JOSE AVE
COUNTRY CLUB DR SF 12 B3
BETWEEN SUNSET BLVD AND
SKYLINE BLVD
S OF SLOAT BLVD
COVENTRY CT SF 13 C2
N FROM CRESTA VISTA DR
ONE BLK E OF BELLA VISTA
COVENTRY LN SF 13 C2
EXTENSION OF COVENTRY CT
COWELL PL SF 3 B2
S FROM S VALLEJO ST BETWEEN
BATTERY ST AND SANSOME ST
COWLES ST SF 1 A2
IN PRESIDIO
CRAGMONT AV SF 13 B1
S FROM ROCKRIDGE DR BETWEEN
10TH AV AND 12TH AV
TO QUINTARA ST
CRAGS CT SF 14 A2
NW FROM BERKELEY WY W OF
DIAMOND HEIGHTS BLVD
CRAN PL SF 6 B3
N FROM MCALLISTER ST BETWEEN
FILLMORE ST AND WEBSTER ST
CRANE ST SF 21 B1
S FROM PAUL AV BETWEEN WHEAT ST
AND EXETER ST
CRANLEIGH DR SF 13 A3
W FROM LAGUNITAS DR ONE
BLOCK W OR PORTOLA DR
CRANSTON RD SF 1 A2
IN PRESIDIO
NW FROM MERCHANT RD
CRAUT ST SF 14 B3
S FROM TRUMBULL ST
E OF MISSION ST TO SILVER AV
2 CANAL ST
100 TRUMBULL ST
200 NEY ST
300 MAYNARD ST
END SILVER AVE
CRESCENT AV SF 14 C3
E FROM MISSION ST S
OF RICHLAND ST TO PUTNAM ST
2 MISSION ST
LEESE ST
100 AGNON AVE
200 MURRAY ST
ARNOLD AVE
300 ROSCOE ST
PORTER ST
BACHE ST
400 ANDOVER ST
500 MOULTRIE ST
600 ANDERSON ST
700 ELLSWORTH ST
800 GATES ST
900 FOLSOM ST
1000 BANKS ST
1100 PRENTISS ST
NEVADA ST
PUTNAM ST
BRONTE ST
BRADFORD ST
CRESPI DR SF 19 A2
NE FROM JUAN BAUTISTA CIRCLE
BETWEEN GRIJALVA DR
AND FUENTE AV TO SERRANO DR
CRESTA VISTA DR SF 13 B3
W FROM BELLA VISTA WY TO BAXTER
AL & CASITAS AV, 4 BLKS N OF
MONTEREY BLVD
BELLA VISTA WY
COVENTRY CT
LULU AL
EMIL LN
GLOBE AL
BAXTER AL
END CASITAS AVE
CRESTLAKE DR SF 12 B2
FROM 800 SLOAT BLVD W
TO 34TH AV AND WAWONA ST
CRESTLINE DR SF 13 C1
W FROM BURNETT AV 3 BLKS
N OF PORTOLA DR TO PARKRIDGE DR
CRESTMONT DR SF 9 B3
W FROM CHRISTOPHER DR ONE
BLK FROM GLENHAVEN LN
CRESTWELL WK SF 9 A3
OFF JUNCTION OF NORIEGA
ST AND 15TH AV
CRISP RD SF 17 A1
N FROM SPEAR AV TO PALOU AV
IN HUNTERS PT NAVAL RESERVATION
CRISSY FIELD AV SF 1 A2
E FROM LINCOLN BLVD TO MASON ST
CROSS ST SF 20 A2
SW FROM POPE ST NEAR
MISSION ST TO CONCORD ST
CROSS OVER DR SF 8 C
IN GOLDEN GATE PARK
CROWN TER SF 9 C3
S FROM S CLARENDON AV
TO PEMBERTON PL
CRYSTAL ST SF 19 B
N FROM DE LONG ST TO ALEMANY BLV
CUBA AL SF 14 A
EAST FROM THE INTERSECTION OF
MARIETTA DR, MOLIMO DR AND
TERESITA BLVD
CUESTA CT SF 14 A
ONE BLK N FROM CORBETT AND
MARKET ST JUNCTION
CULEBRA TER SF 2 C
N FROM A POINT N OF LOMBARD ST
BETWEEN LARKIN ST AND POLK ST TO
A POINT S OF FRANCISCO ST
2 LOMBARD ST
100 CHESTNUT ST
END FRANCISCO ST
CUMBERLAND ST SF 10 E
W FROM S GUERRERO ST BETWEEN
19TH ST AND 20TH ST
TO A POINT E OF NOE ST
3 GUERRERO ST
DOLORES ST
200 CHURCH ST
300 SANCHEZ ST
END NOE ST
CUNNINGHAM PL SF 10
W FROM S VALENCIA ST BETWEEN
19TH ST AND 20TH ST
CURTIS ST SF 20
S FROM S ROLPH ST BETWEEN
POPE ST AND NEWTON ST
TO PRAGUE ST
2 ROLPH ST
100 MORSE ST
200 BRUNSWICK ST
END PRAGUE ST
CUSHMAN ST SF 3
FROM CALIFORNIA ST TO
SACRAMENTO ST BETWEEN MASON ST
AND TAYLOR ST
CUSTER AV SF 15
NW FROM 3RD ST TO RANKIN ST
CUSTOM HOUSE PL SF 3
N FROM S WASHINGTON ST BETWEEN
BATTERY ST AND SANSOME ST
TO JACKSON ST
CUTLER AV SF 12
W FROM 47TH AV TO THE GREAT
HIGHWAY BETWEEN WAWONA ST
AND VICENTE ST
CUVIER ST SF 14
S FROM SAN JOSE AV BETWEEN
MARSILLY ST AND MILTON ST
CYPRESS ST SF 14
S FROM S 24TH ST BETWEEN
SOUTH VAN NESS AV AND
CAPP ST S TO 26TH ST
CYRUS PL SF 2
S FROM S BROADWAY BETWEEN
LEAVENWORTH ST AND HYDE ST
D ST SF 17
S FROM VAN KEUREN AV TO SPEAR

IN HUNTERS POINT
DAGGETT ST SF 11 B1
NE FROM 1000 16TH ST TO 7TH ST
300 7TH ST
END 16TH ST
DAKOTA ST SF 11 B3
SE FROM 23RD ST TO TEXAS ST
E OF CONNECTICUT ST
DALE PL SF 6 C3
S FROM S GOLDEN GATE AV BETWEEN
LEAVENWORTH ST AND HYDE ST
DALEWOOD WY SF 13 B2
W FROM MYRA ST TO LANSDALE AV
DANL BURNHAM CT SF 6 B2
BETWEEN VAN NESS AV AND
FRANKLIN ST
DANTON ST SF 14 B3
NW FROM CAYUGA AV W OF
LYELL ST
DANVERS ST SF 10 A2
S FROM CORBETT AV TO 19TH ST
2 CORBETT AVE
MERRITT ST
18TH ST
100 MARKET ST
200 CASELLI AVE
END 19TH ST
DARIEN WY SF 13 B3
E FROM JUNIPERO SERRA BLVD
TO KENWOOD WY
2 JUNIPERO SERRA BL
100 SAN RAFAEL WAY
200 SAN FERNANDO WAY
300 SAN LEANDRO WAY
400 SANTA ANA AVE
500 SAN BENITO WAY
APTOS AVE
600 SAN ALESO AVE
700 WESTGATE DR
800 MANOR DR
900 NORTH GATE DR
END KENWOOD WAY
DARRELL PL SF 3 A2
N FROM 200 FILBERT ST BETWEEN
MONTGOMERY ST AND SANSOME ST
DARTMOUTH ST SF 15 A3
DARTMOUTH ST SF 21 A1
S FROM SWEENY ST W OF BOWDOIN ST
TO A POINT S OF MANSELL ST
SWEENY ST
2 SILVER AVE
100 SILLIMAN ST
FELTON ST
RESERVOIR
600 WOOLSEY ST
700 DWIGHT ST
800 OLMSTEAD ST
END MANSELL ST
DAVIDSON AV SF 15 C1
S FROM POINT NW OF RANKIN ST
TO 3RD ST
DAVIS ST SF 3 B3
N FROM S MARKET ST BETWEEN
DRUMM ST AND FRONT ST
TO THE BAY
2 MARKET ST
PINE ST
100 CALIFORNIA ST
200 SACRAMENTO ST
COMMERCIAL ST
300 CLAY ST
400 WASHINGTON ST
500 JACKSON ST
600 PACIFIC AVE
700 BROADWAY
800 VALLEJO ST
GREEN ST
END THE EMBARCADERO
DAWNVIEW WY SF 14 A1
W FROM BURNETT AV TO GLENVIEW DR
DAWSON PL SF 3 A3
E FROM 1000 MASON ST BETWEEN
SACRAMENTO ST AND CLAY ST
DAY ST SF 14 B3
W FROM S SAN JOSE AV
BETWEEN 29TH ST AND 30TH ST
TO A POINT W OF CASTRO ST
2 SAN JOSE AVE
100 DOLORES ST
200 CHURCH ST
300 SANCHEZ ST
400 NOE ST
END CASTRO ST
DEARBORN ST SF 10 C2
FROM S S 17TH ST BETWEEN
VALENCIA ST AND GUERRERO ST
TO 18TH ST
DE BOOM ST SF 7 B3
E FROM S 2ND ST BETWEEN
BRYANT ST AND BRANNAN ST
DECATUR ST SF 11 A1
SE FROM S BRYANNT ST BETWEEN
7TH ST AND 8TH ST
DECKER AL SF 7 A3
W FROM S 7TH ST BETWEEN
FOLSOM ST AND HARRISON ST
DEDMAN CT SF 15 C2
W OFF CASHMERE ST ONE BLOCK S
OF HUDSON AV
DEEMS RD SF 1 B3
IN PRESIDIO
W FROM WASHINGTON BLVD
DEFOREST WY SF 10 A2
W FROM BEAVER ST W OF
CASTRO ST TO FLINT ST
DE HARO ST SF 11 B1
S FROM DIVISION BETWEEN RHODE
ISLAND ST AND CAROLINA ST
TO 26TH ST
2 DIVISION ST
BERRY ST
100 ALAMEDA ST
200 15TH ST
300 16TH ST
400 17TH ST
500 MARIPOSA ST
600 18TH ST
700 19TH ST
800 20TH ST
SOUTHERN HTS AVE
1000 22ND ST
1200 23RD ST
1300 24TH ST
1400 25TH ST
END 26TH ST
DEHON ST SF 10 B2
S FROM 3415 16TH ST BETWEEN
CHURST ST AND SANCHEZ ST
TOWARDS 17TH ST
DELANO AV SF 20 A2
E OF SAN JOSE AV S FROM
S SANTA YSABEL AV TO
OTTAWA AV
2 SANTA YSABEL AVE
100 SAN JUAN AVE
200 SANTA YNEZ AVE
RUDDEN AVE
MEDA AVE
400 OCEAN AVE
500 ONEIDA AVE
600 SENECA AVE
NAVAJO AVE
700 GENEVA AVE
SEMINOLE AVE
800 NIAGARA AVE
SHAWNEE AVE
900 MT VERNON AVE
NAHUA AVE
END OTTOWA AVE
DELGADO PL SF 2 C3
E FROM S HYDE ST BETWEEN
GREEN ST AND UNION ST
DELLBROOK AV SF 9 C3
DELLBROOK AV SF 13 C1
S OFF OLYMPIA WY E
AND N TO PALO ALTO AV
DELMAR ST SF 10 A1
S FROM S WALLER ST BETWEEN
MASONIC AV AND ASHBURY ST
TO PIEDMONT ST
2 WALLER ST
100 FREDERICK ST
END PIEDMONT ST
DEL MONTE ST SF 20 A2
N FROM OTTAWA AV TO A POINT
NE OF MT VERNON AV
W OF MISSION ST
5200 MISSION ST
2 NIAGARA AVE
100 MT VERNON AVE
END OTTAWA AVE
DE LONG ST SF 19 B3
W FROM SAN JOSE AV NEAR
COUNTY LINE TO JOHN DALY BLVD
2 SAN JOSE AVE
LIEBIG ST
RICE ST
GOETHE ST
RHINE ST
100 CRYSTAL ST
WILSON ST
200 ORIZABA AVE
FLOURNOY ST
300 HEAD ST
SHAKESPEARE ST
SANTA CRUZ AVE
SAN LUIS AV
SAN MATEO AV
END SAN DIEGO AV
DEL SUR AV SF 13 C2
E FROM 901 PORTOLA DR
TO CHAVES AV
DELTA PL SF 7 A2
NE FROM 600 MASON ST BETWEEN
SUTTER ST AND BUSH ST
DELTA ST SF 21 A2
BETWEEN ELLIOTT ST AND RUTLAND ST
S FROM ANKENY ST TO SUNNYDALE AV
2 WILDE AVE
TIOGA AVE
TUCKER AVE
100 CAMPBELL AVE
200 TEDDY AVE
300 ARLETA AVE
400 RAYMOND AVE
500 LELAND AVE
600 VISITACION AVE
END SUNNYDALE AVE
DEL VALE AV SF 13 C2
SE FROM EVELYN WY TO
OSHAUGHNESSY BLVD
DEMING ST SF 10 A2
E FROM CLAYTON ST TO A
POINT E OF URANUS TER
DE MONTFORT AV SF 19 B1
W FROM MIRAMAR AV TO ASHTON AV
2 MIRAMAR AVE
100 CAPITOL AVE
200 FAXON AVE
300 JULES AVE
END ASHTON AVE
DENSLOWE DR SF 19 A2
E FROM 19TH AV AND S TO
BANBURY DR PARALLEL WITH 19TH AV
DENT RD SF 1 A3
IN PRESIDIO S FROM
COMPTON RD TO WASHINGTON BLVD
DERBY ST SF 7 A2
W FROM S MASON ST BETWEEN
GEARY ST AND POST ST TO
TAYLOR ST
DESMOND ST SF 21 A3
W OF SAN BRUNO AV FROM
LELAND AV TO SUNNYDALE AV
DE SOTO ST SF 19 B1
BETWEEN CORONA ST AND
VICTORIA ST FROM HOLLOWAY
AV N TO URBANO DR
DETROIT ST SF 14 A3
N FROM CIRCULAR AV TO
STILLINGS AV
2 CIRCULAR AVE
100 JUDSON AVE
200 STAPLES AVE
300 FLOOD AVE
400 HEARST AVE
500 MONTEREY BLVD
600 JOOST AVE
700 MANGELS AVE
800 MELROSE AVE
END STILLINGS AVE
DEVONSHIRE WY SF 9 B3
E FROM WARREN DR BETWEEN
OAKHURST LN & CHRISTOPHER DR
TO CRESTMONT DR
DEWEY BLVD SF 13 B1
S FROM LAGUNA HONDA BLVD S
TO CLAREMONT BLVD
DE WOLF ST SF 19 C3
W FROM LAWRENCE ST NEAR
SAN JOSE AV TO SICKLES AV
DIAMOND ST SF 10 A3
DIAMOND ST SF 14 A2
S FROM S 17TH ST BETWEEN
COLLINGSWOOD ST AND
EUREKA ST TO CIRCULAR AV
2 17TH ST
MARKET ST
100 18TH ST
200 19TH ST
300 20TH ST
400 21ST ST
500 22ND ST
ALVARADO ST
600 23RD ST
700 ELIZABETH ST
800 24TH ST
900 JERSEY ST
1000 25TH ST
1100 CLIPPER ST
1200 26TH ST
1300 ARMY ST
1400 27TH ST
1500 DUNCAN ST
1600 28TH ST
1700 VALLEY ST
1800 29TH ST
2590 ARBOR ST
SUSSEX ST
SURREY ST
2790 CHENERY ST
2870 BOSWORTH ST
END CIRCULAR AV
DIAMOND HTS BL SF 14 A1
S FROM CLIPPER ST AT PORTOLA
DR TO ARBOR ST
DUNCAN ST
GOLDMINE DR
DIAMOND ST
ADDISON ST
BERKELEY WAY
END ARBOR ST
DIANA ST SF 15 B3
S FROM THORNTON AV TO
WILLIAMS AV
DIAZ AV SF 19 A2
W FROM GONZALES DR TO
JUAN BAUTISTA CIR
DICHA AL SF 5 C2
S FROM LUPINE AV W OF LAUREL ST
TO WOOD ST
DICHIERA CT SF 19 C2
N FROM ELLINGTON 3 BLKS E OF
MISSION ST
DIGBY ST SF 14 B2
S FROM ADDISON ST 3
BLKS E OF DIAMOND HEIGHTS BLVD
TO EVERSON ST
DIKEMAN SF 7 A2
W FROM S 14TH ST BETWEEN
OFARRELL ST AND ELLIS ST
DIVISADERO ST SF 2 A3
DIVISADERO ST SF 6 A3
DIVISADERO ST SF 10 A1
FROM N S 14TH ST BET
SCOTT ST AND BRODERICK ST
TO MARINA BLVD
2 14TH ST
100 DUBOCE ST
200 WALLER ST
250 HAIGHT ST
300 PAGE ST
400 OAK ST
500 FELL ST
600 HAYES ST
700 GROVE ST
800 FULTON ST
900 MCALLISTER ST
1000 GOLDEN GATE AVE
1100 TURK ST
1200 EDDY ST
1300 ELLIS ST
1400 OFARRELL ST
1500 GEARY ST
GARDEN ST
1600 POST ST
1700 SUTTER ST
1800 BUSH ST
1900 PINE ST
2000 CALIFORNIA ST
2100 SACRAMENTO ST
2200 CLAY ST
2300 WASHINGTON ST
2500 PACIFIC AVE
2600 BROADWAY
2700 VALLEJO ST
2800 GREEN ST
2900 UNION ST
3000 FILBERT ST
3100 GREENWICH ST
3200 LOMBARD ST
3300 CHESTNUT ST
3400 FRANCISCO ST
3500 BAY ST
3600 NORTH POINT ST
3700 BEACH ST
3800 JEFFERSON ST
END MARINA BLVD
DIVISION ST SF 11 B1
W FROM KING ST AND DE HARO ST
TO FLORIDA ST
2 KING ST
DE HARO ST
100 TOWNSEND ST
KANSAS ST
VERMONT ST
SAN BRUNO AVE
200 9TH ST
UTAH ST
BRANNAN ST
POTRERO AVE
300 10TH ST
YORK ST
450 BRYANT ST
END FLORIDA ST
DIXIE AL SF 10 A3
W FROM CORBETT AV TO BURNETT AV
TO BURNETT AV
DODGE PL SF 6 C2
S FROM S TURK ST BETWEEN

1988 SAN FRANCISCO COUNTY CROSS STREET INDEX

HYDE ST AND LARKIN ST
DOLORES ST SF 10 B1
DOLORES ST SF 14 B1
S FROM S MARKET ST BETWEEN
GUERRERO ST AND CHURCH ST
TO SAN JOSE AV
2 MARKET ST
CLINTON PARK
100 14TH ST
HIDALGO TER
200 15TH ST
230 ALERT AL
300 16TH ST
CHULA LN
400 17TH ST
DOLORES TER
DORLAND ST
18TH ST
19TH ST
CUMBERLAND ST
700 20TH ST
750 LIBERTY ST
800 21ST ST
900 22ND ST
1000 23RD ST
1100 24TH ST
1150 JERSEY ST
1200 25TH ST
1250 CLIPPER ST
1300 26TH ST
1350 ARMY ST
1400 27TH ST
1450 DUNCAN ST
1500 28TH ST
1550 VALLEY ST
1600 29TH ST
1650 DAY ST
1700 30TH ST
END SAN JOSE AVE
DOLORES TER SF 10 B2
OFF 401 DOLORES ST BETWEEN
17TH ST AND DORLAND ST
DOLPHIN CT SF 17 A1
N FROM KIRKWOOD AV IN
HUNTERS PT
DONAHUE ST SF 16 B3
DONAHUE ST SF 17 A1
SW FROM LOCKWOOD TO A POINT S
OF KIRKWOOD AV
KING AVE
HUDSON AVE
INNES AVE
JERROLD AVE
END KIRKWOOD AVE
DONNER AV SF 15 B3
SE FROM BAYSHORE BLVD & QUINT ST
DONNER AV SF 21 B1
SE FROM 3RD ST, FROM JENNINGS ST
TO INGALLS ST, & FROM FITCH ST
DORADO TER SF 19 B1
N FROM OCEAN AV 2 BLOCKS W
OF MIRAMAR AV
DORANTES AV SF 13 B1
W FROM S MAGELLAN AV AND THEN
PARALLEL WITH MAGELLAN AV TO A
POINT W OF CORTES AV
DORCAS WY SF 13 C2
N FROM FOERSTER ST TO
BELLA VISTA DR
DORCHESTER WY SF 13 B2
NW FROM 1300 PORTOLA DR
TO CLAREMONT BLVD
PORTOLA DR
ULLOA ST
END CLAREMONT BLVD
DORE ST SF 11 A1
S FROM S HOWARD ST BETWEEN
9TH ST AND 10TH ST TO BRANNAN ST
2 HOWARD ST
100 FOLSOM ST
SHERIDAN ST
200 HARRISON ST
300 BRYANT ST
END BRANNAN ST
DORIC AL SF 3 A3
S FROM 901 JACKSON ST BETWEEN
POWELL ST AND MASON ST
DORLAND ST SF 10 B2
W FROM S GUERRERO ST BETWEEN
17TH ST AND 18TH ST W TO
SANCHEZ ST
2 GUERRERO ST
100 DOLORES ST
200 CHURCH ST
END SANCHEZ ST
DORMAN AV SF 15 A2
SW FROM PALOU ST BETWEEN
APPAREL WY AND INDUSTRIAL ST TO
BARNEVELD AV
DORMITORY RD SF 16 A3
S FROM NORTHRIDGE RD TO
KISKA RD
DOUBLE ROCK ST SF 21 C1
E FROM CAMERON WY
2 BLKS N OF FITZGERALD ST
DOUGLASS ST SF 10 A3
DOUGLASS ST SF 14 A1
S FROM A POINT N OF 17TH ST
TO 28TH ST
2 ORD CT
100 CORBETT AVE
17TH ST
MARKET ST
200 18TH ST
230 CASELLI AVE
300 19TH ST
324 CARSON ST
366 SEWARD ST
20TH ST
CORWIN ST
400 ROMAIN ST
500 21ST ST
600 22ND ST
ALVARADO ST
700 23RD ST
750 ELIZABETH ST
800 24TH ST
JERSEY ST
900 25TH ST
1000 CLIPPER ST
1100 26TH ST
1200 ARMY ST
1300 27TH ST
1400 DUNCAN ST
END 28TH ST
DOVE LOOP SF 1 A2
IN PRESIDIO
DOVER ST SF 7 C2
N FROM S BRANNAN ST BETWEEN
1ST ST AND 2ND ST
DOW PL SF 7 B2
SW FROM 2ND ST BETWEEN FOLSOM ST
AND HARRISON ST
DOWNEY ST SF 9 C2
S FROM S WALLER ST BETWEEN
ASHBURY ST AND CLAYTON ST
TO ASHBURY ST
2 WALLER ST
100 FREDERICK ST
END ASHBURY ST
DOYLE DR SF 1 B2
IN PRESIDIO
DRAKE ST SF 20 A3
S FROM S MUNICH ST TO
BALTIMORE WY
2 MUNICH ST
100 PRAGUE ST
200 WINDING WAY
END COUNTY LINE
DRUMM ST SF 3 B3
N FROM S MARKET ST BETWEEN
THE EMBARCADERO AND DAVIS ST
TO JACKSON ST
2 MARKET ST
CALIFORNIA ST
100 SACRAMENTO ST
COMMERCIAL ST
200 CLAY ST
300 WASHINGTON ST
400 JACKSON ST
DRUMMOND AL SF 15 B2
E FROM S QUINT ST BETWEEN
OAKDALE AV AND PALOU AV
TO DUNSHEE ST
DUBLIN ST SF 20 B2
S FROM S PERSIA AV E OF
PRAGUE ST TO A POINT S OF
RUSSIA ST
100 PERSIA AVE
200 RUSSIA AVE
END PT S OF RUSSIA AVE
DUBOCE AV SF 10 B1
FROM MISSION ST N OF 14TH
ST W TO BUENA VISTA AV
2 MISSION ST
OTIS ST
WOODWARD ST
STEVENSON ST
100 VALENCIA ST
132 ELGIN PARK
170 PEARL ST
200 GUERRERO ST
MARKET ST
300 BUCHANAN ST
392 WEBSTER ST
400 CHURCH ST
402 FILLMORE ST
BELCHER ST
SANCHEZ ST
STEINER ST
WALTER ST
NOE ST
700 SCOTT ST
CASTRO ST
800 DIVISADERO ST
900 ALPINE TERR
END BUENA VISTA AVE
DUDLEY RD SF 1 B3
IN PRESIDIO
S OF WASHINGTON BLVD
DUKES CT SF 15 C2
N OFF CASHMERE ST ONE BLOCK N
OF LA SALLE AV
DUNBAR AL SF 3 A3
S FROM WASHINGTON ST BETWEEN
MONTGOMERY ST AND KEARNY ST
TO MERCHANT ST
DUNCAN ST SF 14 B1
W FROM S TIFFANY AV BETWEEN
ARMY ST AND MISSION ST
TO DIAMOND HEIGHTS BLVD
TIFFANY AVE
SAN JOSE AVE
100 GUERRERO ST
200 DOLORES ST
300 CHURCH ST
400 SANCHEZ ST
500 NOE ST
600 CASTRO ST
NEWBERG ST
700 DIAMOND ST
800 DOUGLASS ST
END CLIPPER ST
DUNCOMBE AL SF 3 A3
N FROM S JACKSON ST BETWEEN
GRANT AV AND STOCKTON ST
DUNNES AL SF 3 A3
E FROM 1100 KEARNY ST BETWEEN
BROADWAY ST AND VALLEJO ST
DUNSHEE ST SF 15 B3
S FROM S DRUMMOND AL BETWEEN
PHELPS ST AND QUINT ST
TO PALOU AV
DUNSMUIR ST SF 15 A3
S FROM SWEENY ST BETWEEN
DARTMOUTH ST AND COLBY ST
TO SILVER AV
DWIGHT ST SF 21 A1
SW FROM SAN BRUNO AV S OF
WOOLSEY ST TO UNIVERSITY ST
2 SAN BRUNO AVE
100 GIRARD ST
200 BRUSSELS ST
300 GOTTINGEN ST
600 HAMILTON ST
700 BOWDOIN ST
800 DARTMOUTH ST
900 COLBY ST
END UNIVERSITY ST
DYNAMITE RD SF 1 A2
IN PRESIDIO
W FROM RALSTON AV
E ST SF 17 B1
SE FROM MORRELL ST TO MANSEAU
ST IN HUNTERS PT
EAGLE ST SF 10 A3
W FROM YUKON ST TO MARKET ST
2 YUKON ST
100 MONO ST
END MARKET ST
EARL ST SF 17 A1
SW FROM A POINT N OF INNES AV
TO NAVY RD
EASTMAN ST SF 2 C2
N FROM S GREEN ST BETWEEN
HYDE ST AND LARKIN ST
TO ALLEN ST
2 GREEN ST
RUSSELL ST
ROCKLAND ST
100 UNION ST
END ALLEN ST
EASTWOOD DR SF 19 B1
E AND N FROM MIRAMAR AV
TO MIRAMAR AV
2 MIRAMAR AVE
100 WILDWOOD AVE
MONTECITO AVE
END MIRAMAR AVE
EATON PL SF 3 A3
S FROM 701 GREEN ST BETWEEN
POWELL ST AND MASON ST
ECKER ST SF 7 B1
FROM STEVENSON STS TO
MISSION ST AND FROM
CLEMENTINA ST TO FOLSOM ST
BETWEEN 1ST ST AND 2ND ST
EDDY ST SF 6 A3
EDDY ST SF 7 A2
FROM MARKET ST & POWELL ST W
TO ST JOSEPHS AV
2 MARKET & POWELL STS
5TH ST
100 MASON ST
200 TAYLOR ST
300 JONES ST
WAGNER AL
400 LEAVENWORTH ST
500 HYDE ST
600 LARKIN ST
700 POLK ST
800 VAN NESS AVE
900 FRANKLIN ST
1000 GOUGH ST
1100 OCTAVIA ST
1200 LAGUNA ST
1300 BUCHANAN ST
1400 WEBSTER ST
1500 FILLMORE ST
1600 STEINER ST
BOURBIN ST
1700 PIERCE ST
FARREN ST
1800 SCOTT ST
1900 DIVISADERO ST
2000 BRODERICK ST
END ST JOSEPHS AV
EDGAR PL SF 19 C1
S FROM BRUCE AV NEAR
HAROLD AV
EDGARDO PL SF 3 A2
FROM 1701 GRANT AV BETWEEN
GREENWICH ST AND LOMBARD ST
EDGEHILL WY SF 13 B2
S FROM S GARCIA AV SW AND
NW TO GARCIA AV
EDGEWOOD AV SF 9 C2
S FROM FARNSWORTH LN W BLK W OF
WILLARD ST
100 FARNSWORTH ST
200 BELMONT AVE
EDIE RD SF 1 C2
IN PRESIDIO
S OF GORGAS AV
EDINBURGH ST SF 20 B2
SW FROM SILVER AV BETWEEN
MADRID ST AND NAPLES ST
TO GENEVA AV
2 SILVER AVE
100 PERU AVE
200 AVALON AVE
300 EXCELSIOR AVE
400 BRAZIL AVE
500 PERSIA AVE
600 RUSSIA AVE
700 FRANCE AVE
800 ITALY AVE
900 AMAZON AVE
END GENEVA AVE
EDITH ST SF 3 A2
FROM 1701 GRANT AV BETWEEN
GREENWICH ST AND LOMBARD ST
EDNA ST SF 19 C1
N FROM HAVELOCK ST TO
MELROSE AV BETWEEN DETROIT ST
AND FOERSTER ST
2 HAVELOCK ST
100 MARSTON AVE
200 JUDSON AVE
300 STAPLES AVE
400 FLOOD AVE
500 HEARST AVE
600 MONTEREY BLVD
700 JOOST AVE
800 MANGELS AVE
900 MELROSE AVE
EDWARD ST SF 5 B3
W FROM WILLARD ST TO
ARGUELLO BLVD N OF TURK ST
EGBERT AV SF 21 B1
SE FROM BAYSHORE BL NW
TO HAWEST ST
INGALLS ST
JENNINGS ST
KEITH ST
3RD ST
NEWHALL ST
PHELPS ST
END BAYSHORE BLVD
EL CAMINO DEL MARSF 4 A2
W FROM 24TH AV TO LINCOLN PARK
25TH AVE
300 26TH AVE
400 27TH AVE
28TH AVE
MCLAREN AVE
30TH AVE
LAKE ST
32ND AVE
GEARY BLVD

END 48TH AVE
EL DORADO ST SF 11 C1
E OF 1700 3RD ST
ELGIN PARK SF 10 C1
S FROM MCCOPPIN ST BETWEEN
VALENCIA ST AND MARKET ST
S TO DUBOCE AV
ELIM AL SF 7 B1
W FROM S 1ST ST BETWEEN
JESSIE ST AND MISSION ST
ELIZABETH ST SF 10 A3
W FROM S SAN JOSE AV BETWEEN
23RD ST AND 24TH ST TO BURNHAM ST
2 SAN JOSE AVE
GUERRERO ST
200 CHURCH ST
NELLIE ST
VICKSBURG ST
BLANCHE ST
400 SANCHEZ ST
500 NOE ST
600 CASTRO ST
700 DIAMOND ST
800 DOUGLASS ST
900 HOFFMAN AVE
MARKET ST
END GRAND VIEW AV
ELK ST SF 14 A3
N FROM BOSWORTH ST TO ARBOR ST
ELKHART ST SF 7 C2
W FROM S MAIN ST BETWEEN
FOLSOM ST AND HARRISON ST
ELLERT ST SF 14 C2
E FROM BOCANA ST NEAR HOLLY
PARK CIRCLE TO ANDOVER ST
2 BOCANA ST
100 BENNINGTON ST
END ANDOVER ST
ELLINGTON AV SF 19 C3
W OF MISSION ST NEAR
COUNTY LINE FROM S OF NIAGARA AV
AV SW TO MISSION ST
2 NIAGARA AVE
100 MT VERNON AVE
200 OTTAWA AVE
SALA TERR
300 FOOTE AVE
400 NAGLEE AVE
500 WHIPPLE AVE
END MISSION ST
ELLIOT ST SF 21 A2
BETWEEN DELTA ST AND BRITTON ST
S FROM CAPBELL AV TO LELAND AV
2 CAMPBELL AVE
100 TEDDY AVE
200 ARLETA AVE
300 RAYMOND AVE
END LELAND AVE
ELLIS ST SF 6 A3
ELLIS ST SF 7 A2
W FROM MARKET ST AND STOCKTON ST
TO ST JOSEPHS AV
2 MARKET & STOCKTON STS
100 POWELL ST
5TH ST
200 MASON ST
300 TAYLOR ST
400 JONES ST
500 LEAVENWORTH ST
COHEN PL
600 HYDE ST
700 LARKIN ST
800 POLK ST
900 VAN NESS AVE
1000 FRANKLIN ST
1100 GOUGH ST
1200 OCTAVIA ST
1300 LAGUNA ST
HOLLIS ST
1500 WEBSTER ST
FOLGER AL
1600 FILLMORE ST
1700 STEINER ST
BOURBIN ST
1800 PIERCE ST
FARREN ST
1900 SCOTT ST
BEIDEMAN ST
2000 DIVISADERO ST
2100 BRODERICK ST
END ST JOSEPHS AV
ELLSWORTH ST SF 14 C2
S FROM S BENRAL HTS BLVD
BETWEEN ANDERSON ST AND GATES ST
TO ALEMANY BLVD
2 ESMERALDA AVE
100 POWHATTAN AVE
200 EUGENIA AVE
300 CORTLAND AVE
400 JARBOE AVE
500 TOMPKINS AVE
600 OGDEN AVE
700 CRESCENT AVE
END PT S OF CRESCENT AV
ELM ST SF 6 B3
W FROM S POLK ST BETWEEN
GOLDEN GATE AV AND TURK ST
TO SCOTT ST
2 POLK ST
200 VAN NESS AVE
300 FRANKLIN ST
GOUGH ST
JEFFERSON SQUARE
PIERCE ST
END SCOTT ST
ELMHURST DR SF 13 A3
E AND S FROM ROSSMOOR DR
TO ROSSMOOR DR S OF OCEAN AV
ELMIRA ST SF 15 A3
FROM INDUSTRIAL ST S TO
THORNTON AV
INDUSTRIAL ST
TOLAND ST
100 HELENA ST
200 AUGUSTA ST
300 SILVER AVE
END THORNTON AVE
EL MIRASOL PL SF 12 C3
N FROM SLOAT BLVD TO CREST
LAKE DR
ELMWOOD WY SF 19 B1
N OF OCEAN AV AND W FROM
WESTWOOD DR
EL PLAZUELA WY SF 19 A1
E FROM 501 JUNIPERO SERRA BLVD
EL POLIN LOOP SF 1 C3
IN PRESIDIO
AT S END OF MACARTHUR ST
EL SERENO CT SF 14 A2
E FROM TERESITA BLVD TO
MARIETTA DR
ELSIE ST SF 14 C2
FROM COSO AV S OF ARMY ST TO
HOLLY PARK CIR
2 COSO AVE
100 ESMERALDA AVE
VIRGINIA AVE
200 EUGENIA AVE
300 CORTLAND AVE
320 SANTA MARINA AVE
APPLETON ST
END HOLLY PARK CIRCLE
EL VERANO WY SF 13 B3
N FROM 1100 MONTREY BLVD
TO ST ELMO WY
ELWOOD ST SF 7 A2
N FROM 200 O FARRELL ST BETWEEN
POWELL ST AND MASON ST
AND W TO MASON ST
EMBARCADERO SWY SF 3 B3
N FROM BAY BRIDGE TO
BROADWAY AND SANSOME ST
EMBARCADERO, THE SF 3 A2
EMBARCADERO, THE SF 7 C2
FROM BERRY ST PARALLEL
WITH THE SEA WALL TO TAYLOR ST
BERRY ST
KING ST
1ST ST
TOWNSEND ST
FREMONT ST
BRANNAN ST
BEALE ST
MAIN ST
BRYANT ST
SPEAR ST
SF-OAKLAND BAY BR/I-80
HARRISON ST
STEUART ST
FOLSOM ST
HOWARD ST
MISSION ST
EMBARCADERO SKWY RAMPS
WASHINGTON ST
PACIFIC AVE
BROADWAY
VALLEJO ST
GREEN ST
FRONT ST
FILBERT ST
GREENWICH ST
LOMBARD ST
BATTERY ST
CHESTNUT ST
SANSOME ST
BAY ST
KEARNY ST
NORTH POINT ST
GRANT AV
BEACH ST
JEFFERSON ST
POWELL ST
END TAYLOR ST
EMERALD LN SF 12 B3
W FROM RIVERTON DR TO
EVERGLADE DR
S OF SLOAT BLVD
EMERSON ST SF 5 C2
N FROM GEARY BLVD
EMERY LN SF 3 A3
N FROM 700 VALLEJO ST BETWEEN
STOCKTON ST AND POWELL ST
EMIL LN SF 13 C3
S FROM CRESTA VISTA DR TO
LOS PALMOS DR BETWEEN GLOBE
AL AND LULU AL
EMMA ST SF 7 A1
E FROM 500 STOCKTON ST BETWEEN
BUSH ST AND PINE ST
EMMETT CT SF 14 C1
S FROM S PRECITA AV BETWEEN
COSO AV AND SHOTWELL ST
TO MIRABEL AV
EMPRESS LN SF 21 A2
NE FROM SAN BRUNO AV
3 BLKS N OF BAYSHORE BLVD
ENCANTO AV SF 6 A3
N FROM ANZAVISTA AV TO
TERRA VISTA AV NEAR FORTUNA ST
ENCINAL WK SF 9 A3
E FROM 15TH AV JUST N OF
MORAGA ST
ENCLINE CT SF 13 C2
FROM POINT E OF DEL VALE
AV TO MARIETTA DR S OF
O SHAUGHNESSY BLVD
ENGLISH ST SF 16 B3
HUNTERS POINT
SW FROM LOCKWOOD ST
ENNIS RD SF 1 A3
IN PRESIDIO
S FROM COMPTON ST
ENTERPRISE ST SF 10 C2
E FROM S FOLSOM ST BETWEEN
16TH ST AND 17TH ST
ENTRADA CT N SF 19 B1
ENTRADA CT S SF 19 B1
W FROM BORICA ST BETWEEN URBANO
DR N AND S
ERIE ST SF 10 C1
W FROM S FOLSOM ST BETWEEN
13TH ST AND 14TH ST TO
MISSION ST
2 FOLSOM ST
100 SOUTH VAN NESS AVE
END MISSION ST
ERKSON CT SF 6 A2
N FROM S POST ST BETWEEN
DIVISADERO ST AND BRODERICK ST
ERVINE ST SF 21 A2
BETWEEN ALBERTA ST AND DELTA ST
FROM CAMPBELL AV N TO WILDE AV
WILDE AV
ESCOLTA WY SF 12 B2
FROM 30TH AV W TO WAWONA
ST W OF 1901 VICENTE ST
ESCONDIDO AV SF 12 B3
FROM CONSTANSO WY W TO
34TH AV
ESMERALDA AV SF 14 C2
ESMERALDA AV SF 15 A2
FROM COLERIDGE ST SE AND
E TO HOLLADAY AV
2 COLERIDGE ST
LUNDYS LN
100 PROSPECT AVE
200 WINFIELD ST
300 ELSIE ST
400 BONVIEW ST
BOCANA ST
500 ANDOVER ST
600 MOULTRIE ST
650 ANDERSON ST
SHOTWELL ST
700 ELLSWORTH ST
750 GATES ST
800 FOLSOM ST
BANKS ST
PRENTISS ST
NEVADA ST
900 ROSENKRANS ST
BERNAL HTS BLVD
ALABAMA ST
BRADFORD ST
1000 PERALTA ST
1100 FRANCONIA ST
BREWSTER ST
END HOLLADAY AVE
ESPANOLA ST SF 16 A3
W OF INGALKLS ST BETWEEN ROSIE
LEE LN AND BEATRICE LN
ESQUINA DR SF 20 C3
S FROM PARQUE DR BETWEEN
CIELITO DR AND CARRIZAL ST
TO GENEVA AV
ESSEX ST SF 7 B2
S FROM S FOLSOM ST BETWEEN
1ST ST AND 2ND ST TO HARRISON
ESTERO AV SF 19 A1
SE FROM JUNIPERO SERRA
BLVD TO ALVISO ST
EUCALYPTUS DR SF 12 C3
W FROM JUNIPERO SERRA
BLVD S OF OCEAN AV TO
CLEARFIELD DR
EUCLID AV SF 5 B2
W FROM S PRESIDIO AV BETWEEN
CALIFORNIA ST AND GEARY BLVD
TO ARGUELLO BLVD
PRESIDIO AVE
MASONIC AVE
LAUREL ST
COLLINS ST
MANZANITA AVE
IRIS AVE
HEATHER AVE
SPRUCE ST
PARKER AVE
COMMONWEALTH AVE
JORDAN AVE
PALM AVE
ARGUELLO BLVD
EUGENIA AV SF 14 C2
SE FROM MISSION ST NEAR 30TH ST
AND E TO A POINT E OF
NEVADA ST
2 MISSION ST
100 COLERIDGE ST
200 PROSPECT AVE
300 WINFIELD ST
400 ELSIE ST
VIRGINIA AVE
500 BONVIEW ST
600 BOCANA ST
BENNINGTON ST
700 WOOL ST
800 ANDOVER ST
900 MOULTRIE ST
1000 ANDERSON ST
1100 ELLSWORTH ST
1200 GATES ST
1300 FOLSOM ST
1400 BANKS ST
1500 PRENTISS ST
END PT S OF PRENTISS ST
EUREKA PL SF 6 C2
E OFF S LARKIN BETWEEN BUSH ST
AND PINE ST
EUREKA ST SF 10 A2
S FROM S 17TH ST BETWEEN
DIAMOND ST AND DOUGLASS ST
TO 23RD ST
2 17TH ST
MARKET ST
100 18TH ST
200 19TH ST
300 20TH ST
400 21ST ST
500 22ND ST
END 23RD ST
EVA TER SF 10 B1
N FROM OAK ST BETWEEN
STEINER ST AND PIERCE ST
EVANS AV SF 15 B1
NW FROM JENNINGS ST TO ARMY ST
KEITH ST
MENDELL ST
NEWHALL ST
3RD ST
PHELPS ST
QUINT ST
RANKIN ST
SO-EMBARCADERO FRWY
NAPOLEON ST
TOLAND ST
MARIN ST
END ARMY ST
EVELYN WY SF 13 C2
NW FROM DEL VALE AV
TO 801 PORTOLA DR
EVERGLADE DR SF 12 B3
S FROM SOAT BLVD TO GELLERT DR
E OF HAVENSIDE DR
EVERSON ST SF 14 B2
E FROM ADDISON ST BETWEEN
DIGBY ST AND ADDISON ST
TO AMATISTA LN
EWER PL SF 3 A3
W FROM S MASON ST BETWEEN
SACRAMENTO ST AND CLAY ST

EWING TER SF 5 C3
W OF MASONIC AV S OF
ANZA ST AND N OF TURK ST
EXCELSIOR AV SF 20 B1
SW FROM MISSION ST BETWEEN
AVALON AV AND BRAZIL AV
TO PRAGUE ST
2 MISSION ST
100 LONDON ST
200 PARIS ST
300 LISBON ST
400 MADRID ST
500 EDINBURGH ST
600 NAPLES ST
700 VIENNA ST
800 ATHENS ST
900 MOSCOW ST
1000 MUNICH ST
END PRAGUE ST
EXCHANGE PL SF 7 B1
S OFF S PINE ST BETWEEN
MONTGOMERY ST & SANSOME ST
EXECUTIVE PK BL SF 21 B3
N FROM ALANA WY E OF BAYSHORE FWY
THEN E & S TO HARNEY WY
EXETER ST SF 21 B1
S FROM PAUL AV BETWEEN GOULD ST
AND CRANE ST TO SALINAS AV
NEAR SAN BRUNO AV
EXPOSITION DR SF 3 C1
NW FROM 13TH ST TO GATEVIEW AV
TREASURE ISLAND
FAIR AV SF 14 C1
SE FROM 3201 MISSION ST OPPOSITE
VALENCIA ST TO PROSPECT ST
2 MISSION ST
100 COLERIDGE ST
LUNDY S LN
END PROSPECT ST
FAIRBANKS ST SF 10 A2
E FROM JUNCTION OF
ROOSEVELT & MUSEUM WYS
FAIRFAX AV SF 15 B1
FROM KEITH ST NW TO RANKIN ST
KEITH ST
MENDELL ST
NEWHALL ST
3RD ST
PHELPS ST
QUINT ST
END RANKIN ST
FAIRFIELD WY SF 19 B1
N FROM 1950 OCEAN AV TO
KENWOOD WY
FAIRMOUNT ST SF 14 B2
W FROM ARLINGTON ST TO
MIGUEL ST
ARLINGTON ST
100 CHENERY ST
200 WHITNEY ST
300 LAIDLEY ST
END MIGUEL ST
FAIR OAKS ST SF 10 B3
S FROM S 21ST ST BETWEEN
GUERRERO ST AND DOLORES ST
TO 26TH ST
2 21ST ST
100 22ND ST
200 23RD ST
300 24TH ST
400 25TH ST
END 26TH ST
FAITH ST SF 15 A1
NW FROM A POINT E OF HOLLADAY AV
TO A POINT W OF HOLLADAY AV
FALLON PL SF 3 A3
E FROM S TAYLOR ST BETWEEN
BROADWAY ST AND VALLEJO ST
FALMOUTH ST SF 7 A3
S FROM S FOLSOM ST BETWEEN
5TH ST AND 6TH ST TO
SHIPLEY ST
FANNING WY SF 13 A1
FROM 14TH AV TO JUNCTION
OF 15TH AV AND QUINTARA ST
FARALLONES ST SF 19 B2
W FROM SAN JOSE AV
TO ORIZABA AV BETWEEN
LOBOS ST AND BROAD ST
2 SAN JOSE AVE
100 PLYMOUTH AVE
200 CAPITOL AVE
END ORIZABA AVE
FARGO PL SF 11 A1
SW FROM BOARDMAN PL BETWEEN
BRYANT ST AND BRANNAN ST
FARNSWORTH LN SF 9 C2
W FROM WILLARD ST S OF
PARNASSUS AV
FARNUM ST SF 14 B2
SE FROM DIAMOND ST
ST W OF CASTRO ST
2 31ST ST
100 MORELAND ST
END MOFFIT ST
FARRAGUT AV SF 19 C3
NW FROM MISSION ST TO
ALAMANY BLVD
2 MISSION ST
100 HURON AVE
200 WINNIPEG AVE
END SAN JOSE AVE
FARVIEW CT SF 9 C3
W FROM MARVIEW WY TO
POINT SW OF FREDELA LN
FAXON AV SF 19 B1
N FROM MONTANA ST TO
MONTEREY BLVD
2 MONTANA ST
200 LAKE VIEW AVE
300 GRAFTON AVE
400 HOLLOWAY AVE
500 DE MONTFORD AVE
600 OCEAN AVE
700 ELMWOOD WAY
800 WILDWOOD WAY
900 PIZARRO WAY
KENWOOD WAY
END MONTEREY BLVD
FEDERAL ST SF 7 B2
W FROM S 1ST ST BETWEEN
BRYANT & BRANNAN STS TO 2ND ST
FELIX AV SF 19 A2
E FROM CAMBON DR
W OF JUNIPERO SERRA BLVD
FELL ST SF 6 C3
FELL ST SF 9 C1
FELL ST SF 10 A1
W FROM JUNCTION MARKET ST
AND POLK ST BETWEEN OAK ST
& HAYES ST TO STANYAN ST
2 MARKET ST
POLK ST
100 VAN NESS AVE
200 FRANKLIN ST
300 GOUGH ST
400 OCTAVIA ST
500 LAGUNA ST
600 BUCHANAN ST
700 WEBSTER ST
800 FILLMORE ST
900 STEINER ST
1000 PIERCE ST
1100 SCOTT ST
1200 DIVISADERO ST
1300 BRODERICK ST
1400 BAKER ST
1500 LYON ST
1600 CENTRAL AVE
1700 MASONIC AVE
1800 ASHBURY ST
1900 CLAYTON ST
2000 COLE ST
2100 SHRADER ST
END STANYAN ST
FELLA PL SF 7 A1
NE FROM 600 POWELL ST BETWEEN
BUSH ST AND PINE ST
FELTON ST SF 20 C1
W FROM SAN BRUNO AV BETWEEN
SILLIMAN ST AND BURROWS
ST TO PERU AV
2 BAY SHORE BLVD
100 GIRARD ST
200 BRUSSELS ST
300 GOETTINGEN ST
400 SOMERSET ST
500 HOLYOKE ST
600 HAMILTON ST
700 BOWDOIN ST
800 DARTMOUTH ST
900 COLBY ST
1000 UNIVERSITY ST
1100 PRINCETON ST
1200 AMHERST ST
1300 YALE ST
1400 CAMBRIDGE ST
1500 OXFORD ST
1600 HARVARD ST
1700 GAMBIER ST
1800 MADISON ST
END PERU AV
FENTON LN SF 14 A1
W FROM PORTOLA DR NEAR 25TH ST
TO BURNETT AV
FERN ST SF 6 B2
W FROM S LARKIN ST BETWEEN
SUTTER ST AND BUSH ST
TO GOUGH ST
2 LARKIN ST
100 POLK
200 VAN NESS AVE
300 FRANKLIN ST
END GOUGH ST
FERNANDEZ ST SF 1 C3
IN PRESIDIO
SE FROM BARNARD AV
FERNWOOD DR SF 13 B3
N FROM EL VERANO WY TO
RAVENWOOD DR
FIELDING ST SF 3 A2
FROM 1901 STOCKTON ST BETWEEN
LOMBARD AND CHESTNUT STS
TO POWELL ST
FILBERT ST SF 2 A3
FILBERT ST SF 3 A2
FROM THE BAY BETWEEN UNION ST
AND GREENWICH ST W TO
LYON ST
THE EMBARCADERO
2 FRONT ST
100 BATTERY ST
200 SANSOME ST
NAPIER PL
DARRELL PL
300 MONTGOMERY ST
400 KEARNY ST
GENOA PL
VARENNES ST
HARDWOOD AL
500 GRANT AVE
MEDAU PL
JASPER PL
KRAUSGRILL AL
600 STOCKTON ST
700 POWELL ST
COLUMBUS AVE
SCOTLAND ST
800 MASON ST
900 TAYLOR ST
ROACH ST
REDFIELD AL
1000 JONES ST
ATTRIDGE AL
1100 LEAVENWORTH ST
1200 HYDE ST
1300 LARKIN ST
1400 POLK ST
1500 VAN NESS AVE
1600 FRANKLIN ST
1700 GOUGH ST
1800 OCTAVIA ST
1900 LAGUNA ST
2000 BUCHANAN ST
AHLERS CT
2100 WEBSTER ST
2200 FILLMORE ST
2300 STEINER ST
2400 PIERCE ST
2500 SCOTT ST
2600 DIVISADERO ST
2700 BRODERICK ST
2800 BAKER ST
END LYON ST
FILLMORE ST SF 2 A3
FILLMORE ST SF 6 B3
FILLMORE ST SF 10 B1
N FROM S DUBOCE AV BETWEEN
WEBSTER ST AND STEINER ST
TO THE BAY
2 DUBOCE AVE
100 HERMANN ST
130 GERMAINIA ST
200 WALLER ST
LAUSSAT ST
300 HAIGHT ST
400 PAGE ST
500 OAK ST
600 FELL ST
700 HAYES ST
800 GROVE ST
900 FULTON ST
1000 MCALLISTER ST
1100 GOLDEN GATE AVE
1200 TURK ST
1300 EDDY ST
1400 ELLIS ST
BYINGTON ST
1500 O FARRELL ST
1600 GEARY ST
1700 POST ST
1800 SUTTER ST
1900 BUSH ST
WILMOT ST
2000 PINE ST
CALUMET PL
2100 CALIFORNIA ST
2200 SACRAMENTO ST
2300 CLAY ST
2400 WASHINGTON ST
JACKSON ST
PACIFIC AVE
BROADWAY
2800 VALLEJO ST
2900 GREEN ST
3000 UNION ST
3100 FILBERT ST
PIXLEY ST
3200 GREENWICH ST
MOULTON ST
3300 LOMBARD ST
3400 CHESTNUT ST
CERVANTES BLVD
3600 BAY ST
NORTH POINT ST
3800 BEACH ST
JEFFERSON ST
END MARINA BLVD
FISHER AL SF 3 A3
E FROM 1300 POWELL ST BETWEEN
PACIFIC AV AND BROADWAY
FISHER AV SF 17 B1
SW FROM ROBINSON E OF
HORNEL AV TO SPEAR AV
FISHER LOOP SF 1 B3
IN PRESIDIO
W OF INFANTRY TER
FITCH ST SF 16 A3
SW FROM INNES AV
FITCH ST SF 17 A1
FITCH ST SF 21 C2
SW FROM PALOU AV TO THOMAS AV &
FROM CARROL AV TO GILMAN AV
PALOU AV
QUESADA AV
REVERE AV
SHAFTER AV
THOMAS AV
UNDERWOOD AV
VAN DYKE AV
CARROL AV
DONNER AV
END GILMAN AV
FITZGERALD AV SF 21 B1
NW FROM A POINT E OF GRIFFITH ST
TO BAYSHORE BLVD
GRIFFITH ST
CAMERON WY
HAWES ST
INGALLS ST
JENNINGS ST
END 3RD ST
FLINT ST SF 10 A2
NW FROM 16TH ST NEAR CASTRO
ST TO A POINT NW OF DEFOREST WY
FLOOD AV SF 13 C3
FLOOD AV SF 14 A3
W FROM CIRCULAR AV BETWEEN
HEARST AV AND STAPLES AV
TO HAZELWOOD AV
2 CIRCULAR AVE
100 CONGO ST
200 DETROIT ST
300 EDNA ST
400 FOERSTER ST
500 GENNESSEE ST
PHELAN AVE
RIDGEWOOD ST
END HAZELWOOD AVE
FLORA ST SF 15 B3
FROM BAY VIEW ST BETWEEN
POMONA ST AND NEWHALL ST
S TO THORNTON AVE
FLORENCE ST SF 2 C3
S FROM VALLEJO ST BETWEEN
TAYLOR ST AND JONES ST
FLORENTINE ST SF 20 A2
S FROM 5401 MISSION ST
TO BRUNSWICK ST
2 MISSION ST
100 MORSE ST
END BRUNSWICK ST
FLORIDA ST SF 11 A1
FLORIDA ST SF 15 A1
S FROM A POINT N OF DIVISION ST
BETWEEN BRYANT ST AND
ALABAMA ST TO PERALTA AV
2 PT N OF DIVISION ST
DIVISION ST
100 ALAMEDA ST
200 15TH ST
300 16TH ST
400 17TH ST
500 MARIPOSA ST
600 18TH ST
700 19TH ST
800 20TH ST
900 21ST ST
1000 22ND ST
1100 23RD ST

1200 24TH ST
1300 25TH ST
1400 26TH ST
1500 ARMY ST
1600 PRECITA ST
END PERALTA AVE
FLOURNOY ST SF 19 B3
SE FROM DE LONG ST TO
COUNTY LINE
FLOWER ST SF 15 A2
FROM LOOMIS ST S OF
OAKDALE AV W TO BAYSHORE BLVD
FOERSTER ST SF 13 C3
N FROM JUDSON AV BETWEEN EDNA ST
AND GENESSEE ST TO
TERESITA BLVD
2 JUDSON AVE
100 STAPLES AVE
200 FLOOD AVE
300 HEARST AVE
400 MONTEREY BLVD
500 JOOST AVE
600 MANGELS AVE
700 MELROSE AVE
END TERESITA BLVD
FOLSOM ST SF 7 B2
FOLSOM ST SF 10 C1
FOLSOM ST SF 11 A1
FOLSOM ST SF 15 A2
SW FROM THE BAY BETWEEN HOWARD ST
AND HARRISON ST
AND TO A POINT S OF
CRESCENT AV
2 THE EMBARCADERO
50 STEUART ST
100 SPEAR ST
200 MAIN ST
300 BEALE ST
ZENO PL
400 FREMONT ST
BALDWIN CT
GROTE PL
500 1ST ST
ECKER ST
ESSEX ST
600 2ND ST
654 HAWTHORNE ST
HAMPTON PL
700 3RD ST
800 4TH ST
900 5TH ST
FALMOUTH ST
1000 6TH ST
HARRIET ST
COLUMBIA SQ
1078 RUSS ST
SHERMAN ST
MOSS ST
1100 7TH ST
LANGTON ST
HALLAM ST
1138 RAUSCH ST
RODGERS ST
1200 8TH ST
1300 9TH ST
DORE ST
1400 10TH ST
JUNIPER ST
1500 11TH ST
NORFOLK ST
1600 12TH ST
1700 13TH ST
1732 ERIE ST
1800 14TH ST
1900 15TH ST
2000 16TH ST
ENTERPRISE ST
2100 17TH ST
2200 18TH ST
2300 19TH ST
2400 20TH ST
2500 21ST ST
2600 22ND ST
2700 23RD ST
2800 24TH ST
2900 25TH ST
3000 26TH ST
3100 ARMY ST
3200 BESSIE ST
PRECITA AVE
3300 STONEMAN ST
3400 RIPLEY ST
3500 ESMERALDA AVE
BERNAL HTS BLVD
3600 POWHATTAN AVE
3700 EUGENIA AVE
3800 CORTLAND AVE
3900 JARBOE AVE
4000 TOMPKINS AVE
4100 OGDEN AVE
4200 CRESCENT AVE
END PT S OF CRESCENT AVE
FONT BLVD SF 18 C1
FONT BLVD SF 19 A2
FROM JUAN BAUTISTA CIR
NW TO LAKE MERCED BLVD
AND SE TO JUNIPERO SERRA BLVD
FOOTE AV SF 19 C2
NW FROM S MISSION ST NEAR
COUNTY LINE BETWEEN OTTAWA AV
& NAGLEE AV TO SAN JOSE AV
2 MISSION ST
100 ELLINGTON AVE
200 HURON AVE
ALEMANY BLVD
CAYUGA AVE
END SAN JOSE AVE
FORD ST SF 10 B2
W FROM S SANCHEZ ST BETWEEN
17TH ST AND 18TH ST TO
NOE ST
FOREST KNOLLS DR SF 9 C3
FROM CHRISTOPHER DR SOUTH
TO A POINT S OF GLENHAVEN LN
ONE BLK W OF CLARENDON AV
FOREST SIDE AV SF 13 A2
N FROM VICENTE ST TO
TARAVAL ST
VICENTE ST
ULLOA ST
END TARAVAL ST
FOREST VIEW DR SF 12 C3
S FROM SLOAT BLVD BETWEEN
MEADOWBROOK DR AND INVERNESS DR
TO EUCALYPTUS DR
FORTUNA AV SF 6 A3
N FROM ANZAVISTA AV BETWEEN
BAKER ST AND ENCANTO AV
TO TERRA VISTA AV
FOUNTAIN ST SF 14 A1
S FROM S 24TH ST BETWEEN
HOFFMAN AV AND GRAND VIEW AV
TO CLIPPER ST
2 24TH ST
100 25TH ST
END CLIPPER ST
FOWLER AV SF 13 C1
FROM 701 PORTOLA DR SW
OF TERESITA BLVD
FRANCE AV SF 20 B2
SE FROM 4901 MISSION ST S OF
RUSSIA AV TO A POINT E
OF MOSCOW ST
2 MISSION ST
100 LONDON ST
200 PARIS ST
300 LISBON ST
400 MADRID ST
500 EDINBURGH ST
600 NAPLES ST
700 VIENNA ST
800 ATHENS ST
MOSCOW ST
END PT S OF MOSCOW ST
FRANCIS ST SF 20 B1
NW FROM 4440 MISSION ST BETWEEN
COTTER ST AND SANTA ROSA AV
TO ALEMANY BLVD
FRANCISCO ST SF 2 A2
FRANCISCO ST SF 3 A2
W FROM MONTGOMERY ST BETWEEN
CHESTNUT & BAY STS TO LAGUNA ST &
FROM SCOTT ST TO THE PRESIDIO
50 MONTGOMERY ST
100 KEARNY ST
200 GRANT AVE
MIDWAY ST
BELLAIR PL
300 STOCKTON ST
WORDEN ST
400 POWELL ST
500 MASON ST
600 TAYLOR ST
COLUMBUS AVE
700 JONES ST
BRET HARTE TER
800 LEAVENWORTH ST
900 HYDE ST
RESERVOIR
1000 LARKIN ST
1100 POLK ST
1200 VAN NESS AVE
1300 FRANKLIN ST
1400 GOUGH ST
1500 OCTAVIA ST
LAGUNA ST
2200 SCOTT ST
2300 DIVISADERO ST
2400 BRODERICK ST
2500 BAKER ST
RICHARDSON AVE
END LYON ST
FRANCONIA ST SF 15 A2
S FROM 151 PERALTA AV TO
A POINS S OF POWHATTAN AV
2 PERALTA AVE
MULLEN AVE
200 MONTCALM ST
300 RUTLEDGE ST
MASSASOIT ST
SAMOSET ST
CABOT ST
STAR ST
400 ESMERALDA AVE
500 MAYFLOWER ST
END POWHATTAN AVE
FRANK ST SF 7 A1
W FROM 801 MASON ST BETWEEN
PINE ST AND CALIFORNIA ST
FRANKLIN ST SF 2 B2
FRANKLIN ST SF 6 B1
N FROM S MARKET ST BETWEEN
VAN NESS AV AND GOUGH ST
TO FORT MASON
2 MARKET ST
PAGE ST
LILY ST
100 OAK ST
HICKORY AVE
200 FELL ST
LINDEN ST
300 HAYES ST
IVY ST
400 GROVE ST
500 FULTON ST
600 MCALLISTER ST
REDWOOD ST
700 GOLDEN GATE AVE
730 ELM ST
800 TURK ST
LARCH ST
900 EDDY ST
WILLOW ST
1000 ELLIS ST
OLIVE ST
1100 O FARRELL ST
MYRTLE ST
1200 GEARY ST
1300 POST ST
HEMLOCK ST
1400 SUTTER ST
FERN ST
1500 BUSH ST
AUSTIN ST
1600 PINE ST
1700 CALIFORNIA ST
1800 SACRAMENTO ST
1900 CLAY ST
2000 WASHINGTON ST
2100 JACKSON ST
2200 PACIFIC AVE
2300 BROADWAY
2400 VALLEJO ST
2500 GREEN ST
2600 UNION ST
2700 FILBERT ST
2800 GREENWICH ST
BLACKSTONE ST
2900 LOMBARD ST
3000 CHESTNUT ST
3100 FRANCISCO ST
BAY ST
END FORT MASON
FRATESSA CT SF 21 B2
W FROM SAN BRUNO AV
1 BLK N OF CAMPBELL AV
FREDELA LN SF 9 C3
N FROM MARVIEW WY TO
FARVIEW CT
FREDERICK ST SF 9 C2
W FROM BUENA VISTA AV S OF
WALLER ST W TO ARGUELLO
AV
2 BUENA VISTA AVE
100 MASONIC AVE
124 DELMAR ST
200 ASHBURY ST
250 DOWNEY ST
300 CLAYTON ST
352 BELVEDERE ST
400 COLE ST
450 SHRADER ST
500 STANYAN ST
600 WILLIAR ST
END ARGUELLO BLVD
FREDSON CT SF 20 A2
SE FROM HURON AV BETWEEN
FOOTE AV AND NAGLEE AV
FREELON ST SF 7 B3
SW FROM ZOE ST BETWEEN
BRYANT ST AND BRANNAN ST
TO A POINT W OF 4TH ST
2 ZOE ST
100 4TH ST
END PT W OF 4TH ST
FREEMAN CT SF 3 A3
S FROM 1001 CLAY ST BETWEEN
POWELL ST AND MASON ST
FREEMAN ST SF 1 B2
IN PRESIDIO
SW OF LINCOLN BLVD
FREMONT ST SF 7 B1
SE FROM S MARKET ST BETWEEN
BEALE ST AND 1ST ST
TO THE EMBARCADERO
2 MARKET ST
100 MISSION ST
NATOMA ST
200 HOWARD ST
300 FOLSOM ST
END THE EMBARCADERO
FRENCH CT SF 1 C2
IN PRESIDIO
N FROM LINCOLN BLVD
FRESNO ST SF 3 A3
E FROM GRANT AV BETWEEN
BROADWAY AND VALLEJO ST
FRIEDELL ST SF 17 A1
IN HUNTERS PT
SW FROM HUDSON AV
FRONT ST SF 3 B2
N FROM S MARKET ST BETWEEN
DAVIS ST AND BATTERY ST
TO THE EMBARCADERO
2 MARKET ST
100 PINE ST
200 CALIFORNIA ST
HALLECK ST
300 SACRAMENTO ST
COMMERCIAL ST
400 CLAY ST
600 JACKSON ST
700 PACIFIC AVE
800 BROADWAY
900 VALLEJO ST
1000 GREEN ST
COMMERCE ST
1100 UNION ST
FILBERT ST
END THE EMBARCADERO
FUENTE AV SF 19 A2
N FROM JUAN BAUTISTA CIR
TO SERRANO DR
FULTON ST SF 6 A3
FULTON ST SF 8 A1
FULTON ST SF 9 A1
SW FROM HYDE ST BETWEEN
GROVE ST AND MCALLISTER ST
TO GREAT HIGHWAY
HYDE ST
CIVIC CENTER
200 VAN NESS AVE
300 FRANKLIN ST
400 GOUGH ST
500 OCTAVIA ST
600 LAGUNA ST
700 BUCHANAN ST
800 WEBSTER ST
900 FILLMORE ST
1000 STEINER ST
1100 PIERCE ST
1200 SCOTT ST
1300 DIVISADERO ST
1400 BRODERICK ST
1500 BAKER ST
1600 LYON ST
1700 CENTRAL AVE
1800 MASONIC AVE
ATAYLA TERR
ASHBURY ST
HEMWAY TERR
CLAYTON ST
LOYOLA TERR
COLE ST
2200 PARKER AVE
SHRADER ST
2300 STANYAN ST
2344 PARSONS ST
2400 WILLARD ST
2500 ARGUELLO BLVD
2600 2ND AVE
2700 3RD AVE
2800 4TH AVE
2900 5TH AVE
3000 6TH AVE
3100 7TH AVE
3200 8TH AVE
3300 9TH AVE
3400 10TH AVE
3500 11TH AVE

3600 12TH AVE
FUNSTON AVE
PARK PRESIDIO BLVD
3800 14TH AVE
3900 15TH AVE
4000 16TH AVE
4100 17TH AVE
4200 18TH AVE
4300 19TH AVE
4400 20TH AVE
4500 21ST AVE
4600 22ND AVE
4700 23RD AVE
4800 24TH AVE
4900 25TH AVE
5000 26TH AVE
5100 27TH AVE
5200 28TH AVE
5300 29TH AVE
5400 30TH AVE
5500 31ST AVE
5600 32ND AVE
5700 33RD AVE
5800 34TH AVE
5900 35TH AVE
6000 36TH AVE
6100 37TH AVE
6200 38TH AVE
6300 39TH AVE
6400 40TH AVE
6500 41ST AVE
6600 42ND AVE
6700 43RD AVE
6800 44TH AVE
6900 45TH AVE
7000 46TH AVE
7100 47TH AVE
7200 48TH AVE
7300 LA PLAYA ST
END GREAT HIGHWAY
FUNSTON AV SF 1 C3
FUNSTON AV SF 5 A2
FUNSTON AV SF 9 A2
FUNSTON AV SF 13 A1
S BETWEEN 12TH AV AND 14TH AV
FROM MOUNTAIN LAKE PARK
TO ULLOA ST
2 MOUNTAIN LAKE PARK
100 LAKE ST
200 CALIFORNIA ST
300 CLEMENT ST
400 GEARY BLVD
500 ANZA ST
600 BALBOA ST
700 CABRILLO ST
FULTON ST
GOLDEN GATE PARK
1200 LINCOLN WAY
1300 IRVING ST
1400 JUDAH ST
1500 KIRKHAM ST
LURLINE ST
ALOHA AVE
1600 LAWTON ST
1700 MORAGA ST
1800 NORIEGA ST
1900 ORTEGA ST
ROCKRIDGE DR
2400 TARAVAL ST
END ULLOA ST
GABILAN WY SF 12 C3
N FROM SLOAT BLVD E OF
PARAISO PL TO CRESTLAKE DR
GAISER CT SF 10 B2
E FROM S GUERRERO ST BETWEEN
16TH ST AND CAMP ST
GALE ST SF 7 C3
SE OFF TOWNSEND ST
TO KING ST
GALEWOOD CIR SF 9 C3
W FROM CLARENDON AV BETWEEN
ASHWOOD N & OLYMPIA WY
GALINDO AV SF 19 A2
E FROM CHUMASERO AV TO A POINT
W OF JUNIPERO SERRA BLVD
GALLAGHER LN SF 7 A3
S FROM TEHAMA ST BETWEEN 4TH ST &
5TH ST TO CLEMENTINA ST
GALVEZ AV SF 15 B2
N FROM MENDELL
ST TO TOLAND ST
PT S OF MENDELL ST
MENDELL ST
NEWHALL ST
3RD ST
PHELPS ST
QUINT ST
RANKIN ST
SELBY ST
END TOLAND ST
GALVEZ AV SF 16 A3
NW FROM HORNE AV TO A POINT
NW OF DONAHUE ST IN HUNTERS PT
GAMBIER ST SF 20 C1
S FROM SILVER AV TO BURROWS ST
2 SILVER AVE
100 PIOCHE ST
200 SILLIMAN ST
300 FELTON ST
END BURROWS ST
GARCES DR SF 18 C2
FROM A POINT S OF VIDAL DR
N AND E TO GONZALES DR
GARCIA AV SF 13 B2
SW FROM 401 VASQUEZ AV
AND NW TO MERCED AV
GARDEN ST SF 6 A2
W FROM S DIVISADERO ST BETWEEN
GEARY ST AND POST ST
TO BRODERICK ST
GARDENSIDE DR SF 10 A3
S FROM BURNETT AV TO
PARKRIDGE DR & BURNETT AV
GARFIELD ST SF 19 A2
W FROM ORIZABA AV BETWEEN
HOLLOWAY AV AND SHIELDS ST
TO JUNIPERO SERRA BLVD
2 ORIZABA AVE
100 BRIGHT ST
200 HEAD ST
300 VICTORIA ST
400 RAMSELL ST
500 ARCH ST
600 VERNON ST
700 RALSTON ST
800 BIXBY ST
900 MONTICELLO ST
1000 BEVERLY ST
END JUNIPERO SERRA BLVD
GARLINGTON CT SF 15 C3
S OFF LA SALLE AV ONE BLOCK E
OF NECOMB AV
GARRISON AV SF 21 A3
S FROM SUNNYDALE ONE
BLK W OF SCHWERIN ST
GATES ST SF 15 A2
FROM S BERNAL HTS BLVD
NEAR ELLSWORTH S TO POINT
S OF CRESCENT AVE
2 BERNAL HT BLVD
100 POWHATTAN AVE
GATEVIEW AV SF 3 C1
NW FROM 13TH ST & AV H TO
LESTER CT ON TREASURE ISLAND
13TH ST
EXPOSITION DR
MARINER DR
NORTH POINT DR
BAYSIDE DR
MARINER DR
OZBORN CT
REEVES CT
MASON CT
13TH ST
END LESTER CT
GATEVIEW CT SF 13 B1
N FROM MENDOSA AV BETWEEN
QUINTARA ST AND 9TH AV
GAVEN ST SF 15 A3
W FROM 2300 SAN BRUNO AV
TO A POINT N OF COLBY ST
GAVIOTA WY SF 13 C2
S FROM TERESITA BLVD TO
BELLA VISTA WY
GEARY BLVD SF 4 B3
GEARY BLVD SF 5 C2
GEARY BLVD SF 6 A2
GEARY BLVD SF 7 A2
W FROM MARKET TO
PT LOBOS AV AT 40TH AV
1100 VAN NESS AV
1200 FRANKLIN ST
1300 GOUGH ST
1500 LAGUNA ST
1700 WEBSTER ST
1800 FILLMORE ST
STEINER
2100 SCOTT ST
2200 DIVISADERO ST
2400 BAKER ST
2500 LYON ST
2600 PRESIDIO
2800 EMERSON ST
2900 WOOD ST
3000 COLLINS ST
3100 BLAKE ST
3200 COOK ST
BOYCE ST
PARKER AVE
COMMONWEALTH AVE
STANYAN ST
3500 JORDAN AVE
3600 PALM AVE
3700 ARGUELLO BLVD
3800 2ND AVE
3900 3RD AVE
4000 4TH AVE
4100 5TH AVE
4200 6TH AVE
4300 7TH AVE
4400 8TH AVE
4500 9TH AVE
4600 10TH AVE
4700 11TH AVE
4800 12TH AVE
FUNSTON AVE
PARK PRESIDIO BLVD
5000 14TH AVE
5100 15TH AVE
5200 16TH AVE
5300 17TH AVE
5400 18TH AVE
5500 19TH AVE
5600 20TH AVE
5700 21ST AVE
5800 22ND AVE
5900 23RD AVE
6000 24TH AVE
6100 25TH AVE
6200 26TH AVE
6300 27TH AVE
6400 28TH AVE
6500 29TH AVE
6600 30TH AVE
6700 31ST AVE
6800 32ND AVE
6900 33RD AVE
7000 34TH AVE
7100 35TH AVE
7200 36TH AVE
7300 37TH AVE
7400 38TH AVE
7500 39TH AVE
7600 40TH AVE
7700 41ST AVE
7800 42ND AVE
7900 43RD AVE
8000 44TH AVE
8100 45TH AVE
8200 46TH AVE
8300 47TH AVE
END 48TH AVE
2 MARKET ST
KEARNY ST
100 GRANT AVE
STOCKTON ST
300 POWELL ST
400 MASON ST
500 TAYLOR ST
SHANNON ST
600 JONES ST
700 LEAVENWORTH ST
800 HYDE ST
900 LARKIN ST
1000 POLK ST
END VAN NESS
GELLERT DR SF 12 B3
N AND S OF OCEAN AV E OF
SUNSET BLVD
GENEBERN WY SF 14 B3
SE OF MISSION ST AND SW FROM
COLLEGE AV S TO JUSTIN DR
DR
2 COLLEGE AVE
100 MURRAY ST
200 BENTON AVE
END JUSTIN DR
GENEVA AV SF 19 C1
GENEVA AV SF 20 A2
SE FROM OCEAN AV AND PHELAN AV TO
SANTOS ST
2 PT W OF HOWTH ST
100 HOWTH ST
200 LOUISBURG ST
TARA ST
500 SAN JOSE AVE
600 DELANO AVE
CAYUGA AVE
BAYWOOD CT
BANNOCK ST
ALEMANY BLVD
GLORIA CT
900 MISSION ST
LONDON ST
1000 PARIS ST
LISBON ST
1100 MADRID ST
EDINBURGH ST
1200 NAPLES ST
VIENNA ST
1300 ATHENS ST
MOSCOW ST
HILL BLVD S
1400 MUNICH ST
1500 PRAGUE ST
1600 LINDA VISTA STEPS
BROOKDALE AVE
WALBRIDGE ST
CARTER ST
PARQUE DR
CIELITO DR
ESQUINA DR
CARRIZAL ST
SANTOS ST
COUNTY LINE
GENNESSEE ST SF 13 C3
N FROM JUDSON AV BETWEEN
FOERSTER ST AND PHELAN AV
TO MELROSE AV
2 JUDSON AVE
100 STAPLES AVE
200 FLOOD AVE
300 HEARST AVE
400 MONTEREY ST
500 JOOST AVE
600 MANGELS AVE
END MELROSE AVE
GENOA PL SF 3 A2
N FROM 400 UNION ST BETWEEN
KEARNY ST AND GRANT AV
TO FILBERT ST
GEORGE CT SF 15 C3
W OFF INGALLS ST BETWEEN
LA SALLE AV AND OAKDALE AV
GERKE AL SF 3 A2
E FROM 1600 GRANT AV BETWEEN
FILBERT ST AND GREENWICH ST
GERMANIA ST SF 10 B1
W FROM S WEBSTER ST BETWEEN
HERMANN ST AND WALLER ST
TO STEINER ST
GETZ ST SF 19 C2
SW FROM MT VERNON AV W OF
HOWTH ST TO HAROLD AV
GIANTS DR SF 21 C2
SW FROM GILMAN AV
TO INGERSON AV
GIBB ST SF 3 A3
W FROM S COLUMBUS AV BETWEEN
WASHINGTON ST AND JACKSON ST
GIBSON RD SF 4 C2
OFF BOWLEY ST AT LINCOLN BLVD
GILBERT ST SF 11 B1
SE FROM S BRYANT ST BETWEEN
6TH ST AND 7TH ST TO
A POINT S OF BRANNAN ST
GILLETTE AV SF 21 B3
N FROM LATHROP AV TO A
POINT NE OF BLANKEN AV
GILMAN AV SF 21 B1
NW FROM WATER FRONT TO
3RD ST
GRIFFITH ST
INGALLS ST
JENNINGS ST
END 3RD ST
GILROY ST SF 21 B2
S FROM S INGERSON AV E
OF GRIFFITH ST TO
JAMESTOWN AV
GIRARD RD SF 1 C2
IN PRESIDIO
NE FROM LINCOLN BLVD
GIRARD ST SF 15 A3
S FROM SILVER AV S TO FRATESSA CT
BETWEEN SAN BRUNO AV
AND BRUSSELS ST
2 SILVER AVE
100 SILLIMAN ST
300 BURROWS ST
400 BACON ST
500 WAYLAND ST
600 WOOLSEY ST
700 DWIGHT ST
800 OLMSTEAD ST
900 MANSELL ST
1000 ORDWAY ST
1100 WARD ST
1200 HARKNESS AVE
1300 WILDE AVE
END SAN BRUNO AVE
GLADEVIEW WY SF 13 C1
N OFF SKYVIEW WY BETWEEN
KNOLLVIEW WY AND SKYVIEW WY
TO PANORAMA DR
GLADIOLUS LN SF 13 A
S FROM EUCALYPTUS DR BETWEEN
19TH AV AND JUNIPERO SERRA BLVD
TO ELMHURST DR
GLADSTONE DR SF 14 C

E AND N FROM MAYNARD ST
TO TRUMBULL ST
GLADYS ST SF 14 C2
S FROM SANTA MARINA ST NEAR
MISSION ST TO APPLETON ST
GLENBROOK AV SF 9 C3
SW FROM MOUNTAIN SPRINGS AV TO
PALO ALTO AV
STANYAN
GLENDALE ST SF 10 A3
W FROM MARKET ST BETWEEN COPPER
AL AND ROMAIN ST TO
CORBETT AV
GLENHAVEN LN SF 9 B3
FROM CHRISTOPHER DR EAST
GLENVIEW DR SF 13 C1
N FROM 400 PORTOLA DR TO
BURNETT AV
GLOBE AL SF 13 B3
N FROM HAZELWOOD AV
TO LANDSDALE AV
GLORIA CT SF 20 A2
NE FROM 840 GENEVE AV
GLOVER ST SF 2 C3
W FROM S JONES BETWEEN VALLEJO ST
AND BROADWAY TO
LEAVENWORTH ST
GODEUS ST SF 14 C2
FROM 3351 MISSION ST NEAR
30TH ST TO COLERIDGE ST
GOETHE ST SF 19 B3
NW FROM MISSION ST
TO DE LONG ST
2 COUNTY LINE
100 SAN JOSE AVE
END DE LONG ST
GOETTINGEN ST SF 15 A3
GOETTINGEN ST SF 21 A1
S FROM S SILVER AV TO
CAMPBELL AV
2 SILVER AVE
100 SILLIMAN ST
200 FELTON ST
300 BURROWS ST
400 BACON ST
500 WAYLAND ST
600 WOOLSEY ST
700 DWIGHT ST
800 OLMSTEAD ST
900 MANSELL ST
1000 ORDWAY ST
1100 WARD ST
1200 HARKNESS AVE
1300 ALPHA ST
END CAMPBELL AVE
GOLD ST SF 3 A3
W FROM 701 SANSOME ST BETWEEN
JACKSON ST AND PACIFIC AV
TO MONTGOMERY ST
GOLDEN CT SF 2 C3
S FROM S SACRAMENTO ST BETWEEN
JONES AND LEAVENWORTH STS
GOLDEN GATE AV SF 5 B3
GOLDEN GATE AV SF 6 A3
W FROM JUNCTION MARKET ST
AND TAYLOR ST BETWEEN
MCALLISTER AND TURK STS
TO ARGUELLO BLVD
2 MARKET ST
TAYLOR ST
100 JONES ST
200 LEAVENWORTH ST
DALE PL
300 HYDE ST
400 LARKIN ST
500 POLK ST
600 VAN NESS AVE
700 FRANKLIN ST
GOUGH ST
OCTAVIA ST
1000 LAGUNA ST
1100 BUCHANAN ST
CRAM PL
1200 WEBSTER ST
1300 FILLMORE ST
1400 STEINER ST
1500 PIERCE ST
1700 DIVISADERO ST
1800 BRODERICK ST
1900 BAKER ST
2000 LYON ST
2100 CENTRAL AVE
MASONIC AVE
ANNAPOLIS TERR
TAMALPAIS TERR
ROSLYN TERR
KITTREDGE TERR
CHABOT TERR
TEMESCAL TERR
PARKET AVE
2700 STANYAN ST
2800 WILLARD ST
END ARGUELLO BLVD
GOLDING LN SF 10 A3
W FROM MARKET ST OPPOSITE
ELIZABETH TO BURNETT AV
2 MARKET ST
100 CORBETT AVE
END BURNETT AVE
GOLD MINE DR SF 14 A2
W FROM DIAMOND HGTS BLVD
N & E TO DIAMOND HEIGHTS BLVD
GOLETA AV SF 12 C3
N FROM SLOAT BLVD BETWEEN
VALE AND PARAISO PL TO
CRESTLAKE DR
GONZALEZ DR SF 18 C2
GONZALEZ DR SF 19 A2
E FROM ARBALLO DR S OF
SERRANO DR TO CASTELO AV
GORDON ST SF 11 A1
N FROM S HARRISON ST BETWEEN
8TH ST AND 9TH ST
GORGAS AV SF 1 C2
IN PRESIDIO
S OF RICHARDSON AV
GORHAM ST SF 14 B3
W FROM CAYUGA AV
N OF TINGLEY ST
GOUGH ST SF 2 B3
GOUGH ST SF 6 B1
GOUGH ST SF 10 C1
N FROM S MARKET ST BETWEEN
FRANKLIN AND OCTAVIA STS
TO FORT MASON
2 MARKET ST
HAIGHT ST
ROSE ST
100 PAGE ST
LILY ST
200 OAK ST
HICKORY ST
300 FELL ST
LINDEN ST
400 HAYES ST
IVY ST
500 GROVE ST
600 FULTON ST
ASH ST
700 MCALLISTER ST
800 GOLDEN GATE AVE
ELM ST
900 TURK ST
1000 EDDY ST
WILLOW ST
1100 ELLIS ST
1300 GEARY ST
1400 POST ST
1500 SUTTER ST
FERN ST
1600 BUSH ST
AUSTIN ST
1700 PINE ST
1800 CALIFORNIA ST
1900 SACRAMENTO ST
2000 CLAY ST
2100 WASHINGTON ST
2200 JACKSON ST
2300 PACIFIC AVE
2400 BROADWAY
2500 VALLEJO ST
2600 GREEN ST
2700 UNION ST
2800 FILBERT ST
2900 GREENWICH ST
3000 LOMBARD ST
3100 CHESTNUT ST
3200 FRANCISCO ST
BAY ST
END FORT MASON
GOULD ST SF 21 B1
S FROM PAUL AV BETWEEN CARR AND
EXETER STS TO SALINAS AV
GRACE ST SF 10 C1
S FROM S MISSION ST BETWEEN
9TH AND 10TH STS TO
HOWARD ST
GRAFTON AV SF 19 B2
W FROM HAROLD AV TO ORIZABA AV
2 HAROLD AVE
100 LEE AVE
200 BRIGHTON AVE
300 PLYMOUTH AVE
400 GRANADA AVE
500 MIRAMAR AVE
600 CAPITOL AVE
700 FAXON AVE
800 JULES AVE
900 ASHTON AVE
END ORIZABA AVE
GRAHAM ST SF 1 B3
IN PRESIDIO
NE FROM MORAGA AV
GRANADA AV SF 19 B2
N FROM LAKE VIEW AV TO
SOUTHWOOD DR BETWEEN PLYMOUTH
AND MIRAMAR AVES
2 LAKE VIEW AVE
100 GRAFTON AVE
200 HOLLOWAY AVE
300 OCEAN AVE
END SOUTHWOOD DR
GRANAT CT SF 9 B1
E OFF S 9TH AV BETWEEN FULTON
ST AND CABRILLO ST
GRAND VIEW AV SF 10 A3
GRAND VIEW AV SF 14 A1
S FROM MARKET ST AND YUKON ST
TO 23RD ST
2 MARKET ST
STANTON ST
GRAND VIEW TERR
ACME AL
100 ROMAIN ST
200 21ST ST
246 MORGAN AL
HOFFMAN ST
ALVARADO ST
23RD ST
ELIZABETH ST
24TH ST
25TH ST
END CLIPPER ST
GRANDVIEW TER SF 10 A3
N FROM GRAND VIEW AV BETWEEN
ACME AL AND STANTON ST
GRANT AV SF 3 A2
GRANT AV SF 7 A1
N FROM S MARKET ST BETWEEN
KEARNY AND STOCKTON STS
TO BEACH ST
2 MARKET ST
OFARRELL ST
100 GEARY ST
MAIDEN LN
200 POST ST
ASHBURTON PL
CAMPTON PL
TILLMAN PL
300 SUTTER ST
HARLAN PL
400 BUSH ST
500 PINE ST
VINTON CT
600 CALIFORNIA ST
700 SACRAMENTO ST
COMMERCIAL ST
800 CLAY ST
900 WASHINGTON ST
1000 JACKSON ST
1100 PACIFIC AVE
ADLER ST
BROADWAY
1200 COLUMBUS AVE
FRESNO ST
1300 VALLEJO ST
1400 GREEN ST
1500 UNION ST
NOBLES AL
1600 FILBERT ST
GERKE AL
PARKEE AL
1700 GREENWICH ST
EDITH PL
EDGARDO PL
1800 LOMBARD ST
WHITING ST
1900 CHESTNUT ST
PFEIFFER ST
2000 FRANCISCO ST
GRANVILLE WY SF 13 B2
NW FROM 1200 PORTOLA DR TO
CLAREMONT BLVD
2 PORTOLA DR
100 ULLOA ST
END CLAREMONT BLVD
GRATTAN ST SF 9 C2
W FROM BELVEDERE ST NEAR
ALMA ST TO STANYAN ST
2 BELVEDERE ST
100 COLE ST
200 SHRADER ST
END STANYAN ST
GRAYSTONE TER SF 9 C3
S FROM S PEMBERTON PL TO
CORBETT AV
100 PEMBERTON PL
200 IRON AL
300 COPPER AL
END CORBETT AVE
GREAT HWY SF 8 A3
GREAT HWY SF 12 A1
S FROM TERMINATION OF POINT
LOBOS AV ALONG THE OCEAN
BEACH TO SLOAT BLVD
600 END OF PT LOBOS AVE
700 BALBOA ST
800 CABRILLO ST
FULTON ST
JFK DR
1200 LINCOLN WAY
1300 IRVING ST
1400 JUDAH ST
1500 KIRKHAM ST
1600 LAWTON ST
1700 MORAGA ST
1800 NORIEGA ST
1900 ORTEGA ST
2000 PACHECO ST
2100 QUINTARA ST
2200 RIVERA ST
2300 SANTIAGO ST
TARAVAL ST
ULLOA ST
VICENTE ST
WAWONA ST
END SLOAT BLVD
GREEN PL SF 2 C3
GREEN ST SF 2 A3
GREEN ST SF 3 B2
FROM THE EMBARCADERO BETWEEN
VALLEJO ST AND UNION ST
TO PRESIDIO RESERVATION
2 THE EMBARCADERO
DAVIS ST
50 FRONT ST
100 BATTERY ST
GAINES ST
200 SANSOME ST
CALHOUN ST
300 MONTGOMERY ST
CASTLE ST
WINDSOR PL
400 KEARNY ST
SONOMA ST
VARENNES ST
500 GRANT AVE
BANNAM PL
JASPER PL
600 COLUMBUS AVE
STOCKTON ST
700 POWELL ST
AUGUST AL
EATON PL
800 MASON ST
ALTA VISTA TER
900 TAYLOR ST
1000 JONES ST
1100 LEAVENWORTH ST
NEW ORLEANS AVE
1200 HYDE ST
EASTMAN ST
1300 LARKIN ST
1400 POLK ST
1500 VAN NESS AVE
1600 FRANKLIN ST
1700 GOUGH ST
1800 OCTAVIA ST
1900 LAGUNA ST
2000 BUCHANAN ST
2100 WEBSTER ST
2200 FILLMORE ST
2300 STEINER ST
2400 PIERCE ST
2500 SCOTT ST
2600 DIVISADERO ST
2700 BRODERICK ST
2800 BAKER ST
END LYON ST
GREENOUGH AV SF 1 A2
IN PRESIDIO
N FROM KOBBE AV
GREENVIEW CT SF 9 C3
E FROM S DELLBROOK ONE BLK S
OF PANORAMA DR
GREENWICH ST SF 2 A3
GREENWICH ST SF 3 B2
W FROM THE EMBARCADERO BETWEEN
FILBERT AND LOMBARD STS
TO PRESIDIO RESERVATION
2 THE EMBARCADERO
100 BATTERY ST
200 SANSOME ST
TELEGRAPH HILL BLVD
400 KEARNY ST
CHILD ST
500 GRANT AVE
KRAMER PL
600 STOCKTON ST
700 POWELL ST

1988 SAN FRANCISCO COUNTY CROSS STREET INDEX

GROVER PL
COLUMBUS AVE
800 MASON ST
JANSEN ST
900 TAYLOR ST
ROACH ST
1000 JONES ST
1100 LEAVENWORTH ST
GREENWICH TER
SOUTHARD PL
1200 HYDE ST
1300 LARKIN ST
1400 POLK ST
1500 VAN NESS AVE
1600 FRANKLIN ST
IMPERIAL AL
1700 GOUGH ST
1800 OCTAVIA ST
1900 LAGUNA ST
2000 BUCHANAN ST
2100 WEBSTER ST
2200 FILLMORE ST
2300 STEINER ST
2400 PIERCE ST
2500 SCOTT ST
2600 DIVISADERO ST
2700 BRODERICK ST
2800 BAKER ST
END LYON ST
GREENWOOD AV SF 19 C1
W FROM JUNCTION OF HAZELWOOD AV
OPPOSITE JUDSON AV TO
PLYMOUTH AV
2 HAZELWOOD AVE
50 VALDEZ AVE
100 COLON AVE
END PLYMOUTH AVE
GRENARD TER SF 2 B2
N FROM 1412 GREENWICH ST
GRIFFITH ST SF 21 C2
SW FROM NAVY RD TO
JAMESTOWN AV
NAVY RD
OAKDALE AVE
PALOU AVE
QUESADA AV
REVERE AV
SHAFTER AV
THOMAS AV
UNDERWOOD AV
VAN DYKE AV
CAMERON WY
FITZGERALD AVE
GILMAN AVE
INGERSON AV
END JAMESTOWN AVE
GRIJALVA DR SF 19 A2
SW FROM JUAN BAUTISTA CIR
TO GARCES DR
GROTE PL SF 7 B2
S FROM S FOLSOM ST BETWEEN
FREMONT ST AND 1ST ST
GROVE ST SF 6 A3
GROVE ST SF 9 C1
W FROM S MARKET ST AT HYDE ST
BETWEEN HAYES ST AND FULTON ST
TO STANYAN ST
MARKET ST
LARKIN ST
POLK ST
200 VAN NESS AVE
300 FRANKLIN ST
400 GOUGH ST
500 OCTAVIA ST
600 LAGUNA ST
700 BUCHANAN ST
800 WEBSTER ST
900 FILLMORE ST
STEINER ST
ALAMO SQUARE

1200 SCOTT ST
1300 DIVISADERO ST
1400 BRODERICK ST
1500 BAKER ST
1600 LYON ST
1700 CENTRAL AVE
1800 MASONIC AVE
1900 ASHBURY ST
2000 CLAYTON ST
2100 COLE ST
2200 SHRADER ST
END STANYAN ST
GROVER PL SF 3 A2
S FROM 701 GREENWICH ST TO
COLUMBUS AV
GUERRERO ST SF 10 C1
GUERRERO ST SF 14 C1
S FROM S MARKET ST BETWEEN
VALENCIA AND DOLORES STS
TO SAN JOSE AV
2 MARKET ST
100 DUBOCE AVE
132 CLINTON PARK
BROSNAN ST
200 14TH ST
300 15TH ST
400 16TH ST
GAISER CT
CAMP ST
500 17TH ST
DOLORES TER
550 DORLAND ST
600 18TH ST
700 19TH ST
800 20TH ST
850 LIBERTY ST
900 21ST ST
HILL ST
1000 22ND ST
ALVARADO ST
1100 23RD ST
ELIZABETH ST
1200 24TH ST
1300 25TH ST
JURI ST
1400 26TH ST
1454 ARMY ST
1500 27TH ST
1550 DUNCAN ST
1600 28TH ST
END SAN JOSE AVE
GUTTENBERG ST SF 20 A3
SE FROM 5501 MISSION ST
TO COUNTY LINE
2 MISSION ST
100 MORSE ST
200 BRUNSWICK ST
300 HANOVER ST
END COUNTY LINE
GUY PL SF 7 B2
W FROM S 1ST ST BETWEEN
FOLSOM ST AND HARRISON ST
H ST SF 17 B1
SE FROM SPEAR AV IN
HUNTERS POINT
HAHN ST SF 20 C3
N FROM SUNRISE WY TO LELAND AV
HAIGHT ST SF 9 C1
HAIGHT ST SF 10 A1
W FROM JUNCTION MARKET AND
GOUGH STS BETWEEN WALLER AND
PAGE STS TO STANYAN ST
2 MARKET ST
GOUGH ST
100 OCTAVIA ST
200 LAGUNA ST
300 BUCHANAN ST
400 WEBSTER ST
500 FILLMORE ST
600 STEINER ST

700 PIERCE ST
800 SCOTT ST
900 DIVISADERO ST
1000 BRODERICK ST
BUENA VISTA AVE
1100 BAKER ST
1200 LYON ST
BUENA VISTA AVE
1300 CENTRAL AVE
1400 MASONIC AVE
1500 ASHBURY ST
1600 CLAYTON ST
BELVEDERE ST
1700 COLE ST
1800 SHRADER ST
END STANYAN ST
HALE ST SF 15 A3
W FROM 2300 SAN BRUNO AV
TO BOWDOIN ST
2 SAN BRUNO AVE
100 BARNEVELD ST
200 MERRILL ST
300 BOYLSTON ST
END BOWDOIN ST
HALLAM ST SF 7 A3
S FROM S FOLSOM ST BETWEEN
7TH AND 8TH STS
HALLECK ST SF 1 C2
IN PRESIDIO
N FROM LINCOLN BLVD
HALLECK ST SF 3 B3
W FROM 201 FRONT ST BETWEEN
CALIFORNIA AND SACRAMENTO STS
TO LEIDESDORFF ST
2 FRONT ST
100 BATTERY ST
200 SANSOME ST
END LIEDESDORFF ST
HALYBURTON CT SF 3 C1
N FROM 13TH ST BET HUTCHINS CT &
BIGELOW CT, TREASURE ISLAND
HAMERTON AV SF 14 A3
BETWEEN BURNSIDE AV AND
CHILTON AV FROM CHENERY ST S
THEN N FROM MANGELS AV
HAMILTON ST SF 1 A2
IN PRESIDIO
S FROM MARINE DR
HAMILTON ST SF 21 A1
S FROM SILVER AV TO DELTA ST
2 SILVER AVE
100 SILLIMAN ST
200 FELTON ST
300 BURROWS ST
400 BACON ST
500 WAYLAND ST
600 WOOLSEY ST
700 DWIGHT ST
900 MANSELL ST
END DELTA ST
HAMPSHIRE ST SF 11 A2
S FROM ALAMEDA ST BETWEEN
PORTERO AV AND YORK ST
TO PERALTA AV
100 ALAMEDA ST
200 15TH ST
16TH ST
400 17TH ST
500 MARIPOSA ST
600 18TH ST
700 19TH ST
800 20TH ST
900 21ST ST
1000 22ND ST
1100 23RD ST
1200 24TH ST
1300 25TH ST
26TH ST
1500 ARMY ST
END PERALTA AVE

HANCOCK ST SF 10 B2
W FROM S CHURCH ST BETWEEN
18TH & 19TH STS TO NOE ST
2 CHURCH ST
100 SANCHEZ ST
END NOE ST
HANOVER ST SF 20 A3
SW FROM 300 BLOCK OF
POPE ST S OF BRUNSWICK ST
TO COUNTY LINE
50 POPE ST
100 ALLISON ST
200 WATT AVE
CONCORD ST
300 GUTTENBERG ST
400 LOWELL ST
END COUNTY LINE
HARBOR RD SF 16 A3
NW FROM NORTHRIDGE RD AND
INGALLS ST BETWEEN INNES AV
AND HUDSON AV
HARDIE PL SF 7 A1
E FROM 200 KEARNY ST BETWEEN
SUTTER ST AND BUSH ST
HARDIE RD SF 1 B3
IN PRESIDIO
S OF MORAGA AV
HARDING RD SF 18 A1
SE FROM SKYLINE BLVD S
FROM LAKE MERCED BLVD
HARE ST SF 16 A3
E FROM MIDDLE PT RD ONE BLK
N OF INNES AV
HARKNESS AV SF 21 A2
W FROM 3500 SAN BRUNO AV
BETWEEN WILDE AND WARD ST
TO DELTA ST
2 SAN BRUNO AVE
100 GIRARD ST
300 GOETTINGEN ST
SPARTA ST
BISHOP ST
RUTLAND ST
400 ALDER ST
MILL ST
DELTA ST
BOWDOIN ST
END MANSELL ST
HARLAN PL SF 7 A2
W FROM MARK LN BETWEEN BUSH
AND SUTTER STS
HARLEM AL SF 6 C2
N FROM S O FARRELL ST BETWEEN
LEAVENWORTH ST AND HYDE ST
HARLOW ST SF 10 B2
S FROM 3465 16TH ST BETWEEN
CHURCH ST AND SANCHEZ ST
TOWARDS 17TH ST
HARNEY WY SF 21 B3
SW FROM JAMESTOWN AV AT
CANDLESTICK PARK
HAROLD AV SF 19 C2
N FROM GETZ ST NEAR GRAFTON AV
TO OCEAN AV
2 GETZ ST
GRAFTON AVE
HOLLOWAY AVE
200 BRUCE ST
END OCEAN AVE
HARPER ST SF 14 B2
S FROM 30TH ST NEAR NOE ST
TO LAIDLEY ST
2 30TH ST
RANDALL ST
END LAIDLEY ST
HARRIET ST SF 7 A3
HARRIET ST SF 11 B1
SE FROM 1001 HOWARD ST BETWEEN
6TH AND 7TH STS TO A
POINT S OF BRANNAN ST

2 HOWARD ST
100 FOLSOM ST
200 HARRISON ST
300 BRYANT ST
400 BRANNAN ST
END PT S OF BRANNAN ST
HARRINGTON ST SF 20 A1
NW FROM S MISSION ST BETWEEN
SANTA ROSA ST AND NORTON ST
TO ALEMANY BLVD
HARRIS PL SF 2 B2
S FROM E S LAGUNA ST BETWEEN
FILBERT AND GREENWICH STS
HARRISON BLVD SF 1 A3
IN PRESIDIO
S OF KOBBE AV
HARRISON ST SF 7 A3
HARRISON ST SF 11 A2
HARRISON ST SF 15 A1
W FROM THE BAY BETWEEN FOLSOM
AND BRYANT STS AND S
TO RIPLEY ST
THE EMBARCADERO
2 STEUART ST
100 SPEAR ST
200 MAIN ST
300 BEALE ST
400 FREMONT ST
500 1ST ST
RINCON ST
ESSEX ST
STERLING ST
BRADLEY CT
600 2ND ST
VASSAR PL
650 HAWTHORNE ST
700 3RD ST
LAPU LAPU
800 4TH ST
900 5TH ST
MERLIN ST
OAK GROVE ST
MORRIS ST
1000 6TH ST
HARRIET ST
COLUMBIA SQUARE
SHERMAN ST
1100 7TH ST
1126 LANGTON ST
CHESLEY ST
BERWICK PL
HAYWARD ST
1200 8TH ST
GORDON ST
1300 9TH ST
DORE ST
1400 10TH ST
JUNIPER ST
1500 11TH ST
NORFOLK ST
1600 12TH ST
1700 13TH ST
1800 14TH ST
ALAMEDA ST
1900 15TH ST
16TH ST
2000 TREAT AVE
2100 17TH ST
MARIPOSA ST
2200 18TH ST
2300 19TH ST
2400 20TH ST
2500 21ST ST
2600 22ND ST
2700 23RD ST
2800 24TH ST
25TH ST
3000 26TH ST
3100 ARMY ST
3200 PRECITA AVE

3300 NORWICH ST
END RIPLEY ST
HARRY ST SF 14 B2
SW FROM LAIDLEY ST TO BEACON ST
HARTFORD ST SF 10 B2
S FROM S 17TH ST BETWEEN NOE
& CASTRO STS TO 20TH ST
2 17TH ST
100 18TH ST
200 19TH ST
END 20TH ST
HARVARD ST SF 20 C1
S FROM SILVER AV BETWEEN
OXFORD ST AND BAMBIER ST
TO BACON ST
2 SILVER AVE
100 PIOCHE ST
200 SILLIMAN ST
300 FELTON ST
400 BURROWS ST
END BACON ST
HARWOOD AL SF 3 A2
S OFF 451 FILBERT ST BETWEEN
GRANT AV AND VARENNES ST
HASTINGS TER SF 2 C2
E FROM S HYDE ST BETWEEN
UNION ST AND FILBERT ST
HATTIE ST SF 10 A2
S FROM CORBETT AV W OF ORD ST
TO 18TH ST
HAVELOCK ST SF 19 C1
W FROM SAN JOSE AV 2
BLKS N OF OCEAN AV
TO A POINT W OF
EDNA ST
HAVENS ST SF 2 C2
W FROM S LEAVENWORTH ST
BETWEEN UNION AND FILBERT STS
HAVENSIDE DR SF 12 B3
S FROM OCEAN AV TO
EUCALYPTUS DR E OF
WESTMOORLAND DR
HAWES ST SF 21 C1
FROM PALOU AV SW TO JAMESTOWN AV
PALOU AVE
QUESADA AVE
REVERE AVE
SHAFTER AV
THOMAS AV
UNDERWOOD AV
VAN DYKE AV
YOSEMITE AV
ARMSTRONG AV
BANCROFT AV
CARROL AV
EGBERT AV
FITZGERALD AV
GILMAN AV
HOLLISTER AV
END JAMESTOWN AV
HAWTHORNE ST SF 7 B2
S FROM S HOWARD ST BETWEEN
2ND AND 3RD ST TO
HARRISON ST
HAYES ST SF 6 A3
HAYES ST SF 9 C1
W FROM JUNCTION MARKET ST
AND LARKIN ST BETWEEN FELL ST
& GROVE ST TO STANYAN ST
MARKET ST
LARKIN ST
100 POLK ST
200 VAN NESS AVE
300 FRANKLIN ST
400 GOUGH ST
500 OCTAVIA ST
600 LAGUNA ST
700 BUCHANAN ST
800 WEBSTER ST
900 FILLMORE ST
STEINER ST
PIERCE ST
1200 SCOTT ST
1300 DIVISADERO ST
1400 BRODERICK ST
1500 BAKER ST
1600 LYON ST
1700 CENTRAL AVE
1800 MASONIC AVE
1900 ASHBURY ST
2000 CLAYTON ST
2100 COLE ST
2200 SHRADER ST
END STANYAN ST
HAYWARD PL SF 11 A1
S FROM S HARRISON ST BETWEEN
7TH ST AND 8TH ST
HAZELWOOD AV SF 13 C3
E OF VALDEZ AV AND NW FROM
JUDSON AV TO YERBA BUENA AV
2 JUDSON AVE
GREENWOOD AVE
34 STAPLES AVE
66 FLOOD AVE
100 MONTECITO AVE
200 MONTEREY BLVD
JOOST AVE
300 MANGELS AVE
400 BRENTWOOD AVE
END YERBA BUENA AVE
HEAD ST SF 19 B2
W OF SAN JOSE AV NEAR
COUNTY LINE FROM
RANDOLPH N AND NE
TO ASHTON AV
400 RANDOLPH ST
500 SARGENT ST
600 SHIELDS ST
700 GARFIELD ST
800 HOLLOWAY AVE
END ASHTON AVE
HEARST AV SF 13 C3
HEARST AV SF 14 A3
W FROM CIRCULAR AV BETWEEN
MONTEREY BLVD AND FLOOD AV
TO RIDGEWOOD ST
2 CIRCULAR AVE
100 BADEN ST
200 CONGO ST
300 DETROIT ST
400 EDNA ST
500 FOERSTER ST
600 GENNESSEE ST
END RIDGEWOOD ST
HEATHER AV SF 5 C2
N FROM EUCLID AV TO
MAYFAIR DR W OF IRIS AV
HELEN ST SF 6 C1
S FROM S CALIFORNIA ST
BETWEEN LEAVENWORTH AND HYDE STS
HELENA ST SF 15 A2
E OF SAN BRUNO AV NEAR
SILVER AV N OF AUGUSTA ST
E FROM BAYSHORE BLVD
HEMLOCK ST SF 6 B2
W FROM S LARKIN ST BETWEEN
POST ST AND SUTTER ST
TO A POINT W OF LAGUNA ST
2 LARKIN ST
100 POLK ST
VAN NESS AVE
FRANKLIN ST
600 LAGUNA ST
END PT W OF LAGUNA ST
HEMWAY TER SF 5 C3
N FROM 1900 FULTON ST W OF
MASONIC AV
HENRY ST SF 10 B2
W FROM S SANCHEZ ST BETWEEN
14TH AND 15TH STS TO A
POINT W OF CASTRO ST
2 SANCHEZ ST
100 NOE ST
200 CASTRO ST
END PT W OF CASTRO ST
HERMANN ST SF 10 B1
W FROM MARKET ST BETWEEN WALLER
ST AND DUBOCE AV TO STEINER ST
2 MARKET ST
LAGUNA ST
100 BUCHANAN ST
200 WEBSTER ST
CHURCH ST
300 FILLMORE ST
END STEINER ST
HERNANDEZ AV SF 13 B1
W FROM WOODSIDE AV TO
MERCED AV
2 WOODSIDE AVE
100 LAGUNA HONDA BLVD
200 VASQUEZ ST
END WOODSIDE AVE
HERON ST SF 11 A1
W FROM S BERWICK PL BETWEEN
FOLSOM AND HARRISON STS
TO 8TH ST
HESTER AV SF 21 B2
SE AND W FROM BAY SHORE
BLVD TO BAY SHORE BLVD
HEYMAN AV SF 14 C2
SE FROM 200 BLOCK COLERIDGE AV
TO PROSPECT AV
HICKORY ST SF 10 B1
W FROM S VAN NESS AV BETWEEN
OAK ST & FELL ST TO WEBSTER ST
2 VAN NESS AVE
100 FRANKLIN ST
200 GOUGH ST
300 OCTAVIA ST
LAGUNA ST
BUCHANAN ST
END WEBSTER ST
HICKS RD SF 1 B3
E OF ARGUELLO BLVD, PRESIDIO
HIDALGO TER SF 10 B2
E FROM S DOLORES BETWEEN 14TH ST
AND 15TH ST
HIGH ST SF 14 A1
S FROM 25TH ST W OF GRAND VIEW AV
TO CLIPPER ST
HIGHLAND AV SF 14 B2
E FROM ARLINGTON ST NEAR
CHARLES ST TO ANDOVER ST
ARLINGTON ST
100 MISSION ST
PATTON ST
300 HOLLY PARK CIR
BENNINGTON ST
END ANDOVER ST
HIGUERA AV SF 18 C2
W FROM ARBALLO DR TO
LAKE MERCED BLVD
HILIRITAS AV SF 14 A2
N FROM ARBOR ST TO DIAMOND ST
HILL BLVD S SF 20 B3
SE FROM S GENEVA TO COUNTY LINE
HILL DR SF 17 B1
HUNTERS POINT RES
HILL ST SF 10 B3
W FROM S VALENCIA ST BETWEEN
21ST ST & 22ND ST W TO CASTRO ST
2 VALENCIA ST
END GUERRERO ST
300 CHURCH ST
400 SANCHEZ ST
500 NOE ST
END CASTRO ST
HILLCREST CT SF 13 C3
S FROM MYRA WY E OF SHERWOOD CT
HILLPOINT AV SF 9 C2
N FROM PARNASSUS AV BETWEEN
WILLARD ST AND HILLWAY AV
HILLWAY AV SF 9 C2
N FROM PARNASSUS AV BETWEEN
WILLARD ST AND ARGUELLO BLVD
TO CARL ST
HILTON ST SF 15 A2
S FROM CORTLAND AV BETWEEN
BAYSHORE BLVD AND JAMES LICK FRWY
HIMMELMAN PL SF 2 C3
N FROM S PACIFIC AV BETWEEN
MASON ST & TAYLOR ST TO BROADWAY
HITCHCOCK ST SF 1 A2
E FROM HARRISON BLVD, PRESIDIO
HOBART AL SF 7 A2
E FROM S TAYLOR ST BETWEEN
POST ST AND SUTTER ST
HODGES AL SF 3 A2
N FROM 300 VALLEJO ST BETWEEN
SANSOME ST AND MONTGOMERY ST
HOFF ST SF 10 C2
S FROM S 16TH ST BETWEEN
MISSION ST AND VALENCIA ST
TO 17TH ST
HOFFMAN AV SF 10 A3
HOFFMAN AV SF 14 A1
S FROM GRAND VIEW AV TO
CLIPPER ST 1 BLK E OF MARKET ST
GRAND VIEW AV
2 22ND ST
100 ALVARADO ST
200 23RD ST
300 ELIZABETH ST
400 24TH ST
500 25TH ST
END CLIPPER ST
HOFFMAN ST SF 1 A2
S OF LINCOLN BLVD, PRESIDIO
HOLLADAY AV SF 15 A1
S FROM PERALTA AV S OF ARMY ST
TO MAYFLOWER ST
100 PERALTA AV
WRIGHT ST
YORK ST
300 RUTLEDGE ST
COSTA ST
FAITH ST
JOY ST
400 ESMERALDA AV
END MAYFLOWER ST
HOLLAND CT SF 7 A2
NW FROM S HOWARD ST BETWEEN
4TH ST AND 5TH ST
HOLLIS ST SF 6 B2
N FROM S ELLIS ST BETWEEN
LAGUNA ST AND WEBSTER ST TO
O'FARRELL ST
HOLLISTER AV SF 21 B1
FROM A POINT SE OF HAWES ST
NW TO 3RD ST
HAWES ST
INGALLS ST
JENNINGS ST
END 3RD ST
HOLLOWAY AV SF 19 B1
W FROM HAROLD AV TO TAPIA DR
2 HAROLD AV
100 LEE AV
200 BRIGHTON AV
300 PLYMOUTH AV
400 GRANADA AV
500 MIRAMAR AV
600 CAPITOL AV
700 FAXON AV
800 JULES AV
900 ASHTON AV
ORIZABA AV
BRIGHT ST
1100 HEAD ST
1200 VICTORIA ST
RAMSELL ST
1300 DE SOTO ST
ARCH ST
1400 CORONA ST
VERNON ST
1500 BORICA ST
RALSTON ST
1600 ALVISO ST
BIXBY ST
1700 MONTICELLO ST
1800 LUNADO WY
BEVERLY ST
JUNIPERO SERRA BLVD
STRATFORD DR
DENSLOWE DR
19TH AV
VARELA AV
CARDENAS AV
ARELLANO AV
END TAPIA DR
HOLLY PARK CIR SF 14 C2
SURROUNDING HOLLY PARK
ELSIE ST
BOCANA ST
NEWMAN ST
HIGHLAND AV
PARK ST
MURRAY ST
PARK ST
HIGHLAND AV
END APPLETON ST
HOLLYWOOD CT SF 20 A2
E OFF S POPE ST BETWEEN MORSE ST
AND MISSION ST
HOLYOKE ST SF 21 A1
S FROM SILVER AV BETWEEN
HAMILTON ST & SOMERSET ST TO
ANKENY ST, AND S FROM CAMPBELL AV
2 SILVER AV
END SILLIMAN ST
200 FELTON ST
300 BURROWS ST
400 BACON ST
500 WAYLAND ST
600 WOOLSEY ST
END KAREN CT
900 MANSELL ST
END ANKENY ST
CAMPBELL AV
HOMER ST SF 11 A1
SW FROM CHELSEY ST BETWEEN
HARRISON ST & BRYANT ST
AND 7TH ST AND 8TH ST
HOMESTEAD ST SF 14 A1
S FROM S 24TH ST BETWEEN
DOUGLASS ST AND HOFFMAN AV
TO CLIPPER ST
2 24TH ST
100 25TH ST
END CLIPPER ST
HOMEWOOD CT SF 19 B1
N FROM WILDWOOD WY BETWEEN
KEYSTONE WY & FAXON AV
HOOKER AL SF 7 A2
E FROM 700 MASON ST BETWEEN
PINE ST AND BUSH ST
HOOPER ST SF 11 B1
S FROM 1100 - 7TH ST
TO 8TH ST
HOPKINS AV SF 10 A3
NW FROM CORBETT AV NEAR 23RD ST
TO BURNETT AV
HORACE ST SF 15 A1
S FROM 25TH ST BETWEEN FOLSOM ST
AND SHOTWELL ST TO 26TH ST
HORNE AV SF 17 B1
SW FROM ROBINSON ST BETWEEN
FISHER AV AND COLEMAN ST
TO SPEAR AV
ROBINSON ST

1988 SAN FRANCISCO COUNTY CROSS STREET INDEX

GALVEZ AV
END SPEAR AV
HOTALING PL SF 3 B3
N FROM WASHINGTON ST BETWEEN
MONTGOMERY ST AND SANSOME ST
TO JACKSON ST
HOUSTON ST SF 2 C2
W FROM 1001 COLUMBUS AV BETWEEN
CHESTNUT ST AND FRANCISCO ST
TO JONES ST
HOWARD RD SF 4 C2
E FROM LINCOLN BLVD, PRESIDIO
HOWARD ST SF 7 A3
HOWARD ST SF 10 C1
SW FROM THE EMBARCADERO BETWEEN
MISSION ST AND FOLSOM ST
TO SOUTH VAN NESS AV
2 THE EMBARCADERO
50 STEUART ST
100 SPEAR ST
200 MAIN ST
300 BEALE ST
400 FREMONT ST
500 1ST ST
MALDEN AL
600 2ND ST
656 NEW MONTGOMERY ST
HAWTHORNE ST
700 3RD ST
800 4TH ST
HOLLAND CT
900 5TH ST
MARY ST
1000 6TH ST
HARRIET ST
RUSS ST
MOSS ST
1100 7TH ST
LANGTON ST
RAUSCH ST
SUMNER ST
1200 8TH ST
1300 9TH ST
WASHBURN ST
DORE ST
GRACE ST
1400 10TH ST
1500 11TH ST
LAFAYETTE ST
1600 12TH ST
END SOUTH VAN NESS AV
HOWE RD SF 1 A2
SW OF STOREY AV, PRESIDIO
HOWTH ST SF 19 C2
SW FROM 810 OCEAN AV TO RIDGE LN
2 OCEAN AV
100 GENEVA AV
200 NIAGARA AV
300 MT VERNON AV
END RIDGE LN
HUBBELL ST SF 11 B2
SW FROM 1300 7TH ST TO 16TH ST
HUDSON AV SF 15 B1
HUDSON AV SF 16 A3
NW FROM A POINT E OF INGALLS ST
TO TOLAND ST
INGALLS ST
BERTHA LN
WHITNEY YOUNG CIR
ARDATH CT
WESTBROOK CT
CASHMERE ST
REUEL CT
KEITH ST
MENDELL ST
NEWHALL ST
3RD ST
END PHELPS ST
SELBY ST
END TOLAND ST
HUGO ST SF 9 B2
FROM ARGUELLO BLVD BETWEEN
LINCOLN WY & IRVING ST TO 7TH AV
2 ARGUELLO BLVD
100 2ND AV
200 3RD AV
300 4TH AV
400 5TH AV
500 6TH AV
END 7TH AV
HULBERT AL SF 7 B3
N & S OFF CLARA ST BETWEEN
4TH ST AND 5TH ST
HUMBOLDT ST SF 11 C3
E FROM ILLINOIS ST BETWEEN
22ND ST AND 23RD ST
HUNT ST SF 7 B2
BETWEEN MISSION ST AND HOWARD ST
NORTHEAST FROM 3RD ST
HUNTERS PT BLVD SF 16 A2
SE FROM 1000 EVANS SE TO INNES ST
HUNTERS PT EXWY SF 21 C2
END OF JAMESTOWN AV AT
CANDLESTICK PARK
HUNTINGTON DR SF 12 B3
OFF COUNTRY CLUB DR
HURON AV SF 19 C2
SW FROM ALEMANY BL TO MISSION ST
ALEMANY BLVD
OTTAWA AV
SALA TER
FOOTE AV
FREDSON CT
NAGLEE AV
MONETA WY
WHIPPLE AV
MILAN TER
FARRAGUT AV
LAURA ST
LAWRENCE ST
SICKLES AV
END MISSION ST
HUSSEY ST SF 17 B1
SE FROM SPEAR AV, HUNTERS POINT
HUTCHINS CT SF 3 C1
N FROM 13TH ST BETWEEN KEPPLER CT
& HALYBURTON CT, TREASURE ISLAND
HYDE ST SF 2 C2
HYDE ST SF 6 C2
N FROM S MARKET AT GROVE ST
TO THE BAY
MARKET ST
GROVE ST
FULTON ST
2 MCALLISTER ST
100 GOLDEN GATE AV
200 TURK ST
300 EDDY ST
400 ELLIS ST
500 OFARRELL ST
MABEL AL
600 GEARY ST
700 POST ST
800 SUTTER ST
900 BUSH ST
1000 PINE ST
1100 CALIFORNIA ST
1200 SACRAMENTO ST
TROY AL
1300 CLAY ST
1400 WASHINGTON ST
1500 JACKSON ST
1600 PACIFIC AV
LYNCH ST
1700 BROADWAY ST
1800 VALLEJO ST
1900 GREEN ST
DELGADO PL
RUSSELL ST
WARNER PL
2000 UNION ST
ALLEN ST
HASTINGS TER
2100 FILBERT ST
2200 GREENWICH ST
2300 LOMBARD ST
2400 CHESTNUT ST
2500 FRANCISCO ST
2600 BAY ST
BERGIN PL
2700 NORTH POINT ST
2800 BEACH ST
2900 JEFFERSON
I ST SF 17 A1
SE FROM SPEAR AV TO J ST
IN HUNTERS POINT
ICEHOUSE AL SF 3 B2
N FROM 100 GREEN ST BETWEEN
BATTERY ST AND SANSOME ST
TO UNION ST
IDORA AV SF 13 B2
W FROM WOODSIDE AV TO GARCIA AV
IGNACIO ST SF 21 C2
S OF INGERSON AV OFF GILROY ST
ILLINOIS ST SF 11 C1
ILLINOIS ST SF 15 C1
S FROM 4TH ST TO TULARE ST
4TH ST
MERRIMAC ST
ALAMEDA ST
EL DORADO ST
16TH ST
17TH ST
MARIPOSA ST
18TH ST
19TH ST
20TH ST
22ND ST
HUMBOLDT ST
23RD ST
24TH ST
END 25TH ST
ARMY ST
MARIN ST
END TULARE ST
ILS LN SF 3 A3
OFF COLUMBUS AV BETWEEN
JACKSON ST AND WASHINGTON ST
IMPERIAL AV SF 2 B2
S FROM S GREENWICH ST BETWEEN
FRANKLIN ST AND GOUGH ST
INA CT SF 20 B1
EXTENSION OF MUNICH TO
LAGRANDE AV
INDIANA ST SF 11 C2
INDIANA ST SF 15 C1
S FROM MARIPOSA ST BETWEEN
MINNESOTA ST AND I-280
TO TULARE ST
500 MARIPOSA ST
600 18TH ST
700 19TH ST
800 20TH ST
1000 22ND ST
TUBBS ST
1200 23RD ST
1400 25TH ST
1500 26TH ST
1600 ARMY ST
MARIN ST
END TULARE ST
INDUSTRIAL ST SF 15 A2
SW FROM OAKDALE AV TO BAYSHORE BL
INFANTRY TER SF 1 B3
IN PRESIDIO
INGALLS ST SF 16 A3
INGALLS ST SF 21 C1
SW FROM INNES AV TO JAMESTOWN AV
INNES AV
HARBOR RD
HUDSON AV
NORTHRIDGE RD
ROSIE LEE LN
KISKA RD
BEATRICE LN
LA SALLE AV
WHITFIELD CT
GEORGE CT
OAKDALE AV
PALOU AV
QUESADA AV
REVERE AV
SHAFTER AV
THOMAS AV
UNDERWOOD ST
VAN DYKE AV
WALLACE AV
YOSEMITE AV
ARMSTRONG AV
BANCROFT AV
CARROLL AV
DONNER AV
EGBERT AV
FITZGERALD AV
GILMAN AV
HOLLISTER AV
INGERSON AV
END JAMESTOWN AV
INGERSON AV SF 21 B1
NW FROM GIANTS DR TO 3RD ST
GIANTS DR
GILROY ST
GRIFFITH ST
CORONADO ST
HAWES ST
REDONDO ST
INGALLS ST
JENNINGS ST
END 3RD ST
INNES AV SF 15 B1
INNES AV SF 16 A3
NW FROM COLEMAN ST TO
TO MILTON ROSS ST
COLEMAN ST
FRIEDELL ST
DONAHUE ST
EARL ST
FITCH ST
HUNTERS PT BLVD
END MIDDLE PT RD
MENDELL ST
3RD ST
NEWHALL ST
END PHELPS ST
RANKIN ST
END MILTON ROSS ST
INVERNESS DR SF 12 C3
S FROM SLOAT BLVD BETWEEN
FOREST VIEW DR AND 26TH AV
TO EUCALYPTUS DR
IOWA ST SF 11 C3
S FROM 22ND ST BETWEEN INDIANA AV
AND PENNSYLVANIA AV TO 23RD ST
700 22ND ST
900 23RD ST
IRIS AV SF 5 C2
N FROM EUCLID AV TO MAYFAIR DR
IRON AL SF 10 A3
S FROM CLAYTON ST
TO GRAYSTONE TER
IRVING ST SF 8 A2
IRVING ST SF 9 A2
W FROM ARGUELLO BLVD S OF
LINCOLN WY TO THE GREAT HIGHWAY
2 ARGUELLO BLVD
100 2ND AV
200 3RD AV
300 4TH AV
400 5TH AV
500 6TH AV
600 7TH AV
700 8TH AV
800 9TH AV
900 10TH AV
1000 11TH AV
1100 12TH AV
1200 FUNSTON AV
1300 14TH AV
1400 15TH AV
1500 16TH AV
1600 17TH AV
1700 18TH AV
1800 19TH AV
1900 20TH AV
2000 21ST AV
2100 22ND AV
2200 23RD AV
2300 24TH AV
2400 25TH AV
2500 26TH AV
2600 27TH AV
2700 28TH AV
2800 29TH AV
2900 30TH AV
3000 31ST AV
3100 32ND AV
3200 33RD AV
3300 34TH AV
3400 35TH AV
3500 36TH AV
SUNSET BLVD
3600 37TH AV
3700 38TH AV
3800 39TH AV
3900 40TH AV
4000 41ST AV
4100 42ND AV
4200 43RD AV
4300 44TH AV
4400 45TH AV
4500 46TH AV
4600 47TH AV
4700 48TH AV
END LA PLAYA ST
IRWIN ST SF 11 B2
S FROM 2700 7TH ST TO 8TH ST
TO 8TH ST
ISIS ST SF 10 C1
S FROM 12TH ST BETWEEN FOLSOM ST
AND HARRISON ST TO 13TH ST
ISLAIS ST SF 15 C1
E FROM THE END OF NAPOLEON ST
TO ARTHUR AV
ISOLA WY SF 13 C2
SW FROM TERESITA BLVD
TO ROCKDALE DR
ITALY AV SF 20 A2
SE FROM 5001 MISSION ST S OF
FRANCE AV TO MOSCOW ST
2 MISSION ST
100 LONDON ST
200 PARIS ST
300 LISBON ST
400 MADRID ST
500 EDINBURGH ST
600 NAPLES ST
700 VIENNA ST
800 ATHENS ST
END MOSCOW ST
IVY ST SF 6 B3
W FROM FRANKLIN ST BETWEEN HAYES
ST AND GROVE ST W TO WEBSTER ST
200 FRANKLIN ST
300 GOUGH ST
500 LAGUNA ST
600 BUCHANAN ST
END WEBSTER ST
J ST SF 17 A1
S OFF SPEAR ST
SPEAR AV

6TH AV
3RD AV
I ST
MAHAN ST
JACKSON ST SF 2 A3
JACKSON ST SF 3 A3
JACKSON ST SF 5 B2
W FROM THE BAY BETWEEN PACIFIC AV
AND WASHINGTON ST TO ARGUELLO BL
DRUMM ST
100 DAVIS ST
200 FRONT ST
300 BATTERY ST
CUSTOM HOUSE PL
400 SANSOME ST
BALANCE ST
HOTALING PL
500 MONTGOMERY ST
COLUMBUS AV
600 KEARNY ST
COOPER AL
WENTWORTH PL
BECKETT ST
700 GRANT AV
ST LOUIS PL
JASON CT
ROSS AL
DUNCOMBE AL
800 STOCKTON ST
BEDFORD PL
JAMES AL
STONE ST
ADELE CT
900 POWELL ST
DORIC AL
1000 MASON ST
MARCY PL
AUBURN ST
1100 TAYLOR ST
1200 JONES ST
1300 LEAVENWORTH ST
WALL PL
1400 HYDE ST
1500 LARKIN ST
1600 POLK ST
1700 VAN NESS AV
1800 FRANKLIN ST
1900 GOUGH ST
2000 OCTAVIA ST
2100 LAGUNA ST
2200 BUCHANAN ST
2300 WEBSTER ST
2400 FILLMORE ST
2500 STEINER ST
2600 PIERCE ST
2700 SCOTT ST
2800 DIVISADERO ST
2900 BRODERICK ST
3000 BAKER ST
3100 LYON ST
3200 PRESIDIO AV
3300 WALNUT ST
3400 LAUREL ST
3500 LOCUST ST
3600 SPRUCE ST
3700 MAPLE ST
3800 CHERRY ST
END ARGUELLO BLVD
JADE PL SF 14 A2
W FROM GOLDMINE DR 3 BLKS W
OF DIAMOND HEIGHTS BLVD
JAMES AL SF 3 A3
S FROM JACKSON ST BETWEEN
STOCKTON ST AND POWELL ST
JAMES LICK FRWY SF 15 A2
JAMES LICK FRWY SF 21 A1
JAMES LICK SKWY SF 11 A1
JAMESTOWN AV SF 21 C3
FROM HUNTERS PT EXPWY N W
TO SALINAS AV

HUNTERS PT EXPWY
HARNEY WY
GILROY ST
GRIFFITH ST
CORONADO ST
HAWES ST
REDONDO ST
INGALLS ST
JENNINGS ST
3RD ST
KEY ST
END SALINAS AV
JANSEN ST SF 2 C2
N FROM 800 GREENWICH ST BETWEEN
MASON & TAYLOR STS TO LOMBARD ST
JARBOE AV SF 14 C2
E FROM 300 MOULTRIE ST
TO PERALTA AV
100 MOULTRIE ST
200 ANDERSON ST
300 ELLSWORTH ST
400 GATES ST
500 FOLSOM ST
600 BANKS ST
700 PRENTISS ST
800 NEVADA ST
900 PUTNAM ST
1000 BRONTE ST
1100 BRADFORD ST
1200 PERALTA AV
JASON CT SF 3 A3
OFF 700 JACKSON ST BETWEEN
GRANT AV AND STOCKTON ST
JASPER PL SF 3 A3
N FROM 500 GREEN ST BETWEEN
GRANT AV AND STOCKTON ST
TO FILBERT ST
2 GREEN ST
100 UNION ST
END FILBERT ST
JAVA ST SF 10 A2
SW FROM BUENA VISTA AV
TO MASONIC AV
JEAN WY SF 5 C3
NW FROM EWING TER TO ANZA ST
S OF GEARY BLVD
JEFFERSON ST SF 2 A2
W FROM THE BAY N OF BEACH ST
TO THE PRESIDIO
2 POWELL ST
THE EMBARCADERO
100 MASON ST
200 TAYLOR ST
300 JONES ST
400 LEAVENWORTH ST
END HYDE ST
WEBSTER ST
END FILLMORE ST
1800 SCOTT ST
1900 DIVISADERO ST
2000 BRODERICK ST
END BAKER ST
JENNINGS ST SF 16 A2
JENNINGS ST SF 21 B1
SW FROM CARGO WY TO LARKSPUR AV
CARGO WY
END HUNTERS POINT BLVD
PALOU AV
QUESADA AV
REVERE AV
SHAFTER AV
THOMAS AV
UNDERWOOD AV
VAN DYKE AV
WALLACE AV
YOSEMITE AV
ARMSTRONG AV
BANCROFT AV
CARROLL AV
DONNER AV

EGBERT AV
FITZGERALD AV
GILMAN AV
HOLLISTER AV
INGERSON AV
JAMESTOWN AV
KEY AV
LE CONTE AV
MEADE AV
END NELSON AV
JEROME AL SF 3 A3
S FROM 501 PACIFIC AV BETWEEN
MONTGOMERY ST AND KEARNY ST
JERROLD AV SF 15 B1
JERROLD AV SF 16 A3
JERROLD AV SF 17 A1
NW FROM MENDELL ST TO BAYSHORE BL
MENDELL ST
NEWHALL ST
3RD ST
PHELPS ST
QUINT ST
RANKIN ST
SELBY ST
MILTON ROSS ST
LETTUCE LN
TOLAND ST
UPTON ST
NAPOLEON ST
BARNEVELD AVE
BAY SHORE BLVD
JERSEY ST SF 14 A1
W FROM S DOLORES ST BETWEEN
24TH ST AND 25TH ST
TO DOUGLASS ST
2 DOLORES ST
CHATTANOOGA ST
100 CHURCH ST
VICKSBURG ST
200 SANCHEZ ST
300 NOE ST
400 CASTRO ST
500 DIAMOND ST
END DOUGLASS ST
JESSIE ST SF 6 C3
JESSIE ST SF 7 A2
JESSIE ST SF 10 C1
W FROM S 1ST ST BETWEEN MARKET ST
AND MISSION ST SW TO A POINT
S OF MCCOPPIN ST
2 1ST ST
ECKER ST
ANTHONY ST
100 2ND ST
NEW MONTGOMERY ST
188 ANNIE ST
END 3RD ST
300 4TH ST
END 5TH ST
400 MINT ST
END 6TH ST
END 7TH ST
800 9TH ST
900 10TH ST
JEWETT ST SF 7 B3
SW FROM 4TH ST BETWEEN KING ST
& TOWNSEND ST TO 5TH ST
JOHN ST SF 3 A3
W FROM 1201 POWELL ST BETWEEN
JACKSON ST AND PACIFIC AV
TO MASON ST
J F KENNEDY DR SF 8 A1
IN GOLDEN GATE PARK
J F KENNEDY DR SF 9 A1
IN GOLDEN GATE PARK
J F SHELLEY DR SF 20 C1
IN JOHN MCLAREN PARK
JOHN MUIR DR SF 18 B2
SE FROM SKYLINE BLVD TO
LAKE MERCED BLVD

JOHNSTONE DR SF 9 C3
N FROM CLARENDON AV ONE BLK
W OF STANYAN
JOICE ST SF 3 A3
N FROM 700 PINE BETWEEN
STOCKTON ST AND POWELL ST
TO CLAY ST
2 PINE ST
100 CALIFORNIA ST
200 SACRAMENTO ST
END CLAY ST
JONES ST SF 2 C2
JONES ST SF 7 A2
N FROM S MARKKET ST BETWEEN
TAYLOR ST AND LEAVENWORTH ST
TO THE BAY
2 MARKET ST
MCALLISTER ST
100 GOLDEN GATE AV
200 TURK ST
300 EDDY ST
400 ELLIS ST
ANTONIO ST
STEVELOE PL
500 OFARRELL ST
600 GEARY ST
COLIN PL
700 POST ST
COSMO PL
800 SUTTER PL
900 BUSH ST
1000 PINE
1100 CALIFORNIA ST
1200 SACRAMENTO ST
PLEASANT ST
1300 CLAY ST
1400 WASHINGTON ST
1500 JACKSON ST
1600 PACIFIC AV
BERNARD ST
1700 BROADWAY
GLOVER ST
1800 VALLEJO ST
1900 GREEN ST
MACONDRAY ST
2000 UNION ST
2100 FILBERT ST
VALPARAISO ST
2200 GREENWICH ST
2300 LOMBARD ST
2400 CHESTNUT ST
HOUSTON ST
2500 FRANCISCO ST
COLUMBUS AV
2600 BAY ST
2700 NORTH POINT ST
2800 BEACH ST
2900 JEFFERSON ST
END THE EMBARCADERO
JOOST AV SF 13 C3
N FROM CIRCULAR AV AND DIAMOND ST
TO HAZELWOOD AV
2 CIRCULAR AV
BROMPTON AV
LIPPARD AV
100 ACADIA ST
200 BADEN ST
300 CONGO ST
400 DETROIT ST
500 EDNA ST
600 FOERSTER ST
700 GENNESSEE ST
800 RIDGEWOOD AV
END HAZELWOOD AV
JORDAN AV SF 5 C2
S FROM S CALIFORNIA ST BETWEEN
COMMONWEALTH AV AND PALM AV
TO GEARY ST
2 CALIFORNIA ST
100 EUCLID AV

END GEARY ST
JOSEPHA AV SF 19 A2
S FROM JUAN BAUTISTA CIR
TO GONZALES DR
JOSIAH AV SF 19 C2
BETWEEN MARGARET AV AND LEE AV
CROSSING LAKE VIEW AV SW FROM
RIDGE LN
JOY ST SF 15 A2
FROM BREWSTER ST TO A POINT E OF
HOLLADAY AV
JUAN BATSTA CIR SF 19 A2
CIRCLE W OF JUNIPERO SERRA BLVD
N OF BROTHERHOOD WY
FONT BLVD
FUENTE AV
CRESPI DR
DIAZ AV
FONT BLVD
JOSEPHA AV
GRIJALVA DR
BUCARELI DR
JUANITA WY SF 13 B2
SW FROM TERESITA BLVD TO
MIRALOMA DR
2 TERESITA BLVD
FOWLER AV
100 EVELYN WY
200 DEL SUR AV
250 REX AV
300 MARNE AV
LANSDALE AV
END MIRALOMA DR
JUDAH ST SF 8 A2
JUDAH ST SF 9 A2
FROM 5TH AVE BET IRVING
AND KIRKHAM STS W TO
GREAT HIGHWAY
2 5TH AV
100 6TH AV
200 7TH AV
300 8TH AV
400 9TH AV
500 10TH AV
600 11TH AV
700 12TH AV
800 FUNSTON AV
900 14TH AV
1000 15TH AV
1100 16TH AV
1200 17TH AV
1300 18TH AV
1400 19TH AV
1500 20TH AV
1600 21ST AV
1700 22ND AV
1800 23RD AV
1900 24TH AV
2000 25TH AV
2100 26TH AV
2200 27TH AV
2300 28TH AV
2400 29TH AV
2500 30TH AV
2600 31ST AV
2700 32ND AV
2800 33RD AV
2900 34TH AV
3000 35TH AV
PINO AL
3100 36TH AV
SUNSET BLVD
3200 37TH AV
3300 38TH AV
3400 39TH AV
3500 40TH AV
3600 41ST AV
3700 42ND AV
3800 43RD AV
3900 44TH AV

4000 45TH AV
4100 46TH AV
4200 47TH AV
4300 48TH AV
LA PLAYA ST
END GREAT HIGHWAY
JUDSON AV SF 19 C1
FROM DETROIT ST BET
STAPLES AND MARSTON AVES
W TO HAZELWOOD AVE
100 DETROIT ST
200 EDNA ST
300 FOERSTER ST
400 GENNESSEE ST
500 PHELAN AV
END HAZELWOOD AV
JULES AV SF 19 B1
N FROM LAKE VIEW AV BETWEEN
FAXON AV AND ASHTON AV TO
OCEAN AV
2 LAKE VIEW AV
100 GRAFTON AV
200 HOLLOWAY AV
300 DE MONTFORD AV
END OCEAN AV
JULIA ST SF 7 A3
S FROM S MISSION ST BETWEEN
7TH ST & 8TH ST TO NATOMA ST
2 MISSION ST
44 MINNA ST
END NATOMA ST
JULIAN AV SF 10 C1
S FROM S 14TH ST BETWEEN
2 14TH ST
MISSION ST AND VALENCIA
ST TO 16TH ST
100 15TH ST
END 16TH ST
JULIUS ST SF 3 A2
N FROM 300 LOMBARD ST BETWEEN
KEARNY ST AND GRANT AV
JUNIOR TER SF 20 A2
E AND N FROM CAYUGA AV
NEAR ALEMANY BLVD
JUNIPER ST SF 11 A1
S FROM S FOLSOM ST BETWEEN
10TH ST AND 11TH ST
TO BRYANT ST
2 FOLSOM ST
100 HARRISON ST
END BRYANT ST
JUNIPRO SRRA BL SF 19 A2
S FROM ST FRANCIS BLVD TO
COUNTY LINE
ST FRANCIS BLVD
SLOAT BLVD
WOODACRE DR
MONTEREY BLVD
DARIEN WY
300 OCEAN AV
ROSSMOOR DR
MONCADA WY
PALOMA AV
STONECREST DR
EL PLAZUELA WY
WINSTON DR
MERCEDES WY
STONECREST DR
LYNDHURST DR
800 ESTERO AV
WYTON LN
HOLLOWAY AV
GARFIELD ST
1000 STRATFORD DR
SHIELDS ST
19TH AV
FONT BLVD
BROTHERHOOD WY
PALMETTO AV
COUNTY LINE
JURI ST SF 14 C1
W FROM SAN JOSE AV BETWEEN
25TH ST AND 26TH ST
JUSTIN DR SF 14 B3
S FROM 301 COLLEGE AV
AND W TO ALEMANY BLVD
2 COLLEGE AV
AGNON AV
100 MURRAY ST
200 BENTON AV
300 COLLEGE AV
400 GENEBERN WY
END ALEMANY BLVD
KANSAS ST SF 11 A1
S FROM DIVISION ST BETWEEN
RHODE ISLAND AND VERMONT
STS TO MARIN ST
2 DIVISION ST
100 ALAMEDA ST
200 15TH ST
300 16TH ST
400 17TH ST
500 MARIPOSA ST
600 18TH ST
700 19TH ST
END 20TH ST
1000 22ND ST
1200 23RD ST
1300 24TH ST
1400 25TH ST
END 26TH ST
1600 ARMY ST
END MARIN ST
KAPLAN LN SF 7 B2
FROM CLEMENTINA ST NEAR
3RD ST BET HOWARD ST
AND FOLSOM ST
KAREN CT SF 21 A1
S OF WOOLLSEY STREET BETWEEN
HAMILTON AND GOETTINGEN STREET
KATE ST SF 11 A1
S FROM S BRYANT ST BETWEEN
7TH ST AND 8TH ST
KEARNY ST SF 3 A2
KEARNY ST SF 7 A1
N FROM S MARKET ST BETWEEN
MONTGOMERY ST AND GRANT AV
TO THE EMBARCADERO
2 MARKET ST
GEARY ST
MAIDEN LN
100 POST ST
VER MEHR PL
200 SUTTER ST
HARDIE PL
300 BUSH ST
400 PINE ST
500 CALIFORNIA ST
600 SACRAMENTO ST
COMMERCIAL ST
700 CLAY ST
MERCHANT ST
800 WASHINGTON ST
900 JACKSON ST
COLUMBUS AV
1000 PACIFIC AV
NOTTINGHAM PL
1100 BROADWAY
DUNNES AL
FRESNO ST
1200 VALLEJO ST
1300 GREEN ST
1400 UNION ST
END FILBERT ST
1700 LOMBARD ST
END LA FERRERA TER
1900 FRANCISCO ST
2000 BAY ST
N POINT ST
END THE EMBARCADERO
KEITH ST SF 15 C2
KEITH ST SF 21 B2
FROM EVANS AV SW TO 3RD ST
EVANS AV
FAIRFAX AV
END HUDSON AV
NEWCOMB AV
1400 OAKDALE AV
1500 PALOU AV
1600 QUESADA AV
1700 REVERE AV
1800 SHAFTER AV
1900 THOMAS AV
2000 UNDERWOOD AV
2100 VAN DYKE AV
2200 WALLACE AV
2300 YOSEMITE AV
2400 ARMSTRONG AV
BANCROFT AV
END CARROLL AV
END 3RD ST
KELLOCH AV SF 21 A3
W FROM SCHWERIN ST TWO
BLKS S OF SUNNYDALE AV
KEMPTON AV SF 19 B3
N FROM ALEMANY BLVD TWO
BLKS E OF JUNIPERO SERRA
KENNEDY AV SF 1 C2
IN PRESIDIO
SW OF RICHARDSON AV
KENNY AL SF 20 A2
FROM 4901 BLOCK OF
MISSION ST BETWEEN FRANCE AV
AND ITALY AV TO LONDON ST
KENSINGTON WY SF 13 B2
FROM 1096 PORTOLA DR TO
CLAREMONT BLVD
2 PORTOLA DR
100 ULLOA ST
300 VASQUEZ ST
MERCED AV
END CLAREMONT BLVD
KENT ST SF 3 A2
W FROM 1802 MASON ST BETWEEN
UNION ST AND FILBERT ST
KENWOOD WY SF 19 B1
W FROM FAXON AV N
OF WILDWOOD WY TO SAN ALESO AV
2 FAXON AV
DARIEN WY
100 KEYSTONE WY
200 FAIRFIELD WY
300 MANOR DR
400 PINEHURST WY
END WESTGATE DR
KEPPLER CT SF 3 C1
S FROM 13TH ST BETWEEN GATEVIEW
AV & HUTCHINS CT, TREASURE ISLAND
KERN ST SF 14 B3
W FROM DIAMOND ST TO
BROMPTON AV N OF BOSWORTH ST
KEY AV SF 21 B2
NW FROM A POINT S OF JENNINGS ST
TO LANE ST & BAYSHORE BLVD
SOUTH OF LE CONTE AV
LE CONTE AV
JENNINGS ST
3RD ST
KEITH ST
LANE ST
END BAY SHORE BLVD
KEYES AL SF 3 A3
N FROM 900 PACIFIC AV BETWEEN
POWELL ST AND MASON ST
KEYES AV SF 1 B2
IN PRESIDIO
S FROM LINCOLN BLVD
KEYSTONE WY SF 19 B1
N FROM 1900 OCEAN AV N TO
KENWOOD WY
KEZAR DR SF 9 B2
WESTERLY END OF WALLER ST
TO LINCOLN WY
KIMBALL PL SF 2 C3
N FROM 1400 SACRAMENTO ST AND S
BETWEEN LEAVENWORTH & HYDE STS
KING ST SF 11 B1
SW FROM THE BAY BETWEEN BERRY AND
TOWNSEND STS TO
DIVISION ST
2 THE EMBARCADERO
GALE ST
100 2ND ST
200 3RD ST
300 4TH ST
400 5TH ST
500 6TH ST
600 7TH ST
END DIVISION ST
KINGSTON ST SF 14 C2
E FROM 837 SAN JOSE AV TO
PROSPECT AV
2 SAN JOSE AV
100 MISSION ST
200 COLERIDGE AV
END PROSPECT AV
KINZEY ST SF 1 A2
IN PRESIDIO
N OF RALSTON AV
KIRKHAM ST SF 8 A3
KIRKHAM ST SF 9 A2
W FROM 4TH AV RO LA PLAYA
2 4TH AV
100 5TH AV
200 6TH AV
300 7TH AV
400 8TH AV
500 9TH AV
600 10TH AV
700 11TH AV
800 12TH AV
900 FUNSTON AV
1000 14TH AV
1100 15TH AV
1200 16TH AV
1300 17TH AV
1400 18TH AV
1500 19TH AV
1600 20TH AV
1700 21ST AV
1800 22ND AV
1900 23RD AV
2000 24TH AV
2100 25TH AV
2200 26TH AV
2300 27TH AV
2400 28TH AV
2500 29TH AV
2600 30TH AV
2700 31ST AV
2800 32ND AV
2900 33RD AV
3000 34TH AV
3100 35TH AV
PINO AL
3200 36TH AV
SUNSET BLVD
3300 37TH AV
3400 38TH AV
3500 39TH AV
3600 40TH AV
3700 41ST AV
3800 42ND AV
3900 43RD AV
4000 44TH AV
4100 45TH AV
4200 46TH AV
4300 47TH AV
4400 48TH AV
END GREAT HIGHWAY
KIRKWOOD AV SF 15 B2
NW FROM A POINT SW OF MENDELL
ST TO TOLAND ST
MENDELL ST
3RD ST
NEWHALL ST
END PHELPS ST
SOUTH OF RANKIN ST
RANKIN ST
SELBY ST
MILTON ROSS ST
LETTUCE LN
END TOLAND ST
SE FROM END TOLAND ST TO A POINT
SE OF FRIEDELL ST
KISKA RD SF 16 A3
FROM INGALLS ST TO KIRKWOOD
AV S OF NORTHRIDGE RD
KISSLING ST SF 10 C1
W FROM POINT E OF 11TH ST
BETWEEN HOWARD ST AND FOLSOM ST
TO 12TH ST
KITTREDGE TER SF 5 C3
S FROM TURK ST TO GOLDEN
GATE AV E OF CHABOT TER
KNOLLVIEW WY SF 13 C1
N FROM CITY VIEW WY
TO PANORAMA DR
3 BLKS N OF TWIN PEAKS BLVD
KNOTT CT SF 20 A3
W FROM WATT AV 1 BLK S
OF HANOVER ST
KOBBE AV SF 1 A3
IN PRESIDIO
N OF HITCHCOCK ST
KOHALA RD SF 11 B2
E S AND W FROM CAROLINA
ST TO CAROLINA ST S OF
18TH ST
KONA RD SF 15 B1
S FROM 2200 ARMY ST TO KANSAS ST
KRAMER PL SF 3 A2
S FROM 501 GREENWICH ST BETWEEN
GRANT AV AND STOCKTON ST
KRAUSGRILL PL SF 3 A2
N FROM 500 FILBERT ST BETWEEN
GRANT AV AND STOCKTON ST
KRONQUIST CT SF 14 B1
N FROM S 27TH ST BETWEEN
CASTRO AND DIAMOND STS
LA AVANZADA SF 9 C3
SW FROM PALO ALTO AV BETWEEN
GLENBROOK AV AND CLARENDON AV
LA BICA WY SF 13 C2
S FROM AGUA WY TO ST CROIX DR
LAFAYETTE ST SF 10 C1
SE FROM S MISSION ST BETWEEN
11TH AND 12TH STS TO HOWARD ST
LA FERRERA TER SF 3 A2
W FROM S KEARNY ST BETWEEN
LOMBARD AND CHESTNUT STS
LA GRANDE AV SF 20 B2
FROM PERU AV SW TO PERSIA AV
100 AVALON AV
INCA CT
MANSFIELD ST
END BURROWS ST
300 BRAZIL AV
DUBLIN ST
400 PERSIA AV
RUSSIA AV
END S OF RUSSIA AV
LAGUNA ST SF 2 B3
LAGUNA ST SF 6 B3
LAGUNA ST SF 10 B1
N FROM S MARKET ST BETWEEN
OCTAVIA ST AND BUCHANAN ST
TO BEACH ST
2 MARKET ST
HERMANN ST

100 WALLER ST
200 HAIGHT ST
230 ROSE ST
300 PAGE ST
312 LILY ST
400 OAK ST
550 HICKORY ST
500 FELL ST
516 LINDEN ST
600 HAYES ST
650 IVY ST
700 GROVE ST
750 BIRCH ST
600 FULTON ST
ASH ST
900 MCALLISTER ST
REDWOOD ST
1000 GOLDEN GATE AV
1100 TURK ST
1200 EDDY ST
1250 WILLOW ST
1300 ELLIS ST
1350 CLEARY CT
END GEARY ST
1600 POST ST
1650 HEMLOCK ST
1700 SUTTER ST
1750 FERN ST
1800 BUSH ST
1900 PINE ST
2000 CALIFORNIA ST
2100 SACRAMENTO ST
2200 CLAY ST
2300 WASHINCTON ST
2400 JACKSON ST
2500 PACIFIO AV
2600 BROADWAY
2700 VALLEJO ST
2800 GREEN ST
2900 UNION ST
3000 FILBERT ST
HARRIS PL
3100 GREENWICH ST
3200 LOMBARD ST
MAGNOLIA ST
3300 CHESTNUT ST
3400 FRANCISCO ST
BAY ST
NORTH POINT ST
END BEACH ST

LAGUNA HONDA BL SF 13 B1
SE FROM 7TH AV TO DEWEY BLVD
7TH AV
CLARENDON AV
PLAZA DR
END DEWEY BLVD

LAGUNITAS DR SF 13 A3
SW FROM SLOAT BLVD TO
OCEAN AV E OF 19TH AV

LAIDLEY ST SF 14 B2
S FROM S 30TH ST BETWEEN NOE
AND CASTRO STS TO CASTRO ST
2 30TH ST
NOE ST
100 HARRY ST
HARPER ST
200 FAIRMOUNT ST
300 MIGUEL ST
400 MATEO ST
500 ROANOKE ST
END CASTRO ST

LAKE ST SF 4 B2
LAKE ST SF 5 A2
W FROM ARGUELLO BLVD N OF
CALIFORNIA ST TO
EL CAMINO DEL MAR
2 ARGUELLO BLVD
100 2ND AV
200 3RD AV
300 4TH AV
400 5TH AV
500 6TH AV
600 7TH AV
700 8TH AV
800 9TH AV
900 10TH AV
1000 11TH AV
1100 12TH AV
FUNSTON AV
PARK PRESIDIO BLVD
1300 14TH AV
1400 15TH AV
1500 16TH AV
1600 17TH AV
1700 18TH AV
1800 19TH AV
1900 20TH AV
2000 21ST AV
2100 22ND AV
2200 23RD AV
2300 24TH AV
2400 25TH AV
2500 26TH AV
2600 27TH AV
2700 28TH AV
2800 29TH AV
2900 30TH AV
END EL CAMINO DEL MAR

LAKE FOREST CT SF 9 B3
N FROM OAK PARK DR BETWEEN
DEVONSHIRE & CHRISTOPHER DR

LAKE MERCED BL SF 12 B3
LAKE MERCED BL SF 18 C2
SE FROM SKYLINE BLVD
S TO ALEMANY BLVD

LAKE MERCED HILL SF 18 C3
E FROM LAKE MERCED BLVD
WITHIN SF GOLF CLUB

LAKE SHORE DR SF 12 B3
OFF OCEAN AV - S OF SLOAT
BLVD - CIRCULAR

LAKE SHORE PZ SF 12 B3
S FROM SLOAT BLVD E OF 34TH AV

LAKEVIEW AV SF 19 B2
NW FROM SAN JOSE AV AND
W TO ORIZABA AV
2 SAN JOSE AV
100 CAINE AV
200 MAJESTIC AV
300 MARGARET AV
400 JOSIAH AV
500 LEE AV
SUMMIT ST
550 BRIGHTON AV
600 PLYMOUTH AV
636 GRANADA AV
672 MIRAMAR AV
700 CAPITOL AV
730 FAXON AV
756 JULES AV
ASHTON AV
END ORIZABA AV

LAKEWOOD AV SF 19 B1
N FROM 2000 OCEAN AV TO
FAIRFIELD WY

LAMARTINE ST SF 14 B2
N FROM CAYUGA AV W OF
DANTON ST

LAMSON LN SF 10 A3
N FROM 19TH ST TO CASELLI AV
S OF MARKET ST

LANCASTER LN SF 12 B3
E FROM LAKESHORE DR ONE BLK
N OF LAKE MERCED BLVD

LANDERS ST SF 10 B2
S FROM S 14TH ST BETWEEN
DOLORES ST AND CHURCH ST
TO 16TH ST
2 14TH ST
100 15TH ST
ALERT AL
END 16TH ST

LANE ST SF 15 C3
LANE ST SF 21 B2
SW FROM LA SALLE AV TO ARMSTRONG
AV & FROM SALINAS AV TO
BAYSHORE BLVD
LA SALLE AV
MCKINNON AV
NEWCOMB AV
OAKDALE AV
PALOU AV
QUESADA AV
REVERE AV
SHAFTER AV
THOMAS AV
UNDERWOOD AV
VAN DYKE AV
3RD ST
WALLACE AV
YOSEMITE AV
END ARMSTRONG AV
SALINAS AV
KEY AV
BAYSHORE BLVD

LANGDON CT SF 1 A2
IN PRESIDIO
NW FROM LINCOLN BLVD

LANGTON ST SF 7 A3
S FROM S HOWARD ST BETWEEN
7TH AND 8TH STS TO HARRISON ST
2 HOWARD ST
100 FOLSOM ST
DECKER ST
200 HARRISON ST

LANSDALE AV SF 13 B2
S FROM JUANITA WY

LANSING ST SF 7 B2
W FROM S 1ST ST BETWEEN
FOLSOM ST AND HARRISON ST

LAPHAM WY SF 20 B3
SE OFF CHICAGO WY NE OF
SOUTH HILL BLVD

LAPIDGE ST SF 10 C2
S FROM S 18TH ST BETWEEN
VALENCIA ST AND GUERRERO ST
ST TO 19TH ST

LA PLAYA SF 8 A1
S FROM SUTRO HEIGHTS TO
JUDAH ST
600 SUTRO HEIGHTS
700 BALBOA ST
800 CABRILLO ST
FULTON ST
PARK
1200 LINCOLN WY
1300 IRVING ST
END JUDAH ST

LAPU LAPU ST SF 7 B3
SE FROM BONIFACIO ST TO
HATTISON ST BETWEEN
BONIFACIO ST
RIZAL ST
END HARRISON ST

LARCH ST SF 6 C3
W FROM S VAN NESS AV BETWEEN
TURK ST AND EDDY ST TO
FRANKLIN ST
200 VAN NESS AVE
END FRANKLIN ST

LARKIN ST SF 2 C2
LARKIN ST SF 6 C2
N FROM S MARKET ST BETWEEN
HYDE AND POLK STS TO
BEACH ST
2 MARKET ST
HAYES ST
GROVE ST
FULTON ST
300 MCALLISTER ST
REDWOOD ST
400 GOLDEN GATE AV
500 TURK ST
600 EDDY ST
WILLOW ST
700 ELLIS ST
OLIVE ST
800 OFARRELL ST
800 MYRTLE ST
900 GEARY ST
CEDAR ST
1000 POST ST
HEMLOCK ST
1100 SUTTER ST
FERN ST
1200 BUSH ST
EUREKA PL
AUSTIN ST
1300 PINE ST
1400 CALIFORNIA ST
1500 SACRAMENTO ST
1600 CLAY ST
1700 WASHINGTON ST
1800 JACKSON ST
1900 PACIFIC AV
2000 BROADWAY
2100 VALLEJO ST
2200 GREEN ST
ROCKLAND ST
2300 UNION ST
2400 FILBERT ST
2500 GREENWICH ST
2600 LOMBARD ST
2700 CHESTNUT ST
2800 FRANCISCO ST
2900 BAY ST
3000 NORTH POINT ST
END BEACH ST

LARKSPUR AV SF 21 B2
SW FROM MEADE AV ONE BLK E
OF 3RD ST

LA SALLE AV SF 15 C2
FROM INGALLS ST NW TO PHELPS ST
INGALLS ST
WHITFIELD CT
OSCEOLA LN
GARLINGTON CT
NEWCOMB AV
LANE ST
CASHMERE ST
1600 MENDELL ST
1690 3RD ST
1700 NEWHALL ST
END PHELPS ST

LASKIE ST SF 7 A3
N FROM S MISSION ST BETWEEN
8TH ST AND 9TH ST

LATHAM PL SF 7 A2
W FROM S MASON ST BETWEEN
OFARRELL ST AND ELLIS ST

LATHROP AV SF 21 B3
E FROM TUNNEL AV TO US-101 FRWY

LATONA ST SF 15 B3
S FROM BAY VIEW ST BETWEEN 3RD ST
AND POMONA ST TO
THORNTON AV

LAURA ST SF 19 C3
BETWEEN LAWRENCE AV AND
FARRAGUT AV FROM 5700 MISSION ST
MISSION NW TO ALEMANY BLVD

LAUREL ST SF 5 C1
S OF PACIFIC AV BETWEEN
WALNUT ST AND LOCUST ST
TO EUCLID AV
100 JACKSON ST
200 WASHINGTON ST
300 CLAY ST
400 SACRAMENTO ST
CALIFORNIA ST
MAYFAIR DR
END EUCLID AV

LAUSSAT ST SF 10 B1
W FROM S BUCHANAN ST BETWEEN
WALLER ST AND HAIGHT ST
TO STEINER ST
2 BUCHANAN ST
WEBSTER ST
200 FILLMORE ST
END STEINER ST

LAWRENCE AV SF 19 C3
NW FROM 5800 BLOCK MISSION ST
NW TO SAN JOSE AV NEAR
COUNTY LINE
2 MISSION ST
100 HURON AV
SEARS ST
ALEMANY BLVD
END DE WOLF ST

LAWTON ST SF 8 A3
LAWTON ST SF 9 A3
W FROM LOCKSLEY AV S OF
KIRKHAM ST TO GREAT HIGHWAY
2 LOCKSLEY AV
100 7TH AV
200 8TH AV
300 9TH AV
400 10TH AV
500 11TH AV
600 12TH AV
700 FUNSTON AV
800 14TH AV
900 15TH AV
LOMITA AV
1000 16TH AV
1100 17TH AV
1200 18TH AV
1300 19TH AV
1400 20TH AV
1500 21ST AV
1600 22ND AV
1700 23RD AV
1800 24TH AV
1900 25TH AV
2000 26TH AV
2100 27TH AV
2200 28TH AV
2300 29TH AV
2400 30TH AV
2500 31ST AV
2600 32ND AV
2700 33RD AV
2800 34TH AV
2900 35TH AV
3000 36TH AV
SUNSET BLVD
3100 37TH AV
3200 38TH AV
3300 39TH AV
3400 40TH AV
3500 41ST AV
3600 42ND AV
3700 43RD AV
3800 44TH AV
3900 45TH AV
4000 46TH AV
4100 47TH AV
4200 48TH AV
END GREAT HIGHWAY

LEAVENWORTH ST SF 2 C2
LEAVENWORTH ST SF 6 C2
LEAVENWORTH ST SF 7 A3
N FROM MCALLISTER ST BETWEEN
HYDE STS TO THE BAY
FULTON ST
50 MCALLISTER ST
100 GOLDEN GATE AV
200 TURK ST
300 EDDY ST
400 ELLIS ST
500 O'FARRELL ST

600 GEARY ST
700 POST ST
800 SUTTER ST
900 BUSH ST
1000 PINE ST
PANTON AL
1100 CALIFORNIA ST
ACORN AL
1200 SACRAMENTO ST
1300 CLAY ST
1400 WASHINGTON ST
1500 JACKSON ST
1600 PACIFIC AV
LYNCH ST
BERNARD ST
1700 BROADWAY
GLOVER ST
WALDO AL
1800 VALLEJO ST
1900 GREEN ST
MACONDRAY ST
2000 UNION ST
HAVENS ST
2100 FILBERT ST
2200 GREENWICH ST
LURMONT TER
2300 LOMBARD ST
2400 CHESTNUT ST
2500 FRANCISCO ST
2600 BAY ST
NORTH POINT ST
2700 COLUMBUS AV
2800 BEACH ST
END JEFFERSON ST
LECH WALESA SF 6 C3
BETWEEN HAYES ST AND GROVE ST W
FROM POLK ST TO VAN NESS AV
LE CONTE AV SF 21 B2
NW FROM KEY AV TO KEITH ST
KEY AV
JENNINGS ST
3RD ST
END KEITH ST
LEDYARD ST SF 15 B3
SE FROM SILVER AV W OF
SCOTIA AV
LEE AV SF 19 C2
N FROM LAKE VIEW AV TO OCEAN AV
2 LAKE VIEW AV
100 GRAFTON AV
200 HOLLOWAY AV
END OCEAN AV
LEESE ST SF 14 C2
SE FROM PARK ST NEAR HIGHLAND AV
TO CRESCENT AV
PARK ST
100 RICHLAND AV
END CRESCENT AV
LEGION CT SF 19 B1
FROM OCEAN AV SW TO URBANO DR
LEGION HONOR DR SF 4 B2
FROM CLEMENT ST N TO
EL CAMINO DEL MAR BETWEEN 32ND AV
AND 36TH AV
LEIDESDORFF ST SF 3 B3
FROM 300 PINE ST BETWEEN
SANSOME ST AND MONTGOMERY ST
N TO CLAY ST
2 PINE ST
100 CALIFORNIA ST
HALLECK ST
200 SACRAMENTO ST
COMMERCIAL ST
END CLAY ST
LELAND AV SF 21 A2
BETWEEN RAYMOND AV AND
VISITACION AV FROM BAYSHORE BLVD
W TO HAHN ST
BAY SHORE BLVD
DESMOND ST

100 ALPHA ST
PEABODY ST
200 RUTLAND ST
CORA ST
300 DELTA ST
SCHWERIN ST
REY ST
400 ELLIOT ST
BRITTON ST
LOEHR ST
500 SAWYER ST
END HAHN ST
LENOX WY SF 13 B2
FROM 51 TARAVAL ST S TO
ULLOA ST
LEO ST SF 20 A1
W FROM 4700 BLOCK MISSION ST
BETWEEN ONONDAGA AV AND RUTH ST
LEONA TER SF 6 A2
W FROM LYON ST BETWEEN GEARY BLVD
AND POST ST
LEROY PL SF 2 C3
FROM SACRAMENTO ST N & S BETWEEN
JONES ST AND LEAVENWORTH ST
LESSING ST SF 19 C3
W OF MISSION ST NE FROM LIEBIG ST
BETWEEN MISSION ST & SAN JOSE AV
LESTER CT SF 3 C1
W FROM GATEVIEW AV, TREASURE ISLD
LETTERMAN DR SF 1 C3
S OF LETTERMAN GEN HOSP BETWEEN
PRESIDIO BLVD AND LOMBARD ST
LETTUCE LN SF 15 B2
S W FROM JERROLD AV BET
TOLAND ST AND SELBY ST
LEVANT ST SF 10 A2
N OF 17TH ST FROM LOWER TER
TO FAIRBANKS ST
LEXINGTON ST SF 10 C2
FROM SYCAMORE ST BETWEEN
VALENCIA ST AND MISSION ST
S TO 21ST ST
2 SYCAMORE AVE
100 18TH ST
200 19TH ST
300 20TH ST
END 21ST ST
LIBERTY ST SF 10 B3
W FROM S VALENCIA ST BETWEEN
20TH & 21ST STS W TO CASTRO ST
2 VALENCIA ST
100 GUERRERO ST
200 DOLORES ST
300 CHURCH ST
400 SANCHEZ ST
END RAYBURN ST
500 NOE ST
END CASTRO ST
LICK PL SF 7 B2
FROM POST ST BETWEEN KEARNY ST
AND MONTGOMERY ST N TO SUTTER ST
LIEBIG ST SF 19 C3
FROM SAN JOSE AV SE TO THE
COUNTY LINE BETWEEN REGENT ST
AND RICE ST
LT ALLEN ST SF 1 C2
N OF DOYLE DR BETWEEN
CPL ZAVOVITZ ST & SGT MITCHELL ST
LT JAUSS ST SF 1 C2
E OF CPL ZAVOVITZ ST BETWEEN
MARINE DR AND LT ALLEN ST
LIGGETT AV SF 1 C3
S FROM PRESIDIO BLVD BETWEEN
CLARKE ST AND SIBLEY RD
LILAC ST SF 14 C1
S FROM 24TH ST BETWEEN CAPP ST
AND MISSION ST S TO 26TH ST
LILLIAN ST SF 15 C3
W OF INGALLS ST BETWEEN
ROSIE LEE LN & BEATRICE LN

LILY ST SF 10 B1
W FROM S FRANKLIN ST BETWEEN
PAGE ST & OAK ST W TO BUCHANAN ST
2 FRANKLIN ST
100 GOUGH ST
200 OCTAVIA ST
300 LAGUNA ST
END BUCHANAN ST
LINARES AV SF 9 B3
FROM S END OF 8TH AV SE TO A
POINT E OF VENTURA AV
LINCOLN BLVD SF 1 A3
LINCOLN BLVD SF 4 C1
LINCOLN CT SF 20 A3
W OF NADELL CT TWO BLOCKS
S OF BRUNSWICK
LINCOLN WY SF 8 A2
LINCOLN WY SF 9 A2
S OF GOLDEN GATE PARK FROM
ARGUELLO BLVD W TO GREAT HIGHWAY
1 ARGUELLO BLVD
100 2ND AV
200 3RD AV
300 4TH AV
400 5TH AV
500 6TH AV
600 7TH AV
700 8TH AV
800 9TH AV
900 10TH AV
1000 11TH AV
1100 12TH AV
1200 FUNSTON AV
1300 14TH AV
1400 15TH AV
1500 16TH AV
1600 17TH AV
1700 18TH AV
1800 19TH AV
1900 20TH AV
2000 21ST AV
2100 22ND AV
2200 23RD AV
2300 24TH AV
2400 25TH AV
2500 26TH AV
2600 27TH AV
2700 28TH AV
2800 29TH AV
2900 30TH AV
3000 31ST AV
3100 32ND AV
3200 33RD AV
3300 34TH AV
3400 35TH AV
3500 36TH AV
SUNSET BLVD
3600 37TH AV
3700 38TH AV
3800 39TH AV
3900 40TH AV
4000 41ST AV
4100 42ND AV
4200 43RD AV
4300 44TH AV
4500 46TH AV
4600 47TH AV
4700 48TH AV
LA PLAYA ST
END GREAT HIGHWAY
LINDA ST SF 10 C2
S FROM 18TH ST BETWEEN
LAPIDGE ST AND GUERRERO ST
LINDA VISTA LN SF 20 B3
OFF GENEVA AV S TO CHICAGO WY
LINDEN ST SF 6 B3
W FROM FRANKLIN ST BETWEEN
FELL ST AND HAYES ST TO A
POINT W OF BUCHANAN ST
200 FRANKLIN ST

300 GOUGH ST
400 OCTAVIA ST
500 LAGUNA ST
600 BUCHANAN ST
LIPPARD AV SF 14 A3
FROM SURREY ST S TO JOOST AV
2 SURREY ST
CHENERY ST
100 BOSWORTH ST
END JOOST AV
LISBON ST SF 20 A2
FROM SILVER AV S W TO GENEVA AV
2 SILVER AV
PERU AV
100 AVALON AV
200 EXCELSIOR AV
300 BRAZIL AV
400 PERSIA AV
500 RUSSIA AV
600 FRANCE AV
700 ITALY AV
800 AMAZON AV
END GENEVA AV
LIVINGSTON ST SF 1 B2
N FROM MASON ST TO MARINE DR
LLOYD ST SF 10 A1
W FROM S SCOTT ST BETWEEN
DUBOCE AV AND WALLER ST
LOBOS ST SF 19 B2
W OF SAN JOSE AV NEAR THE
COUNTY LINE FROM CAINE ST
W TO ORIZABA AV
2 CAINE ST
100 PLYMOUTH AV
200 CAPITOL AV
END ORIZABA AV
LOCKSLEY AV SF 9 B3
S OFF KIRKHAM ST AND
ONE BLOCK E OF 7TH AV
LOCKWOOD ST SF 17 B1
SE FROM DONAHUE ST TO NIMITZ AV
LOCUST ST SF 5 C2
FROM PACIFIC AV BETWEEN LAUREL ST
AND SPRUCE ST S TO CALIFORNIA ST
2 PACIFIC AV
100 JACKSON ST
200 WASHINGTON ST
300 CLAY ST
400 SACRAMENTO ST
END CALIFORNIA ST
LOEHR ST SF 20 C3
W OF BAYSHORE BLVD N & S OF
VISITACION AV BETWEEN
BRITTON ST AND SAWYER ST
LOMA VISTA TER SF 10 A2
S FROM UPPER TER TO ROOSEVELT WY
LOMBARD ST SF 2 A2
LOMBARD ST SF 3 A2
FROM THE BAY BETWEEN GREENWICH ST
AND CHESTNUT ST W TO LYON ST
THE EMBARCADERO
2 BATTERY ST
100 SANSOME ST
200 MONTGOMERY ST
WINTHROP ST
300 KEARNY ST
CHILD ST
JULIUS ST
400 GRANT AV
500 STOCKTON ST
TUSCANY AL
600 POWELL ST
700 MASON ST
NEWELL ST
COLUMBUS AV
JANSEN ST
800 TAYLOR ST
900 JONES ST
1000 LEAVENWORTH ST
MONTCLAIR TER

1100 HYDE ST
1200 LARKIN ST
1300 POLK ST
1400 VAN NESS AV
1500 FRANKLIN ST
1600 GOUGH ST
1700 OCTAVIA ST
1800 LAGUNA ST
1900 BUCHANAN ST
2000 WEBSTER ST
2100 FILLMORE ST
2200 STEINER ST
2300 PIERCE ST
2400 SCOTT ST
2500 DIVISADERO ST
2600 BRODERICK ST
2700 BAKER ST
END LYON ST
LOMITA AV SF 9 A3
FROM LAWTON ST AND 15TH AV
S TO MORAGA ST
LONDON ST SF 20 B1
FROM AVALON AV SW TO GENEVA AV
AVALON AV
200 EXCELSIOR AV
300 BRAZIL AV
400 PERSIA AV
500 RUSSIA AV
600 FRANCE AV
700 ITALY AV
800 AMAZON AV
END GENEVA AV
LONE MTN TER SF 5 C3
E FROM ROSSI AV BETWEEN ANZA ST
AND TURK ST TO PARKER AV
LONG AV SF 1 A1
FROM MARINE DR S TO LINCOLN BLVD
LONGVIEW CT SF 13 C1
E FROM PANORAMA DR BETWEEN
CITYVIEW WY AND MOUNTVIEW CT
LOOMIS ST SF 15 A2
FROM INDUSTRIAL ST N OF
MCKINNON AV AT BARNEVELD AV
LOPEZ AV SF 13 B1
N FROM CASTENADA AV PARALLEL WITH
SANTA RITA AV N TO PACHECO ST
LORAINE CT SF 5 B3
N FROM ANZA ST BETWEEN ALMADEN CT
AND STANYAN ST
LORI LN SF 9 C3
E FROM CLARENDON AV ONE BLK
N OF PANORAMA
LOS PALMOS DR SF 13 C3
FROM TERESITA BLVD W TO
HAZELWOOD AV
TERESITA BLVD
VERNA ST
FOERSTER ST
STANFORD HEIGHTS AV
BELLA VISTA WY
LULU AL
EMIL LN
GLOBE AL
END HAZELWOOD AV
LOTTIE BENNT LN SF 4 A1
IN ST FRANCIS SQ S FROM GEARY BL
W OF LAGUNA ST
LOUISBURG ST SF 19 C2
FROM GENEVA AV W OF TARA ST
S TO RIDGE LN
100 GENEVA AV
200 NIAGARA AV
300 MT VERNON AV
END RIDGE LANE
LOWELL ST SF 20 A3
FROM 5600 BLOCK OF MISSION ST
SE TO COUNTY LINE
2 MISSION ST
100 MORSE ST
200 BRUNSWICK ST

BYRON ST
300 HANOVER ST
END COUNTY LINE
LOWER TER SF 10 A2
FROM SATURN ST N OF 17TH ST NEAR
ORD ST AND E OF ROOSEVELT WY
LOYOLA TER SF 5 C3
FROM 1900 FULTON ST N BETWEEN
HEMWAY TER AND KITTREDGE TER
LUCERNE ST SF 11 B1
BETWEEN 6TH ST AND 7TH ST FROM
BRANNAN ST S
LUCKY ST SF 15 A1
S FROM 24TH ST BET TREAT AV &
FOLSOM ST TO 26TH ST
LUCY ST SF 15 B3
FROM THRONTON AV BETWEEN 3RD ST
AND CERES ST S TO WILLIAMS AV
LUDLOW AL SF 13 B2
S FROM JUANITA WY TO CASITAS AV
S OF PORTOLA DR
LULU AL SF 13 C3
FROM A POINT N OF CRESTA VISTA DR
S TO MELROSE AV
CRESTA VISTA DR
BURLWOOD DR
LOS PALMOS DR
END MELROSE AV
LUNADO CT SF 19 A1
SE FROM LUNADO WY
S OF MERCEDES WY
LUNADO WY SF 19 A1
FROM HOLLOWAY AV N TO MERCEDES WY
2 HOLLOWAY AV
100 ESTERO AV
END MERCEDES WY
LUNDEEN ST SF 1 C2
N OF DOYLE DR BETWFEN
CPL ZAVOVITZ ST AND PEDESTRIAN WY
LUNDYS LN SF 14 C2
SW FROM COSO AV BETWEEN
COLERIDGE AV AND PROSPECT AV
TO VIRGINIA AV
2 COSO AV
FAIR AV
100 ESMERALDA AV
END VIRGINIA AV
LUPINE AV SF 5 C2
W OF MASONIC AV ONE BLOCK S
OF EUCLID AV
LURLINE ST SF 9 A3
FROM KIRKHAM ST AND 14TH AV S
E TO FUNSTON AV
LURMONT TER SF 2 C2
W FROM LEAVENWORTH ST BETWEEN
GREENWICH ST AND LOMBARD ST
LUSK ST SF 7 B3
NE OF TOWNSEND ST BETWEEN
CLYDE ST AND 4TH ST
LYELL ST SF 14 B3
FROM BOSWORTH ST W OF ROTTECK ST
ST S TO ALEMANY BLVD
LYNCH ST SF 2 C3
SW FROM LEAVENWORTH ST BETWEEN
PACIFIC AV AND BROADWAY
W TO HYDE ST
LYNDHURST DR SF 19 A1
SW FROM JUNIPERO SERRA BLVD
TO DENSLOWE DR
LYON ST SF 1 C3
LYON ST SF 6 A1
LYON ST SF 10 A1
NW FROM HAIGHT ST W OF
BAKER ST N TO MARINA BLVD
2 HAIGHT ST
100 PAGE ST
END OAK ST
300 FELL ST
400 HAYES ST
500 GROVE ST
600 FULTON ST
700 MCALLISTER ST
800 GOLDEN GATE AV
TURK ST
END ANZAVISTA AV
TERRA VISTA AV
OFARRELL ST
1300 GEARY ST
1400 POST ST
1500 SUTTER ST
1600 BUSH ST
1700 PINE ST
1800 CALIFORNIA ST
1900 SACRAMENTO ST
2000 CLAY ST
2100 WASHINGTON ST
2200 JACKSON ST
2300 PACIFIC AV
2400 BROADWAY
2500 VALLEJO ST
2600 GREEN ST
2700 UNION ST
2800 FILBERT ST
2900 GREENWICH ST
3000 LOMBARD ST
3100 CHESTNUT ST
3200 FRANCISCO ST
3300 BAY ST
END MARINA BLVD
LYSETTE ST SF 2 C3
S FROM SACRAMENTO ST BETWEEN
JONES ST AND LEAVENWORTH ST
MABEL AL SF 6 C2
OFF HYDE ST BETWEEN GEARY ST
AND O'FARRELL ST
MABINI ST SF 7 B2
SE FROM FOLSOM ST TO BONIFACIO ST
BETWEEN 3RD ST AND 4TH ST
MAC ARTHUR AV SF 1 C3
FROM PRESIDIO BL S TO EL POLIN LP
MAC ARTHUR AV SF 2 B2
IN FORT MASON N OF BAY ST
MACEDONIA ST SF 15 A1
FROM MONTCALM ST W OF
MULLEN AV SE TO BREWSTER ST
MACONDRAY ST SF 2 C3
FROM 1801 TAYLOR ST BETWEEN
GREEN ST AND UNION ST W TO
LEAVENWORTH ST
2 TAYLOR ST
100 JONES ST
END LEAVENWORTH ST
MACRAE ST SF 1 C3
S OF MACARTHUR ST W OF PORTOLA ST
MADDUX AV SF 15 B3
NE FROM SCOTIA AV TO REVERE AV
BETWEEN BRIDGEVIEW DR & QUINT ST
MADERA ST SF 11 B3
W FROM ARKANSAS ST BETWEEN
22ND ST & 23RD ST TO WISCONSIN ST
MADISON ST SF 20 C1
FROM SILVER AV S TO BURROWS ST
2 SILVER AV
100 ATHENS ST END
PIOCHE ST
VALMAR TER
200 SILLIMAN ST
300 FELTON ST
END BURROWS ST
MADRID ST SF 20 B2
FROM SILVER AV SW TO ROLPH ST
2 SILVER AV
100 PERU AV
200 AVALON AV
300 EXCELSIOR AV
400 BRAZIL AV
500 PERSIA AV
600 RUSSIA AV
700 FRANCE AV
800 ITALY AV
900 AMAZON AV
1000 GENEVA AV
END ROLPH ST
MADRONE AV SF 13 B2
FROM TARAVAL ST SW TO VICENTE ST
2 TARAVAL ST
100 ULLOA ST
END VICENTE ST
MAGELLAN AV SF 13 B1
NE FROM 12TH AV PARALLEL TO
DEWEY BLVD ENDING AT CASTANEDA AV
12TH AV
500 CORTES AV
400 MONTALVO AV
DORANTES AV
300 PACHECO AV
200 SOLA AV
PLAZA
100 MARCELA AV
END CASTENADA AV
MAGNOLIA ST SF 2 B2
BETWEEN LOMBARD ST & CHESTNUT ST
FROM LAGUNA ST W TO WEBSTER ST
MAHAN ST SF 17 B2
SW FROM HUSSEY ST TO J ST BETWEEN
MANSEAU ST AND THE BAY
MAIDEN LN SF 7 A2
W FROM S KEARNY ST BETWEEN
GEARY ST AND POST ST ENDING AT
STOCKTON ST
2 KEARNY ST
100 GRANT AV
END STOCKTON ST
MAIN ST SF 7 B1
S FROM MARKET ST BETWEEN SPEAR ST
AND BEALE ST SE TO THE BAY
2 MARKET ST
100 MISSION ST
200 HOWARD ST
300 FOLSOM ST
ELKHART ST
400 HARRISON ST
500 BRYANT ST
END THE EMBARCADERO
MAJESTIC AV SF 19 C2
BETWEEN CAINE ST AND MARGARET AV
CROSSING LAKEVIEW AV FROM
RIDGE LN S TO SUMMIT AV
2 RIDGE LANE
100 LAKE VIEW AV
END SUMMIT AV
MALDEN AL SF 7 B2
S FROM HOWARD ST BETWEEN 1ST ST
AND 2ND ST SE TO TEHAMA ST
MALLORCA WY SF 2 A2
FROM CHESTNUT ST AND FILLMORE ST
NW TO BEACH ST AND CERVANTES BLVD
2 CHESTNUT ST
100 TOLEDO WAY
200 ALHAMBRA ST
CAPRA WY
END BEACH ST
MALTA DR SF 14 A3
N FROM STILLINGS AV TO
OSHAUGHNESSY BLVD
MALVINA PL SF 3 A3
W FROM S MASON ST BETWEEN CLAY ST
AND SACRAMENTO ST
MANCHESTER ST SF 14 C1
S OF ARMY ST FROM BESSIE ST TO
RIPLEY ST BETWEEN FOLSOM ST
AND SHOTWELL ST
2 BESSIE ST
100 STONEMAN ST
END RIPLEY ST
MANDALAY LN SF 13 A1
FROM PACHECO ST AND 15TH AV
E TO 14TH AV
MANGELS AV SF 13 C3
FROM HAMERTON AV N OF JOOST AV
W TO PLYMOUTH AV
HAMERTON AV
BURNSIDE AV
100 BADEN ST
NORDHOFF ST
200 CONGO ST
300 DETROIT ST
400 EDNA ST
500 FOERSTER ST
600 GENNESSEE ST
700 RIDGEWOOD AV
750 BRENTWOOD AV
800 HAZELWOOD AV
850 VALDEZ AV
900 COLON AV
END PLYMOUTH AV
MANOR DR SF 19 B1
FROM 2060 OCEAN AV N TO DARIEN WY
2 OCEAN AV
100 KENWOOD WY
200 UPLAND DR
END DARIEN WY
MANSEAU ST SF 17 B2
BETWEEN SPEAR AV AND MAHAN ST
MANSELL ST SF 20 C2
MANSELL ST SF 21 A2
FROM 3200 BLOCK OF SAN BRUNO AV
S OF OLMSTEAD ST
W TO JOHN MCLAREN PARK
2 SAN BRUNO AV
100 GIRARD ST
200 BRUSSELS ST
300 GOETTINGEN ST
400 SOMERSET ST
500 HOLYOKE ST
600 HAMILTON ST
700 BOWDOIN ST
800 DARTMOUTH ST
COLBY ST
UNIVERSITY ST
VISITACION AV
JOHN F SHELLEY DR
END PERSIA AV & BRAZIL AV
MANSFIELD ST SF 20 C1
FROM LA GRANDE AV S TO BURROWS ST
MANZANITA AV SF 5 C2
S FROM MAYFAIR DR TO EUCLID AV
W OF COLLINS ST
MAPLE ST SF 5 C2
FROM PRESIDIO RESERVATION
BETWEEN SPRUCE ST AND CHERRY ST
S TO CALIFORNIA ST
2 PRESIDIO RESERVATION
100 JACKSON ST
200 WASHINGTON ST
300 CLAY ST
400 SACRAMENTO ST
END CALIFORNIA ST
MARCELA AV SF 13 B1
E FROM PACHECO ST PARALLEL WITH
CASTANEDA AV TO MAGELLAN AV
PACHECO ST
SOLA AV
END MAGELLAN AV
MARCY PL SF 3 A3
S FROM S JACKSON ST BETWEEN
MASON ST AND TAYLOR ST
MARENGO ST SF 15 A2
E OF JAMES LICK FRWY FROM
WATERLOO ST S TO BAYSHORE BLVD
MARGARET AV SF 19 C2
BETWEEN MAJESTIC AV AND JOSIAH AV
CROSSING LAKE VIEW AV FROM
RIDGE LN S TO SUMMIT AV
MARGRAVE PL SF 3 A2
FROM 500 VALLEJO ST BETWEEN
KEARNY ST AND GRANT AV
MARIETTA DR SF 13 C2
MARIETTA DR SF 14 A2
FROM TERESITA BL SE TO CUBA AL
MARIN ST SF 15 C1
ONE BLK S OF ARMY ST FROM A POINT
E OF MICHIGAN ST TO BAYSHORE BLVD
MARINA BLVD SF 2 C3
FROM BEACH ST AND BUCHANAN ST NW
AND W TO LYON ST
100 BUCHANAN ST
BEACH ST
WEBSTER ST
FILLMORE ST
RETIRO WY
CASA WY
AVILA ST
SCOTT ST
DIVISADERO ST
BRODERICK ST
BAKER ST
END LYON ST
MARINE DR SF 1 B2
W FROM LYON ST ALONG THE COAST TO
MARINER DR SF 3 C1
W FROM GATEVIEW AV 1 BLK NW OF
FORT POINT NATIONAL HISTORIC SITE
13TH ST, REJOINING GATEVIEW NEAR
BAYSIDE DR, TREASURE ISLAND
MARION PL SF 2 C2
N FROM 900 UNION ST BETWEEN
JONES ST AND TAYLOR ST
MARIPOSA ST SF 11 A2
FROM THE BAY BETWEEN 17TH ST
& 18TH ST W TO HARRISON ST
400 ILLINOIS ST
500 3RD ST
600 TENNESSEE ST
700 MINNESOTA ST
800 INDIANA ST
900 IOWA ST
1000 PENNSYLVANIA AV
1100 MISSISSIPPI ST
1200 TEXAS ST
1300 MISSOURI ST
1400 CONNECTICUT ST
ARKANSAS ST
WISCONSIN ST
1700 CAROLINA ST
1800 DE HARO ST
1900 RHODE ISLAND ST
2000 KANSAS ST
2100 VERMONT ST
2200 SAN BRUNO AV
2300 UTAH ST
2400 POTRERO AV
2500 HAMPSHIRE ST
2600 YORK ST
2700 BRYANT ST
2800 FLORIDA ST
2900 ALABAMA ST
END HARRISON ST
MARK LN SF 7 A1
S FROM 401 BUSH ST BETWEEN
KEARNY ST & GRANT AV TO SUTTER ST
MARKET ST SF 7 A3
MARKET ST SF 10 B2
FROM THE BAY SW TO THE JUNCTION
OF 17TH ST AND CASTRO ST, THEN W
TO 24TH ST AND PORTOLA DR
THE EMBARCADERO
STEUART ST
SPEAR ST
CALIFORNIA ST
200 DRUMM ST
MAIN ST
300 DAVIS ST
PINE ST
BEALE ST
400 FRONT ST
FREMONT ST
BUSH ST
500 BATTERY ST
1ST ST

ECKER ST
546 SANSOME ST
SUTTER ST
600 MONTGOMERY ST
NEW MONTGOMERY ST
ANNIE ST
700 KEARNY ST
GEARY ST
3RD ST
750 GRANT AVE
O'FARRELL ST
4TH ST
800 STOCKTON ST
ELLIS ST
900 POWELL ST
EDDY ST
5TH ST
TURK ST
950 MASON ST
6TH ST
1000 TAYLOR ST
GOLDEN GATE AV
1100 JONES ST
MCALLISTER ST
7TH ST
1200 HYDE ST
8TH ST
GROVE ST
1300 LARKIN ST
HAYES ST
9TH ST
10TH ST
1400 POLK ST
FELL ST
11TH ST
1500 VAN NESS AV
12TH ST
1600 FRANKLIN ST
ROSE ST
BRADY ST
HAIGHT ST
1700 GOUGH ST
VALENCIA ST
MCCOPPIN ST
1800 OCTAVIA ST
PEARL ST
GUERRERO ST
1900 LAGUNA ST
HERMANN ST
2000 DUBOCE AV
DOLORES ST
RESERVOIR ST
14TH ST
2100 CHURCH ST
15TH ST
2200 SANCHEZ ST
2300 16TH ST
NOE ST
17TH ST
2400 CASTRO ST
2500 COLLINGWOOD ST
2600 DIAMOND ST
2700 EUREKA ST
2800 DOUGLASS ST
2900 ORD ST
3000 HATTIE ST
MERRITT ST
3100 DANVERS ST
3200 MONO ST
3300 IRON AL
CASELLI AV
EAGLE ST
SHORT ST
3460 COPPER AL
3500 GLENDALE ST
STANTON ST
GRANDVIEW AV
3700 MORGAN AL
3800 DIXIE AL
3878 ARGENT AL
3950 GOLDING LN
MARLIN CT SF 17 A1
SW FROM NAVY RD IN
HUNTERS PT NAVAL RES
MARNE AV SF 13 B2
FROM 1099 PORTOLA DR S TO
JUANITA AV
MARS ST SF 10 A2
S FROM 17TH ST TO CORBETT AV
MARSHALL ST SF 1 C2
SW FROM GORGAS AV IN THE PRESIDIO
MARSILLY ST SF 14 B3
W OF MISSION ST FROM ST MARYS AV
S TO A POINT S OF BOSWORTH ST
MARSTON AV SF 19 C1
FROM CIRCULAR AV W BETWEEN
JUDSON AV AND HAVELOCK ST
MARTHA AV SF 14 A3
FROM CONGO ST SE TO A POINT NEAR
BURNSIDE AV
MARTINEZ ST SF 1 C2
E FROM FUNSTON AV
N OF PRESIDIO BLVD
MARTIN L KING DR SF 8 A2
MARTIN L KING DR SF 9 A2
IN GOLDEN GATE PARK W FROM
E MIDDLE DR TO THE GREAT HWY
E MIDDLE DR
CONCOURSE DR
TEA GARDEN DR
STOW LAKE DR E
19TH AV
MIDDLE DR W
METSON RD
MIDDLE DR W
CHAIN OF LAKES DR E
THE GREAT HWY
MARVEL CT SF 4 B2
W FROM 32ND AV 2 BLKS N OF
GEARY BLVD
MAR VIEW WY SF 9 C3
E FROM PANORAMA DR BETWEEN
CLAIRVIEW CT AND GLADEVIEW WY
MARX MEADOW DR SF 8 C1
NE FROM JFK DR TO CROSS OVER DR
IN GOLDEN GATE PARK
MARY ST SF 7 A3
S FROM S MISSION ST BETWEEN
5TH ST & 6TH ST SE TO HOWARD ST
2 MISSION ST
30 MINNA ST
70 NATOMA ST
END HOWARD ST
MASON CT SF 3 C1
W FROM GATEVIEW AV BETWEEN
OZBORN CT & LESTER CT
ON TREASURE ISLAND
MASON ST SF 1 B2
E FROM HAMILTON ST TO LYON ST
N OF DOYLE DR
MASON ST SF 3 A2
MASON ST SF 7 A2
N FROM S MARKET ST BETWEEN
POWELL ST & TAYLOR ST
N TO THE BAY
2 MARKET ST
TURK ST
100 EDDY ST
200 ELLIS
300 OFARRELL ST
ELWOOD ST
400 GEARY ST
DERBY ST
500 POST ST
600 SUTTER ST
DELTA PL
700 BUSH ST
HOOKER AL
800 PINE ST
FRANK ST
900 CALIFORNIA ST
1000 SACRAMENTO ST
EWER PL
DAWSON PL
MALVINA PL
1100 CLAY ST
TRUETT ST
SHEPHARD PL
1200 WASHINGTON ST
1300 JACKSON ST
JOHN ST
1400 PACIFIC AV
1500 BROADWAY
1600 VALLEJO ST
1700 GREEN ST
WINTER PL
WEBB PL
1800 UNION ST
KENT ST
1900 FILBERT ST
VALPARAISO ST
GREENWICH ST
2000 COLUMBUS AV
2100 LOMBARD ST
2200 CHESTNUT ST
WATER ST
2300 FRANCISCO ST
2400 BAY ST
2500 NORTH POINT ST
2600 BEACH ST
END JEFFERSON ST
MASONIC AV SF 5 C3
MASONIC AV SF 10 A1
FROM PINE ST W OF CENTRAL AV
S TO UPPER TERRACE
PINE ST
EUCLID AV
GEARY BLVD
ANZA ST
EWING TER
300 TURK ST
400 GOLDEN GATE AV
500 MCALLISTER ST
600 FULTON ST
700 GROVE ST
800 HAYES ST
FELL ST
1000 OAK ST
1100 PAGE ST
1200 HAIGHT ST
1300 WALLER ST
1400 FREDERICK ST
1500 JAVA ST
PIEDMONT ST
END UPPER TERRACE
MASSASOIT ST SF 15 A1
FROM FRANCONIA ST N W TO
RUTLEDGE ST
MATEO ST SF 14 B2
FROM BEMIS ST SE TO SAN JOSE AV
2 BEMIS ST
100 LAIDLEY ST
200 CHENERY ST
300 ARLINGTON ST
END SAN JOSE AV
MATTHEW CT SF 16 A3
OFF ESPANOLA ST BETWEEN
BEATRICE LN AND ROSIE LEE LN
MAULDIN ST SF 1 A2
FROM HAMILTON ST SE TO
LIVINGSTON ST BETWEEN MASON ST
AND MARINE DR
MAYFAIR DR SF 5 C2
W FROM LAUREL ST TO SPRUCE ST
S OF CALIFORNIA ST
MAYFLOWER ST SF 15 A2
FROM HOLLADAY AV NEAR
POWHATTAN AV W TO CARVER ST
MAYNARD ST SF 14 B3
FROM 4200 BLOCK MISSION ST NEAR
SILVER AV TO TRUMBULL ST
22 MISSION ST
100 CRAUT ST
200 CONGDON ST
END TRUMBULL ST
MAYWOOD DR SF 13 B3
FROM YERBA BUENA AV S TO
EL VERANO WY
MCALLISTER ST SF 5 C3
MCALLISTER ST SF 6 A3
FROM THE JUNCTION OF MARKET ST
AND JONES ST BETWEEN FULTON ST &
GOLDEN GATE AV W TO ARGUELLO BLVD
2 MARKET ST
JONES ST
7TH ST N
100 LEAVENWORTH ST
200 HYDE ST
BREEN PL
300 LARKIN ST
400 POLK ST
500 VAN NESS AV
600 FRANKLIN ST
700 GOUGH ST
800 OCTAVIA ST
900 LAGUNA ST
1100 WEBSTER ST
CRAN PL
1200 FILLMORE ST
1300 STEINER ST
1400 PIERCE ST
1500 SCOTT ST
1600 DIVISADERO ST
1700 BRODERICK ST
1800 BAKER ST
1900 LYON ST
2000 CENTRAL AV
END MASONIC AV
PARKER AV
2600 STANYAN ST
PARSONS ST
2700 WILLARD ST
END ARGUELLO BLVD
MCCANN ST SF 16 B3
S FROM LOCKWOOD TO ENGLISH ST
MCCARTHY AV SF 20 C3
S FROM ARGONAUT 1 BLK TO BURR AV
MCCOPPIN ST SF 10 C1
FROM OTIS ST BETWEEN GOUGH ST
& DUBOCE AV W TO MARKET ST
2 OTIS ST
JESSIE ST
STEVENSON ST
100 VALENCIA ST
ELGIN PARK
END MARKET ST
MCCORMICK PL SF 2 C3
S FROM PACIFIC AV BETWEEN HYDE ST
AND LARKIN ST
MCDONALD ST SF 1 B2
N FROM MASON ST BETWEEN
HAMILTON ST & LIVINGSTON ST
MCDOWELL AV SF 1 B2
N FROM LINCOLN BLVD TO
CRISSY FIELD AV IN PRESIDIO
MCDOWELL AV SF 2 B2
N FROM SCHOFIELD RD TO THE BAY
MCKINNON AV SF 15 B2
FROM A POINT S OF LANE ST
NW TO BARNEVELD AV
PT S OF LANE ST
LANE ST
MENDELL ST
3RD ST
NEWHALL ST
PHELPS ST
END QUINT ST
RANKIN ST
SELBY ST
TOLAND ST
UPTON ST
END BARNEVELD AV
MCLAREN AV SF 4 B2
W FROM 28TH AV N OF LAKE ST
TO EL CAMINO DEL MAR
MCLEA CT SF 11 A1
E FROM S 9TH ST BETWEEN BRYANT ST
AND HARRISON ST
MEACHAM PL SF 6 C2
S FROM S POST ST BETWEEN HYDE ST
AND LARKIN ST
MEADE AV SF 21 B2
NW FROM LARKSPUR AV TO 3RD ST
LARKSPUR AV
JENNINGS ST
END 3RD ST
MEADOWBROOK DR SF 12 C3
S FROM SLOAT BLVD TO
EUCALYPTUS DR E OF SYLVAN DR
MEDA AV SF 20 A1
NW FROM OTSEGO AV BETWEEN
OCEAN AV & SANTA YNEZ AV W TO
DELANO AV
MEDAU PL SF 3 A2
N FROM 500 FILBERT ST BETWEEN
GRANT AV AND STOCKTON ST
MELBA AV SF 13 A3
S FROM OCEAN AV TO
EUCALYPTUS DR BETWEEN 22ND AV
AND 23RD AV
MELRA CT SF 21 A3
S FROM SUNNYDALE AV
AT DELTA ST
MELROSE AV SF 13 C3
FROM CONGO ST N OF MANGELS AV
W TO LULU AV
2 CONGO ST
100 DETROIT ST
200 EDNA ST
300 FOERSTER ST
400 GENNESSEE ST
END LULU AL
MENDELL ST SF 15 C2
MENDELL ST SF 21 B1
FROM CARGO WY SW TO PALOU AV
AND THEN S FROM WILLIAMS AV
TO CARROLL AV
CARGO WY
NEWHALL ST
EVANS AV
FAIRFAX AV
GALVEZ AV
HUDSON AV
INNES AV
JERROLD AV
KIRKWOOD AV
LA SALLE AV
MCKINNON AV
NEWCOMB AV
OAKDALE AV
PALOU AV
WILLIAMS AV
YOSEMITE AV
ARMSTRONG AV
BANCROFT AV
END CARROLL AV
MENDOSA AV SF 13 B1
W FROM S 9TH AV TO POINT E
OF 12TH AV
MERCATO CT SF 14 A3
N FROM MALTA DR ONE BLK N OF
STILLINGS AV
MERCED AV SF 13 B2
FROM LAGUNA HONDA BLVD SW
TO KENSINGTON WY
2 LAGUNA HONDA BLVD
100 PACHECO ST
END KENSINGTON WY
MERCEDES WY SF 19 A1
W FROM JUNIPERO SERRA BLVD

N TO PALOMA AV
MERCHANT RD SF 1 A2
N FROM LINCOLN BLVD TO
A POINT S OF DOYLE DR
MERCHANT ST SF 3 B3
FROM BATTERY ST BETWEEN CLAY ST
AND WASHINGTON ST W TO
KEARNY ST
400 BATTERY ST
500 SANSOME ST
600 MONTGOMERY ST
END KEARNY ST
MERCURY ST SF 15 B3
S FROM THORNTON AV W OF VESTA ST
MERLIN ST SF 7 B3
S FROM HARRISON ST BETWEEN
5TH ST AND 6TH ST
MERRILL ST SF 15 A3
S FROM GAVEN ST BETWEEN
BARNEVELD AV AND BOYLSTON
ST S TO SILVER AV
MERRIMAC ST SF 11 C1
E FROM 1500 3RD ST
MERRITT ST SF 10 A2
W FROM MARKET ST TO DANVERS ST
MERSEY ST SF 10 B3
FROM PT N OF 23RD ST BETWEEN
DOLORES ST AND CHATTANOOGA
ST S TO 24TH ST
MESA AV SF 1 C2
SW FROM LINCOLN BLVD TO MORAGA AV
BETWEEN FUNSTON AV AND KEYES AV
MESA AV SF 13 B1
W FROM S SANTA RITA AV
TO 2200 9TH AV
METSON RD SF 8 B2
MICHIGAN ST SF 11 C3
S FROM 20TH ST TO MARIN ST
E OF 3RD ST
20TH ST
22TH ST
24TH ST
25TH ST
ARMY ST
MARIN ST
MIDCREST WY SF 13 C1
1 BLK W OF TWIN PEAKS
BLVD E OF PANORAMA DR
MIDDLE DR E SF 9 B1
IN GOLDEN GATE PARK SW FROM
JFK DR TO MARTIN L KING DR
MIDDLE DR W SF 8 C2
FROM A POINT N OF 39TH AV E
TO A POINT N OF 20TH AV
IN GOLDEN GATE PARK
TRANSVERSE RD
OVERLOOK DR
METSON RD
MARTIN L KING DR
MIDDLEFIELD DR SF 12 C3
S FROM SLOAT BLVD
BETWEEN SYLVAN DR AND
RIVERTON DR
MIDDLE POINT RD SF 16 A2
S FROM EVANS AV TO INNES AV
MIDWAY ST SF 3 A2
FROM 200 FRANCISCO ST BETWEEN
GRANT AV AND STOCKTON ST
N TO BAY ST
MIGUEL ST SF 14 B2
FROM BEACON ST SE TO POINT
S OF ARLINGTON ST
2 BEACON ST
100 BEMIS ST
FAIRMOUNT ST
200 LAIDLEY ST
300 CHENERY ST
400 ARLINGTON ST
END PT S OF ARLINGTON ST
MILAN TER SF 19 C3
S FROM MONETA WY W OF
WHIPPLE AV TO HURON AV
MILES ST SF 1 B2
IN PRESIDIO BETWEEN ORD ST AND
TAYLOR RD S OF LINCOLN BLVD
MILEY ST SF 5 C1
E FROM S BAKER ST BETWEEN
FILBERT ST AND GREENWICH ST
MILL ST SF 21 A2
S OF MANSELL ST FROM
ANKENY ST TO HARKNESS AV
MILLER PL SF 3 A3
N FROM 900 SACRAMENTO ST BETWEEN
STOCKTON ST AND POWELL ST
MILLER RD SF 1 A2
IN PRESIDIO E OF LINCOLN BLVD
N OF STOREY AV
MILTON ST SF 14 B3
S FROM SAN JOSE AV BETWEEN
CUVIER ST
AND ROUSSEAU ST
MILTON ROSS ST SF 15 B2
N E FROM KIRKWOOD AV TO INNES
AV BETWEEN TOLAND ST AND SELBY ST
MINERVA ST SF 19 B2
W OF SAN JOSE AV FROM SUMMIT AV
BETWEEN MONTANA ST AND LOBOS ST
W TO ORIZABA AV
2 SUMMIT AV
100 PLYMOUTH AV
200 CAPITOL AV
END ORIZABA AV
MINNA ST SF 7 A3
MINNA ST SF 10 C1
SW FROM 1ST ST BETWEEN MISSION ST
AND HOWARD ST TO 15TH ST
2 1ST ST
SHAW AL
100 2ND ST
130 NEW MONTGOMERY ST
200 3RD ST
300 4TH ST
400 5TH ST
MARY ST
500 6TH ST
RUSS ST
600 7TH ST
JULIA ST
700 8TH ST
9TH ST
900 10TH ST
1000 11TH ST
LAFAYETTE ST
1300 14TH ST
END 15TH ST
MINNESOTA ST SF 11 C2
MINNESOTA ST SF 15 C1
S FROM MARIPOSA ST BETWEEN
TENNESSEE ST AND INDIANA ST
S TO ARMY ST
500 MARIPOSA ST
600 18TH ST
700 19TH ST
800 20TH ST
KENTUCKY PL
1000 22ND ST
1200 23RD ST
1300 24TH ST
1400 25TH ST
1500 26TH ST
END ARMY ST
MINT ST SF 7 A3
W FROM W 5TH ST BETWEEN
MISSION ST AND STEVENSON ST
MIRABEL AV SF 14 C1
E FROM COSO AV TO SHOTWELL
ST S OF ARMY ST
MIRALOMA DR SF 13 B2
S FROM 1151 PORTOLA DR TO
YERBA BUENA AV
MIRAMAR AV SF 19 B2
N FROM LAKE VIEW AV TO
MONTEREY BLVD
2 LAKE VIEW AV
100 GRAFTON AV
200 HOLLOWAY AV
DE MONTFORD AV
300 OCEAN AV
400 SOUTHWOOD DR
500 EASTWOOD DR
WESTWOOD DR
600 WILDWOOD DR
700 EASTWOOD DR
WESTWOOD DR
800 NORTHWOOD DR
END MONTEREY BLVD
MISSION ST SF 6 C3
MISSION ST SF 7 A2
MISSION ST SF 10 C2
MISSION ST SF 14 B3
MISSION ST SF 20 A2
FROM THE BAY BETWEEN HOWARD ST
& MARKET ST SW TO COUNTY LINE
2 THE EMBARCADERO
50 STEUART ST
100 SPEAR ST
200 MAIN ST
300 BEALE ST
400 FREMONT ST
500 1ST ST
ECKER ST
SHAW AL
ANTHONY ST
600 2ND ST
638 NEW MONTGOMERY ST
ANNIE ST
700 3RD ST
800 4TH ST
900 5TH ST
MINT ST
MARY ST
1000 6TH ST
1100 7TH ST
JULIA ST
1200 8TH ST
LASKIE ST
1300 9TH ST
WASHBURN ST
GRACE ST
1400 10TH ST
1500 11TH ST
LAFAYETTE ST
1600 OTIS ST
VAN NESS AVE
12TH ST
PLUM ST
13TH ST
1700 DUBOCE ST
ERIE ST
1800 14TH ST
1900 15TH ST
2000 16TH ST
2100 17TH ST
2120 CLARION AL
2146 SYCAMORE ST
2200 18TH ST
2300 19TH ST
2400 20TH ST
CATHERINE CT
2500 21ST ST
2600 22ND ST
2700 23RD ST
2800 24TH ST
2900 25TH ST
3000 26TH ST
CAPP ST
3100 ARMY ST
COSO AVE
POWERS AV
3200 VALENCIA ST
FAIR AVE
3300 29TH ST
VIRGINIA AV
GODEUS ST
3400 30TH ST
EUGENIA AV
3438 KINGSTON ST
CORTLAND AV
3500 BROOK ST
SANTA MARINA ST
3600 RANDALL ST
APPLETON AV
3700 HIGHLAND AV
LEESE ST
3750 PARK ST
3800 RICHLAND AV
CRESCENT AV
3900 COLLEGE AV
COLLEGE TER
3990 ST MARYS AV
4000 BOSWORTH ST
MURRAY ST
ALEMANY BLVD
TRUMBALL ST
NEY ST
MAYNARD ST
CASTLE MANOR AV
SILVER AV
4300 TINGLEY ST
AVALON AV
4350 THERESA ST
4400 COTTER ST
4434 FRANCIS ST
EXCELSIOR AV
4500 SANTA ROSA AV
4550 HARRINGTON ST
BRAZIL AV
4600 NORTON ST
SAN JUAN AV
OCEAN AV
4700 RUTH ST
PERSIA AV
4723 LEO ST
RUSSIA AV
4800 ONONDAGA AV
FRANCE AV
KENNEY AL
ITALY AV
SENECA AV
AMAZON AV
5100 GENEVA AV
ROLPH ST
5200 NIAGARA AV
POPE ST
5300 MT VERNON AV
ALLISON ST
CONCORD ST
5400 OTTAWA AV
FLORENTINE ST
5500 FOOTE AV
GUTENBERG ST
5600 NAGLEE AV
LOWELL ST
MORSE ST
5650 WHIPPLE AV
WHITTIER ST
5700 FARRAGUT AV
LAURA ST
OLIVER ST
5800 LAWRENCE AV
ACTON ST
5900 SICKLES AV
HURON AV
END COUNTY LINE
MISSION ROCK ST SF 11 B1
AT JCT OF 4TH AND 3RD ST AT
PIER 50
MISSISSIPPI ST SF 11 B2
MISSISSIPPI ST SF 15 B1
FROM 16TH ST BETWEEN TEXAS ST AND
PENNSYLVANIA AV S TO ARMY ST
2 16TH ST
100 17TH ST
200 MARIPOSA ST
300 18TH ST
400 19TH ST
500 20TH ST
700 22ND ST
1000 25TH ST
END ARMY ST
MISSOURI ST SF 11 B2
MISSOURI ST SF 15 B1
FROM 16TH ST BETWEEN TEXAS AND
CONNECTICUT ST S TO ARMY ST
2 16TH ST
100 17TH ST
200 MARIPOSA ST
300 18TH ST
400 19TH ST
500 20TH ST
SIERRA ST
700 22ND ST
900 23RD ST
END ARMY ST
MISTRAL ST SF 11 A2
E FROM TREAT AV TO HARRISON ST
BETWEEN 19TH ST AND 20TH ST
MIZPAH ST SF 14 A3
BETWEEN SWISS AV AND ELK AV
FROM CHENERY ST N TO
SUSSEX ST
MODOC AV SF 19 C2
N FROM CAYUGA AV BETWEEN
FOOTE AV AND NAGLEE AV
MOFFITT ST SF 14 B2
BETWEEN MORELAND ST AND SUSSEX ST
N FROM CASTRO ST
MOJAVE ST SF 15 A2
W FROM PERALTA AV S OF
CORTLAND AV TO BRONTE ST
MOLIMO DR SF 13 C2
FROM BELLA VISTA DR W TO POINT
WEST OF MYRA WY
MONCADA WY SF 13 A3
N FROM URBANO DR TO
JUNIPERO SERRA BLVD
2 URBANO DR
100 CERRITOS AV
200 CEDRO AV
300 PALOMA AV
END JUNIPERO SERRA BLVD
MONETA CT SF 19 C3
NW FROM MONETA WY
MONETA WY SF 19 C3
N FROM HURON AV BETWEEN
NAGLEE AV AND WHIPPLE AV
MONO ST SF 10 A3
FROM MARKET ST N AND W TO
CASELLI AV
2 MARKET ST
100 EAGLE ST
END CASELLI AV
MONROE ST SF 7 A1
N FROM 600 BUSH ST BETWEEN
STOCKTON ST AND POWELL ST
TO PINE ST
MONTAGUE PL SF 3 A2
E FROM 1201 MONTGOMERY ST
BETWEEN GREEN ST AND UNION ST
MONTALVO AV SF 13 B1
FROM DEWEY BLVD N TO CASTENADA AV
MONTANA ST SF 19 B2
W FROM SUMMIT AV BETWEEN
THRIFT ST AND MINERVA ST TO
ORIZABA AV
2 SUMMIT AV
100 PLYMOUTH AV
200 CAPITOL AV
FAXON AV
END ORIZABA AV

MONTCALM AV SF 15 A1
FROM YORK ST W TO ALABAMA ST
YORKS
MULLEN AVE
200 FRANCONIA ST
300 PERALTA AV
END ALABAMA ST
MONTCLAIR TER SF 2 C2
N FROM LOMBARD ST BETWEEN HYDE ST
AND LEAVENWORTH ST
MONTECITO AV SF 13 C3
FROM MONTEREY BLVD SW TO
EASTWOOD DR
2 MONTEREY BLVD
100 HAZELWOOD AV
200 VALDEZ AV
300 COLON AV
400 PLYMOUTH AV
NORTHWOOD AV
END EASTWOOD DR
MONTEREY BLVD SF 13 C3
FROM CIRCULAR AVE AND SAN
JOSE AVE W THROUGH
WESTWOOD PARK AND ST
FRANCIS WOOD TO JUNIPERO
SERRA BLVD
2 CIRCULAR AVE
100 ACADIA ST
200 BADEN ST
300 CONGO ST
400 DETROIT ST
542 EDNA ST
600 FOERSTER ST
700 GENNESSEE ST
800 RIDGEWOOD AV
MONTECITO AV
856 HAZELWOOD AV
900 VALDEZ AV
930 COLON AV
950 PLYMOUTH ST
MIRAMAR AV
1000 YERBA BUENA AV
FAXON AV
1100 ST ELMO WY
1200 SAN FELIPE AV
NO GATE DR
1400 SAN JACINTO WY
1500 SAN ANDREAS WY
SAN ALESO AV
1600 SANTA CLARA AV
1700 SAN BENITO WY
1800 SANTA ANA AV
1900 SAN LEANDRO WY
2000 SAN FERNANDO WY
2100 SAN RAFAEL WY
END JUNIPERO SERRA BLVD
MONTE VISTA DR SF 19 A1
W FROM 19TH AV S OF
EUCALYPTUS DR
MONTEZUMA ST SF 14 C1
FROM COSO AV E TO
SHOTWELL ST
MONTGOMERY ST SF 1 B2
SW FROM LINCOLN BLVD TO
SHERIDAN AV BETWEEN TAYLOR RD AND
ANZA ST
MONTGOMERY ST SF 3 A2
MONTGOMERY ST SF 7 B1
N FROM MARKET ST BETWEEN SANSOME
ST AND KEARNY ST TO FRANCISCO ST
2 MARKET ST
POST ST
100 SUTTER ST
200 BUSH ST
300 PINE ST
400 CALIFORNIA ST
500 SACRAMENTO ST
COMMERCIAL ST
600 CLAY ST
MERCHANT ST
700 WASHINGTON ST
COLUMBUS AV
800 JACKSON ST
GOLD ST
900 PACIFIC AV
VERDI PL
1000 BROADWAY
1100 VALLEJO ST
1200 GREEN ST
MONTAGUE PL
1300 UNION ST
SCHOOL AL
ALTA ST
1400 FILBERT ST
1500 GREENWICH ST
1600 LOMBARD ST
1700 CHESTNUT ST
END FRANCISCO ST
MONTICELLO ST SF 19 A2
N FROM RANDOLPH ST TO ESTERO AV
2 BLKS E OF JUNIPERO SERRA BLVD
19TH AV
100 SARGENT ST
200 SHIELDS ST
300 GARFIELD ST
400 HOLLOWAY AV
END ESTERO AV
MONUMENT WY SF 9 C2
N FROM 17TH ST E OF ROOSEVELT WY
MOORE PL SF 2 C2
N FROM UNION ST BETWEEN HYDE
ST AND LARKIN ST
MORAGA AV SF 1 B3
IN PRESIDIO NE FROM INFANTRY TER
TO FUNSTON AV
MORAGA ST SF 8 A3
MORAGA ST SF 9 A3
FROM LOCKSLEY AV S OF
LAWTON ST W TO GREAT HWY
2 LOCKSLEY AV
100 7TH AV
200 8TH AV
AUTO DR
300 9TH AV
400 10TH AV
500 11TH AV
600 12TH AV
700 FUNSTON AV
800 14TH AV
900 15TH AV
1000 16TH AV
1100 17TH AV
1200 18TH AV
1300 19TH AV
1400 20TH AV
1500 21ST AV
1600 22ND AV
1700 23RD AV
1800 24TH AV
1900 25TH AV
2000 26TH AV
2100 27TH AV
2200 28TH AV
2300 29TH AV
2400 30TH AV
2500 31ST AV
2600 32ND AV
2700 33RD AV
2800 34TH AV
2900 35TH AV
3000 36TH AV
SUNSET BLVD
3100 37TH AV
3200 38TH AV
3300 39TH AV
3400 40TH AV
3500 41ST AV
3600 42ND AV
3700 43RD AV
3800 44TH AV
3900 45TH AV
4000 46TH AV
4100 47TH AV
4200 48TH AV
END GREAT HIGHWAY
MORELAND ST SF 14 B2
W FROM FARNUM ST TO DIAMOND ST
MORGAN AL SF 10 A3
FROM GRAND VIEW AV W TO
CORBETT AV
MORNINGSIDE DR SF 12 B3
N AND S OF OCEAN AV BETWEEN
GELLERT DR AND CLEARFIELD DR
MORRELL PL SF 2 C3
N FROM PACIFIC AV BETWEEN
HYDE ST AND LARKIN ST N TO
BROADWAY
MORRELL ST SF 17 B1
S FROM SPEAR AV TO MANSEAU ST
MORRIS RD SF 1 A3
IN PRESIDIO W FROM AMATURY LOOP
MORRIS ST SF 7 B3
S FROM HARRISON ST BETWEEN
5TH ST AND 6TH ST SE TO
POINT S OF BRYANT ST
MORSE ST SF 20 A3
FROM ROLPH ST S W TO
MISSION ST N W OF
BRUNSWICK ST
2 ROLPH ST
ROYAL DR
100 NEWTON ST
200 CURTIS ST
300 POPE ST
400 ALLISON ST
500 CONCORD ST
FLORENTINE ST
600 GUTENBERG ST
700 LOWELL ST
END MISSION ST
MORTON ST SF 1 C3
IN PRESIDIO SE FROM RODGIGUEZ ST
TO SANCHEZ ST
MOSCOW ST SF 20 B2
FROM MADISON ST SW TO AMAZON AV
100 AVALON AV
200 EXCELSIOR AV
300 BRAZIL AV
400 PERSIA AV
500 RUSSIA AV
600 FRANCE AV
700 ITALY AV
800 AMAZON AV
END GENEVA AV
MOSS ST SF 7 A3
S FROM HOWARD ST BETWEEN 6TH ST
AND 7TH ST SE TO FOLSOM ST
MOULTON ST SF 2 B2
W FROM BUCHANAN ST BETWEEN
GREENWICH ST AND LOMBARD ST
W TO STEINER ST
2 BUCHANAN ST
100 WEBSTER ST
200 FILLMORE ST
END STEINER ST
MOULTRIE ST SF 14 C2
S FROM BERNAL HEIGHTS BLVD
TO A POINT S OF CRESCENT AV
100 BERNAL HEIGHTS BLVD
200 POWHATTAN AV
300 EUGENIA AV
400 CORTLAND AV
500 JARBOE AV
600 TOMPKINS AV
700 OGDEN AV
800 CRESCENT AV
END PT S OF CRESCENT AV
MOUNT LN SF 9 A3
FROM NORIEGA ST AND 15TH
AV E TO 14TH AV
MOUNTAIN SPGS AV SF 9 C3
FROM TWIN PEAKS BLVD S OF
CLARENDON AV TO PT W OF
STANYAN ST
MOUNT VERNON AV SF 19 C2
FROM MISSION ST BETWEEN OTTAWA AV
AND NIAGARA AV NW TO HAROLD AV
MISSION ST
ELLINGTON AV
DEL MONTE ST
ALEMANY BLVD
ROME ST
CAYUGA AV
DELANO AV
OTEGA AV
SAN JOSE AV
SAN MIGUEL ST
TARA ST
LOUISBURG ST
HOWTH ST
WILLIAR AV
END HAROLD AV
MOUNTVIEW CT SF 13 C1
2 BLKS N OF TWIN PEAKS
BLVD E FROM PANORAMA DR
MUIR LOOP SF 1 C3
IN PRESIDIO S OF SIMONDS LOOP
E OF SHAFTER RD
MULFORD AL SF 7 A2
E FROM TAYLOR ST BETWEEN
BUSH ST AND PINE ST
MULLEN AV SF 15 A1
E FROM ALABAMA ST BETWEEN
PRECITA AV AND MONTCALM ST
TO BREWSTER ST
MUNICH ST SF 20 B2
SW FROM EXCELSIOR AV TO CROCKER
AMAZON PLGD, & FROM HILL BLVD TO
NAPLES ST
200 EXCELSIOR AV
300 BRAZIL AV
400 PERSIA AV
500 RUSSIA AV
CROCKER AMAZON PLGD
900 HILL BLVD
1000 ROLPH ST
NAYLOR ST
1100 CORDOVA ST
DRAKE ST
END NAPLES ST
MURRAY ST SF 14 B3
TO HOLLY PARK CIRCLE
2 MISSION ST
100 GENEBERN WY
200 COLLEGE AV
300 JUSTIN DR
400 CRESCENT AV
500 RICHLAND AV
END HOLLY PARK CIRCLE
MUSEUM WY SF 10 A2
S FROM ROOSEVELT WAY
AND FAIRBANKS ST
MYRA WY SF 13 C2
FROM ROCKDALE DR SW TO
POINT S OF MOLINO DR
MYRTLE ST SF 6 C2
W FROM LARKIN ST BETWEEN
O FARRELL ST AND GEARY ST
2 LARKIN ST
100 POLK ST
200 VAN NESS AVE
END FRANKLIN ST
NADELL CT SF 20 A3
E FROM GUTTENBERG 2 BLKS S
OF BRUNSWICK
NAGLEE AV SF 19 C2
FROM 5600 BLOCK OF MISSION
ST NW TO SAN JOSE AV
2 MISSION ST
100 ELLINGTON AV
RAE AV
200 HURON AV
ALEMANY BLVD
CAYUGA AV
END SAN JOSE AVE
NAHUA AV SF 19 C2
SE FROM MT VERNON AV TO
DELANO AV N OF OTTAWA AV
NANTUCKET AV SF 20 A1
W FROM 1800 SAN JOSE AV
NAPIER LN SF 3 A2
N FROM 200 FILBERT ST BETWEEN
SANSOME ST AND MONTGOMERY ST
NAPLES ST SF 20 B2
FROM SILVER AV SW
THROUGH CROCKER AMAZON
TRACT TO CURTIS ST
2 SILVER AV
100 PERU AV
200 AVALON AV
300 EXCELSIOR AV
400 BRAZIL AV
500 PERSIA AV
600 RUSSIA AV
700 FRANCE AV
800 ITALY AV
900 AMAZON AV
1000 GENEVA AV
1100 ROLPH ST
ATHENS ST
ROYAL LN
SEVILLE ST
NEWTON ST
MUNICH ST
END CURTIS ST
NAPOLEON ST SF 15 B1
W FROM ISLAIS ST TO JERROLD AV
NATICK ST SF 14 C3
S FROM CHENERY ST TO SAN JOSE AV
NATOMA ST SF 7 A3
NATOMA ST SF 10 C1
FROM W S FREMONT ST BETWEEN
MISSION AND HOWARD ST SW
TO 15TH ST
2 FREMONT ST
20 1ST ST
100 2ND ST
144 NEW MONTGOMERY ST
TO A POINT N OF 3RD ST
400 5TH ST
MARY ST
500 6TH ST
RUSS ST
600 7TH ST
700 8TH ST
9TH ST
WASHBURN ST
GRACE ST
900 10TH ST
1000 11TH ST
LAFAYETTE ST
1300 14TH ST
END 15TH ST
NAUMAN RD SF 1 B3
IN PRESIDIO N FROM WASHINGTON
BLVD TO A POINT E OF AMATURY LOOP
NAUTILUS CT SF 17 A1
N FROM KIRKWOOD AV IN
HUNTERS PT NAVAL RES
NAVAJO AV SF 20 A1
FROM A POINT NW OF DELANO AV S E
TO CAYUGA AV
NAVY RD SF 16 A3
NAVY RD SF 17 A1
FROM A POINT NW OF GRIFFITH ST
SE TO EARL ST
GRIFFITH ST
EARL ST
END KIRKWOOD AV
NAYLOR ST SF 20 B3

S FROM MUNICH ST E OF CORDOVA ST
SE TO BALTIMORE WY
2 MUNICH ST
100 PRAGUE ST
200 WINDING WY
300 CHICAGO WY
END BALTIMORE WY
NEBRASKA ST SF 15 A2
FROM POWHATTAN ST S TO
CORTLAND AV
NELLIE ST SF 10 B3
N FROM ELIZABETH ST TO
POINT N OF 23RD ST W OF
CHURCH ST
NELSON AV SF 21 B2
NW FROM LARKSPUR AV
NEPTUNE ST SF 15 B3
FROM THORNTON AV S TO WILLIAMS AV
NEVADA ST SF 15 A2
FROM BERNAL HEIGHTS BLVD BETWEEN
PRENTISS ST AND ROSENKRANZ ST
S TO CRESCENT AV
BERNAL HEIGHTS BLVD
100 POWHATTAN AV
200 CORTLAND AV
300 JARBOE AV
400 TOMPKINS AV
500 OGDEN AV
END CRESCENT AV
NEWBURG ST SF 14 A1
FROM 27TH ST BETWEEN CASTRO ST
AND DIAMOND ST S TO DUNCAN ST
NEWCOMB AV SF 15 B2
FROM WHITNEY YOUNG CIR N OF
OAKDALE AV NW TO BARNEVELD AV
SOUTH RIDGE RD
LANE ST
MENDELL ST
3RD ST
NEWHALL ST
PHELPS ST
QUINT ST
RANKIN ST
SELBY ST
TOLAND ST
END BARNEVELD AV
NEWELL ST SF 2 C2
N FROM 700 LOMBARD ST BETWEEN
MASON ST AND TAYLOR ST
NEWHALL ST SF 15 B3
NEWHALL ST SF 21 B1
FROM JENNINGS ST NW TO MENDELL
ST & W TO EVANS AV THEN SW TO
EGBERT AV
JENNINGS ST
MENDELL ST
EVANS AV
FAIRFAX AV
GALVEZ AV
HUDSON AV
INNES AV
3RD ST
JERROLD AV
KIRKWOOD AV
LA SALLE AV
MCKINNON AV
NEWCOMB AV
OAKDALE AV
PALOU AV
QUESADA AV
REVERE AV
BAY VIEW AV
TOPEKA AV
WILLIAMS AV
YOSEMITE AV
ARMSTRONG AV
CARROLL AV
END EGBERT AV
NEWMAN ST SF 14 C2
E FROM HOLLY PARK CIRCLE BETWEEN
ELLERT ST AND HIGHLAND AV
TO ANDOVER ST
2 HOLLY PARK CIRCLE
100 BENNINGTON ST
END ANDOVER ST
NEW MONTGMRY ST SF 7 B2
S FROM MARKET ST BETWEEN 2ND ST
AND 3RD ST SE TO HOWARD ST
2 MARKET ST
STEVENSON ST
JESSIE ST
ALDRICH AL
100 MISSION ST
140 MINNA ST
NATOMA ST
END HOWARD ST
NEWTON ST SF 20 A2
S FROM S ROLPH ST NE OF
CURTIS ST SE TO NAPLES ST
2 ROLPH ST
100 MORSE ST
BRUNSWICK ST
END NAPLES ST
NEY ST SF 14 B3
E FROM S MISSION ST TO TRUBULL ST
2 MISSION ST
100 CRAUT ST
200 CONGDON ST
END TRUMBULL ST
NIAGARA AV SF 19 C2
N FROM 5200 BLOCK MISSION ST
BETWEEN GENEVA AV AND MOUNT
VERNON AV TO EDGAR PL
2 MISSION ST
ALEMANY BLVD
CAYUGA AV
300 DELANO AV
400 SAN JOSE AV
500 SAN MIGUEL AV
600 TARA ST
700 LOUISBURG ST
800 HOWTH ST
WILLIAR AV
END EDGAR PL
NIANTIC AV SF 19 B3
SW FROM PANAMA ST TO
ST CHARLES AV RUNNING
PARALLEL WITH SOUTHERN FRWY
NIBBI CT SF 21 B3
E FROM GILLETTE AV
NICHOLS WY SF 21 C2
E FROM CAMERON WY ONE
BLK N OF FITZGERALD ST
NIDO AV SF 5 C3
N FROM TURK ST TO VEGA ST
BETWEEN ANZAVISTA AV AND
MASONIC AV
NIMITZ AV SF 17 B1
E FROM BLANDY ST TO A ST S
OF SPEAR AV IN HUNTERS POINT
NOB HILL CIR SF 7 A1
NE CORNER OF PINE ST AND MASON ST
NOBLES AL SF 3 A2
FROM 1500 GRANT AV BETWEEN
UNION ST AND FILBERT ST
NOE ST SF 10 B1
NOE ST SF 14 B1
S FROM DUBOCE AV BETWEEN
SANCHEZ ST AND CASTRO ST S
TO LAIDLEY ST
2 DUBOCE AV
100 14TH ST
150 HENRY ST
200 15TH ST
250 BEAVER ST
16TH ST
300 MARKET ST
400 17TH ST
FORD ST
500 18TH ST
HANCOCK ST
600 19TH ST
700 20TH ST
750 LIBERTY ST
800 21ST ST
850 HILL ST
900 22ND ST
950 ALVARADO ST
1000 23RD ST
1050 ELIZABETH ST
1100 24TH ST
1150 JERSEY ST
1200 25TH ST
1250 CLIPPER ST
1300 26TH ST
1350 ARMY ST
1400 27TH ST
1500 28TH ST
1550 VALLEY ST
1600 29TH ST
1650 DAY ST
1700 30TH ST
END LAIDLEY ST
NORDHOFF ST SF 14 A3
BETWEEN BADEN AV AND CONGO AV
FROM STILLINGS ST S ONE BLK
NORFOLK ST SF 10 C1
S FROM FOLSOM ST BETWEEN
11TH ST AND 12TH ST SE TO
HARRISON ST
NORIEGA ST SF 8 A3
NORIEGA ST SF 9 A3
FROM 8TH AV S OF MORAGA
ST W TO GREAT HIGHWAY
2 7TH AV
100 8TH AV
200 9TH AV
300 10TH AV
400 11TH AV
500 12TH AV
600 FUNSTON AV
700 14TH AV
800 15TH AV
900 16TH AV
1000 17TH AV
1100 18TH AV
1200 19TH AV
1300 20TH AV
1400 21ST AV
1500 22ND AV
1600 23RD AV
1700 24TH AV
1800 25TH AV
1900 26TH AV
2000 27TH AV
2100 28TH AV
2200 29TH AV
2300 30TH AV
2400 31ST AV
2500 32ND AV
2600 33RD AV
2700 34TH AV
2800 35TH AV
2900 36TH AV
SUNSET BLVD
3000 37TH AV
3100 38TH AV
3200 39TH AV
3300 40TH AV
3400 41ST AV
3500 42ND AV
3600 43RD AV
3700 44TH AV
3800 45TH AV
3900 46TH AV
3000 47TH AV
4100 48TH AV
END GREAT HIGHWAY
NORMANDIE TER SF 2 A3
N FROM BROADWAY BETWEEN SCOTT ST
AND DIVISADERO ST TO VALLEJO ST
NORTH GATE DR SF 13 B3
FROM 1199 MONTEREY BLVD S
TO UPLAND DR
NORTH POINT DR SF 3 C1
LOOP EXTENDING N FROM GATEVIEW AV
2 BLKS NW OF 13TH ST, TREASURE
ISLAND
NORTH POINT ST SF 2 A2
NORTH POINT ST SF 3 A2
FROM THE BAY BETWEEN BAY ST AND
BEACH ST W TO BAKER ST
THE EMBARCADERO
2 KEARNY ST
100 GRANT AV
200 STOCKTON ST
300 POWELL ST
400 MASON ST
500 TAYLOR ST
JONES ST
700 COLUMBUS AV
LEAVENWORTH ST
800 HYDE ST
900 LARKIN ST
1000 POLK ST
VAN NESS AV
FORT MASON
1500 LAGUNA ST
1600 BUCHANAN ST
WEBSTER ST
1266 FILLMORE ST
2100 SCOTT ST
2200 DIVISADERO ST
2300 BRODERICK ST
END BAKER ST
NORTHRIDGE RD SF 16 A3
E FROM INGALLS ST TO JERROLD AV
NORTH VIEW CT SF 2 C2
S FROM BAY ST BETWEEN POLK ST AND
LARKIN ST
NORTHWOOD DR SF 13 B3
WESTERLY FROM MONTECITO
AV TO PIZARRO WY S OF
MONTEREY BLVD
2 MONTECITO AV
100 MIRAMAR AV
END PIZARRO WY
NORTON ST SF 20 A1
FROM 4600 BLOCK MISSION ST
BETWEEN HARRINGTON ST AND
SAN JUAN ST
NORWICH ST SF 15 A1
W FROM S ALABAMA ST NEAR
RIPLEY ST W TO POINT NEAR
TREAT AV
NOTTINGHAM PL SF 3 A3
FROM 1000 KEARNY ST BETWEEN
PACIFIC AV AND BROADWAY
NUEVA AV SF 21 B3
FROM LATHROP AV NE TO A POINT
NE OF BLANKEN AV
OAK ST SF 10 A1
FROM JUNCTION MARKET ST
AND VAN NESS AV BETWEEN PAGE ST
AND FELL ST W TO STANYAN ST
2 MARKET ST
VAN NESS AV
100 FRANKLIN ST
200 GOUGH ST
300 OCTAVIA ST
400 LAGUNA ST
500 BUCHANAN ST
600 WEBSTER ST
700 FILLMORE ST
800 STEINER ST
EVA TERR
900 PIERCE ST
1000 SCOTT ST
1100 DIVISADERO ST
1200 BRODERICK ST
BAKER ST
LYON ST
CENTRAL AV
MASONIC AV
ASHBURY ST
CLAYTON ST
COLE ST
SHRADER ST
END STANYAN ST
OAKDALE AV SF 15 B2
FROM GRIFFITH ST NW TO
BAYSHORE BLVD
GRIFFITH ST
BALDWIN CT
INGALLS ST
KEITH ST
LANE ST
MENDELL ST
3RD ST
NEWHALL ST
PHELPS ST
QUINT ST
RANKIN ST
SELBY ST
INDUSTRIAL ST
TOLAND ST
BARNEVELD AVE
LOOMIS ST
PATTERSON ST
END BAY SHORE BLVD
OAK GROVE ST SF 7 B3
S FROM S HARRISON ST BETWEEN
5TH ST AND 6TH ST SE TO BRYANT ST
OAKHURST LN SF 9 B3
FROM WARREN AV E BETWEEN
LOCKSLEY AV AND DEVONSHIRE WY
OAK PARK DR SF 9 B3
S FROM GLENHAVEN LN AND
WARREN DR W OF CLARENDON AV
OAKWOOD ST SF 10 B2
S FROM 18TH ST BETWEEN
GUERRERO AND DOLORES ST
OCEAN AV SF 19 C1
FROM 4700 MISSION ST W TO
COUNTRY CLUB DR
2 MISSION ST
PERSIA AV
WATSON PL
ALEMANY BLVD
100 SANTA YNEZ AV
CAYUGA AV
WANDA ST
200 OTSEGO AV
ONONDAGA ST
300 DELANO AV
400 SAN JOSE AV
TARA ST
920 HOWTH ST
1000 PHELAN AV
HAROLD AV
LEE AV
BRIGHTON AV
1300 PLYMOUTH AV
1400 GRANADA AV
1500 MIRAMAR AV
1600 CAPITOL AV
1700 FAXON AV
1800 JULES AV
ASHTON AV
KEYSTONE WY
FAIRFIELD WY
VICTORIA ST
2100 LAKEWOOD AV
MANOR DR
PINEHURST WY
CORONA ST
CERRITOS AV
WEST GATE DR
CEDRO AV
2200 APTOS AV

1988 SAN FRANCISCO COUNTY CROSS STREET INDEX

SAN BENITO WY
PALOMA AV
SANTA ANA AV
SAN LEANDRO WY
SAN FERNANDO WY
JUNIPERO SERRA BLVD
EUCALYPTUS DR
2500 WOODACRE DR
LAGUNITAS DR
19TH AV
20TH AV
21ST AV
22ND AV
MELBA AV
23RD AV
24TH AV
25TH AV
26TH AV
INVERNESS DR
FOREST VIEW DR
MEADOWBROOK DR
SYLVAN DR
MIDDLEFIELD DR
RIVERTON DR
SPRINGFIELD DR
EVERGLADE DR
HAVENSIDE DR
WESTMOORLAND DR
CLEARFIELD DR
MORNINGSIDE DR
GELLERT DR
SUNSSET BLVD
LAKE SHORE DR
END COUNTRY CLUB DR
OCTAVIA ST SF 2 B2
OCTAVIA ST SF 6 B3
OCTAVIA ST SF 10 B1
N FROM MARKET ST BETWEEN
GOUGH AND LAGUNA ST N TO
FORT MASON
2 MARKET ST
WALLER ST
100 HAIGHT ST
ROSE ST
200 PAGE ST
LILY ST
300 OAK ST
HICKORY ST
400 FELL ST
LINDEN ST
500 HAYES ST
IVY ST
600 GROVE ST
BIRCH ST
700 FULTON ST
ASH ST
800 MCALLISTER ST
GOLDEN GATE AV
1600 SUTTER ST
1700 BUSH ST
AUSTIN ST
1800 PINE ST
1900 CALIFORNIA ST
SACRAMENTO ST
2200 WASHINGTON ST
2300 JACKSON ST
2400 PACIFIC AV
2500 BROADWAY
2600 VALLEJO ST
2700 GREEN ST
2800 UNION ST
2900 FILBERT ST
3000 GREENWICH ST
3100 LOMBARD ST
3200 CHESTNUT ST
3300 FRANCISCO ST
END FORT MASON
OFARRELL ST SF 6 A3
OFARRELL ST SF 7 A2
FROM JUNCTION MARKET ST
AND GRANT AV BETWEEN ELLIS ST
AND GEARY ST W TO MASONIC AV
2 MARKET ST
GRANT AVE
SAVINGS UNION PL
100 STOCKTON ST
200 POWELL ST
CYRIL MAGIN ST
ELWOOD ST
300 MASON ST
400 TAYLOR ST
SHANNON ST
500 JONES ST
600 LEAVENWORTH ST
HARLAM AL
ADA CT
700 HYDE ST
800 LARKIN ST
900 POLK ST
1000 VAN NESS AV
FRANKLIN ST
HOLLIS ST
1600 WEBSTER ST
1700 FILLMORE ST
STEINER ST
PIERCE ST
2000 SCOTT ST
BEIDEMAN ST
2100 DIVISADERO ST
2200 BRODERICK ST
ST JOSEPHS AV
LYON ST
ANZAVISTA AV
END MASONIC AV
OGDEN AV SF 14 C2
E FROM 601 ANDOVER ST TO
PUTNAM ST
2 ANDOVER ST
100 MOULTRIE ST
200 ANDERSON ST
300 ELLSWORTH ST
400 GATES ST
500 FOLSOM ST
600 BANKS ST
700 PRENTISS ST
800 NEVADA ST
END PUTNAM ST
OLD CHINA TN LN SF 3 A3
N FROM WASHINGTON ST BETWEEN
STOCKTON ST AND GRANT AV
OLIVE ST SF 6 C2
W FROM LARKIN ST BETWEEN
ELLIS ST AND O FARRELL ST
2 LARKIN ST
100 POLK ST
200 VAN NESS AV
END FRANKLIN ST
OLIVER ST SF 19 C3
SE FROM 5800 MISSION ST
NEAR COUNTY LINE
OLMSTEAD ST SF 21 A2
SW FROM 3100 SAN BRUNO AV S
OF DWIGHT ST TO UNIVERSITY ST
2 SAN BRUNO AV
100 GIRARD ST
200 BRUSSELS ST
300 GOETTINGEN ST
700 BOWDOIN ST
800 DARTMOUTH ST
900 COLBY ST
END UNIVERSITY ST
OLYMPIA WY SF 13 C1
W OFF PANORAMA DR TO
CLARENDON AV
OMAR WY SF 13 C2
W FROM SEQUOIA WY TO MYRA WY
ONEIDA AV SF 20 A1
FROM ALEMANY BLVD NW TO
SAN JOSE AV
ALEMANY BLVD
100 CAYUGA AV
200 OTSEGO AV
300 DELANO AV
END SAN JOSE AV
ONIQUE LN SF 14 A2
W FROM GOLD MINE DR TO
TO BERKELEY WY
ONONDAGA AV SF 20 A1
NW FROM 4800 MISSION ST
TO OCEAN AV
2 MISSION ST
ALEMANY BLVD
ROSELLA CT
100 CAYUGA AV
WANDA ST
200 OTSEGO AV
END OCEAN AV
OPAL PL SF 7 A2
E FROM S TAYLOR ST BETWEEN
MARKET ST AND TURK ST
OPALO LN SF 14 A2
N FROM GOLD MINE DR ONE
BLK W OF DIAMOND HEIGHTS BLVD
OPHIR AL SF 6 C2
N FROM POST ST BETWEEN JONES
ST AND TAYLOR ST
ORA WY SF 14 A2
S FROM GOLD MINE DR TWO
BLKS W OF DIAMOND HEIGHTS BLVD
ORANGE ST SF 14 C1
S FROM POINT N OF 24TH ST
BETWEEN VALENCIA ST AND BARTLETT
ST TO 26TH ST
ORBEN PL SF 6 B1
N FROM PINE ST BETWEEN
WEBSTER ST AND FILLMORE ST
TO CALIFORNIA ST
ORD CT SF 10 A2
FROM DOUGLASS ST WESTERLY
N OF VULCAN ST
ORD ST SF 1 B2
IN PRESIDIO N OF SHERIDAN AV
TO MILES ST
ORD ST SF 10 A2
N FROM 18TH ST ONE BLK
W OF DOUGLASS
MARKET ST
100 17TH ST
126 CORBETT AV
SATURN ST
VALCAN ST
END ORD CT
ORDWAY ST SF 21 A2
W FROM 3300 SAN BRUNO AV S
OF MANSELL ST TO ANKENY ST
2 SAN BRUNO AV
100 GIRARD ST
200 BRUSSELS ST
300 GOETTINGEN ST
400 SOMERSET ST
END ANKENY ST
OREILLY AV SF 1 C2
IN PRESIDIO N FROM TORNEY AV
TO EDIE RD
ORIENTE ST SF 20 C3
S FROM VELASCO ST TO
COUNTY LINE E OF ACACIA ST
ORIOLE WY SF 13 B1
FROM PACHECO ST BETWEEN 10TH AV
AND 11TH AV SW TO ROCKRIDGE DR
ORIZABA AV SF 19 B2
W OF SAN JOSE AV FROM DE LONG ST
N TO HOLLOWAY AV
2 DE LONG ST
50 PALMETTO AV
100 SAGAMORE ST
150 SADOWA ST
STANLEY ST
200 BROAD ST
250 FARALLONES ST
RANDOLPH ST
300 LOBOS ST
350 MINERVA ST
SARGENT ST
400 MONTANA ST
450 THRIFT ST
SHIELDS ST
500 LAKE VIEW AV
GARFIELD ST
600 GRAFTON AV
END HOLLOWAY AV
ORTEGA ST SF 12 A1
ORTEGA ST SF 9 B3
W FROM POINT E OF 8TH AV S
OF NORIEGA ST TO THE OCEAN
100 8TH AV
200 9TH AV
300 10TH AV
400 11TH AV
AERIAL WY
SELMA WY
CASCADE WK
700 14TH AV
600 FUNSTON AV
800 15TH AV
900 16TH AV
1000 17TH AV
1100 18TH AV
1200 19TH AV
1300 20TH AV
1400 21ST AV
1500 22ND AV
1600 23RD AV
1700 24TH AV
1800 25TH AV
1900 26TH AV
2000 27TH AV
2100 28TH AV
2200 29TH AV
2300 30TH AV
2400 31ST AV
2500 32ND AV
2600 33RD AV
2700 34TH AV
2800 35TH AV
2900 36TH AV
SUNSET BLVD
3000 37TH AV
3100 38TH AV
3200 39TH AV
3300 40TH AV
3400 41ST AV
3500 42ND AV
3600 43RD AV
3700 44TH AV
3800 45TH AV
3900 46TH AV
4000 47TH AV
4100 48TH AV
END GREAT HIGHWAY
ORTEGA WY SF 9 A3
E FROM ORTEGA ST AND 15TH
AV TO 14TH AV
OSAGE ST SF 14 C1
FROM POINT N OF 24TH ST
BETWEEN MISSION ST AND
BARTLETT ST S TO 26TH ST
OSCAR AL SF 7 B2
N FROM CLEMENTINA ST BETWEEN
1ST ST AND 2ND ST
OSCEOLA LN SF 15 C3
LOOP EXTENDING S FROM LA SALLE AV
GARLINGTON CT AND WHITFIELD CT
OSGOOD PL SF 3 B3
N FROM 400 PACIFIC AV BETWEEN
SANSOME ST AND MONTGOMERY
ST TO BROADWAY
OSHAUGHNESSY BL SF 13 C1
OSHAUGHNESSY BL SF 14 A2
FROM 600 PORTOLA DR S TO
BOSWORTH ST
PORTOLA DR
EVELYN WY
DEL VALE AV
MALTA DR
END BOSWORTH ST
OTEGA AV SF 19 C2
SW FROM MOUNT VERNON AV E OF
SAN JOSE AV TO OTTAWA AV
OTIS ST SF 10 C1
FROM MISSION AND 12TH STS
SW TO MCCOPPIN ST THEN
S TO MISSION ST AND DUBOCE AV
2 12TH ST
MISSION ST
70 BRADY ST
GOUGH ST
100 MCCOPPIN ST
MISSION ST
END DUBOCE AV
OTSEGO AV SF 20 A1
FROM SANTA YSABEL AV SW
TO ONEIDA AV
2 SANTA YSABEL AV
100 SAN JUAN AV
200 SANTA YNEZ AV
RUDDEN AV
MEDA AV
300 OCEAN AV
400 ONONDAGA AV
END ONEIDA AV
OTTAWA AV SF 20 A2
NW FROM 5400 MISSION ST
TO SAN JOSE AV NEAR
COUNTY LINE
2 MISSION ST
24 ELLINGTON AV
DEL MONTE ST
100 HURON AV
ALEMANY BLVD
ROME ST
CAYUGA AV
DELANO AV
OTEGA AV
END SAN JOSE AV
OVERLOOK DR SF 8 C1
IN GOLDEN GATE PARK N FROM MIDDLE
DR W TO TRANSVERSE RD
OWEN ST SF 1 B2
IN PRESIDIO SE FROM ANZA ST
TO GRAHAM ST
OWENS ST SF 11 B1
SW FROM CHANNEL ST
AND S TO 16TH ST
OXFORD ST SF 20 C1
FROM SILVER AV S TO WAYLAND ST
2 SILVER AV
PIOCHE ST
100 SILLIMAN ST
200 FELTON ST
300 BURROWS ST
400 BACON ST
END WAYLAND ST
OZBORN CT SF 3 C
NW FROM GATEVIEW AV 1 BLK SW OF
BAYSIDE DR, TREASURE ISLAND
PACHECO ST SF 9 A
PACHECO ST SF 12 A
PACHECO ST SF 13 A
FROM MERCED AV N AND NW TO
JUNCTION OF PACHECO ST
PROPER THEN WESTERLY TO
THE OCEAN
2 MERCED AV
100 DEWEY BLVD
200 MAGELLAN AV
266 MARCELA AV
DORANTES AV
300 CASTENADA AV
325 LOPEZ AV

400 ALTON AV
500 9TH AV
600 10TH AV
700 11TH AV
ORIOLE WY
800 12TH AV
900 FUNSTON AV
1000 14TH AV
1100 15TH AV
1200 16TH AV
1300 17TH AV
1400 18TH AV
1500 19TH AV
1600 20TH AV
1700 21ST AV
1800 22ND AV
1900 23RD AV
2000 24TH AV
SUNSET RESERVOIR
2400 28TH AV
2500 29TH AV
2600 30TH AV
2700 31ST AV
2800 32ND AV
2900 33RD AV
3000 34TH AV
3100 35TH AV
3200 36TH AV
SUNSET BLVD
37TH AV
SUNSET COMMUNITY CTR
3700 41ST AV
3800 42ND AV
3900 43RD AV
4000 44TH AV
4100 45TH AV
4200 46TH AV
4300 47TH AV
END 48TH AV
PACIFIC AV SF 2 A3
PACIFIC AV SF 3 B3
FROM THE BAY BET JACKSON
& BROADWAY W TO THE PRESIDIO
2 THE EMBARCADERO
50 DRUMM ST
100 DAVIS ST
200 FRONT ST
300 BATTERY ST
400 SANSOME ST
OSGOOD PL
500 MONTGOMERY ST
JEROME AL
KEARNY ST
600 COLUMBUS AV
BECKETT ST
700 GRANT AV
JASON CT
PELTON PL
800 STOCKTON ST
CORDELIA ST
TRENTON ST
900 POWELL ST
KEYES AL
WAYNE PL
1000 MASON ST
AUBURN ST
SALMON ST
HIMMELMANN PL
1100 TAYLOR ST
PHOENIX TER
1200 JONES ST
1300 LEAVENWORTH ST
BURGOYNE PL
1400 HYDE ST
MORRELL PL
MCCORMICK ST
1500 LARKIN ST
1600 POLK ST
1700 VAN NESS AV
1800 FRANKLIN ST

1900 GOUGH ST
2000 OCTAVIA ST
2100 LAGUNA ST
2200 BUCHANAN ST
2300 WEBSTER ST
2400 FILLMORE ST
2500 STEINER ST
2600 PIERCE ST
2700 SCOTT ST
2800 DIVISADERO ST
RAYCLIFF TER
2900 BRODERICK ST
3000 BAKER ST
3100 LYON ST
3200 PRESIDIO AV
WALNUT ST
LAUREL ST
LOCUST ST
END PRESIDIO
PACIFIC AV W SF 5 B2
BEGINNING WALNUT
LAUREL ST
LOCUST ST
SPRUCE ST
MAPLE ST
CHERRY ST
ARGUELLO BLVD
END 8TH AV
PAGE ST SF 9 C1
PAGE ST SF 10 B1
FROM JUNCTION MARKET ST
AND FRANKLIN ST BETWEEN HEIGHT ST
AND OAK ST W TO STANYAN ST
2 MARKET ST
FRANKLIN ST
100 GOUGH ST
200 OCTAVIA ST
300 LAGUNA ST
400 BUCHANAN ST
500 WEBSTER ST
600 FILLMORE ST
700 STEINER ST
800 PIERCE ST
900 SCOTT ST
1000 DIVISADERO ST
1100 BRODERICK ST
1200 BAKER ST
1300 LYON ST
1400 CENTRAL AV
1500 MASONIC AV
1600 ASHBURY ST
1700 CLAYTON ST
1800 COLE ST
1900 SHRADER ST
END STANYAN ST
PAGODA PL SF 7 A1
N FROM 1800 SACRAMENTO ST BETWEEN
STOCKTON ST AND GRANT AV
PALACE DR SF 1 C2
S FROM MARINA BLVD AROUND
THE PALACE OF FINE ARTS
TO BAY ST
PALI RD SF 15 B1
FROM NS OF 26TH ST BET
DE HARO ST AND WISCONSIN ST
PALM AV SF 5 B2
FROM CALIFORNIA ST S TO
GEARY BLVD BETWEEN JORDAN AV
AND ARGUELLO BLVD
2 CALIFORNIA ST
100 EUCLID AV
END GEARY BLVD
PALMETTO AV SF 19 B3
W FROM HEAD ST TO
JUNIPERO SERRA BLVD
SERRA BLVD
300 HEAD ST
VICTORIA ST
RAMSELL ST
WORCESTER AV

600 ST CHARLES AV
700 CHESTER AV
END JUNIPERO SERRA BLVD
PALO ALTO AV SF 9 C3
E FROM LA AVANZADA TO A POINT
W OF BURNETT AV
PALOMA AV SF 19 A1
W FROM OCEAN AV TO
JUNIPERO SERRA BLVD
2 OCEAN AV
100 MONCADA WY
MERCEDES WY
END JUNIPERO SERRA BLVD
PALOS PL SF 12 C3
N FROM SLOAT BLVD BETWEEN
VALE AV AND EL MIRASOL PL
PALOU AV SF 15 B2
FROM FITCH ST NW TO BARNEVELD AV
FITCH ST
1000 GRIFFITH ST
1100 HAWES ST
1200 INGALLS ST
1300 JENNINGS ST
1400 KEITH ST
1500 LANE ST
1600 3RD ST
MENDELL ST
1700 NEWHALL ST
1800 PHELPS ST
DUNSHEE ST
1900 QUINT ST
SILVER AV
2000 RANKIN ST
2100 SELBY ST
INDUSTRIAL ST
DORMAN AV
END BARNEVELD AV
PANAMA ST SF 19 A3
W OF SO EMBARCADERO FRWY
FROM NIANTIC AV
PANORAMA DR SF 9 C3
PANORAMA DR SF 13 C1
N FROM TWIN PEAKS BLVD TO
CLARENDON AV 1 BLK N OF
PORTOLA DR
PANTON AL SF 6 C1
E FROM LEAVENWORTH ST BETWEEN
CALIFORNIA ST AND PINE ST
PARADISE AV SF 14 A3
SE FROM ELK ST BETWEEN
CHENERY ST AND BOSWORTH ST
TO BURNSIDE AV
PARAISO PL SF 12 C3
FROM SLOAT BLVD N TO
CRESTLAKE DR
PARAMOUNT TER SF 5 C3
W FROM STANYAN ST BETWEEN
GOLDEN GATE AV AND MCALLISTER ST
PARDEE AL SF 3 A2
FROM 1601 GRANT AV BETWEEN
FILBERT ST AND GREENWICH ST
PARIS ST SF 20 A2
FROM AVALON AV SW TO ROLPH ST
AVALON ST
200 EXCELSIOR AV
300 BRAZIL AV
400 PERSIA AV
500 RUSSIA AV
600 FRANCE AV
700 ITALY AV
800 AMAZON AV
900 GENEVA AV
END ROLPH ST
PARK BLVD SF 5 A2
IN PRESIDIO PARALLEL TO
PARK PRESIDIO BLVD
PARK ST SF 14 B2
FROM SAN JOSE AV TO ANDOVER ST
MISSION ST
100 LEESE ST

300 HOLLY PARK CIRCLE
END ANDOVER ST
PARKER AV SF 5 C2
S FROM CALIFORNIA ST OPPOSITE
MAPLE ST S TO FULTON ST
CALIFORNIA ST
EUCLID AV
200 GEARY BLVD
ANZA ST
600 TURK ST
GOLDEN GATE AV
MCALLISTER ST
END FULTON ST
PARK HILL AV SF 10 A2
N FROM ROOSEVELT WY BETWEEN
BUENA VISTA AV AND BUENA
VISTA TER
PARKHURST AL SF 3 A3
N FROM 900 CLAY ST BETWEEN
STOCKTON ST AND POWELL ST
PARK PRESIDIO BL SF 5 A3
N FROM FULTON ST TO LAKE ST
BETWEEN FUNSTON AV AND 14TH AV
FULTON ST
CABRILLO ST
BALBOA ST
ANZA ST
GEARY BLVD
CLEMENT ST
CALIFORNIA ST
END LAKE ST
PARKRIDGE DR SF 14 A1
N FROM BURNETT AV 4
BLKS N OF PORTOLA DR
PARNASSUS AV SF 9 B2
FROM CLAYTON ST BETWEEN CARL ST
AND GRATTON ST W TO 5TH AV
W TO 5TH AVE
2 CLAYTON ST
BELVEDERE ST
100 COLE ST
164 SHRADER ST
200 STANYAN ST
WOODLAND AV
300 WILLARD ST
HILL POINT ST
374 HILLWAY ST
400 ARGUELLO BLVD
500 2ND AV
600 3RD AV
700 4TH AV
END 5TH AV
PARQUE DR SF 20 C3
N FROM CARRIZAL ST TO GENEVA AV
PARSONS ST SF 9 C1
N FROM FULTON ST BETWEEN
STANYAN ST AND WILLARD ST
PASADENA ST SF 20 C3
FROM VELASCO AV TO GENEVA AV
PATTEN RD SF 1 B2
IN PRESIDIO E FROM MCDOWELL AV
TO LINCOLN BLVD
PATTERSON ST SF 15 A2
E OF BAYSHORE BLVD FROM
FLOWER ST NE
PATTON ST SF 14 C2
FROM APPLETON AV S TO
HIGHLAND AV E OF MISSION ST
PAUL AV SF 21 B1
FROM 3RD ST AND GILMAN AV
NW TO SAN BRUNO AV
3RD ST
CARR ST
GOULD ST
EXETER ST
CRANE ST
500 WHEAT ST
BAYSHORE BLVD
END SAN BRUNO AV
PAULDING ST SF 20 A1

FROM W S SAN JOSE AV BETWEEN
NANTUCKET AV AND HAVELOCK ST
PAYSON ST SF 19 A3
N OF PALMETTO AV FROM ST CHARLES
AV TO CHESTER AV
PEABODY ST SF 21 A3
W OF BAYSHORE BLVD FROM LELAND AV
COUNTY LINE
PEARCE ST SF 1 A2
IN PRESIDIO E FROM HAMILTON ST
BETWEEN MARINE DR AND HAMILTON ST
PEARL ST SF 10 C1
S FROM MARKET ST BETWEEN
ELGIN PARK AND GUERRERO ST
S TO DUBOCE AV
PEDESTRIAN WY SF 1 C2
N FROM MARINA BLVD AT
ST FRANCIS YACHT CLUB
PELTON PL SF 3 A3
N FROM 700 PACIFIC AV BETWEEN
GRANT AV AND STOCKTON ST
PEMBERTON PL SF 9 C3
SW FROM CLAYTON ST AND CORBETT AV
TO BURNETT AV
PENA ST SF 1 B3
IN PRESIDIO NW FROM MESA AV
PENINSULA AV SF 21 B3
BETWEEN WHEELER AV AND TOCOLOMA
AV FROM HESTER AV TO
POINT S OF LATHROP AV
PENNINGTON ST SF 1 B2
IN PRESIDIO N FROM MASON ST
TO MAULDIN ST
PENNSYLVANIA AV SF 11 B3
FROM 16TH ST BETWEEN IOWA ST AND
MISSISSIPPI ST S TO ARMY ST
16TH ST
100 17TH ST
200 MARIPOSA ST
300 18TH ST
400 19TH ST
500 20TH ST
700 22ND ST
900 23RD ST
1100 25TH ST
END ARMY ST
PERALTA AV SF 15 A1
FROM HOLLADAY AV S OF
ARMY ST SW AND S T A POINT S
OF OGDEN AV
2 HOLLADAY AV
16 HAMPSHIRE ST
100 YORK ST
FRANCONIA ST
200 FLORIDA ST
220 MULLEN ST
300 MONTCALM ST
400 RUTLEDGE ST
SAMOSET ST
500 RIPLEY ST
ESMERALDA AV
MAYFLOWER ST
700 POWHATTAN AV
800 CORTLAND AV
MOJAVE ST
900 JARBOE AV
TOMPKINS AV
END PUTNAM ST
PEREGO TER SF 14 A1
E FROM BURNETT 4 BLKS N OF
PORTOLA DR
PERINE PL SF 6 A2
W FROM STEINER ST BETWEEN
CALIFORNIA ST AND SACRAMENTO ST
TO PIERCE ST
PERRY ST SF 7 B2
FROM POINT W OF 2ND ST BETWEEN
HARRISON ST AND BRYANT ST
SW TO 5TH ST
2 PT W OF 2ND ST

1988 SAN FRANCISCO COUNTY CROSS STREET INDEX

100 3RD ST
200 4TH ST
END 5TH ST
PERSHING DR SF 4 C1
IN PRESIDIO
PERSIA AV SF 20 B1
FROM OCEAN AV BETWEEN
ALEMANY BLVD AND MISSION ST SE TO
BRAZIL AV AND MANSELL ST
OCEAN AV
2 MISSION ST
100 LONDON ST
200 PARIS ST
300 LISBON ST
400 MADRID ST
500 EDINBURGH ST
600 NAPLES ST
700 VIENNA ST
800 ATHENS ST
900 MOSCOW ST
1000 MUNICH ST
1100 PRAGUE ST
DUBLIN ST
LA GRANDE AV
SUNNYDALE AV
END MANSELL ST & BRAZIL AV
PERU AV SF 20 B1
SE FROM LISBON ST TO BURROWS ST
100 LISBON ST
200 MADRID ST
300 EDINBURG ST
400 NAPLES ST
500 VIENNA ST
600 ATHENS ST
VALMAR TER
AVALON AV
FELTON ST
END BURROWS ST
PETERS AV SF 14 C2
SW FROM FAIR AV BETWEEN
MISSION ST AND COLERIDGE ST
PETER YORKE WY SF 6 B2
N FROM GEARY ST BETWEEN GOUGH ST
AND FRANKLIN ST
PETRARCH PL SF 7 B1
FROM 301 PINE ST BETWEEN
SANSOME ST AND MONTGOMERY ST
PFEIFFER ST SF 3 A2
FROM POINT E OF GRANT AV BETWEEN
CHESTNUT ST AND FRANCISCO ST W TO
STOCKTON ST
2 POINT E OF GRANT AV
100 GRANT AV
BELLAIR PL
END STOCKTON ST
PHELAN AV SF 19 C1
FROM OCEAN AV N TO FLOOD AV
W OF BALBOA PARK
2 OCEAN AV
200 JUDSON AV
300 STAPLES AV
END FLOOD AV
PHELPS ST SF 15 B2
PHELPS ST SF 21 B1
S FROM DAVIDSON AV AND 3RD ST TO
BAYSHORE BLVD
DAVIDSON AV
400 EVANS AV
500 FAIRFAX AV
600 GALVEZ AV
700 HUDSON AV
800 INNES AV
900 JERROLD AV
1000 KIRKWOOD AV
1100 LA SALLE AV
1200 MCKINNON AV
1300 NEWCOMB AV
1400 OAKDALE AV
1500 PALOU AV
1600 QUESADA AV

2500 BANCROFT AV
2600 CARROLL AV
2700 DONNER AV
2800 EGBERT AV
END BAYSHORE BLVD
PHOENIX TER SF 2 C3
S OF PACIFIC AV BETWEEN
TAYLOR ST AND JONES ST
PICO AV SF 19 B1
FROM ASHTON AV W BETWEEN
HOLLOWAY AV AND OCEAN AV
PIEDMONT ST SF 10 A2
FROM MASONIC AV S OF FREDERICK ST
W TO ASHBURY ST
2 MASONIC AV
100 DELMAR ST
END ASHBURY ST
PIERCE ST SF 2 A3
PIERCE ST SF 6 A1
PIERCE ST SF 10 B1
FROM DUBOCE PARK BETWEEN
STEINER ST AND SCOTT ST N TO
BEACH ST
2 DUBOCE PARK
100 WALLER ST
200 HAIGHT ST
300 PAGE ST
400 OAK ST
500 FELL ST
HAYES
ALAMO SQUARE
800 FULTON ST
900 MCALLISTER ST
1000 GOLDEN GATE AV
ELM ST
1100 TURK ST
1200 EDDY ST
1300 ELLIS ST
O'FARRELL ST
HAMILTON SQUARE
1600 POST ST
1700 SUTTER ST
1800 BUSH ST
1900 PINE ST
2000 CALIFORNIA ST
PERINE PL
2100 SACRAMENTO ST
CLAY ST
ALTA PLAZA
2400 JACKSON ST
2500 PACIFIC AV
2600 BROADWAY
2700 VALLEJO ST
2800 GREEN ST
2900 UNION ST
3000 FILBERT ST
3100 GREENWICH ST
3200 LOMBARD ST
3300 CHESTNUT ST
TOLEDO WY
3400 ALHAMBRA ST
3500 CAPRA WY
END BEACH ST
PILGRIM AV SF 14 A3
S FROM MONTEREY BLVD TO
SAN JOSE AV
PINE ST SF 3 B3
PINE ST SF 6 A2
FROM JUNCTION MARKET ST
AND DAVIS ST BETWEEN BUSH ST
AND CALIFORNIA ST W TO
PRESIDIO AV
2 MARKET ST
DAVIS ST
100 FRONT ST
200 BATTERY ST
CENTURY PL
300 SANSOME ST
LEIDESDORFF ST
EXCHANGE PL

PETRARCH PL
400 MONTGOMERY ST
BELDEN ST
500 KEARNY ST
ST GEORGE AL
QUINCY ST
600 GRANT AV
700 STOCKTON ST
JOICE ST
MONROE ST
800 POWELL ST
900 MASON ST
VINE TERR
1000 TAYLOR ST
1100 JONES ST
TOUCHARD ST
1200 LEAVENWORTH ST
1300 HYDE ST
1400 LARKIN ST
1500 POLK ST
1600 VAN NESS AV
1700 FRANKLIN ST
1800 GOUGH ST
1900 OCTAVIA ST
2000 LAGUNA ST
2100 BUCHANAN ST
2200 WEBSTER ST
ORBEN PL
2300 FILLMORE ST
2400 STEINER ST
2500 PIERCE ST
2600 SCOTT ST
2700 DIVISADERO ST
2800 BRODERICK ST
2900 BAKER ST
3000 LYON ST
END PRESIDIO AV
PINEHURST WY SF 19 B1
FROM 2000 OCEAN AV N TO UPLAND DR
2 OCEAN AV
100 KENWOOD WY
END UPLAND DR
PINK AL SF 10 B1
FROM PEARL ST BETWEEN MARKET ST
AND DUBOCE AV
PINO AL SF 8 C2
FROM JUDAH ST BETWEEN 35TH AV AND
36TH AV
PINTO AV SF 18 C2
W FROM TAPIA DR NEAR FONT BLVD
TO ARBALLO DR
PIOCHE ST SF 20 B1
FROM CAMBRIDGE ST W TO MADISON ST
100 CAMBRIDGE ST
200 OXFORD ST
300 HARVARD ST
400 GAMBIER ST
END MADISON ST
PIPER LOOP SF 1 B3
IN PRESIDIO LOOP EXTENDING NW
FROM WASHINGTON BLVD
PIXLEY ST SF 2 A3
W FROM BUCHANAN ST BETWEEN
FILBERT ST AND GREENWICH
ST TO STEINER ST
2 BUCHANAN ST
100 WEBSTER ST
200 FILLMORE ST
END STEINER ST
PIZARRO WY SF 13 B3
FROM WESTWOOD DR TO FAXON
AV JUST S OF MONTEREY BLVD
PLAZA ST SF 13 B1
E FROM MAGELLAN AV TO
LAGUNA HONDA BLVD
PLEASANT ST SF 2 C3
W FROM TAYLOR ST BETWEEN
SACRAMENTO ST AND CLAY ST
W TO JONES ST
PLUM ST SF 10 C1

E FROM MISSION ST TO
S VAN NESS AV BETWEEN 12TH ST AND
13TH ST
PLYMOUTH AV SF 19 C2
FROM SAN JOSE AV AT
JUNCTION OF PALMETTO AV
N TO YERBA BUENA AV
SAN JOSE AV
100 SAGAMORE ST
200 SADOWA ST
300 BROAD ST
400 FARALLONES ST
500 LOBOS ST
600 MINERVA ST
700 MONTANA ST
800 THRIFT ST
900 LAKEVIEW AV
1000 GRAFTON AV
1100 HOLLOWAY AV
1200 OCEAN AV
1300 SAN RAMON WY
1400 WILDWOOD WY
GREENWOOD AV
1500 MONTECITO AV
1600 MONTEREY BLVD
MANGELS AV
END YERBA BUENA AV
POINT LOBOS AV SF 4 A3
FROM JUNCTION OF GEARY
BLVD AND 40TH AV NW W AND
S TO GREAT HIGHWAY
GEARY BLVD
40TH AV
41ST AV
42ND AV
100 43RD AV
200 44TH AV
300 45TH AV
400 46TH AV
ALTA MAR WY
500 47TH AV
600 48TH AV
END GREAT HIGHWAY
POLARIS WY SF 20 A3
E FROM POPE ST 2 BLKS S OF
HANOVER ST
POLK ST SF 2 C2
POLK ST SF 6 C3
N FROM MARKET ST BETWEEN
VAN NESS AV AND LARKIN ST N TO
BEACH ST
2 MARKET ST
FELL ST
HAYES ST
LECH WALESA
GROVE ST
MCALLISTER ST
430 REDWOOD ST
500 GOLDEN GATE AV
ELM ST
600 TURK ST
700 EDDY ST
730 WILLOW ST
800 ELLIS ST
830 OLIVE ST
900 OFARRELL ST
930 MYRTLE ST
1000 GEARY ST
1030 CEDAR ST
1100 POST ST
1130 HEMLOCK ST
1200 SUTTER ST
1230 FERN ST
1300 BUSH ST
1330 AUSTIN ST
1400 PINE ST
1500 CALIFORNIA ST
1600 SACRAMENTO ST
1700 CLAY ST
1800 WASHINGTON ST

1900 JACKSON ST
2000 PACIFIC AV
2100 BROADWAY
2200 VALLEJO ST
BONITA ST
2300 GREEN ST
2400 UNION ST
2500 FILBERT ST
2600 GREENWICH ST
2700 LOMBARD ST
2800 CHESTNUT ST
2900 FRANCISCO ST
3000 BAY ST
3100 NORTH POINT ST
END BEACH ST
POLLARD PL SF 3 A2
FROM 500 VALLEJO ST BETWEEN
KEARNY ST AND GRANT AV
POMONA ST SF 15 B3
FROM BAY VIEW ST BETWEEN
LATONA ST AND FLORA ST S TO
THORNTON AV
POND ST SF 10 B2
S FROM 16TH ST BETWEEN NOE ST
AND SANCHEZ ST TO 17TH ST
POPE RD SF 2 B2
IN FORT MASON N FROM SHOFIELD RD
POPE ST SF 1 A2
IN PRESIDIO N FROM KOBBE AV
BETWEEN GREENOUGH AV AND TODD ST
POPE ST SF 20 A2
FROM 5200 MISSION OPPOSITE
NIAGARA AV S TO BELLEVUE WY
2 MISSION ST
HOLLYWOOD CT
100 CROSS ST
200 MORSE ST
300 BRUNSWICK ST
HANOVER ST
BALTIMORE WY
POLARIS WY
END BELLEVUE WY
POPLAR ST SF 14 C1
FROM POINT N OF 24TH ST BETWEEN
VALENCIA ST AND SAN JOSE AV
S TO 26TH ST
2 PT N OF 24TH ST
100 24TH ST
200 25TH ST
END 26TH ST
POPPY LN SF 14 A2
NE FROM CONRAD ST TO A POINT W OF
CASTRO ST N OF SUSSEX ST
BEMIS ST AND N OF SUSSEX ST
PORTAL PATH SF 13 B2
S FROM PORTOLA DR TO
SANTA MONICA AV W OF
SAN LORENZO WY
PORTER ST SF 14 C3
S FROM CRESCENT AV BETWEEN
ROSCOE ST AND BACHE ST
PORTOLA DR SF 13 B2
FROM DIAMOND HEIGHTS BLVD
AND SW TO JUNIPERO SERRA BLVD
DIAMOND HEIGHTS BLVD
TURQUOISE WY
O'SHAUGHNESSY BLVD
TERESITA BLVD
700 WOODSIDE AV
800 SYDNEY WY
FOWLER AV
EVELYN WY
900 LAGUNA HONDA BLVD
DEL SUR AV
1000 WAITHMAN PL
REX AV
MARNE AV
1100 KENSINGTON WY
MIRALOMA DR
1200 GRANVILLE WY

SAN PABLO AV
SANTA PAULA AV
1300 DORCHESTER WY
SAN LORENZO WY
1370 CLAREMONT BLVD
PORTAL PATH
1400 VICENTE ST
SANTA CLARA AV
1500 14TH AV
TERRACE DR
SANTA ANA AV
SAN ANSELMO AV
SAN LEANDRO WY
1600 15TH AV
SAN FERNANDO WY
END JUNIPERO SERRA BLVD
PORTOLA ST SF 1 C3
IN PRESIDIO S FROM MACARTHUR ST
PARALLEL TO RODRIGUEZ ST
POST ST SF 6 A2
POST ST SF 7 A2
FROM JUNCTION MARKET ST AND
MONTGOMERY ST BETWEEN GEARY ST
AND SUTTER ST W TO PRESIDIO AV
2 MARKET ST
MONTGOMERY ST
LICK PL
100 KEARNY ST
ROBERT KIRK LN
200 GRANT AV
300 STOCKTON ST
400 POWELL ST
500 MASON ST
600 TAYLOR ST
AGATE AL
SHANNON ST
OPHIR AL
700 JONES ST
800 LEAVENWORTH ST
900 HYDE ST
MEACHAM PL
1000 LARKIN ST
1100 POLK ST
1200 VAN NESS AV
1300 FRANKLIN ST
1400 GOUGH ST
1600 LAGUNA ST
1700 BUCHANAN ST
1800 WEBSTER ST
1900 FILLMORE ST
AVERY ST
2000 STEINER ST
2100 PIERCE ST
2200 SCOTT ST
2300 DIVISADERO ST
ERKSON CT
2400 BRODERICK ST
2500 BAKER ST
2600 LYON ST
END PRESIDIO AV
POTOMAC ST SF 10 B1
FROM 549 WALLER ST S TO
DUBOCE PARK BETWEEN STEINER ST
AND PIERCE ST
POTRERO AV SF 11 A3
FROM DIVISION ST BETWEEN UTAH ST
AND HAMPSHIRE ST S TO ARMY ST
2 DIVISION ST
100 ALAMEDA ST
200 15TH ST
300 16TH ST
400 17TH ST
500 MARIPOSA ST
600 18TH ST
700 19TH ST
800 20TH ST
900 21ST ST
1000 22ND ST
1100 23RD ST
1200 24TH ST

1300 25TH ST
END ARMY ST
POWELL ST SF 3 A1
POWELL ST SF 7 A2
N FROM MARKET ST BETWEEN
STOCKTON ST AND MASON ST N TO
THE EMBARCADERO
2 MARKET ST
EDDY ST
100 ELLIS ST
200 OFARRELL ST
GEARY ST
400 POST ST
500 SUTTER ST
ANSON PL
600 BUSH ST
FELLA PL
700 PINE ST
800 CALIFORNIA ST
900 SACRAMENTO ST
1000 CLAY ST
1100 WASHINGTON ST
1200 JACKSON ST
JOHN ST
1300 PACIFIC AV
FISHER AL
1400 BROADWAY
1500 VALLEJO ST
1600 GREEN ST
1700 UNION ST
COLUMBUS AV
1800 FILBERT ST
1900 GREENWICH ST
2000 LOMBARD ST
FIELDING ST
2100 CHESTNUT ST
2200 FRANCISCO ST
VANDEWATER ST
2300 BAY ST
2400 NORTH POINT ST
2500 BEACH ST
JEFFERSON ST
END THE EMBARCADERO
POWERS AV SF 14 C1
FROM MISSION ST S OF
PRECITA AV SE TO COLERIDGE ST
POWHATTAN AV SF 15 A2
FROM BOCANA ST BETWEEN EUGENIA
AV AND ESMERALDA AV E TO
HOLLADAY AV
BOCANA ST
2 WOOL ST
100 ANDOVER ST
200 MOULTRIE ST
300 ANDERSON ST
400 ELLSWORTH ST
500 GATES ST
600 FOLSOM ST
700 BANKS ST
800 PRENTISS ST
900 NEVADA ST
ROSENKRANZ ST
1000 NEBRASKA ST
1100 BRADFORD ST
1200 PERALTA AV
FRANCONIA ST
END HOLLADAY AV
PRADO ST SF 2 A2
W FROM CERVANTES BLVD TO SCOTT ST
PRAGUE ST SF 20 B2
FROM EXCELSIOR AV BETWEEN
MUNICH ST AND DUBLIN ST SW TO
HANOVER ST
2 EXCELSIOR AV
100 BRAZIL AV
200 PERSIA AV
300 RUSSIA AV
CROCKER AMAZON PLGD
GENEVA AV
HILL BLVD

700 ROLPH ST
800 NAYLOR ST
900 CORDOVA ST
1000 DRAKE ST
1100 CURTIS ST
WINDING WY
END POPE ST & HANOVER ST
PRECITA AV SF 14 C1
FROM COSO AV S OF ARMY ST
E TO ARMY ST AND YORK ST
100 COSO AV
EMMETT CT
252 SHOTWELL ST
300 FOLSOM ST
400 HARRISON ST
500 ALABAMA ST
600 FLORIDA ST
BRYANT ST
700 YORK ST
HAMPSHIRE ST
END ARMY ST
PRENTISS ST SF 15 A2
FROM BERNAL HEIGHTS BLVD BETWEEN
BANKS ST AND NEVADA ST S TO
POINT S OF CRESCENT AV
2 BERNAL HTS BLVD
CHAPMAN ST
100 POWHATTAN AV
200 EUGENIA AV
300 CORTLAND AV
400 JARBOE AV
500 TOMPKINS AV
600 OGDEN AV
700 CRESCENT AV
END PT S OF CRESCENT AV
PRESCOTT CT SF 3 B2
FROM 301 VALLEJO ST BETWEEN
SANSOME ST AND MONTGOMERY ST
PRESIDIO AV SF 5 C1
W OF LYON ST FROM PRESIDIO
RESERVATION S TO GEARY BLVD
2 PACIFIC AV
100 JACKSON ST
200 WASHINGTON ST
300 CLAY ST
400 SACRAMENTO ST
500 CALIFORNIA ST
600 PINE ST
700 BUSH ST
800 SUTTER ST
900 POST ST
END GEARY BLVD
PRESIDIO BLVD SF 1 C3
IN PRESIDIO N FROM PACIFIC AV TO
MESA AV
PRESIDIO TER SF 5 B2
LOOP EXTENDING FROM W END OF
WASHINGTON ST S OF PRESIDIO
PRETOR WY SF 20 A3
E FROM GUTTENBERG ST 3 BLKS S OF
MISSION ST
PRICE ROW SF 3 A2
S FROM 501 UNION ST BETWEEN
GRANT AV AND STOCKTON ST
PRIEST ST SF 2 C3
S FROM WASHINGTON ST TO
A POINT N OF CLAY ST
AND LEAVENWORTH ST
PRINCETON ST SF 20 C1
FROM SILVER AV TO WAYLAND ST
2 SILVER AV
100 SILLIMAN ST
200 FELTON ST
BACON ST
END WAYLAND ST
PROSPECT AV SF 14 C2
S FROM COSO AV BETWEEN
WINFIELD ST AND COLERIDGE ST TO
SANTA MARINA ST
2 COSO AV

FAIR AV
100 ESMERALDA AV
200 VIRGINIA AV
HEYMAN AV
300 EUGENIA AV
KINGSTON ST
400 CORTLAND AV
END SANTA MARINA ST
PROSPER ST SF 10 B2
S FROM 16TH ST BETWEEN SANCHEZ ST
AND NOE ST TO 17TH ST
PUEBLO ST SF 20 C3
FROM VELASCO AV TO COUNTY LINE
PUTNAM ST SF 15 A2
S FROM CORTLAND AV BETWEEN
BRONTE ST AND NEVADA ST S TO
CRESCENT AV
2 CORTLAND AV
100 JARBOE AV
200 TOMPKINS AV
300 OGDEN AV
END CRESCENT AVE
QUANE ST SF 10 B3
S FROM 21ST ST BETWEEN
DOLORES ST AND FAIR OAKS ST
TO 24TH ST
QUARRY RD SF 5 B1
E OF ARGUELLO S FROM FERNANDEZ ST
IN THE PRESIDIO
QUARTZ WY SF 14 A1
W OF AMBER DR JUST S OF
PORTOLA DR
QUESADA AV SF 15 B2
FROM FITCH ST NW TO INDUSTRIAL ST
BETWEEN PALOU AV AND REVERE AV
FITCH ST
GRIFFITH ST
1200 HAWES ST
1300 INGALLS ST
1400 JENNINGS ST
1500 KEITH ST
1600 LANE ST
1700 3RD ST
1800 NEWHALL ST
1900 PHELPS ST
2000 QUINT ST
SILVER AV
2100 RANKIN ST
2200 SELBY ST
END INDUSTRIAL ST
QUINCY ST SF 3 A3
FROM A POINT S OF PINE ST BETWEEN
KEARNY ST AND GRANT AV N
TO CALIFORNIA ST
QUINT ST SF 15 B2
FROM CARGO WY SW TO REVERE AV
AND BANCROFT AV S TO BAYSHORE BL
2 CARGO WY
200 CUSTER AV
300 DAVIDSON AV
400 EVANS AV
500 FAIRFAX AV
600 GALVEZ AV
700 HUDSON AV
800 INNES AV
900 JERROLD AV
1000 KIRKWOOD AV
1200 MCKINNON AV
1300 NEWCOMB AV
1400 OAKDALE AV
1500 PALOU AV
1600 QUESADA AV
REVERE AV
THOMAS AV
TOPEKA AV
SANTA FE ST
SCOTIA ST
2500 BANCROFT AV
2600 CARROLL AV
END BAYSHORE BLVD

QUINTARA ST SF 12 A1
QUINTARA ST SF 13 A1
FROM A POINT E OF 10TH AV S
OF PACHECO ST W TO THE
GREAT HIGHWAY
2 PT E OF 10TH AV
100 10TH AV
CRAGMONT AV
300 12TH AV
FUNSTON AV
14TH AV
600 15TH AV
700 16TH AV
800 17TH AV
900 18TH AV
1000 19TH AV
1100 20TH AV
1200 21ST AV
1300 22ND AV
1400 23RD AV
1500 24TH AV
1600 25TH AV
1700 26TH AV
1800 27TH AV
1900 28TH AV
2000 29TH AV
2100 30TH AV
2200 31ST AV
2300 32ND AV
2400 33RD AV
2500 34TH AV
2600 35TH AV
2700 36TH AV
SUNSET BLVD
2800 37TH AV
3000 39TH AV
3100 40TH AV
3200 41ST AV
3300 42ND AV
3400 43RD AV
3500 44TH AV
3600 45TH AV
3700 46TH AV
3800 47TH AV
3900 48TH AV
END GREAT HIGHWAY
RACCOON DR SF 9 C3
FROM PEMBERTON PL S TO
PALO ALTO AV
RACINE LN SF 21 B2
SW FROM BEEMAN LN TO BRUNO AV
W OF BAYSHORE BLVD
RADIO TER SF 13 A1
FROM ROCKRIDGE ST NW TO 14TH AV
RAE AV SF 19 C3
SW FROM NAGLEE AV TO FARRAGUT AV
2 NAGLEE AV
100 WHIPPLE AV
END FARRAGUT AV
RALEIGH ST SF 20 A1
FROM PAULDING ST TO A POINT N
OF HAVELOCK ST
RALSTON AV SF 1 A2
LOOP EXTENDING S FROM STOREY AV
IN THE PRESIDIO
RALSTON ST SF 19 A2
FROM HOLLOWAY AV TO A POINT S OF
RANDOLPH ST
400 GARFIELD ST
300 SHIELDS ST
200 SARGENT ST
100 RANDOLPH ST
RAMONA ST SF 10 B2
S FROM 14TH ST TO 15TH ST BETWEEN
GUERRERO ST AND DOLORES ST
RAMSELL ST SF 19 B2
S FROM HOLLOWAY AV BETWEEN
ARCH ST & VICTORIA ST TO A POINT
S OF RANDOLPH ST, AND FROM
ALEMANY BLVD TO PALMETTO AV AND

WORCESTER AV
2 PALMETTO & WORCESTER AVS
100 ALEMANY BLVD
200 RANDOLPH ST
300 SARGENT ST
400 SHIELDS ST
500 GARFIELD ST
END HOLLOWAY AV
RANDALL ST SF 14 B2
FROM 3550 MISSION ST S OF
30TH ST W TO HARPER ST
2 MISSION ST
32 SAN JOSE AV
100 CHENERY ST
150 CHURCH ST
200 WHITNEY ST
250 SANCHEZ ST
END HARPER ST
RANDOLPH ST SF 19 B2
W OF SAN JOSE AV NEAR COUNTY LINE
W FROM ORIZABA AV BETWEEN
STANLEY ST AND SARGENT ST W TO A
POINT W OF CHESTER AV
2 ORIZABA AV
100 BRIGHT ST
200 HEAD ST
300 VICTORIA ST
400 RAMSELL ST
500 ARCH ST
600 VERNON ST
700 RALSTON ST
19TH AV
900 CHESTER AV
END PT W OF CHESTER AV
RANKIN ST SF 15 B2
FROM ISLAIS SW TO REVERE AV
BETWEEN QUINT ST & SELBY ST
2 ISLAIS ST
CUSTER AV
DAVIDSON AV
300 EVANS AV
400 FAIRFAX AV
500 GALVEZ AV
700 INNES AV
800 JERROLD AV
900 KIRKWOOD AV
1100 MCKINNON AV
1200 NEWCOMB AV
1300 OAKDALE AV
1400 PALOU AV
1500 QUESADA AV
1600 REVERE AV
RAUSCH ST SF 7 A3
S FROM HOWARD ST BETWEEN 7TH ST
& 8TH ST SE TO FOLSOM ST
RAVENWOOD DR SF 13 B3
FROM 200 YERBA BUENA AV SW
TO MAYWOOD DR
RAWLES ST SF 1 C3
FROM PRESIDIO BL TO SIMONDS LOOP
IN THE PRESIDIO
RAYBURN ST SF 10 B3
S FROM LIBERTY ST TO 21ST ST
BETWEEN SANCHEZ ST AND NOE ST
RAYCLIFF TER SF 2 A3
N FROM PACIFIC AV BETWEEN
BRODERICK ST & DIVISADERO ST
RAYMOND AV SF 21 A2
FROM BAY SHORE BLVD W TO
A POINT W OF SAWYER ST
BAY SHORE BLVD
100 ALPHA ST
200 RUTLAND ST
300 DELTA ST
400 ELLIOT ST
500 SAWYER ST
END PT W OF SAWYER ST
REARDON RD SF 16 A3
S FROM KISKA RD IN HUNTERS PT
REDDY ST SF 15 B3
FROM THORNTON AV S TO WILLIAMS AV
REDFIELD AL SF 2 C2
FROM 1901 TAYLOR ST BETWEEN
UNION ST AND FILBERT ST
TURNING N TO FILBERT ST
REDONDO ST SF 21 B2
SW FROM INGERSON ST TO
JAMESTOWN ST BETWEEN HAWES ST
AND INGALLS ST
RED ROCK WY SF 14 A1
E FROM DUNCAN ONE BLK S OF
DIAMOND HEIGHTS BLVD
REDWOOD ST SF 6 C3
W FROM POLK ST BETWEEN
MCALLISTER ST AND GOLDEN GATE AV
TO A POINT W OF LAGUNA
100 POLK ST
200 VAN NESS AV
300 FRANKLIN ST
600 LAGUNA ST
REED ST SF 2 C3
N FROM CLAY ST BETWEEN JONES ST
AND LEAVENWORTH ST N TO
WASHINGTON ST
REEVES CT SF 3 C1
SE FROM GATEVIEW AV 1 BLK SW OF
BAYSIDE DR, TREASURE ISLAND
REGENT ST SF 19 C3
FROM CAYUGA AV NW TO SAN JOSE AV
BETWEEN SICKLES AV AND LIEBIG ST
RENO PL SF 3 A2
S FROM 301 GREEN ST BETWEEN
MONTGOMERY ST AND KEARNY ST
REPOSA WY SF 13 C2
FROM MARIETTA DR SW TO MYRA WY
RESERVOIR ST SF 10 B1
W FROM MARKET ST BETWEEN 14TH ST
& DUBOCE AV TO CHURCH ST
RESTANI WY SF 20 A2
NW OFF ALEMANY BLVD BETWEEN
GENEVA AV AND NIAGARA AV
RETIRO WY SF 2 A2
FROM BEACH ST N AND NE TO
MARINA BLVD
REUEL CT SF 15 C2
E FROM HUDSON AV JUST N OF
CASHMERE ST
REVERE AV SF 15 B2
N FROM FITCH ST W TO
INDUSTRIAL ST
FITCH ST
GRIFFITH ST
1200 HAWES ST
1300 INGALLS ST
1400 JENNINGS ST
1500 KEITH ST
1600 LANE ST
1700 3RD ST
1800 NEWHALL ST
2000 SILVER AV
2100 RANKIN ST
2200 SELBY ST
END INDUSTRIAL ST
REX AV SF 13 C2
OFF PORTOLA DR S TO JUANITA WY
REY ST SF 21 A3
W OF BAYSHORE BLVD N FROM
SUNNYDALE AV TO LELAND AV
RHINE ST SF 19 B3
S FROM DE LONG ST SW TO
SHAKESPEARE ST
RHODE ISLAND ST SF 11 B1
FROM DIVISION ST BETWEEN
DE HARO ST AND KANSAS ST S TO
26TH ST
2 DIVISION ST
8TH ST
100 ALAMEDA ST
200 15TH ST
300 16TH ST
400 17TH ST
500 MARIPOSA ST
600 18TH ST
700 19TH ST
800 20TH ST
S HEIGHTS AV
1000 22ND ST
1200 23RD ST
1300 24TH ST
1400 25TH ST
END 26TH ST
RICE ST SF 19 B3
FROM THE COUNTY LINE NW TO
DE LONG ST
2 COUNTY LINE
100 SAN JOSE AVE
END DE LONG ST
RICHARDSON AV SF 1 C2
NW FROM LOMBARD ST TO A
POINT NW OF LYON ST
RICHLAND AV SF 14 C2
E FROM SAN JOSE AV TO ANDOVER ST
SAN JOSE AVE
100 MISSION ST
200 LEESE ST
300 MURRAY ST
END ANDOVER ST
RICKARD ST SF 15 A3
W FROM SAN BRUNO AV NEAR
EMBARCADERO FRWY
RICO WY SF 2 A2
FROM RETIRO WY NW TO AVILA ST
RIDGE LN SF 19 C2
FROM SAN JOSE AV S OF
MOUNT VERNON AV W TO JOSIAH AV
RIDGEWOOD AV SF 13 C3
FROM FLOOD AV W OF GENESEE ST
N TO MANGLES AV
2 FLOOD AV
100 HEARST AV
200 MONTEREY BLVD
300 JOOST AV
END MANGLES AV
RILEY AV SF 1 B2
N FROM SHERIDAN AV TO LINCOLN BL
IN THE PRESIDIO
RINCON ST SF 7 C2
FROM HARRISON ST BETWEEN 1ST ST
& 2ND ST SE TO FEDERAL ST
2 HARRISON ST
100 BRYANT ST
END FEDERAL ST
RINGOLD ST SF 11 A1
W FROM 8TH ST BETWEEN FOLSOM ST
& HARRISON ST SW TO 9TH ST
RIO CT SF 14 A2
OFF TERESITA BLVD E TO
EL SERRENO CT
RIO VERDE ST SF 20 C3
FROM VELASCO AV S TO
COUNTY LINE
RIPLEY ST SF 15 A2
FROM MANCHESTER ST S OF
STONEMAN ST E TO PERALTA AV
MANCHESTER ST
100 FOLSOM ST
HARRISON ST
200 ALABAMA ST
END PERALTA AV
RITCH ST SF 7 B3
S FROM BRYANT ST BETWEEN 3RD ST
& 4TH ST SE TO TOWNSEND ST
200 BRYANT ST
300 BRANNAN ST
END TOWNSEND ST
RIVAS AV SF 18 C2
S FROM GONZALES DR TO VIDAL DR
E OF ARABALLO DR
RIVERA ST SF 12 A1
RIVERA ST SF 13 A1
FROM 14TH AV S OF QUINTARA ST
W TO GREAT HIGHWAY
400 14TH AV
500 15TH AV
600 16TH AV
700 17TH AV
800 18TH AV
900 19TH AV
1000 20TH AV
1100 21ST AV
1200 22ND AV
1400 24TH AV
1500 25TH AV
1600 26TH AV
1700 27TH AV
1800 28TH AV
1900 29TH AV
2000 30TH AV
2100 31ST AV
2200 32ND AV
2300 33RD AV
2400 34TH AV
2500 35TH AV
2600 36TH AV
SUNSET BLVD
2700 37TH AV
2800 38TH AV
2900 39TH AV
3000 40TH AV
3100 41ST AV
3200 42ND AV
3300 43RD AV
3400 44TH AV
3500 45TH AV
3600 46TH AV
3700 47TH AV
3800 48TH AV
END GREAT HIGHWAY
RIVERTON DR SF 12 C3
S FROM SLOAT BLVD BETWEEN
SPRINGFIELD DR & MIDDLEFIELD DR
RIVOLI ST SF 9 C2
FROM BELVEDERE ST BETWEEN ALMA ST
AND 17TH ST TO STANYAN ST
2 BELVEDERE ST
100 COLE ST
200 SHRADER ST
END STANYAN ST
RIZAL ST SF 7 B3
SW FROM LAPU LAPU ST TO
TANDANG SORA BETWEEN FOLSOM ST
AND HARRISON ST
ROACH ST SF 2 C2
N FROM 900 FILBERT ST BETWEEN
TAYLOR ST AND JONES ST N TO
GREENWICH ST
ROANOKE ST SF 14 B2
FROM BEMIS ST SE TO A POINT S OF
ARLINGTON ST
2 BEMIS ST
100 LAIDLEY ST
200 CHENERY ST
300 ARLINGTON ST
ROBBLEE AV SF 15 B3
W FROM MADDUX AV TO THOMAS AV
S OF SILVER AV
ROBINHOOD DR SF 13 B2
SW OF MT DAVIDSON PK FROM
LANDSDALE AV TO LANDSDALE AV
ROBINSON DR SF 20 B3
S OFF LAPHAM WY TO COUNTY LINE
ROBINSON ST SF 17 B1
E FROM GALVEZ AV TO LOCKWOOD
IN HUNTERS POINT NAVAL
RESERVATION
ROCK AL SF 13 B2
N FROM ROCKAWAY AV TO
IDORA ST E OF GARCIA AV
ROCKAWAY AV SF 13 B2
W FROM LAGUNA HONDA BLVD
N OF PORTOLA DR
ROCKDALE DR SF 13 C2
FROM JUANITA WY SE TO
BELLA VISTA DR
ROCKLAND ST SF 2 C3
E FROM LARKIN ST BETWEEN
GREEN ST AND UNION ST
ROCKRIDGE DR SF 13 A1
FROM 12TH AV NEAR PACHECO ST
A CIRCLE AROUND SUNSET HTS PK
ROCKWOOD CT SF 13 B2
S FROM ROCKAWAY AV W OF ULLOA ST
ROD RD SF 1 A2
E OF RUCKMAN AV, IN THE PRESIDIO
RODGERS ST SF 11 A1
S FROM FOLSOM ST BETWEEN 7TH ST
AND 8TH ST
RODRIGUEZ ST SF 1 C3
S FROM MACARTHUR ST BETWEEN
PORTOLA ST AND SANCHEZ ST
IN THE PRESIDIO
ROEMER WY SF 20 A3
BETWEEN WHITTIER ST AND LOWELL ST
S FROM BRUNSWICK ST
ROLPH ST SF 20 A2
FROM 5201 MISSION ST S OF
GENEVA AV E TO A POINT E OF
LINDA VISTA STEPS
2 MISSION ST
100 CURTIS ST
PARIS ST
200 NEWTON ST
MADRID ST
MORSE ST
NAPLES ST
300 CORDOVA ST
400 ATHENS ST
SEVILLE ST
500 MUNICH ST
PRAGUE ST
600 SOUTH HILL BLVD
700 LINDA VISTA STEPS
END E OF LINDA VISTA STEPS
ROMAIN ST SF 10 A3
FROM DOUGLASS ST NEAR 20TH ST
W TO MARKET ST THEN SW TO
CORBETT AV
2 DOUGLASS ST
100 GRAND VIEW AV
200 MARKET ST
END CORBETT AV
ROME ST SF 19 C2
ROME ST SF 20 A2
SW FROM NIAGARA AV 1 BLK W OF
ALEMANY BLVD
ROMOLO ST SF 3 A3
N FROM 500 BROADWAY BETWEEN
GRANT AV AND KEARNY ST TO
VALLEJO ST
RONDEL PL SF 10 C2
S FROM 16TH ST BETWEEN HOFF ST
AND VALENCIA ST
ROOSEVELT WY SF 10 A2
FROM INTERSECTION OF 14TH ST &
ALPINE TER SW TO 17TH ST
2 14TH ST
100 BUENA VISTA TER
200 PARK HILL AV
15TH ST
400 LOMA VISTA TER
CLIFFORD TER
484 LOWER TER
560 SATURN ST
END 17TH ST
ROSCOE ST SF 14 C3
S FROM CRESCENT AV 3 BLKS E OF
MISSION ST TO BENTON AV
ROSE ST SF 10 B1
N FROM MARKET ST BETWEEN PAGE ST
AND HAIGHT ST W TO LAGUNA ST

2 MARKET ST
100 GOUGH ST
200 OCTAVIA ST
END LAGUNA ST
ROSELLA CT SF 20 A1
N FROM ONONDAGA 1 BLK W OF
ALEMANY BLVD
ROSELYN TER SF 5 C3
N FROM GOLDEN GATE AV TO TURK ST
ROSEMARY CT SF 12 C2
E FROM 25TH AV ONE BLK S OF
VICENTE ST
ROSEMONT PL SF 10 B1
N FROM 14TH ST BETWEEN
GUERRERO ST AND DOLORES ST
ROSENKRANZ ST SF 15 A2
S FROM BERNAL HTS BLVD TO
POWHATTAN AV
ROSEWOOD DR SF 13 B3
FROM RAVENWOOD DR S TO
BRENTWOOD AV
ROSIE LEE LN SF 15 C3
OFF INGALLS ST BETWEEN HUDSON AV
AND BEATRICE LN
ROSS AL SF 3 A3
FROM 800 WASHINGTON ST BETWEEN
GRANT AV AND STOCKTON ST
N TO JACKSON ST
ROSSI AV SF 5 C3
N FROM TURK ST TO ANZA ST
E OF ARGUELLO BLVD
ROSSMOOR DR SF 13 A3
E FROM 19TH AV TO JUNIPERO
SERRA BLVD S OF EUCALYPTUS DR
ROTTECK ST SF 14 B3
FROM BOSWORTH ST W OF
ROUSSEAU ST S TO CAYUGA AV
ROUSSEAU ST SF 14 B3
FROM SAN JOSE AV BETWEEN
MILTON ST AND ROTTECK ST S TO
ALEMANY BLVD
100 BOSWORTH ST
END ALEMANY BLVD
ROYAL LANE CT SF 20 A2
N FROM NAPLES 2 BLKS S OF
GENEVA AV
RUCKMAN AV SF 1 A2
E FROM RALSTON AV TO STOREY AV
IN THE PRESIDIO
RUDDEN AV SF 20 A1
FROM 250 DELANO AV TO OSTEGO AV
BETWEEN SANTA YNEZ AV & OCEAN AV
RUGER ST SF 1 C3
S FROM LOMBARD ST, SIMONDS LOOP
IN THE PRESIDIO
RUSS ST SF 7 A3
S FROM MINNA ST BETWEEN 6TH ST
AND 7TH ST SE TO FOLSOM ST
2 MINNA ST
48 NATOMA ST
100 HOWARD ST
END FOLSOM ST
RUSSELL ST SF 2 C3
W FROM HYDE ST BETWEEN GREEN ST
AND UNION ST TO EASTMAN ST
EASTMAN ST
RUSSIA AV SF 20 A1
FROM 4801 MISSION ST SE TO
LA GRANDE AV
2 MISSION ST
100 LONDON ST
200 PARIS ST
300 LISBON ST
400 MADRID ST
500 EDINBURGH ST
600 NAPLES ST
700 VIENNA ST
800 ATHENS ST
900 MOSCOW ST
1000 MUNICH ST
1100 PRAGUE ST
1200 DUBLIN ST
END LA GRANDE AV
RUSSIAN HILL PL SF 2 C3
N FROM VALLEJO ST BETWEEN
JONES ST AND TAYLOR ST
RUTH ST SF 20 A1
FROM 4700 MISSION ST BETWEEN
OCEAN AV AND LEO ST
RUTLAND ST SF 21 A3
FROM HARKNESS AV S TO A POINT S
OF SUNNYDALE AV
2 HARKNESS AV
100 WILDE AV
200 TIOGA AV
300 TUCKER AV
400 CAMPBELL AV
500 TEDDY AV
600 ARLETA AV
700 RAYMOND AV
800 LELAND AV
900 VISITACION AV
END SUNNYDALE AV
RUTLEDGE ST SF 15 A1
FROM HOLLADAY AV W TO
1700 ALABAMA ST
2 HOLLADAY AV
100 BREWSTER ST
FRANCONIA ST
PERALTA AV
END ALABAMA ST
SABIN PL SF 3 A3
N FROM 700 CALIFORNIA ST BETWEEN
GRANT AV AND STOCKTON ST
SACRAMENTO ST SF 2 C3
SACRAMENTO ST SF 3 A3
SACRAMENTO ST SF 5 B2
SACRAMENTO ST SF 6 A3
FROM THE BAY BETWEEN CALIFORNIA
AND CLAY STS W TO ARGUELLO BLVD
100 DRUMM ST
200 DAVIS ST
300 FRONT ST
400 BATTERY ST
500 SANSOME ST
LEIDESDORFF ST
600 MONTGOMERY ST
SPRING ST
700 KEARNY ST
800 GRANT AVE
WAVERLY PL
PAGODA PL
BROOKLYN PL
900 STOCKTON ST
JOICE ST
MILLER PL
1000 POWELL ST
1100 MASON ST
CUSHMAN ST
1200 TAYLOR ST
1300 JONES ST
LYSETTE ST
LEROY PL
GOLDEN CT
1400 LEAVENWORTH ST
KIMBALL PL
1500 HYDE ST
1600 LARKIN ST
1700 POLK ST
1800 VAN NESS AV
1900 FRANKLIN ST
GOUGH ST
OCTAVIA ST
2200 LAGUNA ST
2300 BUCHANAN ST
2400 WEBSTER ST
2500 FILLMORE ST
2600 STEINER ST
2700 PIERCE ST
2800 SCOTT ST
2900 DIVISADERO ST
3000 BRODERICK ST
3100 BAKER ST
3200 LYON ST
3300 PRESIDIO AV
3400 WALNUT ST
3500 LAUREL ST
3600 LOCUST ST
3700 SPRUCE ST
3800 MAPLE ST
3900 CHERRY ST
END ARGUELLO BLVD
SADOWA ST SF 19 B2
W OF SAN JOSE AV TO ORIZABA AV
2 SAN JOSE AV
100 PLYMOUTH AV
200 CAPITOL AV
END ORIZABA AV
SAFFOLD RD SF 1 A2
E OF LINCOLN BLVD BETWEEN
KOBBE AV AND DYNAMITE RD
IN THE PRESIDIO
SAFIRA LN SF 14 A1
E FROM DIAMOND HEIGHTS BLVD
TO 27TH ST
SAGAMORE ST SF 19 B3
W FROM SAN JOSE AV TO ALEMANY BL
2 SAN JOSE AV
100 PLYMOUTH AV
200 CAPITOL AV
ORIZABA AV
END ALEMANY BLVD
ST CHARLES AV SF 19 A3
FROM 19TH AV NEAR RANDOLPH ST
S TO BELLE AV
ST CROIX DR SF 13 C2
S FROM LA BREA WY TO MYRA WY
ST ELMO WY SF 13 B3
FROM 1000 MONTEREY BLVD N
TO YERBA BUENA AV
ST FRANCIS BLVD SF 13 B3
E FROM JUNIPERO SERRA BLVD
BETWEEN PORTOLA DR AND
MONTEREY BLVD OPPOSITE SLOAT BLVD
TO SAN ANSELMO AV
2 JUNIPERO SERRA BLVD
SAN RAFAEL WY
100 SAN FERNANDO WY
200 SAN LEANDRO WY
300 SANTA ANA AV
400 SAN BENITO WY
500 SANTA CLARA AV
600 SAN BUENAVENTURA WY
END SAN ANSELMO AV
ST GEORGE AL SF 3 A3
FROM 400 BUSH ST BETWEEN GRANT AV
AND KEARNY ST N TO PINE ST
ST GERMAIN AV SF 9 C3
W FROM TWIN PEAKS BLVD
ONE BLK S FROM MOUNTAIN SPRINGS
OFF GLENBROOK AV
ST JOSEPHS AV SF 6 A3
N FROM TURK ST BETWEEN BAKER ST
AND BRODERICK ST N TO GEARY BLVD
2 TURK ST
100 EDDY ST
200 ELLIS ST
300 OFARRELL ST
END GEARY BLVD
ST LOUIS PL SF 3 A3
FROM 701 JACKSON ST BETWEEN
GRANT AV AND STOCKTON ST
ST MARYS AV SF 14 B3
W FROM 3990 MISSION ST S
OF COLLEGE AV TO ARLINGTON ST
2 MISSION ST
MARSILLY ST
100 COLLEGE AV
END ARLINGTON ST
SAL ST SF 1 B2
S OF LINCOLN BLVD BETWEEN
GRAHAM ST AND KEYES AV, PRESIDIO
SALA TER SF 20 A2
FROM HURON AV SE TO ELLINGTON AV
SALINAS AV SF 21 B1
FROM 3RD ST OPPOSITE INGERSON AV
W TO SAN BRUNO AV
2 3RD ST
100 CARR ST
150 GOULD ST
JAMESTOWN AVE
200 EXETER ST
KEY ST
BAYSHORE BLVD
SALMON ST SF 3 A3
N FROM PACIFIC AV BETWEEN
MASON ST AND TAYLOR ST N
TO BROADWAY
SAMOSET ST SF 15 A1
W FROM FRANCONIA ST TO PERALTA AV
SAN ALESO AV SF 13 B3
N FROM UPLAND DR TO MONTEREY BLVD
DARIEN WY
END MONTEREY BLVD
SAN ANDREAS WY SF 13 B3
FROM THE JUNCTION OF
SAN ANSELMO AV & ST FRANCIS BLVD
S TO 1500 MONTEREY BLVD
SAN ANSELMO AV SF 13 B2
S FROM PORTOLA DR TO MONTEREY BL
SAN BENITO WY SF 13 B3
S FROM SAN ANSELMO AV BETWEEN
SANTA CLARA AV AND SANTA ANA AV
S TO OCEAN AV
2 SAN ANSELMO AV
100 ST FRANCIS BLVD
200 MONTEREY BLVD
300 DARIEN WY
END OCEAN AV
SAN BRUNO AV SF 11 A2
SAN BRUNO AV SF 15 A3
SAN BRUNO AV SF 21 A1
FROM DIVISION ST BETWEEN UTAH ST
AND VERMONT ST S TO COUNTY LINE
2 DIVISION ST
100 ALAMEDA ST
200 15TH ST
300 16TH ST
400 17TH ST
MARIPOSA ST
1200 23RD ST
1300 24TH ST
1400 25TH ST
ARMY ST
ALEMANY
RICKARD ST
2300 GAVEN ST
SWEENY ST
HALE ST
2400 SILVER AV
2450 SILLIMAN ST
2500 FELTON ST
2600 BURROWS ST
2700 BACON ST
2800 WAYLAND ST
2900 WOOLSEY ST
3000 DWIGHT ST
3100 OLMSTEAD ST
3200 MANSELL ST
3300 ORDWAY ST
3500 HARKNESS AV
3600 WILDE AV
FRATESSA CT
CAMPBELL AV
BEEMAN LN
SOMERSET ST
EMPRESS LN
WABASH TER
RACINE LN
END BAYSHORE BLVD
SN BUENAVNTRA WY SF 13 B3
FROM SAN ANSELMO AV TO
ST FRANCIS BLVD E OF
SANTA CLARA AV
SAN CARLOS ST SF 10 C2
FROM SYCAMORE ST BETWEEN
MISSION ST AND VALENCIA ST
S TO 21ST ST
2 SYCAMORE ST
100 18TH ST
200 19TH ST
300 20TH ST
END 21ST ST
SANCHES ST SF 1 C3
S OF PRESIDIO BLVD BETWEEN
MACARTHUR ST AND MORTON ST
IN THE PRESIDIO
SANCHEZ ST SF 5 C1
S FROM MORTON ST, PRESIDIO
SANCHEZ ST SF 10 B2
S FROM DUBOCE AV BETWEEN
CHURCH ST AND NOE ST
TO RANDALL ST
2 DUBOCE AV
100 14TH ST
150 HENRY ST
15TH ST
200 MARKET ST
300 16TH ST
400 17TH ST
DORLAND ST
450 FORD ST
500 18TH ST
550 HANCOCK ST
600 19TH ST
650 CUMBERLAND ST
700 20TH ST
750 LIBERTY ST
800 21ST ST
850 HILL ST
900 22ND ST
950 ALVARADO ST
1000 23RD ST
1050 ELIZABETH ST
1100 24TH ST
1150 JERSEY ST
1200 25TH ST
1252 CLIPPER ST
1300 26TH ST
1350 ARMY ST
1400 27TH ST
1450 DUNCAN ST
1500 28TH ST
1550 VALLEY ST
1600 29TH ST
1650 DAY ST
1700 30TH ST
END RANDALL ST
SAN DIEGO AV SF 19 B3
W OF SANTA CRUZ AV FROM
DE LONG ST TO THE COUNTY LINE
SAN FELIPE AV SF 13 B3
N FROM 1100 MONTEREY BLVD TO
SAN JACINTO WY
SAN FERNANDO WY SF 13 A3
S FROM PORTOLA DR BETWEEN
SAN RAFAEL WY AND SAN LEANDRO WY
TO OCEAN AV
2 PORTOLA DR
100 ST FRANCIS BLVD
200 MONTEREY BLVD
300 DARIEN WY
END OCEAN AV
SAN GABRIEL AV SF 20 A1
SW FROM CAPISTRANO AV TO
SANTA ROSA AV ONE BLK E OF
SAN JOSE AV
SAN JACINTO WY SF 13 B3
S FROM THE JUNCTION OF
SANTA PAULA AV AND SAN ANSELMO AV

1988 SAN FRANCISCO COUNTY CROSS STREET INDEX

TO MONTEREY BLVD
SAN JOSE AV SF 10 C3
SAN JOSE AV SF 14 B2
SAN JOSE AV SF 19 C2
SAN JOSE AV SF 20 A1
S FROM 22ND ST BETWEEN
VALENCIA ST AND GUERRERO ST
TO THE COUNTY LINE
2 22ND ST
50 ALVARADO ST
100 23RD ST
ELIZABETH ST
200 24TH ST
300 25TH ST
JURI ST
400 26TH ST
500 ARMY ST
550 27TH ST
600 DUNCAN ST
658 GUERRERO ST
672 VALLEY ST
700 29TH ST
DAY ST
800 30TH ST
KINGSTON ST
BROOK ST
DOLORES ST
RANDALL ST
CHARLES ST
HIGHLAND AV
PARK ST
RICHLAND AV
CRESCENT AV
MATEO ST
ST MARYS AV
CUVIER ST
MILTON ST
ROUSSEAU ST
CIRCULAR AV
BOSWORTH ST
GORHAM ST
TINGLEY ST
THERESA ST
COTTER ST
CAPISTRANO AV
STANDISH AV
PILGRM AV
1800 SANTA ROSA AV
COLONIAL WY
SANTA YSABEL AV
NANTUCKET AV
1884 PAULDING ST
SAN JUAN AV
HAVELOCK ST
SANTA YNEZ AV
BALBOA PARK
2100 OCEAN AV
ONEIDA AV
SENECA AV
GENEVA AV
2400 NIAGARA AV
2500 MOUNT VERNON AV
2524 RIDGE LN
2600 LAKEVIEW AV
NAGLEE ST
2700 FARRALLONES ST
2800 BROAD ST
2900 SADOWA ST
SICKLES AV
3000 PLYMOUTH AV
SAGAMORE ST
ALEMANY BLVD
REGENT ST
3100 LIEBIG ST
DE LONG ST
RICE ST
3200 GOETHE ST
END COUNTY LINE
SAN JUAN AV SF 20 A1
FROM MISSION ST AND OCEAN AV
NW TO SAN JOSE AV
2 MISSION ST
100 ALEMANY BLVD
200 CAYUGA AV
300 CAPISTRANO AV
400 OTSEGO AV
500 DELANO AV
END SAN JOSE AV
SAN LEANDRO WY SF 13 A3
S FROM PORTOLA DR BETWEEN
SAN FERNANDO WY AND SANTA ANA AV
TO OCEAN AV
2 PORTOLA DR
100 ST FRANCIS BLVD
200 MONTEREY BLVD
300 DARIEN WY
END OCEAN AV
SAN LORENZO WY SF 13 B2
S FROM PORTOLA DR BETWEEN
SANTA CLARA AV AND SANTA PAULA AV
TO SANTA MONICA AV
SAN LUIS AV SF 19 B3
W FROM DE LONG ST NEAR
THE COUNTY LINE
SAN MARCOS AV SF 13 B1
NW FROM DORANTES AV
SAN MATEO AV SF 19 B3
W FROM DE LONG ST NEAR
THE COUNTY LINE
SAN MIGUEL ST SF 19 C2
S FROM NIAGARA AV BETWEEN TARA ST
AND SAN JOSE AV S TO RIDGE LN
300 NIAGARA AV
400 MOUNT VERNON AV
END RIDGE LANE
SAN PABLO AV SF 13 B2
S FROM PORTOLA DR TO
YERBA BUENA AV
SAN RAFAEL WY SF 13 A3
S FROM ST FRANCIS BLVD BETWEEN
JUNIPERO SERRA BLVD AND
SAN FERNANDO WY TO DARIEN WY
2 ST FRANCIS BLVD
100 MONTEREY BLVD
END DARIEN WY
SAN RAMON WY SF 19 C1
N OF OCEAN AV FROM EASTWOOD DR
SANSOME ST SF 3 B2
N FROM MARKET ST BETWEEN
BATTERY ST AND MONTGOMERY ST
TO THE BAY
2 MARKET ST
SUTTER ST
100 BUSH ST
200 PINE ST
300 CALIFORNIA ST
HALLECK ST
400 SACRAMENTO ST
COMMERCIAL ST
500 CLAY ST
MERCHANT ST
600 WASHINGTON ST
700 JACKSON ST
GOLD ST
800 PACIFIC AV
STEVENS AL
900 BROADWAY
1000 VALLEJO ST
1100 GREEN ST
1200 UNION ST
1300 FILBERT ST
1400 GREENWICH ST
1500 LOMBARD ST
CHESTNUT ST
END THE EMBARCADERO
SANTA ANA AV SF 13 B3
S FROM PORTOLA DR BETWEEN
SAN BENITO WY AND SAN LEANDRO WY
TO OCEAN AV
2 PORTOLA DR
100 ST FRANCIS BLVD
200 MONTEREY BLVD
300 DARIEN WY
END OCEAN AV
SANTA BARBARA AV SF 19 B3
S FROM DE LONG ST TO COUNTY LINE
MERLA CT
SANTA CLARA AV SF 13 B3
S FROM PORTOLA DR BETWEEN
SAN BENITO WY AND
SAN BUENAVENTURA WY TO
MONTEREY BLVD
2 PORTOLA DR
YERBA BUENA AV
100 TERRACE DR
200 SAN ANSELMO AV
300 ST FRANCIS BLVD
END MONTEREY BLVD
SANTA CRUZ AV SF 19 B3
S FROM DE LONG ST NEAR
THE COUNTY LINE
SANTA FE AV SF 15 B3
SE FROM SILVER AV TO QUINT ST
BETWEEN TOPEKA ST AND SCOTIA AV
SANTA MARINA ST SF 14 C2
FROM 3525 MISSION ST NEAR
CORTLAND AV E TO ELSIE ST
2 MISSION ST
GLADYS ST
PROSPECT AV
END ELSIE ST
SANTA MONICA WY SF 13 B2
FROM SANTA CLARA AV S OF
PORTOLA DR E TO SAN PABLO AV
SANTA CLARA AV
100 SANTA PAULA AV
END SAN PABLO AV
SANTA PAULA AV SF 13 B3
S FROM 1251 PORTOLA DR TO
SAN ANSELMO AV
2 PORTOLA DR
SANTA MONICA WY
100 YERBA BUENA AV
END SAN ANSELMO AV
SANTA RITA AV SF 13 B1
S FROM SOTELO AV W OF LOPEZ AV
TO SAN MARCOS AV
2 SOTELO AV
50 MESA AV
END SAN MARCOS AV
SANTA ROSA AV SF 20 A1
FROM 4500 MISSION ST BETWEEN
FRANCIS ST AND HARRINGTON ST
TO A POINT W OF SAN JOSE AV
2 MISSION ST
100 ALEMANY BLVD
CAYUGA AV
200 CAPISTRANO AV
SAN GABRIEL AV
300 SAN JOSE AV
SANTA YNEZ AV SF 20 A1
FROM CAYUGA AV BETWEEN
SAN JUAN AV AND OCEAN AV NW TO
SAN JOSE AV
2 CAYUGA AV
CAPISTRANO AV
100 OTSEGO AV
200 DELANO AV
END SAN JOSE AV
SANTA YSABEL AV SF 20 A1
SE FROM SAN JOSE AV TO
CAPISTRANO AV BETWEEN
SANTA ROSA AV AND SAN JUAN AV
SANTIAGO ST SF 12 A1
SANTIAGO ST SF 13 A1
W FROM 14TH AV TO GREAT HIGHWAY
BETWEEN RIVERA ST AND TARAVAL ST
300 14TH AV
400 15TH AV
CECILIA AV
500 16TH AV
600 17TH AV
700 18TH AV
800 19TH AV
900 20TH AV
1000 21ST AV
1100 22ND AV
1300 24TH AV
1400 25TH AV
1500 26TH AV
1600 27TH AV
1700 28TH AV
1800 29TH AV
1900 30TH AV
2000 31ST AV
2100 32ND AV
2200 33RD AV
2300 34TH AV
2400 35TH AV
2500 36TH AV
SUNSET BLVD
2600 37TH AV
2700 38TH AV
2800 39TH AV
2900 40TH AV
3000 41ST AV
3100 42ND AV
3200 43RD AV
3300 44TH AV
3400 45TH AV
3500 46TH AV
3600 47TH AV
3700 48TH AV
END GREAT HIGHWAY
SANTOS ST SF 20 C3
FROM SUNNYVALE AV TO COUNTY LINE
SARGENT ST SF 19 B2
W FROM ORIZABA AV TO 19TH AV
2 ORIZABA AV
100 BRIGHT ST
200 HEAD ST
300 VICTORIA ST
400 RAMSELL ST
500 ARCH ST
600 VERNON ST
700 RALSTON ST
800 BIXBY ST
900 MONTICELLO ST
END 19TH AV
SATURN ST SF 10 A2
FROM ROOSEVELT WY N OF 17TH ST
E TO LOWER TERRACE
ROOSEVELT WY
100 TEMPLE ST
END LOWER TERRACE
SAWYER ST SF 20 C3
FROM RAYMOND AV S TO
VISITACION AV
200 RAYMOND AV
300 LELAND AV
400 VISITACION AV
SCENIC WY SF 4 C2
FROM 25TH AV W TO 26TH AV BETWEEN
EL CAMINO DEL MAR AND SEACLIFF AV
SCHOFIELD RD SF 1 A2
S FROM APPLETON ST, PRESIDIO
SCHOFIELD RD SF 2 B2
N OF MACARTHUR AV, FORT MASON
SCHOOL AL SF 3 A2
E FROM 1301 MONTGOMERY ST BETWEEN
UNION ST & FILBERT ST
SCHWERIN ST SF 21 A3
S FROM LELAND AV
6 BLKS W OF BAYSHORE BLVD
SCOTIA AV SF 15 B3
FROM SILVER AV SE TO THORNTON AV
SCOTLAND ST SF 3 A2
FROM 700 FILBERT ST BETWEEN
POWELL ST AND MASON ST N
TO COLUMBUS AV
SCOTT ST SF 2 A3
SCOTT ST SF 6 A3
SCOTT ST SF 10 B1
N FROM DUBOCE AV BETWEEN
PIERCE ST AND DIVISADERO ST
TO MARINA BLVD
2 DUBOCE AV
LLOYD ST
100 WALLER ST
200 HAIGHT ST
300 PAGE ST
400 OAK ST
500 FELL ST
HAYES ST
GROVE ST
800 FULTON ST
900 MCALLISTER ST
1000 GOLDEN GATE AV
ELM ST
1100 TURK ST
1200 EDDY ST
1300 ELLIS ST
1400 OFARRELL ST
GEARY BLVD
1600 POST ST
1700 SUTTER ST
1800 BUSH ST
1900 PINE ST
2000 CALIFORNIA ST
2100 SACRAMENTO ST
CLAY ST
WASHINGTON ST
2400 JACKSON ST
2500 PACIFIC AV
2600 BROADWAY
2700 VALLEJO ST
2800 GREEN ST
2900 UNION ST
3000 FILBERT ST
3100 GREENWICH ST
3200 LOMBARD ST
3300 CHESTNUT ST
FRANCISCO ST
3400 ALHAMBRA ST
BAY ST
3500 CAPRA WY
NORTH POINT ST
3700 BEACH ST
3800 PRADO ST
JEFFERSON ST
CERVANTES BLVD
END MARINA BLVD
SEA CLIFF AV SF 4 B2
S FROM 25TH AV W TO 30TH AV N OF
EL CAMINO DEL MAR
SEAL ROCK DR SF 4 A3
W FROM 45TH AV TO
EL CAMINO DEL MAR N OF
POINT LOBOS AV
SEARS ST SF 19 C3
S FROM LAWRENCE ST TO A POINT
S OF SICKLES AV
SEAVIEW TER SF 4 B2
FROM 249 30TH AV W TO A POINT
W OF 31ST AV
SECURITY PAC PL SF 7 A2
N FROM OFARRELL ST W OF GRANT AV
SELBY ST SF 15 B2
FROM ISLAIS ST SW TO
WATERVILLE ST
200 EVANS AV
400 GALVEZ AV
500 HUDSON AV
600 INNES AV
700 JERROLD AV
KIRKWOOD AV
MCKINNON AV
NEWCOMB AV
1200 OAKDALE AV
1300 PALOU AV

1400 QUESADA AV
1500 REVERE AV
END WATERVILLE ST
SELMA WY SF 9 A3
FROM NORIEGA ST AT 12TH AV
SW TO ORTEGA ST
SEMINOLE AV SF 20 A2
FROM 750 DELANO AV E TO CAYUGA AV
SENECA AV SF 20 A1
FROM MISSION ST NW TO SAN JOSE AV
MISSION ST
BERTITA ST
ALEMANY BLVD
BANNOCK ST
CAYUGA AV
DELANO AV
END SAN JOSE AV
SEQUOIA WY SF 13 C2
FROM TERESITA BLVD S TO
BELLA VISTA WY
SGT MITCHELL SF 1 C2
N FROM MASON ST TO LT ALLEN ST
IN THE PRESIDIO
SERPENTINE AV SF 15 A1
E FROM POTRERO AV 1 BLK S
OF 25TH ST
SERRANO DR SF 18 C2
SERRANO DR SF 19 A2
W FROM GRIJALVA DR TO
ARBALLO DR S OF HOLLOWAY AV
SERVICE ST SF 2 A3
W FROM STEINER ST BETWEEN
LOMBARD ST AND GREENWICH ST
SEVERN ST SF 10 B3
N FROM 23RD ST BETWEEN
CHATTANOOGA ST AND CHURCH ST
SEVILLE ST SF 20 A3
S FROM ROLPH ST BETWEEN ATHENS ST
AND MUNICH ST W TO NAPLES ST
TO NAPLES ST
2 ROLPH ST
100 CORDOVA ST
END NAPLES ST
SEWARD ST SF 10 A3
FROM 358 DOUGLASS ST NW TO
19TH ST
2 DOUGLASS ST
ACME ALLEY
END 19TH ST
SEYMOUR ST SF 6 A3
FROM GOLDEN GATE AV BETWEEN
SCOTT ST AND DIVISADERO ST N
TO TURK ST
SHAFTER AV SF 15 C3
SHAFTER AV SF 21 C1
FROM FITCH ST NW TO 3RD ST AND
FROM SELBY ST TO INDUSTRIAL ST
FITCH ST
GRIFFITH ST
1200 HAWES ST
1300 INGALLS ST
1400 JENNINGS ST
1500 KEITH ST
1600 LANE ST
3RD ST
2200 SELBY ST
INDUSTRIAL ST
SHAFTER RD SF 1 C3
NW FROM RAWLES ST, PRESIDIO
SHAKESPEARE ST SF 19 B3
FROM DE LONG ST SE TO COUNTY LINE
SHANGRILA WY SF 13 B2
FROM 300 ULLOA ST N TO
EDGEHILL WY E OF KENSINGTON WY
SHANNON ST SF 7 A2
N FROM O'FARRELL ST BETWEEN
TAYLOR ST AND JONES ST TO POST ST
2 O'FARRELL ST
100 GEARY ST
END POST ST

SHARON ST SF 10 B2
S FROM 15TH ST BETWEEN CHURCH ST
AND SANCHEZ ST TO 16TH ST
SHARP PL SF 2 C2
S FROM UNION ST BETWEEN HYDE ST
AND LEAVENWORTH ST
SHAW AL SF 7 B2
S FROM MISSION ST BETWEEN 1ST ST
AND 2ND ST TO MINNA ST
SHAWNEE AV SF 20 A2
FROM SAN JOSE AV SE TO CAYUGA AV
SHEPHARD PL SF 3 A3
E FROM 1100 MASON ST BETWEEN
CLAY ST AND WASHINGTON ST
SHERIDAN AV SF 1 B2
S FROM LINCOLN BLVD TO TAYLOR RD
IN THE PRESIDIO
SHERIDAN ST SF 11 A1
FROM 9TH ST BETWEEN FOLSOM ST AND
HARRISON ST SW TO 10TH ST
SHERMAN RD SF 1 C3
S OF LOMBARD ST BETWEEN
LINCOLN BLVD AND RUGER ST
IN THE PRESIDIO
SHERMAN ST SF 7 A3
S FROM FOLSOM ST BETWEEN 6TH ST
AND 7TH ST SE TO HARRISON ST
SHERWOOD CT SF 13 C3
S FROM LANSDALE AV ONE
BLK E OF ROBINHOOD DR
SHIELDS ST SF 19 A2
FROM ORIZABA AV W TO
JUNIPERO SERRA BLVD
2 ORIZABA AV
100 BRIGHT ST
200 HEAD ST
300 VICTORIA ST
400 RAMSELL ST
500 ARCH ST
600 VERNON ST
700 RALSTON ST
800 BIXBY ST
900 MONTICELLO ST
1000 BEVERLY ST
END JUNIPERO SERRA BLVD
SHIPLEY ST SF 7 A3
FROM 4TH ST BETWEEN FOLSOM ST AND
CLARA ST SW TO 6TH ST
100 4TH ST
200 5TH ST
FALMOUTH ST
END 6TH ST
SHORE VIEW AV SF 4 B3
S FROM 36TH AV BETWEEN CLEMENT ST
AND GEARY BLVD W TO 38TH AV
SHORT ST SF 10 A3
FROM YUKON ST W TO MARKET ST
OFF 3401 MARKET ST
SHOTWELL ST SF 10 C2
SHOTWELL ST SF 14 C1
S FROM 14TH ST BETWEEN FOLSOM ST
AND S VAN NESS AV TO
BERNAL HEIGHTS BLVD
2 14TH ST
100 15TH ST
200 16TH ST
300 17TH ST
400 18TH ST
500 19TH ST
600 20TH ST
700 21ST ST
800 22ND ST
900 23RD ST
1000 24TH ST
1100 25TH ST
1200 26TH ST
1300 ARMY ST
PRECITA AV
BESSIE ST
MIRABEL AV

1420 MONTEZUMA ST
BERNAL HTS BLVD
SHRADER ST SF 9 C1
S FROM FULTON ST BETWEEN COLE ST
AND STANYAN ST TO BELGRAVE AV
2 FULTON ST
100 GROVE ST
200 HAYES ST
FELL ST
400 OAK ST
500 PAGE ST
600 HAIGHT ST
700 WALLER ST
800 BEULAH ST
FREDERICK ST
1000 CARL ST
1100 PARNASSUS AV
1200 GRATTAN ST
1300 ALMA ST
1400 RIVOLI ST
1500 17TH ST
1550 CARMEL ST
END BELGRAVE AV
SIBERT LOOP SF 1 B3
N FROM ARGUELLO BLVD, PRESIDIO
SIBLEY RD SF 1 C3
S FROM MORTON ST BETWEEN
LIGGETT AV AND SANCHEZ ST
IN THE PRESIDIO
SICKLES AV SF 19 C3
FROM 5900 MISSION ST NW TO
SAN JOSE AV NEAR THE COUNTY LINE
2 MISSION ST
100 HURON AV
SEARS ST
CAYUGA AV
ALEMANY BLVD
DE WOLF ST
END SAN JOSE AV
SIERRA ST SF 11 B3
FROM TEXAS ST TO MISSOURI ST
BETWEEN 20TH ST AND 22ND ST
SILLIMAN ST SF 15 A3
SILLIMAN ST SF 20 C1
FROM 2450 SAN BRUNO AV S OF
SILVER AV W TO VALMAR TER
2 SAN BRUNO AV
100 GIRARD ST
200 BRUSSELS ST
300 GOETTINGEN ST
400 SOMERSET ST
500 BOYSTON ST
600 HAMILTON ST
700 BOWDOIN ST
800 DARTMOUTH ST
900 COLBY ST
1000 UNIVERSITY ST
1100 PRINCETON ST
1200 AMHERST ST
1300 YALE ST
1400 CAMBRIDGE ST
1500 OXFORD ST
1600 HARVARD ST
1700 GAMBIER ST
1800 MADISON ST
END VALMAR TER
SILVER AV SF 14 B3
SILVER AV SF 15 A3
FROM ALEMANY BL E TO SAN BRUNO AV
THEN NE TO PALOU AV
200 ALEMANY BLVD
CAMELLIA AV
300 MISSION ST
LISBON ST
400 CRAUT ST
MADRID ST
EDINBURGH ST
500 CONGDON ST
NAPLES ST
VIENNA ST

MADISON ST
GAMBIER ST
HARVARD ST
SUNGLOW LN
OXFORD ST
CAMBRIDGE ST
YALE ST
AMHERST ST
1000 PRINCETON ST
UNIVERSITY ST
COLBY ST
DUNSMUIR ST
DARTMOUTH ST
1200 BOWDOIN ST
HAMILTON ST
BOYLSTON ST
1300 SOMERSET ST
MERRILL ST
1400 GOETTINGEN ST
BRUSSELS ST
1500 BARNEVELD AV
GIRARD ST
SAN BRUNO AV
BAYSHORE BLVD
CHARTER OAK AV
1700 ELMIRA ST
LEDYARD ST
WATERVILLE ST
SCOTIA AV
CONKLING ST
SANTA FE AV
TOPEKA AV
THOMAS AV
REVERE AV
QUESADA AV
END PALOU AV & QUINT ST
SIMONDS LOOP SF 1 C3
E FROM PRESIDIO BLVD JUST S OF
SHERMAN RD, IN THE PRESIDIO
SKYLINE BLVD SF 18 A1
S FROM SLOAT BLVD TO THE
COUNTY LINE E OF LAKE MERCED BLVD
SKYVIEW WY SF 9 C3
N FROM TWIN PEAKS BLVD TO
MAR VIEW WY
SLOAN AL SF 7 B2
OFF TENNY PL NEAR 201 1ST ST
BETWEEN HOWARD ST AND FOLSOM ST
SLOAT BLVD SF 12 A3
FROM PORTOLA DR W TO
GREAT HIGHWAY
2 PORTOLA DR
CRANLEIGH DR
ARDENWOOD WY
LAGUNITAS DR
BEACHMONT DR
100 AVON WY
300 19TH AV
20TH AV
500 21ST AV
700 23RD AV
24TH AV
25TH AV
GABILAN WY
800 CRESTLAKE DR
26TH AV
1000 PARAISO PL
SYLVAN DR
1300 EL MIRASOL PL
MIDDLEFIELD DR
RIVERTON DR
SPRINGFIELD DR
1600 CONSTANSO WAY
EVERGLADE DR
LAKESHORE PLAZA
1700 34TH AV
CLEARFIELD DR
35TH AV
1800 36TH AV
SUNSET BLVD

37TH AV
39TH AV
SKYLINE BLVD
41ST AV
42ND AV
43RD AV
2600 44TH AV
2700 45TH AV
2800 46TH AV
2800 47TH AV
48TH AV
END GREAT HIGHWAY
SOLA AV SF 13 B1
FROM MAGELLAN AV NW TO MARCELA AV
JUST S OF LAGUNA HONDA BLVD
SOMERSET ST SF 15 A3
SOMERSET ST SF 21 A1
S FROM SILVER AV TO KAREN CT
MANSELL ST TO ANKENY ST & FROM
CAMPBELL AV TO BAYSHORE BLVD
BETWEEN GOETTINGEN & HOLYOKE STS
2 SILVER AV
100 SILLIMAN ST
200 FELTON ST
300 BURROWS ST
400 BACON ST
500 WAYLAND ST
600 WOOLSEY ST
KAREN CT
900 MANSELL ST
ANKENY ST
CAMPBELL AV
SAN BRUNO AV
WABASH TER
TEDDY AV
RACINE LN
BAYSHORE BLVD
SONOMA ST SF 3 A2
FROM 400 GREEN ST BETWEEN
KEARNY ST AND GRANT AV N
TO UNION ST
SONORA LN SF 6 A3
S FROM O'FARRELL ST TO
ELLIS ST E OF ANZAVISTA AV
SOTELO AV SF 13 B1
E FROM 9TH AV S OF ALTON AV
E & S TO LOPEZ AV
SOUTHARD PL SF 2 C2
N FROM GREENWICH ST BETWEEN
LEAVENWORTH ST AND HYDE ST
SOUTHERN HTS AV SF 11 B3
FROM CAROLINA ST BETWEEN 20TH ST
AND 22ND ST TO RHODE ISLAND ST
2 CAROLINA ST
100 DE HARO ST
SOUTH GOUGH ST
END RHODE ISLAND ST
SOUTH HILL BLVD SF 20 B3
S FROM GENEVA AV SE TO
THE COUNTY LINE
SOUTH PARK AV SF 7 B3
W FROM 2ND ST BETWEEN BRANT ST
AND BRANNAN ST SW TO 3RD ST
S VAN NESS AV SF 10 C1
S FROM 13TH ST TO ARMY ST
BETWEEN SHOTWELL ST AND CAPP ST
200 13TH ST
251 ERIE ST
300 14TH ST
400 15TH ST
ADAIR ST
500 16TH ST
600 17TH ST
18TH ST
19TH ST
900 20TH ST
1000 21ST ST
1100 22ND ST
1200 23RD ST
24TH ST

1988 SAN FRANCISCO COUNTY CROSS STREET INDEX

1400 25TH ST
26TH ST
END ARMY ST
SOUTHWOOD DR SF 19 B1
W FROM PLYMOUTH AV TO FAXON AV
PLYMOUTH AV
2 SAN RAMON WY
100 MIRAMAR WY
ELMWOOD WY
END FAXON AV
SPARROW ST SF 10 C2
E FROM VALENCIA ST BETWEEN
15TH ST & 16TH ST TO CALEDONIA ST
SPARTA ST SF 21 A2
E OF BISHOP ST FROM ANKENY ST
S TO HARKNESS AV
SPEAR AV SF 17 B1
E FROM J ST TO A ST, HUNTERS PT
SPEAR ST SF 7 B1
S FROM MARKET ST BETWEEN
STEUART ST AND MAIN ST SE
TO THE BAY
2 MARKET ST
100 MISSION ST
200 HOWARD ST
300 FOLSOM ST
400 HARRISON ST
BRYANT ST
END BAY OF S F
SPENCER ST SF 10 B2
N FROM 16TH ST BETWEEN
GUERRERO ST & DOLORES ST
SPOFFORD ST SF 3 A3
FROM 800 CLAY ST BETWEEN GRANT AV
AND STOCKTON ST N TO
WASHINGTON ST
SPRECKLES LK DR SF 8 B1
S OF FULTON ST BETWEEN 36TH AV
AND 30TH AV IN GOLDEN GATE PARK
SPRING ST SF 3 A3
FROM CALIFORNIA ST BETWEEN
MONTGOMERY ST AND KEARNY ST
N TO SACRAMENTO ST
SPRINGFIELD DR SF 12 C3
S FROM SLOAT BLVD BETWEEN
RIVERTON DR AND EVERGLADE DR
SPROULE LN SF 3 A3
S FROM CLAY ST BETWEEN MASON ST
AND TAYLOR ST
SPRUCE ST SF 5 C2
FROM PRESIDIO RESERVATION
BETWEEN LOCUST ST AND MAPLE ST
S TO ANZA ST
2 PRESIDIO RESERVATION
100 JACKSON ST
200 WASHINGTON ST
300 CLAY ST
400 SACRAMENTO ST
CALIFORNIA ST
MAYFAIR DR
EUCLID AV
GEARY BLVD
END ANZA ST
STANDISH AV SF 14 A3
W OFF 1700 SAN JOSE AV
STANFORD ST SF 7 C3
S FROM BRANNAN ST BETWEEN 2ND ST
AND 3RD ST S TO TOWNSEND ST
STANFORD HTS AV SF 13 C3
FROM LOS PALMOS DR S TO
MELROSE AV
STANLEY ST SF 19 B2
W OF SAN JOSE AV NEAR THE
COUNTY LINE FROM ORIZABA AV
W TO HEAD ST
STANTON ST SF 10 A3
N FROM MARKET ST BETWEEN YUKON ST
AND GRANDVIEW TER
STANYAN ST SF 5 C3
STANYAN ST SF 9 C1
FROM GEARY BLVD S TO
MOUNTAIN SPRINGS AV
GEARY BLVD
ANZA ST
LONE MTN TER
2 TURK ST
GOLDEN GATE AV
PARAMOUNT TER
100 MCALLISTER ST
200 FULTON ST
300 HAYES ST
FELL ST
400 OAK ST
500 PAGE ST
600 HAIGHT ST
700 WALLER ST
800 BEULAH ST
900 FREDERICK ST
1000 CARL ST
1100 PARNASSUS AV
1134 GRATTAN ST
1174 ALMA ST
1200 RIVOLI ST
1226 17TH ST
1300 BELGRAVE AV
CLAREDON AV
END MOUNTAIN SPRINGS AV
STAPLES AV SF 13 C3
W FROM CIRCULAR AV BETWEEN
FLOOD AV AND JUDSON AV TO
HAZELWOOD AV
2 CIRCULAR AV
100 DETROIT ST
200 EDNA ST
300 FOERSTER ST
400 GENNESSE ST
500 PHELAN AV
END HAZELWOOD AV
STARK ST SF 3 A3
FROM 1200 STOCKTON ST BETWEEN
PACIFIC AV AND BROADWAY
STARR KING WY SF 6 C2
S FROM GEARY ST BETWEEN GOUGH ST
AND FRANKLIN ST
STARVIEW WY SF 13 C1
NE FROM PANORAMA DR 6 BLKS N OF
PORTOLA DR
STATE DR SF 18 C1
E FROM LAKE MERCED BLVD
BETWEEN FONT BLVD AND WINSTON DR
STATES ST SF 10 A2
W FROM CASTRO ST BETWEEN 16TH ST
AND 17TH ST W TO LEVANT ST
2 CASTRO
200 DOUGLASS ST
END LEVANT ST
STEINER ST SF 2 A3
STEINER ST SF 6 B3
STEINER ST SF 10 B1
S FROM DUBOCE AV BETWEEN
FILLMORE ST AND PIERCE ST
N TO CHESTNUT ST
2 DUBOCE AV
100 HERMANN ST
130 GERMANIA ST
200 WALLER ST
230 LAUSSAT ST
300 HAIGHT ST
400 PAGE ST
500 OAK ST
600 FELL ST
700 HAYES ST
800 GROVE ST
900 FULTON ST
1000 MCALLISTER ST
1100 GOLDEN GATE AV
1200 TURK ST
1300 EDDY ST
1400 ELLIS ST
1500 O'FARRELL ST
1600 GEARY BLVD
1700 POST ST
1800 SUTTER ST
1900 BUSH ST
WILMOT ST
2000 PINE ST
2100 CALIFORNIA ST
PERINE PL
2200 SACRAMENTO ST
2300 CLAY ST
2400 WASHINGTON ST
2500 JACKSON ST
2600 PACIFIC AV
2700 BROADWAY
2800 VALLEJO ST
2900 GREEN ST
3000 UNION ST
3100 FILBERT ST
3150 PIXLEY ST
3200 GREENWICH ST
3250 MOULTON ST
SERVICE ST
3300 LOMBARD ST
END CHESTNUT ST
STERLING ST SF 7 B2
S FROM HARRISON ST BETWEEN 1ST ST
AND 2ND ST SE TO BRYANT ST
STEUART ST SF 7 B1
S FROM MARKET ST BETWEEN
THE EMBARCADERO AND SPEAR ST
SE TO THE BAY
2 MARKET ST
100 MISSION ST
200 HOWARD ST
300 FOLSOM ST
HARRISON ST
END BAY OF S F
STEVELOE PL SF 7 A2
E FROM JONES ST BETWEEN ELLIS ST
AND O'FARRELL ST
STEVENS AL SF 3 B3
E FROM SANSOME ST BETWEEN
BROADWAY AND PACIFIC AV
STEVENSON ST SF 6 C3
STEVENSON ST SF 7 A3
STEVENSON ST SF 10 C1
S FROM 1ST ST BETWEEN MARKET ST
AND JESSIE ST SW TO 14TH ST
2 1ST ST
ECKER ST
100 2ND ST
NEW MONTGOMERY ST
192 ANNIE ST
200 3RD ST
4TH ST
400 5TH ST
500 6TH ST
600 7TH ST
700 8TH ST
800 9TH ST
10TH ST
1100 12TH ST
1200 BRADY ST
GOUGH ST
1300 MCCOPPIN ST
DUBOCE AV
1400 CLINTON PARK
END 14TH ST
STILL ST SF 14 B3
E FROM ADMIRAL AV TO ROUSSEAU ST
PARALLEL TO I-280 FRWY
STILLINGS AV SF 14 A3
E FROM 600 TERESITA BLVD
TO MARTHA AV
STILLMAN ST SF 7 B3
W FROM 2ND ST BETWEEN BRYANT ST
AND HARRISON ST SW TO 4TH ST
2 2ND ST
100 3RD ST
END 4TH ST
STILWELL DR SF 4 C1
E FROM LINCOLN BLVD TO
PERSHING DR, IN THE PRESIDIO
STOCKTON ST SF 3 A2
STOCKTON ST SF 7 A1
N FROM MARKET ST BETWEEN GRANT AV
AND POWELL ST TO THE EMBARCADERO
2 MARKET ST
ELLIS ST
100 OFARRELL ST
200 GEARY ST
MAIDEN LN
300 POST ST
CAMPTON PL
400 SUTTER ST
500 BUSH ST
EMMA ST
600 PINE ST
700 CALIFORNIA ST
800 SACRAMENTO ST
900 CLAY ST
1000 WASHINGTON ST
1100 JACKSON ST
1200 PACIFIC AV
STARK ST
1300 BROADWAY
1400 VALLEJO ST
CARD AL
COLUMBUS AV
1500 GREEN ST
1600 UNION ST
1700 FILBERT ST
1800 GREENWICH ST
1900 LOMBARD ST
FIELDING ST
2000 CHESTNUT ST
PFEIFFER ST
2100 FRANCISCO ST
2200 BAY ST
2300 NORTH POINT ST
2400 BEACH ST
END THE EMBARCADERO
STONE ST SF 1 A2
BETWEEN RALSTON AV AND STOREY AV
IN THE PRESIDIO
STONE ST SF 3 A3
N FROM 900 WASHINGTON ST BETWEEN
STOCKTON ST AND POWELL ST
N TO JACKSON ST
STONECREST DR SF 19 A1
LOOP EXTENDING W FROM JUNIPERO
SERRA BLVD N & E OF 19TH AV
STONEMAN ST SF 15 A1
FROM 3300 FOLSOM ST W TO
SHOTWELL ST
STONESTOWN SF 13 A3
N FROM 20TH AV NEAR WINSTON DR
STONEYBROOK AV SF 14 C3
S FROM CAMBRIDGE ST TO
GLADSTONE DR NEAR SILVER AV
STONEYFORD AV SF 14 C3
S FROM CAMBRIDGE ST TO
GLADSTONE DR NEAR SILVER AV
STOREY AV SF 1 A2
SE FROM LINCOLN BL, IN PRESIDIO
STORRIE ST SF 10 A2
NE FROM 18TH ST
STOW LAKE DR SF 9 A1
S FROM JOHN F KENNEDY DR IN
GOLDEN GATE PARK
STOW LAKE DR E SF 9 A1
S FROM STOW LAKE DR TO MARTIN L
KING DR IN GOLDEN GATE PARK
STRATFORD DR SF 19 A1
SE FROM LYNDHURST DR TO
JUNIPERO SERRA BLVD E OF
DENSLOWE DR
SUMMIT ST SF 19 C2
FROM MAJESTIC AV W OF SAN JOSE AV
NW TO LAKE VIEW AV
SUMNER AV SF 1 C3
E FROM MACARTHUR ST TO
PRESIDIO BLVD, IN THE PRESIDIO
SUMNER ST SF 7 A3
S FROM HOWARD ST BETWEEN 7TH ST
AND 8TH ST TO CLEMENTINA ST
SUNBEAM LN SF 20 A2
E FROM CAYUGA AV BETWEEN
ONEIDA AV AND JUNIOR TER
SUNGLOW LN SF 14 C3
S FROM GLADSTONE DR TO
SILVER AV NEAR CAMBRIDGE ST
SUNNYDALE AV SF 20 B2
SUNNYDALE AV SF 21 A3
FROM PERSIA ST S TO COUNTY LINE
SANTOS ST
HAHN ST
SAWYER ST
GARRISON AV
REY ST
SCHWERIN ST
DELTA ST
CORA ST
RUTLAND ST
PEABODY ST
TALBERT ST
DESMOND ST
BAY SHORE BLVD
END COUNTY LINE
SUNNYSIDE TER SF 13 C3
E FROM FOERSTER ST BETWEEN
STAPLES AV AND JUDSON AV
SUNRISE WY SF 20 C3
FROM POINT E OF SAWYER ST
TO POINT W OF HAHN ST N OF
VELASCO AV
SUNSET BLVD SF 8 B2
SUNSET BLVD SF 12 B1
S FROM LINCOLN WY BETWEEN
36TH AV AND 37TH AV TO OCEAN AV
LINCOLN WAY
IRVING ST
JUDAH ST
KIRKHAM ST
LAWTON ST
MORAGA ST
NORIEGA ST
ORTEGA ST
PACHECO ST
QUINTARA ST
RIVERA ST
SANTIAGO ST
TARAVAL ST
ULLOA ST
VICENTE ST
WAWONA ST
YORBA ST
SLOAT BLVD
END OCEAN AV
SUNVIEW DR SF 13 C1
N FROM PORTOLA DR
SURREY ST SF 14 A3
FROM CHENERY ST NW TO SWISS AV
LIPPARD AV
292 VAN BUREN ST
END SWISS AV
SUSSEX ST SF 14 B2
NW FROM CASTRO ST NEAR BEMIS ST
TO ELK ST
2 CASTRO ST
100 DIAMOND ST
VAN BUREN ST
300 CONRAD ST
400 SWISS AVE
MIZPAH ST
END ELK ST
SUTRO HTS AV SF 4 A3
BETWEEN ANZA ST AND BALBOA ST
FROM 46TH AV TO 48TH AV
SUTTER ST SF 6 A3

SUTTER ST SF 7 A2
FROM THE JUNCTION OF MARKET ST
AND SANSOME ST BETWEEN POST ST
& BUSH ST W TO PRESIDIO AV
2 MARKET ST
SANSOME ST
100 MONTGOMERY ST
TRINITY ST
LICK PL
200 KEARNY ST
CLAUDE LN
MARK LN
300 GRANT AV
400 STOCKTON ST
500 POWELL ST
600 MASON ST
700 TAYLOR ST
800 JONES ST
900 LEAVENWORTH ST
1000 HYDE ST
1100 LARKIN ST
1200 POLK ST
1300 VAN NESS AV
1400 FRANKLIN ST
1500 GOUGH ST
1600 OCTAVIA ST
1700 LAGUNA ST
1800 BUCHANAN ST
1900 WEBSTER ST
COTTAGE ROW
2000 FILLMORE ST
2100 STEINER ST
2200 PIERCE ST
2300 SCOTT ST
2400 DIVISADERO ST
2500 BRODERICK ST
2600 BAKER ST
2700 LYON ST
END PRESIDIO AVE
SWEENY ST SF 15 A3
FROM SAN BRUNO AV NEAR ISLAIS CK
W TO CAMBRIDGE ST
2 SAN BRUNO AV
100 BARNEVELD ST
200 MERRILL ST
300 BOYLSTON ST
BOWDOIN ST
DARTMOUTH ST
DUNSMUIR ST
COLBY ST
UNIVERSITY ST
PRINCETON ST
END CAMBRIDGE ST
SWISS AV SF 14 A3
BETWEEN CONRAD ST AND MIZPAH AV
FROM ARBOR ST TO SURREY ST
2 ARBOR ST
50 SUSSEX ST
END SURREY ST
SYCAMORE ST SF 10 C2
W FROM MISSION ST BETWEEN 17TH ST
AND 18TH ST TO VALENCIA ST
SYDNEY WY SF 13 C1
FROM IDORA AV S ACROSS
ULLOA ST TO PORTOLA DR
SYLVAN DR SF 12 C3
S FROM SLOAT BLVD TO OCEAN AV
E OF MIDDLEFIELD DR
TABER PL SF 7 B3
FROM 2ND ST BETWEEN BRYANT ST AND
SOUTH PARK AV SW TO 3RD ST
TACOMA ST SF 5 A3
W FROM 15TH AV BETWEEN
GEARY BLVD AND CLEMENT ST
TALBERT CT SF 21 A3
N FROM TALBERT ST & VISITACION AV
2 BLKS W OF BAYSHORE BLVD
TALBERT ST SF 21 A3
SW FROM VISITACION AV TO COUNTY
LINE, 2 BLKS W OF BAYSHORE BLVD

TAMALPAIS TER SF 5 C3
N FROM GOLDEN GATE AV TO TURK ST
BETWEEN ANNAPOLIS TER AND
ROSLYN TER
TAMPA LN SF 15 B3
S FROM QUESADA AV TO
BRIDGEVIEW DR BETWEEN QUINT ST
AND NEWHALL ST
TANDANG SORA SF 7 B3
SE FROM BONIFACIO ST TO RIZAL ST
BETWEEN 3RD ST AND 4TH ST
TAPIA DR SF 18 C1
S FROM ARBALLO DR TO SERRANO DR
E OF LAKE MERCED BLVD
TARA ST SF 19 C2
S FROM GENEVA AV TO RIDGE LN
1 BLK W OF I-280 FRWY
100 GENEVA AV
200 NIAGARA AV
300 MT VERNON AV
END RIDGE LN
TARAVAL ST SF 12 A2
TARAVAL ST SF 13 A2
W FROM DEWEY BLVD TO 48TH AV
BETWEEN SANTIAGO ST & ULLOA ST
2 DEWEY BLVD
LENOX WY
WAWONA ST
100 CORTES ST
MADRONE AV
FOREST SIDE AV
200 12TH AV
300 FUNSTON AV
400 14TH AV
500 15TH AV
600 16TH AV
700 17TH AV
800 18TH AV
900 19TH AV
1000 20TH AV
1100 21ST AV
22ND AV
23RD AV
1400 24TH AV
1500 25TH AV
1600 26TH AV
1700 27TH AV
1800 28TH AV
1900 29TH AV
2000 30TH AV
2100 31ST AV
2200 32ND AV
2300 33RD AV
35TH AV
2500 35TH AV
2600 36TH AV
SUNSET BLVD
2700 37TH AV
2800 38TH AV
2900 39TH AV
3000 40TH AV
3100 41ST AV
3200 42ND AV
3300 43RD AV
3400 44TH AV
3500 45TH AV
3600 46TH AV
3700 47TH AV
END 48TH AV
TAYLOR RD SF 1 B2
S FROM LINCOLN BLVD TO BLISS RD
BETWEEN ORD ST AND MONTGOMERY ST
IN THE PRESIDIO
TAYLOR ST SF 2 C1
TAYLOR ST SF 7 A1
N FROM MARKET ST BETWEEN MASON ST
AND JONES ST TO THE BAY
2 MARKET ST
GOLDEN GATE AV
OPAL PL

100 TURK ST
200 EDDY ST
300 ELLIS ST
400 O'FARRELL ST
500 GEARY ST
DERBY PL
ADELAIDE PL
600 POST ST
COSMO PL
HOBART AL
700 SUTTER ST
800 BUSH ST
MULFORD AL
900 PINE ST
1000 CALIFORNIA ST
1100 SACRAMENTO ST
PLEASANT ST
1200 CLAY ST
1300 WASHINGTON ST
1400 JACKSON ST
1500 PACIFIC AV
BERNARD ST
1600 BROADWAY
FALLON PL
1700 VALLEJO ST
1800 GREEN ST
MACONADRAY ST
1900 UNION ST
ALADDIN TER
2000 FILBERT ST
VALPARAISO ST
2100 GREENWICH ST
2200 LOMBARD ST
COLUMBUS AV
2300 CHESTNUT ST
WATER ST
2400 FRANCISCO ST
2500 BAY ST
2600 NORTH POINT ST
2700 BEACH ST
2800 JEFFERSON ST
END THE EMBARCADERO
TEA GARDEN DR SF 9 A1
S FROM JOHN F KENNEDY DR TO
MARTN L KING DR IN GOLDEN GATE PK
TEDDY AV SF 21 A2
FROM 4100 SAN BRUNO AV BETWEEN
CAMPBELL AV AND ARLETA AV
W TO ELLIOT ST
2 SAN BRUNO AV
100 ALPHA ST
200 RUTLAND ST
300 DELTA ST
400 ELLIOT ST
TEHAMA ST SF 7 A3
W FROM 1ST ST BETWEEN HOWARD ST
AND CLEMENTINA ST SW TO 9TH ST
2 1ST ST
MALDEN AL
100 2ND ST
400 5TH ST
6TH ST
700 8TH ST
END 9TH ST
TELEGRAPH PL SF 3 A2
N OF GREENWICH ST BETWEEN
KEARNY ST AND GRANT AV
TELEGRAPH HL BL SF 3 A2
S FROM LOMBARD ST TO
FILBERT ST AND N TO
GREENWICH ST
TEMESCAL TER SF 5 C3
N FROM GOLDEN GATE AV TO
TURK ST BETWEEN PARKER AV AND
CHABOT TER
TEMPLE ST SF 10 A2
FROM 17TH ST N TO SATURN ST 1 BLK
E OF ROOSEVELT WY
TENNESSEE ST SF 11 C2
TENNESSEE ST SF 15 C1

FROM MARIPOSA ST BETWEEN 3RD ST
AND MINNESOTA ST S TO TULARE ST
600 MARIPOSA ST
700 18TH ST
800 19TH ST
900 20TH ST
1100 22ND ST
TUBBS ST
1200 23RD ST
24TH ST
1500 25TH ST
1600 26TH ST
ARMY ST
MARIN ST
END TULARE ST
TENNY PL SF 7 B2
E FROM 1ST ST BETWEEN HOWARD ST
AND FOLSOM ST
TERESITA BLVD SF 13 C1
FROM 561 PORTOLA DR S TO
FOERSTER ST
PORTOLA DR
100 FOWLER AV
200 EVELYN WY
MARIETTA DR
AGUA WY
300 ISOLA WY
REPOSA WY
SEQUOIA WY
400 GAVIOTA WY
500 ARROYO WY
EL SERENO CT
RIO CT
BELLA VISTA WAY
MARIETTA DR
CUBA AL
FOERSTER ST
600 LOS PALMOS DR
STILLINGS AV
MELROSE AV
EDNA ST
VERNA ST
END FOERSTER ST
TERRACE DR SF 13 B2
FROM 1499 PORTOLA DR SE TO A
POINT E OF SANTA CLARA AV
TERRACE WALK SF 13 B2
SW FROM YERBA BUENA AV TO
SAN ANSELMO AV W OF
SANTA PAULA AV
TERRA VISTA AV SF 6 A3
E FROM ANZAVISTA AV TO
ST JOSEPHS AV BETWEEN
O'FARRELL ST AND TURK ST
TEXAS ST SF 11 B2
FROM 17TH ST BETWEEN MISSOURI ST
AND MISSISSIPPI ST S TO 25TH ST
100 17TH ST
200 MARIPOSA ST
300 18TH ST
400 19TH ST
500 20TH ST
SIERRA ST
900 23RD ST
1100 25TH ST
THERESA ST SF 14 A3
FROM 4400 MISSION ST BETWEEN
TINGLEY ST AND COTTER ST TO
SAN JOSE AV
2 MISSION ST
ALEMANY BLVD
200 CAYUGA AV
END SAN JOSE AV
THOMAS AV SF 1 B3
FROM INFANTRY TER S TO
SIBERT LOOP IN THE PRESIDIO
THOMAS AV SF 15 A2
THOMAS AV SF 21 C1
FROM FITCH ST NW TO 3RD ST AND
FROM MADDUX AV TO A POINT W OF

SELBY ST
FITCH ST
GRIFFITH ST
HAWES ST
1300 INGALLS ST
1400 JENNINGS ST
1500 KEITH ST
1600 LANE ST
3RD ST
2000 MADDUX AV
QUINT ST
ROBBLEE AV
2100 SILVER AV
SELBY ST
END PT W OF SELBY ST
THOMAS MELLON DR SF 21 B3
N FROM ALANA WY AND HARNEY WY
TO EXECUTIVE PARK BLVD
THOMAS MORE WY SF 19 A3
S OF BROTHERHOOD WY 2 BLKS W OF
JUNIPERO SERRA BLVD
THOR AV SF 14 B3
N FROM CHENERY ST TO SURREY ST
THORNBURG RD SF 1 C2
NW FROM KENNEDY AV TO GIRARD RD
IN THE PRESIDIO
THORNE WY SF 15 B3
SE FROM BRIDGEVIEW DR BETWEEN
BRIDGEVIEW DR & TOPEKA AV
THORNTON AV SF 15 B3
FROM 5200 3RD ST W TO BAYSHORE BL
2 3RD ST
LATONA ST
LUCY ST
100 POMONA ST
CERES ST
FLORA ST
REDDY ST
TOPEKA AV
DIANA ST
NEPTUNE ST
VENUS ST
APOLLO ST
BRIDGEVIEW DR
600 SCOTIA ST
VESTA ST
MERCURY ST
700 WATERVILLE ST
QUINT ST
ELMIRA ST
CARROLL AV
END BAYSHORE BLVD
THORP LN SF 10 A3
N FROM 19TH ST AND CLOVER ST
THRIFT ST SF 19 B2
S FROM SUMMIT ST TO ORIZABA AV
2 SUMMIT ST
100 PLYMOUTH AV
200 CAPITOL AV
FAXON AV
END ORIZABA AV
TIFFANY AV SF 14 C1
FROM THE JUNCTION OF VALENCIA ST
AND DUNCAN ST SW TO 29TH ST
TILLMAN PL SF 7 A2
W FROM 201 GRANT AV BETWEEN
SUTTER ST AND POST ST
TINGLEY ST SF 14 B3
FROM 4300 MISSION ST NEAR
SILVER AV NW TO SAN JOSE AV
2 MISSION ST
100 ALEMANY BLVD
200 CAYUGA AV
END SAN JOSE AV
TIOGA AV SF 21 A2
BETWEEN TUCKER AV AND WILDE AV
FROM ALPHA ST W TO DELTA ST
TISDALE RD SF 16 A3
FROM 616 JERROLD AV E IN A SEMI-
CIRCLE BETWEEN EARL ST

AND DONAHUE ST
TOCOLOMA AV SF 21 B3
BETWEEN PENINSULA AV AND NUEVA AV
TODD ST SF 1 A2
FROM POPE ST TO HITCHCOCK ST
IN THE PRESIDIO
TOLAND ST SF 15 B2
FROM EVANS AV SW TO OAKDALE AV
2 EVANS AV
200 GALVEZ AV
300 HUDSON AV
400 INNES AV
JERROLD AV
KIRKWOOD AV
MCKINNON AV
NEWCOMB AV
OAKDALE AV
TOLEDO WY SF 2 A2
W FROM MALLORCA WY TO PIERCE ST
TOMASO CT SF 21 A3
W OF BAYSHORE BLVD
S OF SUNNYDALE AV
TOMPKINS AV SF 14 C2
FROM ANDOVER ST BETWEEN JARBOE AV
& OGDEN AV E TO PERALTA AV
2 ANDOVER ST
100 MOULTRIE ST
200 ANDERSON ST
300 ELLSWORTH ST
400 GATES ST
500 FOLSOM ST
600 BANKS ST
700 PRENTISS ST
800 NEVADA ST
900 PUTNAM ST
1000 BRONTE ST
1100 BRADFORD ST
END PERALTA AV
TOPAZ WY SF 14 A2
S FROM GOLDMINE DR 2 BLKS W
OF DIAMOND ST
TOPEKA AV SF 15 B3
S FROM SILVER AV TO
THRONTON AV E OF SANTA FE AV
TORNEY AV SF 1 C2
SE FROM LINCOLN BLVD TO
LETTERMAN HOSPITAL IN PRESIDIO
TORRENS CT SF 2 C3
N FROM CLAY ST BETWEEN HYDE ST
AND LARKIN ST
TOUCHARD ST SF 6 C1
S FROM 1101 PINE ST BETWEEN
JONES ST AND LEAVENWORTH ST
TOWNSEND ST SF 7 C3
TOWNSEND ST SF 11 B1
FROM THE BAY BETWEEN BRANNAN ST
AND KING ST SW TO 8TH ST
BAY OF S F
2 1ST ST
GALE ST
COLIN P KELLY JR ST
100 2ND ST
STANFORD ST
CLARENCE PL
200 3RD ST
236 RITCH ST
CLYDE ST
LUSK ST
300 4TH ST
400 5TH ST
500 6TH ST
600 7TH ST
700 8TH ST
END DIVISION ST
TOYON LN SF 20 B3
E FROM BALTIMORE WY TO
SOUTH HILL BLVD
TRACY PL SF 3 A3
S FROM 601 VALLEJO ST BETWEEN
COLUMBUS AV & STOCKTON ST

TRAINOR ST SF 10 C1
N FROM 14TH ST BETWEEN FOLSOM ST
AND HARRISON ST
TRANSVERSE RD SF 8 C1
S FROM CROSSOVER DR TO
MIDDLE DR W IN GOLDEN GATE PARK
TREASURY PL SF 3 B3
N FROM 200 BUSH ST BETWEEN
SANSOME ST AND MONTGOMERY ST
TREAT AV SF 11 A2
TREAT AV SF 15 A1
FROM FLORIDA ST SW TO 18TH ST
THEN S BETWEEN FOLSOM ST AND
HARRISON ST TO A POINT S
OF PRECITA AV
2 FLORIDA ST
ALAMEDA ST
100 ALABAMA ST
200 15TH ST
300 HARRISON ST
16TH ST
400 17TH ST
18TH ST
600 19TH ST
MISTRAL ST
700 20TH ST
800 21ST ST
900 22ND ST
1000 23RD ST
1100 24TH ST
1200 25TH ST
1300 26TH ST
PRECITA AV
END PT S OF PRECITA AV
TRENTON ST SF 3 A3
FROM 900 WASHINGTON ST BETWEEN
STOCKTON ST AND POWELL ST
N TO JACKSON ST
2 WASHINGTON ST
100 JACKSON ST
TRINITY ST SF 7 B1
FROM 100 SUTTER ST BETWEEN
MONTGOMERY ST AND KEARNY ST
N TO BUSH ST
TROCADERO DR SF 12 C2
E FROM THE JUNCTION OF WAWONA ST
AND CRESTLAKE IN PINE LAKE PARK
TROY AL SF 2 C3
W FROM 1201 HYDE ST BETWEEN
CLAY ST AND SACRAMENTO ST
TRUBY ST SF 1 C2
S FROM GORGAS AV IN THE PRESIDIO
TRUETT PL SF 3 A3
W FROM MASON ST BETWEEN CLAY ST
AND WASHINGTON ST
TRUMBULL ST SF 14 B3
FROM 4101 MISSION ST NEAR
SILVER AV TO CAMBRIDGE ST
2 MISSION ST
100 CRAUT ST
200 CONGDON ST
NEY ST
MAYNARD ST
STONEYBROOK AV
STONEYFORD AV
GLADSTONE DR
CAMBRIDGE ST
TUBBS ST SF 11 C3
E FROM INDIANA ST TO TENNESSEE ST
BETWEEN 22ND ST AND 23RD ST
TUCKER AV SF 21 A2
W FROM ALPHA ST TO DELTA ST
BETWEEN CAMPBELL AV & TIOGA AV
TULANE ST SF 14 C3
W FROM PRINCETON ST BETWEEN
SWEENY ST AND SILVER AV
TULARE ST SF 15 C1
FROM 3RD ST W TO INDIANA ST
TULIP AL SF 7 A3
OFF RUSS ST BETWEEN MINNA ST

AND NATOMA ST
TUNNEL AV SF 21 B3
FROM BAY SHORE BLVD S TO A
POINT S OF THE COUNTY LINE
TURK ST SF 5 C3
TURK ST SF 6 A3
TURK ST SF 7 A2
FROM THE JUNCTION OF MARKET ST
& MASON ST BETWEEN GOLDEN GATE AV
AND EDDY ST W TO ARGUELLO BLVD
2 MARKET ST
MASON ST
100 TAYLOR ST
200 JONES ST
300 LEAVENWORTH ST
400 HYDE ST
DODGE PL
500 LARKIN ST
600 POLK ST
700 VAN NESS AVE
800 FRANKLIN ST
GOUGH ST
LAGUNA ST
1300 WEBSTER ST
1400 FILLMORE ST
STEINER ST
1600 PIERCE ST
1700 SCOTT ST
SEYMOUR AVE
1800 DIVISADERO ST
1900 BRODERICK ST
1938 ST JOSEPHS AV
2000 BAKER ST
2100 LYON ST
2200 CENTRAL AV
2300 MASONIC AV
ANNAPOLIS TER
TAMALPAIS TER
ROSELYN TER
KITTREDGE TER
CHABOT TER
TEMESCAL TER
PARKER AV
BEAUMONT AV
STANYAN ST
ROSSI AV
3100 WILLARD ST
END ARGUELLO BLVD
TURNER TER SF 11 B3
SE OFF MISSOURI ST BETWEEN
22ND ST AND 23RD ST
TURQUOISE WY SF 14 A2
SW FROM AMBER DR ONE BLK S
OF DUNCAN ST
TUSCANY AL SF 3 A2
S FROM 501 LOMBARD ST BETWEEN
STOCKTON ST AND POWELL ST
TWIN PEAKS BLVD SF 9 C3
FROM CARMEL ST AND CLAYTON ST
S AND SW TO BURNETT AV
100 CARMEL ST
CLAYTON ST
200 CLARENDON AV
MT SPRING AV
ST GERMAIN AV
RACCOON DR
BURNETT AV
300 PALO ALTO AV
VISTA LN
END PORTOLA DR
ULLOA ST SF 12 A2
ULLOA ST SF 13 A2
FROM WOODSIDE AV SW AND W TO
THE GREAT HWY S OF TARAVAL ST
OF TARAVAL ST
2 WOODSIDE AV
SYDNEY WY
300 LAGUNA HONDA BLVD
ROCKAWAY AV
WAITHMAN WY

SHANGRILA WY
500 KENSINGTON WY
600 GRANVILLE WY
650 ALLSTON WY
700 DORCHESTER WY
800 CLAREMONT BLVD
900 LENOX WY
WEST PORTAL AV
1000 WAWONA ST
1100 MADRONE AV
1200 FORESTSIDE AV
1202 FUNSTON AV
1300 14TH AV
1400 15TH AV
1500 16TH AV
1600 17TH AV
1700 18TH AV
1800 19TH AV
1900 20TH AV
2000 21ST AV
2100 22ND AV
2200 23RD AV
2300 24TH AV
2400 25TH AV
2500 26TH AV
2600 27TH AV
2700 28TH AV
2800 29TH AV
2900 30TH AV
3000 31ST AV
3100 32ND AV
3200 33RD AV
3300 34TH AV
3400 35TH AV
36TH AV
SUNSET BLVD
3600 37TH AV
3700 38TH AV
3800 39TH AV
3900 40TH AV
4000 41ST AV
4100 42ND AV
4200 43RD AV
4300 44TH AV
4400 45TH AV
4500 46TH AV
4600 47TH AV
48TH AV
END GREAT HIGHWAY
UNDERWOOD AV SF 21 C1
FROM HAWES ST NW TO 3RD ST
HAWES ST
INGALLS ST
JENNINGS ST
1500 KEITH ST
1600 LANE ST
END 3RD ST
UNION ST SF 2 A3
UNION ST SF 3 A2
FROM THE EMBARCADERO BETWEEN
GREEN & FILBERT STS W TO LYON ST
2 THE EMBARCADERO
50 FRONT ST
100 BATTERY ST
KEHOUSE AL
200 SANSOME ST
CALHOUN ST
300 MONTGOMERY ST
CASTLE ST
400 KEARNY ST
GENOA PL
SONOMA ST
VARENNES ST
500 GRANT AV
BANNAM PL
CADELL AL
550 JASPER PL
PRICE ROW
STOCKTON ST
COLUMBUS AV

700 POWELL ST
800 MASON ST
900 TAYLOR ST
MARION PL
1000 JONES ST
BLACK PL
1100 LEAVENWORTH ST
SHARP PL
1200 HYDE ST
EASTMAN ST
MOORE PL
1300 LARKIN ST
1400 POLK ST
1500 VAN NESS AV
1600 FRANKLIN ST
1700 GOUGH ST
1800 OCTAVIA ST
1900 LAGUNA ST
CHARLTON CT
2000 BUCHANAN ST
2100 WEBSTER ST
2200 FILLMORE ST
2300 STEINER ST
2400 PIERCE ST
2500 SCOTT ST
2600 DIVISADERO ST
2700 BRODERICK ST
2800 BAKER ST
END LYON ST
UNITD NATIONS PZ SF 6 C3
E FROM HYDE ST BETWEEN GROVE ST
AND MCALLISTER ST W TO MARKET ST
UNIVERSITY ST SF 21 A1
FROM SWEENY ST S TO MANSELL ST
SWEENY ST
2 SILVER AV
100 SILLIMAN ST
200 FELTON ST
BURROW ST
BACON ST
500 WAYLAND ST
600 WOOLSEY ST
700 DWIGHT ST
800 OLMSTEAD ST
END MANSELL ST
UPLAND DR SF 13 B3
FROM KENWOOD WY WESTERLY TO
SAN BENITO WY
KENWOOD WY
NORTH GATE DR
MANOR DR
PINEHURST WY
WESTGATE DR
SAN ALESO AV
APTOS AV
END SAN BENITO WY
UPPER TER SF 10 A2
FROM BUENA VISTA AV SW TO
MONUMENT WY
2 BUENA VISTA AV
100 MASONIC AV
ASHBURY TER
200 CLIFFORD TER
END MONUMENT WY
UPPER SERVICE RD SF 9 B2
N FROM JOHNSTONE DR IN SUTRO
FOREST
UPTON AV SF 1 A2
N FROM KOBBE AV TO RUCKMAN AV
IN THE PRESIDIO
UPTON ST SF 15 B2
S FROM JERROLD AV TO MCKINNON AV
N OF TOLAND ST
URANUS TER SF 9 C2
S FROM 17TH ST TO DEMING ST
BETWEEN MARS ST & CLAYTON ST
URBANO DR N SF 19 B1
URBANO DR S SF 19 B1
A CIRCULAR STREET STARTING S OF
OCEAN AV CROSSING VICTORIA ST,

DE SOTO ST, CORONA ST AND
BORICO ST, BOTH E AND W
LEGION CT
2 PICO AV
100 VICTORIA ST
DE SOTO ST
200 CORONA ST
BORICA
ALVISO ST
300 MONCADA WY
500 BORICO ST
600 CORONA ST
700 DE SOTO ST
800 VICTORIA ST
UTAH ST SF 11 A3
FROM DIVISION ST BETWEEN
SAN BRUNO AV AND POTRERO AV S TO
18TH ST & FROM 23RD ST TO A POINT
S OF 25TH ST
2 DIVISION ST
100 ALAMEDA ST
200 15TH ST
300 16TH ST
400 17TH ST
500 MARIPOSA ST
18TH ST
1200 23RD ST
1300 24TH ST
1400 25TH ST
END PT S OF 25TH ST
VALDEZ AV SF 13 C3
N FROM GREENWOOD AV BETWEEN
COLON AV AND HAZELWOOD AV TO
BRENTWOOD ST
2 GREENWOOD AVE
100 MONTECITO AVE
200 MONTEREY BLVD
300 MANGELS AVE
END BRENTWOOD ST
VALE AV SF 12 C3
N FROM SLOAT BLVD TO TROCADERO DR
VALENCIA ST SF 10 C1
VALENCIA ST SF 14 C1
S FROM MARKET ST BETWEEN
MISSION ST AND GUERRERO ST
S TO MISSION ST
2 MARKET ST
100 MC COPPIN ST
200 DUBOCE AVE
240 CLINTON PARK
260 BROSNAN ST
300 14TH ST
400 15TH ST
500 16TH ST
600 17TH ST
CLARION AL
SYCAMORE ST
700 18TH ST
800 19TH ST
CUNNINGHAM PL
900 20TH ST
950 LIBERTY ST
1000 21ST ST
1050 HILL ST
1100 22ND ST
1200 23RD ST
1300 24TH ST
1400 25TH ST
1500 26TH ST
1534 ARMY ST
DUNCAN ST
1600 TIFFANY ST
END MISSION ST
VALERTON CT SF 20 A1
SE FROM CAYUGA AV BETWEEN
ONONDAGA AV AND OCEAN AV
VALLEJO ST SF 1 B2
W FROM SGT MITCHELL ST, PRESIDIO
VALLEJO ST SF 2 C3
VALLEJO ST SF 3 A3
FROM THE EMBARCADERO BETWEEN
BROADWAY & GREEN ST W TO LYON ST
2 THE EMBARCADERO
50 DAVIS ST
100 FRONT ST
200 BATTERY ST
COWELL PL
300 SANSOME ST
PRESCOTT CT
HODGES AL
BARTOL ST
400 MONTGOMERY ST
500 KEARNY ST
SAN ANTONIO ST
ROMOLO ST
POLLARD PL
MARGRAVE PL
600 GRANT AVE
COLUMBUS AVE
TRACY PL
700 STOCKTON ST
EMERY LN
CHURCHILL ST
800 POWELL ST
WASHOE PL
900 MASON ST
VALLEJO TER
VISTA TER
1000 TAYLOR ST
FLORENCE ST
RUSSIAN HILL PL
1100 JONES ST
1200 LEAVENWORTH ST
1300 HYDE ST
WHITE ST
1400 LARKIN ST
1500 POLK ST
1600 VAN NESS AV
1700 FRANKLIN ST
1800 GOUGH ST
1900 OCTAVIA ST
2000 LAGUNA ST
2100 BUCHANAN ST
2200 WEBSTER ST
2300 FILLMORE ST
2400 STEINER ST
2500 PIERCE ST
2600 SCOTT ST
NORMANDY TER
2700 DIVISADERO ST
2800 BRODERICK ST
2900 BAKER ST
END LYON ST
VALLEJO TER SF 3 A3
OFF 927 VALLEJO ST BETWEEN
MASON ST AND TAYLOR ST
VALLETA CT SF 14 A2
NW FROM MALTA DR ONE BLK N OF
STILLINGS AV
VALLEY ST SF 14 B1
W FROM SAN JOSE AV BETWEEN
28TH ST AND 29TH ST TO DIAMOND ST
2 SAN JOSE AVE
100 DOLORES ST
200 CHURCH ST
300 SANCHEZ ST
400 NOE ST
500 CASTRO ST
END DIAMOND ST
VALMAR TER SF 20 B1
S OFF 600 PERU AV
VALPARAISO ST SF 2 C2
FROM 1901 MASON ST BETWEEN
FILBERT ST AND GREENWICH ST
W TO TAYLOR ST AND FROM ROACH ST
TO JONES ST
VAN BUREN ST SF 14 A3
W OF DIAMOND ST S FROM SUSSEX ST
TO SURREY ST
VANDEWATER ST SF 3 A2
W FROM 2201 POWELL ST BETWEEN
BAY ST & FRANCISCO ST
W TO MASON ST
VAN DYKE AV SF 21 B1
N FROM HAWES ST TO 3RD ST
HAWES ST
INGALLS ST
JENNINGS ST
1500 KEITH ST
1600 LANE ST
END 3RD ST
VAN KEUREN AV SF 17 B1
E FROM FISHER AV TO LOCKWOOD ST
N OF SPEAR AV
VAN NESS AV SF 2 B2
VAN NESS AV SF 6 C2
N FROM MARKET ST BETWEEN POLK ST
AND FRANKLIN ST TO BEACH ST
2 MARKET ST
OAK ST
HICKORY ST
100 FELL ST
LINDEN ST
200 HAYES ST
LECH WALESA
GROVE ST
500 MC ALLISTER ST
530 REDWOOD ST
600 GOLDEN GATE AV
630 ELM ST
700 TURK ST
LARCH ST
800 EDDY ST
830 WILLOW ST
900 ELLIS ST
930 OLIVE ST
1000 O FARRELL ST
1030 MYRTLE ST
1100 GEARY ST
1130 CEDAR ST
1200 POST ST
1230 HEMLOCK ST
1300 SUTTER ST
1330 FERN ST
1400 BUSH ST
1430 AUSTIN ST
1500 PINE ST
1600 CALIFORNIA ST
1700 SACRAMENTO ST
1800 CLAY ST
1900 WASHINGTON ST
2000 JACKSON ST
2100 PACIFIC AV
2200 BROADWAY
2300 VALLEJO ST
2400 GREEN ST
2500 UNION ST
2600 FILBERT ST
2700 GREENWICH ST
2800 LOMBARD ST
2900 CHESTNUT ST
3000 FRANCISCO ST
3100 BAY ST
3200 NORTH POINT ST
END BEACH ST
VARELA AV SF 19 A1
S FROM HOLLOWAY AV TO SERRANO DR
W OF 19TH AV
VARENNES ST SF 3 A2
N FROM 400 GREEN ST BETWEEN
KEARNY ST AND GRANT AV TO
FILBERT ST
2 GREEN ST
100 UNION ST
END FILBERT ST
VARNEY PL SF 7 B3
SW FROM CENTER PL BETWEEN
SOUTH PARK AV AND BRANNAN ST
TO 3RD ST
VASQUEZ AV SF 13 B2
FROM WOODSIDE AV SW TO
KENSINGTON WY
2 WOODSIDE AV
50 LAGUNA HONDA BLVD
100 HERNANDEZ AV
GARCIA AV
END KENSINGTON WY
VASSAR PL SF 7 B2
S FROM HARRISON ST BETWEEN 2ND ST
AND 3RD ST
VEGA ST SF 5 C3
W FROM ANZAVISTA AV TO MASONIC AV
BETWEEN TURK ST AND O'FARRELL ST
VELASCO AV SF 20 C3
FROM SCHWERIN ST AND THE
COUNTY LINE W TO CARRIZAL ST
VENARD AL SF 3 A2
S FROM 501 CHESTNUT ST BETWEEN
POWELL ST AND MASON ST
VENTURA AV SF 13 B1
SE FROM LINARES AV TO
CASTENADA AV
VENUS ST SF 15 B3
FROM THORNTON AV S TO WILLIAMS AV
VERDI PL SF 3 A3
W FROM 901 MONTGOMERY ST BETWEEN
PACIFIC AV AND BROADWAY
VERDUN WY SF 13 B2
FROM CLAREMONT BLVD S OF
TARAVAL ST W TO LENOX WY
VERMEHR PL SF 7 A2
E FROM 100 KEARNY ST BETWEEN
POST ST AND SUTTER ST
VERMONT ST SF 11 A1
VERMONT ST SF 15 B1
FROM DIVISION ST BETWEEN
SAN BRUNO AV AND KANSAS ST
S TO 26TH ST
2 DIVISION ST
100 ALAMEDA ST
200 15TH ST
300 16TH ST
400 17TH ST
500 MARIPOSA ST
600 18TH ST
700 19TH ST
20TH ST
900 21ST ST
1000 22ND ST
1200 23RD ST
1300 24TH ST
1400 25TH ST
END 26TH ST
VERNA ST SF 13 C3
S FROM LOS PALMOS DR
TO MELROSE AV E OF FOERSTER ST
VERNON ST SF 19 B2
W OF SAN JOSE AV AND S FROM
HOLLOWAY AV TO A POINT S OF
RANDOLPH ST
100 RANDOLPH ST
200 SARGENT ST
300 SHIELDS ST
400 GARFIELD ST
END HOLLOWAY AVE
VESTA ST SF 15 B3
S FROM THORNTON AV TO WILLIAMS AV
& PHELPS ST
VICENTE ST SF 12 A2
VICENTE ST SF 13 A2
W FROM PORTOLA DR TO GREAT HWY
1 BLK S OF ULLOA ST
2 PORTOLA DR
100 WEST PORTAL AVE
200 WAWONA ST
MADRONE AVE
260 FOREST SIDE AVE
300 14TH AVE
400 15TH AVE
500 16TH AVE
600 17TH AVE
700 18TH AVE
800 19TH AVE
900 20TH AVE
1000 21ST AVE
1100 22ND AVE
1200 23RD AVE
1300 24TH AVE
1400 25TH AVE
1500 26TH AVE
1600 27TH AVE
1700 28TH AVE
1800 29TH AVE
1900 30TH AVE
2000 31ST AVE
2100 32ND AVE
2200 33RD AVE
2300 34TH AVE
2400 35TH AVE
2500 36TH AVE
SUNSET BLVD
2600 37TH AVE
2700 38TH AVE
2800 39TH AVE
2900 40TH AVE
3000 41ST AVE
3100 42ND AVE
3200 43RD AVE
3300 44TH AVE
3400 45TH AVE
3500 46TH AVE
3600 47TH AVE
END GREAT HIGHWAY
VICKSBURG ST SF 10 B3
VICKSBURG ST SF 14 B1
S FROM 22ND ST BETWEEN CHURCH ST
AND SANCHEZ ST TO 25TH ST
VICTORIA ST SF 19 B2
N FROM PALMETTO AV TO ALEMANY BL
& FROM S OF RANDOLPH ST
TO OCEAN AV
2 PALMETTO AVE
ALEMANY BLVD
200 RANDOLPH ST
300 SARGENT ST
400 SHIELDS ST
500 GARFIELD ST
600 HOLLOWAY AVE
700 URBANO DR S
URBANO DR N
END OCEAN AVE
VIDAL DR SF 18 C2
S FROM FONT BLVD TO RIVAS DR
VIENNA ST SF 20 B2
FROM SILVER AV SW TO GENEVA AV
2 SILVER AVE
100 PERU AVE
200 AVALON AVE
300 EXCELSIOR AVE
400 BRAZIL AVE
500 PERSIA AVE
600 RUSSIA AV
700 FRANCE AVE
800 ITALY AVE
900 AMAZON AVE
END GENEVA AVE
VILLA TER SF 10 A3
SE FROM TWIN PEAKS BLVD TO
GRAYSTONE TER
2 TWIN PEAKS BLVD
100 PEMBERTON PL
END GRAYSTONE TER
VINE TER SF 7 A1
N FROM PINE ST BETWEEN MASON ST
AND TAYLOR ST
VINTON CT SF 3 A3
W FROM 501 GRANT AV BETWEEN
PINE ST AND CALIFORNIA ST
VIRGIL ST SF 14 C1
S FROM 25TH ST BETWEEN SOUTH

VAN NESS AV & SHOTWELL ST
VIRGINIA AV SF 14 C2
SE FROM 3351 MISSION ST NEAR
30TH ST TO ELSIE ST AND
EUGENIA AV
2 MISSION ST
100 COLERIDGE AV
LUNDYS LANE
200 PROSPECT AV
300 WINFIELD ST
400 ELSIE ST
END EUGENIA AV
VISITACION AV SF 20 C2
VISITACION AV SF 21 A3
FROM A POINT E OF BAYSHORE BLVD
NEAR COUNTY LINE TO MANSELL ST
BAYSHORE BLVD
700 DESMOND ST
TALBERT CT
900 PEABODY ST
948 RUTLAND ST
CORA ST
DELTA ST
SCHWERIN ST
REY ST
BRITTON ST
LOEHR ST
SAWYER ST
HAHN ST
END MANSELL ST
VISTA LN SF 10 A3
W FROM BURNETT AV 5
BLKS N OF PORTOLA DR
VISTA VERDE CT SF 14 A3
N FROM STILLINGS AV BETWEEN
TERESITA BLVD & MALTA DR
VULCAN ST SF 10 A2
FROM POINT W OF ORD ST TO
LEVANT ST N OF LOWER TER
WABASH TER SF 21 B2
NE FROM SAN BRUNO AV TO
BEEMAN LN W OF BAYSHORE BLVD
WAGNER AL SF 6 C2
WAGNER AL SF 7 A3
S FROM EDDY ST BETWEEN JONES ST
AND LEAVENWORTH ST
WAGNER RD SF 1 A2
FROM STOREY AV SE TO HOWE RD
IN THE PRESIDIO
WAITHMAN WY SF 13 B2
FROM 1000 PORTOLA DR N TO ULLOA S
WALBRIDGE ST SF 20 B3
W FROM THE INTERSECTION OF
GENEVA AV AND PARQUE DR
WALDO AL SF 2 C3
W FROM LEAVENWORTH ST BETWEEN
BROADWAY AND VALLEJO ST
WALL PL SF 2 C3
N FROM JACKSON ST BETWEEN HYDE ST
AND LEAVENWORTH ST
WALLACE AV SF 21 B1
FROM POINT S OF INGALLS ST
NW TO 3RD ST
INGALLS ST
JENNINGS ST
KEITH ST
LANE ST
END 3RD ST
WALLEN CT SF 1 B3
SW FROM MACARTHUR ST, PRESIDIO
WALLER ST SF 9 C1
WALLER ST SF 10 A1
FROM THE JUNCTION OF MARKET ST
& OCTAVIA ST W TO STANYAN ST
2 MARKET ST
8 OCTAVIA ST
LAGUNA ST
200 BUCHANAN ST
300 WEBSTER ST
400 FILLMORE ST
500 STEINER ST
POTOMAC ST
600 PIERCE ST
CARMELITA ST
700 SCOTT ST
800 DIVISADERO ST
ALPINE TER
900 BRODERICK ST
1100 BUENA VISTA AVE
1200 CENTRAL AVE
1300 MASONIC AVE
DELMAR ST
1400 ASHBURY ST
DOWNEY ST
1500 CLAYTON ST
1550 BELVEDERE ST
1600 COLE ST
1700 SHRADER ST
END STANYAN ST
WALNUT ST SF 5 C1
FROM PACIFIC AV BETWEEN
PRESIDIO AV AND LAUREL ST S TO
CALIFORNIA ST
2 PACIFIC AVE
100 JACKSON ST
200 WASHINGTON ST
300 CLAY ST
400 SACRAMENTO ST
END CALIFORNIA ST
WALTER ST SF 10 B1
S FROM DUBOCE AV BETWEEN
SANCHEZ ST & NOE ST TO 14TH ST
WALTER LUM PL SF 3 A3
BRENHAM PL SF 3 A3
N FROM S CLAY ST BETWEEN GRANT AV
AND KEARNY ST TO WASHINGTON ST
WALTHAM ST SF 15 A2
W FROM ALABAMA ST NEAR
ESMERALDA AV
WANDA ST SF 20 A1
N FROM ONONDAGA AV BETWEEN
CAYUGA AV AND OTSEGO AV N TO
OCEAN AV
WARD ST SF 21 A2
W FROM SAN BRUNO AV TO SPARTA ST
BETWEEN ORDWAY ST AND HARKNESS AV
WARNER PL SF 2 C2
E FROM HYDE ST BETWEEN GREEN ST
AND UNION ST
WARREN DR SF 9 B3
SE FROM LAWTON ST & LOCKSLEY AV
PARALLEL TO 7TH AV
WASHBURN ST SF 11 A1
S FROM MISSION ST BETWEEN 9TH ST
AND 10TH ST SE TO HOWARD ST
WASHINGTON BLVD SF 1 B3
E FROM LINCOLN BL TO ARGUELLO BL
IN THE PRESIDIO
WASHINGTON ST SF 2 A3
WASHINGTON ST SF 3 B3
WASHINGTON ST SF 5 C2
WASHINGTON ST SF 6 A2
WASHINGTON ST SF 7 B1
FROM THE EMBARCADERO BETWEEN
CLAY ST AND JACKSON ST W
TO ARGUELLO BLVD
2 THE EMBARCADERO
100 DRUMM ST
200 DAVIS ST
400 BATTERY ST
CUSTOM HOUSE PL
500 SANSOME ST
HOTALING PL
MONTGOMERY ST
600 COLUMBUS AVE
DUNBAR AL
700 KEARNY ST
WALTER LUM PL
WENTWORTH PL
800 GRANT AVE
WAVERLY PL
ROSS AL
OLD CHINA TOWN LN
SPOFFORD ST
900 STOCKTON ST
TRENTON ST
STONE ST
1000 POWELL ST
CODMAN PL
WETMORE ST
1100 MASON ST
1200 TAYLOR ST
1300 JONES ST
PRIEST ST
REED ST
1400 LEAVENWORTH ST
1500 HYDE ST
1600 LARKIN ST
1700 POLK ST
1800 VAN NESS AV
1900 FRANKLIN ST
2000 GOUGH ST
2100 OCTAVIA ST
2200 LAGUNA ST
2300 BUCHANAN ST
2400 WEBSTER ST
2500 FILLMORE ST
STEINER ST
2800 SCOTT ST
2900 DIVISADERO ST
3000 BRODERICK ST
3100 BAKER ST
3200 LYON ST
3300 PRESIDIO AVE
3400 WALNUT ST
3500 LAUREL ST
3600 LOCUST ST
3700 SPRUCE ST
3800 MAPLE ST
3900 CHERRY ST
END ARGUELLO BLVD
WASHOE PL SF 3 A3
S FROM 800 VALLEJO ST BETWEEN
POWELL ST AND MASON ST
WATCHMAN WY SF 11 B3
SE OFF MISSOURI ST BETWEEN
22ND ST & 23RD ST
WATER ST SF 2 C2
FROM 2201 MASON ST BETWEEN
CHESTNUT ST AND FRANCISCO ST
W TO TAYLOR ST
WATERLOO ST SF 15 A2
FROM E S BAY SHORE BLVD
N OF INDUSTRIAL ST
WATERVILLE ST SF 15 B2
FROM SELBY ST E OF ELMIRA ST S TO
THORNTON AV
2 HELENA ST
SILVER AVE
END THORNTON AVE
WATSON PL SF 20 A1
SW FROM OCEAN AV 1 BLK E OF
ALEMANY BLVD
WATT AV SF 20 A3
S FROM HANOVER ST TO
BELLEVUE ST E OF GUTTENBERG ST
WAVERLY PL SF 3 A3
FROM 800 SACRAMENTO ST BETWEEN
GRANT AV AND STOCKTON ST
N TO WASHINGTON ST
2 SACRAMENTO ST
100 CLAY ST
END WASHINGTON ST
WAWONA ST SF 12 B3
WAWONA ST SF 13 A2
FROM TARAVAL ST S AND W TO
GREAT HIGHWAY
2 TARAVAL ST
100 ULLOA ST
200 VICENTE ST
300 14TH AVE
400 15TH AVE
500 16TH AVE
600 17TH AVE
18TH AV
800 19TH AVE
900 20TH AVE
1000 21ST AVE
1100 22ND AVE
1200 23RD AVE
1300 24TH AVE
1400 25TH AVE
26TH AVE
1700 28TH AVE
1900 30TH AVE
2200 33RD AVE
2300 34TH AVE
2400 35TH AVE
2500 36TH AVE
SUNSET BLVD
2600 37TH AVE
2700 38TH AVE
2800 39TH AVE
2900 40TH AVE
3000 41ST AVE
3100 42ND AVE
3200 43RD AVE
3300 44TH AVE
3400 45TH AVE
3500 46TH AVE
3600 47TH AVE
48TH AV
END GREAT HIGHWAY
WAYLAND ST SF 20 C1
WAYLAND ST SF 21 A1
FROM SAN BRUNO AV S OF BACON ST
W TO OXFORD ST
100 SAN BRUNO AV
200 GIRARD ST
300 BRUSSELS ST
400 GOETTINGEN ST
500 SOMERSET ST
600 HOLYOKE ST
700 HAMILTON ST
800 BOWDOIN ST
1100 UNIVERSITY ST
1200 PRINCETON ST
1300 AMHERST ST
1400 YALE ST
1500 CAMBRIDGE ST
END OXFORD ST
WAYNE PL SF 3 A3
FROM 900 PACIFIC AV BETWEEN
POWELL ST AND MASON ST N TO
BROADWAY
WEBB PL SF 3 A2
W FROM 1701 MASON ST BETWEEN
GREEN ST AND UNION ST
WEBSTER ST SF 2 B3
WEBSTER ST SF 6 B3
WEBSTER ST SF 10 B1
N FROM DUBOCE AV BETWEEN
BUCHANAN ST AND FILLMORE ST
TO A POINT N OF MARINA BLVD
2 DUBOCE AV
50 HERMANN ST
GERMANIA ST
100 WALLER ST
LAUSSAT ST
200 HAIGHT ST
300 PAGE ST
LILY ST
400 OAK ST
HICKORY ST
500 FELL ST
512 LINDEN ST
600 HAYES ST
614 IVY ST
700 GROVE ST
800 FULTON ST
900 MCALLISTER ST
1000 GOLDEN GATE AV
1100 TURK ST
1200 EDDY ST
1300 ELLIS ST
1400 O FARRELL ST
1500 GEARY ST
1600 POST ST
1700 SUTTER ST
1800 BUSH ST
WILMOT ST
1900 PINE ST
2000 CALIFORNIA ST
2100 SACRAMENTO ST
2200 CLAY ST
2300 WASHINGTON ST
2400 JACKSON ST
BROMLEY PL
2500 PACIFIC AVE
2600 BROADWAY
2700 VALLEJO ST
2800 GREEN ST
2900 UNION ST
3000 FILBERT ST
PIXLEY ST
3100 GREENWICH ST
MOULTON ST
3200 LOMBARD ST
MAGNOLIA ST
CHESTNUT ST
BAY ST
NORTH POINT ST
3700 BEACH ST
JEFFERSON ST
3800 MARINA BLVD
END PT N OF MARINA BLVD
WELSH ST SF 7 B3
W FROM ZOE ST BETWEEN BRANT ST
& BRANNAN ST SW TO 5TH ST
2 ZOE ST
100 4TH ST
END 5TH ST
WENTWORTH PL SF 3 A3
FROM 733 WASHINGTON ST BETWEEN
KEARNY ST AND GRANT AV N
TO JACKSON ST
WESTBROOK CT SF 15 C3
BETWEEN CASHMERE ST AND ARDATH CT
OFF HUDSON AV
WEST CLAY ST SF 4 C2
W FROM 22ND AV ONE BLOCK N
OF LAKE ST
WESTGATE DR SF 13 B3
FROM 2100 OCEAN AV N TO
MONTEREY BLVD
2 OCEAN AV
100 KENWOOD WY
200 UPLAND DR
300 DARIEN WY
END MONTEREY BLVD
WESTMOORLAND DR SF 12 B3
S FROM OCEAN AV TO EUCALYPTUS DR
WEST POINT RD SF 16 A2
A LOOP EXTENDING W FROM
MIDDLEPOINT RD
WEST PORTAL AV SF 13 A2
FROM ULLOA ST SW TO PORTOLA DR
2 ULLOA ST
100 VICENTE ST
300 14TH AVE
400 15TH AVE
END PORTOLA DR
WEST VIEW AV SF 14 C3
E FROM CAMBRIDGE ST BETWEEN
SWEENY ST AND ALEMANY BLVD
WESTWOOD DR SF 19 B1
W & N FROM MIRAMAR AV TO
MIRAMAR AV
2 MIRAMAR AVE
100 WILDWOOD AVE

PIZARRO WAY
END MIRAMAR AVE
WETMORE ST SF 3 A3
FROM 1000 CLAY ST BETWEEN
POWELL ST AND MASON ST N
TO WASHINGTON ST
WHEAT ST SF 21 B1
FROM PAUL AV BETWEEN CRANE ST
& BAYSHORE BLVD S TO SALINAS AV
WHEELER AV SF 21 B3
FROM HESTER AV TO A POINT S OF
LATHROP AV
WHIPPLE AV SF 19 C3
FROM MISSION ST NW TO SAN JOSE AV
NEAR THE COUNTY LINE
WHITE ST SF 2 C3
N FROM VALLEJO ST BETWEEN HYDE ST
AND LARKIN ST
WHITFIELD CT SF 15 C3
OFF LA SALLE AV BETWEEN
OSEOLA LN AND INGALLS ST
WHITING ST SF 3 A2
E FROM 1800 GRANT AV BETWEEN
LOMBARD ST & CHESTNUT ST
WHITNEY ST SF 14 B2
FROM 30TH ST E OF SANCHEZ ST
S TO CHENERY ST
2 30TH ST
100 RANDALL ST
200 FAIRMOUNT ST
END CHENERY ST
WHITNEY YOUNG CIRSF 15 C3
S FROM CASHMERE ST TO HUDSON AV
WHITTIER ST SF 19 C3
SE FROM 5701 MISSION ST
2 MISSION ST
CASSANDRA CT
100 BRUNSWICK ST
COUNTY LINE
WIESE ST SF 10 C2
FROM 1601 15TH ST BETWEEN
MISSION ST & JULIAN AV S TO
16TH ST
WILDE AV SF 21 A2
FROM 3600 SAN BRUNO AV BETWEEN
CAMPBELL AV & HARNESS AV W TO
ERVINE ST
2 SAN BRUNO AVE
100 GIRARD ST
200 BRUSSELS ST
300 GOETTINGEN ST
400 RUTLAND ST
DELTA ST
END ERVINE ST
WILDER ST SF 14 B3
FROM POINT E OF CARRIE ST
S OF CHENERY ST W TO DIAMOND ST
WILDWOOD WY SF 19 B1
FROM A POINT E OF PLYMOUTH AV
BETWEEN GREENWOOD AV AND
SAN RAMON WY W TO A POINT W
OF FAXON AV
100 PLYMOUTH AVE
200 EASTWOOD DR
300 MIRAMAR AVE
400 WESTWOOD DR
500 FAXON AVE
HOMEWOOD CT
END PT W OF HOMEWOOD CT
WILLARD ST SF 9 C2
FROM GOLDEN GATE PARK S TO
WOODLAND AV
1200 FREDERICK ST
1300 CARL ST
1400 PARNASSUS AVE
FARNSWORTH ST
1500 BELMONT AVE
END WOODLAND AVE
WILLARD ST N SF 5 B3
FROM EDWARD ST E OF
ARGUELLO BLVD SW TO FULTON ST
2 EDWARD ST
100 TURK ST
200 GOLDEN GATE AVE
300 MCALLISTER ST
END FULTON ST
WILLIAMS AV SF 15 B3
FROM 3RD ST NEAR VAN DYKE AV
W TO PHELPS ST & VESTA ST
2 3RD ST
34 LUCY ST
66 CERES ST
MENDELL ST
100 REDDY ST
150 DIANA ST
200 NEPTUNE ST
NEWHALL ST
250 VENUS ST
300 APOLLO ST
PHELPS ST
END VESTA ST
WILLIAR AV SF 19 C2
W OF 2400 SAN JOSE AV OFF
800 NIAGARA AV S TO MT VERNON AV
WILLOW ST SF 6 B3
W FROM LARKIN ST BETWEEN EDDY ST
AND ELLIS ST W TO BUCHANAN ST
2 LARKIN ST
100 POLK ST
200 VAN NESS AVE
300 FRANKLIN ST
GOUGH ST
600 LAGUNA ST
END BUCHANAN ST
WILLS ST SF 16 A3
E FROM MIDDLE POINT RD IN
HUNTERS POINT
WILMOT ST SF 6 B2
W FROM WEBSTER ST BETWEEN BUSH ST
& PINE ST W TO STEINER ST
2 WEBSTER ST
100 FILLMORE ST
END STEINER ST
WILSON ST SF 19 B3
FROM MISSION ST S OF COUNTY LINE
NW TO DE LONG ST
COUNTY LINE
200 RHINE ST
END DE LONG ST
WINDING WY SF 20 A3
FROM ROLPH ST AND SOUTH HILL BLVD
SW AND WESTERLY TO PRAGUE ST
TO PRAGUE ST
2 ROLPH ST
100 NAYLOR ST
200 CORDOVA ST
300 DRAKE ST
END PRAGUE ST
WINDSOR PL SF 3 A2
N FROM 300 GREEN ST BETWEEN
MONTGOMERY ST AND KEARNY ST
WINFIELD ST SF 14 C2
FROM COSO AV BETWEEN PROSPECT AV
AND ELSIE ST SW TO CORTLAND AV
2 COSO AVE
100 ESMERALDA AVE
200 VIRGINIA AVE
300 EUGENIA AVE
END CORTLAND AVE
WINSTON DR SF 19 A1
W FROM JUNIPERO SERRA BLVD
TO LAKE MERCED BLVD
WINTER PL SF 3 A2
E OFF 1700 MASON ST BETWEEN
UNION ST AND GREEN ST
WINTHROP ST SF 3 A2
N FROM 200 LOMBARD ST BETWEEN
MONTGOMERY ST AND KEARNY ST
TO CHESTNUT ST
WISCONSIN ST SF 11 B2
FROM 16TH ST BETWEEN ARKANSAS ST
& CAROLINA ST S TO 26TH ST
100 16TH ST
17TH ST
300 MARIPOSA ST
500 19TH ST
600 20TH ST
800 22ND ST
MADERA ST
1000 23RD ST
CONNECTICUT ST
1200 25TH ST
26TH ST
WISER CT SF 1 A3
E FROM THE INTERSECTION OF
HITCHCOCK ST AND WRIGHT LOOP
IN THE PRESIDIO
WOOD ST SF 5 C2
FROM A POINT E OF EMERSON ST
W & S BETWEEN EMERSON ST AND
COLLINS ST S TO ANZA ST
PT E OF EMERSON ST
EMERSON ST
GEARY BLVD
END ANZA ST
WOODACRE DR SF 13 A3
NE FROM OCEAN AV TO
JUNIPERO SERRA BLVD NEAR
PORTOLA DR
WOODHAVEN CT SF 9 C3
W FROM FOREST KNOLLS DR 1
BLK S OF CHRISTOPHER DR
WOODLAND AV SF 9 C2
FROM 249 PARNASSUS AV BETWEEN
STANYAN ST AND WILLARD ST
S TO WILLARD ST
WOODSIDE AV SF 13 B1
FROM PORTOLA DR W TO DEWEY BLVD
WOODWARD ST SF 10 C1
S FROM DUBOCE AV BETWEEN
MISSION ST AND VALENCIA ST
TO 14TH ST
WOOL CT SF 1 A2
S FROM UPTON AV, IN THE PRESIDIO
WOOL ST SF 14 C2
FROM POWHATTAN AV AND BOCANA ST
S TO CORTLAND AV
2 BOCANA ST
POWHATTAN AVE
100 EUGENIA AVE
END CORTLAND AVE
WOOLSEY ST SF 21 A1
FROM SAN BRUNO AV S OF WAYLAND ST
W TO UNIVERSITY ST
100 SAN BRUNO AVE
200 GIRARD ST
300 BRUSSELS ST
400 GOETTINGEN ST
500 SOMERSET ST
600 HOLYOKE ST
700 HAMILTON ST
800 BOWDOIN ST
900 DARTMOUTH ST
1000 COLBY ST
END UNIVERSITY ST
WORCESTER AV SF 19 B3
SE FROM ALEMANY BLVD TO
PALMETTO AV
WORDEN ST SF 3 A2
N FROM 300 FRANCISCO ST BETWEEN
STOCKTON ST AND POWELL ST
WORTH ST SF 10 A3
FROM 4301 21ST ST S TO
22ND ST W OF DOUGLASS ST
WRIGHT LOOP SF 1 A3
S FROM HITCHCOCK ST, PRESIDIO
WRIGHT ST SF 15 A1
W FROM HOLLADAY AV
TO MONTCALM ST
WYTON LN SF 19 A1
W FROM JUNIPERO SERRA BLVD
TO 19TH AV N OF HOLLOWAY AV
YALE ST SF 20 C1
S FROM SILVER AV TO WAYLAND ST
2 SILVER AVE
100 SILLIMAN ST
200 FELTON ST
END 500 WAYLAND ST
YERBA BUENA AV SF 13 B2
SE FROM SANTA CLARA AV TO
MONTEREY BLVD
2 SANTA CLARA AVE
SANTA MONICA WY
TERRACE WK
100 SANTA PAULA AVE
SAN PABLO AV
MIRALOMA DR
MAYWOOD DR
200 RAVENWOOD DR
BAXTER AL
HAZELWOOD AV
300 BRENTWOOD AVE
400 ST ELMO WAY
END MONTEREY BLVD
YORBA LN SF 12 B3
W FROM 40TH AV TO 41ST AV BETWEEN
SLOAT BLVD AND WAWONA ST
YORBA ST SF 12 B3
FROM CRESTLAKE DR W TO 40TH AV
2200 CRESTLAKE DR
2300 34TH AVE
2400 35TH AVE
2500 36TH AVE
SUNSET BLVD
2600 37TH AVE
2700 38TH AVE
2800 39TH AVE
END 40TH AV
YORK ST SF 11 A2
YORK ST SF 15 A1
FROM A POINT S OF MARIPOSA ST
BETWEEN HAMPSHIRE ST & BRYANT ST
S TO HOLLADAY AV
500 MARIPOSA ST
600 18TH ST
700 19TH ST
800 20TH ST
900 21ST ST
1000 22ND ST
1100 23RD ST
1200 24TH ST
1300 25TH ST
1400 26TH ST
ARMY ST
1500 PRECITA AVE
1600 PERALTA AVE
1700 WRIGHT ST
END HOLLADAY AVE
YOSEMITE AV SF 21 B1
FROM HAWES ST NW TO NEWHALL ST
HAWES ST
INGALLS ST
JENNINGS ST
1600 KEITH ST
1700 3RD ST
LANE ST
MENDELL ST
END NEWHALL ST
YOUNG ST SF 1 C2
W OF HALLECK ST, IN THE PRESIDIO
YUKON ST SF 10 A3
FROM CASELLI AV S TO
GRAND VIEW AV
2 CASELLI AVE
100 EAGLE ST
END GRAND VIEW AVE
ZENO PL SF 7 B2
S FROM FOLSOM ST BETWEEN BEALE ST
AND FREMONT ST
ZIRCON PL SF 14 B2
S FROM 29TH ST BETWEEN BACON ST
AND CASTRO ST
ZOE ST SF 7 B3
S FROM BRYANT ST BETWEEN 3RD ST
AND 4TH ST TO BRANNAN ST
ZOO RD SF 12 A3
E FROM GREAT HIGHWAY TO
SKYLINE BLVD S OF SLOAT BLVD
1ST ST SF 3 C1
NE FROM AVENUE A AT ENTRANCE TO
TREASURE ISLAND
1ST ST SF 7 B1
S FROM MARKET ST BETWEEN 2ND ST
AND FREMONT ST TO THE EMBARCADERO
2 MARKET ST
STEVENSON ST
JESSIE ST
ELIM ALLEY
100 MISSION ST
MINNA ST
NATOMA ST
200 HOWARD ST
TEHEMA ST
TENNY PL
CLEMENTINA ST
300 FOLSOM ST
GUY PL
LANSING ST
400 HARRISON ST
500 BRYANT ST
FEDERAL ST
600 BRANNAN ST
TOWNSEND ST
END THE EMBARCADERO
2ND AV SF 5 B2
2ND AV SF 9 B2
FROM POINT N OF LAKE ST S
TO PARNASSUS AV
NUMBERS THE SAME AS 19TH AV
2ND ST SF 7 B2
S FROM MARKET ST BETWEEN 1ST ST
& 3RD ST SE TO THE BAY
2 MARKET ST
STEVENSON ST
JESSIE ST
100 MISSION ST
MINNA ST
NATOMA ST
200 HOWARD ST
TEHAMA ST
CLEMENTINA ST
300 FOLSOM ST
DOW PL
400 HARRISON ST
STILLMAN ST
500 BRYANT ST
TABER PL
FEDERAL ST
SOUTH PARK AV
DE BOOM ST
600 BRANNAN ST
700 TOWNSEND ST
KING ST
BERRY ST
END BAY OF S F
3RD AV SF 5 B2
3RD AV SF 9 B2
FROM POINT N OF LAKE ST S
TO PARNASSUS AV
NUMBERS THE SAME AS 19TH AV
3RD AV SF 17 A2
SE FROM SPEAR AV TO MAHAN ST
3RD STIN HUNTERS POINT
3RD ST SF 3 C1
NE FROM AVENUE A TO AVENUE B AND
FROM AVENUE D TO AVENUE N
TREASURE ISLAND
AV A
AV B
AV D

AV F
AV H
AV M
END AV N
3RD ST SF 7 B2
3RD ST SF 11 C1
3RD ST SF 15 C2
3RD ST SF 21 B1
SE FROM MARKET ST BETWEEN 2ND ST & 4TH ST TO CHANNEL, THEN S & SW TO BAYSHORE BLVD
2 MARKET ST
STEVENSON ST
ALDRICH ST
100 MISSION ST
134 MINNA ST
HUNT ST
200 HOWARD ST
CLEMENTINA ST
300 FOLSOM ST
ST FRANCIS PL
400 HARRISON ST
PERRY ST
STILLMAN ST
500 BRYANT ST
TABER PL
SOUTH PARK AV
VARNEY PL
600 BRANNAN ST
700 TOWNSEND ST
800 KING ST
900 BERRY ST
CHINA BASIN ST
ROCK ST
4TH ST
1800 16TH ST
1900 17TH ST
2000 MARIPOSA ST
2100 18TH ST
2200 19TH ST
2300 20TH ST
2500 22ND ST
2700 23RD ST
2800 24TH ST
2900 25TH ST
3000 26TH ST
3100 ARMY ST
3200 MARIN ST
3300 TULARE ST
3400 ARTHUR AVE
CARGO WY
BURKE ST
3600 CUSTER AVE
3700 DAVIDSON AVE
PHELPS ST
3800 EVANS AVE
3900 FAIRFAX AVE
4000 GALVEZ AVE
4100 HUDSON AVE
4200 INNES AVE
NEWHALL ST
4300 JERROLD AVE
4400 KIRKWOOD AVE
4500 LA SALLE AVE
4600 MCKINNON AVE
4700 NEWCOMB AVE
4800 OAKDALE AVE
MENDELL ST
4900 PALOU AVE
5000 QUESADA AVE
REVERE AVE
5100 BAYVIEW ST
SHAFTER AVE
THOMAS AVE
5200 THORNTON AVE
UNDERWOOD AVE
VAN DYKE AVE
5300 WILLIAMS AVE
LANE ST
WALLACE AVE
5500 YOSEMITE AVE
5600 ARMSTRONG AVE
5700 BANCROFT AVE
5800 CARROLL AVE
DONNER AVE
EGBERT AVE
FITZGERALD AV
GILMAN AVE
6200 PAUL AVE
HOLLISTER AVE
INGERSON AVE
6300 SALINAS AVE
6400 JAMESTOWN AVE
6500 KEY AVE
6600 LE CONTE AVE
KEITH ST
6700 MEADE AVE
END BAYSHORE BLVD
4TH AV SF 5 B2
4TH AV SF 9 B2
FROM 100 LAKE ST S TO PARNASSUS AV
NUMBERS THE SAME AS 19TH AV
4TH ST SF 3 C1
NE FROM AVENUE H TO AVENUE N TREASURE ISLAND
AV H
AV M
END AV N
4TH ST SF 7 B2
4TH ST SF 11 C1
S FROM MARKET ST BETWEEN 3RD ST AND 5TH ST SE TO 3RD ST
2 MARKET ST
PIONEER CT
STEVENSON ST
JESSIE ST
100 MISSION ST
134 MINNA ST
200 HOWARD ST
CLEMENTINA ST
300 FOLSOM ST
SHIPLEY ST
CLARA ST
400 HARRISON ST
PERRY ST
STILLMAN ST
500 BRYANT ST
WELSH ST
FREELON ST
600 BRANNAN ST
BLUXOME ST
700 TOWNSEND ST
JEWETT ST
800 KING ST
900 BERRY ST
CHANNEL
MISSION ROCK ST
END 3RD ST
5TH AV SF 5 B2
5TH AV SF 9 B2
FROM PRESIDIO RESERVATION S TO LOCKSLEY AV
NUMBERS THE SAME AS 19TH AV
5TH ST SF 3 C1
NE FROM AVENUE M TO AVENUE N, ONE BLK NW OF 4TH ST, TREASURE ISLAND
5TH ST SF 7 A2
S FROM MARKET ST BETWEEN 4TH ST AND 6TH ST SE TO CHANNEL
2 MARKET ST
STEVENSON ST
MINT ST
JESSIE ST
100 MISSION ST
136 MINNA ST
NATOMA ST
200 HOWARD ST
TEHAMA ST
268 CLEMENTINA ST
300 FOLSOM ST
SHIPLEY ST
368 CLARA ST
400 HARRISON ST
500 BRYANT ST
WELSH ST
600 BRANNAN ST
BLUXOME ST
700 TOWNSEND ST
JEWETT ST
800 KING ST
900 BERRY ST
END CHANNEL
6TH AV SF 5 B2
6TH AV SF 9 B2
FROM PRESIDIO S TO LOCKSLEY AV
NUMBERS THE SAME AS 19TH AV
6TH AV SF 17 A1
NE FROM J ST TO SPEAR AV
6TH ST SF 3 C1
NE FROM AVENUE H TO AVENUE M TREASURE ISLAND
AV H
AV I
END AV M
6TH ST SF 7 A3
6TH ST SF 11 B1
S FROM MARKET ST BETWEEN 5TH ST AND 7TH ST TO 16TH ST
2 MARKET ST
32 STEVENSON ST
JESSIE ST
100 MISSION ST
132 MINNA ST
162 NATOMA ST
200 HOWARD ST
TEHAMA ST
CLEMENTINA ST
300 FOLSOM ST
SHIPLEY ST
CLARA ST
400 HARRISON ST
AHERN WY
500 BRYANT ST
600 BRANNAN ST
BLUXOME ST
700 TOWNSEND ST
800 KING ST
900 BERRY ST
1000 CHANNEL
END 16TH ST
7TH AV SF 5 B2
7TH AV SF 9 B2
FROM PRESIDIO S TO CLARENDON AV & LAGUNA HONDA BLVD
NUMBERS THE SAME AS 19TH AV
7TH ST SF 7 A3
7TH ST SF 11 B1
S FROM MARKET ST BETWEEN 6TH ST AND 8TH ST TO 17TH ST AND PENNSYLVANIA AV
2 MARKET ST
STEVENSON ST
JESSIE ST
100 MISSION ST
134 MINNA ST
168 NATOMA ST
200 HOWARD ST
300 FOLSOM ST
DECKER AL
CLEVELAND ST
400 HARRISON ST
500 BRYANT ST
600 BRANNAN ST
700 TOWNSEND ST
800 KING ST
900 BERRY ST
1000 CHANNEL
1100 HOOPER ST
1200 IRWIN ST
1300 HUBBELL ST
1400 DAGGETT ST
1500 16TH ST
MISSISSIPPI ST
17TH ST
END PENNSYLVANIA AVE
8TH AV SF 5 B2
8TH AV SF 9 B2
FROM MOUNTAIN LAKE PARK S TO PACHECO ST
NUMBERS SAME AS 19TH AV
8TH ST SF 3 C1
NE FROM AVENUE I TO AVENUE N TREASURE ISLAND
AV I
AV M
END AV N
8TH ST SF 7 A3
8TH ST SF 11 B1
S FROM MARKET ST BETWEEN 7TH ST & 9TH ST SE TO TOWNSEND ST
2 MARKET ST
STEVENSON ST
100 MISSION ST
MINNA ST
NATOMA ST
200 HOWARD ST
TEHAMA ST
CLEMENTINA ST
300 FOLSOM ST
320 RINGOLD ST
HERON ST
400 HARRISON ST
500 BRYANT ST
600 BRANNAN ST
END TOWNSEND ST
9TH AV SF 5 B2
9TH AV SF 9 B3
9TH AV SF 13 B1
FROM MOUNTAIN LAKE PARK S TO 12TH AV
NUMBERS THE SAME AS 19TH AV
9TH ST SF 3 C1
NE FROM AVENUE D TO AVENUE M TREASURE ISLAND
AV D
AV E
AV F
AV H
AV I
END AV M
9TH ST SF 11 A1
S FROM MARKET ST BETWEEN 8TH ST & 10TH ST SE TO DIVISION ST
2 MARKET ST
STEVENSON ST
JESSIE ST
100 MISSION ST
MINNA ST
NATOMA ST
200 HOWARD ST
TEHAMA ST
CLEMENTINA ST
300 FOLSOM ST
RINGOLD ST
SHERIDAN ST
400 HARRISON ST
BLACKWOOD ST
MCLEA CT
500 BRYANT ST
600 BRANNAN ST
END DIVISION ST
10TH AV SF 5 A2
10TH AV SF 9 B2
10TH AV SF 13 B1
FROM MOUNTAIN LAKE PARK S TO MENDOSA AV
NUMBERS SAME AS 19TH AV
10TH ST SF 3 C1
NE FROM AVENUE M TO AVENUE N
BETWEEN 9TH ST & 11TH TREASURE ISLAND
10TH ST SF 10 C1
S FROM MARKET ST BETWEEN 9TH ST & 11TH ST SE TO DIVISION ST
2 MARKET ST
STEVENSON ST
JESSIE ST
100 MISSION ST
MINNA ST
NATOMA ST
200 HOWARD ST
300 FOLSOM ST
SHERIDAN ST
400 HARRISON ST
500 BRYANT ST
END DIVISION ST
11TH AV SF 5 A2
11TH AV SF 9 B2
FROM MOUNTAIN LAKE PARK S TO PACHECO ST
NUMBERS SAME AS 19TH AV
11TH ST SF 3 C1
NE FROM AV D TO AV M, TREASURE ISLAND
AV D
AV E
AV H
AV I
END AV M
11TH ST SF 10 C1
S FROM MARKET ST BETWEEN 10TH ST AND 12TH ST SE TO BRYANT ST AND DIVISION ST
2 MARKET ST
100 MISSION ST
MINNA ST
NATOMA ST
200 HOWARD ST
238 KISSLING ST
298 BURNS PL
300 FOLSOM ST
400 HARRISON ST
BRYANT ST
END DIVISION ST
12TH AV SF 5 A2
12TH AV SF 9 A3
12TH AV SF 13 B1
FROM MOUNTAIN LAKE PARK S TO TARAVAL ST NUMBERS THE SAME AS 19TH AV
12TH ST SF 3 C1
NE FROM AVENUE B TO AVENUE H TREASURE ISLAND
AV B
AV D
AV E
END AV H
12TH ST SF 10 C1
S FROM MARKET ST BETWEEN 11TH ST AND BRADY ST SE TO HARRISON ST
2 MARKET ST
STEVENSON ST
100 MISSION ST
200 HOWARD ST
KISSLING ST
300 FOLSOM ST
ISIS ST
BERNICE ST
END HARRISON ST
13TH ST SF 3 C1
E FROM GATEVIEW AV TO AVENUE E, THEN NE TO AV N, TREASURE ISLAND
GATEVIEW AV
KEPPLER CT
HUTCHINS CT
HALYBURTON CT
BIGELOW CT
AV E
AV H & GATEVIEW AV

1988 SAN FRANCISCO COUNTY CROSS STREET INDEX

EXPOSITION DR
AV I
AV M
END AV N
13TH ST SF 10 C1
W OFF CENTRAL SKYWAY TO
MISSION ST
14TH AV SF 5 A2
14TH AV SF 9 A2
14TH AV SF 13 A1
FROM PRESIDIO S TO PORTOLA DR
NUMBERS SAME AS 19TH AV
14TH ST SF 10 B1
W FROM HARRISON ST BETWEEN
13TH ST AND 15TH ST TO
BUENA VISTA TER
2 HARRISON ST
TRAINOR ST
100 FOLSOM ST
SHOTWELL ST
S VAN NESS AV
NATOMA ST
MINNA ST
300 MISSION ST
328 WOODWARD ST
JULIAN AVE
STEVENSON ST
400 VALENCIA ST
500 GUERRERO ST
RAMONA AVE
ROSEMONT PL
600 DOLORES ST
LANDERS ST
MARKET ST
700 CHURCH ST
750 BELCHER ST
BOYNTON CT
800 SANCHEZ ST
850 WALTER ST
900 NOE ST
1000 CASTRO ST
1034 DIVISADERO ST
1058 ALPINE TER
END BUENA VISTA TERR
15TH AV SF 5 A2
15TH AV SF 9 A3
15TH AV SF 13 A1
FROM PRESIDIO RESERVATION
S TO PORTOLA DR
NUMBERS SAME AS 19TH AV
15TH ST SF 10 A2
15TH ST SF 11 A2
FROM CAROLINA ST BETWEEN 16TH ST
& ALAMEDA ST W TO PARKHILL AV
2 CAROLINA ST
100 DE HARO ST
200 RHODE ISLAND ST
300 KANSAS ST
400 VERMONT ST
500 SAN BRUNO AVE
600 UTAH ST
700 POTRERO AVE
1000 BRYANT ST
FLORIDA ST
ALABAMA ST
1300 HARRISON ST
1400 FOLSOM ST
1450 SHOTWELL ST
S VAN NESS AV
1536 NATOMA ST
CAPP ST
1572 MINNA ST
1600 MISSION ST
WIESE ST
1660 JULIAN AVE
1680 CALEDONIA ST
1700 VALENCIA ST
ALBION ST
1800 GUERRERO ST
1840 RAMONA AVE
AILEEN ST
1900 DOLORES ST
1950 LANDERS ST
2000 CHURCH ST
SHARON ST
MARKET ST
2100 SANCHEZ ST
2200 NOE ST
2300 CASTRO ST
BEAVER ST
2500 BUENA VISTA TER
END PARKHILL AV
16TH AV SF 5 A3
16TH AV SF 9 A2
16TH AV SF 13 A1
FROM PRESIDIO S TO WAWONA ST
NUMBERS SAME AS 19TH AV
16TH ST SF 10 B2
16TH ST SF 11 A2
FROM THE BAY BETWEEN 15TH ST
& 17TH ST W TO FLINT ST
300 ILLINOIS ST
3RD ST
600 6TH ST
OWENS ST
PENNSYLVANIA AV
BARSTOW ST
MISSISSIPPI ST
900 7TH ST
1000 DAGGETT ST
MISSOURI ST
CONNECTICUT ST
1100 HUBBELL ST
ARKANSAS ST
1200 8TH ST
1300 WISCONSIN ST
1400 CAROLINA ST
1500 DE HARO ST
1600 RHODE ISLAND ST
1700 KANSAS ST
1800 VERMONT ST
1900 SAN BRUNO AVE
2000 UTAH ST
2100 POTRERO AVE
2200 HAMPSHIRE ST
2300 YORK ST
2400 BRYANT ST
2500 FLORIDA ST
2600 ALABAMA ST
TREAT AVE
2700 HARRISON ST
2800 FOLSOM ST
2850 SHOTWELL ST
2900 SOUTH VAN NESS AVE
2950 CAPP ST
3000 MISSION ST
3050 WIESE ST
HOFF ST
3060 JULIAN AVE
RONDEL PL
CALEDONIA ST
3100 VALENCIA ST
ALBION ST
3200 GUERRERO ST
SPENCER ST
3300 DOLORES ST
3350 LANDERS ST
3400 CHURCH ST
HARLOW ST
3450 SHARON ST
DEHON ST
3500 SANCHEZ ST
PROSPER ST
POND ST
3600 NOE ST
MARKET ST
3700 CASTRO ST
FLINT ST
END 1 BLK BEYOND
17TH AV SF 5 A2
17TH AV SF 9 A2
FROM PRESIDIO S TO WAWONA ST
NUMBERS SAME AS 19TH AV
17TH ST SF 9 C2
17TH ST SF 10 A2
17TH ST SF 11 A2
FROM PENNSYLVANIA AV BETWEEN
16TH ST AND MARIPOSA ST W
TO STANYAN ST
1000 PENNSYLVANIA AVE
1100 MISSISSIPPI ST
1200 TEXAS ST
1300 MISSOURI ST
1400 CONNECTICUT ST
1500 ARKANSAS ST
1600 WISCONSIN ST
1700 CAROLINA ST
1800 DE HARO ST
1900 RHODE ISLAND ST
2000 KANSAS ST
2100 VERMONT ST
2200 SAN BRUNO AVE
2300 UTAH ST
2400 POTRERO AVE
HAMPSHIRE ST
2700 BRYANT ST
2800 FLORIDA ST
2900 ALABAMA ST
3000 HARRISON ST
TREAT AVE
3100 FOLSOM ST
3150 SHOTWELL ST
3200 SOUTH VAN NESS AVE
3250 CAPP ST
3300 MISSION ST
3338 HOFF ST
3400 VALENCIA ST
3444 ALBION ST
DEARBORN ST
3500 GUERRERO ST
3600 DOLORES ST
ABBEY ST
3700 CHURCH ST
3800 SANCHEZ ST
3854 PROSPER ST
3870 POND ST
3900 NOE ST
HARTFORD ST
MARKET ST
4000 CASTRO ST
COLLINGWOOD ST
DIAMOND ST
EUREKA ST
4200 DOUGLASS ST
CORBETT AVE
4300 ORD ST
CORBIN PL
4400 TEMPLE ST
MARS ST
URANUS TERR
ROOSEVELT WY
MONUMENT WY
ASHBURY ST
4600 CLAYTON ST
4700 BELVEDERE ST
4800 COLE ST
4900 SHRADER ST
END STANYAN ST
18TH AV SF 5 A2
18TH AV SF 9 A2
18TH AV SF 13 A1
FROM PRESIDIO S TO WAWONA ST
NUMBERS SAME AS 19TH AV
18TH ST SF 10 A2
18TH ST SF 11 A2
FROM THE BAY BETWEEN MARIPOSA ST
& 19TH ST W TO DANVERS ST
AT MARKET ST
500 ILLINOIS ST
600 3RD ST
700 TENNESSEE ST
800 MINNESOTA ST
900 INDIANA ST
1000 IOWA ST
1100 PENNSYLVANIA AVE
1200 MISSISSIPPI ST
1300 TEXAS ST
1400 MISSOURI ST
1500 CONNECTICUT ST
1600 ARKANSAS ST
1800 CAROLINA ST
1900 DE HARO ST
2000 RHODE ISLAND ST
2100 KANSAS ST
2200 VERMONT ST
2300 SAN BRUNO AVE
2400 UTAH ST
2500 POTRERO AVE
2600 HAMPSHIRE ST
2700 YORK ST
2800 BRYANT ST
2900 FLORIDA ST
3000 ALABAMA ST
3100 HARRISON ST
TREAT AVE
3200 FOLSOM ST
3250 SHOTWELL ST
3300 SOUTH VAN NESS AVE
3350 CAPP ST
3400 MISSION ST
3426 SAN CARLOS ST
3466 LEXINGTON ST
3500 VALENCIA ST
LAPIDGE ST
DEARBORN ST
LINDA ST
3600 GUERRERO ST
OAKWOOD ST
3700 DOLORES ST
3800 CHURCH ST
3900 SANCHEZ ST
4000 NOE ST
4050 HARTFORD ST
4100 CASTRO ST
4200 COLLINGWOOD ST
4300 DIAMOND ST
4400 EUREKA ST
4500 DOUGLASS ST
4548 ORD ST
4600 HATTIE ST
CLOVER ST
END DANVERS ST
19TH AV SF 5 A3
19TH AV SF 9 A2
19TH AV SF 13 A1
19TH AV SF 19 A1
FROM PRESIDIO S TO PT S OF
RANDOLPH ST
2 PRESIDIO
100 LAKE ST
200 CALIFORNIA ST
300 CLEMENT ST
400 GEARY BLVD
500 ANZA ST
600 BALBOA ST
700 CABRILLO ST
FULTON ST
MARTIN L KING DR
1200 LINCOLN WY
1300 IRVING ST
1400 JUDAH ST
1500 KIRKHAM ST
1600 LAWTON ST
1700 MORAGA ST
1800 NORIEGA ST
1900 ORTEGA ST
2000 PACHECO ST
2100 QUINTARA ST
2200 RIVERA ST
2300 SANTIAGO ST
2400 TARAVAL ST
2500 ULLOA ST
2600 VICENTE ST
2700 WAWONA ST
BRIARCLIFF TER
SLOAT BLVD
OCEAN AVE
EUCALYPTUS DR
ROSSMOOR DR
MONTE VISTA DR
WINSTON DR
BUCKINGHAM WY
DENSLOWE DR
WYTON LANE
HOLLOWAY AVE
CRESPI DR
BANBURY DR
CARDENAS AVE
JUNIPERO SERRA BLVD
BEVERLY ST
SARGENT ST
MONTICELLO ST
CHESTER AVE
BYXBEE ST
RANDOLPH ST
ST CHARLES AV
VERNON ST
19TH ST SF 10 A2
19TH ST SF 11 B2
FROM THE BAY BETWEEN 18TH ST AND
20TH ST W TO CORBETT AV
500 ILLINOIS ST
600 3RD ST
700 TENNESSEE ST
800 MINNESOTA ST
900 INDIANA ST
SO EMBARCADERO FRWY
1100 PENNSYLVANIA AVE
1200 MISSISSIPPI ST
1300 TEXAS ST
1400 MISSOURI ST
1500 CONNECTICUT ST
1600 ARKANSAS ST
1700 WISCONSIN ST
1800 CAROLINA ST
1900 DE HARO ST
2000 RHODE ISLAND ST
2100 KANSAS ST
2200 VERMONT ST
2300 SAN BRUNO AVE
2500 POTRERO AVE
2600 HAMPSHIRE ST
2700 YORK ST
2800 BRYANT ST
2900 FLORIDA ST
3000 ALABAMA ST
3100 HARRISON ST
3150 TREAT AVE
3200 FOLSOM ST
3250 SHOTWELL ST
3300 SOUTH VAN NESS AVE
3350 CAPP ST
3400 MISSION ST
3428 SAN CARLOS ST
3464 LEXINGTON ST
3500 VALENCIA ST
3546 LAPIDGE ST
LINDA ST
3600 GUERRERO ST
OAKWOOD ST
DOLORES ST
3800 CHURCH ST
3900 SANCHEZ ST
4000 NOE ST
4050 HARTFORD ST
4100 CASTRO ST
4200 COLLINGWOOD ST
4300 DIAMOND ST
4400 EUREKA ST
4500 DOUGLASS ST

1988 SAN FRANCISCO COUNTY CROSS STREET INDEX

LAWSON LN
SEWARD ST
4612 CLOVER LANE
YUKON ST
DANVERS ST
CASELLI AV
MARKET ST
END CORBETT AVE
20TH AV SF 4 C2
20TH AV SF 9 A2
20TH AV SF 13 A1
FROM PRESIDIO S TO BUCKINGHAM WY
NUMBERS SAME AS 19TH AV
20TH ST SF 10 A3
20TH ST SF 11 A2
FROM THE BAY BETWEEN 19TH ST
& 21ST ST W TO DOUGLASS ST
500 MICHIGAN ST
600 ILLINOIS ST
700 3RD ST
800 TENNESSEE ST
900 MINNESOTA ST
1000 INDIANA ST
1100 IOWA ST
1200 PENNSYLVANIA AVE
1300 MISSISSIPPI ST
1400 TEXAS ST
1500 MISSOURI ST
1600 CONNECTICUT ST
1700 ARKANSAS ST
1800 WISCONSIN ST
1900 CAROLINA ST
2000 DE HARO ST
2100 RHODE ISLAND ST
2200 KANSAS ST
2300 VERMONT ST
2400 SAN BRUNO AVE
2600 POTRERO AVE
2700 HAMPSHIRE ST
2800 YORK ST
2900 BRYANT ST
3000 FLORIDA ST
3100 ALABAMA ST
3200 HARRISON ST
3250 TREAT AVE
3300 FOLSOM ST
3350 SHOTWELL ST
3400 SOUTH VAN NESS AVE
3450 CAPP ST
3500 MISSION ST
3532 SAN CARLOS ST
3572 LEXINGTON ST
3600 VALENCIA ST
3700 GUERRERO ST
DOLORES ST
3900 CHURCH ST
4000 SANCHEZ ST
4100 NOE ST
4150 HARTFORD ST
4200 CASTRO ST
4300 COLLINGWOOD ST
4400 DIAMOND ST
4500 EUREKA ST
END DOUGLASS ST
21ST AV SF 4 C2
21ST AV SF 9 A2
21ST AV SF 13 A1
FROM PRESIDIO S TO EUCALYPTUS DR
NUMBERS SAME AS 19TH AV
21ST ST SF 10 B3
21ST ST SF 11 A3
FROM POTRERO AV BETWEEN 20TH ST &
22ND ST W TO GRAND VIEW AV
2600 POTRERO AVE
2650 HAMPSHIRE ST
2700 YORK ST
2750 BRYANT ST
2800 FLORIDA ST
2850 ALABAMA ST
2900 HARRISON ST
2950 TREAT AVE
3000 FOLSOM ST
3050 SHOTWELL ST
3100 SOUTH VAN NESS AVE
3150 CAPP ST
3200 MISSION ST
3238 SAN CARLOS ST
BARTLETT ST
3266 LEXINGTON ST
3300 VALENCIA ST
3400 GUERRERO ST
AMES ST
FAIR OAKS ST
QUANE ST
3500 DOLORES ST
CHATTANOOGA ST
3600 CHURCH ST
3700 SANCHEZ ST
RAYBURN ST
3800 NOE ST
3900 CASTRO ST
4000 COLLINGWOOD ST
4100 DIAMOND ST
4200 EUREKA ST
4300 DOUGLASS ST
WORTH ST
END GRAND VIEW AVE
22ND AV SF 4 C2
22ND AV SF 8 C2
22ND AV SF 13 A1
FROM PRESIDIO S TO EUCALYPTUS DR
NUMBERS SAME AS 19TH AV
22ND ST SF 10 A3
22ND ST SF 11 A3
FROM THE BAY BETWEEN 21ST ST
& 23RD ST W TO GRAND VIEW AV
50 MICHIGAN
600 ILLINOIS ST
700 3RD ST
800 TENNESSEE ST
900 MINNESOTA ST
1000 INDIANA ST
1100 IOWA ST
1200 PENNSYLVANIA AVE
1300 MISSISSIPPI ST
1500 MISSOURI ST
1600 CONNECTICUT ST
1700 ARKANSAS ST
1800 WISCONSIN ST
1900 CAROLINA ST
2000 DE HARO ST
2100 RHODE ISLAND ST
KANSAS ST
2400 SAN BRUNO AVE
UTAH ST
2600 POTRERO AVE
2650 HAMPSHIRE ST
2700 YORK ST
2750 BRYANT ST
2800 FLORIDA ST
2850 ALABAMA ST
2900 HARRISON ST
2950 TREAT AVE
3000 FOLSOM ST
3050 SHOTWELL ST
3100 SOUTH VAN NESS AVE
CAPP ST
3200 MISSION ST
3250 BARTLETT ST
3300 VALENCIA ST
SAN JOSE AVE
3400 GUERRERO ST
3426 AMES ST
3450 FAIR OAKS ST
QUANE ST
3500 DOLORES ST
3550 CHATTANOOGA ST
3600 CHURCH ST
VICKSBURG ST
3700 SANCHEZ ST
3800 NOE ST
3900 CASTRO ST
3966 COLLINGWOOD ST
4000 DIAMOND ST
4100 EUREKA ST
4200 DOUGLASS ST
WORTH ST
HOFFMAN AVE
END GRAND VIEW AVE
23RD AV SF 4 C2
23RD AV SF 8 C2
23RD AV SF 12 C1
23RD AV SF 13 A3
FROM LAKE ST S TO EUCALYPTUS DR
NUMBERS SAME AS 19TH AV
23RD ST SF 10 A3
23RD ST SF 11 A3
FROM THE BAY BETWEEN 22ND ST
& 24TH ST W TO CORBETT AV
700 ILLINOIS ST
800 3RD ST
900 TENNESSEE ST
1000 MINNESOTA ST
1100 INDIANA ST
1200 IOWA ST
1300 PENNSYLVANIA AVE
1600 MISSOURI ST
1700 DAKOTA ST
1800 ARKANSAS ST
1900 WISCONSIN ST
2000 CAROLINA ST
2100 DE HARO ST
2200 RHODE ISLAND ST
2300 KANSAS ST
2400 VERMONT ST
SAN BRUNO AVE
UTAH ST
2700 POTRERO ST
2750 HAMPSHIRE ST
2800 YORK ST
2850 BRYANT ST
2900 FLORIDA ST
2950 ALABAMA ST
3000 HARRISON ST
3050 TREAT AVE
3100 FOLSOM ST
3150 SHOTWELL ST
3200 SOUTH VAN NESS AVE
3250 CAPP ST
3300 MISSION ST
3350 BARTLETT ST
3400 VALENCIA ST
3500 SAN JOSE AVE
3600 GUERRERO ST
3628 AMES ST
3650 FAIR OAKS ST
QUANE ST
3700 DOLORES ST
MERSEY ST
3750 CHATTANOOGA ST
SEVERN ST
3800 CHURCH ST
NELLIE ST
3850 VICKSBURG ST
BLANCHE ST
3900 SANCHEZ ST
4000 NOE ST
4100 CASTRO ST
4200 DIAMOND ST
4250 EUREKA ST
4300 DOUGLASS ST
4400 HOFFMAN AVE
GRAND VIEW AVE
4500 MARKET ST
END CORBETT AVE
24TH AV SF 4 C2
24TH AV SF 8 C2
24TH AV SF 12 C1
FROM PRESIDIO S TO EUCALYPTUS DR
100 PRESIDIO
W CLAY
200 LAKE ST
300 CALIFORNIA ST
400 CLEMENT ST
500 GEARY BLVD
600 ANZA ST
700 BALBOA ST
800 CABRILLO ST
FULTON ST
1200 LINCOLN WY
1300 IRVING ST
1400 JUDAH ST
1500 KIRKHAM ST
1600 LAWTON ST
1700 MORAGA ST
1800 NORIEGA ST
1900 ORTEGA ST
2000 PACHECO ST
2100 QUINTARA ST
2200 RIVERA ST
SANTIAGO ST
2400 TARAVAL ST
2500 ULLOA ST
2600 VICENTE ST
WAWONA ST
SLOAT BLVD
OCEAN AV
END EUCALYPTUS DR
24TH ST SF 10 A3
24TH ST SF 11 A3
FROM THE BAY TO MINNESOTA ST AND
FROM DE HARO ST BETWEEN 23RD ST
AND 25TH ST W TO PORTOLA DR
MICHIGAN ST
ILLINOIS ST
3RD ST
TENNESSEE ST
MINNESOTA ST
2100 DE HARO ST
2200 RHODE ISLAND ST
KANSAS ST
2400 VERMONT ST
2500 SAN BRUNO AVE
2600 UTAH ST
2700 POTRERO AVE
2750 HAMPSHIRE ST
2800 YORK ST
2850 BRYANT ST
2900 FLORIDA ST
2950 ALABAMA ST
3000 HARRISON ST
BALMY ST
3050 TREAT AVE
LUCKY ST
3100 FOLSOM ST
3150 SHOTWELL ST
3200 SOUTH VAN NESS AVE
CYPRESS ST
3250 CAPP ST
LILAC ST
3300 MISSION ST
OSAGE AL
3350 BARTLETT ST
ORANGE AL
3400 VALENCIA ST
POPLAR ST
3500 SAN JOSE AVE
3600 GUERRERO ST
3652 FAIR OAKS ST
QUANE ST
3700 DOLORES ST
MERSEY ST
3750 CHATTANOOGA ST
3800 CHURCH ST
3850 VICKSBURG ST
3900 SANCHEZ ST
4000 NOE ST
4100 CASTRO ST
4200 DIAMOND ST
4300 DOUGLASS ST
HOMESTEAD ST
4400 HOFFMAN AVE
FOUNTAIN ST
4500 GRAND VIEW
END PORTOLA DR
25TH AV SF 4 C2
25TH AV SF 8 C3
25TH AV SF 12 C1
S FROM SEACLIFF AV TO EUCALYPTUS
DR NUMBERS SAME AS 24TH AV
25TH ST SF 14 A1
25TH ST SF 15 A1
FROM MICHIGAN ST BETWEEN 24TH ST
AND 26TH ST W TO PORTOLA DR
MICHIGAN ST
ILLINOIS ST
900 3RD ST
1000 TENNESSEE ST
1000 MINNESOTA ST
1200 INDIANA ST
1300 IOWA ST
1400 PENNSYLVANIA AVE
1500 MISSISSIPPI ST
1600 TEXAS ST
1800 CONNECTICUT ST
2000 WISCONSIN ST
PALI RD
2200 DE HARO ST
2300 RHODE ISLAND ST
KANSAS ST
2500 VERMONT ST
2600 SAN BRUNO AVE
2700 UTAH ST
2800 POTRERO AVE
2850 HAMPSHIRE ST
2900 YORK ST
2950 BRYANT ST
3000 FLORIDA ST
3050 ALABAMA ST
3100 HARRISON ST
BALMY ST
3150 TREAT AVE
LUCKY ST
3200 FOLSOM ST
HORACE ST
3250 SHOTWELL ST
VIRGIL AVE
3300 SOUTH VAN NESS AVE
3326 CYPRESS ST
3350 CAPP ST
LILAC ST
3400 MISSION ST
OSAGE AL
3450 BARTLETT ST
ORANGE AL
3590 VALENCIA ST
POPLAR ST
3600 SAN JOSE AVE
3700 GUERRERO ST
3750 FAIR OAKS ST
3800 DOLORES ST
3900 CHURCH ST
3950 VICKSBURG ST
4000 SANCHEZ ST
4100 NOE ST
4200 CASTRO ST
4300 DIAMOND ST
4400 DOUGLASS ST
4500 HOMESTEAD ST
4600 HOFFMAN AVE
4700 FOUNTAIN ST
4800 GRAND VIEW
HIGH ST
END PORTOLA DR
26TH AV SF 4 C2
26TH AV SF 8 C2
26TH AV SF 12 C1
S FROM SEACLIFF AV TO EUCALYPTUS
DR NUMBERS SAME AS 24TH AV
26TH ST SF 14 A1

26TH ST SF 15 A1
FROM 3RD ST BETWEEN 25TH ST AND
ARMY ST W TO DOUGLASS ST
800 3RD ST
900 TENNESSEE ST
1000 MINNESOTA ST
1100 INDIANA ST
CONNECTICUT ST
WISCONSIN ST
PALI RD
DE HARO ST
RHODE ISLAND ST
KANSAS ST
VERMONT ST
2800 HAMPSHIRE ST
2900 YORK ST
2950 BRYANT ST
3000 FLORIDA ST
3050 ALABAMA ST
3100 HARRISON ST
3150 TREAT AVE
LUCKY ST
3200 FOLSOM ST
HORACE ST
3250 SHOTWELL ST
VIRGIL AVE
3300 SOUTH VAN NESS AVE
CYPRESS ST
3350 CAPP ST
LILAC ST
3400 MISSION ST
OSAGE AL
3450 BARTLETT ST
ORANGE ST
3500 VALENCIA ST
POPLAR ST
3600 SAN JOSE AVE
3700 GUERRERO ST
3750 FAIR OAKS ST
3800 DOLORES ST
3900 CHURCH ST
4000 SANCHEZ ST
4100 NOE ST
4200 CASTRO ST
4300 DIAMOND ST
END DOUGLASS ST
27TH AV SF 4 C2
27TH AV SF 12 C1
FROM SEACLIFF AV S TO VICENTE ST
NUMBERS SAME AS 24TH AV
27TH ST SF 14 A1
W FROM SAN JOSE AV BETWEEN
ARMY ST AND DUNCAN ST W TO
DIAMOND HEIGHTS BLVD
2 SAN JOSE AVE
100 GUERRERO ST
200 DOLORES ST
300 CHURCH ST
400 SANCHEZ ST
500 NOE ST
600 CASTRO ST
NEWBURG ST
KRONQUIST CT
700 DIAMOND ST
END 800 DOUGLASS ST
28TH AV SF 4 C3
28TH AV SF 8 C2
28TH AV SF 12 C1
FROM EL CAMINO DEL MAR S TO
WAWONA ST
NUMBERS SAME AS 24TH AV
28TH ST SF 14 B1
W FROM GUERRERO ST BETWEEN
DUNCAN ST AND VALLEY ST TO
DOUGLASS ST
2 GUERRERO ST
100 DOLORES ST
CHURCH ST
300 SANCHEZ ST
400 NOE ST
500 CASTRO ST
600 DIAMOND ST
END 700 DOUGLASS ST
29TH AV SF 4 B3
29TH AV SF 8 C2
29TH AV SF 12 C1
FROM MCLAREN AV S TO VICENTE ST
NUMBERS SAME AS 24TH AV
29TH ST SF 14 B2
FROM 3300 MISSION ST BETWEEN
DAY ST & VALLEY ST
W TO DIAMOND ST
2 MISSION ST
80 TIFFANY AVE
100 SAN JOSE AVE
200 DOLORES ST
300 CHURCH ST
400 SANCHEZ ST
500 NOE ST
600 CASTRO ST
ZIRCON PL
END 700 DIAMOND ST
30TH AV SF 4 B3
30TH AV SF 8 C2
30TH AV SF 12 C1
FROM EL CAMINO DEL MAR S TO
WAWONA ST
NUMBER SAME AS 24TH AV
30TH ST SF 14 B2
FROM 3400 MISSION S OF 29TH ST
W TO CASTRO ST
2 MISSION ST
100 SAN JOSE AVE
200 DOLORES ST
CHENERY ST
300 CHURCH ST
WHITNEY ST
400 SANCHEZ ST
HARPER ST
500 NOE ST
LAIDLEY ST
END CASTRO ST
31ST AV SF 4 B2
31ST AV SF 8 B2
31ST AV SF 12 C1
FROM SEA VIEW TER S TO
ESCOLTA WY
SEA VIEW TERR
300 CALIFORNIA ST
400 CLEMENT ST
500 GEARY BLVD
700 BALBOA ST
800 CABRILLO ST
FULTON ST
1200 LINCOLN WY
1300 IRVING ST
1400 JUDAH ST
1500 KIRKHAM ST
1600 LAWTON ST
1700 MORAGA ST
1800 NORIEGA ST
1900 ORTEGA ST
2000 PACHECO ST
2100 QUINTARA ST
2200 RIVERA ST
2300 SANTIAGO ST
2400 TARAVAL ST
2500 ULLOA ST
2600 VICENTE ST
END ESCOLTA WY
32ND AV SF 4 B3
32ND AV SF 8 B2
32ND AV SF 12 B1
FROM EL CAMINO DEL MAR S TO
VICENTE ST
NUMBERS ARE THE SAME AS 31ST AV
33RD AV SF 4 B3
33RD AV SF 8 B2
33RD AV SF 12 B1
FROM CLEMENT ST S TO WAWONA ST
NUMBERS SAME AS 31ST AV
34TH AV SF 4 B3
34TH AV SF 8 B2
34TH AV SF 12 B1
FROM CLEMENT ST S TO SLOAT BLVD
NUMBERS SAME AS 31ST AV
35TH AV SF 4 B3
35TH AV SF 8 B2
35TH AV SF 12 B1
FROM CLEMENT ST S TO SLOAT BLVD
NUMBERS SAME AS 31ST AV
36TH AV SF 4 B3
36TH AV SF 8 B3
36TH AV SF 12 B1
FROM CLEMENT ST S TO SLOAT BLVD
NUMBERS SAME AS 31ST AV
37TH AV SF 4 B3
37TH AV SF 8 B2
37TH AV SF 12 B1
FROM SHORE VIEW TER S TO SLOAT BL
NUMBERS SAME AS 31ST AV
38TH AV SF 4 B3
38TH AV SF 8 B2
38TH AV SF 12 B1
FROM CLEMENT ST S TO YORBA ST
400 CLEMENT ST
SHORE VIEW AVE
500 GEARY BLVD
600 ANZA ST
700 BALBOA ST
800 CABRILLO ST
FULTON ST
1200 LINCOLN WY
1300 IRVING ST
1400 JUDAH ST
1500 KIRKHAM ST
1600 LAWTON ST
1700 MORAGA ST
1800 NORIEGA ST
1900 ORTEGA ST
2100 QUINTARA ST
2200 RIVERA ST
2300 SANTIAGO ST
2400 TARAVAL ST
2500 ULLOA ST
2600 VICENTE ST
2700 WAWONA ST
END YORBA ST
39TH AV SF 4 B3
39TH AV SF 8 B2
39TH AV SF 12 B1
FROM CLEMENT ST S TO SLOAT
BLVD NUMBERS SAME AS 38TH AV
40TH AV SF 4 A3
40TH AV SF 8 B2
40TH AV SF 12 B1
FROM CLEMENT ST S TO YORBA ST
NUMBERS SAME AS 38TH AV
41ST AV SF 4 A3
41ST AV SF 8 A1
41ST AV SF 12 B1
FROM CLEMENT ST S TO SLOAT BLVD
NUMBERS SAME AS 38TH AV
42ND AV SF 4 A3
42ND AV SF 8 A2
42ND AV SF 12 A1
FROM CLEMENT ST S TO SLOAT BLVD
NUMBERS SAME AS 38TH AV
43RD AV SF 4 A3
43RD AV SF 8 A2
43RD AV SF 12 A1
FROM CLEMENT ST S TO SLOAT BLVD
NUMBERS SAME AS 38TH AV
44TH AV SF 4 A3
44TH AV SF 8 A1
44TH AV SF 12 A1
FROM CLEMENT ST S TO SLOAT BLVD
NUMBERS SAME AS 38TH AV
45TH AV SF 4 A3
45TH AV SF 8 A1
45TH AV SF 12 A1
FROM CLEMENT ST S TO SLOAT BLVD
NUMBERS SAME AS 38TH AV
46TH AV SF 4 A3
46TH AV SF 8 A1
46TH AV SF 12 A1
FROM SEAL ROCK DR TO SLOAT BLVD
NUMBERS SAME AS 38TH AV
47TH AV SF 4 A3
47TH AV SF 8 A1
47TH AV SF 12 A1
FROM PT LOBOS AV TO SLOAT BLVD
NUMBERS SAME AS 38TH AV
48TH AV SF 4 A3
48TH AV SF 8 A2
48TH AV SF 12 A1
FROM PT LOBOS AV TO SLOAT BLVD
NUMBERS SAME AS 38TH AV

18553

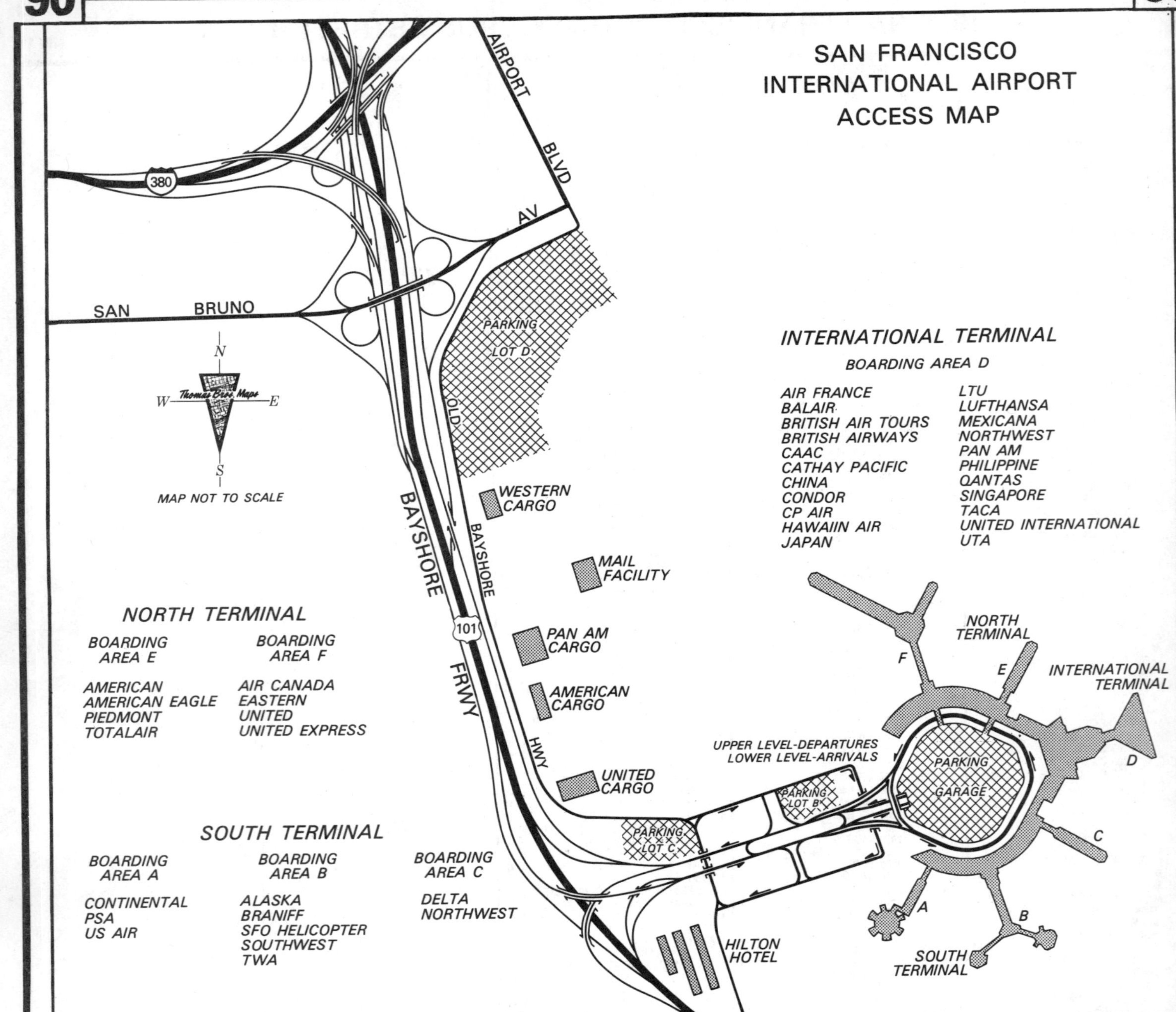
SAN FRANCISCO
INTERNATIONAL AIRPORT
ACCESS MAP
380
AIRPORT
BLVD
AV
SAN
BRUNO
N
W
E
S
Thomas Bros. Maps
MAP NOT TO SCALE
PARKING
LOT D
OLD
BAYSHORE
HWY
BAYSHORE
101
FRWY
WESTERN
CARGO
MAIL
FACILITY
PAN AM
CARGO
AMERICAN
CARGO
UNITED
CARGO
INTERNATIONAL TERMINAL
BOARDING AREA D
AIR FRANCE
BALAIR
BRITISH AIR TOURS
BRITISH AIRWAYS
CAAC
CATHAY PACIFIC
CHINA
CONDOR
CP AIR
HAWAIIN AIR
JAPAN
LTU
LUFTHANSA
MEXICANA
NORTHWEST
PAN AM
PHILIPPINE
QANTAS
SINGAPORE
TACA
UNITED INTERNATIONAL
UTA
NORTH TERMINAL
BOARDING
AREA E
BOARDING
AREA F
AMERICAN
AMERICAN EAGLE
PIEDMONT
TOTALAIR
AIR CANADA
EASTERN
UNITED
UNITED EXPRESS
SOUTH TERMINAL
BOARDING
AREA A
BOARDING
AREA B
BOARDING
AREA C
CONTINENTAL
PSA
US AIR
ALASKA
BRANIFF
SFO HELICOPTER
SOUTHWEST
TWA
DELTA
NORTHWEST
NORTH
TERMINAL
INTERNATIONAL
TERMINAL
F
E
D
C
A
B
UPPER LEVEL-DEPARTURES
LOWER LEVEL-ARRIVALS
PARKING
LOT B
PARKING
LOT C
PARKING
GARAGE
HILTON
HOTEL
SOUTH
TERMINAL